W9-CNF-777

Human Resource Management in Public Service

Fifth Edition

For Dira

—EMB

For Loretta

—JSB

For Colleen

—JPW

For Paul

—MVW

Human Resource Management in Public Service

Paradoxes, Processes, and Problems

Fifth Edition

Evan M. Berman

Victoria University of Wellington, New Zealand

James S. Bowman

Florida State University

Jonathan P. West

University of Miami

Montgomery R. Van Wart

California State University at San Bernardino

University of Hong Kong (Visiting)

Los Angeles | London | New Delhi
Singapore | Washington DC | Boston

Los Angeles | London | New Delhi
Singapore | Washington DC | Boston

FOR INFORMATION:

SAGE Publications, Inc.
2455 Teller Road
Thousand Oaks, California 91320
E-mail: order@sagepub.com

SAGE Publications Ltd.
1 Oliver's Yard
55 City Road
London EC1Y 1SP
United Kingdom

SAGE Publications India Pvt. Ltd.
B 1/I 1 Mohan Cooperative Industrial Area
Mathura Road, New Delhi 110 044
India

SAGE Publications Asia-Pacific Pte. Ltd.
3 Church Street
#10-04 Samsung Hub
Singapore 049483

Acquisitions Editor: Maggie Stanley
Editorial Assistant: Nicole Mangano
Production Editor: Libby Larson
Copy Editor: Judy Selhorst
Typesetter: C&M Digitals (P) Ltd.
Proofreader: Theresa Kay
Indexer: Wendy Allex
Cover Designer: Glenn Vogel
Marketing Manager: Liz Thornton

Printed in the United States of America

Cataloging-in-publication data is available from the Library of Congress.

978-1-4833-4003-6

This book is printed on acid-free paper.

15 16 17 18 19 10 9 8 7 6 5 4 3 2 1

Brief Contents

Detailed Contents

2. Legal Rights and Responsibilities: Laws Governing the Workplace   50

Sally Gertz

9. Training, Learning, and Development: Exploring New Frontiers   349

SAGE was founded in 1965 by Sara Miller McCune to support the dissemination of usable knowledge by publishing innovative and high-quality research and teaching content. Today, we publish more than 750 journals, including those of more than 300 learned societies, more than 800 new books per year, and a growing range of library products including archives, data, case studies, reports, conference highlights, and video. SAGE remains majority-owned by our founder, and after Sara's lifetime will become owned by a charitable trust that secures our continued independence.

Los Angeles | London | Washington DC | New Delhi | Singapore | Boston

Preface

*H*uman Resource Management in Public Service: Paradoxes, Processes, and Problems introduces managers and aspiring managers to this personally relevant and professionally exciting field. Not only do all people encounter human capital processes, but also these issues frequently are found in headline news reports. Execrable or exemplary, such cases make this an unusually interesting area to study. Whether the topic is genetic testing in the recruitment and selection function, pay reform initiatives in compensation, employee and management competencies in training and development, novel ways to evaluate individuals in the appraisal process, or the right to strike in labor–management relations, there is no shortage of controversy. Added to this are challenges of managing under tight budgets, which bring attention to hiring freezes, layoffs, frustrations of too few to do too much, challenges to civil service safeguards, and union activism.

This fifth edition retains the essential qualities and purposes of earlier editions while incorporating numerous revisions, updates, and refinements. Specifically, because employees and managers alike regularly confront human resource problems, the book probes such issues from both employee and managerial viewpoints. It discusses these problems, explains how they arise, and suggests what can be done about them. It continues to offer paradoxical perspectives about the inherent challenges, as well as the unique political and legal context, of the public sector management within which they take place.

Furthermore, this edition offers

- updated and expanded treatment of many issues;
- new or enhanced sections on "merit-light" systems, job management techniques using *Moneyball*-style human resource analytics, talent management, employee engagement and motivation, differential pay, the "new male mystique" in workforce benefits, evolving domestic partner benefits, contemporary labor–management history, collective bargaining changes, pension and health mutations, labor–management partnerships, and the future of civil service reform; and
- additional skill-building exercises and revised exercises.

In short, our team—combining more than 100 years of professional and academic experience (we are much too young to be that old!)—has crafted a volume that

- assumes that readers are or will be generalist line managers;
- presents a comprehensive range of topics and issues;

- illustrates these discussions with a blend of examples from local, state, federal, and international jurisdictions; and
- encourages students not merely to peruse the material but also to apply it.

As longtime members of the American Society for Public Administration who have published widely in the field (see "About the Authors"), we believe that an agency, commission, department, or government enterprise is shaped by its people and how they are managed. That belief motivated us to write the type of text described below.

The Introduction, after articulating the importance of human resource management, sets out the book's provocative theme that baffling paradoxes pervade the field; it then shows how those paradoxes can be explored and addressed. The chapters that follow feature learning objectives, coverage of essential knowledge and skills, pertinent editorial exhibits, lists of key terms, telling endnotes, and management exercises. Our intent is to make the material user-friendly and accessible by highlighting dilemmas, challenging readers to resolve them, and enticing them to go beyond the text to discover and confront other dilemmas. The idea is not to stuff but rather to stretch minds.

Part I, Context and Challenges, showcases two topic areas. Chapter 1, on the heritage of public service, takes an unusual approach: It examines the normative and ethical underpinnings of the field by discussing reform movements from past generations to the present day. Knowledge of what has gone before is helpful for understanding contemporary issues and for avoiding repetition of past mistakes—which themselves were often reincarnations of earlier errors. Paradoxes abound. For example, both the "thickening" of "top" government and the "hollowing" of "big" government (the increase in political appointees, the decrease in career public servants) have been occurring at the same time. Since much of human resource management is framed by law, Chapter 2 introduces legal obligations that agencies and their employees must recognize—not merely to conform with the law, but also to grasp its spirit. Thus, what is legal may not be ethical and vice versa: Law represents minimally acceptable behavior, but ethics inspires exemplary action.

With these foundations established, we turn our attention to the core management functions in Part II, Processes and Skills. Rife with ironies, these chapters are sequenced to reflect the stages of employment, from start to finish. Thus, employees encounter recruitment and selection first, followed by being placed into the organization, motivated, compensated, trained, and evaluated. In the process, they face issues with certain uncertainty, such as the following:

- The quasi-science of employee selection
- The often-unrecognized importance of position management
- The enigma of human motivation
- The difficulty of knowing how much someone should be paid
- The important yet tenuous nature of "employee-friendly" policies, policies that can be quite unfriendly
- The challenges involved in creating training and development policies
- The contradictions of personnel evaluation

The critical approach found in these chapters—stalking, contesting, and seeking resolution to paradoxes—is a distinctive feature of this work.

The final two chapters explore labor–management relations as the capstone of human resource management. That is, both the foundations of the field and its functions have been—and will be—affected by the relationship between public employers and their employees. The key conundrum: The framework undergirding this relationship actually undermines it, a fact that is largely unrecognized. The volume closes with conclusions and provocations about emergent technologies, human competencies, civil service reform, and the drama of personal excellence. Changes in the years ahead will increase not only in speed and intensity but also in unpredictability; pupils, pollsters, pundits, personnel, and prognosticators are sure to be dazzled by paradoxes that prance and posture through the workplace. A glossary and indexes will assist inquisitive readers in exploring the material and discovering new resources. As they do so, we hope that they will contact us with suggestions for further improvements in the book.

Welcome to human resource management in a text that is, paradoxically, both conventional and unconventional in its coverage of issues affecting the future of all readers in their careers.

—*Evan M. Berman*

—*James S. Bowman*

—*Jonathan P. West*

—*Montgomery R. Van Wart*

Acknowledgments

We are pleased to recognize the many individuals who helped us in this work. We thank Lisa Shaw and MaryAnn Vail at SAGE as well as colleagues in the American Society for Public Administration for their encouragement and support. We are grateful to Barbara Moore and Christine Ulrich of the International City/County Management Association as well as the Council of State Governments, the AFL-CIO, the International Personnel Management Association, the American Society for Public Administration, the Families and Work Institute, and the National Academy of Public Administration. In addition, the following provided helpful advice: Doris Jui, the University of Miami, School of Business Administration Librarian; City of Riverside, California, HR Department; and Alex Najera, Riverside County, California. All of us have benefited from our students and graduate assistants, with special appreciation to Marcia A. Beck, Kristan Brown, Alexander Ades, Susan Spice, Victor Munoz, Shane Markowitz, Martha Medina, David J. Miller, Michael Kennedy, Josh Kornfield, Paola Conte, and Rachael Sullivan. Finally, but not least, we want to thank the numerous colleagues and students who, through their feedback and adoption decisions, have helped to make this book successful.

SAGE would also like to thank the following reviewers for their time and editorial insight:

Galia Cohen, *The University of Texas at Dallas*

Joseph C. De Laduranty, *California State University, Northridge*

Craig P. Donovan, *Kean University*

Kurt Fenske, *Northern Arizona University-Yuma Branch Campus*

Paula Holoviak, *Kutztown University*

Yeonsoo Kim, *University of Nevada Las Vegas*

Eric Otenyo, *Northern Arizona University*

Beth M. Rauhaus, *University of North Georgia*

Anna Marie Schuh, *Roosevelt University*

Becky J. Starnes, *Austin Peay State University*

Melvin Rogers, *University of Central Florida*

Introduction

If there are two courses of action, you should always pick the third.

—Proverb

There are two questions virtually everyone asks: "Why is managing people so hard?" and "Why do people dislike management so much?" The answers to both questions involve *paradoxes*—seemingly incompatible ideas and practices that have to be made to work well together in organizations. Working well means, on one hand, that they are efficient and effective at achieving their intended purposes and, on the other, that they are the kinds of places where people would like to be. This book, written for current and future public managers, not personnel technicians, highlights paradoxes in human resource management and invites you to join the search to improve work life in organizations. While human resource management may start with identifying workplace problems—the subject of scathing criticism over the past century and the "Dilbert" cartoons of today—the purpose is ultimately to find ways to make life better for employees and to enhance performance of public institutions as a whole.

In so doing, this text seeks to both "build in" (Latin: *instruere*) and "draw out" (*educare*). That is, most people benefit from an integrated, structured knowledge base more than from disconnected facts and ideas. Yet learning is not simply instruction—it is also an unpredictable process of exploring and questioning, a process that draws out the best in the human mind. Accordingly, you should truly "own" this publication by annotating these pages with *your* ideas, disputes, satisfactions, discomforts, experiences, comparisons, applications, inventions, and paradoxes. Then interact with other readers in a live or virtual classroom to stretch your thinking about the management of work. The way to get the most *out* of the book is to get *into* it! Ask more of yourself than anyone can ever ask of you; that way you will always be ready for anything. Nothing is as exhausting as underachieving. Become knowledgeable, for without knowledge progress is doomed; be prepared to contribute, because giving ensures growth.

MANAGING PEOPLE

What, then, is *human resource management*? If an organization can be defined as a group of people working toward a goal, and management can be defined as the process of accomplishing these goals through other people, then the subject of this volume is the

1

development of policies for effective use of human resources in an organization. Stated differently, all decisions affecting the relationship between the individual and the organization can be seen as dimensions of personnel management. Psychological and productivity goals are pivotal to this relationship. That is, the work performed must be meaningful to employees as well as to the institution. Not surprisingly, these two goals are interactive, reciprocal—and sometimes contradictory.

Human resource management, in short, is a titanic force that shapes the conditions in which people find themselves. Its daily practice is an area that administrators are responsible for and can have a genuine impact on. Human resource management *matters*. Indeed, the most important job of an administrator is to help the organization use its most valuable asset—people—productively. From deciding how individuals will be recruited to how they are then compensated, trained, and evaluated, human resource administration has a significant, even definitive, effect on the careers of all employees and employers. Legislative officials and chief executives may have authority to design new programs and approve budgets, but it is managers who hire, place, pay, develop, and appraise subordinates. They spend more time on managing people than on anything else. Nothing is of more consequence; nothing is more difficult.

And it is not going to get easier. Not only have personnel specialists in many jurisdictions been "downsized," but also organizations are experimenting with entirely new approaches to human resource management, including far-reaching civil service reform. Managers are being required to do more with less, despite the fact that human resource issues are becoming—as this text demonstrates—more numerous and increasingly complicated. Clearly, a supervisor who regards personnel concerns as a nuisance to be endured will be overwhelmed by additional responsibilities and the need to deal with them. As one wise official stated, "Put human resource management first because it is the most important." The unimpeachable fact is that a leader who does not take care of his or her people will have no one to lead. Fail to honor people, and they will fail to honor you. The tragedy: Few are trained to manage employees.

THE PARADOX PUZZLE

An inexorable element of the world is that it evolves and becomes more complex, making management of organizations more difficult. Rapid and spastic change spawns confusing, contradictory, absurd—and true—paradoxes. Existing in a twilight zone between the rational and irrational, a **paradox** (from the Greek *para,* or beyond, and *doxa,* or belief) is an anomalous juxtaposition of incongruous, incredible, and sometimes burlesque contentions. Such seeming absurdities and tantalizing riddles contradict oversimplifications and overrationalizations in conventional thinking. In so doing, they produce humility, vitality, and surprise; the beginning of wisdom is the realization of ignorance. These gnarly predicaments jolt the brain, alternatively puzzling and inspiring people to wring further understanding from understanding by making the unknown known (Rescher, 2001). This creates a deeper comprehension of the principles behind the paradoxes, furnishes valuable insights, and provides unexpected solutions to thinking about people and institutions.

Indeed, the recognition of ambiguities, equivocations, and unstated assumptions inherent in paradoxes has led to significant advances in science, philosophy, mathematics, and other fields. "The true test of a first-rate mind," F. Scott Fitzgerald said, "is the ability to hold two contradictory ideas at the same time and still function." Some of the best-led organizations, likewise, are those that achieve a balance between seemingly contradictory opposites.

Full of paradoxes, the management of human capital embodies clashes between apparent truths that sow confusion and tax the ability of administrators. These truthful contradictions lurk and mock both study and practice. Everyone agrees in principle that people are essential, for example, but often they are taken for granted in organizations. One key conundrum, as obvious as it is ignored, is the paradox of democracy. Citizens have many civil rights in the conduct of public affairs (e.g., the freedoms of speech, elections, and assembly), but employees experience precious few such rights in organizations (e.g., subordinates seldom choose superiors). One part of American culture stresses individualism, diversity, equality, participation, and a suspicious attitude toward power, but another emphasizes conformity, uniformity, inequality, and submission to authority. In fact, the unity of opposites revealed by paradoxes is embedded in the human condition—birth and death, night and day, happiness and misery, good and evil, as each defines the other.

People may value freedom very highly, but in the end they work in organizations that significantly reduce it. As Rousseau observed, "Man is free, but everywhere he is in chains." Political democracy lies uneasily alongside economic authoritarianism. While "we the people" mandates sovereignty over political and economic life, political power has been democratized to serve the many, but economic power nonetheless serves the few (Kelly, 2001)—which includes relentless pressures to turn concerned citizens into mindless consumers. "We stress the advantages of the free enterprise system," Robert E. Wood, former chief executive of Sears, has been quoted as saying, "but in our individual organizations, we have created more or less a totalitarian system." Because capitalism and democracy are mutually exclusive concepts, the manner in which this contradiction is resolved greatly affects quality of life. Does the economy exist for society, or vice versa? Does America belong to citizens or to corporations? In a democratic society, should there be an arbitrary distinction such that people have a voice in political decisions but not in economic decisions?

A related fundamental riddle is the paradox of needs—individuals and organizations need one another, but human happiness and organizational rationality are as likely to conflict as they are to coincide. Many institutions today remain predicated on the machine model of yesteryear; indeed, the vast majority of them were created in the Machine Age of the industrial era. A top-down, command-and-control approach, revealed by the hierarchical organization chart, seeks to impose static predictability, demand efficiency, and expect self-sacrifice—the hallmarks of bureaucratization. But human beings, by definition, are premised not on a mechanical model but rather on an organic one. They are everything machines are not: dynamic, growing, spontaneous problem solvers. Thus, not only do people surrender their democratic liberties, but they also give them up to work in organizations quite unlike themselves. Human flourishing is no mean task in such conditions.

The cardinal human resource management problem is this: Do organizational processes and procedures help or hinder the resolution of these two grand, bittersweet paradoxes in democratic and work life? To put it bluntly, what difference does it make if people function efficiently in a schizophrenic civic culture and in dysfunctional work organizations? Such issues cannot be left unaddressed by institutions whose stated purpose is to champion public, not private, interests—ultimately, government by, for, and of the people. Human resource management in democracy is simply too important to be left to those who would see it as a technical problem. Because most of the nation's wealth is in the form of human capital, the talents of employees offer more value to the overall well-being of the country than anything else. Staffed by men and women, the public service makes it possible on a day-to-day basis for democracy to succeed (Goodsell, 2015). Public administration has always been about governance, not merely management. Unmasking the false clarity found in taken-for-granted operational assumptions can bring about a broader view of the role of citizens in society and organizations.

"There is," then, "nothing like a paradox to take the scum off your mind" (Justice Oliver Wendell Holmes Jr., as quoted in Vaill, 1991, p. 83). Starting with a "clean slate" (Exhibit 0.1) is a vital position from which to reconcile points of view that often seem, and sometimes are, irreconcilable. In fact, dealing with contradictions defines much of a manager's job. Nonetheless, contemplating ironic, ambivalent, inconsistent, poisonous paradoxes is something few employees and managers relish; attempting to make sense out of what seems wholly illogical is generally avoided.

Exhibit 0.1   "Close Enough for Government Work": A Linguistic Hijacking

There is much to be said for forcing people to rethink the basic assumptions of how they run their operations by starting with a clean slate. We all "know," however, certain things that may not be true. Some are all too willing to chuckle after some imperfection is found and say, "Close enough for government work." The phrase originated with government contractors who were making uniforms for the military 150 years ago. Because government standards for uniforms were so high at that time, saying that something was "close enough" meant that it was genuinely first-rate quality. How far we've come! It's all too easy to let the "can't do" types in the office beat down our optimism and desire for change. Starting with a clean slate challenges assumptions about how work is done and how it might be changed.

SOURCE: Adapted from Linden (1994, p. 155).

Yet it is precisely because paradoxes reveal the tensions in operating assumptions that exciting opportunities for investigation, discovery, insight, and innovation exist in managing organizations. Using paradoxes as a way to think about human resource administration is hardly a panacea, however. What it will provide is an occasion for reflection on and questioning of perplexing organizational routines. While there may be no solutions qua solutions, the right queries can provoke interesting, different, and—sometimes—quite suitable responses. If nothing else, a deeper understanding of dilemmas will be achieved, which is, of course, the first step toward their resolution.

Ways to embrace paradoxes include inquiring into the bases of clashing perspectives, identifying and appreciating the best of different viewpoints, and striving to create new viewpoints that incorporate a balance of divergent opinions. Predicaments, then, require integrative thinking, "the ability to face constructively the tension of opposing ideas and, instead of choosing one at the expense of the other, generate a creative resolution of the tension in the form of a new idea that contains elements of the opposing ideas but is superior to each," in the words of scholar Thomas C. Chamberlin, as quoted by Martin (2009, p. 15). "Phenomena," Martin continues, quoting Chamberlin, "appear to become capable of being viewed analytically and synthetically at once" (p. 23).

In other words, systematic, **dialectic** reasoning juxtaposes contradictory opposing ideas (theses and antitheses) and seeks to resolve them by creating new syntheses. A dialectic, then, is a method of reasoning that compares opposing viewpoints in order to seek a reconciliation that integrates the best of both. There can be unity in diversity. Jazz, for instance, "beautifully expresses the dialectic between hope and despair," the tension between individual freedom, and the greater good (Hertsgaard, 2002, p. 59). Leaving your "comfort zone" to engage in this mode of thinking should be as challenging as it is rewarding; change is inevitable, growth is optional. "You cannot solve the problem," Einstein once said, "with the same kind of thinking that created the problem." In short, a key question facing managers is less "What should I do?" and more "How should I think?"

Developing a capacity to manage—and even thrive on—paradoxes is important because they will only multiply in the years ahead with the expansion of the information superhighway, the virtual workplace, and a demographically diverse workforce. Make no mistake about it: Any changes in how people are managed are unlikely to be effective without recognition of the paradoxes born in the 21st century (Heller, 2003). Know, too, the paradox that embodies all such paradoxes: As contradictions proliferate, the expectations to resolve them become increasingly intense.

PATHWAYS THROUGH PARADOXES: CARPE DIEM

Reading is a commitment to the future, an odyssey characterized by the unexpected. To facilitate the journey, this text includes critical questions for you and your organization, be it a governmental agency, nonprofit organization, or educational institution. It reveals logical inconsistencies and conflicting assumptions in human capital management; in so doing, it offers intriguing opportunities to position problems in quite different ways. The charge is to recognize and use this fact—that is, to manage conflicts for mutual benefit. *Human Resource Management in Public Service: Paradoxes, Processes, and Problems* is a reality check on management and the workplace intended to enrich the organization's human capital.

Louis Pasteur once said, "Chance favors the prepared mind." Since the trends discussed in this volume will change you whether or not you read it, you are now presented with an authentic opportunity to "seize the day" and think creatively about managing people. To do this, use the text as a springboard and amplify the example of Leonardo da Vinci (Exhibit 0.2) by developing your own techniques of discovery. The analysis here will spark but seldom settle discussions about how to "do" human resource management. Revealing useful insights does not necessarily lead to easy answers. Reader learning, instead, will develop as much, we hope more, from personal reflection as from pedagogical suggestion.

Exhibit 0.2 Leonardo's Parachute

"There is no use in trying," said Alice; "one can't believe impossible things." "I dare say you haven't had much practice," said the Queen. "When I was your age, I always did it for half an hour a day. Why, sometimes I've believed as many as six impossible things before breakfast."

—Lewis Carroll, *Through the Looking Glass*

The example of Leonardo da Vinci—an accomplished painter, inventor, sculptor, engineer, architect, botanist, and physicist—has inspired people for hundreds of years to tap into their creativity (Gelb, 1998). For instance, by studying the science of art, Leonardo created a masterpiece, the *Mona Lisa*, that reveals how many different truths can be held, and enjoyed, simultaneously. Conversely, by studying the art of science, he invented a perfectly designed parachute—centuries before the airplane. To wit, as long as you are going to think anyway, you may as well think big!

In doing so, resist your first impulse, as jumping to conclusions stifles creativity. "I don't know" is often one of the wisest things that can be said as a prelude to contemplation. A mind is like Leonardo's parachute (it can function only when it is open), and paradoxes will never be adequately addressed without the creativity of a nimble mind. Ask yourself, for instance, "What would I attempt to do if I knew I could not fail?" "If the obvious ways to deal with a problem did not exist, then what would I do?" Answers may not be immediate, specific actions, but rather may evolve from a different perspective, a changed basis for choices, or an alternative way of thinking. As John Lennon once said, "Reality leaves a lot to the imagination."

The act of discovery, in short, consists not of finding new lands but of seeing with new eyes. (For instance, what color are apples? White, of course, once you get inside.) To nurture this capacity to "think outside the box," do at least one of the following every day:

- Take a 5-minute "imagination break."
- Look into a kaleidoscope.
- Pretend to be the secretary of a major government agency.
- Make odd friends.
- Develop a new hobby.
- Read things that you do not normally read.
- Defer judgments and let your ideas incubate.
- Talk to someone from a different walk of life about a challenging problem.
- Use healthy snacks (chocolate, some claim, is not a vegetable) as imaginary "brain pills."
- Form a team and use the "25 in 10" brainstorming approach: Aim for 25 ideas to solve a problem in 10 minutes.

In other words, look where others are not looking to see what they are not seeing (Burrus, 2013). Be the person who "sees a glass not as half full or half empty, but as twice the size that it needs to be and considers designing a vessel with different dimensions" (Rothfeder, 2014).

It is no surprise that Japanese workers are encouraged to learn flower arranging, practice the highly ritualized tea ceremony, and play team sports to appreciate the value of beauty, precision, and cooperation in producing goods and services.

Indeed, we hope to change you from thinking as you normally do, but fall far short of telling you what to think. This book is peppered with precipitous, pernicious, persnickety, pugnacious, perfidious paradoxes designed to propel you toward reflection on and resolution of work/life puzzles. Complete escape from paradoxes, however, is unlikely, because pathways through them, ironically, may generate new problems. But paradoxes also create unique opportunities and, together with the tools and strategies presented here, a chance to achieve democratic freedom in organizations and a matching of individual and institutional needs. "The best way out," wrote Robert Frost, "is always through."

And now for the adventure!

KEY TERMS

Dialectic

Paradox

Paradox of democracy

Paradox of needs

REFERENCES

Burrus, D. (2013, November 11). 10 things you can do to increase your creativity. *Quartz*. Retrieved from http://qz.com/146278/10-things-you-can-do-to-increase-your-level-of-creativity

Gelb, M. J. (1998). *How to think like Leonardo da Vinci*. New York: Delacorte.

Goodsell, C. T. (2015). *The new case for bureaucracy*. Thousand Oaks, CA: CQ Press.

Heller, R. (2003). *The fusion manager*. London: Profile Books.

Hertsgaard, M. (2002). *The eagle's shadow: Why America fascinates and infuriates the world*. New York: Farrar, Straus and Giroux.

Kelly, M. (2001). *The divine right of capital: Dethroning the corporate aristocracy*. San Francisco: Berrett-Koehler.

Linden, R. (1994). *Seamless government*. San Francisco: Jossey-Bass.

Martin, R. (2009). *The opposable mind*. Cambridge, MA: Harvard Business School Press.

Rescher, N. (2001). *Paradoxes: Their roots, range, and resolution*. Chicago: Open Court.

Rothfeder, J. (2014, July 28). How Honda drives its workforce. *Newsweek*. Retrieved from http://www.newsweek.com/how-honda-drives-its-workforce-261814

Vaill, P. B. (1991). *Managing as a performing art*. San Francisco: Jossey-Bass.

Context and Challenges

CHAPTER 1

The Public Service Heritage

People, Process, and Purpose

good people, good systems, good intentions

When government has the right people, and the right system, and the right intentions, many good things are possible. The trick is knowing which ones they are.

—Alan Ehrenhalt

After studying this chapter, you should be able to

- understand the changing structure, environment, key principles, and operating characteristics of public human resource management;
- distinguish the various tides of reform that are part of the public service heritage;
- identify the paradoxes and contradictions in public service history;
- recognize how legacies from the past affect human resource management in the present;
- assess the contributions of recent reforms to effective management;
- show how values influence managers in addressing human resource issues; and
- describe ethical judgments required in human resource management and use guiding questions to make such decisions.

Concern about good government has deep roots in the United States. It has long been recognized that for government to be effective, good people must be hired, trained, and rewarded. There is also a well-established tradition that a properly designed system for managing people is critical to good government. Indeed, two schools of thought have emerged over time: One argues that breakdown in government performance is an "incompetent people" problem, and the other argues that it is an "evil system" problem (Ehrenhalt, 1998).

Others have pointed to an "ethics" problem that demands attention if confidence in government is to be restored (West & Berman, 2004). As the opening quotation suggests, good intentions and the ethical actions that ideally result from them are critical to the creation of a high-performance workplace.

These three things in combination—good people, good systems, and good intentions—are the focus of this chapter. Good people are needed to manage government's most important resource—its employees. A few work in the human resource department, but the vast majority are line and staff managers. Their abilities are critical to the performance and achievement of public purpose. The system in which these people operate is also crucial to the achievement of results. Managing human resources has taken many forms over time and involves activities such as recruitment, classification, compensation, training, and evaluation. The third component, intentions, encompasses the tasks that the people propose to accomplish and the values guiding the effort. Intentions of employees and managers, informed by individual and organizational values and ethics, guide their actions for good or ill. Admirable intentions are key to government performance, especially given today's emphasis on citizen service.

This chapter begins by providing a glimpse into a human resource manager's day. Although this textbook focuses on HRM for all managers, it is important to have some insight into the specialists' world of HRM. Then the discussion moves to the first of the three themes of the chapter: good people. A section identifies some of the broad contemporary challenges of getting and managing the right people, which provides a brief context for the rest of the book. Next are several sections on the second theme: good systems. What are some basic definitions of HRM and related terms? What are the different ways in which human resource support systems are organized? How have such systems changed over time, and what is the philosophical reasoning behind the major waves of changes? Lastly, the third theme is addressed: good intentions. This is covered in two sections. One discusses how all public managers in their human resource capacity must understand and balance four principles. The final section follows up the discussion of the principles by looking specifically at the importance of ethics and its application, moral management, as the mainstay of public service. Throughout, there is no shortage of paradoxes.[1] Knowledge of the public sector heritage provides a foundation for more specialized chapters to follow.

A DAY IN THE LIFE OF MARIA HERNANDEZ

Maria Hernandez is the human resource director of a large southeastern city. She heads a department organized into five divisions—Examinations, Development and Training, Classification, Employee Relations, and Compensation and Benefits. Like most large-city human resource directors, Hernandez faces a thorny set of issues that creates challenges, threats, and opportunities for her and for city government. Her work life is complicated by a rapidly changing workforce, an increasingly cumbersome legal and regulatory environment, declining budgets, heightened citizen complaints, pressures for higher productivity, outsourcing, restive unions, and pending layoffs. In addition, she faces the frequent turnover of political leadership, the increasing impact of technology, and the visible and public way in which government decisions are made. Hernandez earned her MPA degree with a concentration in personnel management more than 20 years ago. She has been working for the city since that time, progressing up the ranks to human resource director, a position she has held for the past 10 years.

After rising at 6:00 A.M., Hernandez is dressed and having morning coffee when she hears the local TV news report an increase in the area's unemployment rate. This development will increase the number of people seeking work with the city, and pending municipal layoffs will add to the unemployment problem. These upcoming layoffs are linked to the city's decision to contract with the private sector for services in two areas: transportation, and tree trimming and planting. Many city department heads have contacted her about the best way to deal with the people issues associated with privatization. Several department heads are especially concerned about avoiding litigation that might arise from layoffs.

Hernandez also reads in the newspaper that the mayor is taking a hard line in negotiations with the city's sanitation workers' union by insisting on increases in employee contributions for health and pension benefits and limits on overtime. The union, in turn, is reluctant to endorse the city manager's proposal for productivity improvements and further privatization efforts. Labor unrest among the city's sanitation workers could spill over and affect other unionized employees who are still at the bargaining table hammering out next year's agreement. Hernandez is meeting later today with the city's negotiating team to get an update and to strategize in hopes of averting a strike. The department heads expect that she will help resolve this problem.

In addition, the newspaper contains a story in the local section detailing some of the facts involved in a lawsuit filed against a city supervisor who has been charged with sexually harassing one of his employees. This is not the first time this particular person has run into difficulties of this type; Hernandez is concerned about the potential fallout from this case. Her office has been conducting mandated online sexual harassment training for a number of years. Although this helps reduce the city's legal exposure (i.e., strict liability), she must still be on top of potentially litigious situations. Her department has been given the responsibility to investigate all sexual harassment complaints even when they do not involve managers (i.e., vicarious liability); she has made it her policy to be informed of any significant complaints.

Hernandez arrives at work at 7:30 A.M., having dropped off her children at school and carpooled to work with fellow city workers. The carpool conversation reveals concerns among dual-career couples with youngsters and the need for on-site child care as well as more flexible working conditions. This is an issue Hernandez has tried to address by proposing to the city manager a set of employee-friendly initiatives. Action on this item has been slow and piecemeal, but many employees and a newly elected city councilperson have been pushing for it. Some administrators have also told her that adoption of the initiatives would make the city more competitive in its recruitment and retention.

Hernandez reviews her day's schedule (see Exhibit 1.1). Many of the topics under consideration can potentially move the city forward and help its employees and managers to be more productive. Although her day is tightly structured around a series of meetings, she tries to set aside a block of time each day to consider the longer-range initiatives she is

Exhibit 1.1   Maria Hernandez's Monday Schedule

8:00: Staff meeting with human resource professionals

9:00: Conduct employee orientation for new hires

10:00: Meeting with department heads—implementing new performance measurement program

11:30: Meeting with assistant city manager, budget officer, and department reps (discuss recruitment plan and increasing personnel costs)

12:00: Lunch with legal counsel—review status of pending lawsuits and sexual harassment charge

1:45: Meeting with labor negotiating team—update on bargaining issues and impasses

2:30: Media briefing—tout elements of employee-friendly policy initiative for city employees

4:00: Meeting with university contractors—review design of training program regarding computer network and pension reform

5:30: Meeting with administrative assistant—review plans for updating all job descriptions

advocating, including a new plan to implement performance measurement in key departments, incentive pay for selected workers, online access to human resource policies and procedures, succession planning in light of pending retirements, and a cafeteria-style employee benefit plan. She also hopes to start a preretirement training program for all employees over age 55, to broaden the description of job classes, and to work with a consultant on pension reform. Nevertheless, human resource issues are sometimes unpredictable, and she knows that she will be interrupted many times as managers and employees ask her opinion on ways to deal with them. When she leaves the office at 6:30 P.M., Hernandez picks up her children at the child care center. After dinner, she reviews two reports on subjects that will occupy her attention at work early the next morning.

Hernandez's day shows the broad range of issues that might be encountered by today's human resource director. These include coping firsthand with worker unrest, labor shortages, productivity and performance measurement, and errant employees. They also involve crafting employee-sensitive policies, dealing with the insecurities of those employees vulnerable to layoffs, and feeling the pressures for greater efficiency. Note how much of Hernandez's time is spent meeting with both executives and line managers. Indeed, today it is critical to realize that much of what HR specialists do is support managers as they carry out HR functions. It is generally managers who must hire, promote, discipline, and fire workers. They have to respond to grievances, evaluate performance, recommend pay rates, approve job reclassifications, and motivate their charges. The constitutional rights of employees must be respected, and officials must be careful not to run afoul of legal requirements (e.g., those dealing with affirmative action, sexual harassment, and age, gender, or handicap status). The challenges faced by HR specialists and managers are discussed next.

SOME CHALLENGES IN GETTING AND MANAGING THE RIGHT PEOPLE

Managers today need to be mindful of important trends in the government environment that affect the context in which personnel decisions are made. The bulleted items below highlight just some of the developments that will have impacts on human resource management for the foreseeable future.

- *Changing workforce.* The workforce is becoming, paradoxically, both grayer and younger. On one hand, as the members of the Baby Boom generation are entering retirement, the average age of many seasoned employees and managers is rising. There is an obvious need for employees who can immediately fill their shoes, but such workforce candidates are often lacking. Demographically, **Generation X (Gen-X)** workers (those born between 1960 and 1980) who might replace them are fewer in number, which has contributed to a graying of the workforce in past decades. On the other hand, the very large cohort of **New Millennials** (those born after 1980) has now begun to enter the workforce; they are the latest job entrants. In a few years, they will experience increasing job opportunities. These new entrants reduce the average age of the workforce. At the same time, many authors have commented on how the career and working styles of Gen-X and New Millennial workers are different from those of Baby Boomers and the members of other preceding generations: Members of the newer generations are more likely than their predecessors to change careers and sectors often, demonstrate less loyalty to their employers, be comfortable with new technology, be independent, be comfortable working on multiple projects, and seek balance between their work and personal lives (Hannon & Yordi, 2011; Marston, 2007; Sauser & Sims, 2012; West, 2012). Exhibit 1.2 lists some reasons young people choose public service work. Beyond these factors, the workforce is also increasingly composed of women and minorities (Condrey, 2010; Guy & Newman, 2010; Kellough, 2009).

- *Declining confidence in government.* With the exception of a brief spike in 2001 after the terrorist attacks on New York City and Washington, D.C., on September 11, opinion polls since the 1960s have shown steady erosion in confidence and trust in government at all levels. In the early 1960s, six out of ten Americans claimed to trust the federal government most of the time. By 2010, only two in ten made that claim (Robinson, 2010). While the majority of Americans think that federal spending can and should be deeply cut, there is no agreement on what wasteful spending is or where to reduce it and no commitment to shared sacrifice to lower the national debt (Swanson & Blumenthal, 2013). Although trust in state and local government is higher than that in the federal government, declining confidence is evident at those levels as well. This can erode the morale of the civil service and impede performance. Rebuilding trust is an important challenge facing the public sector at all levels.

- *Declining budgets, leading to increased use of alternative work arrangements.* A combination of tax limitation measures, budget cuts, and political pressures to curb future expenditures has occurred throughout government. Government policy

---

Exhibit 1.2   Reasons Young People Choose Public Service

- To make a difference in a wide variety of leadership positions in the nonprofit and for-profit sectors; different branches of local, state, regional, and federal governments; and the international arena
- To become engaged intellectually in the challenges facing their communities
- To establish career and personal development skills that they can use throughout their lives
- To build a better future for the world and to solve big problems
- To create communication links within and between different communities
- To gain a sense of responsibility for others and the causes they care about

SOURCES: Education Development Center. (2002). Service-learning satisfies young people's desire for public service; Light, P. C. (2008). A government ill executed: The decline of the federal service and how to reverse it. Cambridge, MA: Harvard University Press.

makers, mindful of the impending exodus of Baby Boomers and attempting to keep costs down, are paying increased attention to alternative work arrangements. One variant, noted by Thompson and Mastracci (2005) and Barr (2005), involves use of the core-ring staffing model, with the core comprising full-time workers in permanent jobs and the ring comprising employees in contingent or alternative arrangements (e.g., contractors, temporary workers, and part-time staff). Paul Light (1999) has estimated that federal civilian employees are supported by about four times as many nonfederal workers via contracts and grants. Exhibit 1.3 on page 17 provides examples of such a blended workforce in various governmental settings.

- *Rightsizing and downsizing despite population growth.* The size of the federal civilian workforce was 2.1 million in 2012, which was 100,000 fewer than in 1946, 66 years earlier (U.S. Office of Personnel Management, 2014). Even so, 68% of the civilian workforce is devoted to defense- and security-related agencies, including the Department of Homeland Security (Partnership for Public Service, 2014). This reduction has been accomplished through periodic downsizings, which took place in the 1950s and from 1993 to 2007. The most recent downsizing left line managers with additional, burdensome administrative tasks. The combination of federal downsizing, scandal, and the war on waste led Paul Light (1999, 2008) to warn of a looming brain drain and to predict further decreases in government-centered public service with a corresponding increase in multisectored service. By contrast, the size of the state and local government workforce has increased, primarily because of population growth. Despite this overall trend, many individual jurisdictions have experienced workforce reductions in specific areas linked to privatization, deregulation, budget or service cuts, and program terminations—trends that are likely to continue well into the future.
- *Demands for productivity gains.* Jurisdictions at all levels are under pressure to improve performance without raising costs. A survey by the U.S. Merit Systems Protection Board of 9,700 managers and employees found that three of four

supervisors assumed additional responsibilities, but only one in five detected any new flexibility in taking personnel actions (Hornestay, 1999), although more recently this has begun to change (Bowman & West, 2007; Thompson, 2007). The federal Human Capital Survey, however, found in 2004 that just 30% of employees believed awards programs offered them incentive to do their best (U.S. Office of Management and Budget [U.S. OMB], 2004). This trend has led to numerous reform and reengineering initiatives aimed at establishing new approaches to the delivery of goods and services, as discussed later in this chapter.

- *Emerging virtual workplaces and virtual government.* With the advent of new information technologies, innovative organizations are replacing some traditional 9-to-5 workplaces with fixed central office locations with more flexible arrangements (telecommuting, flexi-place). This development alters relationships between employers and employees and raises questions about how human resource professionals give support to the variety of work arrangements in virtual workplaces (Milakovich, 2012; West & Berman, 2001). In addition, virtual workplaces alter the relationship between citizens and government. Numerous federal government initiatives begun in the mid-1990s enable citizen transactions to be conducted electronically. Indeed, the 1998 Government Paperwork Elimination Act states that federal agencies must allow people the option of submitting information or transacting electronically. These are just a few ways that new information technology can influence the public workplace (discussed further in Chapter 8). Key websites of government agencies and professional associations are listed in Exhibit 1.4.

- *Decentralization and increased managerial flexibility.* Typically, administrators at the operational level now have greater flexibility and discretion in the acquisition, development, motivation, and maintenance of human resources. Recent civil service reforms at all levels of government have loosened restrictions and increased managerial discretion over matters of pay, hiring, discipline, and termination. At the federal level, this has been evident in changes attempted at the U.S. Department of Homeland Security (DHS) and the U.S. Department of Defense (DOD); at the state and local levels, it is reflected in New Public Management reforms and the move in some jurisdictions toward at-will employment (Bowman & West, 2007; Klingner, 2009).

The trends described above influence the ways officials carry out their functions. Each trend has important implications for human resource management, and the relevance of each is considered in detail in this book.

SOME BASIC DEFINITIONS

The traditional term **personnel administration** is now used only narrowly, in reference to internal processes—staffing, position management, pay systems, benefits management, training, appraisal and discipline, and contract management, and so on—and the efficient application of the rules and procedures of the civil service system. This term connotes a technical approach to these numerous functions that are vital to any organization, often

Exhibit 1.3   Blended Workforces in U.S. Government Settings

Naval Research Lab

The Naval Research Lab has established contractual arrangements that provide for flexibility in the workforce for various special research projects. In this system, the hiring and firing of employees and layoff procedures are left to the contractor; they take place outside the federal personnel system, allowing for quick downsizing if necessary. Other advantages to the system include the ability to evaluate contract workers and hire the best-performing ones for long-term employment. The Naval Research Lab has also taken advantage of part-time work arrangements to create a family-friendly work environment, which has reduced the turnover rate in the workforce. In addition, the lab has created student positions with the goal of transitioning students into permanent employment.

Transportation Security Administration

After the 9/11 attacks—with the need to respond quickly to the requirements of the Aviation and Transportation Security Act of 2001—the Transportation Security Administration pursued flexible policies in hiring and maintaining its workforce. It has taken advantage of indirect-hire arrangements with contractors that have allowed the agency to use workers for specific purposes when required. The Transportation Security Administration has also made part-time work a priority, with 16% of its workforce serving in this role. Part-time work allows the agency to schedule staff when they are most needed, particularly peak flight times in the morning and afternoon, and allows officials to screen for exceptional workers to become permanent full-time employees in the future.

National Aeronautics and Space Administration

NASA has focused extensively on creating flexible arrangements for personnel who seek to use them. The Glenn Research Center, for example, has allowed full-time employees to change to part-time status for health, family, education, or other reasons. It has used term appointments to hire workers for defined periods of time, most particularly for work on special research projects. NASA has also used student employment programs that allow for transition into long-term employment, with 80% of students remaining with NASA after program completion.

SOURCES: Barr, S. (2005, June 8). Government should consider temporary workers, professors say. The Washington Post. Thompson, J., & Mastracci, S. (2005). The blended workforce: Maximizing agility through nonstandard work arrangements. Washington, DC: IBM Center for the Business of Government.

Exhibit 1.4   Key Websites of Government Agencies and Professional Associations

Government Agencies	
Bureau of Labor Statistics	www.stats.bls.gov
Federal Labor Relations Authority	www.flra.gov
National Labor Relations Board	www.nlrb.gov

(Continued)

Exhibit 1.4 (Continued)

U.S. Merit Systems Protection Board	www.mspb.gov
U.S. Office of Personnel Management	www.opm.gov
Professional Associations	
American Society for Public Administration	www.aspanet.org
Council of State Governments	www.csg.org
Ethics Section, American Society for Public Administration	www.aspaonline.org
International City/County Management Association	www.icma.org
National Academy of Public Administration	www.napawash.org
National Association of Counties	www.naco.org

with a relatively sharp divide between the responsibilities of HR specialists and operational managers, which is rare today. The contemporary term human resource management, or HRM, embraces a broader focus and has relevance for HR specialists, line managers, and executives. It encompasses all decisions affecting the relationship between the individual and the organization, with an eye to optimizing effectiveness from the view of both. In addition to technical operations, it includes actively seeking to recruit and select the best employees (talent management), adjusting positions to meet evolving needs (job design), blending strategies of pay for optimal compensation policies, providing cost-effective benefits packages that provide maximum value for employees (family-friendly benefits), building on technical training to include employee development, helping employees to improve their own performance, proactively managing employee–employer relations, and tracking organizational accountability and ensuring that health and safety issues are included (Abramson & Gardner, 2002). When human resource management is most global and long-term in its perspective and includes issues such as workforce planning and overall organizational design issues, it is often called strategic human resource management (SHRM). SHRM "may be regarded as an approach to the management of human resources that provides a strategic framework to support long-term business goals and outcomes. The approach is concerned with longer-term people issues and macro-concerns about structure, quality, culture, values, commitment and matching resources to future need" (Chartered Institute of Personnel and Development, 2013). For simplicity, in this text we use the single term *human resource management* to refer to the relevant technical, managerial, and strategic issues. Exhibit 1.5 compares the traditional system and assumptions with the newer, competing system and assumptions.

The term civil service refers to the government employees in permanent public service, excluding legislative, judicial, or uniformed military; positions typically are filled based on competitive examinations, and a professional career public service exists with protection against political influence and patronage. While the overwhelming bulk of most

Exhibit 1.5   Shifting From a Traditional Public Sector System to a System for the 21st Century

Traditional Public Sector System	Public Service for the 21st Century
Single system in theory; in reality, multiple systems not developed strategically	Recognition of multiple systems, strategic approach to system development, definition and inclusion of core values
Definition of *merit* that had the outcome of protecting people and equated fairness with sameness	Definition of *merit* that has the outcome of encouraging better performance and allows differentiation between varied levels of talent
Emphasis on process and rules	Emphasis on performance and results
Hiring/promotion of talent based on technical expertise	Hiring, nurturing, and promotion of talent to the right places
Treatment of personnel as a cost	Treatment of human resources as an asset and an investment
Job for life/lifelong commitment	Inners and outers who share core values
Protection justifies tenure	Employee performance and employer need justify retention
Performance appraisal based on individual activities	Performance appraisal based on demonstrated individual contribution to organizational goals
Labor–management relationship based on conflicting goals, antagonistic relationship, and ex post disputes and arbitration on individual cases	Labor–management partnership based on mutual goals of successful organization and employee satisfaction, ex ante involvement in work design
Central agency that fulfilled the personnel function for agencies	Central agency that enables agencies, especially managers, to fulfill the personnel function for themselves

SOURCE: Adapted from Ingraham, P., Selden, S., & Moynihan, D. (2000). People and performance: Challenges for the future public service—The report from the Wye River Conference. *Public Administration Review, 60*(1), 58. Reprinted with permission of the American Society for Public Administration, 1120 G Street NW, Suite 700, Washington, DC 20005.

managers' attention on personnel issues is related to civil service employees, managers also often need to be familiar with the non–civil service personnel because of contracting out, the use of consultants, and so on.

The next section provides some background on the challenges that all managers face in responding to the need to establish and retain a high-quality workforce.

THE STRUCTURE AND ROLE OF HUMAN RESOURCE DEPARTMENTS

Even though the focus of this book is human resource management for nonspecialists, it is helpful to have a little background on the array of institutional structures, functions, and placements of human resource departments. These departments are key staff units in all but the smallest jurisdictions, along with departments of budget, finance, facilities, legal affairs, communications, public relations, and so forth. Human resource offices combine both rule promulgation and rule implementation for some of the most important and visible policies in their organizations. That is, most of the personnel-related actions occurring in an organization follow rules codified under the HR department, frequently requiring its preapproval and often requiring its postapproval sign-off. When human resource departments provide direct services, which they frequently do, they have supportive and educative roles. When most human resource services are provided by a single department, HR is considered *centralized*. An example might be a single HR department for a small city in which HR does most interviewing except for the most senior jobs. When many human resource services and responsibilities are shared with managers, as is common today, a *devolved model of HR* is in place. There might be a single HR department for an entire city, for instance, but it is the managers who carry out most recruitment, selection, and promotion functions, albeit with guidelines and monitoring by the HR department. Larger organizations or governmental systems frequently have *decentralized* modes of HR in which a central human resource management agency sets policies, and freestanding agencies (or large divisions) have specialized human resource departments or units. To illustrate, the federal government moved to a decentralized model in 1978, with functional responsibilities going to different line agencies. Another example would be a large state agency that has a small HR unit in every division. Under such circumstances, HR may be both decentralized and devolved. On occasion, agencies will have multiple *specialized HR units* responding to the differing needs of employee groups, such as faculty and staff who are handled separately by a department in academic affairs (for hiring and promotion) and the traditional HR department (for all functions except faculty hiring and promotion). Still another possibility is an *outsourced HR model,* which sometimes occurs with service functions such as payroll, training and development, employee assistance programs, and classification studies, to name some of the more prominent areas. These five alternatives are illustrated in Exhibit 1.6.

The various functions discussed in this book may or may not be part of an HR department per se. For example, some jurisdictions still have separate civil service commissions for hiring purposes, labor relations may be done exclusively out of the executive office,

Exhibit 1.6   Placement of HR Specialists in Medium- and Large-Sized Organizations: Five Common Models

Centralized HR Department	Devolved HR Model	Decentralized HR Model	Specialized HR Departments	Outsourced HR
All HR experts are in a centralized unit, and HR does most HR functions, including the hiring of line employees.	A central HR unit does most policy work, but most functional responsibilities are accomplished by line managers and operational units.	The centralized HR department is smaller and more policy oriented; it oversees smaller HR units in different areas of the system.	There is a core HR department, but it is accompanied by specialist HR units for hiring and promotions, such as a unit of academic personnel in universities for faculty.	There is a small centralized HR unit, but many functions are privatized, such as payroll or training.

training and development may be its own department, payroll may be a part of the finance department, and a variety of organizational policy areas (such as telework programs) may operate under a separate office or authority. See Exhibit 1.7 for an array of places where the functions may be shared or housed. No matter the exact structure and particular set of roles, however, HR functions are the backbone of any organization. Never is this truer than with public sector organizations, in which personnel often make up 80% of the budget, and legal and fiduciary obligations to the law and public are extraordinary.

Today, HR services are provided in a variety of ways. Some functions are performed in the same way they were in the 1960s, relying on traditional subfunctions of employment, compensation, and training; others might be organized differently, with a cross-functional HR professional assigned to provide ongoing services to a team or group in a matrix organization. A shared-services model has increased in prominence recently, whereby HR specialists offer services to the organization on an as-required basis, with charges going to the functional area receiving service. Here, the HR department functions as an in-house consulting service. As noted, some or all HR functions are currently being outsourced, either to shared service centers within government or to outside contractors, where it is deemed that others might perform these functions more effectively and economically.

Exhibit 1.7   Sharing of Common HRM Functions

Common Functions in HR Departments	Function Generally Shared With	Function Sometimes Shared With	Function Sometimes a Separate Unit Under
Employment law	The organization's counsel (lawyer)	Executive oversight officers	
Recruiting	Line managers		Civil service commission
Selection of employees	Line managers		Civil service commission
Position management	Line managers		
Creation of a positive work environment	Line managers		
Compensation	Line managers, separate payroll office		
Benefits		Line managers	
Training and development	Line managers	Units providing in-depth technical training	Sometimes freestanding departments in large organizations
Appraisal	Line managers		
Labor relations	Executive team (bargaining), line managers (grievances)		Frequently a freestanding unit under CEO when numerous bargaining units

The most common placement of HR departments is right under the chief executive officer, with the human resource director serving in the executive's cabinet. In large organizations, it is not uncommon for HR to be combined with other staff units under an executive director of some sort (e.g., an assistant city manager or deputy mayor). In the smallest agencies, the CEO or an executive officer often doubles as the human resource director. The strategic and executive leadership roles of HR departments vary extensively. In some cases, the department plays a relatively dominant role because of the need for workforce planning, avoidance of litigation, contentious labor relations, and management consultation. Yet in some organizations, HR's strategic policy and planning roles have been absorbed by chief executive offices, budget offices, or legal departments, leaving a more service and consultative role for HR along with frontline enforcement functions.

HISTORICAL AND INSTITUTIONAL CONTEXT

Tides of Reform

A useful framework for considering the history of government reform efforts is provided by Paul Light in his 1997 book *The Tides of Reform*. Light identifies four reform philosophies, each of which has its own goals, implementation efforts, and outcomes: scientific management, war on waste, watchful eye, and liberation management. Although Light's analysis focuses on these four tides as they influence the overall performance of government, we use his framework here to highlight the implications of these four philosophies for human resource management with both federal and local examples.

Scientific Management

The first tide is scientific management. Here the focus is on hierarchy, microdivision of labor, specialization, and well-defined chains of command. This philosophy, usually associated with Frederick Taylor, is particularly manifest in the bureaucratic organizational form, with its emphasis on structure, rules, and search for "the one best way." Technical experts in this environment apply the "scientific" principles of administration (e.g., unity of command and POSDCORB—planning, organizing, staffing, directing, coordinating, reporting, and budgeting). The scientific management approach is evident in the recommendations made by two presidential commissions: the Brownlow Committee (1936–1937), which advocated changing the administrative management and government structure to improve efficiency; and the first Hoover Commission (1947–1949), which suggested reorganizing agencies around an integrated purpose and eliminating overlapping services. Herbert Hoover is the "patron saint" of scientific management, and the National Academy of Public Administration's Standing Panel on Executive Organization is a patron organization. Two important reorganizations that occurred in the federal executive branch, one in 1939, the Reorganization Act (establishing the Executive Office of the President), and the other in 2002, the creation of the Department of Homeland Security, are both examples of legislative action. Additional examples include legislation rationalizing centralized control and planning, such as the consolidation of financial controls in federal agencies in 1990 and the requirements for increased use of performance management and strategic planning under the Government Performance and Results Modernization Act of 2010.

Scientific management has implications for human resources. It emphasizes conformity and predictability of employees' contributions to the organization (machine model), and it sees human relationships as subject to management control. Current emphasis on productivity measurement, financial incentives, and efficiency reflects the continuing influence of scientific management. The scientific management of unity of HR command was strengthened by the Chief Human Capital Officers Act of 2002. Much of the foundational structure of government, covered in Title 5 of the U.S. Code, rests on principles of hierarchy, chain of command, consistency, and standardization. While at one time scientific management principles overwhelmingly dominated government philosophy, some hallmarks of scientific management, such as job design (characterized by standard procedures, narrow span of control, and specific job descriptions instituted to improve efficiency), may actually impede achievement of quality performance in today's organizations, where customization, innovation, autonomous work teams, and empowerment are required. Similarly, various human resource actions mirroring scientific management differ from avant-garde practices. For example, training is changing from a nearly exclusive emphasis on functional, technical, job-related competencies to a broader range of skills, cross-functional training, and diagnostic, problem-solving capabilities. Performance measurement and evaluation have been shifting from individual goals and supervisory review to team goals and multiple reviewers (citizen, peer, supervisory). In addition to individually based merit increases, some organizations now include team- or group-based rewards—both financial and nonfinancial.

War on Waste

The second reform tide is the war on waste, which emphasizes economy. Auditors, investigators, and inspectors general are used to pursue this goal. Congressional hearings on welfare fraud are a defining moment in this tide, and the Inspector General Act of 1978 is defining legislation. The 1992 Federal Housing Enterprises Financial Safety and Soundness Act is an expression of the war on waste, with its provisions to fight internal corruption. The patron saints of the war on waste are W. R. Grace, who headed President Reagan's task force (1982–1984) to determine how government could be operated for less; Jack Anderson, the crusading journalist who put a spotlight on government boondoggles; and Senator William Proxmire, who originated the Golden Fleece Award to bring attention to "wasteful, ridiculous or ironic use of the taxpayers' money."

The implications of the war on waste for human resource management are plentiful. Frequently audits, scandals, critical reports, and whistleblowing point out gaps in rules and lax implementation of rules; such revelations often bring needed attention and/or corrective actions. Recent cases of the war on waste include the abolition of the ineffective Minerals Management Service, the federal unit that had been rebuked even before the *Deepwater Horizon* oil rig scandal in the Gulf of Mexico, which it oversaw; and the scandal in Bell, California, in which numerous city officials were found to be in collusion to defraud taxpayers by means of outlandish salaries, resulting in litigation and new transparency laws. Of course, preoccupation with waste also leads to increases in internal controls, oversight and regulations, managerial directives, tight supervision, and concerns about accountability. Thus, it can result in a proliferation of detailed rules, processes, procedures, and multiple reviews that are characteristic of government bureaucracy and that influence personnel management. Critics who detect waste and attribute it to maladministration of public resources or unneeded spending may focus on the deficiencies of employees. Fearful workers seek cover from criticism when they do things strictly by the book. Managers concerned with controlling waste try to minimize idle time, avoid bottlenecks, install time clocks, audit travel vouchers and phone records, inventory office supplies, and monitor attendance and punctuality. Use of temporary rather than permanent staff and service privatization may be ways to contain costs while maintaining performance standards. Clearly, contemporary human resource practices are linked to the heritage of the war on waste, leading to both heightened rigor and not a small amount of administrative red tape.

Watchful Eye

The third tide of reform, the **watchful eye**, emphasizes fairness through openness, transparency, and access. Whistleblowers, the news media, interest groups, and the public need access to information to ensure that the public's rights and the common interest are protected as well as individual rights. Congress and the courts become the institutional champions seeking to ensure fairness. The need for the watchful eye and government that is more open became apparent after the abuses exposed in the Watergate scandal (the Woodward and Bernstein *Washington Post* investigation) and the U.S. involvement in Vietnam (publication of the Pentagon Papers). Although highly controversial, the 2013 leak of thousands of documents by Edward Snowden, a former system administrator for the Central Intelligence Agency and contractor for the National Security Agency, is in this tradition. Another example is the scandal that arose in 2014 concerning the Veterans Administration's falsified waiting list; in this case employees had been receiving bonuses for meeting the goal of providing medical appointments to veterans within two weeks, while thousands of veterans were actually waiting for months (Oppel, 2014). The 1946 Administrative Procedure Act and the **Ethics Reform Act of 1989** are examples of defining legislation. The former is important because it established procedural standards regarding how government agencies must pass rules with public notice, input, and statements of factual basis for decisions. Specific provisions of the latter are efforts to curb lobbying influence and promote ethics in government. John Gardner and Common Cause and Ralph Nader and Public Citizen provide examples of the patron saints and organizations linked to the watchful eye.

The implications of this philosophy for human resource management can be identified as well in the 20th-century legislation related to how hiring, promotion, labor relations, and a host of other activities are conducted. Concern about the fairness of hiring processes leads to requirements for public announcements of jobs as well as the job-related competence of new recruits (e.g., Chapter 33 of U.S. Title 5). Reforms have made the use of hiring criteria based on sex, race, age, and handicap status illegal (U.S. Title 42). Due process requirements minimize arbitrary decisions to terminate employees. Creating an organizational culture of openness, careful record keeping, and compliance with full-disclosure and sunshine requirements are all consistent with the watchful eye philosophy. Adoptions of minimum standards of conduct or codes of ethics along with ethics training are other examples. Union stewards are likely to cast their watchful eyes on negotiated contracts and to blow the whistle when violations occur (such whistle-blowing is protected under U.S. Title 29). Managers should seek congruence between the standards espoused by the organization and the behavior of workers. Calls for integrity at all levels of government reflect the contemporary influence of the watchful eye mentality. Of course, increased reporting and consultation do absorb resources and are a drag on "businesslike" efficiency and executive decisiveness. Perceived excesses of the war on waste and the watchful eye may lead to calls for a reform tide that "liberates" management, as discussed below.

Liberation Management

The final tide of reform is **liberation management**. Its goal is higher performance in government. Buzzwords like *evaluations, outcomes,* and *results* are associated with this tide. Achieving high-performance goals falls to frontline employees, teams, and evaluators. At the national level, the impetus for liberation management is generally the president. The most visible participant, however, was Vice President Al Gore, who promoted various National Performance Review initiatives during his time in office. The 1993 Government Performance and Results Act is a defining statute and expression of this philosophy. Al Gore and Richard Nixon (because of his interest in reorganization) are identified as patron saints of this tide; the Alliance for Redesigning Government is the patron organization.

Liberation management has implications for the management of people in government. Public administration trends toward employee empowerment, reengineering, work teams, continuous improvement, customer service, flattened hierarchies, and self-directed employees reflect a breakdown of the tall hierarchical bureaucracies in many settings and a move toward organizational "liberation." Belief in harmonious relations between labor and management increases the prospects for productive partnerships. Decentralization of personnel management expands authority and discretion of line agencies and gives managers freedom to achieve provable results. Before these strategies are implemented, it is necessary for managers to determine the readiness of employees and units to assume new responsibilities, forge new relationships, and increase outputs. Line administrators can facilitate this state of readiness by identifying likely candidates for training and development and by tailoring incentives to the particular motivational needs of individual employees. Liberation management is sometimes at odds with the war on waste, which advocates high levels of bureaucratic controls, and the watchful eye, which is suspicious of the discretion of civil servants in general. Although the public sector will certainly not banish bureaucracy, greater flexibility is evident at all levels of government and is likely to increase in the future.

Tide Philosophies in Legislation

Two landmark pieces of legislation affecting federal human resource management can be assessed using Light's framework: the **Pendleton Act of 1883**, which introduced the merit system to the federal government, and the **Civil Service Reform Act of 1978 (CSRA)**, which refined the merit system and modified the institutions by which it operates. As Light (1997) notes, the Pendleton Act is "a signal moment in the march of scientific management, but it also involved a war on waste, a bit of watchful eye, and an ultimate hope for liberation management" (p. 18). He observes that the CSRA manifests each of the four tides: *comprehensive*

[A] Senior Executive Service (SES) to strengthen the presidential chain of command (scientific management), a cap on total federal employment to save money (war on waste), whistleblower protection to assure truth telling from the inside (watchful eye), and pay for performance to reward employees for doing something more than just show up for work (liberation management). (p. 71)

Understanding the **tides of reform** helps us to appreciate the public service heritage because the tides highlight recurring themes that characterize such changes (Exhibit 1.8). Paradoxes are also apparent: Two of the reform tides—the war on waste and the watchful eye—are based on mistrust and cynicism regarding government; the two other tides—scientific management and liberation management—reflect trust and confidence in government. The paradox is that reform reflects both trust and distrust in government, and it may cause both as well. As the Pendleton Act and the CSRA demonstrate, however, these conflicting impulses are embedded in these more comprehensive landmark laws dealing with human resource management (and many other statutes as well). Less comprehensive reforms may involve only one or two of the tides of reform.

Institutional structures and procedures are important because managers must operate through them to achieve their objectives. These institutional arrangements have evolved over time, and understanding their purposes, functions, and limitations helps managers to

Exhibit 1.8   The Tides of Reform

Key Characteristics	Scientific Management	War on Waste	Watchful Eye	Liberation Management
Goal	Efficiency	Economy	Fairness	Higher performance
Key input(s)	Principles of administration	Generally accepted practices	Rights	Standards, evaluations
Key products	Structure, rules	Findings (audits, investigations)	Information, legal protections	Outcomes, results

Key Characteristics	Scientific Management	War on Waste	Watchful Eye	Liberation Management
Key participants	Experts	Inspectors general, the media	Whistleblowers, interest groups, the news media, the public, employees	Frontline employees, teams, evaluators
Institutional champion(s)	The presidency	Congressional committees	Congress and the courts	The presidency
Defining moment(s)	Brownlow Committee, first Hoover Commission	Welfare fraud hearings	Vietnam, Watergate	Gore National Performance Review
Defining statutes	1939 Reorganization Act; 1990 Financial Officers Act; 2002 Homeland Security Act	1978 Inspector General Act; 1992 Federal Housing Enterprises Financial Safety and Soundness Act	1946 Administrative Procedure Act; 1989 Ethics Reform Act	1993 Government Performance and Results Act
Patron saint(s)	Herbert Hoover	W. R. Grace, Jack Anderson	John Gardner, Ralph Nader	Richard Nixon, Al Gore
Patron organization(s)	National Academy of Public Administration (Standing Panel on Executive Organization)	Citizens Against Government Waste	Common Cause, Public Citizen	Alliance for Redesigning Government
HRM examples	Principles of hierarchy, chain of command, consistency, and standardization; productivity measurement and efficiency measures	Processes to minimize idle time, install time clocks, audit travel vouchers and phone records, inventory office supplies, and monitor attendance and punctuality	Extensive legislation related to how hiring, promotion, labor relations, and a host of other activities are conducted; promotion of transparency and sunshine requirements	Focus on employee empowerment, reengineering, teams, continuous improvement, customer service, flattened hierarchies, and self-directed employees; more emphasis on results than on processes

SOURCE: Adapted from P. C. Light, *The Tides of Reform: Making Government Work* 1945-1995 (New Haven, CT: Yale University Press), pp. 21, 26, 32, and 37. © Copyright 1997 by Yale University Press.

think strategically about the threats and opportunities in their human resource environments and how to cope with them. Next, we examine the goals and characteristics of these institutions.

Institutional Context

As noted above, the Pendleton Act of 1883 and the CSRA of 1978 established the institutional framework for federal human resource management. The Pendleton Act created the bipartisan Civil Service Commission as a protective buffer against the partisan pressures from the executive and legislative branches. It also served as a model for use by reformers seeking change in subnational governments. The merit system was established as a result of this act (the contemporary version of merit system principles is discussed more fully later in this chapter), but its coverage was initially limited to one in ten federal workers. Competitive practical exams were introduced, and a neutral (nonpartisan), competent, career civil service with legally mandated tenure was expected to carry out the business of government. Entry into the civil service was permitted at any level in the hierarchy, unlike systems where new recruits were required to start at the entry level and work their way up.

The reform movement that led to the Pendleton Act was clear about what it was against but less clear about what it favored. This has led some observers to describe the reformers' efforts as essentially negative. They wanted to get rid of the **spoils system** (appointments based on political favor) and the evils (graft, corruption, waste, incompetence) associated with it. Separating politics from administration was key to accomplishing this objective. Using moralistic arguments, reformers campaigned against what was "bad" in the civil service (politics and spoils) and, to a lesser extent, promoted "good" government (e.g., appointments based on merit) and improved efficiency. (See Chapter 4 for further discussion of this topic.)

Although 95 years of experience with the Pendleton Act's institutional arrangements showed mixed results, by the mid- to late 1970s it was clear that the existing federal personnel system aimed at efficiency was, paradoxically, often inefficient. Among the problems were entrenched civil servants hindering executive initiatives, difficulty in removing incompetent employees, ease of circumventing merit system requirements, managerial frustration at cumbersome rules and red tape, and conflict in the roles of the Civil Service Commission. President Jimmy Carter proposed reforms to address these problems.

The CSRA of 1978 was built on the Pendleton Act and altered the institutional arrangement for federal personnel management. In place of the Civil Service Commission, two new institutions were created: the **U.S. Office of Personnel Management (OPM)** and the **U.S. Merit Systems Protection Board (MSPB)**. The OPM is charged with the "doing" side of human resource management—coordinating the federal government's personnel program. The director is appointed or removed by the president and functions as the president's principal adviser on personnel matters. The MSPB is the adjudicatory side, hearing employee appeals and investigating reported merit system violations. Two other important provisions in the CSRA were the creation of the **Federal Labor Relations Authority (FLRA)** and the establishment of the **Senior Executive Service (SES)**. The FLRA functions as the federal sector counterpart to the private sector's National Labor Relations Board. It is charged with overseeing, investigating, announcing, and enforcing rules pertaining to labor–management relations. The SES comprises top-level administrators—mostly career civil servants and a lesser number of political appointees. It sought (but failed) to establish a European-like professional administrative class of senior executives who may be assigned or reassigned based on performance and ability. The structures created by the CSRA for human resource management are depicted in Exhibit 1.9.

State and local jurisdictions have varied institutional arrangements, but in many cases these governments have patterned their structures after those at the federal level. In some instances, state and local governments have provided models for federal human resource management reforms. Parallelism between federal and subnational governments is seen in the existence of civil service commissions, guardian appeals boards protecting the merit system, executive personnel systems, and employee relations boards, among other features. Civil service reform encompasses the efforts undertaken by groups or individuals to alter the nature of government service. The CSRA and its state and local counterparts have been the subject of recent criticism from those who wish to reform policies and practices. The next section briefly addresses reformer actions and proposals since 1992.

REFORMING GOVERNMENT IN THE CLINTON, BUSH, AND OBAMA YEARS

Federal Level

Administrative change has been a recurring item on the public agenda for the past 25 years. Spurred by David Osborne and Ted Gaebler's 1992 book *Reinventing Government,* reforms at the federal level started in 1993 with the Clinton administration's National Performance Review (NPR; later renamed National Partnership for Reinventing Government). The goal was to achieve government that "works better, costs less, and gets results Americans care about" (Kamensky, 1999). The key focus of reinvention and NPR was to achieve government that would be catalytic, empowering, enterprising, competitive, mission and customer driven, anticipatory, results oriented, decentralized, and market oriented. This very large reform movement was clearly liberation management oriented in thrust, but it also contained smaller elements of scientific management (i.e., reorganizing for greater efficiency), war on waste (i.e., cutting the federal workforce substantially), and watchful eye (i.e., providing enormous publicity around the change process).

Reformers identified the link between performance improvement and the personnel system. In general, they detected flaws in the system rather than in the individual civil servants, and they harshly criticized the counterproductive civil service system, which they viewed as beyond redemption. Bilmes and Neal (2003) summarized the problems facing civil service systems:

> Hiring, firing, promotion, organizational structure, lack of lateral opportunities, insufficient training, poor compensation, limited awards and recognition, few fringe benefits, lack of career development, legalistic dispute resolution, inflexibility, poor performance measurement and evaluation, use of contractors for mission-critical activities, antiquated information technology, and unhealthy, unsanitary office facilities. (pp. 115–116)

Exhibit 1.9 Structures Created by the Civil Service Reform Act of 1978

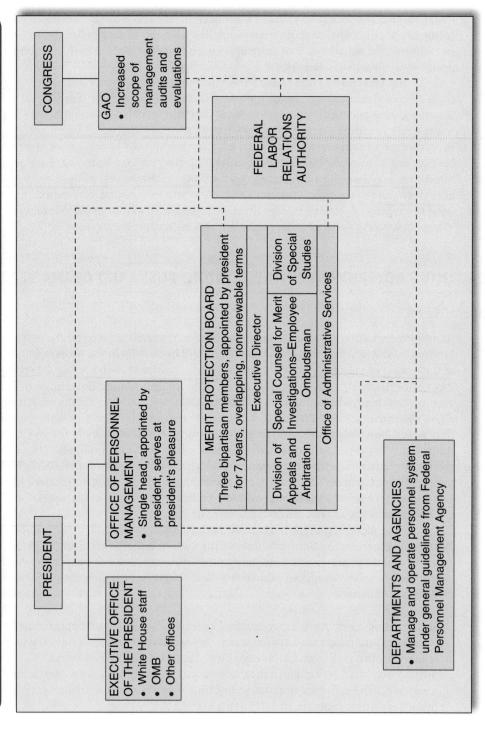

SOURCE: President's Reorganization Project. (1977). Personnel management project: Final staff report. Washington, DC: U.S. Government Printing Office.

Academics and professional groups proposed administrative changes in response to such problems (see, e.g., Donahue & Nye, 2003; National Academy of Public Administration, 2004). Some of these reform proposals echoed past calls for governmentwide reorganization, such as the report of the 1989 National Commission on the Public Service, also known as the Volcker Commission, and anticipated more recent reform recommendations as well, such as those of the 2003 Volcker Commission. The earlier report identified the so-called quiet crisis facing civil service and recommended several familiar changes, including increased salaries, performance-based pay, simplified hiring, fewer political appointees, and improved training. The latter report followed characterizations of the federal civil service as a system at risk (Blunt, 2002; Lane, Wolf, & Woodard, 2003). Indeed, in 2001 U.S. Comptroller General David Walker elevated human capital to the U.S. Government Accountability Office's list of "high-risk government operations" (a designation recently renewed), stating that agencies are vulnerable to mission failure when they lack a focus on human capital development.

A retrospective on civil service reform over the years argues that the 1990s revealed the disaggregation of the federal civil service. This little-noticed phenomenon resulted in slightly fewer than half of all executive branch employees becoming part of the excepted service, thereby relinquishing many traditional civil service protections. In the quest for increased managerial flexibility, the Clinton administration pursued a three-pronged strategy: (1) authorizing personnel demonstration projects, (2) creating "performance-based organizations," and (3) constructing modified personnel systems for malfunctioning agencies (Thompson, 2001, p. 91).

The George W. Bush administration (2001–2009) had its own management reform agenda for addressing management dysfunctions. Five key areas were highlighted: human capital, competitive sourcing, financial performance, e-government, and budget–performance integration. The first two areas are most relevant to human resource management. The administration's initiatives focused on people-related problems, giving greatest attention to the need for organizational restructuring, performance measurement, performance-based pay, hiring and development plans to fill key skill gaps, competitive sourcing, and information technology. For example, the 2001 Freedom to Manage Initiative and Managerial Flexibility Act sought to "eliminate legal barriers to effective management," just as Clinton's NPR reinvention reforms sought to move "from red tape to results." The Federal Activities Inventory Reform Act required agencies to assess the susceptibility to competition of the activities performed by their workforces in anticipation of placing federal workers in competition with the private sector. In the words of one analyst, such reforms "contain the excesses of Madisonian protection" and "promote the opportunity for Hamiltonian performance" (Behn, 2003, p. 199).

The Bush administration stressed the need to manage human capital strategically by obtaining the talent to get the job done, seeking continuity of competent leadership, and creating a results-oriented performance culture (U.S. OMB, 2004). To monitor implementation of the agenda, the administration developed a simple grading system—red, yellow, and green. Key federal agencies were assessed regarding their achievement of the standards for success.

Some of the proposed and adopted reforms were particularly contentious, including the increased flexibility of personnel policies in the Department of Homeland Security and the Department of Defense, the overhaul of pay for the SES, performance-based contracting, modification of the number of political appointees, withdrawal of collective bargaining rights for selected groups of public employees, weakening of the merit system, and the requirement for competitive sourcing (Bowman & West, 2007; Kauffman, 2003; Phinney, 2003; Thompson, 2007). The reforms in DHS and DOD were justified at the time by national security arguments and claims that increasing managerial power and flexibility were necessary to deal with the threat of terrorist attacks (Brook & King, 2008).

While current reform trends in the United States involve weakening formal civil service protections in order to enhance managerial control of the bureaucracy, reformers in some parts of the world, such as developing countries and former communist states, are seeking to strengthen protections to insulate the civil service from political manipulation (see Exhibit 1.10). Civil service reforms in Germany parallel some of the changes in the United States (see Exhibit 1.11).

Among the human resource management reforms of the Obama administration have been a focus on a more rapid hiring process; the Work-Life initiative, which includes job satisfaction and wellness programs; and the Results-Only Work Environment initiative (Berry, 2009).

Exhibit 1.10   The Evolution of Civil Service Systems as They Balance Demands and Needs

Civil service systems have at least three major constituents that they are trying to please. First among these are the *political masters* of the systems, whose primary interest is responsiveness. At a minimum, political masters want responsiveness to the laws that they pass, no matter whether those laws are regarding authorities, expenditures, or reporting requirements. Political executives (e.g., governors and presidents) would like to influence the selection of administrative leaders, and legislators would like to have a say through a confirmation process. Political masters would also like to select rank-and-file public employees, but this practice is highly limited in advanced democracies because it is so prone to corruption and inefficiency. The first step in moving from a relatively primitive administrative system to one that has a reservoir of expertise and continuity is generally to set up hiring and position management systems that elicit and maintain the neutral competence of the sophisticated and complex operations of government. Such systems keep political masters at arm's length from rank-and-file employees. Today, many developing countries and former communist states are grappling with this first phase of anticorruption reform.

The second constituency that a civil service system must please consists of the bureaucracy and *civil servants* themselves, whose primary interest is professionalism. At a minimum, they want to ensure that they are recruited fairly (i.e., based on their technical merits), that their agencies' actions are consistent with widely held professional standards, and that they will be able to use their professional judgment within the confines of legal parameters without political intrusiveness. This dovetails well with the need to keep political elites away from the day-to-day management of personnel or detailed policy implementation. However, over time, problems can seep into civil service systems. Bureaucrats can become too comfortable and secure, resulting in outmoded or poor performance. For example, political elites can set up so many safeguards for performance that the transaction costs of compliance become very high and experimentation is discouraged. Most advanced democracies have been dealing with these issues since the late 1970s. One response is modernization—that is, to update systems technologically, to rationalize and streamline overlapping or outdated legislation, and to require new performance standards. Modernization has been much promoted in continental Europe.

The third constituency to be pleased comprises those being served: *taxpayers and "customers,"* whose primary interests are efficiency and service. Taxpayers want the lowest cost for the most service,

(Continued)

which is to say good value. Customers generally want the best service possible no matter the cost, since they rarely pay directly or their fees are subsidized. In traditional administrative systems, few opportunities for meaningful attention to complaints exist; generally political or judicial remedies are required, and this sets a high bar for complainants. However, other ways to control for efficiency include setting up competition (e.g., contracting out services) and improving service by implementing rigorous customer responsiveness measures. This perspective is representative of the **New Public Management (NPM)**. NPM has been the preferred reform approach of most of the Anglo world and Scandinavia, but it has not left continental Europe untouched, as Exhibit 1.11 illustrates.

Sources of Competing Demands and Values in Reform

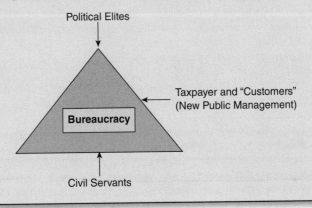

SOURCE: Van Wart, Hondeghem, and Schwella (2014).

Exhibit 1.11   Germany's Civil Service: Prestige or Performance?

The German civil service is based on the concept of the *Rechtsstaat*—the "rule-of-law state" that transcends political divisions and acts in the name of all citizens on the basis of administrative law. After World War II, the system was decentralized to put the focus on regional and local civil service. The German federal bureaucracy is thus relatively small, with the bulk of civil servants working in the 16 *Länder* (states) and local governments.

   The foundations of the German civil service are designed to make public service the most highly respected of all professions (Dahrendorf, 1969, pp. 235–241), since civil servants act in the name of the state and reinforce constitutional principles. As of the late 1990s, there was an "overabundance of candidates for a small number of positions" in German public administration, leading to "a rise in the number of higher educational degrees and thus to an oversupply of highly-qualified persons" (Rothenbacher, 1997, para. 34), due largely, no doubt, to the traditionally high status, pay, and benefits that accompanied public service careers in Germany. Government leaders have been attempting to change what has been considered to be an overly bureaucratic civil service system since the 1970s.

(Continued)

Exhibit 1.11 (Continued)

After the incorporation of the former East Germany into the Federal Republic of Germany (and its inflated bureaucracy) and the consequent financial crises at all levels of government after 1990, reformers in government managed to initiate a series of personnel management reforms in 1997, when the German parliament passed the Civil Service Reform Law. The goal was to improve technical performance and rationalization (modernization) and managerial flexibility and customer focus (NPM) through the following measures:

- Increased employee productivity in the context of reduced costs and personnel downsizing
- Integrated personnel management to enhance staff productivity and satisfaction
- Probationary periods for promoted individuals, with the option of denial of promotion
- Performance measures and personnel evaluations based on results, not process
- The ongoing motivation of employees to excel
- Promotion and pay based on performance, not seniority
- Increased flextime and part-time work
- Soft management techniques to improve organizational culture and leadership development
- Outsourcing of public services to commercial and nonprofit organizations

Not surprisingly, the personal, political, and structural resistance to reforms was great. Civil servants who were used to generous salaries and benefits, as well as clear guidelines about promotion and pay, rebelled against performance-based outcomes and probationary periods, the elimination of their traditional "13th month" paychecks, and reduction in pensions (Zagelmeyer, 1997, pp. 2–3). Germany's public service trade unions, more influential than those in the United States, for example, strongly resisted the reforms that reduced benefits or job security (see Chapter 12). A system based on codified administrative law does not easily adapt to management reforms that emphasize autonomy and creativity in the middle layers of the bureaucracy. Administrative managers tended to view personnel strategies in terms of cost rather than productivity (Kuhlmann & Roeber, 2004, p. 21). Supervisors hesitated to implement pay-for-performance reforms or offer performance bonuses (see Chapter 7) out of concern that this would introduce tension and resentment in the workplace; many civil servants suspected that the reforms were simply an excuse to downsize and reduce pay and benefits (Kuhlmann & Roeber, 2004, pp. 19, 21). Nonetheless, the culture has been made more responsive. Following worldwide trends, the head civil servants (equivalent to permanent secretaries in the British system) now have terms rather than tenure. The privatization of the railway system and the post office and the introduction of e-government are other reforms that have been implemented since 2000. Today the German public service is considerably smaller than it was in the 1990s (Kuhlmann, Bogumil, & Veit, 2014).

Government reformers hope that the features that rendered German civil service the proudest of professions in the past have not hindered contemporary performance in a profession still much revered by the public and one considered to be among the least corrupt in the world (Freedom House, 2013).

Recruitment and selection reforms include process mapping with streamlined, plain-language job announcements, involvement of management in the hiring process, and timely applicant notification. The OPM facilitates the sharing of best practices across agencies and holds training academies to disseminate information on successful hiring strategies. Metrics are used to evaluate manager involvement and satisfaction with the process (Moore, 2014).

In seeking to improve employee satisfaction and promote wellness, the OPM instructs managers to review the Federal Employee Viewpoint Survey (formerly the Federal Human Capital Survey) to identify items and indexes on which their units scored lowest in comparison to the rest of the government and to isolate items and indexes on which employee satisfaction declined in their units since the prior survey. The administrators are then charged with determining the reasons for worker dissatisfaction and work with labor organizations (where appropriate) on strategies to improve worker satisfaction. Managers must create action plans with improvement targets specified. Regarding wellness, managers are expected to inventory current wellness activities (e.g., fitness facilities, health clinics) and to develop agency performance metrics for assessing wellness as well as to collect cost and utilization data. Health and wellness improvement targets and plans are submitted to the OPM with annual budget requests.

The Results-Only Work Environment (ROWE) initiative was first implemented in the private sector at Best Buy and subsequently adapted to government by the Hennepin County, Minnesota, Human Services and Public Health Department. The OPM started the federal government's first ROWE pilot test in 2010. Consistent with the Clinton and Bush administrations' emphasis on results-oriented management, the program expected managers "to manage for results, rather than process. Employees are trusted to get the work done. This is a shift in culture from permission granting to performance guiding," according to a senior adviser to the OPM. In practice, according to the adviser, ROWE means that "each person is free to do whatever they want, whenever they want, as long as the work gets done" (quoted in FedSmith, 2010). Pilot test results were promising, and ROWE was promoted as a model for other units to see whether flexibility can succeed in a federal government setting (see Chapter 10 for additional discussion of ROWE).

State and Local Levels

The National Commission on the State and Local Public Service, commonly known as the Winter Commission, published a report in 1993 outlining an agenda targeting, among other institutions, civil service systems. The human resource portion of this report diagnosed *civil service paralysis* as a problem and prescribed deregulation of government's personnel system. Favoring a more flexible and less rule-bound system, the Winter Commission recommended the following:

- Greater decentralization of the merit system
- Reduced reliance on written tests
- Rejection of the rule of three and other requirements that severely restrict managerial discretion in selecting from a pool of eligible applicants
- Reduction of the weight given to seniority and veterans' preference
- Reduction in the number of job classifications
- Implementation of less cumbersome procedures for removing employees from positions
- Greater portability of pensions, enabling government-to-government mobility
- Greater flexibility to provide financial incentives for exemplary performance by work teams

These recommendations for increased managerial flexibility echoed suggestions from the National Commission on the Public Service (1989, 2003) and resembled parallel observations from the Clinton administration's National Performance Review and the Bush administration's Management Agenda (F. J. Thompson, 1994; J. R. Thompson, 2007). The recommendations of these commissions continue to be relevant, as they guide jurisdictions in shaping human resource management policies.

Subnational reforms have included significant changes to the civil service system, generally reducing civil service protections. The first state to undertake such reforms was Georgia, which withdrew merit protection for all new state employees beginning in 1996; Arizona followed a similar pattern in 2012, making state employment primarily at-will. Florida's substantial reform in 2001 withdrew civil service protection from more than 16,000 managers, making them at-will employees who could be terminated for any or no reason not contrary to law (West & Bowman, 2004). Six other states have also experienced notable reforms (Massachusetts, Minnesota, New Jersey, Ohio, Oklahoma, and South Carolina). Reforms are most common in classification (reduction or increase in the number of job classifications, consolidation or broadbanding of classifications), compensation (pay for performance, noncash incentives, bonuses, incentive-based pay), and performance evaluation (performance plans and standards). Managers' ability to complete their tasks successfully depends, in large measure, on their ability to attract, develop, motivate, and retain top-quality employees—the essential functions of human resource management. Reform efforts are designed to help managers meet these responsibilities. Since the beginning of the Great Recession in 2008, pension reform has been seen in most U.S. states, and many (such as Wisconsin) have introduced reforms limiting the scope of influence of unions.

The prognosis for reform efforts is more mixed than might be expected given the emerging consensus that formed in the mid- to late 2000s. Efforts to reform human resource management have not been without their critics and skeptics (e.g., Bowman & West, 2007; Bowman, West, & Gertz, 2006; Coggburn et al., 2010; Elling & Thompson, 2007; Hays & Sowa, 2007; Kearney & Hays, 1998; Kellough & Nigro, 2010). Following is a sampling of some of the shortcomings of reform efforts, according to critics:

- The role of public servants (e.g., privatization, downsizing) is undermined.
- Results fail to meet expectations (e.g., pay for performance).
- Too few people with the necessary skills (e.g., contract negotiating and auditing) are attracted to public service.
- Performance rewards (bonuses) are underfunded.
- Oversight of the public service (decentralization, deregulation, outsourcing) is reduced, inviting corruption.
- In-service training for continuous learning and planning is frequently inadequate.
- Pursuit of quick successes via downsizing too often takes precedence over improving performance.
- Ideas borrowed from the private sector and accepted blindly often create more problems than solutions.
- Empowerment initiatives frequently have uneven results.

Overall, civil service reform efforts have experienced a combination of success, failure, and something in between (Bowman, 2002; Bowman, Gertz, Gertz, & Williams, 2003; Bowman & West, 2007; Coggburn et al., 2010; Condrey & Maranto, 2001; Kellough & Nigro, 2006; Perry, Wise, & Martin, 1994; Pfiffner & Brook, 2000; Stein, 1994; Suleiman, 2003; West, 2002; U.S. OMB, 2014). One lesson is that when change advocates leave office, reform quickly loses salience as an issue.

The impetus to improve performance and reduce costs, stated goals of the Clinton, Bush, and Obama administrations and implied objectives of the Winter Commission, will remain even if the strategies for achieving such goals change. Similarly, it is likely that various forms of experimentation with new approaches to human resource management will continue. These reforms are part of the public service heritage and continue the ebb and flow of the various tides—scientific management, war on waste, watchful eye, and liberation management.

In the next section of this chapter, the discussion shifts from what is changing to what remains constant.

HUMAN RESOURCE MANAGEMENT PRINCIPLES

Administrators need to be mindful not only of the dynamic environment and the reforms that occur in it but also of overarching principles that endure in human resource management. Four such principles, in particular, should be in the forefront of managerial thinking related to human resource management. These principles are further explored in this and subsequent chapters. Managers must adhere to the following principles:

1. *Understand the values inherent in the career public service.* Public employees, from elected officials to rank-and-file workers, agree that the public's interests must be foremost and the rule of law unquestioned. Yet, because the public's interests are many, there are many roles for public service. Stakeholders expect civil servants to do many different things (ensure effective government performance, implement controversial social policies, respond to political imperatives, and others). Often civil servants are called on to respond to conflicting pressures simultaneously, and managers need to provide leadership in reconciling competing demands (e.g., designing layoffs to balance the budget and simultaneously addressing other factors, such as adhering to the principle of seniority, complying with equal employment opportunity and affirmative action requirements, meeting performance standards, and ensuring organizational effectiveness). An overriding priority of the core of the civil service, however defined, has been and will continue to be an ethos that insulates it from political manipulation in staffing and encourages disclosure of wrongdoing or gross mismanagement.

Merit and merit-light systems dominate advanced democracies, and managers must internalize the rules or principles of these systems. While increased flexibility in hiring and removal has become more common, even the more dramatic reforms do not advocate the elimination of the values that undergird merit principles in general. Merit systems ensure the high-quality hiring processes, fairness, integrity, diligence, and competence so important for the long-term integrity of government. They do this by keeping politics at arm's length, thus providing a permanent workforce defined by **neutral competence** rather than by political loyalty (Bowman, West, & Beck, 2010). An excellent example is the U.S. federal government's set of merit principles, which are laid out in Title 5 of the U.S. Code, Section 2301, and listed here in Exhibit 1.12.

Exhibit 1.12   5 U.S. Code § 2301—Merit System Principles

Federal personnel management should be implemented consistent with the following merit system principles:

1. Recruitment should be from qualified individuals from appropriate sources in an endeavor to achieve a work force from all segments of society, and selection and advancement should be determined solely on the basis of relative ability, knowledge, and skills, after fair and open competition which assures that all receive equal opportunity.

2. All employees and applicants for employment should receive fair and equitable treatment in all aspects of personnel management without regard to political affiliation, race, color, religion, national origin, sex, marital status, age, or handicapping condition, and with proper regard for their privacy and constitutional rights.

3. Equal pay should be provided for work of equal value, with appropriate consideration of both national and local rates paid by employers in the private sector, and appropriate incentives and recognition should be provided for excellence in performance.

4. All employees should maintain high standards of integrity, conduct, and concern for the public interest.

5. The Federal work force should be used efficiently and effectively.

6. Employees should be retained on the basis of the adequacy of their performance, inadequate performance should be corrected, and employees should be separated who cannot or will not improve their performance to meet required standards.

7. Employees should be provided effective education and training in cases in which such education and training would result in better organizational and individual performance.

8. Employees should be—

   (A) protected against arbitrary action, personal favoritism, or coercion for partisan political purposes, and

   (B) prohibited from using their official authority or influence for the purpose of interfering with or affecting the result of an election or a nomination for election.

9. Employees should be protected against reprisal for the lawful disclosure of information which the employees reasonably believe evidences—

   (A) a violation of any law, rule, or regulation, or

   (B) mismanagement, a gross waste of funds, an abuse of authority, or a substantial and specific danger to public health or safety.

Traditional merit systems have emphasized fairness by maximizing consistency with predetermined rules, due process, and pay standardization. **Merit-light systems** function in an orderly way on the basis of qualifications, performance, and competitive selection, but in comparison with full merit systems they allow more managerial discretion in the determination of recruitment, promotion, rewards, and punishments. Full merit systems tend to be somewhat prone to rigidity, whereas merit-light systems are vulnerable to political and managerial cronyism.

2. *Understand and integrate non–civil service systems as appropriate.* Civil servants may have their specialized systems, relying heavily on merit principles internally, but the civil service must work with and integrate other types of non–civil service personnel systems. First and foremost, the civil service is a subordinate part of a larger democratic political system. The political system interprets "merit" largely through the ballot box and appointment for the highest-level policy positions (e.g., a governor and his or her department heads and the division directors under the department heads), rather than through organizational rationality, as is true of the civil service. Understanding and respecting the political system and the role of political masters is critical for managers and leaders in administrative systems. Public services historically have been delivered largely by civil service employees; however, the use of alternative mechanisms has increased (e.g., purchase of service agreements, privatization, franchise agreements, subsidy arrangements, vouchers, volunteers, self-help, regulatory and tax incentives). These arrangements affect managers by redefining relationships with service providers, altering control structures, and reshaping administrative roles (Klingner, 2009). Thus, managers have to work with the private and nonprofit sectors closely, understanding and appreciating their values and strengths, while ensuring that the interests of the public are maintained. This increased attention to reinvigorating the public sector has led to an adjustment in assumptions and working ideals. Managers need to assess the systems in their jurisdictions and adjust their leadership styles as appropriate.

3. *Understand that the public has rights beyond merit principles.* Another distinguishing feature of human resource management is that government decisions are subject to intense public visibility and scrutiny. This influences how work is done, how resources are managed, how decisions are made, and how systems are developed. Unlike the business sector, where decisions usually are made in private (because the Freedom of Information Act does not apply), public administration decision making typically requires citizen access and input. Officials must remember that they are accountable to the populace, but they often face tension between their primary responsibility to all citizens and loyalty to their organizational superiors or their own consciences.

Related to accountability, the principle of transparency is fundamental to effective and ethical government. Open-meeting and open-records laws help to advance the ideal of government transparency and increase citizen trust in policy implementation. Those in public service should be as open as possible about all their decisions and actions, providing rationales for their decisions and restricting information only when sharing it would jeopardize the broader civic interest or compromise legitimate privacy rights.

4. *Provide leadership for the workforce.* Given the labor-intensive characteristics of public organizations, the effective and efficient use of human capital is of paramount importance. Leadership from managers and human resource professionals is a crucial ingredient for achieving the goals and advancing the public service mission of government. Human resource managers must partner with top management in guiding organizational change initiatives. Additionally, high-performing organizations invest in people and pursue best practices. Strategic use of human capital is crucial to the success of organizations like the Government Accountability Office and the Defense Logistics Agency (see Bilmes & Gould, 2009). While the economic downturn limited the extent of human capital investment, the transition from the Bush administration to the Obama administration resulted in renewed emphasis on "insourcing" service provision that had previously been outsourced and on revitalizing partnerships with unions (Ban & Gossett, 2010). While building a people-focused culture is a challenge in many departments, it is a central responsibility of those responsible for the government's human resources.

Building on this brief review of overarching principles, we turn in the next section to a more refined look at values, ethics, and the management of ethics.

VALUES, ETHICS, AND MORAL MANAGEMENT

Values

Managers walk a tightrope as they seek to balance the jurisdiction's basic values, the needs of workers, and the organization's financial resources. When there is uncertainty about fundamental values, no matter whether it is because of reforms or organizational challenges, officials may lack direction in dealing with workplace issues. While reforms rarely shift values and norms dramatically, they can have a subtle impact that managers and HR specialists must understand, incorporate procedurally, and communicate effectively to subordinates.

Clarification of basic values is important, and providing such clarification requires an appreciation of employee values and ethical awareness. There is considerable variation among people regarding the degree of individual or organizational value consciousness. Van Wart (1998) divides value consciousness into three levels: (1) unconsciousness, (2) elementary, and (3) advanced. Administrators at Level 1—values unconsciousness—lack understanding or basic awareness of agency values, missions, or standard operating procedures, and they may knowingly or unconsciously take inappropriate or illegal actions. At Level 2—elementary values consciousness—managers have a basic grasp of the missions, laws, and rules, and they focus on conforming in order to avoid legal violations or inappropriate actions. Managers at Level 3—advanced values consciousness—have a thorough understanding of their units' missions, values, and mandates. They can take actions that reflect the ideals associated with good government, such as efficiency, economy, ethics, fairness, and the common good.

The distinctions among the various levels of values consciousness have important implications. If employees lack awareness of agency values, missions, laws, or standard operating procedures, managers need to educate them. For example, ignorance of sexual harassment laws, affirmative action requirements, or workplace safety procedures (Level 1) can be very costly to an organization; managers must not tolerate such ignorance. Furthermore, mere conformity to laws, rules, and standard operating procedures (Level 2) puts administrators in the role of compliance officers who spend their time detecting and correcting wrongdoing. This is an important role for them, but it should not be their exclusive activity. A more expansive perspective is found at Level 3, where officials are fully conversant with agency values, missions, and requirements and view human resources as precious assets for improving governmental performance.

Conflicts among fundamental values create dilemmas once values are applied. For instance, Americans value both liberty and equality. Nevertheless, programs such as affirmative action may promote equality by preventing discrimination but infringe on the liberty of managers to hire or promote whomever they prefer. Other administrative values are also in tension: change and continuity, unfettered flexibility and unbending centralized control, and responsiveness to elected officials and respect for institutional memory (Smith, 1998). Seeking the proper balance among competing values is a major challenge. For example, timeliness and openness are competing values in hiring that are particularly intractable: It is difficult to hire quickly when jurisdictions require that all citizens have access to jobs. An additional example of conflict is seen in a situation in which a vacancy could be filled quickly because a qualified candidate is already known, but laws and organizational values require public announcement, open competition, and recruiting to ensure a diverse talent pool.

Ethics and Moral Management

Clarifying values, raising consciousness of values, and balancing conflicting values must be accompanied by an emphasis on ethics. Ethics involves behavior that is concerned with doing the right thing or acting on the right values.

Here, too, managers have a difficult task: They must exercise discretion in addressing specific ethical issues. Ethical judgment is required of managers facing complex issues in which there are competing values, such as the following (Brumback, 1991; Grensing-Pophal, 1998; Menzel, 2010; Theedom, 1995):

- Responding to instructions to fire a public health nurse for refusing on religious grounds to distribute birth control (e.g., condoms or birth control pills) to unmarried individuals
- Honoring a request to refuse to consider female job applicants age 30 or older
- Investigating a report by a third party that an employee was abusing legal substances (prescription drugs or alcohol) at work
- Reporting to coworkers who accidentally discovered information about pending layoffs
- Resolving a struggle between the benefits administration and the medical department over the length of time an employee can be absent from work following a surgical procedure

- Disciplining an employee for going on a binge of purchasing activity at the end of the fiscal year
- Reprimanding those who shirk distasteful responsibilities or scapegoat others for their personal failures
- Reporting to supervisors observations of employee loafing and loitering
- Coping with pressure to reassign newly hired minority supervisors because they do not "appear to fit" the prevailing organizational culture
- Questioning the high pay levels and job security given to core staff when employees on the periphery are paid low wages and offered minimal job security

In dealing with issues of legality, ethics, and fairness such as those listed above, managers are indeed required to weigh competing pressures. They are often squeezed from above and below in resolving such matters. Officials are also expected to conform to the organization's stated values and ethics codes. At a minimum, they must communicate the organization's policies and codes to employees (Level 1). Ideally, such policies or codes should be brief, be clear, and provide practical guidance to help managers and employees deal with problems. Typical provisions might include policies regarding conflict of interest, gift giving or receiving, confidentiality, sexual harassment, political activity, equal employment opportunities, and moonlighting (Bowman & West, 2014; Pickard, 1995; Van Wart, 2003; West & Berman, 2006). If policies or codes are adopted, they also need to be observed, so that there is no gap between expectations and behavior.

The strategies for ensuring integrity at work—**moral management**—might differ from setting to setting and from one subsystem to another, but ethics management is an important responsibility for administrators. The following are some of the approaches to ethics management addressed in the personnel literature (Lewis & Gilman, 2012; Menzel, 2007; Richter & Burke, 2007; Svara, 2015; Tenbrunsel, Smith-Crowe, & Umphress, 2003; West, 2009; West & Berman, 2006):

1. Modeling exemplary moral leadership to top officials
2. Adopting an organizational credo that promotes aspirational values
3. Developing and enforcing a code of ethics
4. Conducting an ethics audit
5. Using ethics as a criterion in hiring and promotion
6. Including ethics in employee and management training programs
7. Factoring ethics into performance appraisal

SUMMARY AND CONCLUSION

Managers need to be prepared for a variety of challenges and, as we pointed out at the beginning of the chapter, must make sure that "government has the right people, and the right systems, and ensure the right intentions" (Ehrenhalt, 1998, p. 11). Like Maria Hernandez in the opening section, officials must be able to juggle frenetic work schedules and ensure that personnel issues are not lost in the flurry of daily operations. Administrators must work with (or against) challenging trends such as managing a workforce with highly divergent generational values and expectations, recruiting and motivating a workforce in an antigovernment era, finding ways to innovate and reengineer to counter lean budgetary resources, working within significant personnel shortages, and meeting ever-changing productivity demands. Of course, these constraints are not necessarily unique to government agencies and public sector management.

In terms of systems, we have reviewed the many different ways that human resource management can be organized. Some medium-sized agencies use a centralized model, some devolve responsibilities to HR personnel dispersed in various units, and some use the central HR agency for policy functions and decentralize operations, which is common in larger governmental systems. HR departments typically share responsibilities with line managers, but also occasionally with general counsel, payroll, the executive office or officers, specialized departments such as ones set up for training and development, and/or a civil service commission.

Human resource issues, like other aspects of government, change and evolve. Reforms can emphasize different values and concerns, such as efficiency, economy, fairness, and high performance. The recognition that many issues and the alternatives for addressing them are not new, but rather are recurring manifestations of problems and solutions from earlier historical periods, is fundamental. The waves or "tides" of reform can reflect different corrective emphases—scientific management, war on waste, watchful eye, and liberation management. Good managers are able to retain the best of the past and reform what has become dated or dysfunctional. As Franklin D. Roosevelt observed, "A government without good management is a house built on sand."

Effective human resource problem solving also requires that managers combine appropriate human resource principles with the right intentions. Defining core values and being guided by bedrock principles help administrators make the critical ethical judgments often needed in resolving nettlesome human resource issues. Those principles include understanding how the career public service operates, with its merit approach; understanding non–civil service systems; understanding that the public has rights that relate to human resource management beyond merit principles; and providing leadership for the workforce. Public values are continuously changing, and managers must recognize and guide the change process while being constant in ethics and flexible in method. As Thomas Jefferson said, "In matters of style, swim with the current; in matters of principle, stand like a rock." Managers must decide, amid the turbulence in the public sector environment, when to swim with the current and when to stand against it, not succumbing to pressures that would compromise core values and ethical principles. Further, administrators must be able to help their employees develop the ethical compasses they need to progress from values unconsciousness to advanced values consciousness.

The chapters that follow highlight the practices, paradoxes, problems, and prospects facing those who must function simultaneously as technically skilled managers and as change agents in the 21st-century public service.

KEY TERMS

Civil service
Civil service commission
Civil service reform
Civil Service Reform Act of 1978 (CSRA)
Ethics Reform Act of 1989
Federal Labor Relations Authority (FLRA)
Generation X
Human resource management
Liberation management
Merit-light systems
Merit systems
Moral management
National Partnership for Reinventing
   Government
Neutral competence

New Millennials
New Public Management (NPM)
Pendleton Act of 1883
Personnel administration
POSDCORB
Scientific management
Senior Executive Service (SES)
Spoils system
Strategic human resource management (SHRM)
Tides of reform
U.S. Merit Systems Protection Board (MSPB)
U.S. Office of Personnel Management (OPM)
War on waste
Watchful eye

EXERCISES

Class Discussion

1. Do you think Maria Hernandez is an example of a good human resource director? Why? What advice would you give her? Explain.

2. Identify and discuss some paradoxes and contradictions in the public service heritage. Why are they significant? To what extent do they reflect the two underlying paradoxes discussed in this book's introduction?

3. What are some fundamental differences between the public and private sectors that influence how human resources are managed in these sectors?

4. Using Leonardo da Vinci's parachute (Exhibit 0.2) as inspiration, answer these questions: Which current trends in the government environment are likely to continue in the future? Why? How will future trends influence human resource management?

5. Identify the tides of reform. What are the implications of these four philosophies for human resource management? Evaluate the tides. Which do you consider to be the most valuable philosophy for human resource management?

Team Activities

6. Employing the "25 in 10" technique (Exhibit 0.2), brainstorm the types of ethical dilemmas related to human resource management that you think line and staff managers are likely to encounter at work.

7. Discuss the lessons from each of the four historical tides of reform and how they can influence human resource management decisions.

8. What are the human resource management consequences of different levels of value consciousness?

9. Which ethics management strategies do you think are most effective? Why?

10. Identify the reasons group members are interested in being a part of the public service. Compare your reasons with those listed in Exhibit 1.2.

Individual Assignments

11. Identify several human resource management department websites. Compare what the departments seem to include and how they are organized.

12. Identify several of the recent public sector pension reform initiatives in U.S. states and local governments. Which of the tides of reform are in operation? Look at the federal Chief Human Capital Officers Act of 2002. Which of the tides is in operation for that act?

13. Interview a public manager and ask him or her to describe the most difficult human resource issues he or she has had to deal with. What areas of human resource management did the issues fall into? How were they handled?

14. Compare the U.S. federal merit principles with those of a state government. (For example, the explanation of the merit principles for the state of California are found at http://www.calhr.ca.gov/Training/Pages/performance-management-merit-system-principles.aspx.)

15. Examine an agency's website or interview a knowledgeable manager to discover how many of the moral management techniques discussed in the chapter seem to be operational. Also report on how easy or difficult it is to find information about moral management in the agency you select to examine.

NOTE

1. These paradoxes include, for example, reforms that simultaneously reflect and cause distrust in government, national policies that contradict reform tides, and contradictory restructuring themes embedded in the same statute.

REFERENCES

Abramson, M. A., & Gardner, N. W. (Eds.). (2002). *Human capital 2002*. Lanham, MD: Rowman & Littlefield.

Ban, C., & Gossett, C. W. (2010). The changing role of the human resource office. In S. E. Condrey (Ed.), *Handbook of human resource management in government* (3rd ed., pp. 5–26). San Francisco: Jossey-Bass.

Barr, S. (2005, June 8). Government should consider temporary workers, professors say. *Washington Post*.

Behn, R. D. (2003). Creating leadership capacity for the twenty-first century: Not another technical fix. In J. D. Donahue & J. S. Nye Jr. (Eds.), *For the people: Can we fix public service?* (pp. 191–224). Washington, DC: Brookings Institution Press.

Berry, J. (2009, June 18). *Memorandum for heads of departments and agencies.* Washington, DC: U.S. Office of Personnel Management. Retrieved from http://www.chcoc.gov/Documents/Attachments/Document51.pdf

Bilmes, L. J., & Gould, W. S. (2009). *The people factor: Strengthening America by investing in public service.* Washington, DC: Brookings Institution Press.

Bilmes, L. J., & Neal, J. R. (2003). The people factor: Human resources reform in government. In J. D. Donahue & J. S. Nye Jr. (Eds.), *For the people: Can we fix public service?* (pp. 113–133). Washington, DC: Brookings Institution Press.

Blunt, R. (2002). Organizations growing leaders: Best practices and principles in the public service. In M. A. Abramson & N. W. Gardner (Eds.), *Human capital 2002* (pp. 111–162). Lanham, MD: Rowman & Littlefield.

Bowman, J. S. (2002). At-will employment in Florida government: A naked formula to corrupt public service. *WorkingUSA, 6*(2), 90–102.

Bowman, J. S., Gertz, M. G., Gertz, S. C., & Williams, R. L. (2003). Civil service reform in Florida state government: Employee attitudes 1 year later. *Review of Public Personnel Administration, 23*(4), 286–304.

Bowman, J. S., & West, J. P. (Eds.). (2007). *American public service: Radical reform and the merit system.* New York: Taylor & Francis.

Bowman, J. S., & West, J. P. (2014). *Public service ethics: Individual and institutional responsibilities.* Washington, DC: CQ Press.

Bowman, J. S., West, J. P., & Beck, M. (2010). *Achieving competencies in public service: The professional edge.* Armonk, NY: M. E. Sharpe.

Bowman, J. S., West, J. P., & Gertz, S. C. (2006). Florida's "service first": Radical reform in the Sunshine State. In J. E. Kellough & L. G. Nigro (Eds.), *Civil service reform in the states: Personnel policy and politics at the subnational level* (pp. 145–170). Albany: State University of New York Press.

Brook, D., & King, C. (2008). Federal personnel management reform. *Review of Public Personnel Administration, 28*(3), 205–221.

Brumback, G. (1991). Institutionalizing ethics in government. *Public Personnel Management, 20*(3), 353–363.

Chartered Institute of Personnel and Development. (2013, July). Strategic human resource management: Resource summary. Retrieved from http://www.cipd.co.uk/hr-resources/factsheets/strategic-human-resource-management.aspx

Coggburn, J. D., Battaglio, R. P., Jr., Bowman, J. S., Condrey, S. E., Goodman, D., & West, J. P. (2010). State government human resource professionals' commitment to employment-at-will. *American Review of Public Administration, 40*(2), 189–208.

Condrey, S. E. (Ed.). (2010). *Handbook of human resource management in government* (3rd ed.). San Francisco: Jossey-Bass.

Condrey, S. E., & Maranto, R. (Eds.). (2001). *Radical reform of the civil service.* Lanham, MD: Lexington Books.

Dahrendorf, R. (1969). *Society and democracy in Germany.* New York: Doubleday.

Donahue, J. D., & Nye, J. S., Jr. (Eds.). (2003). *For the people: Can we fix public service?* Washington, DC: Brookings Institution Press.

Education Development Center. (2002, February 1). Service-learning satisfies young people's desire for public service. Retrieved from http://main.edc.org/newsroom/features/LID_report.asp

Ehrenhalt, A. (1998, May). Why governments don't work. *Governing,* pp. 7–11.

Elling, R. C., & Thompson, L. (2007). Dissin' the deadwood or coddling the incompetents? Patterns and issues in employee discipline and dismissal in the states. In J. S. Bowman & J. P. West (Eds.), *American public service: Radical reform and the merit system* (pp. 195–217). New York: Taylor & Francis.

FedSmith. (2010, May 11). "Telework" in the federal government. Retrieved from http://www.fedsmith.com/2010/05/11/telework-federal-government

Freedom House. (2013). *Freedom in the world 2013*. Lanham, MD: Roman & Littlefield.

Grensing-Pophal, L. (1998). Walking the tightrope, balancing risks and gains. *HRMagazine, 11*(43), 112–118.

Guy, M. E., & Newman, M. A. (2010). Valuing diversity: The changing workplace. In S. E. Condrey (Ed.), *Handbook of human resource management in government* (3rd ed., pp. 149–170). San Francisco: Jossey-Bass.

Hannon, S., & Yordi, B. (2011). *Engaging a multi-generational workforce: Practical advice for government managers*. Washington, DC: IBM Center for the Business of Government. Retrieved from http://www .businessofgovernment.org/sites/default/files/Engaging%20a%20Multi-Generational%20Workforce.pdf

Hays, S. W., & Sowa, J. E. (2007). Changes in state civil service systems: A national survey. In J. S. Bowman & J. P. West (Eds.), *American public service: Radical reform and the merit system* (pp. 3–21). New York: Taylor & Francis.

Hornestay, D. (1999, February). The human factor. *Government Executive*. Retrieved from http://www.govexec .com/gpp/0299hr.htm

Ingraham, P. W., Selden, S. C., & Moynihan, D. P. (2000). People and performance: Challenges for the future public service—The report from the Wye River Conference. *Public Administration Review, 60*(1), 54–60.

Kamensky, J. (1999, January). National Partnership for Reinventing Government: A brief history. Retrieved from http://govinfo.library.unt.edu/npr/whoweare/history2.html

Kauffman, T. (2003, April 21). Overhaul at defense: Sweeping personnel authorities proposed for DOD secretary. *Federal Times*, pp. 1, 11.

Kearney, R. C., & Hays, S. W. (1998). Reinventing government: The New Public Management and civil service systems in international perspective. *Review of Public Personnel Administration, 18*(4), 38–54.

Kellough, J. E. (2009). Affirmative action and diversity in the public sector. In S. W. Hays, R. C. Kearney, & J. D. Coggburn (Eds.), *Public human resource management: Problems and prospects* (5th ed., pp. 219–235). New York: Longman.

Kellough, J. E., & Nigro, L. G. (Eds.). (2006). *Civil service reform in the states: Personnel policy and politics at the subnational level*. Albany: State University of New York Press.

Kellough, J. E., & Nigro, L. G. (2010). Civil service reform in the United States: Patterns and trends. In S. E. Condrey (Ed.), *Handbook of human resource management in government* (3rd ed., pp. 73–94). San Francisco: Jossey-Bass.

Klingner, D. E. (2009). Competing perspectives on public personnel administration: Civil service, patronage, and privatization. In S. W. Hays, R. C. Kearney, & J. D. Coggburn (Eds.), *Public human resource management: Problems and prospects* (5th ed., pp. 3–16). New York: Longman.

Kuhlmann, S., Bogumil, J., & Veit, S. (2014). Public service systems at subnational and local levels of government: A British–German–French comparison. In J. C. N. Raadschelders, T. A. J. Toonen, & F. M. Van der Meer (Eds.), *The civil service in the 21st century: Comparative perspectives*. Basingstoke, England: Palgrave Macmillan.

Kuhlmann, S., & Roeber, M. (2004, May 14–15). *Civil service in Germany: Characteristics of public employment and modernization of public personnel management*. Paper presented at the meeting Modernization of State and Administration in Europe: A France–Germany Comparison, Goethe Institute, Bordeaux, France. Retrieved from http://www.uni-konstanz.de/bogumil/kuhlmann/Download/KuhlmannRoeber1.pdf

Lane, L., Wolf, J., & Woodard, C. (2003). Reassessing the human resource crisis in the public service, 1987–2002. *American Review of Public Administration, 33*(2), 123–145.

Lewis, C. W., & Gilman, S. C. (2012). *The ethics challenge in public service: A problem-solving guide* (3rd ed.). San Francisco: Jossey-Bass.

Light, P. C. (1997). *The tides of reform: Making government work, 1945–1995*. New Haven, CT: Yale University Press.

Light, P. C. (1999). *The new public service*. Washington, DC: Brookings Institution Press.

Light, P. C. (2008). *A government ill executed: The decline of the federal service and how to reverse it*. Cambridge, MA: Harvard University Press.

Marston, C. (2007). *Motivating the "What's in it for me?" workforce: Manage across the generational divide and increase profits.* Hoboken, NJ: John Wiley.

Menzel, D. C. (2007). *Ethics management for public administrators: Building organizations of integrity.* Armonk, NY: M. E. Sharpe.

Menzel, D. C. (2010). *Ethics moments in government: Cases and controversies.* New York: Taylor & Francis.

Milakovich, M. E. (2012). *Digital governance: New technologies for improving public service and participation.* New York: Routledge.

Moore, J. (2014, March 26). OPM's focus in hiring reform shifting from speed to quality. Federal News Radio. Retrieved from http://www.federalnewsradio.com/520/3590759/OPMs-focus-in-hiring-reform-shifting-from-speed-to-quality

National Academy of Public Administration. (2004). *Conversations on public service: Performance-based pay in the federal government.* Washington, DC: Author.

National Commission on the Public Service. (1989). *Leadership for America: Rebuilding the public service.* Washington, DC: Author.

National Commission on the Public Service. (2003). *Urgent business for America: Revitalizing the federal government for the 21st century.* Washington, DC: Brookings Institution Press.

National Commission on the State and Local Public Service. (1993). *Hard truths/tough choices: An agenda for state and local reform.* Albany, NY: Rockefeller Institute of Government.

Oppel, R. A., Jr. (2014, June 25). 2 V.A. officials to leave posts as agency seeks to remake itself and rebuild trust. *New York Times.* Retrieved from http://www.nytimes.com/2014/06/26/us/senior-veterans-affairs-officials-to-step-down.html?_r = 0

Osborne, D., & Gaebler, T. (1992). *Reinventing government: How the entrepreneurial spirit is transforming the public sector.* New York: Penguin Books.

Partnership for Public Service. (2014). Federal workforce. Retrieved from http://www.scribd.com/doc/220100041/Federal-Workforce-2014-Key-Figures

Perry, J., Wise, L. R., & Martin, M. (1994). Breaking the civil service mold: The case of Indianapolis. *Review of Public Personnel Administration, 14*(2), 40–54.

Pfiffner, J. P., & Brook, D. A. (Eds.). (2000). *The future of merit: Twenty years after the Civil Service Reform Act.* Baltimore: Johns Hopkins University Press.

Phinney, D. (2003, September 22). Opposition to outsourcing builds in Congress. *Federal Times,* pp. 6–7.

Pickard, J. (1995). Prepare to make a moral judgment. *People Management, 9*(1), 22–31.

President's Reorganization Project. (1977). *Personnel management project: Final staff report.* Washington, DC: Government Printing Office.

Richter, W. L., & Burke, F. (Eds.). (2007). *Combating corruption, encouraging ethics: A practical guide to management ethics* (2nd ed.). Lanham, MD: Rowman & Littlefield.

Robinson, E. (2010, April 20). The eradication of trust. RealClearPolitics. Retrieved from http://www.realclearpolitics.com/articles/2010/04/20/the_eradication_of_trust_105234.html

Rothenbacher, F. (1997). *Public sector employment in Europe: Where will the decline end?* Mannheim, Germany: University of Mannheim, Mannheim Centre for European Social Research, EURODATA.

Sauser, W. I., Jr., & Sims, R. R. (Eds.). (2012). *Managing human resources for the millennial generation.* Charlotte, NC: Information Age.

Smith, C. J. (1998). Reinvigorating our understanding of merit: Introductory comments on Maranto's polemic and the replies thereto. *Administration & Society, 29*(6), 620–622.

Stein, L. (1994). Personnel rules and reforms in an unreformed setting. *Review of Public Personnel Administration, 14*(2), 55–63.

Suleiman, E. (2003). *Dismantling democratic states.* Princeton, NJ: Princeton University Press.

Svara, J. S. (2015). *The ethics primer for public administrators in government and nonprofit organizations* (2nd ed.). Burlington, MA: Jones & Bartlett.

Swanson, E., & Blumenthal, M. (2013, March 18). "Wasteful spending" poll: Few agree on what government waste is, most want to cut it. Huffington Post. Retrieved from http://www.huffingtonpost.com/2013/03/18/wasteful-spending-poll_n_2886081.html

Tenbrunsel, A., Smith-Crowe, K., & Umphress, E. (2003). Building houses on rocks: The role of the ethical infrastructure in organizations. *Social Justice Research, 16*(3), 285–307.

Theedom, R. (1995). Employee recognition and a code of ethics in the public service. *Optimum, 25*(4), 38–40.

Thompson, F. J. (1994). Deregulation and public personnel administration: The Winter Commission. *Review of Public Personnel Administration, 14*(2), 5–10.

Thompson, J. R. (2001). The civil service under Clinton: The institutional consequences of disaggregation. *Review of Public Personnel Administration, 21*(2), 87–113.

Thompson, J. R. (2007). Federal labor–management relations under George W. Bush: Enlightened management or political retribution? In J. S. Bowman & J. P. West (Eds.), *American public service: Radical reform and the merit system* (pp. 233–254). New York: Taylor & Francis.

Thompson, J. R., & Mastracci, S. H. (2005). *The blended workforce: Maximizing agility through nonstandard work arrangements.* Washington, DC: IBM Center for the Business of Government. Retrieved from http://www.businessofgovernment.org/sites/default/files/BlendedWorkforce.pdf

U.S. Office of Management and Budget. (2004). *Progress implementing the president's management agenda.* Washington, DC: Author. Retrieved from http://www.whitehouse.gov/omb/budget/fy2004/progress.html + "federal + human + capital + survey" + OMB

U.S. Office of Management and Budget. (2014). *FY 2014 budget analytic perspectives.* Washington, DC: Author. Retrieved from http://www.whitehouse.gov/omb/performance

U.S. Office of Personnel Management. (2014). Data, analysis & documentation: Federal employment reports. Retrieved from http://www.opm.gov/policy-data-oversight/data-analysis-documentation/federal-employment-reports/historical-tables/executive-branch-civilian-employment-since-1940

Van Wart, M. R. (1998). *Changing public sector values.* New York: Garland.

Van Wart, M. R. (2003). Codes of ethics as living documents: The case of the American society for public administration. *Public Integrity, 5*(4), 331–346.

Van Wart, M. R., Hondeghem, A., & Schwella, E. (2014). *Leadership and culture: Comparative models of top civil servant training.* Basingstoke, England: Palgrave Macmillan.

West, J. P. (2002). Georgia on the mind of radical civil service reformers. *Review of Public Personnel Administration, 21*(2), 79–93.

West, J. P. (2009). Ethics and human resource management. In S. W. Hays, R. C. Kearney, & J. D. Coggburn (Eds.), *Public human resource management: Problems and prospects* (5th ed., pp. 275–289). New York: Longman.

West, J. P. (2012). Employee-friendly policies and development benefits for millennials. In W. I. Sauser Jr. & R. R. Sims (Eds.), *Managing human resources for the millennial generation* (pp. 201–228). Charlotte, NC: Information Age Press.

West, J. P., & Berman, E. M. (2001). From traditional to virtual HR: Is the transition occurring in local government? *Review of Public Personnel Administration, 21*(1), 38–64.

West, J. P., & Berman, E. M. (2004). Ethics training in U.S. cities: Content, pedagogy, and impact. *Public Integrity, 6*(3), 189–206.

West, J. P., & Berman, E. M. (2006). *The ethics edge* (2nd ed.). Washington, DC: International City/County Management Association.

West, J. P., & Bowman, J. S. (2004). Stakeholder analysis of civil service reform in Florida: A descriptive, instrumental, normative human resource management perspective. *State and Local Government Review, 36*(1), 20–34.

Zagelmeyer, S. (1997, July 28). Civil service law reform comes into force on 1 July 1997. European Industrial Relations Observatory. Retrieved from http://www.eurofound.europa.eu/eiro/1997/07/feature/de9707123f.htm

CHAPTER 2

Legal Rights and Responsibilities

Laws Governing the Workplace

Sally Gertz

Your right to swing your arms ends just where the other man's nose begins.

—Zechariah Chafee

After studying this chapter, you should be able to

- explain the sources of human resource management law;
- distinguish between a binding and a persuasive judicial decision;
- determine if a law or proceeding is criminal, civil, or administrative;
- identify the main laws that create the framework for human resource management and explain each one's purpose and basic requirements;
- recognize employment practices that raise legal concerns; and
- spot situations in which a human resource professional or lawyer should be contacted.

People do not have the same rights on their jobs that they have as citizens. Individuals who want to be employed must arrive on time, follow orders, accept limits on their speech and privacy, and conform to a host of other regulations. Those who want to manage must leave their personal prejudices at home and enforce workplace rules, such as safety protocols, even if they decrease productivity. Broadly conceived, the ultimate paradox presented by employment is this: To get something (money, responsibility, opportunity to make a difference), employees must give up something (liberty, time, discretion).

Many workplace obligations and restraints are rooted in the law, and agency leaders must know these principles. The most valued leaders are familiar enough with the law to anticipate and prevent problems from developing into lawsuits in the first place. Even cases that eventually are won consume enormous amounts of time and exact a heavy psychological toll. Hence, another paradox is this: Managers must embrace the law to avoid the law. They must learn the intricacies of the law to ensure they do not spend their careers entangled in it.

Those entrusted with supervising others should master the law for another reason as well—to gain the confidence to make tough personnel decisions, such as when to discharge an employee. These emotionally charged confrontations are difficult enough without the added worry that a lawsuit will result. But the reality is that, if the employee in question possesses a legally protected characteristic (e.g., race, color, religion, sex, national origin, age, or disability) or has engaged in legally protected conduct (e.g., organized a union, filed for workers' compensation, complained of harassment), even the savviest manager will hesitate. An employee may even brandish one of these protections like a shield, seeking to deflect scrutiny. But employment laws do not shield workers from discipline when it is warranted, and supervisors should not yield to the temptation to avoid lawsuits by inaction (or by not hiring women, minorities, or potential agitators in the first place). Failure to hire or discipline someone when it is justified creates problems as well. It is better for managers to learn the law and confidently apply standards uniformly and objectively.

A final, compelling reason for administrators to delve into the law is so that they can capably assist in implementing worthy societal objectives. Equality, fairness, dignity, economic well-being, strong familial relationships, and healthfulness are all goals that employment laws seek to further. In notable instances, the government, the largest employer in the nation, has led the way in complying with new workplace laws and modeling desirable employer behavior, for example, by providing equal opportunities to women, minorities, and the disabled. An administrator who comprehends policy objectives as well as technicalities will reap personal satisfaction along with professional success.

Still, even leaders who diligently stay abreast of legal developments will find themselves perplexed on a regular basis. Another overarching paradox in the legal arena is this: Those in charge are expected to uphold the law, but inherent complexities and uncertainties make complying frustratingly difficult. Five commonly occurring factors explain much of this disconnect:

1. Legal requirements and interpretations of them are voluminous and dynamic, so managers sometimes have the experience that "the more you know, the less you know." A manager who seeks to review all available information on a topic before making a decision may find him- or herself paralyzed. There is always more to know.

2. Supervisors may contact legal counsel for assistance, but formal opinions take time and legal staff may be unwilling to stand behind initial, informal opinions.

3. Applying a statute is rarely straightforward. A law often contains a general principle, such as the admonition in the Americans with Disabilities Act to provide "reasonable accommodation" to disabled employees. But department heads need

answers to concrete questions, such as whether the organization must pay for a sign language interpreter so a deaf employee can participate in a group meeting.

4. Basing decisions on judicial opinions is tricky because cases are decided on specific facts. Managers seldom confront circumstances identical to those in court cases, so they must determine whether minor distinctions should alter outcomes.

5. Legal requirements may be crosscutting, so that compliance with one directive conflicts with the requirements of another. For example, antidiscrimination laws require swift corrective action to stop harassment, but civil service laws require time-consuming, fairness-ensuring procedures prior to discipline.

In light of these many challenges, perhaps the prudent course for a manager to take is to call a human resource professional or attorney with every specific question. Of course, managers should consult with legal experts regularly, but they must make choices daily about how work is to be performed, often with little time for input from others. A basic understanding of the law, which this chapter begins to provide, will help a manager make better snap decisions and recognize when to delay a decision and consult an expert.

No matter how complex employment law on a particular topic appears to be, it typically is grounded in the balance of three often-competing interests: (1) the need of employers to manage their workforces and operations in efficient ways; (2) the rights that employees have to economic security, privacy, and other matters; and (3) the interest of governments to pursue social objectives through public policy. The balance struck varies from situation to situation and changes dynamically over time. Indeed, as attitudes, social norms, and economic conditions change, previously resolved issues may resurface (e.g., health insurance benefits for family members may extend to same-sex partners/spouses) and new areas of contention arise (e.g., whether veterans with posttraumatic stress disorder have a disability that must be accommodated).

In reading this chapter, note its emphasis on the rights and responsibilities of individual employees—in other words, *employment law*. Chapter 11 discusses *labor law*—the collective rights of employees to organize and bargain in public sector workplaces. Since 1960, the trend has been toward more direct government intervention into employees' individual relationships with employers, and the result has been a proliferation of employment law statutes and court decisions. Still, in the United States union membership is higher in the public sector than in the private sector, so the "rules" applied to agency workplace issues are often found in collective bargaining agreements, not the law. In these instances disputes are resolved through grievance procedures, not lawsuits. This chapter's focus on legal processes also means that alternative dispute resolution methods, such as mediation, receive little attention. Yet more than 90% of employment-related disputes initiated in judicial forums settle before trial, often as a result of mediation, so learning these negotiation skills is critical for managers.

The chapter begins with a few foundational principles and then shifts to discussion of specific activities. Disciplinary procedures, speech and political activity, compensation and scheduling, health and safety, and the individual liability of employees are examined. Next, searches, preemployment investigations, and postemployment references are reviewed. The last part of the chapter explains how antidiscrimination and antiretaliation laws affect the employment relationship. For each topic the relevant laws are identified and discussed. After studying this chapter, a student should be able to examine a policy, such as a dress code, explain the legal provisions that apply to it, and determine whether it is permissible. Checking agency decisions against current regulations to ensure they are lawful is an ongoing process. Exhibit 2.1 discusses strategies for staying up-to-date.

Exhibit 2.1   Keeping Abreast

How do administrators stay up-to-date with legal changes? Most prefer to await policy directives from their organizations, and this works well normally, but sometimes employers are behind the curve and managers need current information. The human resource department is usually a good source to tap. Singular situations for line managers are routine events for human resource managers, who have access to networks of specialists and subscribe to niche publications.

Still, it pays to develop an independent perspective. Professional association newsletters and conferences are ideal sources of information about the latest trends. The International Public Management Association (IPMA) publishes a manager-friendly newsletter that covers legal issues. Leading newspapers follow legal developments, and resources abound on the Internet. Of particular note is the Catherwood Library at the Cornell University School of Industrial and Labor Relations, which houses a vast collection of labor and employment law materials accessible through a user-friendly subject guide (http://www.ilr.cornell.edu/library).

Exhibit 2.2   Overview of Selected Federal Employment Laws

42 U.S.C. § 1981 (Civil Rights Act of 1866)	Section 1981 was the first major antidiscrimination employment statute. The act prohibits intentional employment discrimination based on race or ethnicity.
42 U.S.C. § 1983 (Civil Rights Act of 1871)	Section 1983 allows individuals to sue state actors in state or federal courts for civil rights violations. It prohibits public sector employment discrimination based on race, color, religion, sex, or national origin. It is the exclusive tool for challenging employee discharge due to the exercise of freedom of expression.
42 U.S.C. § 1985	Prohibits conspiracies to deprive citizens of equal protection of the law or equal privileges and immunities under the law. Can be used to challenge public sector employment discrimination with Sections 1981 and 1983.
Age Discrimination in Employment Act	Protects workers age 40 and over in hiring, promotion, and termination decisions.

(Continued)

Exhibit 2.2 (Continued)

Americans with Disabilities Act	Prohibits employment discrimination against qualified individuals with disabilities. After the U.S. Supreme Court issued several decisions narrowing the act's scope, Congress amended the act in 2008 and broadened its application.
Civil Rights Act of 1964, Title VII	Prohibits employers from discriminating against employees in hiring, promotion, and termination decisions based on race, color, religion, sex, or national origin.
Civil Rights Act of 1991	For discrimination claims, provides the right to trial by jury and emotional distress damages.
Consolidated Omnibus Budget Reconciliation Act of 1985	Mandates an insurance program giving some employees the ability to continue employers' group health insurance coverage after leaving employment.
Consumer Credit Protection Act	Regulates the use of credit reports by employers. Limits the amount of an employee's earning that may be garnished and protects employees from being discharged because their wages have been garnished.
Electronic Communications Privacy Act	Title I, The Wiretap Act, prohibits employers from intercepting wire, oral, and electronic communications. Title II, the Stored Communications Act, prohibits employers from intentional unauthorized access to stored communications.
Employee Polygraph Protection Act	Limits the uses of lie detectors by private employers with respect to employees and job applicants. The act does not apply to governmental employers.
Employee Retirement Income Security Act	Establishes minimum standards for pension plans in private industry.
Equal Pay Act	Prohibits employers from paying men and women different wage rates for equal work on jobs that require equal skill, effort, and responsibility and are performed under similar working conditions.
Fair Labor Standards Act	Sets minimum wage and overtime pay standards, as well as standards for record keeping in regard to child labor laws.
Family and Medical Leave Act	Requires employers of 50 or more employees and all public agencies to provide up to 12 weeks of unpaid leave to eligible employees for the birth and care of a child, adoption and placement of a child, or serious illness of the employee or immediate family member.
Genetic Information Nondiscrimination Act of 2008	Prohibits employers from discriminating on the basis of genetic information, requiring genetic testing, purchasing or collecting genetic information, and disclosing genetic information.
Health Insurance Portability and Accountability Act	Protects the security and privacy of health data.

Immigration Reform and Control Act	Prohibits employers from knowingly hiring or recruiting immigrants who do not possess lawful work authorization.
Occupational Safety and Health Act	Regulates safety and health conditions, including exposure to a variety of health hazards.
Patient Protection and Affordable Care Act	Requires employers with at least 50 workers to provide health insurance coverage to those working an average of 30 hours per week. Requires individuals to maintain health insurance coverage and provides subsidies.
Pregnancy Discrimination Act	Amendment to Title VII, prohibits discrimination on the basis of pregnancy, childbirth, or related medical conditions.
Rehabilitation Act of 1973, Sections 501 and 505	The first civil rights statute for workers with disabilities.
Uniformed Services Employment and Reemployment Rights Act	Protects the employment rights of National Guard and Reserve members called up to active duty.
Whistleblower Protection Act	Protects personnel from retaliatory adverse action when, in good faith, they object to agency misconduct.

THE FOUNDATIONS OF EMPLOYMENT LAW

Legislation is a major source of employment law in the United States. Exhibit 2.2 lists the main *federal* laws and their purposes, but state statutes and local ordinances affect the employer–employee relationship as well. States and local governments, for example, have created civil service systems, raised the minimum wage above the national minimum, and passed antidiscrimination and antiretaliation laws with broader protections than those found in national laws. Not surprisingly, these laws frequently conflict, and courts must decide whether one government body's law preempts another's. The term *preempt* generally refers to the displacing effect that federal law has on a conflicting or inconsistent state law under the Supremacy Clause of the U.S. Constitution (Article VI, Section 2), but it also refers to the displacing effect state laws have on conflicting local government ordinances. Confusion also occurs when Congress attempts to abrogate *sovereign immunity* by passing laws purportedly giving state employees the right to sue their state employers. The Eleventh Amendment to the U.S. Constitution creates a federal system in which each state is a sovereign entity that can be sued only if it consents to be sued. Congress can abrogate this immunity only if it unequivocally expresses its intent to do so and creates a remedy congruent and proportional to the wrong addressed. In recent years, the Supreme Court has held that the Americans with Disabilities Act (Title I, Employment), Age Discrimination in Employment Act, and the 1938 Fair Labor Standards Act do not pass this test, so state employees may not use these acts to sue their state employers for money damages. Only states, not other political subdivisions, are immune from suits for damages under the Eleventh Amendment.

Judicial opinions are another source of employment law. The United States is a **common-law system**. Not all "rules" are written down in statutes or codes. Instead, "the law" is built up successively, case by case, in written opinions of appellate judges. As a result, to find the law on any given issue, in addition to reading any pertinent legislation, one must read appellate judges' opinions on the matter. In contrast, in a **civil law system** comprehensive statutes or codes enacted by a legislative body cover almost every subject. Increasingly in the United States specialized federal and state statutes do provide comprehensive legal rules on issues, but legislatures still leave gaps for courts to fill, so judicial interpretations remain important in developing and memorializing the law.

A manager seeking to apply the law expressed in a judicial opinion should be aware that only controlling court decisions must be followed. The United States adheres to the principle of **stare decisis**, which means that courts generally should abide by precedents established by superior courts. In essence, the federal and state court systems have a pyramid structure. In the federal system, the U.S. Supreme Court sits at the pinnacle, the 12 federal circuit courts (appellate courts) make up the middle, and the 90 federal district courts (trial courts) constitute the base. For a court's opinion to be a *controlling precedent* or *binding precedent,* it must have been written by a court directly up the pyramid from the lower court. The Supreme Court's interpretation of federal law controls all the circuit and district courts, but a circuit court's opinion binds only the few district courts located directly below it on the pyramid. Of course, a court may choose to embrace a well-reasoned, nonbinding opinion, treating it as a *persuasive precedent.*

Federal and state constitutions create legal rights as well. In the U.S. Constitution, the First, Fourth, Fifth, and Fourteenth Amendments conspicuously shape the employment relationship. Constitutional rights may be asserted both defensively and offensively. The most common defensive use is by criminal defendants. A person asserts a right offensively by bringing a civil suit. In litigation, a constitutional right frequently is paired with a statute implementing that right. For example, 42 U.S.C. § 1983 (commonly referred to as Section 1983) allows a person whose constitutional right has been violated to sue the responsible public official or governmental body for money damages, and it provides attorney's fees for the prevailing party.

With all these potential sources of law, where should a manager who wants to prohibit employees from wearing sagging pants start looking? If a federal agency enforces or administers a statute, the agency's rules, regulations, compliance manuals, and guidances provide detailed explanations about how to apply it. The **Equal Employment Opportunity Commission (EEOC)** and the U.S. Department of Labor are responsible for most federal employment laws, and they publish voluminous materials on those laws. State agencies enforce and administer state employment laws and publish related materials, but they rarely provide the comprehensive assistance that federal agencies do. While an agency's interpretation of a statute is not binding on a court, courts defer to agencies because of their expertise.

As you read this chapter, notice the differences among criminal, civil, and administrative laws and procedures. A criminal law dispute occurs in court and involves the government on one side and a person believed to have violated the criminal code on the other. The government seeks to punish the defendant, and extensive procedures focus on protecting him or her from wrongful conviction: A defendant is entitled to a jury, is provided an attorney if unable to afford one, does not have to testify, and can be found guilty only if the government proves its case very convincingly (beyond a reasonable doubt). Civil law disputes take place in courts, usually but not always before juries, and involve private or government parties seeking to determine their rights vis-à-vis each other under the civil laws; often the goal is to obtain an award of money to compensate for a physical or economic injury. Each party usually pays its own attorney or self-represents. The person bringing the claim must prove it by a comparatively low standard (a preponderance of evidence), but elaborate procedures still allow each side to vigorously present its own allegations and undermine those of the opponent. The emphasis remains on protecting the parties from an erroneous result; consequently, these cases take a long time. Exhibit 2.3 shows the progression of a basic civil lawsuit.

Exhibit 2.3 Basic Civil Lawsuit Flowchart

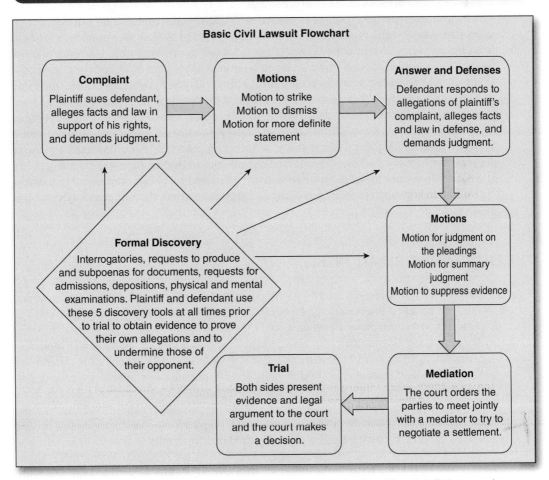

SOURCE: Adapted from a flowchart by the legal self-help company Jurisdictionary (http://www.jurisdictionary.com).

Administrative law disputes are handled by agencies. Typically, an administrative law judge holds an evidentiary hearing to determine the facts, and an agency head makes a final decision. The process permits politically selected agency leaders to influence decisions and shape policy. Disputes involve the government on one side and a person challenging a decision of the government (denying or disciplining a license, enforcing a regulation, denying a benefit) on the other. Procedural rules favor speedy resolution, with short timelines, few motions, and little discovery. Parties pay their own attorneys and employees often self-represent because they cannot afford counsel. Keeping these three types of laws separate analytically can be difficult because an employee may violate all types in one incident. Consider the example of a police officer who unnecessarily strikes and injures a person during an arrest: A prosecutor may charge the crime of battery, the victim may sue for civil money damages, and the police standards commission may discipline the officer's certification. A manager may become involved as a witness or informal source of information in all three proceedings.

The last foundational principle to bear in mind throughout this chapter is the notion of a *remedy.* When evaluating alternative courses of action, for each one a manager should ask, "If a lawsuit is filed and the agency loses, what will the remedy be?" The remedy is the agency's concrete risk. Directing a driver to operate a school bus with faulty brakes could be costly, but firing a habitually tardy nurse who should have been suspended probably means reinstating him. The remedy is determined by the legal claim being made and the losses suffered. Possibilities include hiring, reinstatement, retroactive seniority, reasonable accommodation, back pay, front pay, declaratory statement, injunction, court-ordered affirmative action, medical costs, emotional distress damages, punitive damages, attorney's fees, expert witness fees, and litigation costs. In addition to quantifying the agency's risk, the remedy is illuminating for another reason: It reveals the importance that society places on the right involved. A famous legal maxim holds that "where there is no remedy, there is no right."

THE EMPLOYMENT RELATIONSHIP

An employment relationship is formed when parties exchange promises about duties, wages, hours, and benefits. Employers have policies and forms that define the arrangement, but legislatures and courts have added terms to it. **At-will employment** is the relationship predominantly used by American businesses, and governments use it liberally as well (Bowman & West, 2007). In its pure form it means that if the parties do not specify the duration of employment—and most do not—either party may terminate the employment *at any time, for any reason.* Supporters claim that the relationship upholds freedom of contract and fairly balances the interests of employers and employees because either may sever the relation-ship. But critics point out that many workers need their jobs more than their employers need them, so at-will employment opens the door to abuse. It permits an employer to refuse to hire members of disfavored groups, to engage in opportunistic firings, and to punish employees for behaving in socially desirable ways. It also subjects families to uncertainty and hardship based on employers' whims. To ameliorate these effects, lawmakers and courts have carved out exceptions to at-will employment that make it unlawful for an employer to take adverse action against an employee for specific "bad" reasons. The civil rights laws are the most well-known example. As a result of these exceptions, at-will employment now means something different: If the parties do not specify the duration of employment, either party may terminate it *at any time, for any lawful reason.* From a manager's perspective, this means that even at-will employees have many rights that cannot be violated.

In the public sector, many employees do not serve "at will." Schools and colleges use annual contracts to ensure that teachers stay for the entire academic year, and they use tenure systems to protect teachers' academic freedom. Governments use civil service systems to guard against patronage. In these relationships, employers promise employees that they will be discharged only "for cause." Legislatures and courts have added conditions to these arrangements as well. The Supreme Court has ruled that when a law, rule, or understanding creates an expectation of continued employment in a government job, then employees possess a constitutionally protected "property interest" that cannot be taken away without "due process." The Supreme Court has also ruled that when a public employer takes adverse action against an employee it is "state action," so federal and state constitutional protections apply. As a result, employees who exercise freedom of speech or freedom of association or assert the right to privacy at work cannot be punished if their conduct falls within the ambit of one of these constitutional protections. As you read the next section, consider whether these arrangements in the public sector create a model that, compared with at-will employment, more equitably balances the interests of employees, employers, and the government, or whether they unduly limit the flexibility of government employers.

BALANCING EMPLOYER, EMPLOYEE, AND SOCIETAL INTERESTS

This section examines the law's attempt to balance employer interests, employee rights, and social objectives in six areas: furnishing due process, taking adverse personnel action, safeguarding free speech and political activity, providing compensation and work schedules, protecting health and safety, and holding employees individually liable.

Procedural Due Process and the Taking of Property and Liberty

The Fifth Amendment (applicable to the federal government) and the Fourteenth Amendment (applicable to the states) forbid the taking of "life, liberty, or property without due process of law." Odd as it may seem, based on the definition of the word "property" in these amendments, this includes the right to continued public employment, referred to as *a property interest.* When an employee has a property interest in a job, he or she also has procedural **due process rights.** As a result, the employee may not be disciplined seriously unless procedures designed to guarantee fairness are followed. Managers (and courts) grapple with two questions that flow from this proposition: (1) What guarantees create a property interest? and (2) If one exists, what procedures must be followed to give an employee a fair opportunity to affect the result?

In *Board of Regents v. Roth* (1972), the Supreme Court explained what promises raise government employment to the level of a property interest. The employee must have a legitimate claim of entitlement to continued employment based on codified rules or explicitly agreed-upon contract terms. Generally, academic employees with tenure and classified civil servants with permanent (nonprobationary) status and the statutory right to be discharged only "for cause" fit this description.

As for the procedures required, prior to 1985, it was understood that a government employee with a property interest who was facing serious discipline was entitled to notice of the charges and a *posttermination hearing* in front of a neutral judge. In *Cleveland Board of Education v. Loudermill* (1985), the Supreme Court held that "due process" demanded an additional middle step—*a pretermination hearing*. Before making a decision, the employer must give the employee notice of the charges, an explanation of the evidence, and an opportunity for the employee to present his side of the story. Only in rare situations when an employer must act quickly may a pretermination hearing be omitted.[1]

The Due Process Clause also prohibits governments from depriving citizens of their "liberty" without a fair process. When a public employer discharges someone for a stigmatizing reason, such as an immoral act, and the allegation becomes publicly known, the employee, on request, must be provided a hearing to have the chance to clear her name. Otherwise, her ability to obtain another job is unjustly limited. In practice, this means that sometimes a probationary or exempt civil servant still must be provided a posttermination hearing. If the employee prevails, the discipline is nullified, but she is not reinstated; her remedy is her liberty to seek other jobs with a clean record.

Adverse Action

Formal discipline of an employee (covered in Chapter 10) is referred to as **adverse action**. This term encompasses suspensions, salary reductions, demotions, and terminations. Other measures affect employees (e.g., reprimands, transfers, alteration of duties, changes in schedule, denial of promotion), but they usually do not cause serious enough harm to meet the legal definition of adverse action. The right to challenge adverse action has been created chiefly by statute. It is a critical component of civil service systems designed to ensure that discipline and hiring decisions are based on merit, not patronage. Civil servants in classified (covered) positions have this right. Probationary employees and individuals in unclassified (uncovered or exempt) positions do not, so they are "at will." Staff members who initially have the right to challenge adverse action may lose it by being promoted to an exempt position or by having their positions reclassified as exempt, a practice utilized extensively by some states in recent years (Bowman & West, 2007). Adverse action rights are created by statute, but the procedures also provide the "due process" required by the U.S. Constitution.

Either unsatisfactory performance or misconduct may prompt adverse action. The process followed often differs depending on which is involved. The probationary period is the ideal time to weed out employees who are unable to do their jobs. Once they become permanent, prior to adverse action for unsatisfactory performance, they typically must be notified of deficiencies, provided with an explanation of them, given remedial assistance if necessary, and allowed time to improve. The purpose of the process is to improve performance by reducing deficiencies. Written performance evaluations (discussed in Chapter 10) are critical for showing initial deficiencies as well as improvement or lack thereof.

The process used to punish misconduct often is quicker. Serious discipline usually involves the supervisor, a high-level manager, a representative from the personnel department, and one of the agency's attorneys. This group reviews the supervisor's recommendation for discipline and, if necessary, requests an investigator to interview witnesses, review documents and physical evidence, and prepare a report. After reviewing the information gathered, the group determines whether the employee's conduct violates agency standards—the *cause* question—and, if it does, selects a penalty. If the alleged misconduct is serious, when the employee is apprised of the charges she also may be suspended and perhaps even escorted from the premises.

Typically, a civil service statute or rule lists offenses that provide cause for discipline. Florida's civil service statute, for example, prohibits "poor performance, negligence, inefficiency or inability to perform assigned duties, insubordination, violation of the provisions of law or agency rules, conduct unbecoming a public employee, misconduct, habitual drug abuse, or conviction of any crime" (Florida Statutes, 2013). Agencies maximize their discretion by making lists of offenses open-ended (e.g., "misconduct includes, but is not limited to") and by incorporating standards located outside the statute (i.e., "violation of the provisions of law or agency rules" incorporates all rules, directives, policies, regulations, and internal operating procedures promulgated by the agency and its subdivisions). Wherever they are located, agency "cause" standards should be clear enough to apprise employees of what is prohibited and to prevent unbridled agency discretion (Gertz, 2001).

Public employees may be disciplined for off-duty conduct. Usually the charge is "conduct unbecoming a public employee" or "conviction of any crime." Law enforcement officers and teachers, especially, are held to high standards, but all government leaders worry about their agencies' reputations being sullied by off-duty behavior. Generally, a *nexus,* or demonstrable connection, must exist between the off-duty misconduct and the job. A school employee, for example, likely could be terminated for any off-duty misconduct involving illegal drugs due to the government's strong interest in maintaining drug-free schools.

In civil service systems, the right to challenge adverse action includes the right to an administrative hearing. Governments have created quasi-judicial administrative agencies to hear these disputes, such as the U.S. Merit Systems Protection Board and state civil service commissions. An administrative law judge hears the case and determines what happened, whether those facts justify discipline, and, if they do, whether the penalty chosen is fair. An agency head or panel reviews the decision. Timelines are expedited. Unions provide attorneys for union members; nonmembers in highly compensated positions often hire private attorneys, but nonmembers in lower salary ranges often represent themselves. An employee who prevails will have the discipline nullified or reduced, and may receive back pay and attorney's fees. Sometimes an employee has the choice of challenging adverse action through an administrative hearing or through the grievance procedure in the collective bargaining agreement, but a grievant may have to pay the cost of arbitration.

On a related matter, a person who is terminated may seek partial, temporary replacement wages while seeking another job by filing for **unemployment compensation**.

This federal–state insurance program is funded by employers through a tax on payrolls. Employers with repeated claims pay higher tax rates. An employer may prevent a former employee from obtaining benefits (and raising the employer's tax rate) by proving at a hearing that the individual voluntarily resigned or was discharged "for cause." Accordingly, this administrative hearing often covers the same issues and involves the same parties as the adverse action hearing.

Freedom of Speech

Citizens do not relinquish their **free speech rights** when they enter government employment, but they do accept restrictions on them. The First Amendment, which prohibits the making of any law abridging freedom of speech, protects a citizen's right, in limited circumstances, to speak out on matters of public concern. In *Pickering v. Board of Education* (1968), the leading case in this area, the Supreme Court balanced employees' speech rights against the need for workplace efficiency. The case concerned a teacher who wrote a letter to a local newspaper criticizing the school board's funding priorities and subsequently was dismissed for disloyalty and insubordination. The Court found that the letter addressed a matter of public concern and had not unduly disrupted operation of the school district. Consequently, it held that the board could not fire Pickering. Out of this decision grew the two-part "*Pickering* balancing test." To determine whether an employer may take adverse action, a court asks (1) whether the speech was a matter of public concern and (2) whether the disruptive nature of the speech justifies the adverse personnel action. To enforce his or her First Amendment rights, an employee must file an action in court.

Trying to determine what constituted a "matter of public concern" proved confusing, so in the 1983 case of *Connick v. Myers* the Supreme Court clarified that the speech must relate to a "political, social or other concern of the community." *Connick* centered on a district attorney who was dismissed from his position after he circulated a questionnaire to coworkers soliciting their opinions about office management. His "speech" did not qualify for protection, according to the Court, because it concerned primarily matters of personal grievance, not public policy. After *Connick*, courts repeatedly held that frustrated, disgruntled staff members who vented their personal disagreements were not speaking about matters of public concern.[2]

Confusion also arose about whether a comment made as part of person's job was protected. In *Garcetti v. Ceballos* (2006b) the Supreme Court ruled that an employee's expression "made pursuant to official responsibilities" is not protected by the First Amendment. Ceballos, a district attorney, wrote a memo to his superiors recommending that a case not be prosecuted because he suspected that the sheriff had lied in the affidavit used to secure the search warrant. Ceballos claimed that he was moved to a less desirable position, transferred to a different courthouse, and denied promotion as a result (*Garcetti v. Ceballos*, 2006a). The Court denied his claim because he made the comment as part of his job. In light of *Garcetti*, a supervisor considering disciplining an employee for an expression should ask a preliminary question before applying the *Pickering* balancing test: Was the speech made pursuant to the employee's official responsibilities? If the answer is yes, the First Amendment is no impediment.

Critics of *Garcetti* predict that it will deter employees from raising legitimate concerns, and that **whistleblower statutes** will not overcome this reticence (Gertz, 2007). Almost all jurisdictions have enacted legislation protecting personnel from retaliatory adverse action when, in good faith, they object to agency misconduct. But safeguards are limited. For example, the Whistleblower Protection Act of 1989 shields a federal employee's disclosure of gross mismanagement, waste of funds, illegal acts, misuse of funds, and danger to public safety or health. A victim initially must seek assistance from the U.S. Office of Special Counsel, an agency charged with stopping prohibited personnel practices. If unsatisfied, the whistleblower may request a hearing before the U.S. Merit Systems Protection Board, where the employee must pay for an attorney and prove that the adverse action was retaliatory. An employee may not initiate a civil action for money damages in court. State whistleblower statutes vary, but they likewise protect a narrow range of speech, impose burdensome and expensive procedures on employees when they are out of work, and offer weak remedies.

Political Activity and Affiliation

During the 19th century, public employees routinely campaigned and raised funds for the political parties or executives who appointed them. Now, government workers are limited in the political activity in which they may engage by the federal **Hatch Act of 1939**, as amended, and state and local "little Hatch Acts." These acts restrict a person's First Amendment right to political expression, but they pass muster with courts because they reduce political coercion of the bureaucracy and promote a nonpartisan, efficient government workforce. Congress retreated from some initial broader restrictions because it feared that denying so many Americans their right to engage in political activity was negatively affecting the quality of democracy. The impact of this retreat—whether it is repoliticizing the bureaucracy—is unclear (Bloch, 2005; Bowman & West, 2009). The U.S. Office of Special Counsel publishes guides to the Hatch Act, provides advisory opinions to government employees contemplating political activity, and prosecutes violators. The office divides federal employees into two groups: "Further restricted" employees in intelligence and enforcement-type agencies have little ability to participate in partisan politics; "less restricted" employees face fewer restrictions, as summarized in Exhibit 2.4.

What happens when a victorious political leader takes office and wants to replace current civil servants with loyal party supporters? Classified civil servants, who may be discharged only "for cause," are protected, but exempt civil servants, who serve "at will," are not. Here, the First Amendment potentially bars the way because it forbids adverse action based on beliefs as well as on speech. In *Elrod v. Burns* (1976), the Supreme Court held that *patronage dismissals* are allowed only if the person being discharged occupies a policy-making or confidential position. Later, in *Branti v. Finkel* (1980) the Court refined its ruling and explained that party affiliation must be necessary for effective performance of the job. A decade later, in *Rutan v. Republican Party of Illinois* (1990), the Court extended this holding to personnel actions other than discharge—including hirings, promotions, transfers, and recalls. Now, a government leader who uses party affiliation for any of these decisions must show that it is necessary for job performance.

Exhibit 2.4 The Hatch Act: Permitted and Prohibited Activities for "Less Restricted" Federal and D.C. Employees

"Less restricted" employees may

- Be candidates for public office in nonpartisan elections
- Register and vote as they choose
- Assist in voter registration drives
- Express opinions about candidates and issues
- Contribute money to political organizations
- Attend political fund-raising functions
- Attend and be active at political rallies and meetings
- Join and be active members of a political party or club
- Sign nominating petitions
- Campaign for or against referendum questions, constitutional amendments, municipal ordinances
- Campaign for or against candidates in partisan elections
- Make campaign speeches for candidates in partisan elections
- Distribute campaign literature in partisan elections
- Hold office in political clubs or parties

"Less restricted" employees may not

- Use their official authority or influence to interfere with an election (e.g., may not use official title while engaged in political activity; may not invite subordinates to political events or ask them to undertake partisan political activity)
- Solicit or discourage political activity of anyone with business before their agency
- Solicit or receive political contributions (e.g., may not host or invite anyone to a political fundraiser) (there are exceptions for labor organizations and other employee organizations)
- Be candidates for public office in partisan elections
- Engage in political activity while
  - On duty
  - In a government office
  - Wearing an official uniform
- Using a government vehicle
- Wear partisan political buttons, T-shirts, or other items on duty

SOURCE: U.S. Office of Special Counsel. (2011). Federal less restriction and activities.

Compensation and Scheduling

If a work site is unionized, the collective bargaining agreement likely addresses the matter of wages. The primary statute covering the right to compensation is the **Fair Labor Standards Act of 1938 (FLSA)**, enforced and administered by the U.S. Department of Labor. The act prohibits child labor, mandates a minimum wage, and requires that overtime be paid, at one and a half times the regular rate, for hours more than 40 per week. State and local governments may substitute compensatory time off, at the rate of time and a half, for overtime. The FLSA applies to federal, state, and local employees, but lawsuits against states by private citizens are barred by Eleventh Amendment sovereign immunity. Many states and localities mandate a minimum wage higher than the one in the FLSA.

Certain FLSA provisions regularly are the foci of lawsuits—for example, the *white-collar exemption.* This exemption was created to excuse employers from paying overtime to highly compensated employees. Employees engaged in an executive, administrative, or professional capacity are exempt from both minimum wage and overtime requirements. An exempt individual must be paid on a salary basis, earn at least $455 per week, and meet the duties test. In 2013 more than 7,000 FLSA lawsuits were filed, many of which claimed that an employer misclassified an employee as "white-collar exempt" to avoid paying overtime and minimum wages. In 2014 President Obama sent a memo to the secretary of the Department of Labor directing him to consider how this exemption could be updated. Another way organizations sidestep FLSA requirements is by mislabeling workers as "independent contractors" or "interns" rather than as employees. The Department of Labor has definitions for each category, but the boundaries are blurry and employers exploit the ambiguity.

Conflicts also erupt over whether *idle time* is compensable work time. Waiting time, on-call time, sleep time, travel time, and rest and meal periods all raise this question and require managers to examine the precise facts and to look for specific rules and guidance from the Department of Labor. The FLSA has complicated overtime exemptions for firefighters and law enforcement officers, and agencies with these positions should designate and train personnel to master them. *Off-the-clock* time spent responding to phone calls, texts, and e-mails must be counted as work time and compensated.

The 1963 Equal Pay Act, an amendment to the FLSA, requires employers to pay men and women equal wages for equal work, unless an employer can justify the differential by seniority, merit, piecework, or any factor other than sex. "Equal work" means that the skill, effort, responsibility, and working conditions are equal. The work need not be identical, but significant portions of it should be. A plaintiff must find one opposite-sex "comparator" who is doing equal work at a higher rate and may use statistical evidence of gender-based disparity to buttress a claim. An employer found guilty may comply with the act only by raising the rate of the lower-paid employee. (Chapters 7 and 8 cover pay and benefit programs.)

Public sector pensions are prized by government employees, who see themselves as agreeing to lower wages than they could earn in the private sector in exchange for the promise of a secure retirement, but that "promise" may be illusory. In the past decade state and local governments have cut pension benefits by enacting laws, using ballot initiatives, and declaring bankruptcy. The Employee Retirement Income Security Act (ERISA) is the main federal law governing private sector pensions, but no public sector counterpart exists. As a result, when a government reduces pension benefits, constitutional provisions, state statutes, and court decisions about contract principles and property rights determine legal outcomes. Protection varies from state to state and worker to worker.

Retirees have the greatest rights. Courts have not allowed reductions in base benefits, but Colorado and Minnesota were permitted to reduce scheduled cost-of-living adjustments, and others locales followed suit. For current employees, the situation is less clear; many cases are still wending through the courts. In Arizona, Colorado, and Oregon courts have protected future benefits that had been promised to current employees. But in Maryland, only benefits based on past service have been protected, which means the government could cut future benefits. The state of Florida and the city of Atlanta cut benefits by increasing the percentage of current employees' contributions. Rhode Island raised the retirement age and reduced payments from 80% to 75% of salary. For new hires, governments are free to discontinue or change pension plans (Munnell & Quinby, 2012). Ultimately, the right to a pension is meaningless if there is no money, but public employees have limited ability to ensure that governments adequately fund pension plans, do not raid them, and invest the funds wisely. The Pension Protection Act of 2006 addressed problems with underfunded private pensions, but not public ones. Privatization raises complex legal issues about pension rights that are beyond the scope of this short summary (Ravitch & Lawther, 1999).

Pensions may be lost due to misconduct. Forfeiture laws in at least 13 states allow public employers to withhold pensions from employees for misbehavior. Depending on the state, misbehavior may be defined as a felony conviction, administrative misconduct, or conviction of a particular crime.

Scheduling largely is left to employers' discretion, but workers have some rights. Under the Patient Protection and Affordable Care Act (ACA, popularly known as Obamacare), employees who are nursing mothers must be provided break time and private places to express milk. Discrimination statutes give those with disabilities and religious needs the right to request accommodations (discussed in the "Discrimination" section below). Many part-time workers face the trial of dealing with unpredictable schedules. A writer for the *New York Times* provoked a flurry of responses when he reported the story of Mary Coleman, who, after an hour-long bus commute, arrived for her scheduled shift at a Popeyes in Milwaukee only to be told to go home without clocking in because the store had enough people working (Greenhouse, 2014a, 2014b). A fluctuating schedule makes it impossible for a worker to juggle one job with another, to secure child or elder care, or to take classes, yet many employers demand on-call availability from part-timers. Vermont and San Francisco have adopted laws giving workers the "right to request" predictable schedules, and President Obama has ordered federal agencies to give the right to 2 million workers. Other locales are considering similar measures. These laws require an employer to discuss employees' situations with them and to consider scheduling requests; the employer is not obligated to grant the requests.

Health and Safety

In 2012, there were 453 fatal occupational injuries to government workers in the United States. The injuries occurred most often in the job categories of police protection; national security; construction; and trade, transportation, and utilities (Bureau of Labor Statistics, 2012). The number of nonfatal public sector injuries is unavailable. People may suffer harm on the job because employers create dangerous conditions, employees are careless, someone becomes violent, or nature intervenes, among other reasons.

The Occupational Safety and Health Act of 1970 is the main federal statute protecting federal employees from unsafe working conditions. Twenty-three states have adopted occupational safety and health (OSH) acts for their public and private employees, and a few states have plans that cover only public employees (the Workplace Fairness website provides a comprehensive chart of state OSH acts; www.workplacefairness.org). In general, federal and state OSH acts mandate standards and enforce them through inspections, fines, and closures. They do not give employees the right to sue.

The remedies available to injured persons generally are those in **workers' compensation** acts. In 1908, Congress passed the Federal Employees Compensation Act, and subsequently all states passed workers' compensation laws. These laws demand sacrifices from both employers and employees to ensure that all injured workers receive health care and lost wages. Employees relinquish the right to sue in civil court for on-the-job injuries, which, in some instances, means giving up large money damage awards. Employers forfeit the right to deny benefits to employees whose own negligence caused or contributed to their injuries; these plans are "no fault." Employers must finance these systems through insurance premiums, or by being self-insured and paying claims themselves. Disputes are resolved through an administrative system. Benefits include payment of medical expenses, partial replacement income, and, if an injury is fatal, survivors' benefits. Permanently injured employees who are unable to work also may be eligible for Social Security disability benefits and early pension benefits.[3]

In the United States health insurance is provided primarily by employers. Citizens in other industrialized countries have permanent, portable insurance, but for Americans health insurance usually is tied to their jobs. In the public sector, governments provide wide coverage to their full-time employees and pay most of the premiums. Employed and retired federal employees have access to the well-regarded Federal Employees Health Benefits Program. In 2007, about 85% of those eligible were enrolled, and the federal government paid 72% of the average premium across all plans (U.S. Government Accountability Office, 2007). In 2010, 88% of state and local government workers had access to plans, and their employers paid 89% of the cost of single coverage (Bureau of Labor Statistics, 2010). Most agencies offer coverage to retirees, and many subsidize the premiums, but financing benefits is a challenge, especially as large numbers of workers under age 65—and thus not yet eligible for Medicare—retire.[4]

Extending health insurance coverage has been a major goal of the Obama administration. Part-timers are a large segment of the government workforce, but in 2014 just 24% of part-timers in state and local government had access to employer-sponsored health insurance (Bureau of Labor Statistics, 2014). Starting in 2015, the ACA requires employers with at least 50 employees to offer coverage to people who work an average of 30 hours a week. It is too soon to gauge the law's impact, but some cities, counties, public schools, and community colleges have reduced the hours of part-timers to keep them under the 30-hour threshold (Maciag, 2014). The ACA requires all Americans to maintain health insurance coverage, so part-timers unable to access employers' plans must turn to private insurers or to state or federal exchanges. Many are eligible for subsidies that help to pay their premiums. Both the employer and the individual "mandates" of the law are enforced by fines.

Coverage of young adults, same-sex partners, and those changing jobs also is compelled by law. The Affordable Care Act requires health insurance plans to make dependent coverage available until an adult child reaches the age of 26. Many parents and children who worried about a child losing health insurance after graduation from college no longer have that concern. As for same-sex partners, the federal Defense of Marriage Act defined marriage as a legal union between one man and one woman, but the Supreme Court declared that provision unconstitutional under the Due Process Clause in *United States v. Windsor* (2013). Federal employees with same-sex partners now may enroll them in the Federal Employees Health Benefits Program.[5] In the 14 months following *Windsor,* 19 federal courts ruled on the constitutionality of state bans on same-sex marriages, with 19 victories for those challenging the bans (*Brenner v. Scott,* 2014). Given this trend, it seems likely that soon no government-sponsored plan will be able to exclude same-sex partners. Coverage for those changing jobs was the subject of an older law, the Consolidated Omnibus Budget Reconciliation Act of 1985 (COBRA). It requires employers to offer continued coverage to most former employees for 18 to 36 months, or until coverage of another plan begins, at not more than 102% of cost.

Health insurance laws also address what conditions must be covered and how much companies may charge. The ACA requires coverage to be "affordable" and "adequate" as defined in the statute. It forbids insurers to deny coverage because of a preexisting condition, and it prohibits annual or lifetime limits. Two older acts, the Health Insurance Portability and Accountability Act (HIPAA) and the Genetic Information Nondiscrimination Act (GINA), curtailed some exclusions for preexisting conditions, but they did not limit the premiums that insurers could charge, nor did they require insurers to enroll individuals. The best-known part of HIPAA is its privacy rule—employers must safeguard the privacy and security of personally identifiable health information through a panoply of measures spelled out in the act and its accompanying rules.

In addition to insurance, employees need time off for health problems. The **Family and Medical Leave Act of 1993 (FMLA)** covers local, state, and federal government agencies and provides eligible workers with up to 12 weeks of *unpaid* leave, during any 12-month period, for childbirth or adoption, illness of a family member, or illness of the employee. The U.S. Department of Labor has rules on many contentious issues related to this act, including the definition of a "serious health condition," the use of unscheduled and intermittent leave, and the medical certification process. To enforce the act, an employee may file suit or request the secretary of labor to bring suit. Robust remedies are available, including back pay, money damages, and attorney's fees. In 2003, the Supreme Court held that Congress could abrogate sovereign immunity and give state employees the right to sue their state employers using this act. Approximately half the states have their own family and medical leave laws. Collective bargaining about workplace safety, health, and leave is common. (Chapter 8 examines the effects of health and safety policies.)

Individual and Vicarious Liability

Urban legend has it that prolific bank robber Willie Sutton, when asked why he robbed banks, responded, "Because that's where the money is." Likewise, employees (and the lawyers who advise them) prefer to sue deep-pocketed employers, but occasionally they sue an official in his or her "individual capacity," seeking to hold the official personally responsible for money damages. [Official immunity is a common-law doctrine that shields government employees from individual liability.] It is based on the belief that government actors should not be made hesitant in carrying out their responsibilities by threats of lawsuits and should not be diverted from their duties by litigation. A few kinds of officials, such as judges and legislators, have *absolute immunity* for actions performed in furtherance of their judicial or legislative functions. Most officials, however, have *qualified immunity.* They are immune from liability for discretionary acts in the scope of their duties if they act in good faith (without malice) and reasonably. To act reasonably, they must not violate clearly established rights that a reasonable person would have known about, which generally means not acting egregiously. Consider the example of a school nurse and administrative assistant who strip-searched a 13-year-old girl because they found prescription-strength ibuprofen pills in her notebook. The girl's mother sued the searchers individually, but the court concluded that the student's rights were unclear and the searchers had immunity.

In reality, public employees are shielded from most lawsuits. The Federal Employees Liability Reform and Tort Compensation Act of 1988 gives federal personnel the right to request that suits against them individually be converted into suits against the government. Many states have similar laws. The ability to avoid civil liability does not make officials unaccountable, as they still may be disciplined by their agencies for misconduct, but it relieves them of the anxiety that a wrong decision will imperil their personal savings.

On the flip side, leaders worry about an agency being responsible for the misdeeds of a rogue employee, which raises this question: Under what circumstances is an employer responsible for an employee's acts? *Vicarious liability* is a common-law doctrine that makes one person (or entity) liable for the acts or omissions of another because of a legal relationship between the two. ***Respondeat superior*** (Latin for "let the master answer") is a type of vicarious liability that holds an employer liable for the acts or omissions of an employee committed in the course of employment. It is based on the theory that because the employer controls the employee's behavior, the employer must assume some responsibility for the employee's actions. Whether an act was "in the course of employment" depends on the particular facts. A court may consider the employee's job description or assigned duties; the time, place, and purpose of the employee's act; the extent to which the employee's actions conformed to what he or she was hired to do; and whether such an occurrence could reasonably have been expected. Generally, an employer will not be held liable for an employee's assault or battery, unless the use of force bears some relationship to the work, such as in the case of a police officer. The city of Sacramento, for example, was not vicariously liable for the sexual assault of a woman by several on- and off-duty firefighters, who drove a fire truck to a party, invited the woman onto the truck, and assaulted her.

PRIVACY ISSUES

Searches

Conflicts arise when people feel that managers invade their private affairs or private work spaces. These invisible barriers may be breached unconsciously in the regular course of business, such as when a supervisor calls a subordinate at home or searches her desk for an urgently needed work document. The Fourth Amendment, which limits government's ability to conduct "**unreasonable searches** and seizures," is the main restriction on workplace searches by government employers. In the leading case of *O'Connor v. Ortega* (1987), the Supreme Court held that whether a search violates the Fourth Amendment depends on (1) whether the area is one in which the employee has a reasonable expectation of privacy and (2) whether the search is reasonable under the circumstances.

The Court determined that Ortega, a physician, had a reasonable expectation of privacy in his desk and file cabinet because he was the only one who used the office, he stored only personal materials there, and his hospital-employer had never discouraged him from keeping personal items at work. Next, the Court asked whether the search was reasonable under the circumstances. A reasonable search must balance the governmental interest in the efficient and proper operation of the workplace with the employee's privacy interests. It does not require an employer to obtain a warrant or even to give an employee prior notice. In *Ortega,* the hospital's need to retrieve job-relevant material overrode the doctor's privacy rights, so the search was permissible. Managers may wish for a brighter line, but the reasonableness of an employee's privacy expectations and the reasonableness of a search are determined by the discrete facts of each situation.

Agencies can take steps to increase the likelihood of searches being lawful. They can reduce expectations of privacy by eliminating personal work spaces and adopting policies authorizing searches. (Paradoxically, these measures may erode employee–supervisor trust and impede managing.) Most employers have policies allowing searches of employees' texts, e-mails, and Internet use on the employers' devices and networks. As a result, employees have no expectation of privacy in these domains and searches are permissible. Agencies also may conduct video and telephone surveillance if these policies are communicated in advance. In sum, there are few restrictions on the rights of organizations to monitor personnel at work, especially if employees are told about their lack of privacy up front.[6]

Testing for Alcohol or Drug Use

Urinalysis, the most common drug-testing method, is a search and seizure under the Fourth Amendment (*National Treasury Employees Union v. Von Raab,* 1989). The privacy invasions are considerable. Urinalysis permits an employer to surveil several days of off-duty behavior, forces a person to disclose confidential information about medications being taken (e.g., HIV drugs, antidepressants, Viagra), and compels a person to perform an intimate bodily function with a stranger listening or watching. As with other searches, whether it is lawful depends on whether it is reasonable under the circumstances.

In 1986, President Reagan issued Executive Order 12,564, requiring executive agencies to test approximately 2 million federal employees in "sensitive positions" for illegal drug use. The order authorizes drug testing (1) where there is a reasonable suspicion of illegal drug use, (2) in a postaccident investigation, (3) as part of counseling or rehabilitation for drug use through an employee assistance program, and (4) in the screening of any job applicant. Congress also passed two laws affecting large numbers of private sector employees. The Drug-Free Workplace Act of 1988 covers federal government contractors and grant recipients, and the Omnibus Transportation Employee Testing Act of 1991 requires drug and alcohol testing of 6 million workers in transportation industries. Numerous states and localities followed the federal government's lead and passed drug-testing laws. Court challenges ensued.

In determining whether a test is reasonable, the timing of the test (preemployment, preplacement, periodic, postaccident, promotion, random) is important. Testing is liberally allowed at the preemployment and preplacement stages because applicants and new hires have little right to expect privacy. Return-to-work testing after an accident, periodic testing with advance notice, and testing upon promotion also are likely to be approved because employees expect these tests. At the other extreme, suspicionless, *random testing* of current employees is the most intrusive, and therefore the least permissible.

The nature of the job also matters. For *safety-sensitive* and *security-sensitive* positions, random testing is allowed. Applying this principle, one court allowed the suspicionless testing of the U.S. Army's civilian air traffic controllers, mechanics, police, guards, and drug counselors. Police officers and firefighters may be tested randomly. More surprisingly, a court applied this rationale to allow random testing of a broad group of school staff (principals, assistant principals, teachers, aides, substitute teachers, secretaries, and bus drivers). On the other hand, a court refused to allow random testing of all Forest Service Job Corps Center employees. Current employees in positions that do not affect safety or security may be randomly tested only with *reasonable suspicion,* which means information that would lead a reasonable person to suspect on-the-job drug use, possession, or impairment.

Grooming and Dress Codes

One cannot help but pity the poor manager forced to grapple with **dress and grooming codes** in today's workplace. The landscape is fascinating—bejeweled faces, exposed undergarments, colorful tattoos, plunging necklines, artful hair constructions, and stubbly cheeks pervade the scene. But legal and interpersonal land mines await. People consider their clothes and bodies to reflect their individuality and are sensitive to criticism of them. In the legal arena, grooming and dress codes may be unconstitutional or violate antidiscrimination statutes. This is an area where an administrator almost always should ask a human resource professional for help.

Constitutional Law

The First Amendment (free expression, free exercise of religion) and the Fourteenth Amendment (equal protection, due process) afford employees some rights in grooming and attire choices, but courts generally uphold an employer's rule against a constitutional challenge if it is *rationally related* to a legitimate interest. In *Kelley v. Johnson* (1976), the Supreme Court's principal decision about grooming, a police officer challenged a county policy limiting the length of male officers' hair. The court concluded that the regulation was rationally related to safety because it provided a disciplined and easily recognizable police force and upheld it. Bans on mustaches, goatees, and beards for police also have been upheld because they promote esprit de corps. Prohibitions on beards for firefighters and on mustaches and beards for emergency medical technicians have been upheld for safety reasons.

Agencies should be extra cautious about grooming regulations that may limit the free exercise of religion. The U.S. Fourth Circuit Court of Appeals upheld a rule preventing correctional officers from wearing dreadlocks due to safety concerns, even though the hairstyle was required by an employee's religion. But the Third Circuit struck down a rule prohibiting police officers from wearing beards because the policy prevented a Muslim man from observing his beliefs. The rule allowed an exemption for a medical need and the court reasoned that, by allowing an exemption for a secular but not a religious purpose, the county unlawfully discriminated against those with religious motivations. Because of the exemption, the court applied the *strict scrutiny* standard, which requires a measure to be narrowly tailored and to further a compelling governmental interest.

Dress codes raise similar constitutional issues. The leading dress code case is *Goldman v. Weinberger* (1986), involving the First Amendment's guarantee of free exercise of religion. The U.S. Air Force's dress code prevented an Orthodox Jew from wearing a skullcap while on duty. The Supreme Court determined the policy was lawful because it served the legitimate purpose of encouraging "the subordination of personal preferences and identities in favor of the overall group mission." In 2003, the Third Circuit upheld a county's requirement that all van drivers wear pants against an employee's claim that her religious beliefs required her to wear a skirt. The court applied a rational basis standard and accepted the county's explanation that skirts posed a risk to safety. On the other hand, in 2005 a district court in Kentucky held that a public library violated an employee's free exercise rights by prohibiting her from wearing a necklace with a cross on it.

Antidiscrimination Statutes

Title VII of the Civil Rights Act of 1964 (Title VII) prohibits employers from discriminating in "terms and conditions of employment" based on race, color, religion, sex, or national origin.[7] Grooming policies and dress codes are terms and conditions of employment. The grooming policies attacked as gender discrimination primarily have involved different hair length requirements for men and women. Courts routinely uphold such standards if they reflect cultural norms and do not treat one sex more harshly than the other. The grooming rules challenged as race discrimination mainly have been no-beard rules. About 25% of black men (compared with less than 1% of white men) suffer from a skin disorder caused by clean shaving, so no-beard rules have a disparate negative impact on black men. Some courts have upheld no-beard rules while others have pronounced them unlawful. (Disparate impact is discussed further in the "Discrimination" section later in this chapter.)

Dress codes that treat the sexes differently, such as rules that require men to wear ties, are lawful if they do not favor one gender over the other. On the other hand, rules that require only women to wear revealing or physically uncomfortable uniforms, facial makeup, or contact lenses instead of glasses have been invalidated as discriminatory. (Casinos and restaurants mandated these "sexually appealing" uniforms.) Policies that limit an individual's ability to observe religious customs have been attacked as religious discrimination. In 1990 a court upheld a state statute that prohibited a Muslim public school teacher from wearing a head covering. Likewise, in 2007 the city of Philadelphia's rule prohibiting a Muslim police officer from wearing a head covering was upheld. In both cases, the courts concluded that requiring employers to accommodate these exceptions would impose undue hardship. (Under Title VII, employers must accommodate employees' religious beliefs unless doing so would impose undue hardship, as discussed below.) But in 2008 the New York State Department of Corrections settled a high-profile Title VII case by agreeing to determine on a case-by-case basis whether to grant religious exemptions from uniform and grooming regulations. It also agreed to allow personnel to wear close-fitting, solid dark-blue or black religious skullcaps, provided no undue hardship was posed. (Exhibit 2.5 considers the need for dress and grooming codes in the government workplace.)

Exhibit 2.5   Dress and Grooming Regulations in the Public Service

Clothes make the man. Naked people have little or no influence in society.

—Mark Twain

Written and unwritten dress and grooming codes are common in the private and public sectors because a suitably attired and groomed workforce is an integral part of a professional, productive organization. As vital mediators in social relations, clothing and hairstyle choices can reflect complex feelings about power, money, autonomy, and gender, feelings that often have significant interpersonal consequences. Although few would deny the obvious superiority of character and values as bases for judgment, too much credence may be given to glib assertions that images are without moment; empirical evidence demonstrates that people readily form opinions—right or wrong—about the social and professional desirability of individuals based largely on their appearance.

The government is a highly visible employer; its employment relations practices are observed and emulated. One reason dress and grooming practices matter to public employers is that they have subtle and obvious implications for management philosophies (e.g., participative management), task organization (employee teams), personnel functions (selection, placement, evaluation), quality of work life (self-confidence, mutual respect), and constitutional issues (freedom of speech, equal treatment, sex discrimination). In government, dress and grooming can also represent the mantle of state authority.

Managers also should be aware of the instrumental role played by dress and grooming in communicating personal and organizational credibility and responsibility. In one national sample of state managers, a majority of respondents thought "well-dressed and groomed people are often perceived as more intelligent, hardworking, and socially acceptable than those with a more casual appearance." They rejected the contention that "an employee's appearance is unimportant to the organization." Given this consensus, it is not surprising that an Oklahoma agency dress code codifies these attitudes and affirms that "all employees . . . are representatives of the State . . . and shall dress accordingly, in a manner that presents a good image."

These data suggest that certain norms, or formal and informal dress rules, are part of the fabric of most agency cultures. Ignoring commonly held standards of neatness, demonstrating an inability to adapt to the work environment, and showing insensitivity to one's milieu could affect job performance. For example, an employee of the Equal Employment Opportunity Commission would likely encounter difficulties in rendering service to the public if he or she wore Nazi or Ku Klux Klan insignia to work.

A current social trend is body art and ornamentation. According to the American Academy of Dermatology (2008), 24% of the U.S. population has at least one tattoo, compared with 1% a generation ago. As with dress and grooming standards, employers have wide latitude in developing appearance regulations to address skin decoration, but the rules must be justifiable, consistently enforced, nondiscriminatory, and flexible enough to allow for reasonable accommodation of religious beliefs and disabilities. (These legal requirements are discussed in the "Grooming and Dress Codes" section of this chapter.) To illustrate, the state has a right to promote a disciplined, identifiable, and professional police force by maintaining its uniform as a symbol of impartiality; accordingly, the state can require police officers to cover tattoos that are offensive or disruptive.

A clear, one-size-fits-all standard of dress and grooming is not recommended here. Given wide variations of occupations and agencies, not only would such a code be difficult to promulgate, but it also would be contrary to the agency-initiated, participative management approach needed to develop useful standards. A contingency approach seems warranted.

SOURCES: American Academy of Dermatology (2008), Bowman (1992), pp. 35–51.

PREEMPLOYMENT INVESTIGATIONS: TRUTH, PERSONALITY, HEALTH, CREDIT, AND CRIMINAL RECORDS

The cardinal rule for **preemployment investigations**, including interviews, questionnaires, and record checks, is that they must be job related. Employers should not inquire about personal matters, such as marital status, the willingness of a working spouse to relocate, or if the person has children, because those questions are not germane to the candidate's ability to perform the job. Instead, the interviewer should ask, for example, whether there are any barriers to relocation, and whether adequate child care is available (if the applicant discloses having children). These questions solicit the information the organization actually needs to know. (Chapter 4 reviews the hiring process in detail.)

Once the hiring committee crafts its questions, how can it ascertain if an applicant answers them truthfully? "Scientific" tests are alluring, but the Employee Polygraph Protection Act of 1988 restricts the use of polygraph tests due to concerns about the technology's accuracy. Private businesses rarely are authorized to use such tests. Public agencies are exempt from the act, but the law does not preempt state or local regulation, and about half the states have enacted antipolygraph statutes. Even when testing is not prohibited, it has been challenged in court with success. The Texas Supreme Court held that a state agency's use of mandatory polygraph testing violated the state constitution's right to privacy. And the Montana Supreme Court determined that a state law allowing polygraph testing of law enforcement personnel but not other government employees violated the state constitution's equal protection clause (the Washington Supreme Court reached a contrary result). If polygraph testing is used, questions about characteristics protected by antidiscrimination laws should be avoided because they suggest that hiring decisions will be based on those factors.

Some organizations seek to refine the hiring process by using personality and psychological tests, such as the Myers-Briggs Type Indicator, which provides information about decision-making styles and interpersonal interactions, and the Minnesota Multiphasic Personality Inventory (MMPI), which tests for some adult psychopathologies. Not surprisingly, given the controversial nature of psychological testing, there are legal restraints on its use. If a test is a "medical exam" under the Americans with Disabilities Act (ADA), which some courts have found the MMPI to be, it may not be administered until after a conditional offer of employment has been made. And if a disability is then revealed, such as a tendency toward alcoholism, ADA requirements must be followed. Some states—for example, Massachusetts—prohibit the use of any written exam to assess honesty, which includes the MMPI. In general, psychological and personality exams should be used for public sector applicants only when state laws allow it and when the tests are job related, such as when public safety is involved. Employers should ensure that tests are given at the right point in time, instruments are valid, results are interpreted and used lawfully, and confidentiality is maintained. Agencies may be required to give individuals access to their own test results under state laws mandating disclosure of medical records.

Medical testing of public sector applicants is usually done to detect drug and alcohol use or the presence of communicable diseases. These investigations are subject to legal restrictions as well. Under the ADA, preoffer applicants may not be required to answer medical questionnaires or to take medical tests. Postoffer but preplacement medical exams are permissible and need not be job related. Medical testing of current employees must be job related. For example, an AIDS test may be administered if transmission of HIV is a demonstrable risk. Return-to-work medical exams after disability leave are lawful. The results of such tests must be kept confidential and used in a nondiscriminatory way.

An emerging concern is the use of genetic testing for illnesses that might affect job performance, such as Alzheimer's disease. The Genetic Information Nondiscrimination Act of 2008 (covered in greater detail in Chapter 4) prohibits employers from discriminating on the basis of genetic information. It bars employers from requesting or requiring genetic testing and from purchasing genetic information about employees, applicants, or their family members. Some 35 states also have laws against genetic discrimination in employment. (A list of state laws and analysis of their coverage is available from the National Conference of State Legislatures.) Although these laws aim to prevent employers from acquiring "genetic information," employers still receive it, for example, in a family health history provided as part of a preemployment health exam, or in documentation supporting a leave request (e.g., a prophylactic mastectomy). If genetic information is revealed, agencies must be careful how they use and maintain it.

Does an applicant's financial history reveal whether the person will be a dependable, trustworthy employee? Perhaps, but Congress enacted the Fair Credit Reporting Act of 1970, as amended in 2003, in part to prevent employers from using inaccurate or arbitrary financial information. To obtain a credit report on an applicant, the prospective employer must ask the applicant to authorize one. Before taking adverse action based on a credit report, the employer must provide the applicant with a copy and advise her of her legal rights. About one-third of the states also have laws regulating the use of credit reports, but the Fair Credit Reporting Act may preempt them. Other laws regulate this area as well. The federal Bankruptcy Act prohibits public and private organizations from denying or terminating employment because an individual has declared bankruptcy. *Garnishment* of wages for child support or other reasons places administrative burdens on employers, but many states forbid adverse action due to garnishment, and if the adverse action has a disparate impact, it may violate Title VII.

Applicants' criminal history records are of great moment to government employers. The paradox is that about 92 million people, or one in three adults, have criminal records (U.S. Department of Labor, 2013). Three types of laws address the necessity/permissibility of criminal background checks. In the first category are laws that mandate preemployment criminal record reviews. These laws cover applicants seeking positions with access to vulnerable persons (e.g., children, the elderly, patients, and prisoners) and positions of great trust (e.g., with the lottery, in nuclear power facilities, and in law enforcement). Common-law doctrines also may oblige an agency to take this step. For example, an employer may be liable for "negligent hiring" if it fails to perform a check and, as a result, unreasonably exposes coworkers or others to a dangerous person who harms them. A second group of laws allow but do not require checks. Lastly, a third group of laws restrict access to or use of criminal records or allow applicants to withhold them.

Deciding what to do about criminal records revealed is a separate policy choice. Governments may disqualify persons convicted of certain offenses (e.g., felonies) for certain jobs, either permanently or for a set period, or they may consider each applicant's situation individually. A few states prohibit discrimination against applicants with criminal records. Even in states without laws of this type, constitutions and Title VII provide some protection. For example, a state law prohibiting the hiring of all convicted felons for civil service positions was held to violate the federal Equal Protection Clause, and an agency's refusal to hire individuals with arrest records violated the state constitution. In another case, the blanket rejection of all convicted felons was held to be disparate impact race discrimination under Title VII. Criminal record checks are necessary for many positions, but managers should pay attention to applicable laws, the relationship between the crime and the position, and the time elapsed since the conviction. They also should base restrictions on convictions, not arrests. The EEOC publishes helpful guidance on this topic.

Postemployment References

Should a former employer be able to limit a person's job prospects by providing a negative reference? There is a striking paradox here between the needs of employers and those of employees. Open communication about employees in the job market promotes efficient hiring, but protecting individuals from **defamation** is essential. A job reference is defamatory if it contains a false statement that injures an individual's work reputation. Written defamation is libel; spoken defamation is slander. References with *unfounded* allegations of misconduct, incompetence, poor performance, criminal or other illegal conduct, dishonesty, or falsification of records are defamatory because they impugn the employee's ability or fitness for a job. Employers who provide job references have a common-law *privilege* that broadly protects them from liability for defamation, but they lose that protection if they provide information they know is false, act with reckless disregard for the truth or falsity of the information, communicate the information to persons who are not within the purpose of the privilege, or excessively publish it. In addition to this common-law shield, approximately 36 states have crafted legislation protecting employers who provide job-related information in good faith. Still, some organizations believe the safer approach is to provide abbreviated references, usually job title, dates of employment, and salary history (Cooper, 2001). If an agency allows its supervisors to give references, it should provide them with training on how to compose lawful ones.

DISCRIMINATION

Antidiscrimination Laws

The "big three" federal antidiscrimination statutes—Title VII of the **Civil Rights Act of 1964**, the **Age Discrimination in Employment Act of 1967 (ADEA)**, and the **Americans with Disabilities Act of 1990 (ADA)**—are discussed below. The cumulative effect of these laws is that employers may not discriminate against employees on the basis of race, color, national origin, religion, sex (gender), age (40 years and older), or disability. A host of other federal laws and myriad state and local laws forbid discrimination based on additional criteria, such as sexual orientation, gender identity, marital status, familial status, medical condition, political affiliation, military discharge status, weight, height, and physical appearance.[8]

In public employment, an oft-cited goal of antidiscrimination laws and affirmative action initiatives is a representative bureaucracy. Has this objective been accomplished? A study using data from 2000 found that the federal government employed a higher proportion of African Americans, Asian Americans, and persons categorized as "Native Americans and others" and a lower proportion of Hispanics than would be expected based on the labor pool, leading the authors to conclude that affirmative action programs have increased the overall representation of minorities but benefited certain groups at the expense of others (Kogut & Short, 2007). Other scholars have noted that, as of 2000, women were still grossly underrepresented in high-level positions (Hsieh & Winslow, 2006). More generally, critics contend that current antidiscrimination law is out-of-date because it addresses only conscious prejudice, not unconscious bias, which persists (Cunningham, Preacher, & Banaji, 2001). The demographic changes in America's workforce, the legal erosions of affirmative action, and new understandings derived from psychological and sociological research pose ongoing challenges to those devising future *diversity* efforts, a topic covered in Chapters 3 and 4. (Exhibit 2.6 explains how antidiscrimination laws are enforced in the public sector.)

Exhibit 2.6   It's Good to Be the Government

An employee seeking to enforce Title VII against a private company initially must file a complaint with the Equal Employment Opportunity Commission or a comparable state gatekeeping agency. These agencies investigate discrimination and retaliation claims, determine whether they have merit, try to conciliate disputes, and sometimes prosecute cases themselves. Plaintiffs with meritorious complaints eventually may file civil suits in courts and, if successful, may receive large damage awards, including lost pay, attorneys' fees, compensation for mental anguish, and punitive damages.

In the public sector, governments have enacted more employer-friendly enforcement models for themselves. Both Title VII and the Rehabilitation Act add an extra layer of procedure for federal workers. Every federal agency has an equal employment opportunity counselor who initially must review a complaint. If the counselor cannot resolve it, the agency investigates, holds a hearing if requested, and issues a decision. Only then may an unsatisfied employee file a complaint with the EEOC. If the employee eventually succeeds in court, the government's financial exposure is less; no punitive damages are available against governments.

Congress likewise benefits from unique enforcement provisions. The Congressional Accountability Act of 1995 applied the protections of 11 employment laws to employees of Congress but created special procedures and remedies for them. Following suit, the Judicial Conference of the United States recommended that employees in the federal court system have rights comparable to those in the legislative branch.

Title VII covers state and local governments if they have 15 or more employees, but personal staff, legal advisers, and policy-making assistants have special procedures and minimal remedies. Due to sovereign immunity, employees cannot use the Age Discrimination in Employment Act or the Americans with Disabilities Act to sue state governments.

Intentional Discrimination

Title VII, the ADEA, and the ADA make it unlawful for an employer to make an adverse employment decision *because of* an individual's race, color, religion, sex, national origin, age, or disability. The most straightforward claim is one alleging **disparate treatment discrimination**, also known as intentional discrimination. Under this theory of liability, proving the motivation of the employer is key. But proving a person's state of mind is difficult; a manager's thought process cannot be observed, so her motivation must be inferred from statements and actions. One way a plaintiff may prove discriminatory motivation is with **direct evidence**—a written or oral statement revealing bias—for example, a supervisor calling an employee a "black radical" while firing him. The timing and context of a statement are important. For example, a supervisor's remark that all Italians are "mobsters and goombahs," uttered to a coworker several months before the employee's discharge, was not adequate to prove anti-Italian bias toward the plaintiff at the time of his discharge.

The civil rights laws are decades old, and few supervisors, even if they harbor strong prejudices, are unwise enough to vent them. A more common and more complicated way an employee may prove intentional discrimination is through **indirect evidence**. Here, the plaintiff relies on the employer's actions to support an inference of unlawful motive. First, the plaintiff must present evidence that he or she was treated differently based on a forbidden criterion. (In a hiring case alleging race discrimination, the Supreme Court said the plaintiff could do this by proving that the complainant belongs to a racial minority; that the complainant applied for and was qualified for a job for which the employer was seeking applicants; that, despite the complainant's qualifications, he or she was rejected; and that, after the rejection, the position remained open and the employer continued to seek applicants from persons of the complainant's qualifications. These elements can be adapted to fit promotion, discharge, and other adverse action claims.) Second, the employer can defeat the plaintiff's claim by presenting evidence that it had a *legitimate business reason* for its action. Third, the plaintiff can introduce evidence to show that the employer's stated business reason was a *pretext* to hide its real discriminatory motive. This analytical approach, known as the **McDonnell Douglas burden-shifting framework**, was announced by the Supreme Court in *McDonnell Douglas Corp. v. Green* (1973), and it is used in the vast majority of discrimination cases.

Employers have many defenses available. Typically, an agency argues that the adverse action was prompted by a legitimate business reason and the supervisor had no discriminatory intent. But sometimes the evidence shows that the supervisor had a *mixed motive*, meaning that he or she was motivated by a legitimate business reason *and* an unlawful criterion. Imagine, for example, a boss who fires a prison guard for arriving late and for speaking Spanish to coworkers on breaks. Under Title VII, if an employer proves it would have made the same decision without considering the illegal factor, the victim's remedies are limited to a declaration that the conduct was unlawful, reinstatement, and attorney's fees. Under the ADEA and ADA, a mixed motive is an absolute defense; the plaintiff receives nothing.

Title VII and the ADEA prevent employers from segregating workers in positions on the basis of a proscribed dimension. For example, employers may not limit job applicants for a position to those under 40 years of age. But these acts allow segregation in the rare circumstances where it is an essential requirement of the position, known as a *bona fide occupational qualification* (BFOQ). An example would be auditioning only female actors for a female role. Race is never a BFOQ. Today, BFOQs are seldom utilized because they are difficult to defend. Thus, a men's prison may not make "being male" a job qualification for guards unless it can show that, for job-related reasons, females must be excluded. (Exhibit 2.7 discusses the need to prohibit employers from making decisions based on sexual orientation and gender identity.)

Exhibit 2.7 Inclusive Nondiscrimination Policies: Sexual Orientation and Gender Identity and Expression

Kristin M. Brown, MSW, MPA

Progress is under way in the United States to address employment discrimination affecting gay, lesbian, bisexual, and transgender people. However, many are still without protection from discrimination in local areas and workplaces that have not yet adopted and implemented inclusive nondiscrimination policies. A review of studies has documented ongoing discrimination (Badgett, Sears, Lau, & Ho, 2009).

Federal statutes prohibit job-related discrimination on the basis of race, color, religion, sex, national origin, age, or disability for companies with more than 15 employees. In 1998, Executive Order 13087 outlawed discrimination related to "sexual orientation" in federal civilian employment, except for the Central Intelligence Agency, the National Security Agency, and the Federal Bureau of Investigation; in 2014, President Obama issued Executive Order 11478, which added "gender identity" as a protected category. This order also amended Executive Order 11246 to prohibit discrimination by federal contractors. The Don't Ask, Don't Tell Repeal Act of 2010 sought to improve conditions for gay, lesbian, and bisexual people in the military, but it does not apply to transgender people.

Currently, 21 states and Washington, D.C., prohibit discrimination based on "sexual orientation" (Human Rights Campaign [HRC], 2014c). Of these, 18 states and Washington, D.C., also prohibit discrimination based on "gender identity." So far, 190 local governments prohibit discrimination based on "gender identity" as well as "sexual orientation" throughout their areas (HRC, 2014a). At the time of this writing, 2,211 private sector companies, 175 nonprofit organizations, and 577 universities and colleges include "sexual orientation" as a protected category in their nondiscrimination policies (HRC, 2014b). At least 790 of the private sector companies, 35 of the nonprofit organizations, and 104 of the universities and colleges also include "gender identity" as a protected category (HRC, 2014b). Some of the policies also include "gender expression" as a protected category.

Efforts have been made since 1974 to pass legislation in Congress such as the Employment Non-Discrimination Act (H.R. 1755; S. 815), which includes protections for transgender people; it passed in the Senate in 2013, but not in the House. Policies that prohibit discrimination based on anatomical "sex" and "sexual orientation" do not adequately protect all people from discrimination (Sellers, 2014). *Sexual orientation* refers to attraction, while *gender identity* and *gender expression* refer to individuals' sense of their gender. A transgender person's inner sense of gender identity differs from the gender that individual was assigned at birth. To protect all people from discrimination related to actual or perceived gender and sexual orientation, nondiscrimination policies need to include reference to "gender identity" and "gender expression."

(Continued)

Exhibit 2.7 (Continued)

Simply having inclusive nondiscrimination policies is not adequate; such policies must be implemented. In addition to revising their nondiscrimination statements, employers should update other employment policies (Sellers, 2014). The Affordable Care Act prohibits discrimination on the basis of sexual orientation and gender identity for plans provided through state and federal health insurance marketplaces. Lifetime limits and denial of coverage due to preexisting conditions, such as HIV, also are prohibited. Many health insurance policies specifically exclude medical procedures and prescriptions for transgender persons' health care. Since May 2014, Medicare claims for transgender health care have been processed like other claims and are no longer specifically excluded (National Center for Transgender Equality, 2014). The state of Massachusetts provides health care coverage for low-income and disabled transgender people, and such coverage is provided through Medicaid in California and Vermont. The Human Rights Campaign's website (www.hrc.org) is a good source of information on how employers can put inclusive nondiscrimination policies into action for improvement in the workplace.

Retaliation

The antidiscrimination statutes not only prohibit discrimination but also prohibit reprisal. Title VII, the ADEA, and the ADA make it unlawful to discriminate against an individual because of *opposition* to a prohibited employment practice or because of *participation* in an investigation, proceeding, or hearing. An employee who reports being sexually harassed and is fired as a consequence is a victim of **retaliation**. To prevail on a retaliation claim, a plaintiff must prove that she engaged in a protected activity, that adverse action was taken against her, and that there was a causal connection between the two. As with discrimination claims, the employer's motive may be proven with direct or indirect evidence. Many other laws, including the FLSA, the FMLA, 42 U.S.C. § 1981, whistleblower acts, civil rights acts, and workers' compensation acts, protect employees from retaliation.

In 2013, retaliation claims accounted for approximately 41% of all charges filed with the EEOC. Strategically, such claims offer plaintiffs an advantage: Causation is often easier to prove than in discrimination claims. The time sequence alone—protected activity followed by discipline—may be enough to suggest a cause-and-effect relationship, especially if the events occurred close together. From the employer's perspective, these claims are a disincentive to discipline individuals who recently engaged in protected activity. Exhibit 2.8 demonstrates how an employer might respond to an accusation that it failed to hire an employee for a new position because he previously filed a discrimination complaint.

Harassment

Title VII makes it unlawful for an employee to be subjected, on the basis of a proscribed criterion, to unwelcome **harassment** that is severe or pervasive enough to create an objectively hostile or abusive work environment. Many people associate harassment claims with

Exhibit 2.8   Employer's Response to Charge of Retaliation

June 2, 2010
Mary Stanford
Employment Investigator
Florida Commission on Human Relations
2009 Appalachee Parkway, Suite 200
Tallahassee, FL 32301

Re: Garry Goodwin v. City of Merriton
      FCHR No.: 201001625

Dear Ms. Stanford:

Please accept this letter as the City of Merriton's ("City") Mediation/Position Statement regarding the Charge of Discrimination filed by Mr. Garry Goodwin against the City on May 5, 2010.[1]

The City absolutely denies the allegations in the Charge that it retaliated against Mr. Goodwin because of his previously filed EEOC racial discrimination complaint. Mr. Goodwin's claims that he had better qualifications and better evaluations than the person who was hired are totally false and misleading.

In July 2005, Mr. Goodwin was hired by the City's Underground Utilities Department as a Utility Service Worker and he remains employed in that position. In August 2007, Mr. Goodwin unsuccessfully applied for a position in Electric Distribution Operations. Upon not receiving that position, Mr. Goodwin filed an EEOC complaint and lawsuit against the City alleging discrimination based on race. In June 2009, Mr. Goodwin applied for a Meter Service Technician position with the City's Underground Utilities Department. When he did not receive the Meter Service Technician job, he filed this complaint.

The interview committee for the Meter Service Technician position was made up of three Underground Utilities Department employees. None of the members of the committee knew about the previous EEOC complaint filed by Mr. Goodwin against the City (see affidavits of Janette Inman, Julius Anderson, and Chris Christensen as Exhibit 6). The interview committee asked every interviewee a set of prepared questions. The committee considered the number of correct answers to these questions, and in addition, considered the work ethic and habits of the candidates at their current job position. Two committee members recommended Kevin Stout as their top candidate. The other committee member recommended Peter Goring as her number one candidate. The interview committee did not discuss Mr. Goodwin as being among the most qualified applicants. Tip Tomberlin, Superintendent of the Department, was the hiring authority. Mr. Tomberlin accepted the decision of the majority of the committee that Mr. Stout was the best candidate for the position. Mr. Tomberlin had no knowledge of Mr. Goodwin's previous EEOC complaint (see affidavit of Tip Tomberlin, attached as Exhibit 6).

According to the committee, Mr. Stout was more qualified than the other applicants based on technical knowledge and work ethic. Mr. Stout had slightly more correct answers than Mr. Goodwin did to the set of prepared questions. Additionally, Mr. Stout had better work evaluations at his previous job than did Mr. Goodwin. For example, Mr. Stout completed his employee callback paperwork on a consistent and timely basis, and he completed all employee-mandated training courses. In contrast, Mr. Goodwin consistently had deficiencies in his required callback paperwork and had not completed twenty required training courses at the time of the interview.

(Continued)

Exhibit 2.8 (Continued)

Legal Analysis

To establish a discriminatory retaliation cause of action under the Florida Civil Rights Act of 1992, the charging party must demonstrate the following elements: (1) a statutorily protected expression; (2) an adverse employment action; and (3) a causal connection between the participation in the protected expression and the adverse action. In order to satisfy the "causal connection" element, the charging party must establish that the opposing party was aware of the protected expression at the time the adverse employment action took place.

Moreover, if the time period between the protected activity and the adverse employment action is sufficiently long, and the employee presents no evidence of causation other than the employer's knowledge of the protected activity, the employee has not proven causation. See *Higdon v. Jackson,* 393 F. 3d 1211 (11th Cir. 2004) ("In light of the other evidence in the record, the three and one-half month temporal proximity is insufficient to create a jury issue on causation.").

Here, Mr. Goodwin has not established that the hiring committee or the hiring authority was aware of the previous EEOC complaint he filed against the City. Further, Mr. Goodwin's previous complaint was over a year and a half prior to the selection for the current position, which is too long a time period to establish causation. Regardless, the City had legitimate, non-discriminatory reasons for not hiring Mr. Goodwin: (1) he had not completed training courses that the selected candidate had completed; (2) he had a history of turning in deficient paperwork; (3) he was not impressive in the interview. The Committee did not recommend Mr. Goodwin for hire because he was not one of the most qualified candidates.

In conclusion, the City respectfully requests this Commission to make a finding of "No Cause" and dismiss Mr. Goodwin's charge of retaliation in its entirety. If I can provide any additional information, please do not hesitate to contact me.

Sincerely,
Terry Curry
Assistant City Attorney

[1]Additionally, the City will provide the following documentation that supports its position at mediation.

Exhibit 1   The City's job description of Utility Service Worker.

Exhibit 2   The City's job description of Meter Service Technician.

Exhibit 3   Employment Application of Kevin Stout for the Meter Service Technician position.

Exhibit 4   Employment Application of Peter Goring for the Meter Service Technician position.

Exhibit 5   Employment Application of Garry Goodwin for the Meter Service Technician position.

Exhibit 6   Affidavits of Janette Inman, Julius Anderson, Chris Christensen and Tip Tomberlin.

Exhibit 7   Organizational Chart of City Departments.

Exhibit 8   EEOC Charge dated January 12, 2008.

Exhibit 9   City of Merriton Policies and Procedures on Anti-Discrimination.

Exhibit 10   EEO Analysis of City of Merriton (Citywide on disk) for Period Ending March 31, 2009.

SOURCE: Sally Gertz, Clinical Professor

gender discrimination (i.e., sexual harassment), but a claim is viable if an employee is harassed due to any characteristic listed in Title VII, the ADEA, or the ADA. Typically, it is the behavior of supervisors, coworkers, and others who interact regularly with the employee that creates a **hostile environment**.

Whether objectionable conduct is severe or pervasive enough to be unlawful is often the pivotal question. These laws are not "general civility codes," and they do not provide redress for behavior that is simply rude, abrasive, unkind, or insensitive. Courts look at the gravity, frequency, duration, character, and threatening nature of the conduct. Occasional racial or ethnic slurs are seldom enough to create a hostile environment, but a 6-month period of being called "ayatollah" and "camel jockey" was sufficient to support an Iraqi employee's claim. In another case, a female employee who acquiesced to her supervisor's ongoing unwelcome sexual conduct established a claim. And non-English-speaking workers forced to abide by an employer's English-only rules were successful.

An employer has a defense to a hostile environment claim, the *Ellerth/Faragher* **affirmative defense**, if it exercises reasonable care to prevent and correct the harassment, and if the employee unreasonably fails to use the remedial procedures. An organization can reasonably prevent harassment by adopting adequate policies and procedures, ensuring that all staff members receive the policies, and training supervisors to handle complaints properly. The Virginia Department of Corrections is a good example of an employer that avoided liability by quickly correcting harassment. A supervisor distributed a memo to prison personnel about dress codes and identified the plaintiff as someone who wore attire that was too revealing. After the memo was distributed, coworkers made crude jokes. Managers at the prison prevented public posting of the memo, counseled the supervisor who wrote and distributed it, admonished the employees who made the offensive remarks, and stopped the harassment. When nonsupervisory coworkers or nonemployees (such as customers, contractors, or others sharing the work site) create a hostile work environment, the agency is responsible if it was negligent, meaning if it knew or should have known about the harassment and failed to take prompt and appropriate corrective action.

One of the toughest hostile environment claims to defend against is one that involves **tangible employment action**—a significant change in employment status, such as hiring, firing, failure to promote, reassignment with significantly different responsibilities, or a significant change in benefits. An example would be an administrative assistant who resists a boss's sexual demands and is given less desirable work assignments. If a supervisor takes tangible employment action against a victim based on unwelcome sexual conduct, the employer faces a tough legal battle because the *Ellerth/Faragher* affirmative defense is not available. For managers, the lesson is that all personnel actions should be scanned for improper motivation.

Affirmative Action

Beginning in the early 1960s, many government employers voluntarily adopted **affirmative action** plans to increase the numbers of employees from groups historically excluded from their workplaces. They also adopted rules requiring vendors seeking contracts from the government to adopt such plans. These plans used various means to achieve a more representative workforce, including targeted recruitment and training programs, numerical goals and timetables, and special preferences in hiring and promotion. In the 1980s and 1990s, court decisions raised doubts about the lawfulness of these plans under both Title VII and the Equal Protection Clause, and most were modified or suspended. Even when affirmative action programs are legal they are contentious because they contain a conspicuous paradox: They use race-based decision making to remedy harm caused by race-based decision making. Understandably, critics ask: If race was an unfair criterion to use in the past, how can it be a fair criterion to use now? (Such programs do include women and other minorities, but the debate over affirmative action usually is couched in terms of race.)

Title VII protects all groups, including majority groups, from discrimination. As a result, a white employee, for example, who has been treated disparately on the basis of race due to an affirmative action plan may use Title VII to bring an action for *reverse discrimination*. Additionally, Title VII requires any affirmative action program to be described in a formally adopted plan. The plan must remedy conspicuous racial imbalances in traditionally segregated job categories, it must be temporary, its purpose must be to remedy underrepresentation (not to maintain gender or racial balances indefinitely), and it must not unduly trammel the rights of the majority.

Under the Equal Protection Clause, a government affirmative action program based on race or ethnicity is reviewed using the exacting strict scrutiny standard. It is constitutional only if it is narrowly tailored to further a compelling governmental interest. To date, only the goal of remedying past discrimination has been compelling enough for the Supreme Court to approve a plan. Furthermore, the government adopting the plan must provide convincing proof of its own past discrimination.[9] If an affirmative action program is based on gender rather than on race or ethnicity, it receives less rigorous intermediate judicial scrutiny; it will be approved if it has a substantial relationship to an important governmental interest.

The most prominent case in this area in the recent past did not involve employment. In 2003, the Supreme Court decided in *Grutter v. Bollinger* that the University of Michigan Law School could constitutionally use a race-conscious admissions policy because the law school had a compelling interest in attaining a diverse student body. The impact of this decision in the public employment context is still unclear. Prior to *Grutter*, it was widely accepted that attaining workforce diversity was not a sufficiently compelling reason for a race-based program. But after *Grutter*, the Seventh Circuit approved a plan by the city of Chicago to increase diversity among its police sergeants. The city's compelling reason was its desire to set the proper tone in the department and to earn the trust of the community, which in turn would increase police effectiveness. This is an area where caution and expert advice are necessary. A plan that seeks cultural diversity runs the risk of being denounced as unlawful racial or ethnic balancing.

In rare cases, affirmative action plans may be involuntarily imposed on employers by courts to remedy past discrimination. In 1987, for example, after years of litigation, a federal court ordered the Alabama Department of Public Safety to use quotas to increase the number of minority state troopers. The Supreme Court approved the plan because of the department's history of overt and defiant racism.

Unintentional Discrimination

In addition to intentional discrimination, Title VII, the ADA, and the ADEA prohibit neutral practices that inadvertently produce a disproportionate or disparate impact on a protected group. The Supreme Court first accepted the theory in *Griggs v. Duke Power Co.* (1971), and it was codified in the Civil Rights Act of 1991. **Disparate impact discrimination** claims most frequently challenge hiring and promotion devices, but the theory can be used for layoffs and other employment practices. To aid enforcement, the EEOC requires employers to maintain records of all hiring, promotion, and firing by race, sex, and national origin. Hiring and promotion test scores also must be kept.

To prove disparate impact, an employee must show that a specific selection device had an exclusionary effect. In *Griggs,* a high school graduation requirement and a battery of aptitude tests disproportionately excluded blacks from being hired. There is no "bright line" rule stating how much disparity is unlawful, but the EEOC uses an 80%, or four-fifths, "rule of thumb." If the qualification rates of protected groups are less than 80% of the rate of the highest group, then the selection device is suspect. The Supreme Court has disparaged the EEOC's *80% rule* and has stated that a "case-by-case" approach is necessary because "statistics come in a variety and their usefulness depends on all the surrounding facts and circumstances" (*Watson v. Fort Worth Bank & Trust,* 1988). Still, since the EEOC investigates and determines the merit of claims, and sometimes prosecutes them, agencies should use the 80% rule as a guide.

An employer can defend against a disparate impact claim by showing that a challenged practice is job related and a business necessity. This defense can be used for subjective procedures, such as interviews, and objective procedures, such as tests. To defend tests as job related, agencies must prove their validity. The EEOC adopted the *Uniform Guidelines on Employee Selection Procedures* to assist organizations with this endeavor. If a test is proven to have predictive validity, content validity, or construct validity under these guidelines, then it is job related and its use is justified even if it has a disparate impact. (Chapter 4 explains these validation methods in detail.)

Rather than validating tests, some employers have sought to avoid disparate impact claims by using scores creatively. For example, one agency adopted a cutoff score above which test performance was irrelevant; the court, however, ruled that the cutoff score had to be validated. Another minimized the relative weight of the exam in the selection process; here, the court found the practice to be an unlawful affirmative action plan. Others took the top scores in each racial and gender group, a practice known as **race norming**, now prohibited by the Civil Rights Act of 1991. Still others used **banding**, meaning they treated applicants within a certain range as having identical scores. So far, this process has not been found unlawful, but certain aspects (such as bandwidth) may need to be validated. Finally, the city of New Haven invalidated test results altogether because none of the minority firefighters who passed the exam scored high enough to be considered for the vacant positions, and the city did not want to risk being found guilty of disparate impact discrimination. The Supreme Court held that New Haven's decision to ignore test results violated Title VII.

Age

The ADEA is the main federal statute prohibiting age discrimination. It forbids discrimination against those at least 40 years old, on the basis of age, in the terms and conditions of employment. There is no claim for reverse discrimination by the young. Involuntary retirement generally may not be required, but mandatory retirement is permissible in public safety and executive policy-making positions. Voluntary early retirement incentives are permitted. The act provides a defense for an employer that uses a bona fide seniority system, and in rare instances age may be a bona fide occupational qualification. But employers cannot rely on stereotyped assumptions about older workers' strength, endurance, or speed. Courts have struck down rules that limited the position of flight engineer to those under age 60 and that of bus driver to those under 65.

Disability

The ADA prohibits discrimination against any qualified person with a physical or mental impairment that substantially limits a major life activity. It also protects those with records of impairment, those regarded as impaired, and those who associate with impaired persons. Employers must provide qualified disabled persons with **reasonable accommodation**. The terms "qualified person," "substantially limits," and "major life activity" have spawned considerable litigation. When it was enacted, the ADA was hailed as a major step toward eradicating disability discrimination, but the Supreme Court issued several decisions that sharply limited the scope of the statute (Selmi, 2008). In response, Congress amended the ADA in 2008. The ADA Amendments Act (ADAAA) rejected numerous Supreme Court decisions and EEOC regulations narrowing the act's coverage, and emphasized that the definition of "disability" should be interpreted broadly. One change is that the determination of whether a person has an impairment that qualifies for coverage now is made without any consideration of the impact of mitigating measures, such as medication or prosthetics (the impact of ordinary eyeglasses and contact lenses is considered). Still, even after the amendments, the line between minor conditions that are not covered by the act and substantially limiting impairments that are covered at times is fuzzy. In an attempt to provide more clarity, the EEOC issued regulations with examples of impairments that easily should be concluded to be disabilities, including epilepsy, diabetes, cancer, HIV infection, and bipolar disorder.

To be covered by the ADA, a disabled person must be able to perform essential job functions. This means managers should identify essential job functions in a written job description and ask applicants if they can do them. When an employee requests to be accommodated, managers should make an individualized assessment, with the assistance of the human resource and legal departments, to determine if the person meets threshold conditions to be covered by the act. (Of course, an employer may voluntarily provide accommodation even when it is not legally required.) For qualified persons, accommodations likewise should be determined through individualized assessments. These might include, for example, reserved parking, special equipment, personal aides, part-time or flextime work schedules, and building renovations. Accommodations that cause *undue hardship* to employers are not required.

Religion

Religious employees may request time off for sacred holidays, schedules omitting work on the Sabbath, breaks during the workday to pray and a place to do so, and exceptions to dress and grooming codes. Title VII does more than simply prohibit religious discrimination. Similar to the ADA, it requires employers to make reasonable accommodation for religious beliefs and practices that do not impose undue hardship. "Reasonable accommodation" means that which is minimally necessary for the individual to fulfill his or her religious obligation or conscience. Organizations are not required to compensate workers for time off the job fulfilling religious duties, or to alter work schedules or duty assignments. According to the EEOC (2008), the most common forms of accommodation are (1) flexible scheduling, (2) *voluntary* substitutes or swaps of shifts and assignments, (3) lateral transfer or change of job assignment, and (4) modification of workplace practices, policies, or procedures. The Free Exercise Clause of the First Amendment (as balanced by the Establishment Clause) may expand a public employer's duty to accommodate religiously motivated requests, but the law is unclear. The impact of the Religious Freedom Restoration Act of 1993 on the duty to accommodate also is uncertain. Managers need not accept an employee's suggestion for accommodation, but if the employee offers one, it should be considered. The "Religious Discrimination" section of the *EEOC Compliance Manual* is available online and is a helpful resource for managers responding to accommodation requests (EEOC, 2008).

Preventing and Responding to Discrimination Claims

How can managers prevent discrimination and retaliation claims from occurring and successfully defend those that do arise? Agencies should *have* and be able to *prove* legitimate business reasons for the actions they take. Some basic strategies enable managers to do this. First, agency leaders should not act rashly, but should carefully gather and review all the facts before making personnel decisions. They should consciously articulate and use job-related criteria. By deliberating with other professionals, managers can make sounder and more defensible decisions, as such collective decisions are less likely to have been influenced by any one individual's bad motives. Communication with employees also is essential. Open, two-way communication eliminates surprises, reduces the likelihood of suit, and increases the agency's odds of winning. This should include regular, timely performance evaluations, with positive and negative feedback, and articulation of organizational expectations. When problems arise, supervisors should promptly discuss them with staff members and immediately write summaries of the conferences. Documenting such communication not only underscores management's seriousness but also provides credible evidence. Judges and juries consider contemporaneous business records eminently more reliable than the self-serving testimony of individuals. Organizations should have policies in place prohibiting discrimination, should update them regularly, and should ensure that supervisors and employees receive them. Finally, supervisors and managers should treat all complaints of discrimination and retaliation seriously, regardless of whether complaints are made formally or informally.

SUMMARY AND CONCLUSION

Workplace laws reflect a balance among three competing objectives: managerial efficiency, employee rights, and social aspirations of the law. This balance is not fixed. Rather, it changes to reflect lawmaking and decision making over time. At present, a trend exists to interpret laws in favor of managerial efficiency. Employee rights are becoming ever more narrowly defined.

For example, staff members have few privacy rights at work. "Reasonable" searches of their offices, computers, phones, and excretory fluids are permitted, as is surveillance of their movements. Workers may be required to alter their dress and grooming habits. Applicants for certain jobs may be investigated extensively. Employees must be careful what they say at work. They may be punished for disruptive speech, or for pointing out agency problems they notice as they carry out their duties. Greater numbers of government jobs are being made "at will," so that the people in them can be fired without cause, notice, or explanation.

Still, certain rights remain intact. If an employee has a property interest in employment, he or she cannot be discharged except for cause, and the person must be provided with due process before adverse action can be taken. Certain reasons for taking adverse action remain prohibited: An employer may not discipline an employee for speaking about a matter of public concern in a nondisruptive way (if the comments were not pursuant to the job), for "blowing the whistle" in a manner protected by a whistleblower statute, or for being a member of the "wrong" political party after an election (unless party membership is necessary for the job). An employer cannot retaliate against an individual for participating in a proceeding to enforce a law or for opposing violation of a law. Antidiscrimination laws forbid an employer to intentionally or unintentionally make an employment decision based on a proscribed dimension (and in some areas of the country the list of proscribed dimensions is expanding). Employees must be paid at least a minimum wage and time and a half for overtime (unless they are exempt), must be paid the same as members of the other gender, and must be awarded pensions they already have earned. OSH acts require work sites to meet safety standards, and workers' compensation, health insurance, and FMLA leave provisions provide a safety net for those who become hurt or sick. Public employees rarely are held individually responsible for violating a law.

Of course each "law" described above has conditions, exceptions, and gray areas. Managers who expect the law to provide an exhaustive, well-defined set of prohibited behaviors will be disappointed. Statutes are broad and vague, and court decisions analyze specific conduct under specific conditions. What are administrators to do when the law and their own employers fail to provide definitive guidance? They must form their own judgments. The basis for such judgments is the intent of the law—the values that underlie the cases and statutes discussed in this chapter. For example, if supervisors must respect employees' privacy, then it follows that they should ask permission when they think privacy expectations might be violated, even if they are unsure whether a "right" exists. If employees refuse to cooperate, resolution should be attempted through collaboration, perhaps with assistance from other managers. Cases and laws seldom provide clear-cut answers, but they do provide guideposts that managers can use to ensure that their actions are consistent with the spirit and aims of legislation and court decisions.

KEY TERMS

Adverse action

Affirmative action

Age Discrimination in Employment Act (ADEA)

Americans with Disabilities Act (ADA)

At-will employment

Banding

Civil law system

Civil Rights Act of 1964

Common-law system

Defamation

Direct evidence

Disparate impact discrimination

Disparate treatment discrimination

Dress and grooming codes

Due process rights

Ellerth/Faragher affirmative defense

Equal Employment Opportunity Commission (EEOC)

Fair Labor Standards Act (FLSA)

Family and Medical Leave Act (FMLA)

Free speech rights

Harassment

Hatch Act of 1939

Hostile environment

Indirect evidence

McDonnell Douglas burden-shifting framework

Official immunity

Preemployment investigations

Race norming

Reasonable accommodation

Respondeat superior

Retaliation

Stare decisis

Tangible employment action

Title VII of the Civil Rights Act of 1964

Unemployment compensation

Unreasonable searches

Whistleblower statutes

Workers' compensation

EXERCISES

Class Discussion

1. Some departments in universities believe that their faculty should mirror the demographic composition of the student body and that faculty recruitment should use "diversity" policies to pursue this objective. Assess the merits of this proposition. What laws does it implicate? Can a lawful policy be drafted?

2. Increasingly, people conduct work at home and take care of personal tasks at work. Which privacy rights and responsibilities, if any, does this trend raise, and how might managers deal with them?

3. Many education reformers claim that teacher tenure (in particular the right to be dismissed only "for cause") is an impediment to improvement of primary and secondary schools. Use the test of balancing employee's, employer's, and society's interests to develop a range of possible policies addressing secondary school teacher job security. Which policy strikes the proper balance?

4. A person with a mobility disability applies for a job in your office. Which interview questions can be asked about this disability without violating ADA provisions? Which questions should not be asked? How does this problem exemplify the paradox of needs discussed in the book's introduction?

5. Consider the steps of the hiring process. How can a manager prove that he or she did not discriminate in hiring based on a forbidden criterion but had a legitimate business reason for the choice? What witnesses and documents are available to prove this defense?

Team Activities

6. Design a work group seminar to inform employees about their rights and limits when using social networks, e-mail, texting, and the Internet while at work. What paradoxes exist and how can they be dealt with?

7. A coworker informs you, in confidence, that she feels attracted to another coworker in your office. What legal or policy advice would you give her? If she supervises the person she is attracted to, does that change your advice?

8. An employee requests a leave of absence to attend an event at church. He is important to the success of an effort that you are undertaking as a manager, and the employee's leave is likely to cause some delay and cost. What do you do?

9. A classified civil servant who works as a computer technician for the city was arrested in a sting operation. While off duty, he solicited sex from an undercover male officer in a public restroom. His arrest was reported in the newspaper, where he was identified as "a city employee." No criminal charges were filed. Should the employee be fired for "immorality"?

10. An abuse investigator at the state agency responsible for child protection tells you that she is going to write a letter to the governor and newspaper telling them that the heavy caseloads of investigators are endangering children. How would you advise this coworker?

Individual Assignments

11. Explain the free speech rights of employees. Are there any limits on these rights?

12. For what unlawful actions can public employees be held individually responsible?

13. Define and explain the 80% rule.

14. What substantial interests do public employees have in their jobs?

15. What accommodations must employers make for disabled persons?

16. Based on your experience, give an example of either the paradox of democracy or the paradox of needs using one of the issues raised in this chapter. (Both paradoxes are discussed in the book's introduction.)

17. How may an employer use an applicant's criminal record in a hiring decision? For example, a school district received an application from a man for the position of HVAC engineer.

He appears well qualified, but a criminal background check revealed that 20 years ago he was convicted of possessing half a gram of cocaine, a felony for which he received probation. What laws apply?

18. Roman playwright and carpenter Plautus (254–184 B.C.E.) advised, "Practice what you preach." Do you agree with this advice? Explain your answer using issues from this chapter.

NOTES

1. After *Loudermill,* the Supreme Court ruled that a law enforcement officer who was suspended, rather than discharged, was not entitled to a pretermination hearing because the posttermination hearing was prompt and the loss of income relatively insignificant. To avoid having to determine whether a particular punishment is severe enough to trigger a *Loudermill* predeprivation hearing, many organizations provide such hearings for all adverse actions. Although the Supreme Court predicted that agencies would catch and correct mistakes at pretermination hearings, in practice, employers routinely use them to offer employees the option to resign and avoid being discharged.

2. In 2011, the Supreme Court held that suits under the Petition Clause of the First Amendment, which bars the passing of any law prohibiting petitioning for a governmental redress of grievances, are subject to the same "public concern" test as suits under the Speech Clause. A borough's allegedly retaliatory actions against a police chief who filed and won a grievance did not give rise to liability under the Petition Clause because the grievance did relate to a matter of public concern. Courts are divided over whether the "public concern" test applies to the First Amendment right to freedom of association (the right to association is not explicit, but it has been recognized as protected by the First Amendment). In one case, a youth worker claimed he was fired for retaining an attorney to assist him in a disciplinary matter. The Tenth Circuit Court of Appeals held that the underlying dispute was not an issue of "public concern," so the association was not protected by the First Amendment.

3. Disagreements may arise over whether a condition was preexisting, a treatment is medically necessary, or a treatment is experimental, but most often parties disagree about whether an injury-related disability is permanent and how much money will adequately compensate for it.

4. Government Accounting Standards Board Statements 43 and 45, effective in 2006 and 2007, require public sector employers to report net present liability for future retiree benefits on an accrual basis. A similar accounting change for private sector employers was blamed for a decline in private sector retiree health care coverage. Whether public employers will reduce benefits for retirees remains to be seen.

5. Even before *Windsor,* some executive branch agencies extended health and other federal benefits to same-sex partners. For example, Secretary of State Hillary Clinton directed her agency to extend a variety of relocation, medical, and other benefits to the partners of employees in same-sex, committed relationships (Ginsberg, 2010).

6. Strip searches are in a different category. Employees with public safety duties have a diminished expectation of privacy, but strip searches are so intrusive they must meet a higher standard to be reasonable. The Eighth Circuit Court of Appeals adopted a "reasonable suspicion" standard for strip searches of correctional officers, which means there must be specific objective facts and rational inferences supporting the belief that an employee has contraband hidden on his or her person.

7. The District of Columbia has one of the nation's broadest dress code and grooming statutes. The law prohibits discrimination based on "the outward appearance of any person, irrespective of sex, with regard to bodily condition or characteristics, manner or style of dress, and manner or style of personal grooming,

including, but not limited to, hair style and beards" (District of Columbia Human Rights Act, 2008). An employer violated this statute by discharging a receptionist who had disheveled hair and wore low-cut, tight blouses.

8. The federal laws prohibiting discrimination include the Equal Pay Act, the Rehabilitation Act, the Family Medical Leave Act, Title IX, the 19th-century Civil Rights Acts (§§ 1981, 1983, 1985), the Genetic Information Nondiscrimination Act, the Uniformed Services Employment and Reemployment Act, and the Black Lung Act.

9. Two cases demonstrate how this is possible. In 2003, seven Caucasian police officers sued the city of Boston, alleging that their rights were violated when the police department promoted three African American officers with identical test scores instead of them. The First Circuit found that the department's history of discrimination was well documented by past litigation and records, and the city's evidence of disparity in the promotion of officers to sergeant was strong. In another case in 2007, the Seventh Circuit approved the disadvantaged business enterprises program of Illinois's state transportation agency, which included goal setting. The state relied on the federal government's compelling interest in remedying the effects of past discrimination in the national construction market.

REFERENCES

American Academy of Dermatology. (2008). [Website]. Retrieved from http://www.aad.org

Badgett, M. V. L., Sears, B., Lau, H., & Ho, D. (2009). Bias in the workplace: Consistent evidence of sexual orientation and gender identity discrimination 1998–2008. *Chicago–Kent Law Review, 8,* 559–595.

Bloch, S. J. (2005, Winter). The judgment of history: Faction, political machines, and the Hatch Act. *University of Pennsylvania Journal of Labor & Employment Law, 7,* 255–277.

Board of Regents v. Roth, 408 U.S. 564 (1972).

Bowman, J. (1992). Dress standards in government: A national survey of state administrators. *Review of Public Personnel Administration, 12*(1), 35–51.

Bowman, J. S., & West, J. P. (2007). Lord Acton and employment doctrines: Absolute power and the spread of at-will employment. *Journal of Business Ethics, 74,* 119–130.

Bowman, J. S., & West, J. P. (2009). To "re-Hatch" public employees or not? An ethical analysis of the relaxation of restrictions on political activities in civil service. *Public Administration Review, 69*(1), 52–62.

Branti v. Finkel, 445 U.S. 507 (1980).

Brenner v. Scott, ___ F. 3d ___ (N.D. Fla. 2014).

Bureau of Labor Statistics, U.S. Department of Labor. (2010). National compensation survey: Employee benefits in state and local governments in the United States, March 2010. Economic news release. Retrieved from http://www.bls.gov/news.release/ebs2.nr0.htm

Bureau of Labor Statistics, U.S. Department of Labor. (2012). Census of fatal occupational injuries (CFOI): Current and revised data. Retrieved from http://www.bls.gov/iif/oshcfoi1.htm

Bureau of Labor Statistics, U.S. Department of Labor. (2014). Employee benefits in the United States—March 2014. News release. Retrieved from http://www.bls.gov/ncs/ebs/sp/ebnr0020.pdf

Cleveland Board of Education v. Loudermill, 470 U.S. 532 (1985).

Connick v. Myers, 461 U.S. 138 (1983).

Cooper, M. (2001, Fall). Job reference immunity statutes: Prevalent but irrelevant. *Cornell Journal of Law and Public Policy, 11,* 1–68.

Cunningham, W., Preacher, K. J., & Banaji, M. R. (2001). Implicit attitude measures: Consistency, stability, and convergent validity. *Psychological Science, 12*(2), 163–170.

District of Columbia Human Rights Act, D.C. Code § 2–1401.02 (22) (2008).

Elrod v. Burns, 427 U.S. 347 (1976).

Equal Employment Opportunity Commission. (2008). Section 12: Religious discrimination. In *EEOC compliance manual*. Washington, DC: Author. Retrieved from http://www.eeoc.gov/policy/docs/religion.html

Florida Statutes, § 110.227(1) (2010).

Garcetti v. Ceballos, 126 U.S. 1951 (2006a).

Garcetti v. Ceballos, 547 U.S. 410, 424 (2006b).

Gertz, S. (2001). Florida's civil service appeal process: How "protective" is it? *Justice System Journal, 22*(2), 117–135.

Gertz, S. (2007). At-will employment: Origins, applications, exceptions, and expansions in public service. In J. S. Bowman & J. P. West (Eds.), *American public service: Radical reform and the merit system* (pp. 47–74). New York: Taylor & Francis.

Ginsberg, W. R. (2010). *Federal employee benefits and same-sex partnerships* (CRS Report R41030). Washington, DC: Congressional Research Service. Retrieved from http://assets.opencrs.com/rpts/R41030_20100121.pdf

Greenhouse, S. (2014a, July 15). A push to give steadier shifts to part-timers. *New York Times*. Retrieved from http://www.nytimes.com/2014/07/16/business/a-push-to-give-steadier-shifts-to-part-timers.html?_r = 0

Greenhouse, S. (2014b, July 18). Part-time schedules, full-time headaches. *New York Times*. Retrieved from http://www.nytimes.com/2014/07/19/business/part-time-schedules-full-time-headaches.html?_r = 0

Goldman v. Weinberger, 475 U.S. 503 (1986).

Griggs v. Duke Power Co., 401 U.S. 424 (1971).

Grutter v. Bollinger, 539 U.S. 306 (2003).

Hsieh, C., & Winslow, E. (2006). Gender representation in the federal workforce: A comparison among groups. *Review of Public Personnel Administration, 26*(3), 276–294.

Human Rights Campaign. (2014a). Cities and counties with non-discrimination ordinances that include gender identity. Retrieved from http://www.hrc.org/resources/entry/cities-and-counties-with-non-discrimination-ordinances-that-include-gender

Human Rights Campaign. (2014b). Employer database. Retrieved from http://www.hrc.org/resources/entry/search-our-employer-database

Human Rights Campaign. (2014c). Statewide employment laws and policies. Retrieved from http://hrc-assets.s3-website-us-east-1.amazonaws.com//files/assets/resources/statewide_employment_5-2014.pdf

Kelley v. Johnson, 425 U.S. 347 (1976).

Kogut, C. A., & Short, L. E. (2007). Affirmative action in federal employment: Good intentions run amuck? *Public Personnel Management, 36*(3), 197–206.

Maciag, M. (2014, March). Facing Obamacare mandate, governments may turn to temps. *Governing the States and Localities*. Retrieved from http://www.governing.com/topics/mgmt/gov-government-may-use-temps.html

McDonnell Douglas Corp. v. Green, 411 U.S. 792 (1973).

Munnell, A. H., & Quinby, L. (2012, August). Legal constraints on changes in state and local pensions. *State and Local Pension Plans* (Center for Retirement Research at Boston College), no. 25. Retrieved from http://crr.bc.edu/wp-content/uploads/2012/08/slp_25_508.pdf

National Center for Transgender Equality. (2014, May). *Medicare and transgender people*. Washington, DC: Author. Retrieved from http://transequality.org/PDFs/MedicareAndTransPeople.pdf

National Treasury Employees Union v. Von Raab, 489 U.S. 656 (1989).

Obama, B. (2014, March 13). Memorandum for the secretary of labor: Updating and modernizing overtime regulations. White House, Office of the Press Secretary. Retrieved from http://www.whitehouse.gov/the-press-office/2014/03/13/presidential-memorandum-updating-and-modernizing-overtime-regulations

O'Connor v. Ortega, 480 U.S. 709 (1987).

Pickering v. Board of Education, 391 U.S. 563 (1968).

Ravitch, F., & Lawther, W. (1999). Privatization and public employee pension rights: Treading in unexplored territory. *Review of Public Personnel Administration, 19*(1), 41–58.

Rutan v. Republican Party of Illinois, 497 U.S. 62 (1990).

Sellers, M. D. (2014). Discrimination and the transgender population: Analysis of the functionality of local government policies that protect gender identity. *Administration & Society, 46,* 70–86.

Selmi, M. (2008). Interpreting the Americans with Disabilities Act: Why the Supreme Court rewrote the statute, and why Congress did not care. *George Washington Law Review, 76,* 522–575.

United States v. Windsor, 570 U.S. ___ (2013).

U.S. Department of Justice. (2014). Less restricted employees: Permitted and prohibited activities. Retrieved from http://www.justice.gov/jmd/political-activities

U.S. Department of Labor. (2013). *Office of Federal Contract Compliance Programs Directive 2013-02.* Retrieved from http://www.dol.gov/ofccp/regs/compliance/directives/Dir306_508c.pdf

U.S. Government Accountability Office. (2007, May 18). *Federal Employees Health Benefits Program: Premiums continue to rise, but rate of growth has recently slowed.* Testimony of John E. Dicken, director, Health Care, before the Subcommittee on Oversight of Government Management, the Federal Workforce, and the District of Columbia, Committee on Homeland Security and Governmental Affairs, U.S. Senate. Retrieved from http://www.gao.gov/new.items/d07873t.pdf

Watson v. Fort Worth Bank & Trust, 487 U.S. 977, 995 (1988).

PART II

Processes and Skills

From Start to Finish

Recruitment

From Passive Posting to Social Media Networking

Your recruiting process should say to the candidate, "How'd you like to be part of our community, do neat things together, grow individually and with your peers?"

—Tom Peters

After studying this chapter, you should be able to

- identify the key paradoxes and challenges in recruitment from an organizational viewpoint;
- explain the steps in the civil service staffing process;
- pose preliminary questions such as whether to hire internally or externally and whether to duplicate the previous recruitment process or to restructure the position;
- write a customized job announcement;
- spot the strengths and weaknesses of various strategies and be able to determine effective mixes for specific staffing situations;
- describe some of the "dos and don'ts" of the recruitment process from an applicant's standpoint, as well as enhance the process with effective networking skills; and
- incorporate tactics for enhancing diversity.

Having examined human resource management's context and challenges—the civil service heritage and the legal environment—we now explore the essential functions of human resource management, beginning with recruitment, arguably the most important function of all. From an applicant's perspective, recruitment is often daunting and esoteric. Ultimately, it can be life changing, as the applicant must navigate through what is sometimes a bewildering variety of procedures. From the organization's perspective, recruitment is a process of soliciting the most talented and motivated applicants, and as such it is a bedrock function. Only with highly skilled staff—**human capital**—do organizations have the opportunity to thrive in an era in which work tends to be complex, customized, and rapidly changing. This chapter, then, discusses an array of concerns that agencies and applicants encounter and explains why the public sector confronts unique challenges.

One paradox is that procurement strategies and techniques, despite their importance, may seem relatively insignificant compared with the American sociopolitical environment within which this function takes place. That is, three cultural forces—the historical recruitment philosophy, the social status of public employment, and political leadership—form a powerful context within which government seeks employees. Historically, recruitment has been passive; until the 1950s, it was not legal for the federal government to advertise open employment positions in newspapers. Recruitment has also been highly negative and legalistic, often turning off would-be job applicants and contributing to the perception of excessive red tape in the hiring process (U.S. Merit Systems Protection Board [U.S. MSPB], 2000). Furthermore, the loss of prestige of the public service from its high-water mark in the 1930s and 1940s is a constant concern (Lewis & Frank, 2002). Finally, politicians may make public employment harder by both "bashing the bureaucracy" (which they are in charge of) and starving it of resources needed for high-quality recruitment (such as pay and adequate signing bonuses for hard-to-fill classifications). Indeed, the failure of government is not a problem for some citizens and lawmakers; rather, it is their goal. Critique of public sector employment, its salaries, and its pensions has become particularly pronounced since the beginning of the Great Recession in 2008.

For the job seeker, another stark paradox is the seeming abundance of employment opportunities but the scarcity of desirable positions (or **fast-track positions**). There are several reasons for this. Not only is there a tendency to increase the span of control and eliminate whole layers of middle management, but there is also a propensity to reduce the number of specialists who have management rank and perquisites; as a result, positions with attractive professional opportunities can easily elicit attention from scores of qualified candidates.

Applicants also often are perplexed by the mixed messages. Is recruitment a politically neutral, skill-based process, as it purports to be, or is it frequently conducted through a personalistic, "underground" hiring system with "wired" jobs subject to subtle modern-day patronage? As discussed below, the public service was once largely based on patronage; even today, patronage positions are among the most influential in government. The bulk of those senior positions, however, are supposed to be filled based strictly on technical merit; nonetheless, the influence of "political" or personal factors is common. Below the policy level, however, personal factors cannot be discounted. Local government has always prided itself on a balanced approach using technical merit and a "good fit with the organization." Even at the federal level, entry-level job applicants hear about jobs more frequently from friends and relatives than from any other source (U.S. MSPB, 2008a), and internal promotions are affected by personal factors (U.S. MSPB, 2001). Thus, paradoxically, depending on the position, both perspectives can be true, and the wise applicant is open to the dualistic nature of recruiting—that is, luck, "fit," and connections are often as important as competence.

In addition, should management aspirants prepare themselves as specialists or as generalists? Paradoxically, the answer is sometimes yes. That is, applicants for better positions must be both. Until recently, the American tradition has largely favored specialists. The best caseworkers in social service agencies would often be promoted to supervisors, the best engineers in transportation agencies would be appointed as managers, and good researchers in state universities would become administrators. Those in advanced positions seldom required either generalist management training or experience in rotational assignments to gain broad experience. Although organizations seem to appreciate generalist training, it is usually on top of specialist training—for those few who are advanced in today's flatter hierarchies. Generalist training, however, is critical for managers who deal with diverse functions and who rarely have the time to maintain specialist expertise.

Paradoxes and challenges also exist from an organizational perspective. They start with the notion that recruitment is the most compelling human resource function, but it is generally acknowledged to be the weakest in most organizations (U.S. Government Accountability Office [U.S. GAO], 2003). It is pivotal because if recruitment is done poorly, then all subsequent human resource functions will be negatively affected. It is often weakest because, when done properly, it is a time-consuming, expensive process that busy administrators may try to circumvent. A challenge, given the contemporary demand for well-paying jobs, is that staffing practices may not consistently produce "the best and the brightest." Perceptions of lower pay and lower job quality haunt the public sector even though those perceptions are often empirically incorrect (U.S. MSPB, 2008b). Therefore, recruitment must not depend on pay comparability; public sector pay sometimes outstrips regional private sector pay in rural areas, but it rarely keeps pace with urban and executive positions in the private sector. Best-practice organizations, however, realize that success in a competitive environment cannot occur without, first, entrepreneurial recruitment practices, such as hiring efficiency and test flexibility (Lavigna, 2002), as are afforded through the use of the Internet in disseminating information and gathering and evaluating applicant data (Kauffman & Robb, 2003).

Another challenge is the focus of recruitment: Should it be on current skills or future potential? Traditionally, procuring personnel emphasized technical skills and longevity.[1] More and more, however, organizations are interested in employee potential. The ability to adapt to new responsibilities and positions is critical as agencies reorganize and decentralize decision making. Detecting future ability and flexibility in potential employees requires a staffing process that seeks a different set of skills than was commonly the case in the past (Redman & Mathews, 1997).

Next is the paradox of balancing competing values: the need to recruit in a timely manner—generally the biggest single concern of applicants and hiring supervisors alike—while maintaining lengthy processes in the name of fairness and openness. Although on-the-spot hiring occurs in government (see the discussion of noncompetitive recruitment strategies below), months can elapse between the posting of the job (position) announcement and an offer of employment (U.S. GAO, 2003).

Another paradox centers on what should be emphasized in the recruitment process. Which of the following are most significant: (1) knowledge, skills, and abilities; (2) motivation; (3) diversity and broad representation of minority and protected classes in the workforce; or (4) loyalty? Certainly technical skills are important, but it is quite possible to hire an employee who is well qualified yet who is poorly motivated, contributes to a racial or gender imbalance, and is not loyal. Emphasis on nontechnical aspects has several challenges as well. Motivation is hard to predict, often fading after the probationary period or in the year just before retirement, although certainly nothing can transform a workplace more than energetic employees. Diversity has an important management and ethical dimension, although it is rarely allowed to be more than a "plus" factor in recruiting. Organizations that lack employee loyalty likely lack trust, innovation, and dedication as well. Similarly, there is the dilemma of whether to use open recruitment, which encourages a broader pool of candidates and fresh ideas, or closed recruitment limited to the organization, which rewards service and loyalty. Closed recruitment is also generally faster.

Finally, what responsibility does the organization have to the applicant? Job seekers spend a great deal of energy and time on the process. For example, is it ethical to go through the motions of open recruitment to fulfill a perceived legal requirement when a candidate, usually internal, has already implicitly been selected for the position? **Sham recruitment** processes are infuriating for the rejected candidates and a drain on the resources of the organization. Is it fair to ask for job references in the initial job application process when only those of the most highly ranked candidates will be read?

Such paradoxes illustrate the rich and complex factors that go into a seemingly simple process. Although there are few definitive answers across all situations, an examination of context and proven recruitment principles does lead to numerous best practices, which will be discussed in this chapter. The chapter first identifies the overarching factors affecting recruiting success and then introduces the three specific steps of the **recruitment process**: planning and approval, position announcements, and recruitment strategies. These steps are addressed in detail, followed by additional discussions of recruitment and diversity, the division of recruitment responsibilities, and advice for job seekers. The chapter closes with a summary and concluding recommendations.

FACTORS IN RECRUITMENT: EMPLOYER AND APPLICANT PERSPECTIVES

Recruitment may be seen from two perspectives: that of the employer and that of the applicant. What are the factors that affect success for the organization? And, just as important, what are applicants' perspectives on what a quality process is, even if they are not selected?

High-Quality Recruitment: An Employer's Perspective

At least five major elements influence the effectiveness of recruitment: (1) the breadth and quality of the process, (2) the size of the labor pool and the location of jobs, (3) pay and benefits (discussed in Chapters 7 and 8), (4) job quality, and (5) organizational image.

Having a sound recruitment philosophy means asking the right and wise questions from the outset (Breaugh & Starke, 2000). Is the entire procedure well conceived so that it fully embodies vital organization goals? Are enough—and the correct—strategies used to reach a broad range of persons who might be qualified and interested? Is the process aggressive enough to encourage the best candidates to apply? Is it clear and nonbureaucratic, so that would-be employees will not be discouraged? Is the process free from legal challenges yet not excessively legalistic or stultifying? Do applicants feel good about the recruitment process? Finally, is the overall procedure cost-effective for the position being considered and the recruitment environment, both of which vary enormously (U.S. GAO, 2008a)? The bulk of this chapter is devoted to this pragmatic element: providing an excellent recruitment process.

Although the size of the labor pool and the location of jobs, pay and benefits, job quality, and organizational image are not emphasized in this chapter, these elements have influence on the context within which the technical process operates. Labor pool size and job location together play a role in recruitment (Smith, 2000). For instance, in the last generation, thousands of public sector jobs have been privatized, with the result that they have gone to private domestic and overseas contractors. Economic boom-and-bust cycles also affect recruitment. For school districts, for example, this means that sometimes human resource offices may be inundated with high-quality candidates, but in times of shortages district recruiters may need to travel out of state to job fairs and offer signing bonuses and moving allowances to fill vacancies. Good economic times generally mean that few professionals of all types—lawyers, accountants, doctors, engineers, and others—may be available to apply for open positions; when the economy is weak, employee supply expands to the advantage of employers.

Pay and benefits are often the first factors that potential applicants review and consider. Public pay generally varies from uncompetitive to moderately competitive, depending on the agency, location, and position. Benefits (especially pension and health insurance) in the public sector are generally perceived as on par with or better than those in the private sector on average and thus represent a recruiting strength. The nonprofit sector often suffers from substantially lower pay scales and more limited benefits than either the private or the public sector, and thus must make up for these weaknesses in the intrinsic job quality elements.

Job quality may or may not be an element that applicants are immediately aware of, but top candidates invariably become proficient analysts of the organization they are considering. The best ones investigate with a critical eye such aspects as job security, advancement potential, likelihood of interesting work, working conditions, and professional perquisites such as travel and training. For example, in a survey of federal employment, the most important factors that influenced those accepting employment were job security (28%), advancement opportunities (12%), and challenging and interesting work (10%), with only 10% identifying pay as the key factor (U.S. MSPB, 2008a, p. 37). Although much of a candidate's understanding of job quality is sought and verified in the selection process (Chapter 4), it begins with recruitment. The opportunity to do challenging and interesting work leads among factors for acceptance of employment in the nonprofit sector (Nickson, Warhurst, Dutton, & Hurrell, 2008).

Finally, organizational status plays a significant role (Gatehouse, Gowan, & Lautenschlager, 1993). Being an auditor in a social service agency beleaguered with a series of child protective service and welfare scandals may not be as appealing as working as an auditor in a large accounting firm. When the pay differential is factored in as well, it means that one organization may have Ivy League graduates competing for interviews, whereas the other does not. Laudable as the public service ethic may be, people's attraction to it can wear out if agencies do not contribute to employee welfare in important ways.

To illustrate, although most public defender offices pay poorly and overwork assistant public defenders, some attract fine candidates because the training they afford is excellent and the work is as exciting as it is challenging. Furthermore, because of a short-term surge in the popularity of a strong service ethic after the 9/11 terrorist attacks, interest in public employment increased (Kauffman, 2004). Also, agencies have begun to pay increased attention to polishing their images (a process known as *branding*), often in tandem with recruiting (Bailes, 2002; Davidson, Lepeak, & Newman, 2007). A related trend is organizational ranking, as illustrated by the Partnership for Public Service's (2014) listing of "The Best Places to Work in the Federal Government," which highlights top agencies by size, improvement, class, demographics, and so on.

High-Quality Recruitment: An Applicant's Perspective

According to recruitment expert Sara Rynes (1993), too often employers neglect to think of the applicant's perspective in the recruitment process. Instead of candidates being impressed by an organization whether they are hired or not, most feel resentment because of the cold, unthoughtful, or dilatory treatment they receive. In addition to recommending the use of an efficient and clear recruitment process, Rynes offers four suggestions for employers who want job candidates to have good impressions of their agencies:

1. *Time recruitment steps to minimize anxiety.* Good candidates expect recruitment processes to result in timely notification of being in contention, prompt follow-ups, and enough time to make a reasonable choice among offers.

2. *Provide feedback to optimize scarce job search resources.* "Withholding of negative feedback is often interpreted as 'stringing applicants along' to preserve complete freedom of organizational decision making" (Rynes, 1993, p. 31). In other words, as soon as an agency has eliminated applicants by narrowing the field to a short list, it should consider notifying the eliminated candidates rather than waiting until the final person has been selected.

3. *Offer information that makes distinctions.* People prefer to have information that is detailed enough to allow them to make realistic assumptions about the specific job content rather than the single-sentence descriptions common in many announcements. In the interview process, candidates appreciate a realistic job preview because they understand Malcolm Forbes's view, "If you have a job without aggravation, you don't have a job."

4. *Use enthusiastic, informative, and credible representatives.* In the initial recruitment process, applicants respond much better to warm and enthusiastic recruiters and well-planned interview processes.

Overall, Rynes recommends that employers treat applicants as customers and manage the recruitment process in a professional manner. With the backdrop of these recruitment factors and applicant preferences, we now turn our attention to the technical processes.

RECRUITMENT STEPS

The recruitment process provides information about available positions and encourages qualified candidates to apply. It has three stages: (1) planning and approval of the position, (2) preparation of the position announcement, and (3) selection and use of specific strategies. Recruitment should be seamlessly connected with the selection process (Chapter 4). Together these processes are known as **staffing** (the receipt of applications and the closing date of the position signal the end of recruitment and the beginning of the selection process). The steps of the staffing process are illustrated in Exhibit 3.1.

Generalizations are necessary but difficult, because substantial variations in the recruitment process exist.[2] Thus, the process for an entry-level position may be quite different

Exhibit 3.1   The Civil Service Staffing Process

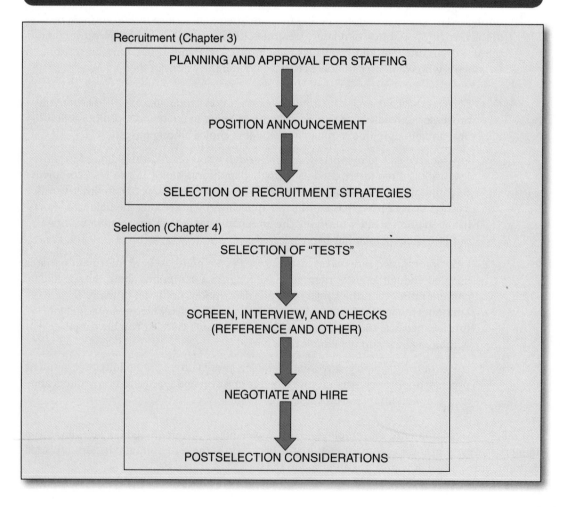

Recruitment (Chapter 3)

PLANNING AND APPROVAL FOR STAFFING

POSITION ANNOUNCEMENT

SELECTION OF RECRUITMENT STRATEGIES

Selection (Chapter 4)

SELECTION OF "TESTS"

SCREEN, INTERVIEW, AND CHECKS (REFERENCE AND OTHER)

NEGOTIATE AND HIRE

POSTSELECTION CONSIDERATIONS

from that used for a midlevel management position, which in turn may be unlike that for a position as an administrative head. Furthermore, recruitment practices vary considerably between small and large organizations. Even in large agencies practices range from centralized to decentralized. Finally, departments often rotate between individual recruitment for particular positions and institutional or pool recruitment to procure many candidates for job classifications such as entry-level secretary, accountant, laborer, forest ranger, or caseworker.

An important long-term trend in public sector recruiting in the 20th century was **procedturalism** (or red tape). It was characterized by processes that became excessively detailed, complicated, protracted, or impersonal (e.g., filling out different forms requesting the same information, having to go to multiple locations, lengthy procedures to complete tasks that could otherwise be accomplished in a short time). Ever since the widespread establishment of civil service systems in the United States, the ideal has been to be as neutral as possible in recruiting to make the process fair and unbiased. To accommodate numerous applicant requests for a large range of positions, centralized systems emerged in the federal government in the 1920s and elsewhere thereafter (Hamman & Desai, 1995, p. 90). Certainly, this was sensible, helping to combat excessive political cronyism and managerial personalism and to overcome a lack of hiring expertise dispersed among various units. It led, however, to rigidity and formalism as well. Adding to proceduralism in the mid-1960s was an interest in providing greater employment accessibility for minorities, women, and other protected classes.[3]

The trend today seeks to ease the effects of proceduralism by decentralizing to allow hiring managers more control and the opportunity to try innovative methods to compete in the new employment environment. Recent government reform initiatives have affected staffing in three ways:

1. There has been a strong drive to decentralize staffing activities in the largest organizations, where extreme centralization historically has been the norm. To the extent feasible, line managers are being allowed greater influence in recruitment and selection efforts. This trend has been particularly evident at the federal and state levels because of their size; it is much less so at the local government level and in the not-for-profit sector, where extreme centralization has not been so widespread.

2. Government appears to be making a sincere effort to simplify and invigorate intake functions. Better agencies are spending more time on selling themselves to prospective workers, and they are devoting more attention to easing new employees' passage into the workforce. However, there is clear evidence that agencies' practices are diverging widely based on both the differences in resources available among agencies and the level of organizational interest, or lack thereof, in this critical function (Davidson et al., 2007).

3. Many human resource offices (with legislative approval) are demonstrating a willingness to use increased flexibility and technological innovations such as on-the-spot hiring, fully online applications, and electronic scaling of applications.

PLANNING AND APPROVAL

At least two different types of planning occur in well-managed organizations (Jacobson, 2010; Mintzberg, 1994). First, such agencies engage in strategic thinking about the future needs, challenges, and opportunities of their incoming workforce. True strategic planning requires research, original thinking, and a willingness to change. Second, these agencies operationalize strategic plans as concrete positions become available. In other words, agencies should be rigorous in asking preliminary, vital questions about available positions before the actual recruitment process takes place (Lavelle, 2007).

Strategic Planning and Management of Vacancies

A plan for staffing begins with a **labor market survey** or specific position parity studies that compare agency job clusters. What are the trends in terms of availability, salaries, and education levels? Statistics and other information regarding the national labor force are available on the website of the Bureau of Labor Statistics (www.bls.gov), and the BLS also offers a useful occupational outlook handbook online (Bureau of Labor Statistics, 2008). Local and regional data can be gathered from each state's bureau of labor as well as from some of the larger jurisdictions. Local job parity studies are often performed by local agencies engaging in job evaluation (see Chapter 5) and by groups of organizations that jointly commission regular studies to benchmark pay trends. Many agencies do not want to be uncompetitive, while others want to be highly competitive. Public organizations often suffer most in tight labor markets because they have difficulty implementing flexible pay policies to compete for workers.

In addition to a market analysis, the organization should conduct a needs assessment. What does the organization anticipate its requirements will be for new positions, restructured positions, and eliminated positions? These issues may crosscut the entire organization, while others may primarily affect a series of jobs. Examples include the following:

- An issue facing organizations today is the retirement of the large Baby Boomer generation (and the last of the traditionalists), as well as the integration of the Generation Xers and New Millennials. Mass retirements always provide challenges, but they can also offer opportunities for renewal if well planned. One important issue frequently raised relates to **succession planning**, which involves an organization's ability to replace its executive and senior management ranks with high-quality talent (U.S. GAO, 2008a). Other related issues are the differences among the generations and the varying needs and preferences of the members of the more recent generations (Bright, 2010), as well as the need to retain or rehire some mature workers past retirement and to hire new older workers who may want reduced schedules through job sharing or part-time work (Armstrong-Stassen & Templer, 2006; Dychtwald & Baxter, 2007; U.S. GAO, 2008b).
- If an agency is required to strengthen its educative or facilitative role and decrease its regulative role (such as occurred at the U.S. Department of Housing and Urban Development in the 1990s), then it will need new skills and even different types of staff.

- The rapid shift in the responsibilities of the U.S. military in recent years—from a traditional war-fighting operation in Desert Storm and the initial invasion in Iraq in 2003 to counterinsurgency and nation building after the fall of Baghdad—caused an enormous strain on organizations that were initially unprepared for an evolution of responsibilities.
- The housing boom after 2000 and the housing bust beginning in 2007 led to dramatic shifts in local-level staffing in code enforcement, building services, and the types of economic development initiatives undertaken. Additionally, dropping home prices have led to automatic tax reductions and thus decreases in public sector revenues (in turn leading to widespread hiring freezes and even reductions in force in some cases), even as the demand for public services is increasing (especially unemployment benefits, job counseling and training, and welfare benefits).
- Given the rapid growth of law enforcement concerns after 9/11 and increasing demand for heightened border security, an enormous wave of federal hiring has made retaining and hiring public safety personnel dramatically more difficult at the state and local levels. It is nevertheless not unusual to find workforces lacking the requisite technical, interpersonal, and problem-solving skills. Such changes in mission or scope of operations are common today. Although the decentralization of human resource functions overall has made planning at the systems level more difficult for states and cities, it has made such planning more flexible at the department and unit levels. (For a guide to strategic workforce planning and an analytic tool to manage this process, see U.S. Office of Personnel Management [U.S. OPM], 2006, Chapter 2.)

Planning can take a number of different forms. Organizations can make sure that the staff intake function is properly funded. They can work on institutional image to affect recruitment positively. Agencies can enhance job quality by offering flexible schedules, family support policies like child care, comparable pay, and technology upgrades. Such planning and action should take place long before any particular position is advertised. A final aspect of planning is to make sure that the process is timely and user-friendly.

Ultimately, each position that opens may present special problems and opportunities. Administrators need to be able to assess whether a routine protocol is best or whether closer examination is necessary. If any of the following red flags are present, the hiring manager should probably give special attention to a new or customized process:

- Applicants for recent positions have been poorly qualified.
- Supervisors complain that new workers do not fit well into the department.
- The best potential candidates do not apply.
- The most desirable applicants have already found jobs by the time the position is offered.

When strategic issues are involved, it is time for managers to consult with the human resource department and colleagues in the agency and other organizations, as well as to consult professional trade journals. Systemic concerns should trigger the use of decision-making tools such as cause-and-effect charts, statistical analysis, and Delphi techniques (i.e., the pooling of expert opinions on a problem or issue) so that solutions can be found.

An example of a strategic problem comes from a midlevel information technology manager arguing with his supervisor about whether to hire an underqualified but high-potential candidate. The supervisor's view was that such an employee would take at least 3 months to have marginal utility and 6 months to perform at standard. Furthermore, some individuals like this candidate would never come up to speed but rather plateau at a low performance level. The midlevel manager's position was that the unit had five open positions, was struggling to keep up with a rapidly expanding workload, and found that fully qualified personnel were simply not applying, despite a new, higher pay level.

By discussing the systemic problem with human resource experts, however, the manager and supervisor uncovered a strategic opportunity. Why not hire five technically underqualified but high-potential candidates (who were relatively plentiful) and offer a special training class? This would be worth the effort because the size of the class would justify a full-time trainer, which, in turn, would ensure higher-quality training than the ad hoc on-the-job training provided to single hires. Furthermore, furnishing a trainer would reduce the demands on the already overworked personnel in the unit for whom training new employees was generally a distraction.

Only with a clear sense of the demographics and competition of the job market, as well as the general direction of the organization, can an agency focus with confidence on a specific position.

Preliminary Decisions About a Specific Position

Before the recruitment for a position begins, some thought must be given to staffing fundamentals. Is it advisable to fill the position at all? Sometimes it is better to leave one position unfilled so that the spare capacity can be used elsewhere in the unit or organization. Another question is whether the position needs to be restructured or if expectations need to be adjusted (see also the discussion of classification in Chapter 5). Has the position become over- or underclassified? Is it too narrowly or too broadly defined? Have the fundamental job skills needed shifted because of technology or program maturation? Sometimes one or two vacancies provide good opportunities to raise such questions.

If the position is not entry level, should it be filled from candidates internal to the organization only, or should it be filled from outside applicants? In very large systems, a third option is to consider candidates outside the agency but within the same governmental system (e.g., federal, state, county, or city). Morale, it is generally argued, is improved by **inside (internal) recruitment**, whereas depth and diversity are improved by **outside (external) recruitment**. Generally, "inside only" decisions are used by departments that rely on rank classification (such as the military and public safety organizations) and by strong union agencies in which priority application provisions for existing employees are tantamount to property rights. At the beginning of the recession of 2008, internal recruiting spiked in both the private and public sectors (Crispin & Mehler, 2011), as jobs became scarce and internal candidates got an edge. This trend was soon followed in the public sector by mass government layoffs and small numbers of new recruitments that were increasingly open searches (external recruitment) for targeted needs (Davidson, 2010).

The type of recruitment process is another issue: **individual versus "pool" hiring or institutional recruitment.** At the federal level, these categories are known as "case examining" versus "standing inventories." Broad, entry-level classifications in moderately large organizations generally use pool hiring. For example, a personnel department may generically advertise for numerous entry-level secretaries, computer programmers, and accountants to be placed on a standing certified list to be used by numerous state agencies in the selection process. The advantages are increased efficiency, low cost, and multiple considerations of qualified applications; the primary disadvantage is the difficulty of keeping the list up-to-date. Common or hard-to-fill positions may be on a continuous list from which candidates are constantly replenished. Individual recruitment is used for most positions above the entry level, jobs in smaller organizations, and less common classifications.

A critical decision concerns the breadth of involvement of those in hiring and related units. Sometimes, typically for entry-level slots, the supervisor is the sole decision maker and works exclusively with the personnel authority. At the other extreme—commonly for senior-level and professional positions—is the use of a search committee that selects the finalists for interviews and recommends a best candidate to the hiring supervisor. A midpoint is often struck for middle-management jobs in which input is solicited from the affected subordinates and colleagues but the final decision is still primarily the domain of the supervisor.

For many positions, especially those involved in first-line management, the question of the generalist versus the specialist arises. Of course, there is no definitive answer; it depends on the needs of the position. Specialists may relate to line workers well and understand technical issues; however, as the philosopher Shunryu Suzuki noted, "In the generalist's mind there are many opportunities; in an expert's mind there are few." Generalists tend to have a broader perspective that is valuable in management positions. On the whole, they can see both the forest and the trees, have superior people skills, and are easier to cross-train. Specialists, on the other hand, can be more efficient because of their technical background, are easier to justify in the budget in frontline supervisory positions, and require relatively little training for the production work that many supervisors today continue to do. The challenge is that frontline positions need specialist abilities, but when those same people are promoted, their new management responsibilities tend to focus on generalist competencies. In the 21st century, it may be less important what one knows and more important what one has in the way of potential to respond to unknown challenges.

The final preliminary issue is getting authority for hiring and approval for any job adjustments that may be needed. Positions are a carefully guarded resource, with hiring freezes instituted directly by presidents, governors, county commissioners, and mayors. Paperwork must be completed carefully and adjustments must be documented; also, acquiring formal union approval or informal approval by colleagues is prudent. Hiring supervisors who are sloppy or impatient with these processes or inarticulate with their rationales may find their hiring opportunities hamstrung by human resource specialists or stymied by superiors. As often as not, managers who demand expedited processes have simply neglected to plan properly or to learn long-established procedures.

In summary, recruitment begins before a position becomes available. An agency that wants to appeal to the best candidates will make sure that it is competitive in terms of pay, reputation, working conditions, and collegiality and that its personnel procurement process has resources to identify and attract the finest people available. As positions open up, proper planning requires that an agency ask a series of preliminary questions related to job currency and restructuring, inside versus outside recruitment, pool versus individual hiring, scope of involvement, specialist versus generalist characteristics, and timeliness. This planning occurs prior to the design of the job announcement, discussed next.

POSITION ANNOUNCEMENTS

Because there are no standard legal requirements concerning minimum information in job (position) announcements, such announcements vary from jurisdiction to jurisdiction, from entry-level to professional recruitment, and from source to source. For example, one jurisdiction may routinely include information about its benefits package, whereas another may not. Or a professional-level announcement in a national trade journal may contain a promotional paragraph about the agency or its jurisdiction that would rarely appear in an entry-level announcement in a local newspaper. Many agencies use advertisements that have relatively little detail; these are aimed at notifying applicants of opportunities that they can explore more fully by requesting more information. A cost-effective compromise may be to post an ad on a national job search website (job board) like Monster.com or Careerpaths.com; such ads include series of questions designed to screen qualified prospective applicants as they read them. In any event, a position announcement should be designed initially using a full format, which subsequently can be modified (see Exhibit 3.2).

Exhibit 3.2 The Elements of a Job Announcement

The following types of information are relatively standard in a full announcement:

1. *Title and agency/organization affiliation.* This can include the official title and/or the working title. The agency/division affiliation is mentioned except when recruitment is being conducted on a centralized basis (e.g., statewide or citywide).

2. *Salary range.* The range generally indicates the starting salary as well as the ceiling. Announcements for professional and executive positions may simply state that a "competitive salary" is offered depending on experience and credentials.

3. *Description of job duties and responsibilities.* This is essentially a short job description. What will the incumbent actually do and be responsible for? Descriptions of supervisory responsibilities, financial duties, and program responsibilities are especially useful for nonentry positions. Work hours are also standard information, although sometimes omitted when conventional.

4. *Minimum qualifications.* What education, skills, and experience are required, as a minimum, to qualify for the job? Education requirements could be a degree in select fields or a specialized certification. Skills could be as specific as typing speed or as general as communication facility. Many positions require specific durations of experience, such as at least 3 years as a planner or 7 years in positions with progressively more responsibility (e.g., managerial). Minimum qualifications must be job related; employers should not arbitrarily raise such qualifications just to reduce the number of job applicants.

5. *Special conditions.* These often signal applicants to aspects of the job that some people (but not necessarily all) may find unappealing. Common special conditions include travel requirements, being stationed at outlying locations, harsh or dangerous work environment, requirements for background checks, unusual hours, and residency requirements.

6. *Application procedures.* What exam methods will be used? If there is a specific test, when is it to be administered? Is the examination to be done through the rating of the education and experience of candidates? To whom and where does one apply, and with what exact materials? A closing date for the recruitment period is necessary, although sometimes positions "remain open until filled" after the closing date.

   Readvertised positions may "begin interviewing immediately." Otherwise, most jurisdictions require 3 weeks or more to close the recruitment period. Minimum periods for advertising are often specified in legal codes or statutes, which should be scrupulously followed. Emergency and temporary hiring practices are always possible, but these generally require exceptional justification and authorization.

7. *Equal opportunity employment.* Standard phrases are used to indicate the organization's commitment to equal opportunity employment and affirmative action.

Beyond these standard types of information, some other kinds are not routine but are nevertheless common:

1. *Classification.* The specific ranking of the position in the organizational system (grade level) is often not included in external postings because it may confuse outsiders. When such a ranking is relatively easy to understand, such as the federal General Schedule, it should be listed. Grade level is invariably of interest to organization members, so internal postings should always include this more technical information.

2. *Career potential.* A good job posting should discourage poorly qualified applicants, but it should also encourage those who are well qualified. Candidates often are looking at not only the position but also its career potential. Mentioning career potential generally helps to attract better and more ambitious applicants. Examples of features that reflect career potential include opportunities for promotion, training and education, and special experience.

3. *Special benefits.* Some positions have special benefits. Examples might be seasonal vacations (such as summers for teachers and university faculty), opportunities for extra pay, availability to work with distinguished people, or exceptional retirement programs (such as those offered in military and paramilitary organizations).

Style and tone matter more in announcements today than in the past because even in an employers' market, the best applicants are picky about whom they will interview with. Although announcements were once expected to be solemn, standardized, and neutral, now they must, at least to some degree, be inviting and interesting (Zeidner, 2001). In an in-depth analysis of vacancy announcements, the U.S. MSPB (2003) criticized federal recruitment in this area:

> Our systematic review of a random sample of vacancy announcements found that at least half of them are poorly written and that they make little or no attempt to sell the government, the agency, or the positions to be filled. Far too often vacancy announcements are difficult to understand and use threatening and insulting language, characteristics that are more likely to drive applicants away than attract them. (p. 7)

Some of the recommendations from the U.S. MSPB (2003) study that apply to all public sector organizations include the following:

- Greatly reduce the length of vacancy announcements.
- Reduce the use of negative, threatening, and legalistic language.
- Design a message to sell the job and the agency and, to the extent possible, to present the agency as the employer of choice.
- Clearly and realistically describe the job and its requirements.
- Require the least amount of information needed to make basic qualification determinations and then request more information as needed later in the process.
- Give straightforward instructions on how to apply.

Finally, announcements should always be reviewed carefully for both accuracy and currency, because misstatements become legally binding and errors make the organization look unprofessional. Of course, an announcement should tie directly to the official job description, which in turn often is based on a formal job analysis (see Chapter 5). Although conceptually job analyses and descriptions precede announcements, it is not unheard-of for preparation of an announcement to spark changes in a description or trigger a new job analysis. Once an announcement is completed and authorized, the department can focus on an appropriate set of recruitment strategies.

RECRUITMENT STRATEGIES

Numerous **recruitment strategies**—methods of contacting and informing potential applicants—are available, but seldom are they all used for any given position. Of course, it is not the sheer number of strategies used that determines a quality intake process but the choice of an appropriate combination. Unfortunately, governments historically have eschewed aggressive recruitment practices. There is a new activism today (U.S. MSPB, 2006), however, which means that agencies are using more approaches and trying to do so with more effect. Ten strategies are discussed below, each of which has strengths and weaknesses and, therefore, various utilization patterns. For each strategy, we identify four major factors: relative ease of use, effectiveness, cost, and common usage.

[handwritten margin notes: easy, transparent, large turnout, cheap]

1. **Job posting** originally consisted of the placing of the announcement on walls in prominent locations such as post offices and city halls. Many civil service systems still require physical posting in a minimum number of public places. Today, however, job posting also includes dissemination of the announcement through in-house job bulletins, newspapers, and other standard communications media. Posting is considered the most basic of all recruitment strategies; it is easy to do because the entire announcement can be used without modification.

Its effectiveness is largely limited to organization members and aggressive job seekers who visit the agency's employment office. For a job that must be filled internally—say, a fire lieutenant's position—posting alone can be sufficient. Many positions, however, are recruited outside the organization, and traditional posting is unlikely to be effective. As Eleanor Trice (1999) of the International Personnel Management Association said, "The days when government organizations could recruit by simply posting a vacancy announcement, then sitting back and assuming that enough qualified applicants would apply, are gone" (p. 10).

2. Today, posting also includes **electronic posting**—listing jobs on (a) agency websites or (b) websites exclusively dedicated to job seekers (also known as job boards). The Internet is an enormously important recruitment tool with minimal cost, so agency website posting has become the "passive" recruitment base, and posting on specialized government job boards has become a very important active strategy.

Electronic posting is now required by law for federal positions that are competitively recruited; the same is true for all but the most specialized jobs and jobs in the smallest agencies in state and local government. Such postings may be located on the websites for human resource or personnel departments, state personnel boards, or civil service commissions. The federal government decentralizes the responsibility for job posting to individual agencies. With a single exception currently, all states allow online applications, and many now require online applications rather than physical applications. Applicants normally are required to register and "build a résumé" in the agency site, and then to either identify specific jobs or request that their competencies be matched with all appropriate jobs. If applicants are interested in specific jobs, it is recommended that they be sure to include key competency phrases that are used in electronic review of résumés. Although the use of such review is not as common in the public sector as in private organizations (Mareschal & Rudin, 2010), many agencies allow applicants to upload their résumés, with the warning that initial screening is invariably from the application résumé, not the uploaded résumé. Uploaded résumés are more useful later in the search process—for example, in the interview phase.

Because ultimately all but a very small number of noncompetitive applicants must go through the agency website, even when other means may be the initial point of reference, the excellence of the website is of vital significance (Cober, Brown, Keeping, & Levy, 2004; Kim & O'Connor, 2009; Selden & Orenstein, 2011). The effectiveness of the recruiting area of an agency website is influenced by such elements as the quality of images, videos, and testimonials about the organization as a place to work; usability; links; feedback capacity; personalization; application tracking; online testing; and job matching (Williamson, King, Lepak, & Sarma, 2010). The availability of detailed information about positions and how to apply is very important for the motivation of high-quality candidates (Breaugh, 2008). Finding the recruitment areas of agency websites is easy; an online search for "[agency name] government jobs" should produce hits with the relevant agency at or near the top of the list. For example, searching for "California state government jobs" will generally quickly locate the California State Personnel Board (www.spb.ca.gov).

A job board is an employment website that focuses on employment opportunities available in general, in a region, or in an industry. Examples of general job boards are CareerBuilder, Yahoo! HotJobs, Monster.com, and Craigslist. Generally the sites that require active employer input are considered more reliable, as opposed to sites that relay secondary information from other sites (an activity called scraping). However, sometimes sites that provide links to local government employment opportunities can be useful (e.g., www.ejobs.com, which provides state-by-state listings) and can provide up-to-date information. The general move for all but the most basic jobs has been to niche sites, those that target regions, industries, and/or professional levels more narrowly (Breaugh, 2008), because of the large numbers of unqualified applicants generic job boards tend to generate. The public sector has avoided using generic, private sector websites that are not themselves sponsored by government organizations. An excellent example of a public sector job board is USAJOBS (www.usajobs.gov), which is an OPM-maintained clearinghouse for all federal jobs. Most state government websites essentially function as job boards for all of their agencies because hiring goes through a centralized personnel agency. Of course state and local government employment offices help facilitate employment primarily targeted at the private sector, but this is through a specialized unemployment division and has a different focus and mission, often including unemployment benefits, retraining programs, and career skills support for the general public. Federal data show that electronic posting is the second most important method, after friends or relatives, through which applicants learn about positions (U.S. MSPB, 2008a, 2008b).

3. **Personal contact recruitment** occurs when potential applicants are personally encouraged to apply for positions. The single most important recruitment source, according to many experts, is employee referrals (Crispin & Mehler, 2011; U.S. MSPB, 2008a, 2008b). Employees often know others who are in the same field; they are often enthusiastic in their recommendations, but they generally provide candidates with useful realistic job previews as well. While there are obvious issues with excessive reliance on employee referrals, such as potentially fostering cronyism, well-managed selection systems with a rigorous sense of merit mitigate these weaknesses.

Another form of personal contact takes place when recruiters, managers, or search panel members attend job fairs, conduct on-campus recruiting, or individually contact top candidates for positions. Recruiters generally travel to such events, perhaps across town but sometimes to other states, or make targeted calls to potential candidates who have not applied. Such tactics are routine for some corporations, professional sports teams, and elite law firms, but they are less common for all but the largest government agencies. Job fairs provide candidates with the chance to talk to prospective employers and give organizations opportunities to increase their visibility and scout for suitable talent. The practice of managers personally contacting executive candidates is typical in business; it is less typical in the public sector, which is considered vulnerable to accusations of cronyism and bias. Nonetheless, job fairs are reported as being more important than postings on USAJOBS for reaching potential candidates under age 30, while older job seekers rely far more heavily on both USAJOBS and agency websites (U.S. MSPB, 2008a). Some federal and large state/local agencies make it a point to participate in job fairs and even campus events (e.g., U.S. GAO, 2011).

Social media are emerging as a major factor in private sector recruiting (Black, 2010; Crispin & Mehler, 2011) but have yet to have a major impact on most public sector employment. Some major agencies are beginning to use Facebook (the more generic social media platform), LinkedIn (the more professionally targeted platform), YouTube, Flickr, and Twitter as information tools and as occasional blogging devices. Social media platforms are rarely the initial or final points of contact; however, they have enormous potential to be part of a powerful cultivation technique, as they provide quick and interesting bursts of information (Flickr and Twitter), video- and context-rich cases and briefings (YouTube), and blog discussions about issues and trends (Facebook and LinkedIn). Unlike other domains, such as advertising and political outreach, these forms of social media are unlikely to be of major interest for public sector agencies in recruiting until the job market tightens up, even though such methods clearly provide value and depth in terms of the tool kit of recruitment strategies.

4. Newspaper recruitment focuses on local or regional openings. The employment section of the largest local Sunday paper is the most common vehicle for job announcements, but some jurisdictions use daily employment sections as well. Advertising in smaller papers may be ideal for local jobs, especially those that are entry level, low paying, or part-time. Despite cost, newspaper advertising can be relatively effective in external recruitment, especially when ads have multiple job listings.

5. Trade journals are the newsletters and magazines that inform members of professions about activities on a regular basis (e.g., *PA Times, ICMA Newsletter,* and *IPMA Newsletter*). The audiences for such publications are narrower than those for newspapers in terms of professional range but broader in terms of national scope. Trade journals are used extensively in recruitment for professional and senior management positions in which high levels of specialized expertise are desired and generally available only on the national market. A federal agency looking for a

senior math statistician, a state agency seeking a director for its lottery department, and a municipality searching for a city manager are all likely to list these positions in relevant journals where candidates can easily scan the entire job market. To the degree that appointive positions use open procedures, trade journals are also a strategy of choice, despite the associated cost.

6. **Mail (and e-mail) recruitment** (custom mailing) is a highly personalized approach in which individuals are encouraged by letter to apply. Aggressive private sector corporations use this strategy to contact students who are in the top few deciles of a handful of institutions identified as sources of exceptional candidates. Even more targeted recruitment occurs when a search committee identifies a select number of individuals who are exceedingly qualified and then personally encourages them. Such an approach "seeds" the recruitment pool with candidates who may not otherwise apply. It is rarely used in the public sector but is a mainstay strategy for Fortune 500 companies. Both sectors use search firms that rely on such personalized approaches. In addition, e-mail provides an inexpensive, informal, and rapid outreach technique.

7. **Institutional capacity recruiting** focuses on ensuring that job seekers consider an agency in general and visit its job application website, rather than on specific jobs. Some organizations (e.g., state universities) use institutional advertising, especially when they have services to sell. This advertising is aimed at increasing awareness and prestige; it does not target select positions. Examples are government-access TV, radio advertisements, billboards, and positive public relations stories, especially "best places to work" media coverage. Government-access TV is frequently used by cities and counties that have controlled-access government stations provided by authorized cable companies. It is common for these stations to list available jobs at various times throughout the day. Governments will sometimes buy advertising space on radio and other media when the job market is very tight. Positive media coverage can have a similar effect on recruitment efforts because of the increased prestige of the agency or department.

8. **Internship recruitment** programs are a common strategy in many midsize and large jurisdictions (see Exhibit 3.3 for two examples of internship recruiting announcements). Elite organizations screen potential interns nearly as closely as job applicants because of program cost and subsequent high hiring rates. Consequently, internship opportunities are a standard element of almost all master's of public administration (MPA) curricula. Program quality in these internships can be quite high. Organizations that make large-scale and effective use of this strategy report that the benefits in terms of training, acculturation, job preview, and job longevity are unequaled by other methods.

9. **Headhunting**, or external recruitment, occurs when the staffing function is farmed out to a third party that makes the initial contact or even provides the hiring contract. Ironically, this method is used most for both the lowest and highest, but not the middle, positions in government. Public agencies contract with

employment firms, especially in a tight labor market, for basic labor, clerical, and temporary positions (generally en masse). At the top end of the spectrum, private sector organizations have long relied on headhunting strategies to fill executive and senior management positions. This strategy is less prevalent in government, which places a premium on open processes from beginning to end. Executive headhunting is on the upswing as an expanded practice in state governments, however, and it has always been common for city and county management positions. Large public agencies may also have specialized internal executive recruiters who actively seek out high-quality candidates. The executive recruiter for the California county of Riverside, for example, handles only searches for deputy director level and up. Departments are required to do job analyses that are more thorough, candidates get more "red carpet" treatment, and the pool normally is seeded with some applicants who have been personally recruited to apply by phone or e-mail.

10. In **noncompetitive recruitment** (also called direct or one-day hiring), a single official completes the process without a formal comparison of candidates. Therefore, recruitment may be "open" for certain jobs or types of applicants. Sometimes this means that immediate hiring is allowed if candidates meet certain standards; at other times the decision maker simply has the authority to select those people deemed appropriate. An illustration of the first instance is when local government recruiters are authorized to hire candidates for hard-to-fill categories on the spot, or when the federal government allows its campus recruiters to hire students immediately if they meet certain grade point standards. Even during periods when the employee pool surges, there are still hard-to-fill categories necessitating standards-based, noncompetitive hiring. An example of the second instance is the process of appointing confidential staff: Elected and senior appointed officials can hire advisers, deputies, and personal assistants without either formal merit or legislative consent processes (at the federal level these are known as Schedule B appointments, which do not require competitive examination). There are a small number of exceptional cases that governments may routinely exempt from competition, such as military spouses at the federal level (Long, 2011). Of course, a noncompetitive process is easier and less costly than other methods. The practice is effective in a limited number of cases, such as hard-to-fill positions where meeting a given standard is sufficient for hiring or where political and personal loyalty is an appropriate factor. However, since it is open to abuse and violates merit principles, noncompetitive recruitment is generally highly restricted and carefully monitored.

Which strategies are best for which jobs? For management positions in police, fire, and paramilitary organizations with strong seniority policies, there is little reason to go much beyond physical and virtual posting. Organizational members wait for these opportunities, and internal recruitment is usually sufficient. The situation is quite different elsewhere, when competition for high-quality candidates can often be fierce. The question is not which but how many strategies to use, given financial and personnel resources. Following

Exhibit 3.3   Examples of Internship Recruiting Announcements

Management Internship

City of Phoenix, Arizona

About the Program

The City of Phoenix Management Intern Program has been attracting outstanding individuals to government service since 1950. If you are interested in a career in public administration, this one-year, full-time program is an excellent opportunity to experience a variety of innovative management systems; gain exposure to many of the issues facing a large, well-run city government; and develop important professional skills. Our program is one of the most respected local government training programs in the United States. It is designed to attract, develop, and retain innovative people in local government.

A Wide Range of Experiences

If selected, you will work in the City Manager's Office, the Budget and Research Department, and a department that provides direct service to the community. You will also work on a wide array of projects and assignments that will develop and refine your professional skills. Past completed projects include

- researching and coordinating outreach activities to increase the diversity of community leaders on public arts boards,
- analyzing best practices to implement a pilot program to apprehend graffiti vandals, and
- developing a department budget.

Professional Development

This program gives you the opportunity to observe firsthand the efforts of a large city government to resolve some of its most pressing issues. You will staff administrative and community committees and attend city council and management policy meetings. You will be able to network with the city's top officials and managers through one-on-one meetings. You also will have the opportunity to attend local and regional professional conferences during the year where you can meet and network with government professionals from throughout the Southwest.

Salary and Benefits

The present salary for 2014–15 is $40,310 annually. City employees who are in a higher salary range would remain at their current rate of pay throughout the program.

- The city's comprehensive benefits package includes medical and dental insurance, city-sponsored training, and seminar/tuition reimbursement. For more information, please visit phoenix.gov/JOBSPECS/bene007.html.

Presidential Management Fellowship

About the Program

Since 1977, the Presidential Management Fellows (PMF) Program and its predecessor, the Presidential Management Intern (PMI) Program, have been attracting outstanding graduate, law, and doctoral students to the federal service. The PMF Program is your passport to a unique and rewarding career experience with the federal government. It provides you with an opportunity to apply the knowledge you acquired from graduate study. As a PMF, your assignments may involve public policy and administration; domestic or international issues; information technology; human resources; engineering, health, and medical sciences; law; financial management; and many other fields in support of public service programs.

Eligibility Graduate students from all academic disciplines who expect to complete an advanced degree (master's, law, or doctoral-level degree) from a qualifying college or university during the current academic year are eligible to be nominated by their schools if they demonstrate the following: breadth and quality of accomplishments, capacity for leadership, and a commitment to excellence in the leadership and management of public policies and programs.

Application Period Application for the PMF Class of 2015 opens via a job opportunity announcement on USAJOBS at www.usajobs.gov; search for "Presidential Management Fellows." Eligible applicants must also complete the on-line assessment prior to the announcement closing.

SOURCES: City of Phoenix website (https://www.phoenix.gov); U.S. Office of Personnel Management website (http://www.opm.gov).

its strategic plan, the U.S. State Department uses both cutting-edge technology and interpersonal relations. By integrating traditional marketing, outreach techniques, and public relations with Web-based technology, its Diplomatic Readiness Initiative made the department's recruitment program a model (Pearson, 2004).

The strengths of public sector recruitment have been in notification strategies—job posting, electronic posting, newspapers, trade journals, and institutional capacity methods. Traditional weaknesses have been the lack of expensive, proactive strategies—well-paid internship programs (with the notable exception of internships with the federal government), systematic personal contacts outside employee referrals, mail recruitment, headhunting, and noncompetitive hiring. Current innovations cluster around increasing timeliness, improved online interfaces (such as provided by the popular program NEOGOV used by many state and local agencies), and flexibility where positions are hard to fill. Agencies engaging in SHRM use the recruitment process as the first step in a self-conscious approach to building the workforce most suited to their needs, as discussions of talent management indicate (see Exhibit 3.4).

A major strength of recruiting for government and not-for-profit organizations has been the passion that many people have for the "doing good" aspect that is intrinsic to much of these sectors (Ng & Gossett, 2013; van der Wal & Oosterbaan, 2013). The nonprofit area often has a humanitarian purpose related to the arts and culture, education, the environment, animals, health, human services, international affairs, public affairs, social benefits, spiritual and psychic health, science and technology, or the social sciences. Not-for-profit organizations also include advocacy groups such as professional associations and political interest groups. While the larger and better-funded nonprofits mirror the practices of most public sector organizations very closely, many of the tens of thousands of smaller ones find it difficult to do so because of funding and other resource constraints. Nonetheless, they often find that they are competing in the same pool for staff and must follow public sector rules because of the obligations required by their government contracts, or to maintain their tax status. These challenges are illustrated in Exhibit 3.5.

Exhibit 3.4 What Is Talent Management?

The term *talent management* has been around for a long time (Schein, 1977), but it has developed new salience in an age of scarce resources and increasing competition. While definitions of **talent management** can vary, all agree that managers and executives play an active role in employee development. Beyond the sense of manager involvement and responsibility, the term can mean two significantly different things.

First, *talent management* can be a synonym for *human capital management* and refer to the idea that employees are generally the most critical factor in providing quality service and in creating an environment of innovation. Because recruiting and training employees is expensive and employees accrue valuable experience, this resource needs to be managed carefully. This definition can be appropriate for the public sector because of the long-term commitment to employees common in government agencies, as well as the higher level of education and training required on average. Human capital management in this sense means well-crafted recruitment, selection, and onboarding, good pay and benefits, and, importantly, a succession of training and education opportunities to foster development of *all* employees (Starks & Brooks, 2009).

Second, the term *talent management* can be used more selectively to refer to attracting, grooming, and promoting exceptional employees for leadership positions or special assignments. Special emphasis is often placed on mentoring and succession planning. This definition, focusing on high-potential management employees, is the more common meaning today (Buckingham & Coffman, 1999). Special hiring authority is granted to recruit the very best and brightest. Special tracks are designed for rapid rotational experiences and promotion. Executive status is largely limited to those who have been nominated for candidacy programs just prior to attaining their senior-level positions. The U.S. government uses this approach with the Presidential Management Fellows (PMF) Program for recruitment, has special promotional tracks for PMF recruits to move through the ranks at an accelerated rate, and has candidate schools for the Senior Executive Service (SES).

As defined here, the human capital management and talent management philosophies neither require nor disqualify one another. Some agencies have an emphasis on the equity of opportunity at all times and follow an egalitarian development model. Others do not provide much support for rank-and-file employees, many of whom may be staff, and provide strong support for high-performing employees, who are usually professionals with credentials. This is a type of "star" system. With a critical mass of resources, an organization can both support development for all employees and provide an extra layer of support for "fast-track" employees. The U.S. federal government fits into this blended model. Of course, it is possible that, because of either lack of resources or poor leadership, an agency may provide neither good general development nor fast-track opportunities, in which case it would follow a model of low employee support and an absence of a viable talent management strategy of any type.

Promoting Diversity in Recruitment

Even though affirmative action has been de-emphasized in recent years, the promotion of diversity in the workforce is both ethical and a management necessity (Armstrong et al., 2010). There are three factors to consider. First, does the agency provide an environment compatible with diversity through its promotion processes and organizational culture? A department that insists on standard working hours, does not provide child care assistance, and subtly penalizes leaves of absence for family reasons does not create a suitable atmosphere for employee-parents. Such issues might be subtle, but attention to them is critical if an optimally productive diverse environment is to be created and maintained.

Exhibit 3.5 Staffing Realities in a Not-for-Profit Organization: Getting the Right Person at the Right Time

Susan Spice, MPA

It goes without saying that one of the best ways to prevent high turnover is to hire the right person for the right job at the right time. Managers face several challenges in trying to achieve this balance, however. For example, recruitment of the "right" person may not be possible unless the position is available, there is funding for it, and, in some cases, there is legislative authority to hire for it. Large agencies have a greater pool in which to fish, whether for employees to promote, employees seeking lateral transfers, or individuals wanting to join the agencies. Public sector recruitment is constrained by specific regulations on when jobs can be posted and how long postings must remain open; nonprofits may have the same constraints if they provide governmental services.

Getting the recruitment process "right" suggests that there is a strategy to be employed. This implies that the agency knows that a vacancy will occur, when it will happen, and that there will be sufficient time and money to recruit the ideal candidate. The reality is that many agencies do not become aware of a pending vacancy until the outgoing employee turns in his or her 2-week notice of intent to leave. This leaves the manager scrambling to get the job advertised and interviews completed in a timely manner. It also leaves the position's supervisor hoping that at least one qualified, desirable potential employee will respond to the posting in time and, if interviewed early in the process, will be willing to wait until the posting closes before being offered the job.

This was an issue, especially with the nursing staff, at the not-for-profit organization (NPO) where I worked from 1998 to 2006. The staff consisted of 13 nurses (who provided case management for approximately 8,000 North Florida children receiving public assistance or who had chronic health problems), four secretaries, and five administrative personnel. On rare occasions a nurse's departure was expected, usually because she was leaving to accompany her husband to his new job in another town. More often than not, the supervisor would learn about an employee's intent to leave when she handed in her resignation.

The administrative assistant generally posted the job announcement within 24 to 48 hours of being told of the imminent departure. As a state-contracted service provider, the agency followed state human resource policies. Because of this, announcements had to remain open for at least 1 month from initial posting. Thus, the challenge was to find a replacement interested in working with pediatric case management who had sufficient qualifications (a BS degree in nursing was required), could receive background and fingerprint clearance, and was interested in working with our client base. Strategic planning and headhunting were not viable options because we rarely knew when positions would become available.

There were similar issues with the secretaries, although it was considerably easier to replace them because of the difference in skill level required. Unfortunately, as an NPO the organization could not offer high salaries. This, and the physical nature of the work (filing hundreds of client charts a day), limited the pool of individuals interested in working with us to young women in their early 20s. However, recent changes in the structure of the "secretarial pool" have radically decreased turnover. Originally four positions, the secretarial pool was cut to three, with the fourth salary (and workload) shared among the remaining employees. This raised their salaries to a level where they could support themselves, which reduced turnover. Also, the increased workload actually raised morale, because the remaining secretaries felt more valued and appreciated.

In a perfect world, all employees would have those same feelings of worth and value. Governmental managers would not only be able to recruit the right personnel but also would actively headhunt for the best. Likewise, NPOs would have sufficient funds to pay competitive salaries, and the right person would always be available at the right time and salary. Unfortunately, the reality is usually that managers have to "satisfice" and recruit the best they can with the resources available.

One illustration of providing a hospitable environment is the creation of spousal assistance programs. Spousal assistance may be offered to help reduce the trauma of relocating families. Such plans are more conventional in the private sphere (28%), especially in large corporations (52%), than in the public sector (Mercer, 1996). For dual-career couples, a transfer or relocation of one spouse is highly disruptive to the other's career plans. This can lead to refusals to accept jobs, promotions, or transfers. Organizations that do not provide spousal assistance may find themselves accepting less-than-ideal candidates for positions because their preferred candidates decline to relocate. Another example of support for diversity involves increasing the participation rate of individuals with disabilities. Some of the elements that promote diversity in this area are top leadership support, regular screening of the workforce to identify potential barriers to employment and work success, the training of staff who do not have disabilities but face barriers that affect their employment and success, offering a flexible work environment, and providing centralized reasonable accommodation funding (U.S. GAO, 2011).

Second, is there a conscious attempt to maintain a well-rounded workforce so that no group, including white males, has a legitimate complaint? Are resources made available to minority members in the organization? All things being equal, qualified women and minorities should be given priority if they are clearly underrepresented in proportion to the available eligible workforce. Research indicates that minorities are highly sensitive to the presence of role models in the recruitment process and to the comparative level of resources available (Gilbert, 2000). Although the public sector has generally done better than business in this regard (see, e.g., U.S. MSPB, 2009), many workplaces are still negligent or lax in promoting diversity successfully. Examples include failure to hire women in paramilitary agencies, traces of a glass ceiling (i.e., cultural barriers impeding groups from executive positions) for women and minorities (U.S. MSPB 2014), lower employment of Hispanics in the federal workforce (U.S. MSPB, 2011; U.S. OPM, 2013), and low representation of African Americans in senior management positions across all levels of government (U.S. MSPB, 2008c).

Third, there should be awareness that where and how recruitment takes place will have an effect (Thaler-Carter, 2001). Sometimes recruitment practices need to target locations where diverse candidates are more likely to congregate (perhaps particular schools or job fairs) and ethnically diverse universities and sources that such individuals are likely to read (such as ethnically oriented newspapers and newsletters).

Dividing Responsibilities

There is no hard-and-fast rule about who is responsible for what aspects of recruitment. As discussed at the Wye River Conference (Ingraham, Selden, & Moynihan, 2000; see Exhibit 1.5 in Chapter 1), the central agency should enable individual units and managers to better perform the human resource function. In large government agencies, the responsibility has been divided among three entities: (1) the centralized human resource office, (2) full-time human resource experts in agencies and departments, and (3) local managers and supervisors. The centralized human resource office is often responsible for (1) overseeing diversity plans, (2) providing a comprehensive listing of recruitment sources, (3) supplying coordination of institutional recruitment (such as mass entry-level positions) and personal procurement (such as job fairs and college recruitment), and (4) furnishing a centralized recruitment source when departments elect not to handle recruitment on their own. These offices function as expert sources of assistance for departments. A second approach is that agencies have either full-time human resource experts or coordinators with personnel responsibilities. These specialists provide support to operational units and monitor hiring practices. Finally, organizations may conduct much of their recruitment directly, especially for midlevel and senior positions. This has the advantage of increased buy-in and involvement from departments in the entire process; it also may mean that there is an opportunity for inappropriate practices if hiring units do not take the responsibility seriously or plan for it properly. Increasingly, line managers are mandated to attend training before being allowed to participate in the hiring process to ensure that organizational and legal requirements are met.

ENHANCING RECRUITMENT PROSPECTS: THE SEEKER'S PERSPECTIVE

The basics of job seeking may be widely known but are not necessarily commonly practiced. Following are several recommendations directed to the job seeker:

- The first suggestion is to know the recruitment process and know what resources are available. Reading this chapter accomplishes the first aspect. Learning where recruitment occurs in a targeted profession includes consulting with practicing professionals who can identify the standard trade journals, knowing which newspapers carry the appropriate advertisements, and exploring to find additional sources through the Internet and elsewhere. Developing personal contacts—networking—can make an enormous difference in discovering good prospects (see Exhibit 3.6).

- Take the time to envision the types of jobs, organizations, and career paths you might be interested in. For those without public sector experience, this may mean a review of lesser-known agencies in order to expand horizons.

- Next, carefully screen jobs before applying. Although it may cost little to send out 100 résumés, it is discouraging to hear nothing from so many, which is likely to happen with a shotgun approach. If one does not already bring some appropriate expertise or some special experience to a job, there is little likelihood of being a finalist. If necessary experience is lacking, there may be a need to either get more experience in an internship or take a lower-level position.

- Be sure to gather all the available information about the job. Short newspaper and trade journal advertisements are generally reduced versions of the full announcements. Contact the appropriate sources to see if additional information is available.

- Take the time to write a customized, flawless cover letter. A letter that is simply "good" will not be noticed. A substantive one is highly focused, responding to the exact points covered in the job announcement. Although all the elements indicated in the announcement may be in the résumé, be sure that they are spelled out in the sequence requested in the cover letter. Failure to do so indicates a lack of seriousness.

- Write a carefully crafted résumé. Certainly you must not make things up, but be sure the résumé has all the relevant experience and that the presentation is professional in content. Résumé writing is an art, and those making distinctions at the reviewing end quickly become master critics. Many how-to guides are available online and in bookstores. Generally, they discuss variations of two types of résumés (the chronological and the functional), as well as presentation styles. You should always have your résumé reviewed by an expert. Be sure to have an electronic copy that can be altered for specific jobs. Use the term *curriculum vitae* (Latin for "course of life") if the job has a research or academic component.

- When selected as a finalist, immediately do research on the organization via the Web and via information provided by the initial point of contact, friends, and any other sources (discussed in Chapter 4). In many cases, failure to have a general knowledge about the organization in the interview is considered to be a demonstration of either a lack of interest or a lack of initiative and constitutes a good reason for a low ranking.

Exhibit 3.6   Recruitment for Job Seekers: Networking

The mantra for any job seeker is networking, networking, networking. Professional acquaintances help job seekers by giving them advance notice of upcoming openings and agency needs. They can also act as advocates for those they would like to see fill positions in their agencies or departments or serve as references who can vouch for the job experience, performance, and personal attributes of job seekers. It is well-known that jobs are sometimes wired for particular people; these people often had networks of advocates working for them. Most professionals belong to several networks. On the national level, for example, you may belong to a national association in your specific line of work. Other networks are statewide or regional associations for more in-depth or frequent interaction with other professionals in your field. And still others are local groups of all types, formal and informal.

Networks are not built overnight. They are often the result of a person's attending professional conferences for several years and building ties with their counterparts in other agencies. Such ties tend to be formed among those with similar professional interests, commitments, and values. Indeed, a basic prerequisite skill for any professional is the ability to articulate his or her interests, commitments, and values in a relatively concise and coherent fashion. People need to know what others stand for. How else do humans form enduring bonds?

It is unclear how large a professional network needs to be in order to be effective, but most professionals who feel part of a network would know about 30 to 60 people fairly well and probably know another 200 by face or name. How does someone get to know so many people? First, most individuals know more people than they realize and even more people who could introduce them to others if only they were asked to do so. Second, building a large network requires a commitment to go to venues such as conferences where people meet others. Attending a conference once may lead to knowing only a very few others, but attending for 4 years may lead to knowing half the attendees. Maintaining a professional network requires an investment of time to keep others informed of your professional self. Third, another great way to network is to volunteer. Often people at lower levels in organizations know what they want to do, but their jobs or bosses do not provide for that. Volunteering for a nonprofit is a great way to gain experience and meet people. Doing good, professional work outside the scope of employment might even get back to a current employer, who then may consider the volunteer "management material" because of the extra commitment shown.

Having a strong network, and helping others in the network, brings numerous rewards. Networking is also helpful for other purposes, such as to increase professional resources for doing one's job (getting advice, help with a problem). Through networking, job seekers also learn about employers: Are they really as good as they claim? Are others happy working there? Or is the department a snake pit, best to be avoided? People in a network often have information about these matters. Find out where people who have similar interests go. Join with them. It will be worth the cost.

Advancing From Job Seeking to Career Development

Midcareer professionals (including most completing MPA degrees) are beyond such basics. They have had one or more positions and perhaps have been a part of the hiring process themselves. Those retooling their skills and looking at entry-level positions are seeking jobs whose career potential is exceptional. They understand that the competition for good management and technical jobs is generally quite intense. For example, in one study of public sector hiring practices, 85% of the hiring managers reported that they use the quality of the candidate's application itself to a great or moderate extent in selection (U.S. MSPB, 2003). For the ambitious midcareer professional, by necessity, job seeking needs to evolve into carefully planned career development. Some tips include the following:

- In addition to passively hunting for positions, the midcareer professional needs to *envision the ideal position*. Such a process requires the candidate to distinguish critical job characteristics from those that are unimportant. It also helps the career developer to focus on the most appropriate prospects.

- At the same time, the midcareer professional needs to *assess his or her strengths and weaknesses candidly*. Of course, the initial question is how to rate one's own technical competence and experience. Technical competence and experience are only part of what employers seek, however (Hicks, 1998). Frequently, the single most desired characteristic is good communication skills (written, oral, listening, persuasiveness). Does the candidate have basic computer literacy skills, such as competence in word processing, spreadsheet programs, Internet usage, and the standard programs utilized in the field? Also high on employers' lists are team skills, facility with interpersonal relations, and the ability to be creative and innovative. Those seriously developing their careers today need to make sure not only that they have developed these skills but also that they can provide examples to demonstrate their competency.

- A rigorous self-assessment should lead *to enhancement of the career developer's ability to demonstrate his or her strengths.* One of the best ways of demonstrating strengths is to develop a portfolio of materials, examples, and references. Copies of successful projects, job evaluations, photographs where visual representations are useful, and letters of reference are examples of the types of materials to be collected and shared as needed.

- The self-assessment should also lead the career developer to *improve in areas where weaknesses recognized.* Deficiencies can be reduced through self-study and reading, training inside or outside the organization, and formal education. Addressing weaknesses takes considerable self-discipline because it is easier to ignore or hide them, but not taking steps to mitigate them damages both job prospects and performance. In a competitive market, lack of exceptional or unusual knowledge, skills, and abilities may be a weakness because basic qualifications are assumed. For instance, although police chiefs (and senior police commanders) in large municipal, county, and state law enforcement agencies may not technically be required to have master's degrees, management and executive training at the FBI and national command schools, and areas of extraordinary competence, the reality is that the agencies seeking to fill such jobs are inundated with exceptional candidates who do possess all these characteristics.

- Pursuing a better job always includes a substantial interview process in which the position is won or, often, lost. *There is no substitute for practice.* When responses are practiced, difficult questions offer a candidate the chance to shine. When unpracticed, these questions are just tough and cause elimination.

- Finally, even before the actual recruitment process begins, those seeking better positions must *be realistic, practical, and disciplined.* Preparation for a position should begin long before the recruitment process. The procedure itself is generally a protracted effort, requiring a long-term devotion of personal resources, numerous attempts, and self-discipline in the face of challenges and disappointments.

SUMMARY AND CONCLUSION

Finding talented workers for the public sector organization is a function involving five elements, of which the quality of the recruitment process per se is only one. Pay, labor pool size, organizational image, and job quality are also important. A first-class intake process can optimize or minimize these other factors substantially. Historically, recruitment has not been a strength in many organizations. Of the seven staffing steps, the first three constituting recruitment often have been the more passively administered, whereas those that constitute selection have been the more rigorously pursued. If competitive candidates are not in the pool, however, then the value of a neutral and precise selection process is limited.

What steps can agencies take to ensure that they attract appropriate applicants? First, they must recognize that quality recruitment is affected by planning. This involves asking and answering key questions, in advance of hiring, so that the recruitment and selection processes do not waste time and resources. Errors include not anticipating vacancies and labor shortages, not providing proper funding for recruitment, not mitigating negative factors, and not effectively identifying agency strengths. Competent planning involves asking pertinent questions about the position, such as whether (1) it is needed at all, (2) it should be hired from within, or (3) it should be restructured, as well as (4) who should be involved in the process and whether necessary forethought has been devoted to the authorization process. The announcement should always be written out fully. It is unwise to rush an advertisement to press before it is carefully crafted and endorsed. The final consideration is which recruitment methods to use in combination, with the goal of producing a customized applicant pool. Strategies include physical posting, electronic posting, personal contact, advertising in newspapers, advertising in trade journals, custom mailings, institutional capacity recruiting, internship programs, headhunting, and noncompetitive recruiting. The variety of methods and the need for a diverse workforce place a major responsibility on the line manager, who is increasingly responsible for organizing and implementing the recruitment process.

Clearly, the recruitment of high-quality human capital is an area that is particularly susceptible to reform for those agencies serious about being "world-class organizations." Traditional passivity must give way to more aggressive strategies in which high-quality candidates are actively sought. There must be an insistence that most recruitment pools include truly exceptional, rather than just acceptable, candidates. This implies that organizations must devote more resources and energy to recruitment, just as the U.S. armed forces did when converting from a draft to a volunteer system in the 1970s. It is unusual for public sector agencies to follow the business example of sending senior managers on annual recruiting trips, but this is a practice they should use more frequently.[4] Finally, it is critical that unit supervisors and employees take seriously their increased responsibilities in decentralized recruiting systems, because they directly affect the quality of the future workforce.

KEY TERMS

Electronic posting
Fast-track positions
Headhunting
Human capital
Individual versus "pool" hiring
Inside (internal) versus outside (external) recruitment
Institutional recruitment
Internship recruitment
Job (position) announcement
Job posting

Labor market survey
Mail (and e-mail) recruitment
Noncompetitive recruitment
Personal contact recruitment
Proceduralism
Recruitment process
Recruitment strategies
Sham recruitment
Staffing
Succession planning
Talent management

EXERCISES

Class Discussion

1. In your area, identify some of the factors affecting recruitment, *excluding the recruitment process itself.* That is, discuss the labor pool, pay and benefits, images of public sector organizations, and perceptions of jobs in government as they affect local agencies' recruitment capacity.

2. How broadly should members of the hiring unit participate in the staffing process? Does the nature of the position (e.g., entry versus midlevel, administrative requiring a master's degree) make a difference? When should a hiring unit vote on the best candidate (such as is common for state university faculty positions)?

3. What examples have you witnessed, if any, of shoddy or inappropriate recruitment practices? How should those practices be modified or improved?

4. What internships are available in the state, county, and cities in your area? Which are paid? How does one apply? Are there any fellowship programs?

5. What is the typical size of the applicant pool for jobs in your organization (be it a public agency, university, or nonprofit organization)? Typically, how many applicants are minimally qualified? Well qualified? Are job searches ever canceled for lack of qualified applicants?

6. Review and compare two public sector websites devoted to employment in an agency or department. Examples of comparison items might include (a) attractiveness, navigation, organization, currency, social media opportunities, and testimonials; (b) quality of job descriptions, completeness of job descriptions, clarity of application process, clarity of pay and benefits, and ability to ask questions and interact with people about job prospects; and (c) quality of supplemental information, such as organizational reputation and friendliness of the process.

Team Activities

7. To what extent would you emphasize future potential over current skills in each of the following jobs: office manager, police recruit, division director, and agency director (appointive but nominated by a committee)?

8. Have group members describe the recruitment strategies they have personally experienced, as well as their perceptions of those sources (e.g., postings versus newspapers versus the Internet).

9. Discuss as a group what agencies would have to do to attract the most outstanding university students.

10. Identify and discuss some paradoxes from your own recruitment experience.

Individual Assignments

11. Rate each of the following factors, by percentage, in terms of importance in recruiting a social service case management supervisor. Current employees in the unit are predominantly white females, and the unit is characterized by low pay, low morale, and high turnover.

    Knowledge, skills, and abilities ___ %

    Motivation ___ %

    Diversity ___ %

    Loyalty ___ %

12. In the preceding example, if you believed that there was only one well-qualified internal candidate who happened to be the only white male in the unit, would you recruit internally or externally? What would your goal be? How would you use recruitment to achieve that goal? How would you publicize that goal to the hiring unit?

13. Clip or print some job advertisements for public sector jobs from several sources, including the local newspaper. What are the variations in format and style that you notice? How might the advertisements be improved?

NOTES

1. See the discussion of rank-in-job versus rank-in-person systems in Chapter 5. Rank-in-job positions have been the most common and emphasize technical skills. Rank-in-person systems (such as the military) emphasize employee development potential.

2. In true patronage positions, elected officials can select whomever they please without review. These often include staff positions. Appointive positions such as department heads and their chief deputies arguably are not true patronage positions because they are reviewed by the appropriate legislative bodies for confirmation. Of course, recruitment in elective positions is generally through the democratic process of primaries.

3. Employment statistics indicate that government has generally been a leader in hiring a diverse workforce. Meeting the requirements and documenting compliance with equal opportunity, affirmative action, age discrimination, and disability accommodation, however, has added to proceduralism.

4. Some examples do exist, of course. For years, the GAO has assigned senior executives to do annual campus visits (Walker, 2007).

REFERENCES

Armstrong, C., Flood, P., Guthrie, J. P., Liu, W., MacCurtain, S., & Mkamwa, T. (2010). The impact of diversity and equality management on firm performance: Beyond high performance work systems. *Human Resources Management, 49*(6), 977–998.

Armstrong-Stassen, M., & Templer, A. J. (2006). The response of Canadian public and private sector human resource professionals to the challenge of the aging workforce. *Public Personnel Management, 35*(3), 247–260.

Bailes, A. L. (2002, Spring). Who says it can't be done? Recruiting the next generation of public servants. *Business of Government,* pp. 51–55.

Black, T. (2010, April 22). How to use social media as a recruiting tool. *Inc.* Retrieved from http://www.inc.com/guides/2010/04/social-media-recruiting.html

Breaugh, J. A. (2008). Employment recruitment: Current knowledge and important areas for future research. *Human Resource Management Review, 18,* 103–118.

Breaugh, J. A., & Starke, M. (2000). Research on employee recruitment: So many studies, so many remaining questions. *Journal of Management, 26*(3), 405–435.

Bright, L. (2010). Why age matters in the work preferences of public employees: A comparison of three age-related explanations. *Public Personnel Management, 39*(1), 1–15.

Buckingham, M., & Coffman, C. (1999). *First, break all the rules: What the world's greatest managers do differently.* New York: Simon & Schuster.

Bureau of Labor Statistics, U.S. Department of Labor. (2008). *Occupational outlook handbook, 2008–09 edition.* Washington, DC: Author. Retrieved from http://www.bls.gov/OCO

Cober, R. T., Brown, D. J., Keeping, L. M., & Levy, P. E. (2004). Recruitment on the net: How do organizational website characteristics influence applicant attraction? *Journal of Management, 30*(5), 623–646.

Crispin, G., & Mehler, M. (2011, March). *10th annual careerXroads source of hire report: By the numbers.* CareerXroads. Retrieved from http://www.careerxroads.com/news/SourcesOfHire11.pdf

Davidson, G., Lepeak, S., & Newman, E. (2007). *Recruiting and staffing in the public sector: Results from the IPMA-HR research series.* Alexandria, VA: International Public Management Association for Human Resources. Retrieved from http://unpan1.un.org/intradoc/groups/public/documents/ipma-hr/unpan027173.pdf

Davidson, P. (2010, July 9). Expect lots of government layoffs at state, local level. *USA Today.* Retrieved from http://www.usatoday.com/money/economy/employment/2010-07-06-jobs06_ST_N.htm

Dychtwald, K., & Baxter, D. (2007). Capitalizing on the new mature workforce. *Public Personnel Management, 36*(4), 325–334.

Gatehouse, R. D., Gowan, M. A., & Lautenschlager, G. J. (1993). Corporate image, recruitment image, and initial job choice decisions. *Academy of Management Journal, 36*(2), 414–428.

Gilbert, J. A. (2000). An empirical examination of resources in a diverse environment. *Public Personnel Management, 29*(2), 175–184.

Hamman, J. A., & Desai, U. (1995). Current issues and challenges in recruitment and selection. In S. W. Hays & R. C. Kearney (Eds.), *Public personnel administration: Problems and prospects* (3rd ed., pp. 89–104). Englewood Cliffs, NJ: Prentice Hall.

Hicks, L. (1998, September 27). Central Iowa labor crisis looms. *Des Moines Sunday Register,* pp. 1G–2G.

Ingraham, P. W., Selden, S. C., & Moynihan, D. P. (2000). People and performance: Challenges for the future public service—The report from the Wye River Conference. *Public Administration Review, 60*(1), 54–60.

Jacobson, W. (2010). Preparing for tomorrow: A case study of workforce planning in North Carolina municipal governments. *Public Personnel Management, 39*(4), 353–377.

Kauffman, T. (2004, July 2). Job seekers favor government, OPM surveys find. *Federal Times.*

Kauffman, T., & Robb, K. (2003, July 14). Online recruitment: New system promises more choice, faster hires. *Federal Times.*

Kim, S., & O'Connor, J. G. (2009). Assessing electronic recruitment implementation in state governments: Issues and challenges. *Public Personnel Management, 38*(1), 47–66.

Lavelle, J. (2007). On workforce architecture, employment relationships and lifecycles: Expanding the purview of workforce planning and management. *Public Personnel Management, 36*(4), 371–385.

Lavigna, R. J. (2002). Best practices in public-sector human resources: Wisconsin state government. *Human Resource Management, 41*(3), 369–384.

Lewis, G. B., & Frank, S. A. (2002). Who wants to work for government? *Public Administration Review, 62*(4), 395–404.

Long, E. (2011, June 29). Employment opportunities for military spouses expand. *Government Executive.* Retrieved from http://www.govexec.com/story_page.cfm?articleid = 48117&oref = todaysnews

Mareschal, P. M., & Rudin, J. P. (2010). E-government versus e-business: A comparison of online recruitment in the public and private sectors. *American Review of Public Administration, 41*(4), 453–467.

Mercer, W. M. (1996). *Mercer work/life and diversity initiatives: Benchmark survey 1996.* Louisville, KY: Author.

Mintzberg, H. (1994, January/February). The fall and rise of strategic planning. *Harvard Business Review,* pp. 107–114.

Ng, E. S. W., & Gossett, C. W. (2013). Career choice in Canadian public service: An exploration of fit with the millennial generation. *Public Personnel Management, 42*(3), 337–358.

Nickson, D., Warhurst, C., Dutton, E., & Hurrell, S. (2008). A job to believe in: Recruitment in the Scottish voluntary sector. *Human Resource Management Journal, 18*(1), 20–35.

Partnership for Public Service. (2014). The best places to work in the federal government. Retrieved from http://bestplacestowork.org/BPTW/rankings/overall

Pearson, R. (2004, July 12). Technology helps state recruit the best. *Federal Times,* p. 21.

Redman, T., & Mathews, B. P. (1997). What do recruiters want in a public sector manager? *Public Personnel Management, 26*(2), 245–256.

Rynes, S. L. (1993). When recruitment fails to attract: Individual expectations meet organizational realities in recruitment. In H. Schuler, J. L. Farr, & M. Smith (Eds.), *Personnel selection and assessment: Individual and organizational perspectives* (pp. 27–40). Hillsdale, NJ: Lawrence Erlbaum.

Schein, E. H. (1977). Increasing organizational effectiveness through better human resources planning and development. *Sloan Management Review, 19*(1), 1–20.

Selden, S., & Orenstein, J. (2011). Content, usability, and innovation: An evaluative methodology for government websites. *Review of Public Personnel Administration, 31*(2), 209–223.

Smith, M. (2000, March). Innovative personnel recruitment/changing workforce demographics. *IPMA News,* pp. 12–14.

Starks, G. L., & Brooks, F. E. (2009). Strategic human capital planning: Recruiting and retaining new federal employees. *Public Manager, 38*(1), 60-67.

Thaler-Carter, R. E. (2001). Diversify your recruitment advertising. *HRMagazine, 46*(6), 92–100.

Trice, E. (1999, June). Timely hiring: Making your agency a best practice. *IPMA News,* pp. 10–11.

U.S. Government Accountability Office. (2003). *Human capital: Opportunities to improve executive agencies' hiring processes.* Washington, DC: Author.

U.S. Government Accountability Office. (2008a). *Federal workforce challenges in the 21st century.* Washington, DC: Author.

U.S. Government Accountability Office. (2008b). *Older workers: Federal agencies face challenges, but have opportunities to hire and retain experienced employees.* Washington, DC: Author.

U.S. Government Accountability Office. (2011). *GAO human capital management: Efforts taken to ensure effective campus recruitment.* Washington, DC: Author.

U.S. Merit Systems Protection Board. (2000). *Competing for federal jobs: Job search experiences of new hires.* Washington, DC: Author.

U.S. Merit Systems Protection Board. (2001). *Attracting quality graduates to the federal government: A view of college recruiting.* Washington, DC: Author.

U.S. Merit Systems Protection Board. (2003). *Help wanted: A review of federal vacancy announcements.* Washington, DC: Author.

U.S. Merit Systems Protection Board. (2006). *Reforming federal hiring: Beyond faster and cheaper.* Washington, DC: Author.

U.S. Merit Systems Protection Board. (2008a). *Attracting the next generation: A look at federal entry-level new hires.* Washington, DC: Author.

U.S. Merit Systems Protection Board. (2008b). *In search of highly skilled workers: A study on the hiring of upper level employees from outside the federal government.* Washington, DC: Author.

U.S. Merit Systems Protection Board. (2008c). *Workforce diversity governmentwide and at the Department of Homeland Security.* Washington, DC: Author.

U.S. Merit Systems Protection Board. (2009). *Fair and equitable treatment: Progress made and challenges remaining.* Washington, DC: Author.

U.S. Merit Systems Protection Board. (2011). *Women in the federal government: Ambitions and achievements.* Washington, DC: Author.

U.S. Merit Systems Protection Board. (2014). *Federal Equal Opportunity Recruitment Program (FEORP) for fiscal year 2012: Report to the Congress.* Washington, DC: Author.

U.S. Office of Personnel Management. (2006). *Career patterns: A 21st century approach to attracting talent.* Washington, DC: Author. Retrieved from http://www.opm.gov/policy-data-oversight/human-capital-management/talent-management/career-patterns-guide.pdf

U.S. Office of Personnel Management. (2013). *Twelfth annual report to the president on Hispanic employment in the federal government.* Washington, DC: Author.

van der Wal, Z., & Oosterbaan, A. (2013). Government or business? Identifying determinants of MPA and MBA students' career preferences. *Public Personnel Management, 42*(2), 239–258.

Walker, D. M. (2007). GAO and human capital reform: Leading by example. *Public Personnel Management, 36*(4), 317–323.

Williamson, I. O., King, J. E., Lepak, D., & Sarma, A. (2010). Firm reputation, recruitment web sites, and attracting applicants. *Human Resource Management, 49*(4), 669–687.

Zeidner, R. (2001, October 1). Do-it-yourself hiring process. *Federal Times.*

CHAPTER 4

Selection

From Civil Service Commissions to Decentralized Decision Making

First-rate people hire first-rate people; second-rate people hire third-rate people.

—Leo Rosten

After studying this chapter, you should be able to

- recognize and seek to resolve paradoxical dimensions in the selection process;
- articulate the different philosophical bases of selection;
- understand the history of civil service commissions and how they continue to affect thinking in employee selection despite their reduced role;
- distinguish historical eras and the current trends in selection;
- discuss the "ideal" stages of the selection process;
- choose appropriate examination methods ("tests") based on six different criteria;
- avoid the use of inappropriate questions in the interview and reference check process;
- determine who will make hiring decisions and how such decisions will be made and documented; and
- ensure successful integration of selected employees.

Selection technically starts when applications have been received. Which of the applicants will be chosen, by what process, and by whom? Certainly the public sector is far stronger for having outgrown the excesses of 19th-century patronage, which permeated jobs at all levels of government and resulted in widespread corruption and graft such as vote racketeering and kickbacks (Mosher, 1982). During the 20th century, merit principles replaced patronage as the most common—but by no means the sole—selection criterion. Today, patronage excesses are relatively rare—far less common than in the private sector— and they constitute little problem for the bulk of positions in government (a position that has been strengthened in Supreme Court cases such as *Branti v. Finkel,* 1980; *Elrod v. Burns,* 1976; and *Rutan v. Republican Party of Illinois,* 1990).[1] Even when mayors, governors, and presidents have strong appointive power and loyalty may initially be a legitimate factor in selection, excessive patronage considerations can get them into trouble, as President Bill Clinton found when he replaced longtime White House travel specialists with Arkansas friends (a scandal known as "Travelgate") and President George W. Bush experienced when he appointed Michael Brown, his former campaign director, to head the Federal Emergency Management Agency, even though Brown lacked any knowledge of emergency management whatsoever.

One challenge in selection is that political appointment—a form of patronage—is the primary selection method for most senior government positions. Appointees are often selected based as much on party and personal affiliations as on technical merit. The U.S. president selects not only all the agency and department heads but also thousands of second- and third-layer executives, including up to 10% of the Senior Executive Service. Governors generally have hundreds of appointive positions under their control. "Strong" mayors and county boards of supervisors also have extensive appointive responsibilities that lend themselves to patronage. Nor is it unheard-of for high-level appointees and elected officials to provide "character references" wherein they "encourage" career supervisors to hire the officials' campaign workers and friends for low-level positions. This paradox—merit systems run by dilettantes—contributes to cynicism among career employees, who often view political appointees as transitory, poorly trained, and inexperienced. Without that occasional fresh administrative leadership, however, the public service might become unresponsive, rigid, and self-serving, just as organizations in the private sector occasionally turn to "outside" CEOs in times of industry transition or organizational decline.

Another irony is that although public sector selection is primarily an open application of merit principles, selection for many positions is determined largely by **internally based hiring**. Such hiring is said to boost internal morale, increase loyalty, reduce training time, and provide recruiting incentives for strong candidates. Nonetheless, this practice reduces full competition and the introduction of outside skills and insights (Grensing-Pophal, 2006). For example, agency policies or union contracts often require a strict ordering in selection rights that results in most of the better jobs being labeled "promotional" and therefore not available to "outside" candidates. Many entry-level and nearly all midlevel vacancies are filled internally. For example, the U.S. Merit Systems Protection Board (U.S. MSPB, 2001a) reported that supervisors filled vacancies with current agency personnel 46% of the time and with other federal employees 25% of the time; only 29% of the time did they select from outside the government. This trend is more severe at the senior levels, at which only 15% are externally hired (U.S. MSPB, 2008b).

Yet another paradox, or tension, lies in the promotion of merit principles with robust testing and the introduction of more flexibility in testing, sometimes at the expense of

[handwritten margin note: succession]

thoroughness (Ingraham, Selden, & Moynihan, 2000). Increased rigor can mean better assessment and higher-quality selection; however, it can also mean that the selection process involves more time, expense, and applicant aggravation, leading to reduced applicant levels and the loss of some of the best applicants to faster-moving competing organizations. Even as the federal government becomes increasingly interested in a competency-based hiring or promotional model, it is more willing to expand the hiring discretion of agencies and their managers. Such discretion may also be abused, whether out of haste or out of ignorance (U.S. MSPB, 2006). State governments are increasing flexibility, too, which opens them up to reducing the rigor of merit (full competition) and even the prospect of illegal practices due to reduced oversight of fragmented systems (Hausser, 2013; McGrath, 2013).

Although participation in the selection process has always been a significant role for managers and supervisors, that role has expanded with the dramatic downsizing of human resource departments throughout government. For instance, the U.S. Office of Personnel Management was downsized by more than 50% as it was being reinvented in the 1990s (U.S. MSPB, 2001b). Therefore, today it is important to recognize that human resource management skills are critical generalist competencies for all managers. The challenge is that the scope and depth of responsibilities have grown over the past generation, making the prospect of a "quick and dirty" hiring process more likely.

In Chapter 3, we alluded to other important pressures concerning whom to recruit; those tensions now resurface in this chapter, which focuses on how candidates are selected and whom the selection process emphasizes. Should it emphasize the potential of newly graduated students or the ability of older candidates? How does an agency encourage diversity in selection while balancing merit principles? Every candidate puts his best foot forward, but average performance on the job may be more important. For example, a talented, brilliant, and charming individual may be highly distractible, lazy, or emotionally temperamental. How does the selection process capture and evaluate the difference between typical and maximal performance?

It is interesting to note that international trends in recruitment and selection are similar and seem to be converging. All emphasize person–job fit and person–unit fit and use methods that are remarkably similar to those discussed here. As one might expect, Australia, Europe, New Zealand, and the United States show the most in common, emphasizing results, decentralization, and past performance in employees. Some Asian countries (e.g., Japan and Taiwan) emphasize potential more than past performance. Many Latin American countries still emphasize family and personal connections (Anderson & Witvliet, 2008; Werbel, Song, & Yan, 2008; Wolf & Jenkins, 2006).

Finally, there is the tension between "selling" the job and educating potential employees about its challenges, drudgery, demands, and constraints related to high stress, late hours, and danger. **Realistic job previews** are opportunities for applicants to learn about both the positive and negative aspects of jobs, so that some may opt out of the selection process or accepting the jobs, but the eventual psychological contracts (discussed in Chapter 6) will be tighter. Ultimately, excitement about the job and eagerness to get started generally fade within 6 months or less, and applicant enthusiasm (as opposed to applicant energy level or past performance and experience) ends up being a poor predictor of long-term job success (Barrick & Zimmerman, 2009).

This chapter begins with a broad discussion of the criteria used in the selection process and how different principles have taken precedence in civil service positions in various historical eras. The majority of the discussion focuses on prominent technical aspects of selection related to application review, testing, interviewing, reference checks, the hiring decision, and posthiring issues. The chapter concludes by reaffirming that this important human resource function is as easy to understand as it is difficult to carry out. Predicting human behavior, a goal in the selection process, is no easy task, as illustrated by the fact that former professional basketball superstar Michael Jordan was cut from his high school basketball team because he lacked potential.

THE BASES AND ORIGIN OF SELECTION

Principles Underlying Selection

Selection is arguably the most momentous and politically sensitive aspect of human resource activities (Ployhart, 2006). Indeed, historical eras of human resource management are largely defined by the underlying philosophy of selection. There are essentially seven possible criteria that can be used, separately or in combination, to provide the basis for the selection decision: (1) electoral popularity, (2) social class, (3) patronage, (4) merit, (5) seniority, (6) representativeness, and (7) character and job fit. All of these, except for social class, are explicitly used in various arenas of the public sector. Although the terms *civil service* and *merit* are often used as synonyms, in common practice *civil service* is a broader term because it embraces elements of seniority and representativeness as well as merit.

Electoral Popularity

Electoral popularity is the basis of representative democracy. Citizens vote for those who they think will do or are doing a good job. What types of positions are reserved for the electoral popularity model? First and foremost, they are policy-making jobs in which responsibilities include crafting laws and defining the broad administrative missions of national, state, and local governments. Such officials occupy the legislative bodies at all levels of government—Congress, state legislatures, county boards of supervisors, city councils, and boards of townships, school districts, and other special units. To a substantially lesser degree, but still common, is the election of judicial personnel: judges, state attorneys general, county attorneys, local justices of the peace, and the like.

Of course, elected executives such as presidents, governors, and mayors are significant and visible in the American democratic system. Although they share a policy role with legislators, they also have a critical administrative role in managing the agencies and departments of government. It should be noted, however, that some elected offices were originally intended to be primarily administrative and are so to this day (e.g., state-level secretaries of state, education, and treasury; county-level sheriffs, treasurers, clerks of court, auditors, and recorders). For instance, in small jurisdictions full-time elected officials may assist their staffs in busy periods by providing direct service to the public. Of course, the bulk of all elected officials serve on school boards and town councils with little or no pay. The strength of the electoral selection philosophy is its support of democratic theory through popular involvement as well as accountability to citizens. The limits of this strategy are also clear: Voters have natural limitations of knowledge, time, and interest. As the numbers of those who run for election increase and as the issues involved become more technical and complex, the attention of citizens becomes diluted, and voter turnout declines. The highly fragmented structure of most county governments is a prime example of the accountability problem.

Social Class

Social class selection, the antithesis of democratic selection, is generally illegal as an explicit selection philosophy in the United States. In many societies, however, the administrative classes were "bred" so that they would have the requisite education to fulfill administrative functions. This remains evident in many European democracies and is one of the distinctive features of some rank-based systems (discussed in Chapter 5). In the United States during the Federalist period access to education was limited, and a strong upper- and upper-middle-class bias existed in administrative roles. In contemporary advanced democracies, with their high literacy rates and widespread access to universities, this philosophical base has limited virtue, although minorities and women often argue that the dominant culture still subtly guides the selection process itself. For example, graduation from certain prestigious educational institutions sometimes becomes a proxy for social class, with classic cases being the U.S. State Department's historical preference for selecting graduates of eastern universities and state governments giving preference to graduates of their flagship universities.

Patronage

Patronage encompasses a broad class of selection decisions in which a single person is responsible for designating officials or employees without a requirement for a formalized application process. Such appointments may or may not be subject to confirmation procedures. As a process, patronage tends to have a negative connotation because it assumes that loyalty will be to the patron, or the person making the selection, rather than to the government at large. This is not always true, however, and it sometimes is not a negative feature. Nominees to the U.S. Supreme Court are often picked because of their political leanings and personal connections to presidents, yet once seated on the Court they sometimes become remarkably independent. A different case is the political adviser who is hired on the public payroll by a political executive for personal loyalty and party-based affinity and whose ideological bias is expected. Ultimately, those using such appointments employ three criteria: (1) political loyalty, (2) personal acquaintance, and (3) technical competence or merit. In the ideal case for a political executive, the pool of possible candidates can be narrowed to those who are of the same party or who have the same political preferences. The executive can identify people he or she has known or worked with in the past and then select people who are still highly experienced in the targeted area and competent for the duties to be assigned.

Problems occur when the first two principles are met but the third is not. For instance, well-connected policy generalists are sometimes installed as directors of large agencies when they lack either the in-depth policy background or the administrative experience to cope with their new responsibilities (e.g., a former Playboy bunny, with no relevant expertise, was appointed to run a large agency in a southern state in the late 1990s). To reduce the political and personal nature of many executive appointments at the city and county levels, professional manager systems have been installed so that competence rather than patronage becomes the primary factor for department heads.

Merit

Merit-based systems emphasize technical qualifications using processes that analyze job competencies and require open application procedures.[2] These systems require "tests," but the tests may consist of education and experience reviews, performance evaluations, or licensure, as well as written tests. **Merit selection** is the primary philosophy for civil service systems that dominate nonexecutive employment. The strengths of merit selection are its fairness to candidates, its availability to scrutiny, and its assurance of minimum competencies and qualifications. It also fits well with notions of democratic access and accountability.

Merit, however, does not always live up to its promise. Selection is often so mechanical and technical that the best potential candidates never apply, diversity of experience is inhibited, there is an excessive emphasis on tangible skills over future potential, and the time required to process an enormous pool of candidates becomes onerous. As the discussion here will highlight, the pursuit of precise and valid indicators of merit is challenging for those who must consider what tests to use and how much weight to give to them. This has led to a decrease in some jurisdictions in the number of "true" merit positions in which a formal competitive process is required. As a typical example, the state of Maryland moved 1,400 management positions from merit to "noncompetitive" and changed their termination rights from "just cause" to "for any reason" in 1996. Likewise, the entire state middle-management corps in Florida was converted in 2001 (see Exhibit 4.1). Yet even though job tenure rights are being curtailed in some jurisdictions (such as Arizona) or for classes of employees (such as managers), most systems contain the bulk of the merit principles related to recruitment and selection.

Seniority

Seniority is also a crucial selection principle in civil service systems. Philosophically, it asserts that those already employed in the agency (1) have been through the merit process once, (2) have been screened in probationary periods and evaluation processes, and (3) have superior organizational insight and loyalty because of their history of employment. Systems that emphasize seniority either limit many job searches to internal candidates or give internal candidates substantial advantages in the process, such as points for years of service or opportunities to fill positions prior to advertisement outside the agency. The effects are that civil service employment occurs primarily in selected entry-level positions and that external hiring is less common at the supervisory level and above. This is particularly noticeable in highly unionized environments and in paramilitary organizations such as those concerned with public safety. Very few organizations follow strict seniority-based selection (following the exact date of hiring) in promotion, but strict seniority often prevails in the case of layoffs and the accompanying "bumping rights" that are sometimes authorized.

Exhibit 4.1 Intriguing Aspects of Civil Service Reform in Florida

The state of Florida's pre-reform personnel system was one of the most productive in the nation based on the number of employees compared to population. The system embraced the negative aspect of the business management model (ready termination of employees) but not its positive dimensions (competitive compensation, the right to strike). Governor Jeb Bush argued that since partisanship, cronyism, nepotism, and favoritism could corrupt the merit system, job safeguards designed to prevent such problems should be abolished. The only independent expert to examine Service First (the governor's civil service reform initiative) prior to legislative passage was a labor mediator special master, who was mandated by law to give the lawmakers nonpartisan advice when collective bargaining negotiations broke down. He concluded that "there was no factual evidence brought forward to show that the (existing) system was broken or dysfunctional" (Special Master, 2001, p. 58) and that Service First would become "Service Worst" because eliminating job protections while simultaneously seeking the most qualified staff "is not logical and will not work" (p. 74). The legislature rejected the recommendations and abolished the special master role in resolving future labor–management impasses.

A Florida Department of Transportation contract inspector observed, "I have been involved in the private sector that Jeb [Bush] so wants to emulate, and if someone proposed a complete overhaul of an existing system without showing any facts or figures to back them up, like the governor is doing, they would earn a quick ticket to 'downsizing'" (quoted in Cotterell, 2001a, p. 2E).

Unions that had endorsed Bush for election were exempted from Service First coverage. They argued that their members needed job protections when making public safety and medical decisions, and without them the unions would have considerable difficulty in recruiting and retaining quality personnel. Other unions, whose members had critical regulatory responsibilities but had not supported the governor in the 1998 election, were unsuccessful in making a similar argument.

The governor's "efficiency czar" resigned in protest the day the bill was signed into law. She argued that she was unable to "slow down the headlong rush to privatize, computerize, and downsize" state jobs, a reckless process that lacked analysis or justification. She was especially concerned about Service First and its expansion of the employment-at-will doctrine to careerists. "I was 'at will,'" she said, "and you can't voice your opinion or be critical in such an environment" (quoted in Cotterell, 2001b, p. 2A).

While some prominent abuses have been reported, widespread abuse (insofar as such things can be readily documented) apparently has not occurred, perhaps because of the practical difficulties of hiring large numbers of employees in a downsizing era and persuading people to work for below-market government salaries. An underlying key reason may be that old-fashioned job patronage is much less appealing to campaign contributors than "pinstripe" patronage found in the awarding of lucrative government contracts.

Despite the value in documenting program successes, no evaluative metrics were written into the legislation. Rather, officials believed that employees would take more pride in their work and that supervisors would report enhanced staff performance. There was a sense that the policy solved the problem, and attention shifted to other, more important issues.

There remains a determined belief in the inherent superiority of business management practices, with their current emphasis on executive leadership at the expense of merit-based neutral competence, despite the continuing corporate management problems from the Enron era through more recent Wall Street debacles. Critics of the shift to business management practices point out that a return to the spoils system of the 19th century is a questionable way to the meet the challenges of the 21st century. Defenders of the trend note that dissatisfaction with public sector stagnation and proceduralism triggered the current reforms.

Seniority systems ensure that organizations demonstrate a sense of loyalty to their staff as well as offer career development paths; however, such systems also tend to lock employees into a single governmental system (often just their own division and unit) for career growth. Organizationally, seniority systems can lead to "inbreeding" and "groupthink," and they can prevent the development of fresh management insights, which is a prime motivation for lateral hiring. Even more insidious is that a strong seniority system can provide a milieu in which the "Peter principle" operates.[3]

Representativeness

The selection principle of **representativeness** can be interpreted in numerous ways, including by geography, social class, gender, race or ethnicity, prior military service, and disability. The U.S. Constitution supports geographic representativeness in electoral issues through the federal system. President Andrew Jackson and his supporters believed too many federal jobs went to easterners and the social elite, and they therefore emphasized appointments of those from western states (of that day) and from less privileged classes. A current debate involves selection (or more generally nonselection) based on sexual orientation. Because veterans have been taken out of the labor force and might have a liability in seeking employment upon leaving the military, they receive a preference in civil service systems. **Veterans' points** (established by such legislation as the Veterans' Preference Act of 1944 and the Veterans' Employment Opportunity Act of 1998) are used in selection by the federal government and in many state governments. Typically, veterans who served during wars are eligible for extra points in ratings systems, and wounded veterans may be eligible for additional points.

In the past half century, there has been an emphasis on gender and racial representativeness, as evidenced by military integration (both African Americans and women), equal opportunity legislation, affirmative action plans, and, more recently, diversity programs. Generally speaking, affirmative action tries to encourage women and minorities to seek positions for which they are qualified, especially where the rate of employment of members of their groups is low. Ceteris paribus—that is, all things being equal—members of the targeted groups should be offered positions in areas of underrepresentation.

That is to say, affirmative action generally has upheld merit as the premier value but has given representativeness a strong second-place consideration when merit principles are followed. In terms of implementation, affirmative action programs also require extensive analysis of disparate impact on women and minorities so that applicant pools can be restructured where underrepresentation appears to be a problem. Although numerically based quota systems are illegal (except when court ordered), chronic underrepresentation of some groups remains an important and legitimate consideration; this is especially true in many formerly male- and white-dominated organizations where occupational segregation has merely given way to tokenism. Representativeness remains a legally appropriate consideration on a case-by-case basis as long as there is equivalent merit and documented imbalance. In more recent diversity programs, numerical representativeness has been replaced by an emphasis on a supportive environment that welcomes employment of different groups and embraces workplace heterogeneity (Hewins-Maroney & Williams, 2013; Sabharwal, 2014). That is, diversity programs are mission driven and derived from internal business needs, not compliance driven and based on social issues as are affirmative action programs (Ewoh, 2013).

Character, Job, and Organization Fit

Even though a person has the right education and technical qualifications, he or she may not be a good "fit," a loose concept that refers to a match of the expectations of the person with those of the job and organization. **Character fit** involves fit in regard to generic work habits, such as conscientiousness, motivation, initiative, resilience, service motivation, and self-discipline. Character fit also encompasses the absence of dysfunctional behaviors such as substance abuse, theft, and violent tendencies. **Job fit** concerns specific traits that lend themselves to particular jobs, such as the ability to handle stress, assertiveness, friendliness, self-confidence, decisiveness, flexibility, willingness to assume responsibility, and similar characteristics, depending on what the job profile is. In a good **organizational fit**, the candidate's personality is well aligned with cultural aspects of the organization, such as the reward and incentive system, notions of organizational citizenship, and departmental values; the individual is likely to exhibit a willingness to strive harder and to have some degree of professional passion for the job (Van Wart, 2011). For an example of the challenges of using the criterion of character and job fit, see Exhibit 4.2, which focuses on the Turkish civil service.

The History of Selection: Six Eras

Administrative selection philosophies have varied over time (Mosher, 1982; Van Riper, 1958), as the discussion of six specific eras below demonstrates. Note that the time frames of the later eras overlap.

Administration by Gentility: 1789–1829

From the time of George Washington's presidency until that of Andrew Jackson, patronage (appointment based on connections and political views) was the primary system for selection in the public sector. It was muted, however, by the ethic of "fitness of character" and genteel education (social class). President Washington was a strong force in shaping a tradition that balanced competence and political neutrality. Although he avoided appointing those openly hostile to his political views, he was careful in selecting candidates from among all the states and from a range of political perspectives. He generally gave preference to those of education—hence those of a higher social class—although he appointed only persons known for integrity and public spirit. He also did sometimes give preference to Revolutionary War military officers. With the evolution of political parties, Thomas Jefferson was faced with replacing enough Federalists to ensure responsiveness to his Democratic-Republican Party. During the presidencies of James Madison, James Monroe, and John Quincy Adams, the ethic of fitness of character and political neutrality generally held sway but increasingly came under pressure as the party ruling Congress urged greater political determination of administrative posts at all levels of government.

Selection by Spoils: 1829–1883

President Jackson insisted on better representation of all social classes and of those from the West, and thought that rotation of government positions was healthy. He advocated

Exhibit 4.2 Turkish Civil Service: Should It Be a Requirement to Record All Interviews?

Ibrahim Dere, MPA

After the Ottoman Empire dissolved, the new Republic of Turkey adopted a civil law system in the 1920s. In addition to the general principle of equality (merit), equal employment opportunity (EEO) in the civil service would eventually become part of the constitution (Yalcindag, 1974). Thus Article 70 of the Turkish constitution states that "every Turk has the right to enter public service" and "no criteria other than the qualifications for the office concerned shall be taken into consideration for recruitment into public service." Representativeness, then, is protected by wider access, not by the use of direct or indirect measures such as quotas or special programs.

Although EEO is not mentioned in the 1965 Civil Service Law, which regulates civil servants' right and responsibilities, historically all career personnel have been recruited through an annual three-tier examination process that—supposedly—promotes EEO (Dodd, 1969; Tutum, 1977). These centralized, comprehensive, and competitive multiple-choice examinations are conducted by the governmental selection and placement center. After being selected from among tens of thousands of applicants (most of whom are new college graduates), successful candidates take another written examination conducted by the hiring ministry. In the final stage of the selection process, the interview or oral examination, committees evaluate candidates based on their knowledge of the field and general culture as well as their expression, attitudes, behaviors, and "presentability." This final stage is an example of the application of the selection criterion of character and job fit.

Allowing an increasing number of interviewees in the third stage in recent years has been part of an effort to broaden management discretion, but it has also led to criticisms of implicit inappropriate discrimination. Many unsuccessful applicants have filed lawsuits against the ministries on the grounds that the interview questions they were asked were not objective. For example, Adnan Özcanan, a failed applicant for junior judge, brought a lawsuit against the Ministry of Justice in 2008. The Fifth Administrative Court of Ankara ruled that the interview violated the rule of law since it was not videotaped, which would have enabled the court to determine its constitutionality. Similarly, an administrative court of appeal ruled against the Ministry of Interior for not recording the interviews of junior city managers. Yet other courts have ruled that failing to tape interviews was not unconstitutional. In short, there has been no definitive decision on the need for recorded interviews.

Three fundamental selection challenges emerge. First, to what degree should managers have the final say in determining which candidates are a "good fit" based on an interview? It is standard in most, but not all, American settings to allow managers such discretion. Second, how much should the interview list be constrained? In the United States, the rule of three has been relaxed in recent years, and this has had both advantages and disadvantages. Third, how does one determine when inappropriate measures have been used in the interview process, such as asking discriminatory or non-job-related questions? Must all interviews be recorded and stored for review to assist in documentation during challenges, as is the trend in some areas, as seen in the installation of cameras on police cars in some jurisdictions in the United States and elsewhere? Or does this lead to excessive second-guessing of managers who have attempted to sift through the nuances of nearly equally qualified applicants?

SOURCES: Dodd (1969); Tutum (1977); Yalcindag (1974).

keeping government jobs as simple as possible so that those with modest education could be eligible. He argued that greater political responsiveness would reduce corruption and complacency. Although he replaced only 20% of the federal workforce (a proportion not substantially greater than that replaced by Jefferson) and was himself not really an advocate of a spoils system (appointment as spoils of victory to those active in the campaign, despite lack of qualifications), he did create the philosophical basis for widespread abuses in the following decades (Van Riper, 1958, p. 42).

Several problems with a solely patronage-based civil service became increasingly clear over the next 50 years, starting in 1829. First, appointments were often assigned with little regard for experience, knowledge, or abilities. Second, inequities in pay were frequent: Compensation was as much a function of connection to a political patron as to specific job responsibilities. Third, it became common to require government workers to campaign for the reelection of politicians in office and to relinquish a portion of their pay to the party in power. Furthermore, spoils appointments often included jobs for those who did not work full-time (or at all) but nevertheless received paychecks.

After the Civil War, rampant corruption spawned a public-driven government reform movement that lasted nearly 50 years. One of the early, if brief, successes was during the administration of President Ulysses S. Grant, when he signed a bill authorizing competitive examinations for some federal positions. The law lapsed only 2 years later for lack of funding because of congressional fears of curbs on patronage opportunities. Many cities where political patronage and corruption were rampant saw the development of civil service reform associations at the municipal level. The pressure continued to build as governmental incompetence and abuse became more blatant and government responsibilities expanded.

Technical Merit Systems: 1883–1912

The Pendleton Act of 1883 signaled a new era in personnel management, although it was more than 50 years before the system evolved into one that was comprehensive in the federal government, widely adopted across other levels of government, and generally rigorously applied. Although the act was prompted by the assassination of President James Garfield by a disappointed job seeker in 1881, it responded to the growing perception that the functions of government had become too large, complex, and important to be handled entirely by a patronage system. The new system incorporated the following:

- Open, competitive examinations based on technical qualifications
- Lists of those eligible or "certified" provided to the hiring authority
- Rules against politicians intervening in civil service selection, coercing civil servants to work in political campaigns, or requiring employees to provide kickbacks for civil government employment
- The independent Civil Service Commission, which administered practical competitive examinations (essentially a central job registry) and acted as a judicial review board for abuses

This new model required bipartisan and independent selection of employees by a commission for covered (or civil service) positions—that is, for those over which the commission had jurisdiction. Initially, only 10% of federal employees were covered (Van Riper, 1958). The proportion gradually increased to around 48% in 1900. By midcentury and continuing today, more than 90% were included in civil service positions, broadly construed.

Expansion of Merit Principles, Along With Employee Rights and Seniority: 1912–1978

Although a few city and state governments were quick to replicate the new reform model, the increase in civil service systems was slow. To facilitate acceptance of civil service models, the federal government conditioned some financial assistance to other levels of government on the use of merit-based employment systems. Especially effective was the Social Security Act of 1935. Other programs continued this requirement, which led to the institution of at least partial or modified civil service systems in all the states, most municipalities, and many counties. The depoliticization of the personnel process was further enhanced by the Hatch Act of 1939 (amended and relaxed in 1993), which strongly prohibited most political activity by federal workers. Subsequently, "little Hatch Acts," modeled on the federal legislation, were enacted by most states (Bowman & West, 2009).

As civil service systems grew in number and size, so too did employee rights. Although the Pendleton Act prohibited political removals at the federal level, it was frequently circumvented. Through an executive order, President William McKinley prohibited removal from the competitive service except for just cause and for reasons given in writing. Furthermore, the person being discharged had to have the basic due process right to respond in writing. This important principle and process was placed into permanent legislation in the Lloyd–La Follette Act of 1912.

Once in the system and protected from political and arbitrary firing, civil servants tended to remain in their positions for long periods, and employee seniority was substantially enhanced. As the legal footing of the seniority principle grew, those outside the service would have access to fewer jobs, and those inside the service would have greater access to promotional selections. With the growth of public sector unions starting in the 1950s, some areas, such as public safety, frequently eliminated lateral selection from outside their agencies.

Expansion of Access: 1964–1990

The era of equal opportunity, which began in the early 1960s, did not replace merit but modified its execution and made hiring more complicated (see Chapter 2). The Civil Rights Act of 1964 addressed discrimination based on race, color, religion, gender, or national origin. The Equal Employment Opportunity Act of 1972 expanded these rights to state and local governments and promoted equal employment opportunity through affirmative action. Other major applicant and employee protections that were enhanced during this period were those against age discrimination (Age Discrimination in Employment Act of 1967, amended in 1974) and disability discrimination (Rehabilitation Act of 1973) for federal employees. At the federal level, the 1978 Civil Service Reform Act (CSRA) established the **80% rule** to provide selection "floors" for protected classes. That is, selection processes should not result in qualification rates of protected groups that are less than 80% of the rate of the highest group.

The burst of attention to representativeness in the 1960s and 1970s, symbolized by widespread use of affirmative action programs to correct imbalances, certainly continued into the 1980s as an organizational way of life. Perhaps the final great push for representation was the Americans with Disabilities Act of 1990, which required reasonable accommodations in the selection process for those with allowable disabilities.

The tide turned in the 1990s when bellwether legal cases produced court rulings that generally required more narrowly tailored and narrowly defined remedies for representational problems. For example, the Civil Rights Act of 1991 disallowed race norming (see Chapter 2). Quotas have always been illegal except when court ordered in response to egregious cases. Although equal opportunity continued to be strongly encouraged, it was increasingly pursued through diversity programs rather than through affirmative action.

Contemporary Selection Trends: 1978–Present

The potential excesses of the civil service system started to emerge as early as the 1930s, when the administration of President Franklin Delano Roosevelt toyed with the idea of major civil service reform. Complaints about the civil service system centered on the following flaws:

- Rigidity (e.g., the restriction of interviews and selection to three top candidates based on technical qualifications)
- Proceduralism, or red tape (e.g., difficulties in hiring rapidly in an applicants' market)
- Isolation from the executive branch (e.g., independent centralized testing agencies apart from the hiring agencies)
- Inadequate accountability (e.g., difficulties in dismissing employees who perform poorly)

Contemporary trends have emphasized flexibility, speed, integration of the selection function with other management responsibilities, and increased employee accountability for productivity. At the federal level, the CSRA reintegrated selection functions into the executive branch through the Office of Personnel Management. It also provided for more managerial latitude. Initially, personnel responsibilities were tightly held by OPM, but the reinventing government initiative begun in 1992 probably had a greater effect on the OPM than on any other agency. By 1996, the OPM was required to decentralize most of its responsibilities to other agencies (a process called *delegated examination authority*). Civil service commissions today (e.g., the U.S. Merit Systems Protection Board) often function as policy and review boards, although in some jurisdictions even these responsibilities have passed to the agencies.

In an important trend, a growing number of agencies or bureaus in departments were able to opt out of the traditional ("competitive") civil service system. This parallel system (the "excepted service," or noncompetitive service) is still required to follow the broad traditions of merit: notification of open positions, reliance on technical merit through minimum established standards, and due process for employees. It allows far more management flexibility and control over selection and employee appraisal, however. The largest example of an entirely excepted service agency is the U.S. Department of Homeland Security. Approximately one-half of all federal new hires are made through excepted service provisions (U.S. MSPB, 2008a). The U.S. Department of Defense began to follow suit in 2006, but it has reduced the scope of this change somewhat due to court and congressional challenges.

At the state and local levels, the move to more flexible, nimble, integrated, and accountable civil service systems mirrored the federal experience, but this trend was far from uniform. Many progressive cities—such as Phoenix, Arizona, and Madison, Wisconsin—never suffered the same degree of rigidity as other jurisdictions and were quick to enhance managerial rationality. Some cities and counties that had traditionally allowed more managerial and political responsiveness found themselves in vogue. However, some school districts, such as that in Washington, D.C., have been taken over by city governments where strong intervention has been seen as desirable or have been privatized outright, leading to radical personnel reforms. Most states had followed the traditional federal pattern but have undergone change in recent years (Bowman & West, 2007; Kellough & Nigro, 2006). Some states, such as Florida, Arizona, and Georgia, have been more radical in their reform efforts (Maynard, 2012), whereas others, such as Maryland, South Carolina, Tennessee, and Washington, have implemented more modest changes. Several states that have attempted major personnel reform, such as California and Rhode Island, have failed to achieve their goals.

The longtime values of civil service systems (technical merit and seniority) seem to have experienced countervailing pressures to expand managerial accountability and flexibility. Some states have abolished or weakened their civil service systems. In relation to selection, the ability to contract out has increased (e.g., the state of Washington). Also, the use of **temporary employees** (those without contracts or tenure rights, and usually without benefits) rose in significance during the 1990s (Hays & Kearney, 1999), but because the Internal Revenue Service insisted that long-term temporary employees are de facto regular employees ("permatemps"), a new trend is toward the use of **term employees**. For example, the federal government is making widespread use of term appointments for 2 to 4 years, with contracts and benefits but without tenure rights. Although such practices allow organizations considerable flexibility, they undermine employee security and increase opportunities for politicization of the civil service. Since 2008, the enormous downturn in the economy and constrained budgets have made personnel change much more politically feasible than it was before.

There has also been an increasing interest in finding opportunities for older workers, many of whom are receiving retirement benefits from one or more sources. These people bring experience and flexibility in that their services can be targeted to specific needs. Often they want part-time or job-sharing positions, and many may be more interested in the benefits package than in remuneration per se. Older employees may be rehired annuitants or workers from outside the hiring agency (Partnership for Public Service, 2008b).

Major changes in recruitment technology have also influenced important trends in selection in two ways. First, not only has Web-based recruitment become a dominant tool (Beagrie, 2013), but also Web-based testing has taken a firm hold and is increasingly accepted by researchers as valid (Nye, Do, Drasgow, & Fine, 2008; Potosky & Bobko, 2004) and by applicants as fair (Dineen, Noe, & Wang, 2004). Furthermore, automated screening has become commonplace as a "first-cut" method wherever large numbers of individuals are applying for positions, from temporary to supervisory (Buckley, Minette, Joy, & Michaels, 2004). Automated screening programs cull either applications or résumés for key phrases, sorting eligibles from ineligibles. If candidates are interested in specific positions, they are wise to ensure that they include in their applications or résumés as many of the key desired elements as possible, using language similar to that in the job vacancy postings. Because the preference in many of these software programs is to use an application format as the initial screening mechanism and to use the résumé attachment as data for in-depth review by human resource specialists or the hiring unit after the first cut, applicants are also wise not to use "see attached" on applications unless directed to do so. Through the use of predictive workforce analytics software, the Oakland A's were able to excel in baseball, as dramatized in the 2011 movie *Moneyball*, with Brad Pitt (see Exhibit 4.3).

Selection, then, potentially is shared by three areas: a civil service commission, a human resource department, and the agency. Up through the 1970s, the most usual model was for the civil service commission to "test" and provide formal review, the personnel department to provide technical assistance such as benefits and salary information, and the hiring

Exhibit 4.3 Staffing Sports Teams and Offices Using Big-Data Technology

The example set by the Oakland Athletics in developing a roster based on human dynamics research has been followed by other teams in Major League Baseball as well as other sports. All National Football League teams, for instance, use analytics in selection—leaving less to chance and subjective judgment—to the point that the best teams now are those making the best use of the data (Nextgov, 2014).

Job-matching technologies are also being adopted in the corporate world. Some firms are testing their current employees to identify traits that make them successful. Such traits (abilities in prioritization, problem solving, multitasking, and learning from mistakes; high levels of creativity and persistence; low levels of ease of distraction) are then keyed to customized video games used to test applicants. Ideally, both individuals and organizations are better served as a result.

Given the dubious records of other selection techniques (in both athletics and the real world), some managers are said to select personnel based on their scores on such video games, not interviews or grade point averages. Improved job-matching technologies may help resolve the paradox of needs (see this book's introduction) if the results are cheaper, faster, and more accurate. Indeed, a major development in people analytics is the creation of algorithms to assess all workers, all the time (see Chapter 10).

Some concerns about the approach are that it may offer a false sense of precision, that it may create "clones" of the present workforce, and that, with so much information about people's limitations, it may stifle creativity. Skeptics also compare the technology to Frederick Taylor's scientific management from a century ago, which was initially "hailed as a progressive force that would free workers from the whim of autocratic bosses and benefit all" but unfortunately was distorted into "speedup dogma used by bosses, and workers hated it" (Lohr, 2014).

department to initiate actions for hiring and to make final selections from short lists of certified applicants. In the 1980s, the most typical model was for personnel departments to provide **certified lists** to hiring units and for the civil service commission to act as administrative judge in disputed cases. By the end of the 1990s, an increasingly common model was for hiring departments to recruit and select applicants directly, following merit principles but having wider discretion in testing practices and interview choices. Human resource departments then provided technical assistance and oversight of legal compliance issues and statistical records, as well as administrative review when necessary. The new model has some definite strengths: greater control and ownership by hiring agencies, greater flexibility, and less red tape as perceived by candidates, who often are interested in specific agencies and positions. Inevitably, there are also weaknesses; these include increased fragmentation of selection practices and less use of economies of scale, less consistency, and more potential for abuse of discretion.

In sum, the eras are defined by their emphasis and de-emphasis of values related to selection: social class, patronage (political responsiveness), merit (technical qualifications, performance criteria), seniority (employee protections and expanded privileges), representativeness, and character, job, and organization fit. Although all the values (except social class) have been explicit in each of the eras, some values have been emphasized at the expense of others. Below is a rough outline of the dominant values in each period:

- *Administration by gentility:* political responsiveness, social class, technical qualifications, fitness of character
- *Selection by spoils:* political responsiveness, performance (though impressionistically defined and evaluated), representativeness
- *Early technical merit:* technical qualifications
- *Expanded merit:* technical qualifications, employee protections, and expanded seniority
- *Expansion of access:* representativeness via affirmative action (superimposed on technical qualifications and seniority)
- *Contemporary trends:* performance criteria (flexibility in hiring, employee accountability), representativeness via diversity, technological efficiency via Web-based and electronic screening methods, fit with the job and organization

CRITERIA IN SELECTING SELECTION TESTS

Critical for all review and test procedures is their relationship to job-related competencies (Connerley et al., 2001). How does the procedure specifically relate to the essential job functions? On one hand, it is important to get good indicators of skills and likely performance. On the other, it is neither appropriate nor legal to pile on job requirements as a screening mechanism. Six criteria for the selection of selection methods are reviewed here: reliability, validity, legality, acceptability, efficiency, and effectiveness. On average, approximately four selection methods are used (DeVaro, 2005), so particular methods may have differing strengths.

Tests that provide consistent results are *reliable*. An unstructured interview has low reliability because the questions vary from one applicant to the next. When tests make good distinctions among the candidates, they are *valid*. As interesting as intelligence tests are, they are extremely poor predictors of job success. Because of affirmative action cases, courts have insisted that all hiring practices, especially written tests, have verifiable connections to core responsibilities and be appropriate predictors of success (see Exhibit 4.4 for a detailed discussion of **test validity**). It is not possible to provide high levels of validity without job analysis, a topic covered in Chapter 5.

Exhibit 4.4 Three Types of Test Validity

The *Uniform Guidelines on Employee Selection Procedures* establish three acceptable validation strategies: content, construct, and criterion. Because of concerns about disparate impact on minorities and women in the 1970s and 1980s, and about applicants with disabilities in the 1990s, test validation has become an important concern in the selection process. For example, the guidelines assert that employers should regularly validate all selection procedures. Where possible, valid selection procedures having less adverse impact on underrepresented groups should be used over those that have more adverse impact. Finally, employers should keep records of all those who applied and were accepted to ascertain whether adverse impact occurs; adverse impact is generally defined as a selection rate of less than 80% of the rate for the group with the highest selection rate.

Demonstrating *content validity* requires showing a direct relationship between the test and the actual job duties or responsibilities. This form of validity is generally the easiest to verify, and content validation is the most common validation procedure. A thorough job analysis of the position is conducted, and its elements are connected to concrete items in the test. Examples are typing tests for clerical positions; written tests that assess specific knowledge needed, such as mathematical skills customarily used by accountants; and actual work samples, such as error analysis of social work cases for supervisory positions.

Demonstrating *criterion validity* involves correlating high test scores (the predictor) with good job performance (the criterion) by those taking the test. For example, perhaps the applicants need few job skills and knowledge prior to employment because subsequent training will be provided (and therefore content validation is inappropriate). How does one predict and select those who will be most suitable? This is the case in entry-level public safety and corrections positions. Criterion validation generally examines aptitudes or cognitive skills for learning and performing well in a given job environment—for example, the aptitude to learn a new language, remember key data, or use logical reasoning.

Demonstrating *construct validity* involves documenting the relationship of select abstract personal traits and characteristics (such as intelligence, integrity, creativity, aggressiveness, industriousness, and anxiety) to job performance. Tests with high construct validity accurately predict future job performance by examining the characteristics of successful job incumbents and judging whether applicants have those characteristics. Construct validation is used for psychological tests that screen candidates based on trait/attitude profiles.

Documenting validity ensures that tests are job related and legally nondiscriminatory. Well-constructed tests can provide an excellent method of identifying and eliminating candidates who lack minimum competencies or are weak in aptitude or predisposition so that other methods can focus on selecting the most qualified from a smaller pool. When integrated with education and experience evaluations, interviews, and reference checks, so that a broad "basket" of indicators is established, content-, criterion-, and construct-based tests can provide a solid base of information from which to make selections.

SOURCE: *Uniform Guidelines on Employee Selection Procedures* (1978).

Some tests are less susceptible to *legal* challenge than others. Tests may be challenged on the basis of inconsistency, disparate impact, or poor relationship to specific job requirements. Lack of a drug test for a public safety position may subject an organization to lawsuits, but drug tests for standard administrative positions may be illegal. Even if tests are legal, another consideration is how well they are *accepted* by the candidates themselves (Forsberg & Shultz, 2009). Candidates expect to fill out application forms but may be put off by integrity tests (see below).

Some tests lend themselves relatively well to the screening of large numbers of applicants without undue expense and thus are *efficient*. For example, electronically submitted applications can be electronically scanned for an initial long list of candidates. While tremendously valued, the interview is not efficient as a preliminary tool when there are scores or hundreds of applicants. *Effectiveness* refers to how well a test functions in either a generic or a targeted purpose within the array of selection methods used. For instance, review of résumés is an effective initial screening device, general skills tests screen for basic communication competence, and background investigations ensure that felons are not put into public safety, child care, or fiduciary positions.

SELECTION: FOUR SCREENING PHASES

Selection processes can be divided into four phases of screening, although sometimes phases are combined for convenience or out of necessity. In Phase 1, the procedure emphasizes discriminating between the qualified and the unqualified. Applicant pools typically have a substantial number of individuals who do not meet basic qualifications and whose applications can be put aside. In eliminating candidates, initial qualifications need to be carefully identified, both from the general job description and from those special needs identified for the position in the job posting. Did the applicant provide a complete packet in the required timeline? Does the person have the required education, job-related experience, licensing, or test score? For example, of the 25 original applicants for a position, 5 may have incomplete applications, 3 may have insufficient educational background, and 6 may not have the required experience. Sometimes, staff or computers do the screening at this point.

In Phase 2, the most highly qualified people are identified and screened. If the initial screening ranked all candidates, it is a simple matter to choose those with the highest scores. In **unassembled tests**, candidates are ranked only on those items that can be submitted by mail or e-mail—applications, résumés, written **work samples**, letters of recommendation, and possibly online or written self-reported assessments. In **assembled tests**, applicants are required to come to a central location or locations to take general aptitude tests (general mental ability tests) or specific work tests (e.g., a typing test), or to provide live work samples in a proctored setting. The idea is to narrow the pool to a number that is practical to interview or test in depth. In the example, 11 candidates were qualified in Phase 1, but 5 were identified to interview in Phase 2. Until a candidate is chosen and has accepted the position, the others are not barred from later consideration.

Invariably, the interview is the centerpiece of this process. Of course, when the **rule of three** applies, the finalists are limited to the top three candidates. In some cases, however, the finalists may be numerous, especially when multiple openings exist. In some unusual cases, the finalists may be limited to one or two clearly exceptional candidates. This is a good time for the agency to require live samples of work and to check references.

Phase 3 results in a single candidate to offer the position to, as well as backup applicants should the individual turn down the offer. Selecting the first choice from the array of candidates may be easy, or in some cases it may be difficult because the top candidates seem equally qualified or bring different types of human assets to the position. Negotiation of salary and benefits may be mechanical, as in the case of frontline positions in which the terms of employment are relatively rigid, or quite flexible, as in the case of many senior positions and hard-to-recruit specialist positions.

During Phase 4 the qualifications and abilities of the candidate are confirmed after the offer. Many offers are conditional on successful drug tests, medical exams, or even background checks. This phase may also include the first period of employment in which the candidate has probationary status and can be terminated without cause. A probationary period is especially warranted in cases where extensive or rigorous schooling is required and some new hires "wash out."

The four-phase approach described above allows for thorough review of applicants and minimal waste of time on unselected candidates. In some limited cases, however, this approach may be too slow in responding to a dynamic applicant pool or too costly for the agency. A reduced or consolidated selection process may sometimes be appropriate, such as the hiring of term employees or entry-level staff workers, or in the event of a situation where hiring must be done as an emergency action.

INITIAL REVIEWING AND TESTING

A wide variety of reviewing and testing mechanisms are available. The cost to organizations and the burden to applicants, however, require restraint in the use of these procedures. Most initial tests (in Phases 1 and 2) are education and experience evaluations, letters of recommendation, self-reported assessments (biodata), general aptitude and trait tests, and performance tests for specific job qualifications.

Education and Experience Evaluations

Education and experience evaluations include application forms, cover letters, and résumés (Carlson, 2003; Udechukwu & Manyak, 2009). Video résumés have fans among some applicants, but these have yet to catch on in the organizational world, especially in the public sector (Jesdanun, 2007), where the legal and technical issues they raise are a concern. Video conferencing may be used in the selection process if distance is an issue. Applicants who want to include video résumés as optional information should keep them very brief and professional for public sector positions. Application forms generally run from one to three pages for job- or agency-specific applications to five or six pages for the "general purpose" forms used by many state governments or large agencies. Such forms generally include requests for biographical data, education, job experiences (asking for organization, address, title, supervisor, and duties), the job title or titles for which the applicant is applying, work location preference (in state systems), work limitations (such as availability), and special qualifications. They also normally provide information about such topics as reasonable accommodation, **diversity policies**, and veterans' points. Finally, applications invariably have certification and authorization statements to be signed. Such statements notify candidates of the consequences of giving false information, inform them that applications are available for public inspection, and authorize background checks. Occasionally, applications are customized for specific positions, and applicants are requested to provide biographical answers to fit specific job-related questions regarding their achievements, education, training, conscientiousness, and work experience (see the "Biodata" section below).

Not all jobs require application forms. Some substitute a cover letter and a résumé, especially for management and executive jobs. Although forms have the benefit of uniformity and provide standard preemployment waivers, they give little insight into the career development, management style, and unique abilities or experiences of candidates. Cover letters provide an opportunity for candidates to explain why they feel they are qualified for an advertised position, and résumés generally provide more specific information about job experience than would fit in an application form. Typically, applicants are asked to provide references—addresses and telephone numbers or sometimes completed letters of recommendation (see the "Letters of Recommendation" section below). Cover letters and résumés create more work for both the applicant and reviewers, but they generally are more informative than applications. Also, sometimes work samples are requested, such as a written work product or visual image of a completed project. Whenever the cover letter and résumé are substituted for the application, the selected candidate is generally required to fill out the form later in the process.

A number of jobs require specific licenses, certificates, or endorsements. These include many medical positions (such as doctors, nurses, and anesthesiologists), engineering and technician positions, teaching positions, legal positions (such as lawyers), jobs requiring special driver's permits (commercial, chauffeur's), and positions in architecture and hazardous material handling. For such positions, licensure is generally the minimum requirement for consideration for hiring. In some cases, certification is required for the position but is provided by the employer as training. In those cases, it is a selection method only to the degree that some candidates drop out or fail the certification process. (Prime examples are positions requiring certified peace officer status and select military occupational programs.)

Although licensure is useful for its definitiveness, it does raise the issue of private control over the process in many occupational settings, sometimes leading to excessive occupational selectivity, which in turn creates a market bottleneck and inflates salaries. Some jurisdictions use emergency and temporary certificates to remedy this situation when it becomes acute.

Letters of Recommendation

Providing letters of recommendation takes considerable effort on the part of candidates and those recommending them, and reading the letters is time-consuming for reviewers. Therefore, such letters should be solicited only with forethought. They are generally most appropriate for those seeking jobs of high potential, such as entry-level professional positions or management posts. Although requests for letters are most easily included in original job postings, increasingly employers are deferring their requests until the finalists have been selected for midlevel and senior positions. Because better jobs require customized letters of recommendation, some highly qualified applicants may choose not to waste a scarce resource on questionable competitions. By postponing this request, the hiring authority often widens the candidate pool. In general, the most useful letters of recommendation are from former employers. The same is true regarding those persons called as references. Former employers can speak to a candidate's abilities, work effectiveness, and work habits most directly.

Biodata—Matching Past Experiences With Current Job Requirements

Because past performance is the best predictor of future performance, one effective assessment technique is to ask candidates to provide detailed examples about themselves on the important accomplishment dimensions (i.e., competencies) of the job. The assessment technique of collecting biographical data related to job competencies is called the **biodata** method, or the behavioral consistency method (U.S. OPM, 1999). Ideally, candidates are asked to report information about five to ten accomplishment dimensions on which they are rated. Critical competencies for a frontline employee might be examples of mastering new skills, work accuracy, work speed, cooperation with colleagues, innovation, perseverance, and commitment. A supervisory position, in contrast, might include monitoring work, operations planning, delegating work, clarifying and informing, developing staff, motivating staff, building teams, managing conflict, and stimulating creativity. Prior to judging the biodata self-reports, the evaluators should have established anchored rating scales. If the competencies are valid and the rating scale is carefully designed, this can be one of the most statistically valid of all selection methods (Schmidt & Hunter, 1998, p. 268). Shortcuts in this method, however, lower the validity significantly, even where the method is encouraged (U.S. MSPB, 2006). Behaviorally anchored questioning (relating specific experience to current job competencies) can be integrated into customized applications, requested as a complementary tool to the biographically oriented résumé, or become the basis for much of a **structured interview**. The biodata method, with its concrete experiential basis, is often compared to other approaches that test for attitudes, subjective judgments, and hypothetical situational decision making (Breaugh, 2009).

General Aptitude and Trait Tests

There are at least three types of aptitude and trait tests: (1) psychological, (2) general skills, and (3) general physical ability.

1. **Psychological tests** examine personality traits and compare them to job requirements (Corcoran, 2005; Lievens, Highhouse, & De Corte, 2005; Scroggins, Thomas, & Morris, 2009). For instance, research has shown that, compared with others with equal knowledge and skill, people who have a low sense of efficacy shy away from difficult tasks, have low aspirations and weak commitment to goals, and give up quickly

in the face of difficulties. For example, the military forces sometimes use psychological hardiness tests to predict resilience under stress (Bartone, Roland, Picano, & Williams, 2008). The challenge is that it can be difficult to demonstrate the necessary validity of such tests for specific positions, given the standards of correlation that the courts have demanded (see Exhibit 4.4). The use of these tests is common only in relation to public safety positions—law enforcement, corrections, emergency services—where job structure and stress justify the research and expense. Noncognitive abilities found to be critical are also assessed, such as motivation, attitude toward people, and sense of responsibility. Although not as prevalent, integrity and civil virtue tests (Viswesvaran, Deller, & Ones, 2007) are used (and seem to be on the rise) to screen out those with attitudes poorly suited to public sector ideals and the particularly high ethical standards required.[4] Honesty and integrity tests are, however, among the least accepted by applicants themselves (Anderson & Witvliet, 2008), and there are concerns about faking and coaching for personality and integrity tests (Miller & Barrett, 2008). Tests measuring very broad psychological constructs such as intelligence might be useful (Ree & Earles, 1994) but generally have been considered to fall far short of contemporary validity requirements. There is a good deal of debate over the use of personality, integrity, and civic virtue tests for selection in both the practitioner and research communities (see, e.g., Morgeson et al., 2007; Ones, Dilchert, Viswesvaran, & Judge, 2007).

2. **General skills tests** provide information about abilities or aptitudes in areas such as reading, mathematics, abstract thinking, spelling, language usage, general problem solving, judgment, proofreading, and memory (Ryan & Tippins, 2004). These tests are frequently used for entry-level positions where commercial vendors have a wide variety of products from which to choose, or where large agencies can create their own tests for large job classes. The measurement of general cognitive skill is used in educational selection in tests such as the SAT, the ACT, and the GRE. In a common case, a 100-item police officer general skills test covers learning and applying law enforcement–related information, remembering details, verbal aptitude, following directions, and using judgment and logic. Although such tests are most often used for broad classification series at the lower end of the administrative hierarchy, they can be purchased or developed for more senior professional positions that justify the expense and effort, such as air traffic controllers (Ackerman & Kanfer, 1993), general skills for middle managers, and for various police and fire commanders. For example, for many years the Immigration and Naturalization Service (INS) had a problem with its Border Patrol training program because more than 10% of candidates were unable to complete the language component successfully. The INS designed and implemented an artificial language test as a selection screen that assessed ability to learn a new language. Subsequently, the failure rate fell 76%, and use of the test produced a $6.5 million savings over 5 years (U.S. MSPB, 2002, p. 9).

3. When general physical ability is a major part of the job, as it is for public safety personnel, tests of physical ability (e.g., strength, agility, eyesight) may be part of a battery of tests used to determine initial job qualification (Arvey, Nutting, & Landon, 1992; Hogan, 1991). Generally, however, medical, physical, and eyesight examinations—when incidental but necessary—are done after a conditional offer has been extended but before employment (see the "Postoffer and Hiring Issues" section below).

Performance Tests for Specific Jobs

Performance tests directly assess the skills necessary for specific jobs.[5] Although tests based on single-factor performance models are somewhat useful and dominated early personnel research and practice, the multifactor nature of performance is better appreciated today (Campbell, 2001). Some jobs involve specific physical skills, such as typing (or keyboarding) or equipment operation, that can be tested. Many job-related knowledge tests use multiple-choice, true-false, and short-answer formats. Sometimes video versions of tests are administered. Occasionally, an essay or an oral presentation is analyzed in the first screening. Knowledge-based tests are also commonly utilized in promotional hiring in public safety and technical positions.

Job-related skills may be tested through work samples or job simulations: Those applicants tested are required to produce samples of the work or demonstrate their skills in a series of simulated activities, generally known as **assessment centers** (Thornton & Gibbons, 2009). Examples include requiring candidates for a trainer position to conduct short workshops, an operator to demonstrate telephone skills, and management applicants to complete a series of activities requiring them to write memoranda, give directions (in writing), and decide on actions to take. Work samples and assessment centers generally are quite effective but are not often used as initial screening devices because of the substantial time and cost involved for customized screening (Thornton & Potemra, 2010). They are used more commonly as part of the process to review the narrowed pool that goes through an interview process or for promotional purposes.

Other Considerations Regarding Reviewing and Testing

Licensure, general aptitude, and performance tests have proliferated over the years. For example, a posting for a civilian detention officer position in an Iowa county sheriff's office listed seven tests, excluding the interview: (1) written exam, (2) physical ability test, (3) polygraph exam, (4) psychological test, (5) medical exam, (6) drug test, and (7) residency requirement. More testing methods and higher-quality testing methods can substantially increase the likelihood of successful hires. Many critics, however, have called for more selection flexibility and a greater reliance on background, education, and experience reviews than on aptitude and performance tests (Gore, 1993; U.S. MSPB, 2004). The reasons are easy to discern. Lengthy testing protocols are expensive to administer and discourage some qualified job seekers from applying. Testing often slows the employment process as applicants wait for test dates and organizations wait for test scores. This is particularly true in a low-unemployment economy. However, the advent of online testing has provided flexibility in this regard. Unproctored versions may be subject to proctored retesting as a post-offer requirement. Also, vendors provide convenient composite tests for job classes that include language, knowledge, aptitude, and attitude questions in a variety of formats, sometimes with performance elements built into them. An example is testing for the ability to multitask by asking applicants to respond to "requests" during the test itself.

Another challenge in using standardized tests is the changing nature of contemporary work (Howard, 1995). Compared with in the past, jobs in general today tend to be broader, change more frequently, require more interpersonal and team skills, need more creativity and self-initiative, and have more demanding performance standards, with broader skill sets required

(Jordan-Nowe, 2007; Van Wart & Berman, 1999). This scenario suggests the need for an increased use of examinations and tests that look for the more abstract characteristics of the job in the applicant. Even with this new need—and although the ability to screen for these skills has increased because of research in affective behavior, general aptitude, and attitude testing—concerns about cost, time, and validity have dampened usage. Thus, in some instances there is a strong countervailing trend to use more tests to increase the rigor. In others there is a tendency to reduce the numbers of exams and avoid testing for abstract constructs.

There is no simple rule of thumb for which or how many tests to use. For example, see Exhibit 4.5, which indicates that although some methods have greater validity, several are necessary at a minimum to provide the degree of assurance appropriate for such important decisions. Factors that lend themselves to larger test batteries include sizable applicant pools and criticality of candidate suitability because of training cost or public safety. Factors that lend themselves to reduced test procedures include difficulties with travel and test administration, the need to move candidates through selection quickly (U.S. MSPB, 2006), and the ability to screen a manageable number of top applicants through interviewing and reference checks (see the discussion of Phase 2 below).

Exhibit 4.5 Validity Scores of Selected Assessment Methods

Assessment Method	Validity Score
Work sample tests	.54
Structured interviews	.51
General mental ability tests	.51
Job knowledge tests	.48
Training and experience (behavioral consistency model)	.45
Job tryout procedures	.44
Unstructured interviews	.38
Biographical data measures	.35
Reference checks	.26
Grade point average	.20
Years of job experience	.18
Training and experience (point method)	.11
Years of education	.10

SOURCE: U.S. MSPB (2008a, p. 24).

INTERVIEWING AND REFERENCE CHECKS: NARROWING THE POOL

For candidates, a selection interview means that they have "made the cut." Interviewees should anticipate that there are one to three other strong candidates, so doing well in the process is key (see Exhibit 4.6).

Interviewing and reference checks are major responsibilities for the hiring manager and involve discretion. Although this discretion is important, unstructured interviews and haphazard reference checks frequently result in low validity, wasted resources, frustrated candidates, and illegal practices (U.S. MSPB, 2003). Generally speaking, only structured interviews (described below) have high validity. (For general discussion of validity issues related to interviewing, see Ryan & Tippins, 2004; Schmidt & Hunter, 1998.) It is especially important to conduct high-quality interviews and reference checks, given the trend toward decreasing use of tests.

The first issue is deciding who will conduct the interviews. The four options are (1) the supervisor, (2) the human resource department or a third party, (3) a panel or committee,

---

Exhibit 4.6   *How Well Do You Interview?*

Management candidates are expected to interview well. Some of the common errors interviewees make include the following:

- *Not practicing:* To a large degree, interviews are performances, and giving a good performance takes practice. It is not acceptable answers that get jobs—it is highly articulate responses. Make up a handful of easy questions and another group of difficult ones. Write out the answers and rehearse them. Although these exact questions may not be asked, similar ones will be.
- *Not knowing the organization and its employees in advance:* Read as much about the agency as possible (certainly the Internet has made this easier). Find out about people on the interview committee and in the hiring unit (generally information will be sent in advance of an interview; if not, ask for it).
- *Not listening:* Candidates are "selling" themselves and talking a lot, but as good salespeople know, it is listening that makes the sale. Good listening shows courtesy, makes others feel satisfied with the interaction, and ensures that you do not miss subtle cues. People can tell the difference between active and passive listening, so do not mistake listening for being quiet without paying attention to others' ideas.
- *Not balancing technical and nontechnical aspects:* Reviewing the technical aspects of a job is certainly key, but just as important are your work philosophy, leadership style, and work-related goals. Do not forget to address the "big picture" while reviewing the details in preparation for an interview.
- *Not dressing the part:* As obvious as it may seem (see Exhibit 2.5), appropriate dress and grooming can make a difference, yet many people merely "make do" in the critical interview. Clothes should be well fitted and relatively new so that they still have crispness.

and (4) a series of interviewers, who may include the immediate supervisor, higher-level supervisors, a committee, a colleague forum, and clients.[6] Although the practice is not common in the public sector outside academe, sometimes the hiring unit acts as the hiring committee due to the increasingly collaborative approach toward work today (Munyon, Summers, & Ferris, 2011). For a nonprofessional entry-level position often a supervisor conducts the interview; in the case of positions with "no minimum education or experience" requirements in which there is high turnover (laundry workers, aides, receptionists, and drivers), professional interviewers in the human resource department conduct the interviews. For entry-level professional positions (such as caseworkers, law enforcement officers, correctional service officers, technicians, engineers, and lawyers) selection panels are frequently used to enhance the diversity of opinions about candidates. Candidates vying for a senior or professional position often have separate interviews with an advisory selection panel and with the hiring supervisor who makes the final selection. Interviewing for high-level positions may also require more resources, as candidates talk with a variety of parties in addition to the selection committee and hiring supervisor.

A second critical question is that of whom to interview (Carlson, 2003). Public sector employment involves two different approaches. One approach is to interview all candidates who meet minimum qualifications, but because this is time-consuming for the reviewers and may unnecessarily inflate the hopes of candidates, it is the less commonly used of the two. Where the applicant pool is small and multiple positions are open, or where the time of interviewers is available, however, such an option may make sense. In other cases, the candidate pool may lack exceptional candidates, and the use of more extensive interviewing may be a logical way to try to discover hidden talent.

By far the most frequently used approach, however, is to interview only the most qualified people. At one time, the rule of three (promulgated by civil service commissions) was commonly followed; it restricted hiring authorities to interviewing the top three candidates who were "certified." This practice was used to keep much-lower-ranked "eligibles" from being selected because of fears of political interference or managerial cronyism. This injunction is still in place in many federal agencies, although it is much criticized (U.S. Government Accountability Office, 2003). In many civil service systems, the allowable number to be certified is often expanded to four, five, or six, or sometimes to the top "tier." Today, the tendency is to give the hiring authority discretion to interview any number it wishes of those deemed to meet the minimum qualifications, making the "eligible" and "certified" lists identical. Nonetheless, there are practical reasons to restrict interviewing. In most cases, the top three or four candidates are obvious, and interviewing more is unlikely to be productive.

Where discretion exists, hiring authorities can consider alternate models. Online or telephone interviews, or both, can rapidly provide a good deal of information and answer many preliminary questions. Likewise, videoconferencing can precede on-site interviews and winnow down the applicant field. Reference checks can be done before the interview process to gather information to help select the most desirable candidates to invite.

GENERAL CONSIDERATIONS FOR THOSE CONDUCTING INTERVIEWS

A good interviewing procedure takes preparation, knowledge of the position, and awareness of the various interviewer biases that may occur. Steps to consider in preparing for and conducting a structured interview are as follows:

1. Plan how it should proceed. Who will meet the applicants? Where will people wait if they do not proceed directly to the interview? Who will explain the general process to be used? If there is more than one interviewer, who will ask which questions?

2. Explain basic facts about the position to the candidate: which department, what division or unit, and the supervisor. Review the job responsibilities.

3. Use the position description and advertisement as guides to ensure that the focus is on essential job functions. In addition, include information about some of the job challenges and opportunities as part of a realistic preview.

4. Hold the interview in a private setting in which distractions are unlikely.

5. Concentrate on listening to the candidate's answers; take notes. Also, be sure that the candidate has opportunities to ask questions during the interview. If only one such opportunity exists and is at the end of the interview, then the candidate may feel rushed if the interview used up most of the allotted time.

6. Use a specific list of written questions that are asked of all candidates, ensuring that the questions have a logical sequence. This list should be reviewed in advance and circulated to relevant parties to ensure balance and appropriateness. In many cases, the human resource department must approve questions in advance. (Use of such a list should not keep the interviewer from asking follow-up questions.)

7. Use behaviorally anchored questions relating past experience to the current position, situational judgment questions to probe thinking processes, or work samples to see minidemonstrations as a part of the process. Following are some examples of behaviorally anchored questions (Krajewski, Goffin, McCarthy, Rothstein, & Johnston, 2006):

   - Tell us about working with a hostile customer and how you resolved the situation.
   - Can you describe a difficult project that you were required to handle?
   - Please describe leading groups in different circumstances, such as when you were the formal leader and when you were not.
   - We have all had to deal with difficult employees. Can you describe one such situation and how you worked with the employee?
   - Tell us how you deal with repeated interruptions and concurrent projects. In other words, can you provide some examples of multitasking in past jobs?

   Situational judgment questions ask the candidate to speculate about how to solve problems that might be encountered on the job (Lievens, Peeters, & Schollaert, 2008; Whetzel & McDaniel, 2009). The following are some examples of situational judgment questions:

- Critique or evaluate something (a program, policy, or procedure, or a report's recommendations, conclusions, decision, or viewpoint).
- Define a relevant problem, identify its causes, develop alternative solutions, decide what to do, and outline an implementation plan.
- Lay out a plan or steps for conducting a study, researching an issue, or reaching a goal.
- Prioritize a number of issues, problems, or activities.
- Solve a hypothetical supervisory problem concerning planning, organizing, assigning, directing, motivating, evaluating, or facilitating the work of others.
- Persuade or convince a hypothetical client or audience of something.
- Respond to a hypothetical complaint or hostile person.
- Role-play a hypothetical work situation.

Cases of work knowledge or samples (which may be done outside the interview with trained raters but in a proximal time frame) could include the following:

- Perform tasks relevant to the position:
  o Demonstrate administration of CPR with a resuscitation dummy.
  o Demonstrate map-reading skills.
  o Troubleshoot a mechanical problem.
  o Write a short business letter.
  o Follow a set of directions.
  o Write or edit written material that is specifically job related.
  o What is the relevant code (statute, or regulation) for . . . ?
  o What are the standard steps in . . . ?
  o Who are the primary experts on . . . ?
  o Deliver an oral presentation (based on information that the candidate is given time to review and prepare, assuming that such presentations are a part of the job).

Although research generally supports behavioral ranking and work samples as having higher validity with job performance, ceteris paribus (Poe, 2003), they are all useful and can be integrated without much difficulty.

8. Be careful that no oral commitments or suggestions about employment prospects are made. Be prepared to give candidates an estimate of when they will receive feedback.

9. Complete the evaluation notes while impressions are fresh, preferably immediately after the interview. Use a predetermined rating system in evaluating answers to the questions.

10. To comply with the Americans with Disabilities Act, be prepared to make accommodations for applicants on request. Even if applicants do not request accommodations for the interview, it is best to ask all individuals: "Can you perform the essential functions of this position with or without a reasonable accommodation?" If accommodation is needed, then consult with human resource specialists. Having to provide accommodation is not an acceptable reason for declining to offer an individual employment.

Finally, it is important that interviewers keep questions focused on the job. Appropriate topics for questions include past work experiences (both paid and volunteer), military experience, education and training, authorization to work in the United States, and personal characteristics related to performing essential functions of the job. Topics to avoid include age, race and ethnicity, disability, national origin, marital status and children, religion, gender (because some jobs are dominated by one gender or the other), arrest record (but not conviction record), credit references, garnishment record, types of military discharges, child care arrangements, height and weight, transportation not explicitly job related, and past workers' compensation claims. Exhibit 4.7 provides a guide to nondiscriminatory interviewing.

Unstructured Interview After or in Addition to Structured Interviews

The research evidence is quite clear that for reliability and content validity, structured interviews are far superior to unstructured interviews (Schmidt & Hunter, 1998). However, when the testing process is meant to be relatively comprehensive, as it is for professional or executive positions, unstructured interviews may be useful for gaining an understanding candidate fit. Such interviews are typical in national searches in which candidates are brought in from around the country for one or more days' worth of meetings and discussions. While the structured interview is conducted early in the process, other informal meetings allow for unstructured interview settings. Often, in longer interview protocols, shared meals offer prime opportunities for conversation. Also, courtesy appointments with executives and experts outside the hiring process, group or public meetings, and meetings with outside constituents are also normally unstructured. It is common for such groups to provide feedback to the hiring manager or panel. Although such unstructured interviews do randomly cover technical competence, those evaluating applicants are as likely to be responding to characteristics such as energy level, social ability, organizational fit, listening ability, and charm. Such information is most useful when the technical competence of candidates is relatively equally balanced.

Reference Checks

References can be verified at different times during the process and in various ways; for example, letters of recommendation are a type of reference check. Although perhaps convenient for the search panel, requiring candidates to obtain letters of recommendation can produce dozens of letters that may not be carefully examined in the search process because candidates are not sufficiently competitive; further, acquiring such letters is a nuisance for applicants and requires them to divulge their interest in new positions before they may be serious candidates. Telephone reference checking can be done prior to interviews, after interviews, and before hiring, or after selection but in advance of the offer (Taylor, Pajo, Cheung, & Stringfield, 2004; U.S. MSPB, 2005). In most cases, it is best to conduct these checks just prior to or after interviews so that the information may add to the selection decision. Where more thorough—and expensive—background investigations are necessary for reasons of public safety (e.g., education, air traffic control, transportation, law enforcement, corrections, child care, elder care), preliminary checking may be appropriate (Hughes, Hertz, & White, 2013). Failure to do so could result in **negligent hiring** lawsuits against the agency should the person hired engage in wrongdoing (Connerley & Bernardy, 2001; Walter, 1992).

Exhibit 4.7 Guide to Nondiscriminatory Interviewing

	Acceptable	Unacceptable
Arrest records	No questions acceptable. (For convictions, see below. Positions in law enforcement may be an exception.)	Unacceptable are inquiries about number of and reasons for arrests.
Availability for work on weekends or evenings	Acceptable if asked of all applicants and it is a business necessity for the person to be available to work weekends or evenings, or both.	Unacceptable are any inquiries about applicant's religious observance.
Child care	No questions acceptable.	Unacceptable are any inquiries about child care arrangements if asked of only one gender of applicants.
Citizenship, birthplace, and national origin	The only legitimate concern here is whether the applicant is eligible to work in the United States under terms of the Immigration Reform and Control Act of 1986. There is a fair and advisable way to obtain this information. The best approach is to ask, Are you either a U.S. citizen or an alien authorized to work in the United States? The yes or no answer that follows provides all needed information while not disclosing which (citizen or alien) the applicant is.	Unacceptable are questions on birthplace, national origin, ancestry, or lineage of applicant, applicant's parents, or applicant's spouse.
Conviction records	Inquiries into convictions, if job related, are acceptable.	Unacceptable are any inquiries about conviction unrelated to job requirements.
Creed or religion	No questions acceptable, except where religion is a bona fide occupational qualification.	Unacceptable are any inquiries about applicant's religious affiliation, church, parish, or religious holidays observed.
Credit records	The interviewer must follow the Fair Credit Reporting Act. This act requires notification of applicants if the interviewer uses outside sources to provide information to make adverse decisions about applicants.	Unacceptable is not informing applicant when interviewer uses information gained from sources outside the hiring organization.
Disability	It is acceptable to ask whether applicant can perform essential functions of the job in question.	Unacceptable are any inquiries that ask applicant to list or describe any disability.
Family status	Acceptable are inquiries as to whether applicant has responsibilities or commitments that will prevent meeting work schedules, if they are asked of all applicants, regardless of sex.	Unacceptable are any inquiries about marital status, number and age of children, or spouse's job.

	Acceptable	Unacceptable
Height and weight	No questions acceptable, unless clearly job related.	Unacceptable are any inquiries unrelated to job requirements.
Language	It is acceptable to ask what language or languages applicant speaks or writes fluently, if job related.	Unacceptable are any inquiries about applicant's native tongue, language used by applicant at home, or how applicant acquired the ability to read, write, or speak a second language.
Marital status	No questions acceptable.	Unacceptable are any inquiries about whether applicant is married, single, divorced, separated, engaged, or widowed.
Military service	Questions on military experience or training are acceptable.	Unacceptable are any inquiries about type or condition of discharge.
Name	Questions on whether applicant has worked under a different name are acceptable.	Unacceptable are any inquiries about the original name of an applicant whose name has been legally changed, or about the national origin of an applicant's name.
Organizations	Questions about applicant's membership in professional organizations, if job related, are acceptable.	Unacceptable are any inquiries about clubs, social fraternities, societies, lodges, or organizations to which applicant belongs.
Photographs	No questions acceptable except after hiring.	Unacceptable are any photographs with application or after interview, but before hiring.
Pregnancy	No questions acceptable.	Unacceptable are any inquiries into applicant's pregnancy, medical history of pregnancy, or family plans.
Race or color	No questions acceptable.	Unacceptable are any inquiries about applicant's race or color of applicant's skin.
References	Asking for names of work references is acceptable.	Unacceptable are any requests for references from applicant's pastor or religious leader.
Relatives or friends	It is acceptable to ask for names of applicant's relatives already employed by the organization or a competitor. Interviewer may not give preference if women and minorities are underrepresented in the workforce, however.	Unacceptable are inquiries about names of friends working for the company or of relatives other than those working for the company.

SOURCE: State of Iowa (2006, pp. 135–137).

Telephone reference checks should be planned as carefully as interviews, especially in the current environment in which employers are increasingly reluctant to provide detailed reference information. Four useful areas to address are (1) verification of employment dates and responsibilities, (2) general assessments of strengths and weaknesses, (3) examples of candidate abilities, and (4) whether the individual was given added responsibilities, was a candidate for advancement, and, most important, would be eligible for rehire. Straying beyond documented facts when providing negative information can expose employers to defamation suits from former employees, but most states have passed laws protecting those responding to job-related reference checks. Despite the relatively constrained nature of reference checks with former employers, they can provide useful information, especially if applicants waive their rights to see any their former employers' comments. Verifying basic information is a requirement of good management. Answers to questions about strengths, successes, and additional responsibilities provide additional depth of knowledge about the candidate's abilities; even muted responses to questions may raise "red flags" to investigate.

Whereas the above focuses on what organizations can do, the appendix for this chapter discusses what job seekers can do to make themselves more attractive to prospective employers and to improve their communications with them. The appendix discusses the professional commitment statement (PCS), a tool for improved communication and focus of an individual's aspirations. Students who develop PCSs often report improved networking and interviewing success.

CHOOSING AND NEGOTIATION

Who determines who the final candidate will be? What if a clear candidate does not emerge from the interviews? How should the offer be made? What documentation is necessary in making the offer?

Most frequently, the supervisor for the position makes the final selection. Often, he or she has a ranked list from a search committee for professional or competitive positions. Supervisors should not overturn search committee recommendations lightly. Although these committees (or whole departments) never technically hire candidates, their decisions may be definitive. For some positions requiring minimum or no qualifications, or where competition for qualified staff is particularly fierce, the hiring authority may essentially be delegated to the human resource department so that immediate selection may take place. In some promotional hiring cases where strong seniority systems and established testing regimens are in place, decisions may be formulaic: The person with the highest score on the required tests gets the position.

Sometimes the interview procedure leaves the supervisor or the search committee bewildered about who is the best candidate; in such cases, a second round of interviewing may be a solution. If the supervisor or committee is confident that the applicant pool is weak, then the search can be continued, with readvertising and interviewing of a second pool, or the search can be closed entirely, to be opened again at a later date. The situation is different, however, if two or three people look highly qualified but would bring different strengths to the position. In such a case, the person doing the hiring should simply make the decision. Delaying decisions with competitive candidates means that they may not be available when needed.

The actual hiring normally begins with an informal phone call. Is the person still interested? Does she understand what the salary is? Does she have any final questions? For entry-level positions, there is usually little ability to negotiate salary or working conditions; senior-level and competitive positions may provide flexibility. Both the organization and the candidate should have a clear idea of how long the agency is willing to wait for the candidate's decision; a period of at least several days is reasonable. Once the candidate orally accepts the position, a letter to confirm the offer (**letter of intent**) usually follows. The person is then generally asked to report to the work site to complete employment forms. This is also done when the starting date of employment is not immediate because of funds availability or because the applicant must give notice at another job. In very senior positions, the letter of intent dictates the special conditions of employment, including retreat rights (to other positions), special travel or equipment allowances, and so on. Only when the organization is confident that the position has been filled are letters (or calls) made to those interviewed but not selected to inform them that the position has been filled.

One significant variation exists when a physical exam or drug test is a part of the hiring process but is conducted after the offer; an offer of employment is then contingent. The terms of such **contingent hiring** must be clearly stipulated. Other possible contingencies include funding availability, job freezes, or completion of training. It is also useful to point out to the new hire that in the probationary period job termination can normally occur without the need for the agency to show either cause or reason.

The final part of the hiring process is the documentation of the process itself. Generally, the human resource department or affirmative action office will require that a form be filled out that confirms the identities of the eligible individuals and the reasons for selection and nonselection. This process is made much easier, and is less subject to challenge, if the hiring authority has done a thorough job of defining essential position functions and then scoring all eligible candidates on the job-related functions.

POSTOFFER AND HIRING ISSUES

Some "tests," as mentioned, occur after the offer, with employment conditional on the candidate's successfully passing them. Such tests are sometimes allowed or required for security purposes or public safety. Although universal drug testing is generally illegal for most positions, it is legal for those conveying passengers and involved in public safety positions (e.g., peace officers, corrections, emergency services; Drug-Free Workplace Act, 1988; Omnibus Transportation Employees Testing Act, 1991). Law enforcement and corrections positions also frequently require extensive background checks and sometimes polygraph examinations, although the questions asked must be carefully screened for job relevance (as stipulated in the Employee Polygraph Protection Act of 1988). Generally, these tests are conducted after an offer but before employment is finalized. It is also legal for governments to impose residency requirements for select positions (*McCarthy v. Philadelphia Civil Service Commission,* 1976), a condition that generally has been modified to distance-from-work requirements for appropriate public safety, public works, and other employees with emergency responsibilities. The Genetic

Information Nondiscrimination Act of 2008, the first civil rights law of the new century, protects workers from having to provide genetic information prior to employment or enrollment in health insurance plans.

Even after the person has accepted the position and documentation on the hiring process has been filed, the selection process is not over. All candidates interviewed or, in some senior-level cases, all persons who applied should be informed that a decision has been made.

Several strategic human resource management issues flow directly from the hiring process. First, the supervisor needs to begin to get ready for the new hire's arrival and integration into the organization. This process is called **onboarding** (Partnership for Public Service, 2008a). It begins with a review of what the new employee will need to be successful and to feel like a valued member of the organization. For example, anticipating any office and equipment needs for the new person helps with a smooth transition.

Next, what are the plans for orientation and training? Orientation includes sessions that inform the new employee of general policies and benefits packages and provides familiarization with facilities. Training provides specific instruction on job-related processes and equipment. The workloads of new employees should be reduced initially whenever possible; they should be informed accordingly. Will the training be conducted by a training department and be part of an established program, or will it be done by the supervisor or an in-house instructor? Although on-the-job training has the virtues of relevance and immediacy when done properly, it is frequently completed in an excessively casual manner that really could be called "you-are-on-your-own training" (Van Wart, Cayer, & Cook, 1993; also see Chapter 9).

A related option to consider is mentoring. Who will make sure that the new employee is introduced to people after the first day, answer questions about the job and culture of the organization, and simply take a special interest in the new person's well-being? The initial period is the most critical in preventing early turnover as well as in establishing a positive bond between the employee and the agency. New employees who realize that the necessary training and support are not being provided are wise to ask for it. Lack of training is generally a simple oversight; even in resource-poor organizations, additional assistance is likely to go to those who ask for it.

Finally, the probationary period itself, where it exists, can be a key part of the selection function. Most organizations set probationary periods at 6 months to a year, although the Canadian government allows up to 36 months in some fields of employment. Generally, termination during probation is difficult to challenge as long as it is for nondiscriminatory reasons; mediocre performance is usually grounds for dismissal, and standards of proof may be minimal. This means that supervisors have an exceptional opportunity, although some let the probationary period elapse as the candidate "gets up to speed." By setting tough standards for probationary employees as an extension of a rigorous selection process, an agency may avoid future performance problems. Federal data indicate that discharges during probation have increased from 4% to 6% in recent years and that challenges to these terminations are extraordinarily low (U.S. MSPB, 2002). Overall, the paradox of probation is that it may be the best selection technique, but for a variety of practical reasons some employers may not take it seriously. When used appropriately, however, it can resolve the paradox of needs.

SUMMARY AND CONCLUSION

Although almost everyone agrees that the single most important class of management decisions is that concerned with hiring the "right" people, there is much less consensus on the basis for deciding who those people are. In fact, democracies require fundamentally different selection processes for different public sector positions. Presidents, governors, and mayors do not take civil service examinations, and midlevel managers are not elected. Technical merit, the focus of this chapter, may be the heart of the civil service system, but most systems pay attention to internal considerations and representativeness as well. Even where merit principles apply—where technically qualified candidates are hired through an open process that scrutinizes the essential job functions and applicants' special knowledge, skills, and abilities—there are different models of implementation. Coming out of an era of excessive patronage, civil service systems originally removed all but the final selection from executive branch agencies to prevent political or managerial tampering. Today, with crass political patronage for nonexecutive jobs relatively uncommon, public sector systems have moved selection functions to agency human resource departments or into the hiring units themselves. Line managers have greater responsibilities. Certification lists are being lengthened to give managers greater discretion, or are sometimes being changed to qualified lists.

Test selection includes many possibilities, from education and experience evaluations to licensure, general aptitude and trait examinations, and performance tests for specific job qualifications. The current tendency has been toward the use of fewer aptitude and performance tests in an environment emphasizing speed and managerial flexibility. However, a stronger employer market provides opportunities for agencies to scrutinize candidates more extensively without fear of losing many good prospects. Interviewing is a complex event with legal pitfalls, yet when it is planned carefully even candidates who are not selected appreciate the opportunity to have been interviewed. The actual hiring decision, also, is made much easier by careful planning, which includes contingency planning should the initial round of interviewing not produce a clear choice. Following through on posthiring issues ensures that the candidate is oriented, trained, and supported so that he or she can pass successfully through the probationary period and become productive.

Increased demands on organizations to be productive, flexible, and responsive—often while only maintaining staff or even losing employees—make selecting the best people critical. More than ever before, line managers need to be informed about and involved in the selection process.

KEY TERMS

Assembled tests

Assessment center

Biodata

Certified lists

Character fit

Civil service commissions

Contingent hiring

Diversity policies

Education and experience evaluations	Psychological tests
80% rule	Realistic job previews
Electoral popularity	Representativeness
General skills tests	Rule of three
Internally based hiring	Seniority
Job fit	Social class selection
Letter of intent	Structured interview
Merit selection	Temporary employees
Negligent hiring	Term employees
Onboarding	Test validity
Organizational fit	Unassembled tests
Patronage	Veterans' points
Performance tests	Work samples

EXERCISES

Class Discussion

1. The paradox of freedom (see the introduction) looms over the selection function, most notably in such areas as drug, polygraph, and genetic testing. Using dialectic reasoning, stalk this paradox using Einstein's famous dictum: "You cannot solve the problem with the same kind of thinking that created it."

2. What is the "best" balance of selection strategies? Should hiring for all civil service jobs be based purely on merit? Should seniority be a major factor in promotional hiring? Should representativeness (both affirmative action and veterans' points) be phased out? Should the number of patronage appointments be decreased or increased?

3. Has anyone in the class taken a civil service examination? What was it like?

4. Who in the class has conducted interviews? What were some of the interviewee "mistakes"? Among the finalists, what was the determining factor: technical competence or interpersonal skills?

Team Activities

5. Discuss what you would do if, in an interview for a merit position, you were asked your political party affiliation. What would you do if later you were asked when you graduated from college? If you refused to answer either of these questions and subsequently were not hired, would you do anything about it? How can the selection process be like a chess match?

6. Assume that you are on the search committee for a new management intern program. It has been determined that interns will be paid between $25,000 and $30,000, will have one-year appointments, and may apply for permanent positions if they receive good evaluations. The recruitment is to be announced nationally, but no travel money will be available; therefore, it is expected that the bulk of the candidates will be local. Design the selection process.

7. You are on the search committee for a public information officer (this is a non–civil service, exempt position in the organization). The last incumbent, although a friend of the agency director and a former reporter, was a disaster. Most of the time, people did not know what he did; when he did organize press conferences he sometimes became more controversial than the issue being discussed. Having learned her lesson, the director has asked you to nominate a slate of three ranked candidates. Design the selection process.

8. If selection techniques for a new or small organization did not exist, what rules would you set up if you had the authority?

9. Investigate three organizations to determine the virtual nature of their recruitment and selection processes. Compare as well as contrast your findings and report them to the entire class.

Individual Assignments

10. You are the hiring supervisor for a junior management position in the city manager's office. The position would largely be responsible for special projects—both analysis (requiring strong quantitative skills) and implementation (mandating interpersonal and coordination skills). The three candidates interviewed, described below, all have recent MPA degrees. Set up a matrix of no more than five factors, give weights to the factors, and score and rank the candidates.

    a. Jill Owens: Good interpersonal skills, pleasant personality, very talkative. Sometimes did not seem to listen very well, mediocre quantitative skills, highly energetic, one internship and one summer job in another city government, the second-best grades of the three, excellent references, and good appearance, manners, and understanding of city government. Former supervisors in the city were quite supportive of her candidacy but admitted that she was not exceptional.

    b. Bruce Hughes: Mediocre interpersonal skills, pleasant personality, quiet but extremely attentive, superb quantitative skills, low energy, one internship in this city, the best grades of the group, below-average appearance, acceptable manners, and unsure about his understanding of city government. Has a rave reference from the supervisor about a program evaluation project completed in his internship that resulted in highly successful changes.

    c. Mary Washington: Excellent interpersonal skills, charming personality, very good listener, weak quantitative skills, high energy, no city experience but a year's experience in state government in a clerical function prior to finishing her graduate degree, the third-best grades among the candidates but still high, quite satisfactory references, very good manners, and little understanding of city government. Talked about her project management skills, using examples from church and volunteer work. She is the only "diversity" candidate.

11. Select a prospective job, perhaps one that you are interested in. Make sure that you have identified a position description (via a vacancy announcement or an organizational job classification description) first, then design a set of interview questions, including biographical, situational judgment, behaviorally anchored, and work knowledge items. The actual interview will be 45 minutes long. Also, decide if a work performance sample outside the interview setting would be useful or critical for a high-quality selection process.

APPENDIX

The Professional Commitment Statement for Job Seekers

Just as in recruitment an agency must design a message to sell the job to prospective employees, so applicants need to design their own messages to sell their abilities to organizations and to their networks. Job candidates have to give people arguments to help them; if they want agencies to make job offers or acquaintances with similar professional interests to introduce them to others, then they have to provide reasons. This is the central point: What matters is not what a job seeker wants, but rather what others want and whether the job seeker can give it to them.

Degrees and accomplishments are not enough to guarantee that a person will get a job. Every year, many graduates of top universities end up without jobs. Why? Because people do not make hiring decisions based on résumés alone. Individuals are hired because others believe that they can help them in some way. This is the central idea that job seekers need to express—the idea that they have something important and useful to offer. Just as we chose this or that item in a store because it promises to be better than the next one, so someone will hire or recommend a person because that individual promises to be better or more helpful than someone else. The job market is a market, after all. Job seekers need to sell themselves. Ask yourself this: If I can't sell myself, then who can?

But people and organizations are not very good at job selection (i.e., hiring others). Of all of the skills in human resource management, this may be the least well mastered; some people think that hiring is akin to flipping a coin, with a 50–50 chance of selecting the best candidate. With so many opportunities to select the wrong person, the process is in part structured around *reducing the risk of making a bad hiring decision.*

Here are four ways organizations reduce the risk:

1. Ensuring that the person hired has a strong and demonstrated commitment to the service area (e.g., economic development or social services). (An agency does not want to hire someone who will leave after 6 months or the slightest setback.)

2. Confirming that the individual has a past record of accomplishment (that is, that the individual is someone who actually get things done—not merely someone who talks a good game.)

3. Ensuring that the person has a record of getting along with others. (No matter how good a person's skills or accomplishments, he or she must also have this quality.)

4. Verifying that the candidate has the necessary (minimum) qualifications for the job.

The writing of a professional commitment statement (PCS) is an exercise designed to help a job seeker address these points. Individuals often use parts of their PCSs in job interviews and in communicating with their networks. A PCS consists of three to four paragraphs in which the job seeker addresses the following questions:

- What difference do you seek to make for an organization? How do you want to make its stakeholders better off?
- What specific kinds of activities would you like to be involved in now, and in a few years?
- How are your answers to these questions consistent with your present or past experiences and commitments? State these experiences and commitments, which can be either professional or personal in nature.
- How did you come to embrace your commitments? Give some pertinent facts about yourself that others should know.
- What are some of the most important accomplishments and successes in your life? How do these relate to your commitments?
- What are some of the strengths required to be successful in that line of work? Show which ones of these you have, and the evidence for this claim. Also, state what you are currently doing to further improve the skills you need to succeed in your area.

Addressing these issues can make for a compelling story about the job seeker. Consider this adapted example of a PCS:[7]

I would like to utilize my background in economics, along with the managerial and analytical skills obtained by my current course work in public administration, to aid in the delivery of quality health care services to individuals of all ages and income levels. In my concentration courses in health care administration, I wish to develop the skills necessary to meaningfully contribute to the efficiency and effectiveness of an organization aiming to provide affordable and accessible health care to individuals. I will commit myself to continuous self-education of current health care trends and policy issues in order to perform my professional duties as diligently as possible.

I wish to bring the same high levels of leadership and commitment to an organization as I have displayed in previous course work, past organizational memberships, and past places of employment. In order to get some valuable exposure to and experience within the health care field, I have recently accepted an internship at State Hospital. I will be exposed to functional areas of the hospital such as quality management, human resources, accounting, and outpatient services. I will also have the opportunity to work on a project involving state hospital accreditation and will be able to sit in on many internal operational meetings with top administrators in order to gain personal insight into emerging issues facing this hospital as well as many others within the state system.

After completing the internship, I will seek employment either at a hospital or within a different type of health care setting, such as an [assisted living facility, home health care service, or state health department]. In order to help me, I will contact some administrators and ask to meet with them for about 15 minutes so more people can know what I seek. I will also ask people I know to make introductions for me. Additionally, other students, faculty members, or full-time employees at my current place of employment can let me know of available job opportunities or place me in contact with individuals who may be able to give me further advice about the health care field or otherwise direct me in my career path.

Such statements are as unique as the individuals who write them. The above PCS is of interest because it is the work of a young graduate student with very little professional experience or background; nonetheless, his commitment and drive are evident. This PCS shows how past course work can be used to buttress claims of commitment, though some additional past, extracurricular accomplishments might have been mentioned as well. Most students need to revise their PCSs a few times to get them right, so that they show a logical thread, substance, and energy. In class, students have the option to share their PCSs, which gives everyone an opportunity to ask questions and learn from feedback. In some classes, students post their initial PCSs online, get feedback from at least two or three other students, and then repost their final PCSs a few weeks later.

A common problem for students in writing PCSs is that they do not know what difference they want to make; they do not yet know what careers they want. Typically, this means that they have a few different ideas that are attractive, but they have not yet pursued any of them. In such cases, we advise students to just choose one and run with it for the sake of the initial PCS. A follow-up assignment is to network with four people by sharing with them their PCSs. This gives further information about the career path, and students can then decide whether they in fact want to pursue it. Sometimes the only way to know what one wants to do is by doing it.

A second problem is that some students are pursuing very large and long-term dreams. An individual might want to be a sheriff, governor, or agency director. That is fine, of course, and big dreams are to be encouraged, but the PCS should focus on next steps, not final destinations. There are also some concerns related to sharing dreams. First, when you state your long-term goals you might be telling others that you want to be their boss, and they may not be ready to hear that. Second, you may sound arrogant and project yourself as an overly ambitious career climber, someone others need to watch out for and even guard against. Third, stating lofty ambitions suggests that you already know that you will not change your mind as new experiences unfold. That sounds unrealistic and shows poor judgment. So, while everyone should have ambitions, it may be best to keep such far-flung expressions to yourself, perhaps sharing them only with those who are very close to you.

How useful is it to have a PCS? It surely helps in developing a good résumé, which needs to reflect and substantiate the PCS. But a PCS also helps with difficult interview questions:

- "Tell me about yourself."
- "Why do you want to work here?"
- "What did you like and dislike about your last job?"
- "What is your biggest accomplishment?"
- "What is your greatest strength? Your largest weakness?"
- "Where do you see yourself in 5 years?"

While some job candidates struggle with these questions, a good PCS makes them a breeze:

- "Tell me about yourself." "I am strongly committed to [whatever is stated in the PCS] . . ."
- "Why do you want to work here?" "Because your organization offers me an opportunity to pursue my commitment to . . ."

- "What did you like and dislike about your last job?" "I liked [disliked] that it gave me [did not give me enough] opportunity to pursue my commitment to . . ."
- "What is your biggest accomplishment?" "I have several, some of them directly related to my commitment to . . ."

A PCS serves as a great basis for succeeding in job interviews. It also helps in networking, providing job seekers with a coherent message and clearly justified reasons for asking others for their support. By supplying their PCSs to members of their networks for comments, job seekers can gain insights and job leads. Some questions they might ask of fellow network members are, "What kinds of jobs are available for what I want to do?" "What advice do you offer for someone pursuing this career?" "What are the ideal qualifications and experiences for these jobs?" "How can I best get these jobs?" Job seekers can proactively contact managers in departments where they would like to work, thereby expanding their networks well before any job interviews. Doing so helps job seekers learn about career opportunities; some of these managers may follow up with the job seekers later, informing them of opportunities that since have become available.

Developing a PCS is an essential task for every job seeker. Many successful officials create such statements, although they may not be formally written down. In the end, the rationale of a strong PCS was well articulated by President John F. Kennedy in his inaugural address: "Ask not what your country can do for you—ask what you can do for your country." Or your prospective employer, as the case may be.

NOTES

1. Patronage certainly has not been wiped out, nor is it ever likely to be. For example, it still exists in Schedule C exceptions (confidential staff for federal executives) and overseas appointments at the federal level. Many state systems have uneven coverage and experience covert intrusion, such as the movement of political appointees to civil service permanent positions through "persuasion" or executive order. Local systems may be merit systems in name only, and very small jurisdictions may be exempted from state civil service requirements entirely.

2. This description refers to "ideal" merit systems. In reality, most have seniority elements infused in them for promotional opportunities. In other words, many merit systems limit promotional hires to agency or governmental personnel, although it is possible that candidates outside the agency might be more meritorious on technical grounds.

3. The Peter principle states that people are promoted until they achieve positions in which they are incompetent (Peter & Hull, 1969).

4. Higher degrees of correlation between the integrity factor measured in the new "honesty tests" and one of the "Big Five" personality factors, conscientiousness, have generally been most highly supported (Viswesvaran et al., 2007).

5. Ultimately, there is considerable overlap among performance tests, aptitude tests, and psychological tests, which rely on a continuum ranging from concrete to abstract predictors.

6. An alternative structure is the self-managed team, which embodies characteristics of both a hiring panel and a hiring supervisor. As in any other group activity, the team has the opportunity to provide a substantially rich experience if the members understand their work and do it well.

7. We thank Michael Kennedy, MPA graduate from Louisiana State University, for allowing us to use this example.

REFERENCES

Ackerman, P. L., & Kanfer, R. (1993). Integrating laboratory and field study for improving selection: Development of a battery to predict air traffic controller success. *Journal of Applied Psychology, 78*(3), 413–432.

Anderson, N., & Witvliet, C. (2008). Fairness reactions to personnel selection methods: An international comparison between the Netherlands, the United States, France, Spain, Portugal, and Singapore. *International Journal of Selection and Assessment, 16*(1), 1–13.

Arvey, R. D., Nutting, S. M., & Landon, T. E. (1992). Validation strategies for physical ability testing in police and fire settings. *Public Personnel Management, 21*(3), 301–312.

Barrick, M. R., & Zimmerman, R. D. (2009). Hiring for retention and performance. *Human Resource Management, 48*(2), 183–206.

Bartone, P. T., Roland, R. R., Picano, J. J., & Williams, T. J. (2008). Psychological hardiness predicts success in US Army Special Force candidates. *International Journal of Selection and Assessment, 16*(1), 78–81.

Beagrie, S. (2013, June). Magnificent seven. *Human Resources,* pp. 34–37.

Bowman, J. S., & West, J. (Eds.). (2007). *American public service: Radical reform and the merit system.* New York: Taylor & Francis.

Bowman, J. S., & West, J. P. (2009). To "re-Hatch" public employees or not? An ethical analysis of the relaxation of restrictions on political activities in civil service. *Public Administration Review, 68*(1), 52–62.

Branti v. Finkel, 445 U.S. 507 (1980).

Breaugh, J. A. (2009). The use of biodata for employee selection: Past research and future directions. *Human Resource Management Review, 19,* 219–231.

Buckley, P., Minette, K., Joy, D., & Michaels, J. (2004). The use of an automated employment recruiting and screening system for temporary professional employees: A case study. *Human Resource Management, 43*(2/3), 233–241.

Campbell, J. P. (2001). *Project A: Exploring the limits of performance improvement through personnel selection and classification.* Hillsdale, NJ: Lawrence Erlbaum.

Carlson, K. D. (2003). The staffing cycles framework: Viewing staffing as a system of decision events. *Journal of Management, 29*(1), 51–78.

Connerley, M. L., Arvey, R. D., Gilliland, S. W., Mae, F. A., Paetzold, R. L., & Sackett, P. R. (2001). Selection in the workplace: Whose rights prevail? *Employee Responsibilities and Rights Journal, 13*(1), 1–13.

Connerley, M. L., & Bernardy, M. (2001). Criminal background checks for prospective and current employees: Current practices among municipal agencies. *Public Personnel Management, 30*(2), 173–183.

Corcoran, C. (2005). Psychometric testing: Can it add value to HR? *Accountancy Ireland, 37*(4), 63–65.

Cotterell, B. (2001a, February 7). Bracing for change. *Tallahassee Democrat,* pp. 1E–2E.

Cotterell, B. (2001b, May 15). State "efficiency" czar resigns in protest. *Tallahassee Democrat,* pp. 1A–2A.

DeVaro, J. (2005). Employer recruitment strategies and the labor market: Outcomes of new hires. *Economic Inquiry, 43*(2), 263–282.

Dineen, B. R., Noe, R. A., & Wang, C. (2004). Perceived fairness of Web-based applicant screening procedures: Weighing the rules of justice and the role of individual differences. *Human Resource Management, 43*(2/3), 127–145.

Dodd, C. H. (1969). *Politics and government in Turkey.* Berkeley: University of California Press.

Drug-Free Workplace Act, P.L. 100–6klj90, 102 Stat. 4304 (1988).

Elrod v. Burns, 427 U.S. 347 (1976).

Ewoh, A. I. E. (2013). Managing and valuing diversity: Challenges to public managers in the 21st century. *Public Personnel Management, 42*(2), 107–122.

Forsberg, A. M., & Shultz, K. S. (2009). Perceived fairness of a background information form and a job knowledge test. *Public Personnel Management, 38*(1), 33–46.

Gore, A. (1993). *Creating a government that works better and costs less: The report of the National Performance Review.* Washington, DC: Government Printing Office.

Grensing-Pophal, L. (2006). Internal solutions. *HRMagazine, 51*(12), 75–79.

Hausser, D. (2013). Does "radical civil service reform" really abandon merit? *Public Administration Review, 73*(4), 649–650.

Hays, S. W., & Kearney, R. C. (1999). *The transformation of public sector human resource management.* Unpublished manuscript.

Hewins-Maroney, B., & Williams, E. (2013). The role of public administrators in responding to changing workforce demographics: Global challenges to preparing a diverse workforce. *Public Administration Quarterly, 37*(3), 456–490.

Hogan, J. (1991). Structure of physical performance in occupational tasks. *Journal of Applied Psychology, 76*(4), 495–507.

Howard, A. (Ed.). (1995). *The changing nature of work.* San Francisco: Jossey-Bass.

Hughes, S., Hertz, G. T., & White, R. J. (2013). Criminal background checks in U.S. higher education: A review of policy developments, process implementations, and post-results evaluation procedures. *Public Personnel Management, 42*(3), 421–437.

Ingraham, P. W., Selden, S. C., & Moynihan, D. P. (2000). People and performance: Challenges for the future public service—The report from the Wye River Conference. *Public Administration Review, 60*(1), 54–60.

Jesdanun, A. (2007, May 6). Video résumés gain fans, but many experts skeptical. *Arizona Republic,* p. E1.

Jordan-Nowe, A. (2007, July 25). "Soft skills" again treasured. *Arizona Republic,* p. E1.

Kellough, J. E., & Nigro, L. G. (Eds.). (2006). *Civil service reform in the states: Personnel policy and politics at the subnational level.* Albany: State University of New York Press.

Krajewski, H. T., Goffin, R. D., McCarthy, J. M., Rothstein, M. G., & Johnston, N. (2006). Comparing the validity of structured interviews for managerial employees: Should we look to the past or focus on the future? *Journal of Occupational and Organizational Psychology, 79*(3), 411–432.

Lievens, F., Highhouse, S., & De Corte, W. (2005). The importance of traits and abilities in supervisors' hirability decisions as a function of method of assessment. *Journal of Occupational and Organizational Psychology, 78,* 453–470.

Lievens, F., Peeters, H., & Schollaert, E. (2008). Situational judgment tests: A review of recent research. *Personnel Review, 37*(4), 426–441.

Lohr, S. (2014, June 22). Unblinking eyes track employees: Workplace surveillance sees good and bad. *New York Times,* p. A1.

Maynard, M. (2012, June 12). Civil service reform passes in 3 states. Stateline. Retrieved from http://www.governing.com/blogs/view/civil-service-reform-passes.html

McCarthy v. Philadelphia Civil Service Commission, 424 U.S. 645 (1976).

McGrath, R. J. (2013). The rise and fall of radical civil service reform in the U.S. states. *Public Administration Review, 73*(4), 638–648.

Miller, C. E., & Barrett, G. V. (2008). The coachability and fakability of personality-based selection tests used for police selection. *Public Personnel Management, 37,* 339–351.

Morgeson, F. P., Campion, M. A., Dipboye, R. L., Hollenbeck, R. L., Murphy, K., & Schmitt, N. (2007). Are we getting fooled again? Coming to terms with limitations in the use of personality tests for personnel selection. *Personnel Psychology, 60*(4), 1029–1049.

Mosher, F. C. (1982). *Democracy and the public service* (2nd ed.). New York: Oxford University Press.

Munyon, T. P., Summers, J. K., & Ferris, G. R. (2011). Team staffing modes in organizations: Strategic considerations on individual and cluster hiring approaches. *Human Resource Management Review, 21*(3), 228–242.

Nextgov. (2014, June 20). What government can learn from NFL's foray into analytics. Retrieved from http://www.nextgov.com/technology-news/2014/06/what-government-can-learn-nfls-foray-analytics/86962

Nye, C. D., Do, B., Drasgow, F., & Fine, S. (2008). Two-step testing in employee selection: Is score inflation a problem? *International Journal of Selection and Assessment, 16*(2), 112–120.

Omnibus Transportation Employees Testing Act, P.L. 102-143, 105 Stat. 952 (1991).

Ones, D. S., Dilchert, S., Viswesvaran, C., & Judge, T. A. (2007). In support of personality assessment in organizational setting. *Personnel Psychology, 69*(4), 995–1027.

Partnership for Public Service. (2008a). *Getting on board.* Washington, DC: Author.

Partnership for Public Service. (2008b). *A golden opportunity: Recruiting Baby Boomers into government.* Washington, DC: Author.

Peter, L. J., & Hull, R. (1969) *The Peter principle.* New York: William Morrison.

Ployhart, R. E. (2006). Staffing in the 21st century: New challenges and strategic opportunities. *Journal of Management, 32*(6), 868–897.

Poe, A. C. (2003). Behavioral interviewing can tell you if an applicant just out of college has traits for the job. *HRMagazine, 48*(10), 95–99.

Potosky, D., & Bobko, P. (2004). Selection testing via the Internet: Practical considerations and exploratory empirical findings. *Personnel Psychology, 57*(4), 1003–1034.

Ree, M. J., & Earles, J. A. (1994). The ubiquitous predictiveness of *g.* In M. G. Rumsey, C. B. Walker, & J. H. Harris (Eds.), *Personnel selection and classification* (pp. 127–136). Hillsdale, NJ: Lawrence Erlbaum.

Rutan v. Republican Party of Illinois, 497 U.S. 62 (1990).

Ryan, A. M., & Tippins, N. T. (2004). Attracting and selecting: What psychological research tells us. *Human Resource Management, 43*(4), 305–318.

Sabharwal, M. (2014). Is diversity management sufficient? Organizational inclusion to further performance. *Public Personnel Management, 43*(2), 197–217.

Schmidt, F. L., & Hunter, J. E. (1998). The validity and utility of selection methods in personnel psychology: Practical and theoretical implications of 85 years of research findings. *Psychological Bulletin, 124*(2), 262–275.

Scroggins, W. A., Thomas, S. L., & Morris, J. A. (2009). Psychological testing in personnel selection: Part III. The resurgence of personality testing. *Public Personnel Management, 38*(1), 67–77.

Special Master. (2001, March 12–14). *In the matter of fact finding between the State of Florida and the American Federation of State, County, and Municipal Employees Council 79 Hearings and Special Master Recommendations.* Tallahassee, FL: Author.

State of Iowa. (2006, December). *Applicant screening manual.* Des Moines, IA: Department of Administrative Services, Human Resources Enterprise.

Taylor, P. J., Pajo, K., Cheung, G. W., & Stringfield, P. (2004). Dimensionality and validity of a structured telephone reference check procedure. *Personnel Psychology, 57*(3), 745–772.

Thornton, G. C., & Gibbons, A. M. (2009). Validity of assessment centers for personnel selection. *Human Resource Management Review, 19,* 169–187.

Thornton, G. C., & Potemra, M. J. (2010). Utility of assessment center for promotion of police sergeants. *Public Personnel Management, 39*(1), 59–69.

Tutum, C. (1977). Politicization of administration and partisanship. *Turkish Public Administration Annual, 4,* 199–232.

Udechukwu, I., & Manyak, T. (2009). Job applicants' perceptions of resumes versus employment application forms in the recruitment process in a public organization. *Public Personnel Management, 38*(4), 79–96.

Uniform guidelines on employee selection procedures. (1978). Title 29. Chapter XIV, Part 1607.

U.S. Government Accountability Office. (2003). *Human capital: Opportunities to improve executive agencies' hiring processes.* Washington, DC: Author.

U.S. Merit Systems Protection Board. (2001a). *The federal merit promotion program.* Washington, DC: Author.

U.S. Merit Systems Protection Board. (2001b). *The U.S. Office of Personnel Management in retrospect.* Washington, DC: Author.

U.S. Merit Systems Protection Board. (2002). *Assessing federal job-seekers in a delegated examining environment.* Washington, DC: Author.

U.S. Merit Systems Protection Board. (2003). *The federal selection interview: Unrealized potential.* Washington, DC: Author.

U.S. Merit Systems Protection Board. (2004). *Managing federal recruitment: Issues, insights, and illustrations.* Washington, DC: Author.

U.S. Merit Systems Protection Board. (2005). *Reference checking in federal hiring: Making the call.* Washington, DC: Author.

U.S. Merit Systems Protection Board. (2006). *Reforming federal hiring: Beyond faster and cheaper.* Washington, DC: Author.

U.S. Merit Systems Protection Board. (2008a). *Attracting the next generation: A look at federal entry-level new hires.* Washington, DC: Author.

U.S. Merit Systems Protection Board. (2008b). *In search of highly skilled workers: A study on the hiring of upper level employees from outside the federal government.* Washington, DC: Author.

U.S. Office of Personnel Management. (1999). *Delegated examining operations handbook: A guide for federal agency examining offices.* Washington, DC: Author.

Van Riper, P. (1958). *History of the United States civil service.* New York: Harper & Row.

Van Wart, M. R. (2011). *Dynamics of leadership in public service: Theory and practice* (2nd ed.). Armonk, NY: M. E. Sharpe.

Van Wart, M. R., & Berman, E. M. (1999). Contemporary public sector productivity values: Narrower scope, tougher standards, and new rules of the game. *Public Productivity & Management Review, 22*(3), 326–347.

Van Wart, M. R., Cayer, N. J., & Cook, S. (1993). *Handbook of training and development for the public sector.* San Francisco: Jossey-Bass.

Viswesvaran, C., Deller, J., & Ones, D. S. (2007). Personality measures in personnel selection: Some new contributions. *International Journal of Selection and Assessment, 15*(3), 354–358.

Walter, R. J. (1992). Public employers' potential liability from negligence in employment decisions. *Public Administration Review, 52,* 491–495.

Werbel, J. D., Song, L. J., & Yan, S. (2008). The influence of external recruitment practices on job search practices across domestic labor markets: A comparison of the United States and China. *International Journal of Selection and Assessment, 16*(2), 93–101.

Whetzel, D. L., & McDaniel, M. A. (2009). Situational judgment tests: An overview of current research. *Human Resource Management Review, 19,* 188–202.

Wolf, A., & Jenkins, A. (2006). Explaining greater test use for selection: The role of HR professionals in a world of expanding regulation. *Human Resource Management Journal, 16*(2), 193–213.

Yalcindag, S. (1974). Notes on the historical evolution of the Turkish administrative system. *Turkish Public Administration Annual, 1,* 169–212.

Position Management

Judicious Plan or Jigsaw Puzzle?

The right people in the right jobs.

—Otto von Bismarck, speech
to the North German Reichstag, 1875

After studying this chapter, you should be able to

- identify the profound trends and paradoxical tensions affecting traditional classification strategies that may remake position management systems in the 21st century;
- differentiate among the three overarching types of personnel systems that are found—generally in layers—in most public sphere organizations;
- write a job description;
- conduct informal job analyses and understand when and how more rigorous methods are used;
- understand the different uses of position classification and know how jobs are grouped together in theory and in practice;
- distinguish between job analysis and job evaluation; and
- differentiate among the various types of tools used in workforce downsizing.

Position management is generally thought to be a dry science of little interest to anyone but a few specialists in human resource departments. Such a notion is full of irony and paradoxes, if not outright misconceptions. First, position classification is as much an art as a science: It is actually composed of different systems, each with distinctly different value biases. Furthermore, the biases of each system shift over time. The art, then, lies in understanding the different values that exist in various systems; the science is found in the rational implementation of that set of values. Unfortunately, when system values become too rigid and when classification and compensation issues are treated as laws based on hard science, an unbalanced characterization of position management exists.[1] Wallace Sayre describes this tendency well in his classic essay "The Triumph of Technique Over Purpose" (1948).

Second, the rational order conveyed by classification systems is generally overstated. Most systems of large organizations are quite fragmented, and sometimes they are haphazard because competing stresses such as politics, market forces, merit, social equity, and union influence distort them over time. The classification systems of most small organizations (including the vast majority of American state and local governments) are actually **piecemeal personnel systems** rather than ideal classification systems.

Third, although formal methods of **job analysis** and **job evaluation** are often preached in management texts and elsewhere, they are not always used in practice. Informal methods are as common, and the skills needed to use such methods are equally important for employees and managers. Finally, although classification may seem to be a subject of little utility to those who are not human resource specialists or managers, it is actually a critical source of knowledge and, by extension, a source of power in agencies. Understanding a system's central organizing structures is as important as understanding budgeting or management principles (Condrey, 1998).

Although classification systems convey a sense of judiciousness, they are probably more accurately viewed as jigsaw puzzles. One should not be put off by this realization, however. Because of their importance to job aspirants, wage earners, status seekers, career strategists, managers, executives, and legislators, classification systems should be considered fascinating cornerstones in the complex organizational universe. Decisions about position management are very important in all professional lives, as well as in the health of organizations. Mastery of a general knowledge of the tools used in classification is a critical competency for today's manager.

THREE TYPES OF PERSONNEL STRATEGIES

The public sector uses three personnel strategies, each of which is represented in a layered fashion in human resource systems. Selection is the core principle in each of these strategies, and it equally affects the subsequent classification and management of positions. The three systems are based on (1) election, (2) appointment, or (3) rules (composed of merit, seniority, and representativeness factors).[2] Although these strategies have been discussed in the preceding chapter, it is important to review them here in the context of position classification.

First, election as a strategy for policy making in personnel selection is the foundation of democratic states. The people choose who will make and execute the laws and, to some degree, who will interpret them. Electoral systems emphasize values, debate, political responsiveness, and generalized (rather than expert) knowledge of government. Elected officials are selected as the leaders of most public sector systems but are required to serve terms and be reelected periodically if they want careers in government. Two types of elected officials are common. The most visible is the full-time official who serves in a major office and whose salary is sufficient to provide a living. The more frequent type, however, is the "citizen-legislator" who serves part-time and whose salary is modest or inconsequential.[3]

A second personnel strategy is appointment by elected officials. Generally, appointed officials serve at the will of those who select them. The most salient appointed officials are those who run agencies as cabinet-level secretaries, directors, and commissioners, and their chief deputies. These employees also typically include policy-related advisers and confidential staff. Ideally, elected officials select individuals for full-time paid jobs who they believe are competent or meritorious in addition to being in general agreement with the officials about their policy positions. Common practice used to allow elected officials to choose appointees in general government service on the spoils principle—either to reward political supporters or to indirectly enhance their own personal situations (such as through the appointment of family members), without regard to competence. Such appointments still occur and sometimes produce well-publicized scandals, but the potential public relations damage (and sometimes legal and electoral consequences) to appointing officials and ethics laws act as restraints. Gross spoils selection at the career level (i.e., civil service) is quite rare today, largely because of court action (Hamilton, 1999), although the "thickening" of government (see the introduction) with numerous high- and midlevel political appointees should not be overlooked. Some of the most common are those who serve as "citizen appointees" on innumerable boards and commissions at all levels of government on a part-time basis for little or no remuneration.

A third strategy is rule-based selection, which affects the bulk of those in the public service and is the primary focus of this chapter. This strategy gives precedence to merit and is based on technical qualifications and competitive selection. Removal from office is often only for cause (see Chapters 2 and 11). Advanced forms of the merit philosophy in organizations evolved in the 19th century. Two fundamental types of merit strategies exist: rank-in-job strategies and rank-in-person strategies (see Exhibit 5.1 for a comparison of the two). **Rank-in-job** personnel strategies (also known as rank-in-position strategies) are the norm in the United States but less common elsewhere. Rank and salary are determined by the position that one holds. Substantial salary increases and higher status are attained only through movement into better jobs (promotion or reclassification), but multiple promotions within an organization are unusual beyond the predetermined job series, such as City Planner I, II, and III. Career development is the responsibility of the incumbent (jobholder), and promotions are normally open competitions, including **lateral entry** from outside the organization (leading to the term **open personnel system**). Merit selection relies heavily on systems with many grades or levels.

Rank-in-person strategies are unusual in the United States except in military and paramilitary organizations such as public safety departments, the foreign service, academic departments, some health agencies, and the federal Senior Executive Service. (Exhibit 5.2 provides some typical examples of occupational ranks.) Rank-in-person emphasizes the development of incumbents over time, especially within the organization, and tends to lead to closed systems. **Closed personnel systems** provide few opportunities for lateral entry by those outside the organization. They allow for more position mobility because personnel carry their ranks with them no matter what their current assignments. Promotions are prized and are expected over time. Closed personnel systems typically have a strong **up-or-out philosophy**—that is, those who are not promoted eventually may be terminated. Ranks may number from as few as three to as many as ten for military officers.

"fitting people to jobs" (handwritten marginal note)

Exhibit 5.1 Job Versus Rank Classification

Job (Open) Merit Strategy	Rank (Closed) Merit Strategy *person*
Focus on work: "Job makes the person."	Focus on individual: "Person makes the job."
Entry is based on technical qualifications only.	Entry is based on general qualifications and long-term potential.
Lateral entry is allowed.	Lateral entry is discouraged or prohibited.
Promotion is based on open competition in most cases.	Promotion is more or less automatic, especially at lower ranks.
Grade level is maintained as long as performance is satisfactory.	Expectation exists that rank will increase over time; an "up-or-out" philosophy will screen out incumbents.
Career development is largely the responsibility of the incumbent.	Career development is planned by the organization through specified career paths.
Tends to focus on/produce specialists.	Tends to focus on/produce generalists.
Elimination of the job means separation of the incumbent.	Elimination of the assignment results in reassignment of the incumbent.

Exhibit 5.2 Three Examples of Occupational Ranks

Army Officer Ranks	Fire Department Ranks	University/Faculty Ranks
Quasi-officers:	Recruit	**Unranked/untenured:**
Cadet	Firefighter	Teaching assistant
Warrant officer	Engineer	Instructor
Company officers:	Medic	Adjunct faculty
Second lieutenant	Lieutenant	**Ranked/untenured:**
First lieutenant	Captain	Assistant professor
Captain	District fire chief	**Ranked/tenured:**
Field officers:	Assistant fire chief	Associate professor
Major	Fire marshal	Full professor
Lieutenant colonel	Deputy fire chief	Professor with special status (distinguished, regent's professor, endowed chair)
Colonel	Fire chief	
General or flag officers:		
Brigadier general		
Major general		
Lieutenant general		
General		
5-star general (general of the army)		

Hybrid or mixed strategies are also possible. In selected cases, public servants are appointed but serve for set terms (examples are state public safety directors and university regents), similar to elected officials. Federal judges and some state judges are appointed for life. In recent years there has been renewed interest in linking rule-based (merit) selection with termination processes similar to those in appointment strategies—that is, at-will employment, in which property rights to jobs are severely limited.[4] Although at-will employment is still the exception rather than the rule in the public sector, this chapter will discuss important contemporary examples of the drive to reform the civil service. The conclusion will focus on this and other trends affecting rank-in-position and rank-in-person systems. (For examples of contributions to this debate, see Bowman & West, 2007a, 2007b; DeSoto & Castillo, 1995; Somma & Fox, 1997.)

THE ORIGINS OF POSITION CLASSIFICATION AND MANAGEMENT

In the first century of public sector employment in the United States, from 1789 to 1883, position classification did not exist as a rational system. Positions tended to be created and salaried in an ad hoc fashion, largely based on a patronage system, social class, and regional representativeness, and only coincidentally by merit. The initial period was relatively elitist and staid, but public service evolved over the 19th century into a tumultuous system. Congress enacted legislation in 1853 establishing four major job classes, with salary rates for each. This legislation was frequently ignored, however, and all levels of government struggled with merit, equity, and consistency problems (Mosher, 1982; Van Riper, 1958).

The civil service reform movement, which started after the Civil War, changed the landscape of position classification and management over time. Nevertheless, the importance of reform should not overshadow other influences. At the same time that political influence was being reduced in recruitment, selection, promotion, discipline, and other personnel processes, principles of modern management were being more generally introduced. By the early 1900s, Frederick Taylor's scientific management, whether or not it was truly "scientific," held great sway over the development of position classification processes. Taylor promoted the idea that there was generally "one best way" to accomplish any given task, a way that could be found thorough work analysis. This effectively combated the Jacksonian notion that the government work was "so plain and simple that men of intelligence may readily qualify themselves" (President Andrew Jackson, quoted in Van Riper, 1958, p. 36).

Work analysis provided the means to select superior methods of performance, to identify those who could perform better, and to provide superior training. Systematic **job descriptions** became commonplace, and work relationships became rationalized. Work analysis highlights differences and breaks work into component parts. Because of this, the scientific management movement then started a long-term trend of "pigeonholing" work, breaking it into hundreds and ultimately thousands of different jobs at dozens of different levels. See, for example, the old and now rarely used *Dictionary of Occupational Titles,* or *DOT* (U.S. Department of Labor, 1991), which had 12,741 occupations listed. The contemporary version is O*NET OnLine, which consolidated the occupational titles to 812 in 2006 (on the validity of the consolidation, see LaPolice, Carter, & Johnson, 2008).[5]

The Classification Act of 1923, capturing the new wisdom of scientific management, provided a model of a rational **position management system**. It established that (1) positions and not individuals were to be classified, (2) **job duties** and responsibilities were to be the distinguishing characteristics of jobs, (3) qualifications were to be a critical factor in determining classification status, and (4) a member of a class would be qualified for all other positions in the class. This act enhanced legislative ability to monitor and control positions in terms of overall employee numbers, grade ceilings, and salary ranges. The Classification Act of 1949 created separate schedules for white-collar and blue-collar workers, a change typical of the trend at the time of dividing personnel systems into occupational clusters. The proliferation of rank-in-position systems promoted the idea of fitting people to jobs. During this period, managerial efficiency and legislative control were emphasized on one hand, and employee procedural rights were increasingly enhanced on the other. Jobs tended to become narrower and less flexible.

Equal opportunity substantially changed position management through legislation addressing discrimination based on race, color, religion, gender, national origin, age, and disability. Particularly important was the passage of the Equal Pay Act of 1963, which addressed gender discrimination in pay. The notion of equal pay for equal work, regardless of personal characteristics of the job incumbent, was taken to its logical legal extension, as was the idea of equal opportunity for employment and advancement. Although unions in the private sector experienced a marked decline by the 1980s, unions in the public sector leveled off beginning in the 1990s.

Even though both equal opportunity and worker representation have obvious benefits, the excesses of the position management systems initiated after the Pendleton Act of 1883 had also become apparent: classification rigidity, extreme specialization and pigeonholing, weak results-oriented accountability, and technical complexity. For example, critics complained that promotion from one **job classification** to another had become positively litigious, the number of different job classifications (2,500) had become excessive, attempting to fire nonperforming employees had become a nightmare, and the technical complexity of nearly three dozen pay systems had become byzantine. State and local government systems tended to demonstrate the same symptoms on a smaller scale. By the mid-1990s, equal opportunity began to recede as the dominant concern in personnel systems (Ewoh & Elliott, 1997).

Although the Civil Service Reform Act of 1978 provided an important initial attempt at reform, the most recent human resource era actually started in the 1990s and continues today with an emphasis on broad employee categories, more procedural flexibility, more rigorous employee accountability, and technical simplification (Hays, 2004).[6] Examples include broadbanding, reinventing government, simplification initiatives in personnel policies and manuals, and revisions in the civil service system. Broadbanding occurs when several grades are combined, creating a wide salary range for a position. Formal promotions are not required for pay movement (as is the case with more traditional—and narrow—classification series), although milestone progress is still required and documented. In some versions, people are ranked in a single classification, such as entry level, journeyman, senior, and specialist, but these designations are determined by the unit rather than by a personnel department or civil service commission. The reinventing government and simplification initiatives in the early 1990s decentralized many personnel functions to the field and, concurrently, streamlined procedures so that field staff (such as those working in field offices, individual departments, or units) could implement them.

Current civil service reform focuses on enhancing employee accountability to meet moderate or definable performance standards (U.S. Merit Systems Protection Board [U.S. MSPB], 1999). The most dramatic examples of this to date are the termination of the civil service system in Georgia in 1996 and in Arizona and Tennessee in 2012, the creation of more flexible personnel systems for the U.S. Department of Homeland Security and U.S. Department of Defense in 2003, and the rise of employment contracts as well as posttenure faculty review processes in state universities (Isfahani, 1998). Although the federal classification system has yet to undergo major changes with respect to the 1949 act, exemptions from it are increasing (Cipolla, 1999), as are recommendations for a moderate to radical overhaul (Kerrigan, 2012; Maynard, 2012; Nelson, 2004; U.S. Government Accountability Office, 2003).

A final historical issue is the effort by human resource experts to utilize a single overarching taxonomy of job titles so that jobs can be compared in and across industries and countries. In practical terms, classification systems ultimately will be customized; the ideal is that they all use a common language and framework, however. That framework is the Standard Occupational Classification. It divides jobs into 23 major groups, 96 minor groups, 449 broad occupations, and 821 detailed occupations (Pollack, Simons, Romero, & Hausser, 2002) and relates closely to the O*NET classification system. It is used by federal departments such as the Bureau of Labor Statistics, in its *Occupational Outlook Handbook* (Bureau of Labor Statistics, 2008); the Bureau of the Census; and the Office of Personnel Management, in its federal classification and job grading systems (U.S. OPM, n.d.). Although the hope is that other levels of government—as well as the private sector, which uses the products of these agencies—will eventually gravitate toward the revised Standard Occupational Classification, such a convergence of systems will be slow to occur because of legacy classification systems.

With this historical background established, the chapter now turns to functional aspects of position management: the basics of job design and how current jobs are analyzed, how technically competent descriptions are written, and how jobs are organized into systems for effective human resource administration.

JOB DESIGN AND JOB ANALYSIS

The fundamental importance of **job design** and job analysis cannot be overestimated. Together, job design (creating balanced jobs in the context of the organizational environment, technology, and resource demands) and job analysis (ensuring that the functions of jobs are rationally presented for internal and external uses) form the basis of most human resource functions. Exhibit 5.3 provides examples that demonstrate how these two skills undergird many other areas.

Exhibit 5.3 Common Examples of Job Design and Analysis

Case 1 (Job Design)

A moderate-size division realizes that a series of functions are being performed at too high a level. The assistant director of the division has come to act as the Web master, information technology (IT) troubleshooter, and public relations officer for the division. These additional roles prevent him from focusing on operations, which is his role according to his job description. Rather than creating a second assistant director position to handle the regular operational workload, the division wants to create specialized functions. The division now interacts with the public a great deal through its Web page, which needs daily maintenance and updates; this role is not yet considered a full-time job. The division also needs a local IT troubleshooter to fix easy systems problems and to manage software purchases; complex problems can be referred to the organization's IT department. Furthermore, because of its Web presence, the division wants to be more proactive in providing good public relations stories as well as educational messages to the public. At first, the hope was that all these functions could be performed by the same person, who would provide excellent job enlargement. However, after talking with people fulfilling similar roles in other organizations, the job analyst found that the array of skills seemed too wide-ranging and was concerned that combining them into one job would diminish job specialization too greatly. The division ultimately decided to hire one person who would be both IT troubleshooter and Web master, as well as a separate public information officer who would take over a number of community outreach responsibilities. The IT–Web master would report to the public information officer, who would in turn report to the assistant director.

Case 2 (Job Analysis)

A fire department has requested that the human resource division review two series—the firefighter series and the emergency management technician (EMT) series. When the fire department expanded into first-responder services in the 1980s, firefighters did not do medical services generally. Personnel were even segregated by vehicles—fire trucks and ambulances. Over time, however, the expectation that new firefighter recruits would be able to perform basic first-responder responsibilities had become routine, and the city could not afford to maintain a large presence exclusively for firefighting when less than 10% of the calls were for fire service—most were for EMTs, and a sizable portion were for various types of rescue services and hazardous materials cleanup. After reviewing existing positions, sending questions to all those affected, conducting focus group interviews, and even performing a number of ride-alongs, the human resource department proposed a new joint firefighter–EMT series. The new series would pay better, but it would also increase the training and job requirements substantially. Hiring would cease in the old series until those classifications had no incumbents, at which time they could be eliminated.

Creating or Re-creating Jobs

Job design is the specification of job features, primarily the duties, the quantity of work expected, and the level of responsibility (Clegg & Spencer, 2007; Sherwood, 2000). The *duties* include major work functions to be accomplished; a key issue is the breadth of those duties. Just how narrow or broad should they be? The *quantity of work* aspect determines the balance of those duties. In many jobs, a single duty may take up more than half of an incumbent's time, with other duties taking up relatively small amounts of time. In other jobs, the work is evenly distributed among the duties. The *level of responsibility* of the job relates to the independence of the incumbent and where the position will be placed in the organizational hierarchy. What types of decisions can the incumbent make independently? At what level and how frequently will the incumbent be reviewed? Also, what will be the scope of the incumbent's decision making? Will the person have subordinates or levels of subordinates? Will the incumbent have responsibility for one or more program areas? Will the individual have fiduciary responsibility or a legal investiture as the "responsible officer"? Other aspects of job design that may or may not be stipulated include when the individual will carry out responsibilities, the order of tasks and how the incumbent will do them, where the individual will carry out the tasks, additional reporting relationships beyond the incumbent's supervisor (if any), competencies the individual will need to perform the job, and the training the individual will need to do the job.

Job design—and redesign—is important for managers at all levels. It is their responsibility to maximize both productivity and employee satisfaction; the creation and changing of jobs is an indispensable tool in that effort (Yan, Peng, & Francesco, 2011). Small and large examples of job design are plentiful: A subordinate wants a reclassification to a higher level, and the manager must decide whether to support the request and how to ensure that the incumbent takes on greater responsibility if approved. A department has grown, and it is time to have employees move from being generalists to being specialists. A division has received a new mandate and must create a new unit to handle the programmatic responsibility. An agency is forced to downsize and must decide how to accommodate its work with fewer people. A new technology creates an opportunity to reassign or redesign work (Institute of Management & Administration, 2003).

Keeping one eye on the efficiency and effectiveness of productivity is a fundamental responsibility in job design; doing so supports the organization's mission and provides the public with high value. The well-known efficiency consideration relates to the narrowness of responsibilities. **Job specialization**—the narrowing of job responsibilities—tends to promote higher levels of task mastery and thus speed, less training, and simpler incumbent replacement. In many situations, job specialization leads to more manageable jobs and greater professionalization. In others, however, job specialization can lead to the perception that employees are being treated as replaceable parts in deadening assembly-line-type jobs. The effectiveness consideration relates to how positions are grouped together and to overall work flow. Ensuring that the flow of work among individuals and units is as rational (smooth and optimal) as possible requires skillful **process management**. Perhaps the work flow has become suboptimal over time, as people and technology have changed. A work flowchart may reveal that there are steps that can be eliminated in a process, tasks that can be reassigned for greater coherence, or a step that needs to be added to ensure a better customer focus. If the changes that need to be made in the work flow are radical, process management becomes **process reengineering**.

Productivity is important, to be sure, but job designers must also keep employee satisfaction in mind. Job satisfaction invariably leads to reductions in employee problems such as grievances and improved retention rates; further, it sometimes—but not always—leads to greater productivity (Kelly, 1992; Vermeeren, Kuipers, & Steijn, 2014). Some of the classic considerations here are task variety, development, and autonomy. **Job enlargement** increases the scope of a job by extending the range of duties and responsibilities. It can sometimes be an antidote to employ dissatisfaction in positions that are perceived as too narrow or stifling, or in which the work is too fragmented from either the worker's or the client's perspective. **Job rotation** is a means of developing employees at all levels so that they understand the "big picture" and become cross-trained. **Job enrichment** attempts to motivate employees by giving them more authority or independence for organizing their work and solving problems. (Exhibit 5.4 illustrates the relationship between job design and job analysis.) Because of the importance of employee satisfaction and the numerous other factors that affect it, Chapter 6 is devoted entirely to this topic.

Analyzing and Describing Current Jobs

Job analysis encompasses a systematic process of collecting data for determining the knowledge, skills, and abilities (KSAs) required to perform a job successfully and to make numerous judgments about it (U.S. OPM, 2006). It typically is used as a key tool for recruitment, classification, selection, training, employee appraisal, and other functions (Jenkins & Curtin, 2006). In terms of recruitment and position classification, job analysis provides up-to-date information for position announcements and a thorough and rigorous basis for the writing of job descriptions and ranking jobs. For selection, analysis is decisive for determining valid selection criteria that are both practical and legally defensible. For training and development, analysis can be indispensable in identifying and detailing the competencies needed as well as the specific gaps that typically exist between those competencies and incumbent performance. In regard to employee appraisal, job analysis can help to define concrete standards and to catalog evaluation criteria. In terms of other human resource functions, job analysis is critical in making reasonable accommodations for disabled persons as well as in redesigning jobs.

Exhibit 5.4   Job Design and Job Analysis Create the Platform for Most HR Functions

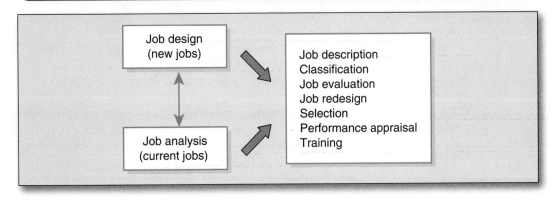

Job analysis is a powerful instrument because it offers a unique opportunity for learning about fundamental aspects of the organization as well as an opportunity for thoughtful examination of current practices. Executives can encourage managers to conduct job analyses to make sure that the organizational structure reflects current practices, technology, and work requirements. It is likely that job analyses will discover such inefficiencies as excessive middle management, outdated hardware, absence of appropriate software, and areas of under- and overstaffing. Managers can target problem jobs or clusters of jobs as opportunities for innovation in job redesign or work flow. Employees can perform informal job analyses to study their colleagues' positions for cross-training or their own positions for better understanding and to recommend changes in their positions. Even students outside the organization can use job analysis methodology as a part of their internship experiences and as a marketable skill, similar to finance management or policy analysis.

Job analyses rely on a combination of four information collection methods: (1) archival data, (2) questionnaires, (3) interviews, and (4) observation (Foster, 1998). The methods chosen tend to depend on the number of jobs to be analyzed, the kind of work being done, and the type of information required. For example, a job analysis of a police sergeant's position intended for use in the development of a selection test for a large urban police department would require strategies from those needed for a job analysis of all the positions in an IT department planning to restructure its operations.

- Use of archival data involves a review of job and **position descriptions**, previous job analyses, performance appraisals, training materials, worker manuals and aids, examples of work products, and other artifacts that help describe and define the position. Ideally, these data are employed before other steps, but in practice they often become available as the process evolves. An array of archival data provides a potentially invaluable wealth of contextual and detailed information.
- Questionnaires can be either open-ended or structured. Open-ended instruments ask incumbents to identify the content of their jobs on their own and quantify the functions by percentage of their time (Exhibit 5.5 provides an example). The surveys are then reviewed by supervisors. The strengths of this method are its low cost, standard form, and use of incumbents' knowledge of the position. Unfortunately, questionnaires generally require significant follow-up to fill in gaps and are susceptible to employee embellishment—or, in some cases, diffidence. Closed-ended or structured instruments provide task lists from which incumbents select. Such questionnaires can provide highly detailed information about the job but require computer-based aggregation and trained staff analysis for effective utilization.
- Interviews can be conducted with individuals or groups. The content of jobs can be analyzed through semistructured or wholly structured question protocols administered to either job incumbents or supervisors. This is a particularly useful method for analyzing managerial, technical, and professional positions. Group methods are useful when a class of positions has relatively little variation or when a list of unstructured elements, such as critical incidents, is being elicited (Foss, Minbaeva, Pederson, & Reinholt, 2009). The primary drawback of interviews is their time-consuming nature.

[handwritten margin notes: no bias, truth, comprehensive, time-consuming, snapshot in time]

- Observation involves watching individuals actually perform their jobs. It is particularly effective for analyzing blue-collar positions for which the activities can be observed; it is less useful for analyzing white-collar occupations. Observation provides the analyst with firsthand experience, which may be enhanced by the analyst's performing the functions.

Formal methods of job analysis are time-consuming and expensive. In practice, they are employed only in small numbers of important cases. Formal job analysis should always be used when a position involves an employment test that can be challenged easily on the grounds of validity. Validity challenges (see Chapter 4) are most common for large, entry-level classifications, especially for jobs that are highly sought because of their professional potential and that require basic knowledge- or skill-based tests. Examples include firefighter and fire lieutenant, police officer and police detective or corporal, sheriff's deputy, FBI agent, IRS investigator, and auditor. Formal analysis is also important to determine reasonable accommodations for those with disabilities. These types of analyses are conducted by personnel specialists but are frequently subcontracted to specialized consulting firms. Some jurisdictions, especially small ones, use off-the-shelf tests that have been validated by vendors.

Formal job analysis may be used in a reclassification when there is pressure to upgrade a position. A reclassification generally is formally requested by the incumbent, must be supported by the supervisor, and is administered and approved by the human resource department. It is highly useful for those requesting, supporting, or discouraging reclassifications to understand formal job analysis methodology. (Note that the questionnaire in Exhibit 5.5 can be used in reclassifications as well as in the classification of new positions.)

Formal job analysis also may be used as a preliminary step in an evaluation study in which the positions of a division or entire organization are being recalibrated. Such studies normally are subcontracted to consulting firms, if only for the neutrality that external assessors are perceived to possess. Except for relatively consistent (but highly generic) job descriptions, however, formal job analysis may supply information of limited value. Finally, formal job analysis is sometimes used for comprehensive training studies. The increased expectation of the posting of formal job descriptions on the organization's website, as well as the development of enhanced tools for displaying job analysis results (Stetz, Button, & Porr, 2009), has breathed new life into descriptive position management systems. To summarize, job analysis can be utilized not only by human resource departments but also by managers and employees. Formal methods of job analysis tend to be practiced by internal experts or consultants, but the ability to perform informal job analyses is now considered a generic management skill.[7]

JOB AND POSITION DESCRIPTIONS

One of the end products of job design or job analysis is the job description or position description. Although these terms are used nearly interchangeably, with *job description* being the collective reference, they actually represent different concepts. It is useful to exaggerate the differences for clarity because job and position descriptions are the building blocks of **position classification systems** and management systems. Both are written

Exhibit 5.5   Example of a Position Description Questionnaire

IOWA DEPARTMENT OF PERSONNEL

POSITION DESCRIPTION QUESTIONNAIRE (PDQ)

FOR AGENCY USE ONLY	FOR IDOP USE ONLY PDQ # _____
M-5# _____	Class Title _____
New position	18-Digit Position # _____
_____ Position review requested	Personnel Officer _____
_____ No position review requested	Response to IDOP request
	Date _____

1. Name of employee (if none, write VACANT)

2. Current 18-digit position # and class title

3. Department, division, bureau, section, and work address

4. Hours worked (shifts, rotations, travel)

5. _____ Full-time (40 hours per week)

   _____ Part-time (list number of hours per week)

6. Have the assigned duties changed since this position was last reviewed for a classification decision? ____ Yes ____ No

   If Yes, place an "X" beside each NEW task written below. Also, describe in detail how those tasks are different from those previously assigned.

7. Name and job classification of the immediate supervisor

8. Description of Work: Describe the work in detail. Make the description so clear that the reader can understand each task exactly. In the TIME/% column, enter the percentage of time spent on each task during an average workweek. List the most important responsibility first. If this is a reclassification request, the previous PDQ must be attached. This PDQ will be returned if any section is incomplete.

TIME/%	WORK PERFORMED
	(ATTACH ADDITIONAL SHEETS IF NECESSARY)

CFN 552-0094-4   R 4/99

9. Is this position considered to be supervisory? _____ Yes _____ No

    If Yes, complete a Supervisory Analysis Questionnaire form (CFN 552-0193) and attach it to this form.

10. For what reasons are you requesting that this position be reviewed? Include, if applicable, significant changes or additions to duties, comparison(s) with other positions, etc. Be specific.

    I certify that I have read the instructions for the completion of this questionnaire, that the answers are my own, and that they are accurate and complete. I understand that falsification or misrepresentation made in regard to any information submitted may lead to discipline up to and including discharge.

Signed _____   _____

       (Incumbent Employee)   (Date)

   If you have not been notified by your department's management of their decision to support or deny this request within 30 days, you may send this request directly to IDOP for review. Address it to: Facilitator, Program Delivery Services, Iowa Department of Personnel, Grimes Building, East 14th & Grand, Des Moines, Iowa 50319-0150.

SUPERVISOR REVIEW OF POSITION DESCRIPTION QUESTIONNAIRE

This section must be completed within 30 days after the PDQ is received from the employee. The employee must be notified of the decision to support or deny the request. Regardless, the request must be forwarded to IDOP. This PDQ will be returned if any section is incomplete.

11. Indicate to what extent, if any, the statements on this form are, in your opinion, not correct or need clarification.

_____

_____

Describe the origin of any new duties, i.e., those marked with an "X" in Item 8. If new duties have been added, where were they performed prior to being assigned to this position? Are these duties performed by anyone else? If so, identify the person(s) and the position classification of their positions.

_____

_____

What is the basic purpose of this position?

_____

_____

(Continued)

Exhibit 5.5 (Continued)

Identify the essential functions that must be performed by the incumbent, with or without reasonable accommodation for disabilities. Identify any certifications or licenses that are required. Refer to the instruction sheet and Section 3.15 of the Managers and Supervisors Manual for more information on essential functions.

_____

_____

Is this position considered to be confidentially or managerially exempt from collective bargaining?
_____ Yes_____ No

If Yes, complete the Bargaining Exemption Questionnaire (CFN 552-0631) and attach it to this form.

Signed _____ _____ _____

       (Supervisor)   (Title and Job Classification) (Date)

APPOINTING AUTHORITY REVIEW OF POSITION DESCRIPTION QUESTIONNAIRE

12. Comments:

_____

_____

Signed   _____ _____

       (Appointing Authority)   (Date)

CFN 552-0094-4   R 4/99

SOURCE: Iowa Department of Personnel (1999).

statements about a job that describe or list the duties, but they often differ significantly in focus, as well as in their uses, writers, and level of specificity.

Job descriptions are statements that codify the typical or average duties (sometimes by using work examples), levels of responsibility, and general competencies and requirements of a job class. They are generally prepared by human resource specialists or personnel consultants. Their primary uses are for systems management (placement of positions in specific classes) and compensation decisions; job descriptions tend to be maintained by the human resource department. The language is usually generic, so that a description covers many positions, and the examples used may or may not apply to a specific position. Although the format varies, the underlying structure of job descriptions does not.

Position descriptions are statements that define the exact duties, level of responsibility, and organizational placement of a specific position (or essentially identical group of positions). Although they are sometimes written by personnel specialists, they are normally written by job incumbents or their supervisors. Their primary purposes are for recruitment (where they are modified as vacancy announcements), reclassification (where the duties and responsibilities tend to be compared to the job classification requested), and performance appraisal (where work standards and accomplishments are emphasized). Because of the wide variety of objectives, their formats vary considerably. Their maintenance is generally dependent on the specific use of or the culture of the local unit; true position descriptions are rarely centrally maintained. An example of a comparison of job and position descriptions, using the class Equipment Operator 2, is located in the appendix to this chapter. The job description is for a class with more than 1,000 positions; the position description was used as part of a successful effort to reclassify the position from an Equipment Operator 1 to an Equipment Operator 2.

Small organizations may not maintain job descriptions and may use position descriptions only occasionally, such as when they need to recruit. Small and medium-size organizations that have overhauled their position classification systems within a decade or so often find that they are able to maintain job descriptions that have many characteristics of position descriptions because the number of incumbents is small in each class. In big organizations with many large classes, job descriptions generally are maintained conscientiously (and used for all purposes even if they prove less than ideal for recruitment and appraisal), whereas position descriptions are created selectively for management and human resource purposes.

Finally, it should be noted that traditional job and position descriptions vary from their contemporary counterparts in two significant regards. The first of these stems from the profound effect on job descriptions, position descriptions, and position announcements of the Americans with Disabilities Act of 1990. Traditionally, jobs were defined as having three to ten major duties, each of which might have two or more **job tasks**.[8] Because the ADA prohibits discrimination against an individual with a disability who, with or without reasonable accommodation, can perform the **essential functions** of the employment position, the language more often used today addresses essential and nonessential functions rather than duties and tasks. Furthermore, physical, manual, and special requirements are now routinely spelled out in job and position descriptions.[9] Second, the new management emphasis on accountability and results has led to the incorporation of performance standards in some cases. It remains to be seen whether results-oriented job and position descriptions will become the norm.

Writing Job Descriptions

Writing job descriptions is a specific skill that takes study to master. In practice, templates are used, but the style invariably is terse. The simple format furnished here as an example (using the job of town accounts payable or payroll clerk) has the following elements or categories: (1) job summary, (2) essential functions, (3) physical and environmental standards required to perform essential functions, and (4) minimum job requirements and qualifications. Most agencies provide instructions for the writing of job descriptions on their websites (see, e.g., HR-Guide, 2000; U.S. Fish and Wildlife Service, 2008).

The job summary begins with the level of responsibility and identifies the department and level of supervision, if any, followed by a list of major duties.

Example: Under general supervision, this position works in the office of the city administrator. This position is responsible for financial support tasks including payroll processing, accounts receivable, accounts payable, bank deposits and reconciliations, and other general clerical support duties for the administrator and council as assigned.

The second category identifies essential functions, generally those that constitute more than 5% of the incumbent's time and are central to the job. Each of the function descriptions starts with a verb followed by an object and sometimes an explanatory phrase. Ideally, five to seven functions are listed, but there may be as few as three and as many as ten. Long, unorganized task lists once were typical but now are considered poor form. Tasks should be clustered into duty areas and combined where necessary. A performance standard may be placed at the end of each statement.

Example: Processes biweekly time sheets and enters payroll information into computer; computes used and accrued sick and vacation time and overtime hours; pays required federal and state taxes; deducts insurance and related payroll costs; prints payroll checks and payroll reports. Extreme accuracy and timeliness are required in performing this critical function.

The third category identifies the physical and environmental standards required to perform essential functions. Physical standards should articulate the exact abilities required to accomplish job tasks as normally constituted, with the understanding that reasonable accommodation may be necessary for a qualified applicant or incumbent who is disabled. Environmental standards include such conditions as working outdoors, dangerous conditions, and nonstandard working hours. Generally, this section employs a format similar to that used for the essential functions.

Example: Requires the ability to handle a variety of documents and use hands in typing, data entry, using a calculator and related equipment; occasionally lift and carry books, ledgers, reports, and other documents weighing less than 25 pounds. Incumbent will use personal automobile in depositing monies at local banks. Requires visual and hearing ability sufficiently correctable to see clients, hear phones, and operate in an office environment that has limited auxiliary support.

The fourth category identifies minimum requirements and qualifications. Here, required KSAs, as well as special certifications, degrees, and training, are identified. Requirements for excessive credentials should be avoided to ensure consistency with merit principles and equal employment opportunity. Acceptable substitutions generally are listed.

Example: Graduation from high school or GED and 3 years of general accounting or bookkeeping experience; substitution of successful completion of a business or accounting curriculum at a recognized college or school may be made for part of the experience requirement. Must also have good interpersonal skills and excellent ability to coordinate and balance numerous, sometimes hectic activities in a calm fashion without letting technical accuracy suffer.

Job design and analysis, then, provide the content of position and job descriptions that are used in a variety of human resource functions, from recruiting to appraisal. Now it is time to turn to the way that these individual efforts are assembled into systems.

FROM JOBS TO JOB SYSTEMS

The Two Primary Uses of Classification Systems

Position classification systems can provide the foundation for job design and support, as well as the basis for management, tracking, and control of employment numbers, costs, and position levels. When the function of position classification systems is job design and support, they provide the basis for the division and coordination of work, recruitment efforts, selection methods, training programs, appraisal systems, and other human resource functions through the analysis and organization of jobs.

Position classification systems are also structures that manage, track, and control employment numbers, costs, and levels of positions; in this context, they are frequently called position *management* systems. Legislators need to know the number of authorized positions versus the number of filled positions and to anticipate total personnel costs so that they can curb the number of positions in specific areas and control position grades or ranks. A position management system typically numbers positions, assigns locations, and determines an exact system of compensation. Positions can be tracked by function, such as transportation, and by specialty, such as engineering. Positions also can be tracked and monitored by grade or rank. For example, the state of Iowa has 57 pay grades and six steps in most grades. A legislator thus can determine how many employees work in what agencies, at what levels, and at what cost. A position classification system from this perspective is ultimately a management tool to support compensation systems and control costs.

Grouping Positions

Position systems start with the duties and responsibilities of a single individual, whose job is called a **position**. Clusters of positions with similar characteristics are organized into a job classification, job class, classification, or simply job or class (terms that are used interchangeably). Technically, the term *jobs* refers to identical positions, whereas *classes* refers to similar positions in which there are equivalent responsibilities and training, although the specific duty assignments may vary. For example, "property appraiser" may be the class, but one individual may be assigned to residential properties and another to commercial. For classification purposes, however, both have generic training with easy rotational opportunities, which is why the concept of job classifications is used (so that excessive numbers of categories will not be created). The number of job classifications varies considerably by organization: The federal government has approximately 2,500, state governments have anywhere from a high of 4,500 (California) to a low of 550 (South Dakota), and very tiny organizations have just a few classifications (Chi, 1998). Classes that are linked developmentally are grouped into class series.[10] For example, the federal government has approximately 450 class series for white-collar workers and another 350 for blue-collar workers. Class series are subsequently grouped into large **occupational families**. Related occupational families, such as all white-collar jobs, are assigned a **pay plan** or schedule in which the grades, steps, and related pay are determined.

As rational as this sounds in theory, practice can produce disorderly systems. The size of the jurisdiction, the number of bargaining units, and the history of the jurisdiction produce very different position classification systems with different sorts of challenges and contradictions. First, systems often have an unnecessary number of pay plans, which are driven more by labor–management negotiations than by rational planning. Separate pay plans are created for each major group: blue-collar, clerical and support staff, public safety, executives, confidential staff, and a variety of professional groups in particular agencies (e.g., health professionals, engineers, lawyers, judges). From a strategic human resource management perspective, they would be grouped together or divided into just a few major groups.

Second, individuals frequently change pay plans as they move up the chain of command. Firefighters may be in one plan, fire captains may be in another for midlevel managers in the city, and the fire chief may be in the plan for city executives. The number of plans seems to increase as the jurisdiction size increases; Exhibit 5.6 presents an example of this problem. Although this may increase responsiveness to market factors and enhance comparability, it can lead to a system that is complex and unwieldy. Note that the one system in the exhibit with a moderate number of pay plans (the judicial branch of Iowa) was comprehensively reorganized in the 1980s. Other problems are

Exhibit 5.6   Increases in Number of Pay Plans as Jurisdiction Size Increases (Examples)

	City of Ames, Iowa	Iowa Judicial Branch[a]	State of Iowa[b]	U.S. Federal Government
Number of positions	522	2,200	19,000	5,000,000
Number of classes	224 (average size: 2.3)	132 (average size: 16.7)	850 (average size: 22.4)	2,500 (average size: 2,000)
Number of pay plans or schedules	8	4	15	36

A. This branch of government was rationalized and streamlined in 1986, when the system was converted to a statewide system.

B. The positions do not reflect the 24,000 regents employees (Iowa State, University of Iowa, and University of Northern Iowa). Each regents institution has separate classification systems for merit, professional and administrative, faculty, and temporary employees.

excessively narrow class definitions (sometimes with only a single job incumbent) and positions that have dual classifications (and different compensation patterns) merely because the identical jobs are found in different organizational or bargaining units of the same government.

Rank-in-person systems reduce the number of job classes through the use of a uniform series of ranks for a multitude of operational positions. "Army captain," "district fire chief," and "assistant professor" are generic job titles for numerous positions identified by a specific army unit, fire district, or university department. Systems with rank are normally closed to lateral entry (entry from outside the organization without completion of a junior or entry-level position), unlike position systems.

In sum, although many small jurisdictions have, and function acceptably with, piecemeal patterns, large jurisdictions need formal position classification systems. Such systems help them track and control positions as well as support those positions by logical groupings called job classes, class series, occupational families, and pay plans. The special case of classification for pay is considered next.

Analyzing Jobs to Set Pay: Job Evaluation

The two most important tools in position classification and management are job analysis (discussed above) and job evaluation. In theory, a job evaluation is a special type of job analysis, one that attaches a dollar value or worth to the position (Siegel, 1998a, 1998b). In practice, job evaluations are often so specialized that they operate as a different function from job analysis.

Position classification systems provide grades or ranks for all merit positions as well as for nonmerit positions. This allows for rational position management systems that assign **authorized salary ranges** to each grade or rank. In the ideal, all merit jobs are thoroughly analyzed for content and rigorously evaluated for relative worth. Furthermore, the system should provide **internal equity** among organization members and **external equity** with those in similar positions outside the organization (see Chapter 7). The system should also furnish an opportunity to reflect seniority, merit, skill, and other specialized **individual equity** concerns (such as locale and shift differences). In reality, position management systems rarely meet such standards, partly because of the expense and effort required to maintain such ideals and partly because of the competing and inconsistent demands placed on these systems (see Chapter 7).

Not all personnel systems are based on formal position classification systems. Piecemeal personnel systems are those that lack grades or ranks and assign salaries on an ad hoc basis. Job relationships may be reflected in an organization chart, and brief job descriptions may exist. Detailed job analyses, well-articulated job series, and civil service protections, however, are partial or nonexistent. Piecemeal personnel systems are still common in small governments. Obvious drawbacks include inconsistency; lack of integration of the human resource functions, such as hiring, appraisal, and promotion; and the possibility of legal challenge regarding hiring and promotional validity. These systems, however, do offer flexibility and a level of informality that may suit small organizations fairly well.

Using Factors and Points for Job Evaluation

Historically, jobs were evaluated using a holistic job methodology: What was a particular job thought to be worth in general terms? Despite the flexibility and immediacy of such systems, they are prone to distortions based on personalism, limited information, and excessive focus on the job incumbent. Position classification ushered in an age of factor systems in which job grades or levels were established. Graded systems took into account (often implicitly) such factors as level of responsibility, job requirements, difficulty of work, nature of relationships, and level of supervision. This led to far more rational and equitable compensation systems. The assignment of points for various factors made these systems still more rigorous.

Today, organizations use the **point factor method** when they find that their position classification systems have become too inconsistent and outdated. In the majority of cases, an external consultant conducts the underlying pay study to design the new system because of the time and expertise required to accomplish such a large task.

A point factor system starts with the assumption that factors should be broad enough to apply consistently to all jobs in an organization or schedule. In practice, four to twelve factors generally are selected. For instance, the Federal Evaluation System (FES) uses nine for the General Schedule (GS). Each factor is then weighted according to a determination of the maximum number of points that can be assigned to it (U.S. OPM, 1991). In the case of the FES, note the tremendous differences in the weights of the different factors, as shown in Exhibit 5.7.

Next, the factors are defined by levels or standards that are used to determine the actual number of points a job classification will receive. In the General Schedule, GS Grade 9 is from 1,855 points to 2,100 points, whereas GS Grade 15 exceeds 4,050 points. Three to five

Exhibit 5.7   Weighting Equivalencies for the Nine Factors Used in the Federal Evaluation System

Factor	Maximum Points	Evaluation Weight (%)
Knowledge required	1,850	41.3
Supervisory controls	650	14.5
Guidelines	650	14.5
Complexity	450	10.0
Scope and effect	450	10.0
Personal contacts	110	2.5
Purpose of contacts	220	4.9
Physical demands	50	1.1
Work environment	50	1.1

SOURCE: U.S. OPM (1991).

standards interpret the various levels; descriptions are provided of what high, medium, and low levels mean in each factor. Factors may be further subdivided into a number of subfactors. All jobs are then evaluated by individuals, committees, or both. This part of the process should provide internal equity because of the consistency of the process. After all jobs have been evaluated and arranged from lowest to highest, point ranges are selected to determine grade levels.

Point factor systems are excellent for internal equity, but they do not ensure external equity. External equity is maintained through the linking of the entire point factor system to compensation comparisons of select jobs outside the organization. A portion of the classifications are chosen as **benchmark jobs**, anchored to general market salary ranges as indicated by reliable compensation survey information.[11] In large organizations, it may be as few as 5% or 10% of the positions; in small organizations it may be as many as 25%. Benchmark jobs are used for each major class series to ensure external equity and to ensure that the entire system is in line with market compensation practices.

As a straightforward example, suppose that an organization finds that its position classification system is dated, that most job descriptions do not reflect ADA standards, and that there is an opportunity to modestly increase salaries, which are currently below the market. An external consulting firm is hired that specializes in government compensation studies. The consultant uses four factors: (1) level of responsibility, (2) complexity of problem solving, (3) degree of accountability, and (4) working conditions.[12] Multiple raters examine 7% of the job classes, using the four factors to ensure reliability. This provides reference points (benchmark jobs) in the evaluation of other jobs.

At that point, all classes are analyzed and evaluated using the factors. (As a by-product of the evaluation process, new job descriptions are generated that provide essential and nonessential duties as well as physical requirements and environmental conditions for compatibility with the ADA.) The evaluation assigns a specific point value to each job class. After all the classes have been arrayed on a point scale from lowest to highest, intervals are selected that determine the grade levels. Those benchmarked jobs are then matched to salary survey data to ensure comparability to market salaries. Throughout the process, the organization has a task force assigned to work with the consultant, which includes the human resource specialist for compensation. After the study is completed, the results are forwarded to the entire organization, and all members have an opportunity to review the analysis and provide further input. The task force presents the study to the governing body, along with its recommendations for adoption (or rejection) and for specific changes. Since such investigations usually represent salary increases, the governing board may or may not accept the study.

Because comprehensive job evaluations (pay studies) are expensive and time-consuming, they occur infrequently.[13] Managers, executives, and legislators need to be aware of how compensation factors were arrived at in the past, how well the compensation system has fared over time, and when a new compensation study and pay plan may be called for, as well as the auxiliary features that such research can produce with planning (see Exhibit 5.8 for a discussion of when to conduct a job evaluation study).

For their part, it is essential for employees and managers to understand job evaluation factors so that they can maximize the prospects for success in petitions for reclassification. Too frequently, a good employee is performing well but has weak grounds for a

Exhibit 5.8 When to Conduct a Job Evaluation Study

Because organization-wide job evaluation studies are expensive, time-consuming, and often controversial, they should not be used as feasibility studies. If the adoption of the final study (with modifications) will not be propitious, it is better not to begin at all. Nor should a comprehensive job evaluation analysis be used if only a few job classifications are at issue; in that event, only those cases or class series should be evaluated.

First, preliminary questions must be asked. How and when were jobs last evaluated (using what methodologies) and by whom? How much controversy does the system seem to generate, and what are its major problems (internal equity such as pay inconsistencies; external equity such as widespread below-market salaries; special problems such as hard-to-recruit and hard-to-retain jobs, excessive job plateauing, inadequate financial incentives)?

Second, the purpose of a proposed study needs to be clearly outlined. Is it for an occupational family, a pay plan, or the entire organization? Would the analysis primarily target internal inequities, overall external inequities such as depressed salaries across the board, more flexible salary plans, merit-based pay systems, or a variety of factors? Who would conduct the evaluation, and how would they be commissioned? What would be the role or input of employee unions? Defining the purposes of the initiative ensures that the organizational or legislative leaders and the evaluators do not have two separate notions of what is to be accomplished (which is not uncommon).

Third, feasibility and political reality must be assessed candidly. If the overall problem with the compensation plan is depressed salaries across the board but government revenues are limited because of economic or financial exigencies (such as a recession or an expensive capital building plan), then a job evaluation study will do little but agitate workers, put executives in an uncomfortable position, and annoy elected officials (who will turn down the plan). Practical questions include the following: Will there be money to both pay for the analysis and increase some or all salaries? Do legislators really understand the underlying need (because the study itself is unlikely to convince them) as well as the general plan of implementation? How can the study be used as a means of enhancing labor–management relations rather than become another bone of contention?

Finally, the jurisdiction needs to be clear if it wants more than just a compensation study conducted. A common outcome desired is a set of job descriptions that have wider human resource utility. Such a by-product must not be assumed and should be carefully spelled out before the process begins.

reclassification, which is based on the nature of the position and not on her particular skills or assignments. Unless grounds can be established that the position itself has been fundamentally and permanently altered, a reclassification request may be turned down (although a classification specialist might assist with a market adjustment, special step increase, bonus, or other pay modification suggestion). Because of this type of problem, as well as the perceived rigidity of position management systems in general today, alternative systems such as broadbanding (discussed in Chapter 7) frequently are recommended.

Substituting a Whole Job Methodology for Job Analysis or Job Evaluation

Whereas formal position classification systems rely on job analysis and point factor systems, piecemeal classification systems and new positions rely instead on whole job methods. **Whole job analysis** does not systematically break a job down into its constituent parts for purposes of grade and classification; rather, it relies on past experience and intuition. **Whole job evaluation** methods do not systematically break a job down into its constituent parts for purposes of compensation; rather, they consider the job in its entirety and make summary judgments based on intuition and past experience. Examples are numerous:

- *Whole job analysis:* A supervisor hires a clerical support person from another unit in the organization; this employee clearly has the appropriate skills and already knows the position in general terms. The supervisor needs someone quickly, so no analysis of the position is conducted. Although identified as a Secretary III position, the generic job description gives almost no insight into the specific position.
- *Whole job analysis:* A manager hires a special project coordinator for a new position. Although a rough description of the job elements is provided, it is really only suggestive of the types of KSAs that might actually be required.
- *Whole job analysis:* An executive appraises a high-performing manager in general terms, without a detailed knowledge of the specific tasks that the person conducts on a daily basis.
- *Whole job evaluation:* A manager in an organization (that does not have a formal position classification system) intuitively selects a salary for a new position that experience indicates will attract competent candidates.

Whole job methods involve simple, summary judgments. Their merits include efficiency and a tendency to honor the decision maker's past experience and wisdom (Van Wart, 2000). The difficulties are that these judgments can be hasty and based on insufficient or inaccurate information. They also may yield little information for various human resource functions and provide inadequate management or legal defense when the decisions are faulty. In systems with large job classifications and typical job valuations, whole job methods are often inappropriate.

Curbing, Cutting, and Eliminating Workforce

The process of reducing the workforce is not the opposite of the process of enlarging it. While adding to the workforce is generally well received and signifies good times, reducing the workforce involves some pain and/or a period of economic constraint (Iverson & Zatzick, 2011). Although the importance of position management becomes more intense during workforce reduction, the philosophy and many of the tools are different. Federal employment dropped from 2010 to 2013 and has since leveled off, and state and local government stopped declining in absolute numbers in 2014. Exhibit 5.9 illustrates the downward trend of public sector employment since 2009, momentarily interrupted by Census Bureau hiring in 2010.

The reasons for curbing, cutting, or eliminating a part of the workforce can be pragmatic, strategic, or both. They include budget shortfalls, program sunsets, retrenchments affected by ideological beliefs, and technological advancements that make employees

Exhibit 5.9   The Downward Trend in Public Sector Employment After a Peak in 2009

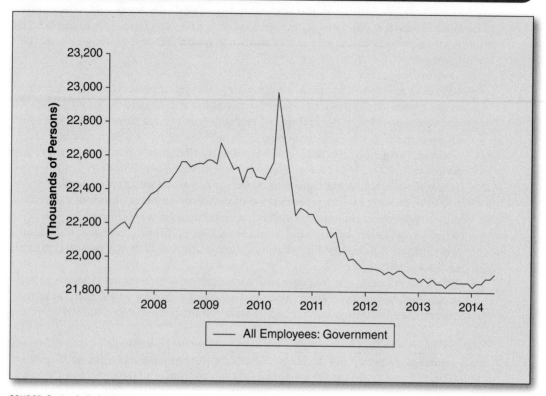

SOURCE: St. Louis Federal Reserve website (http://www.stlouisfed.org).

NOTE: The temporary spike in 2010 reflects the hiring of seasonal Census Bureau employees.

redundant. The most common reason for reducing personnel is budget woes, typically aligned with recessions, such as in 1960, 1969, 1973, 1980, 1990, 2001, and 2008 (National Bureau of Economic Research, 2011). Budget downturns do not affect all governments equally because of regional variations, and light recessions may have little effect on governments where leaders have a more cautious and long-term philosophy. Sometimes, however, as in the recession of 2008, government funding is actually stimulated to offset the economic cycle and to deal with increased service demands, and therefore workforces grow slightly, before a perceived need to cut budgets occurs as the private sector stabilizes. An important budgetary reason for personnel cuts not necessarily related to recessions is the impact on public budgets of tax slumps caused by events such as housing busts or runaway expenditures caused by events such as rapidly increasing health care or prison costs, or wars. Another reason to cut and eliminate jobs is that agencies or specific programs have outlived their usefulness. Finally, sometimes cuts to budgets and personnel have a significant ideological element: the belief that there should be more of a shift to the private sector in specific cases, such as in outsourcing building maintenance, or in general, such as a "shrink government" philosophy. Sometimes technology affects personnel planning, as when computer technology largely eliminates the need for routine secretarial support for all but executives and when military drones and high-tech equipment enable reductions in troop numbers.

The tools that legislators and executives use in reducing the workforce can be more or less severe. Less severe curbs include personnel ceilings, hiring freezes, and buyouts; these approaches put caps on the size of the workforce or reduce it modestly. Such tools are all being used extensively in the public arena across the world today. **Personnel ceilings** set the maximum number of positions that may be budgeted by appropriation unit or for all positions in an organization. When ceilings are lowered, governments generally reduce services. Sometimes, however, services are shifted to nonpermanent workers not covered by the ceilings, nonprofits, or vendors, forestalling significant savings. A related method is the hiring freeze, in which an employer stops hiring for all nonessential positions; a hiring freeze uses the natural attrition caused by retirement and resignations to reduce the workforce. Freezes can be imposed by executive orders or by legislatively lowered ceilings, forcing attrition to occur. Exceptions to hiring freezes must normally be approved at very high levels in an agency or government to ensure compliance; during a "hard" freeze, waivers are highly limited. For example, President Ronald Reagan's civilian hiring freeze in 1981 led to an immediate overall downsizing of the federal government by 35,000 people, even though the military was allowed to grow by 30,000 during the same period. Much of the public sector experienced hiring freezes during the 2010–2014 period. When lowered personnel ceilings or hiring freezes are used, they are effective in getting relatively quick results and reduce the need to use more severe tactics. However, ceilings and freezes are blunt instruments in terms of allowing talented and experienced workers to exit in areas that may be strategic and/or critical (Partnership for Public Service & Booz Allen Hamilton, 2010). Proportionately the public sector has shrunk in recent decades. In 1975 public sector employment was 19.2% of the workforce at its height; by 2013 it had declined to 16% (Mayer, 2014).

Buyouts can be a more strategic approach to workforce reduction, resulting in lower employee stress levels as colleagues leave in better spirits. A buyout plan offers incentives for voluntary separation or retirement. Buyout plans in the public sector are normally adjusted for years of service, but they may also have a base amount. Long-term employees commonly get the equivalent of between 6 months' to 2 years' pay. Buyouts speed the retirement of more expensive, long-term employees and can be limited to specified areas or classifications. Buyouts make the most sense when it is unlikely that overall employee levels will be reduced for at least several years without intervention (Linskey, 2010; Losey, 2011; Trask, 2008); they make less sense when reductions are temporary or the financial condition of the jurisdiction is in crisis and more extreme tools are needed to balance budgets.

The tools used to reduce the workforce more substantially include layoffs, reductions in job costs, and reorganizations. Layoffs are generally called *reductions in force,* or RIFs, in the United States and *redundancies* in Commonwealth countries. Reductions in force authorize agencies to abolish positions and terminate employees; for example, Title 5, Part 351, in the Code of Federal Regulations establishes the procedures in the federal government. In most agencies, employees are covered by regulations using factors such as type of employment (whether or not the position is covered by layoff regulations), tenure of employment, veterans' preference, length of service, and performance ratings. RIFs often allow for "bumping rights," situations in which employees with seniority can displace those with similar positions but less time in the classification or organization. RIFs also sometimes allow employees to downgrade their classifications in order to retain their employment. Although intended to guarantee maximum opportunities for redeployment for employees, RIFs with extensive bumping can be very disruptive to operations while being implemented. Public sector RIFs differ from many business layoffs because the government normally provides much longer notification periods. Sometimes employees must be notified of potential layoffs but the layoffs are later rescinded when the budget is finalized (this is common with teacher layoffs). Ideally, from an organization standpoint, RIFs also allow for long-term redeployment of resources as personnel are shifted from areas with a lack of work to those that have greater need.

Public organizations are increasingly *reducing the pay and benefits* of incumbent and future workers. Temporary reductions in the time and pay of employees were uncommon in the past, but since the Great Recession of 2008 they have been used by thousands of agencies across the country at all levels of government. The term used for involuntary time off for budgetary reasons is *furlough,* which is not to be confused with military furlough (leave that is generally paid) or prison furlough (usually time off a sentence for good behavior). Public organizations impose furloughs while they try to cope with budget shortfalls (but generally only with union support in order to prevent layoffs). Furloughs are most effective when shortfalls are likely to be temporary; they are less effective when agencies have long-term budget challenges. Other types of strategies aimed at trimming employee expenses that are becoming popular are reductions in paid holidays, decreases in employer contributions to health and retirement plans, and increases in the use of part-time and term employees. For instance, more than half of the American professoriat are adjunct faculty (Moser, 2014).

Sometimes *reorganizations* are used to enhance efficiency and therefore provide organizations with personnel savings. At the federal level, attempts to implement large-scale reorganizations to deliver savings have not fared well. President Jimmy Carter did reorganize the personnel agency (OPM), and President George W. Bush did reorganize the Department of Homeland Security (DHS), but neither achieved much cost savings, and the expanding mission of DHS has actually led to dramatic increases in its budget. A number of smaller reorganizations have occurred at the federal level within agencies—such as the reorganization of the ill-famed Minerals Management Service in the Department of the Interior into the Bureau of Ocean Energy in 2010 after the *Deepwater Horizon* oil disaster off the Louisiana coast—but few have achieved personnel savings. City–county consolidations are another form of reorganization that is frequently discussed but rarely implemented. More successful in terms of savings have been reorganizations in education (numerous waves of consolidations of school districts, e.g., from more than 100,000 during World War II to approximately 15,000 currently) and the judicial system (from decentralized county court systems to state-organized systems).

The most extreme methods of personnel reduction are employee termination, program elimination, and privatization. While RIFs occur because of fiscal exigency, insufficient personnel ceilings, or work shortages, *large-scale public sector firing* is caused by contractual or legal partisan differences. In the context of major personnel changes, firing occurs in two primary instances. First, employees may be dismissed by executives who assert themselves when workers have gone on strike and there is a breach of contract. A famous and precedent-setting case was when President Reagan fired air traffic controllers who were members of the Professional Air Traffic Controllers Organization (PATCO) in 1981 for walking off their jobs. He successfully discharged more than 11,000 controllers and banned them from working in the federal government. Second, dismissals may occur in the case of at-will public sector employees such as political appointees, policy advisers, and personal assistants for elected officials. Examples of such firings have involved U.S. inspectors general (President Ronald Reagan), attorneys general (President George W. Bush), and personal travel personnel consultants (President Bill Clinton). In governmental transitions, federal Schedule C personnel (confidential staff) do not expect to be continued, and political appointees know that they lack job security; equivalent changes in personnel occur at the state level following partisan elections. Nonetheless, the termination of large numbers of employees is an unusual event, and mass dismissals other than in transitions are rare (Cauchon, 2011).

Despite grumblings to the contrary (Fahrenthold, 2011), government programs are sometimes shut down. Particularly likely to be eliminated are temporary agencies, such as those created for wartime (e.g., Manhattan Project, Office of Censorship, War Production Board), economic crises (e.g., Reconstruction Finance Corporation, Resettlement Administration, Resolution Trust Corporation), and needs whose time has passed (e.g., Freedman's Bureau, Steamboat Inspection Service, Bureau of Prohibition). Program closures can also occur within agencies or departments, such as military base closures (approximately 350 installations have been closed in five base realignment and closure rounds, in 1989, 1991, 1993, 1995, and 2005), school campus closures, and closure of the famous Walter Reed Army Medical Center in 2011.

Privatization occurs when public responsibilities for services or assets are directly or indirectly shifted to the private sector. There are many methods and types of privatization, but the three that are most important to position management are discussed here.

The least draconian type of privatization takes the form of restricting funds to selected agencies, thereby reducing public services and personnel and increasing demand for private services. This is a viable strategy when moderately priced private sector options exist. A prominent example is the widespread trend in budget cuts to public higher education. This is causing rapidly escalating tuition costs, such as in California, where tuition costs in the 23-campus California State University system tripled from 2001 to 2011. A second type of privatization is contracting out. For instance, in some states, public charter schools can be run by for-profit organizations. Other important areas where contracting out is becoming increasingly common include prisons, social services, and local government services ranging from maintenance, trash collection, and public safety to public works (Bradbury & Waechter, 2009). Privatization of troops means that private military contractors often outnumber U.S. military personnel in war zones (Cole, 2009).

Because governments in the United States have not been as expansive as most of their counterparts around the world, the selling off of enterprises such as oil companies and manufacturing plants has not been as necessary. Nonetheless, some examples of moving government agencies to the private or quasi-private sector have included the conversion of the U.S. Post Office to the U.S. Postal Service (1971), the changing of Fannie Mae from a government agency to a private, shareholder-owned organization (1968), and the occasional selling of public utilities. This area has been particularly troublesome, however, with agencies struggling either because of continuing expectations of public good over private efficiency despite changes in missions and goals or because of financial liabilities. For example, Fannie Mae's private liabilities were reassumed by the federal government in 2008 when the agency was put under government conservatorship due to insolvency.

SUMMARY AND CONCLUSION

Position classification became more of a judicious plan throughout the last century than it ever was before. Outright corruption in the civil service is unusual; rational plans for managing jobs in terms of compensation and other human resource functions exist in all large organizations and are tailored to their needs and histories. In addition, specific tools now exist in this area, such as job analysis and job evaluation, which include both highly sophisticated methodologies and standard methods commonly used by managers. Most small organizations with piecemeal systems follow job analysis and classification methods in spirit, even if they frequently lack the rigor of large agencies.

Nevertheless, the ability to have greater (but not perfect) control, consistency, precision, and rationality (which position classification and management theory and practice have enabled managers to achieve) should not disguise the underlying truth that position management is only partially a science and largely an art. The decisions made in position management systems ultimately are founded on value choices, not universal laws (Van Wart, 1998). Many of the values assumed over the last half century are shifting dramatically because of changed economics, politics, and technology. Furthermore, even at its most rational and ideal, the position classification system of any large organization is a combination of at least three fundamentally different personnel systems based on election, appointment, and rule-based criteria. Indeed, rule-based (i.e., merit) criteria are themselves divided between position-based systems and less common rank-based systems, sometimes occurring in the same organization. Finally, the sheer organizational complexity and level of change in organizations today mean that extensive, expensive, difficult-to-maintain position classification systems naturally tend to become less rational, less consistent, and out-of-date. Paradoxically, then, as much as position classification systems are judicious plans, they are also ever-changing jigsaw puzzles of shifting values, radically different personnel approaches, and competing human resource needs to provide management control on one hand and to support and design jobs on the other (Ingraham & Getha-Taylor, 2005).

The new value changes emanate from elemental transformations in the public sector landscape in terms of what people want public sector organizations to do and how they want them to do it (deLeon & Denhardt, 2000; Yergin & Stanislaw, 1998). Rather than an emphasis on employee rights and internal procedural consistency, there is far greater interest in employee accountability and concrete achievement, translating into an increased reliance on at-will systems (with appointment-based features) and performance standards (Grady & Tax, 1996; U.S. MSPB, 2002). This has certainly prompted extensive debate about the advantages and potential liabilities of contemporary civil service reforms. The emphasis on efficiency and effectiveness is in line with the historic tradition of scientific management and can be seen as a logical progression of the art of position management.

Other trends promise to take position management into new domains and configurations. The demand for agencies that are flexible, flatter, and more entrepreneurial requires not only new organizational structures but also new internal management systems in the United States (Leavitt & Johnson, 1998; Marshall, 1998) and elsewhere in the world (Lodge & Hood, 2005). Such trends will propel institutions to reexamine and simplify their complex systems. Efforts to use broadbanding (fewer classes and enlarged jobs) and work teams are examples, as are attempts to simplify massive management systems. Contemporary initiatives to decentralize responsibility to local managers who will be more accountable for results but will also be allowed more flexibility will further change the landscape. Indeed, some predict the "death of the job" (Crandall & Wallace, 1998; Leonard, 2000) as virtual work designs stretch people beyond narrow, predictable tasks by extending not only their lines of sight (understanding outcomes and how their activities relate to them) but also their lines of impact (confidence stemming from affecting results). Finally, the use of various tools for downsizing has become more commonplace as public sector budgets have come under pressure; these tools include lowered personnel ceilings, hiring freezes, buy-outs, layoffs, reduction of job expectations, reorganizations, wholesale firings, program elimination, and privatization.

However, whether one comes to view position management systems more as judicious plans or as jigsaw puzzles, they will remain the core of the human resource function that managers, employees, and job aspirants cannot afford to mystify or underutilize.

KEY TERMS

Authorized salary range
Benchmark jobs
Broadbanding
Class series
Closed personnel systems
Essential functions
External equity
Individual equity
Internal equity
Job analysis
Job classification

Job descriptions
Job design
Job duties
Job enlargement
Job enrichment
Job evaluation
Job rotation
Job specialization
Job tasks
Lateral entry
Occupational families

Open personnel system

Pay plan

Personnel ceilings

Piecemeal personnel systems

Point factor method

Position

Position classification systems

Position descriptions

Position management system

Privatization

Process management

Process reengineering

Rank-in-job

Rank-in-person

Up-or-out philosophy

Whole job analysis

Whole job evaluation

EXERCISES

Class Discussion

1. Canvass the class to determine if any members have been a part of a reclassification effort or an organization-wide job evaluation. What happened? Was it successful or not?

2. Ask those in the class who now work or have ever worked in the public sector to describe any position management challenges they have experienced.

3. There is perhaps no better example of the grand paradox of needs (see the book's introduction) than position management. Discuss and seek pathways through the paradox as well as subparadoxes found in various position management techniques.

Team Activities

4. Discuss how the position management function can help or hinder in the resolution of the twin paradoxes introduced at the outset of this book.

5. Analyze a public sector organization's classification system. Determine the number of positions, classes, and pay plans. How many of the positions are elected, appointed, and merit appointees? Does the system "work," and does the checkerboard make sense to those using the system?

6. A large, growing county decides to place a new service center in another city. None of the current employees is interested in relocating. Furthermore, there is some concern that many of the county offices are using outdated technology and old-fashioned methods of customer delivery. For example, services related to building permits, licenses, land records, and tax assessment are scattered throughout a variety of buildings in the county seat. The new model of customer service recommends a single service counter for related services, with employees who are cross-trained. Almost all the job descriptions are at least a decade old (some are 25 years old!), and nearly all the "training" is on the job. How might a job analysis study be useful in this situation? Specifically, what functions might be supported by such a study, and how would they be implemented?

7. As a class, determine which members are currently employed in the public sector and then select some of them to be interviewed about their jobs in small groups. After the interviews, each small group must write a job description. The person interviewed should not do any of

the writing, nor should he or she suggest the format to be used. Compare the results across groups as a class and make suggestions for improvements.

8. You are a manager whose best worker has "topped out"; that is, the employee is at the top step of her pay grade. Furthermore, her job is properly classified. Unfortunately, the government jurisdiction for which you both work is 20% to 30% below the market in its pay rates for most positions. You know that the person will leave soon if the situation is not altered. You could assign a few people to report to her to justify a reclassification and pay increase, although this would not make much sense functionally. Take an imagination break (see Exhibit 0.2). What would you do? (Teams should compare and justify their recommendations.)

Individual Assignments

9. The reform of civil service will be an important topic of discussion and debate for the next several decades. What are the implications of the civil service reform initiative in Georgia? Do you think that the movement to replace independent civil service commissions with executive branch personnel agencies is a good one? Do you think that job property rights should be abolished in all public sector systems? Will the widespread use of at-will systems lead to patronage problems again, as it did in the 19th century?

10. What are the similarities and dissimilarities between broadbanding and rank-in-person systems?

11. If you were the analyst looking at the position reclassification request in this chapter's appendix (for the Equipment Operator 2), what would you view as its positive and negative points? Would you grant the request?

APPENDIX

Comparison of Job and Position Descriptions

Sample Job Description[14]

> Equipment Operator 2, Class Code: 08111dy
>
> Definition: Under general supervision, performs specialized and routine roadway and right-of-way maintenance activities including physical laboring activities, the operation of self-propelled mobile equipment, skilled equipment operation, and limited direction of work crews. Performs related work as required.

> ### Work Examples
>
> - Assists a supervisor by performing limited lead work in accordance with set procedures, policies, and standards; and such duties as instructing employees about tasks, answering questions about procedures and policies, and distributing and balancing the workload and checking work. Makes occasional suggestions on appointments, promotions, and reassignments.
> - Works on district paint crew in rotation with other paint crew positions.

- Works on the district bridge crew.
- Acts as a maintenance sign crew leader in maintenance areas where work on signs requires a full-time sign crew.
- Acts as a lighting specialist and may be assigned to the state lighting crew to assist that crew in the maintenance and construction of roadway lights.
- Cleans ditches and culverts, excavates soil, straightens drainage channels, and resets culvert ends using a dragline or hydraulic excavator in a residency or districtwide area.
- Operates a mud pump, grout pump, or high reach in a residency or districtwide area.
- Operates the curb-making machine in a residency.
- Performs herbicide spraying operations in right-of-way areas by using a backpack sprayer, by driving a truck, or by operating a pressure sprayer as required.
- Loads and unloads material, demolishes structures, loads debris, and so on, using a small bulldozer. May be required to run a large erosion dozer for erosion control purposes in districtwide or residency-wide areas.

Competencies Required

- Knowledge of specialized highway maintenance equipment, its operation, and use
- Knowledge of highway maintenance procedures and techniques
- Knowledge of highway maintenance terminology
- Ability to work outdoors during inclement weather and to be on call during emergency situations such as snowstorms, pavement blowups, floods, and so on
- Ability to operate a 90-pound jackhammer in the operation of breaking and removing pavement materials
- Ability to lift and load bagged material weighing up to 95 pounds to a truck bed that is 55 inches above ground
- Ability to drive trucks and other vehicles in a safe and conscientious manner
- Ability to understand and carry out written and oral instructions
- Ability to direct the work of and to train crew members
- Ability to meet customer needs in a consistently helpful and courteous manner
- Ability to work cooperatively with others as part of a team
- Ability to apply personal work attitudes such as honesty, responsibility, and trustworthiness to be a productive employee
- Ability to operate specialized highway maintenance equipment that requires hand, foot, and eye coordination

Education, Experience, and Special Requirements

- The equivalency of one-year full-time experience in the operation of heavy equipment, performing highway or other related maintenance functions, or in subprofessional engineering program areas.
- All positions in this job class require applicants to possess a commercial driver's license, class A, at the time of hire. Endorsements may also be required.

- For designated positions, the appointing authority, with Iowa Department of Personnel prior approval, may request applicants to possess a minimum of twelve semester hours of postsecondary education, 6 months of experience, or a combination of both, or a specific certificate, license, or endorsement in the following areas: air brakes, doubles or triples endorsement, hazardous materials endorsement, or tank vehicles. Applicants wishing to be considered for such designated positions must list applicable course work, experience, certificate, license, or endorsement on the application.

Special Notes

- After accepting an offer of employment, all persons are required to have a physical examination by a doctor of choice verifying the applicant's physical ability to perform the duties described.
- Employees must be available to travel and may be required to stay away from home overnight during assignments.
- Certain designated positions require the employee to be certified by the U.S. Department of Agriculture and Land Stewardship as a Pesticide Applicator.
- Employees must respond to emergency conditions, and so must live within a fifteen-mile distance or be able to report within a 30-minute period of time to their assigned facility.

Sample Position Description (Intended Usage: Reclassification)

Incumbent	John Doe
Agency	Iowa Department of Transportation
Division	Highway Maintenance Division
Unit	District 2
Place of work	Waterloo Maintenance Garage, US 63 and West Ridgeway
Position number and class title of existing position	645 S44 5520 08110 111 Equipment Operator 1
Hours worked	7:00 a.m. through 3:30 p.m., Monday through Friday
Immediate supervisor	Robert Fisck, Highway Supervisor 1
Position requested	Equipment Operator 2

Description of work: List in detail the work you do. List the most important duties first. Indicate the percentage of time or hours in an average workweek spent on each duty.

45%	Grout pump. Operate a grout pump over a districtwide area. Reestablishing pavement support by undersealing. Includes marking and drilling injection holes and injecting a mixture of cement flash grout under low pressure to completely fill any voids under the pavement. Must understand and be able to locate longitudinal subdrains and any other drains located under the pavement to make sure that the drains are not plugged with grout. Must constantly monitor roadway, shoulder, and under the bridge while pumping to make certain not to damage the bridge, shoulder, or roadway in any way. Train and direct a crew of seven to nine operators on the pump and on proper traffic control. Must understand the mechanics of the grout pump so if any problem occurs can take the pump apart and get the grout out of the machine, so as not to have a flash set before a mechanic can get to the job site.
20%	Routine roadway and right-of-way maintenance activities, to include the following:
	Surfaces: patch spalls, seal/fill joints and cracks, remove bumps, fill depressions, remove and replace damaged pavements
	Shoulders: fill edge ruts, operate blading equipment to smooth shoulders, patch paved shoulders, and so on
	Roadsides: pick up litter, cut brush, repair fences, control weeds by mowing and spraying, erect and dismantle snow fences
	Bridges: clean decks, clean and lubricate working members, spot paint
	Traffic services: repair guardrails, flag traffic, maintain lighting, erect and maintain signs
	Drainage: repair and maintain drainage structures and tile lines, clean ditches
	Performance of these tasks includes the use of physical labor and operation of self-propelled mobile equipment such as dump trucks, front-end loaders, tractors, motor graders, and an array of support equipment and hand tools such as chain saws, pneumatic hammers, hand drills, weed eaters, lawn mowers, and shovels.
20%	Snow removal. Operate snow removal equipment such as single-axle dump truck or a tandem-axle dump truck, each of which may be equipped with a tailgate or hopper spreader, a straight blade or V-plow, a wing plow, and underbody ice blade. Procedures include the removal of snow, packed snow, and/or ice by plowing and/or spreading abrasives and de-icing chemicals on the roadway surface.
10%	Equipment maintenance. Service and perform preventive maintenance on all assigned equipment traditionally used in the performance of highway and bridge maintenance.
5%	Other duties. Miscellaneous duties as assigned from time to time.

SOURCE: Iowa Department of Personnel (1999).

NOTES

1. Position management and position classification are related—but not identical—concepts. *Position classification* primarily refers to categorization of positions with a rational set of principles. *Position management* generally refers to the allocation of positions for budgetary purposes. A position classification system is one of the elements of a position management system, but position classification systems can have nonbudgetary purposes as well, such as the fundamental division and

coordination of work, selection, training, and performance appraisal. Position management can have aspects not directly related to classification, such as budget authorization, budget "capping," downsizing, privatization, contracting out, and load shedding.

2. In the past, hereditary selection was common. Although it is less so today, it still exists, even in some advanced democracies.

3. This type includes most city council members, school board members, township trustees, other local board members, and some locally elected commissioners, as well as some county supervisors.

4. In at-will jobs, an employee who is dismissed has a narrow scope of appeal; the incumbent must prove that he or she was removed from the job for an illegal reason, such as discrimination based on race, age, or gender. This puts the burden of proof on the job incumbent. In most civil service positions, the employer must prove "cause" for termination—that is, the incumbent must be documented to be incompetent, to exhibit inappropriate or illegal behavior, or to be unwilling to reform derelict or improper behaviors.

5. O*NET OnLine, the Occupational Informational Network on the Internet (http://www.oneton line.org), is an electronic database commonly used by human resource professionals nationally. It has consolidated the occupational listings from the old *DOT* and analyzes them more fully than they were analyzed in the past.

6. The Civil Service Reform Act of 1978 provided for (a) the bulk of the U.S. Civil Service Commission's routine work to be administered by the Office of Personnel Management, an executive agency; (b) the creation of the Merit Systems Protection Board to be a watchdog of merit employees' rights; (c) the reorganization of the Federal Labor Relations Authority; (d) the creation of the Senior Executive Service, a quasi-rank-based corps that was more flexible and mobile than the former supergrades (General Schedule grades 16–18); (e) the creation of a merit and bonus pay system for GS grades 13–15; and (f) the mandate of performance appraisal systems in the various agencies.

7. Additional online sources for information on job analysis include the U.S. OPM's "Grade Level Guide for Clerical and Assistance Work" (http://www.opm.gov/fedclass/gsadmn.pdf) and the website HR-Guide's personnel selection page (http://www.hr-guide.com/selection.htm) and job analysis page (http://www.job-analysis.net).

8. Job tasks are discrete work activities necessary to performance and that result in an outcome usable to another person. Usage of the term *task* varies. Here it means broad activities such as (with regard to the upcoming example for a payroll clerk) processing time sheets, printing the payroll, and deducting appropriate expenses such as taxes. Another usage (seen in Exhibit 5.4) for the term *task* is as a synonym for "step performed." For example, paying payroll taxes requires the payroll clerk to use different exemptions, distinguish between salary and reimbursements, and control and pay out from a separate tax account. These subtasks are here referred to as *job elements*.

9. Depending on the position and the individual, such physical, manual, or special requirements may require a reasonable accommodation.

10. The terms *class series* and *occupational series* are used interchangeably. Both refer to a normal progression pattern that can be followed by employees, sometimes designated by Roman numerals (Secretary I, II, III, IV) and sometimes by a traditional management series (lead worker, supervisor, manager).

11. Because there is a range in the market, the organization must decide whether it wants to be in the middle of the range, at the top, or at the bottom. This is referred to as the "lead, match, or lag" question (see Chapter 7). Because most governments are labor cost-intensive, small differences can be important in terms of budget outlays.

12. These are the general categories for the well-known Hay system.

13. On the other hand, in larger jurisdictions job evaluation of individual job classes or class series is often constant. This helps with currency but generally leads to inconsistency in the long term in the absence of occasional pay studies to rationalize the overall system.

14. The work examples and competencies listed in this appendix are for illustrative purposes only and are not intended to be the primary basis for position classification decisions.

REFERENCES

Bowman, J. S., & West, J. P. (Eds.). (2007a). *American public service: Radical reform and the merit system.* New York: Taylor & Francis.

Bowman, J. S., & West, J. P. (2007b). Lord Acton and employment doctrines: Absolute power and the spread of at-will employment. *Journal of Business Ethics, 74,* 119–130.

Bradbury, M. D., & Waechter, G. D. (2009). Extreme outsourcing in local government: At the top and all but the top. *Review of Public Personnel Administration, 29*(3), 230–248.

Bureau of Labor Statistics, U.S. Department of Labor. (2008). *Occupational outlook handbook, 2008–09 edition.* Washington, DC: Author. Retrieved from http://www.bls.gov/OCO

Cauchon, D. (2011, July 19). Some federal workers more likely to die than lose jobs. *USA Today.* Retrieved from http://www.usatoday.com/news/washington/2011-07-18-fderal-job-security_n.htm

Chi, K. S. (1998). State civil service systems. In S. E. Condrey (Ed.), *Handbook of human resource management in government* (pp. 35–55). San Francisco: Jossey-Bass.

Cipolla, F. (1999, July 15). Time for the classification system to go. *Federal Times,* p. 15.

Clegg, C., & Spencer, C. (2007). A circular and dynamic model of the process of job design. *Journal of Occupational and Organizational Psychology, 80*(2), 321–339.

Cole, A. (2009, August 22). Afghanistan contractors outnumber troops: Despite surge in U.S. deployments, more civilians are posted in war zone. *Wall Street Journal.* Retrieved from http://online.wsj.com/article/SB125089638739950599.html

Condrey, S. E. (1998). Toward strategic human resource management. In S. E. Condrey (Ed.), *Handbook of human resource management in government* (pp. 1–14). San Francisco: Jossey-Bass.

Crandall, F. N., & Wallace, M. J. (1998). *Work and rewards in the virtual workplace.* New York: AMACOM.

deLeon, L., & Denhardt, R. B. (2000). The political theory of reinvention. *Public Administration Review, 60*(2), 89–97.

DeSoto, W., & Castillo, R. (1995). Police civil service in Texas. *Review of Public Personnel Administration, 15*(1), 98–104.

Ewoh, A. I. E., & Elliott, E. (1997). End of an era? Affirmative action and reaction in the 1990s. *Review of Public Personnel Administration, 17*(4), 38–51.

Fahrenthold, D. (2011, April 20). Even in an era of budget cuts, these government programs won't die. *Washington Post.* Retrieved from http://www.washingtonpost.com/politics/even-in-an-era-of-budget-cuts-these-government-programs-wont-die/2011/04/20/AFYOtwEE_story.html

Foss, N. J., Minbaeva, D. B., Pederson, T., & Reinholt, M. (2009). Encouraging knowledge sharing among employees: How job design matters. *Human Resource Management, 48*(6), 871–893.

Foster, M. R. (1998). Effective job analysis methods. In S. E. Condrey (Ed.), *Handbook of human resource management in government* (pp. 322–348). San Francisco: Jossey-Bass.

Grady, D., & Tax, P. C. (1996). Entrepreneurial bureaucrats and democratic accountability: Experience at the state government level. *Review of Public Personnel Administration, 16*(4), 5–14.

Hamilton, D. K. (1999). The continuing judicial assault on patronage. *Public Administration Review, 59*(1), 54–62.

Hays, S. W. (2004). Trends and best practices in state and local human resource management: Lessons to be learned? *Review of Public Personnel Administration, 24*(5), 256–275.

HR-Guide. (2000). Job analysis: Job descriptions. Retrieved from http://www.job-analysis.net/G051.htm

Ingraham, P. W., & Getha-Taylor, H. (2005). Common sense, competence, and talent in the public sector in the USA: Finding the right mix in a complex world. *Public Administration, 83*(4), 789–803.

Institute of Management & Administration. (2003). Why job descriptions are so necessary for your payroll staff. *IOMA Payroll Manager's Report, 3*(4), 5–8.

Iowa Department of Personnel. (1999). *Position description questionnaire.* Des Moines, IA: Author.

Isfahani, N. (1998). The debate over tenure. *Review of Public Personnel Administration, 18*(1), 80–86.

Iverson, R. D., & Zatzick, C. D. (2011). The effects of downsizing on labor productivity: The value of showing consideration for employees' morale and welfare in high-performance work systems. *Human Resource Management, 50*(1), 29–44.

Jenkins, S. M., & Curtin, P. (2006). Adapting job analysis methodology to improve evaluation practice. *American Journal of Evaluation, 27*(4), 485–494.

Kelly, J. (1992). Does job re-design theory explain job re-design outcomes? *Human Relations, 45*(8), 753–774.

Kerrigan, H. (2012, May 8). Civil service reform comes to Tennessee. *Governing.* Retrieved from http://www.governing.com/topics/public-workforce/col-civil-service-reform-tennessee.html

LaPolice, C. C., Carter, G. W., & Johnson, J. W. (2008). Linking O*NET descriptors to occupational literacy requirements using job component validation. *Personnel Psychology, 61*(2), 405–441.

Leavitt, W. M., & Johnson, G. (1998). Employee discipline and the post-bureaucratic public organization: A challenge in the change process. *Review of Public Personnel Administration, 18*(2), 73–81.

Leonard, S. (2000). The demise of the job description. *HRMagazine, 45*(8), 184–185.

Linskey, A. (2010, December 7). O'Malley offers buyout to state workers: Employees offered $15,000, plus $200 for each year of service. *Baltimore Sun.* Retrieved from http://articles.baltimoresun.com/2010-12-07/news/bs-md-state-worker-buyouts-20101207_1_o-malley-plan-state-workers-buyout-program

Lodge, M., & Hood, C. (2005). Symposium introduction: Competency and higher civil servants. *Public Administration, 83*(4), 779–787.

Losey, S. (2011, June 26). Agencies are turning to buyouts and early retirements to lower personnel expenses and experts say the pace is likely to accelerate. *Federal Times.*

Marshall, G. S. (1998). Whither (or wither) OPM? *Public Administration Review, 58*(3), 280–282.

Mayer, G. (2014). *Selected characteristics of private and public sector workers* (CRS Report R41897). Washington, DC: Congressional Record Service.

Maynard, M. (2012, June 12). Civil service reform passes in 3 states. Stateline. Retrieved from http://www.governing.com/blogs/view/civil-service-reform-passes.html

Moser, R. (2014, January 13). Overuse and abuse of adjunct faculty members threaten core academic values. *Chronicle of Higher Education.* Retrieved from http://m.chronicle.com/article/OveruseAbuse-of-Adjuncts/143951

Mosher, F. C. (1982). *Democracy and the public service* (2nd ed.). New York: Oxford University Press.

National Bureau of Economic Research. (2011). [Website]. Retrieved from http://www.nber.org

Nelson, S. (2004). The state of the federal service today: Aching for reform. *Review of Public Personnel Administration, 24*(3), 202–215.

Partnership for Public Service & Booz Allen Hamilton. (2010). *Beneath the surface: Understanding attrition at your agency and why it matters.* Washington, DC: Partnership for Public Service. Retrieved from http://www.ourpublicservice.org/OPS/publications/viewcontentdetails.php?id=151

Pollack, L. J., Simons, C., Romero, H., & Hausser, D. (2002). A common language for classifying and describing occupations: The development, structure, and application of the Standard Occupational Classification. *Human Resource Management, 41*(3), 297–307.

Sayre, W. (1948, Spring). The triumph of technique over purpose. *Public Administration Review, 8,* 134–137.

Sherwood, C. W. (2000). Job design, community policing, and higher education: A tale of two cities. *Police Quarterly, 3*(2), 191–212.

Siegel, G. B. (1998a). Designing and creating an effective compensation plan. In S. E. Condrey (Ed.), *Handbook of human resource management in government* (pp. 608–626). San Francisco: Jossey-Bass.

Siegel, G. B. (1998b). Work management and job evaluation systems in a government environment. In S. E. Condrey (Ed.), *Handbook of human resource management in government* (pp. 586–607). San Francisco: Jossey-Bass.

Somma, M., & Fox, C. J. (1997). It's not civil service, but leadership and communication: Response to DeSoto and Castillo. *Review of Public Personnel Administration, 17*(1), 84–91.

Stetz, T. A., Button, S. B., & Porr, W. B. (2009). New tricks for an old dog: Visualizing job analysis results. *Public Personnel Management, 38*(1), 91–100.

Trask, M. (2008, December 18). Public sector imitates private buyouts. *Las Vegas Sun*. Retrieved from http://www.lasvegassun.com/news/2008/dec/18/public-sector-imitates-private-buyouts

U.S. Department of Labor. (1991). *Dictionary of occupational titles* (4th ed.). Washington, DC: Author. Retrieved from http://www.oalj.dol.gov/libdot.htm

U.S. Fish and Wildlife Service. (2008). [Website]. Retrieved from http://training.fws.gov

U.S. Government Accountability Office. (2003). *Preliminary observations on DOD's proposed civilian personnel reforms* (Testimony No. 03-7171). Washington, DC: Author.

U.S. Merit Systems Protection Board. (1999). *Federal supervisors and poor performers*. Washington, DC: Author.

U.S. Merit Systems Protection Board. (2002). *Making the public service work: Recommendations for change*. Washington, DC: Author.

U.S. Office of Personnel Management. (1991). *The classifier's handbook*. Washington, DC: Author. Retrieved from http://www.opm.gov/Fedclass/clashnbk.pdf

U.S. Office of Personnel Management. (2006). *Career patterns: A 21st century approach to attracting talent*. Washington, DC: Author.

U.S. Office of Personnel Management. (n.d.). Federal classification and job grading systems. Retrieved from http://www.opm.gov/fedclass

Van Riper, P. P. (1958). *History of the United States civil service*. New York: Harper & Row.

Van Wart, M. R. (1998). *Changing public sector values*. New York: Garland.

Van Wart, M. R. (2000). The return to simpler methods in job analysis: The case of municipal clerks. *Review of Public Personnel Administration, 20*(3), 5–23.

Vermeeren, B., Kuipers, B., & Steijn, B. (2014). Does leadership style make a difference? Linking HRM, job satisfaction, and organizational performance. *Review of Public Personnel Administration, 34*(2), 174–195.

Yan, M., Peng, K. Z., & Francesco, A. M. (2011). The differential effect of job design on knowledge workers and manual workers: A quasi-experimental field study in China. *Human Resource Management, 50*(3), 407–424.

Yergin, D. A., & Stanislaw, J. (1998). *The commanding heights: The battle between government and the marketplace that is remaking the modern world*. New York: Simon & Schuster.

CHAPTER 6

Employee Engagement

Possible, Probable, or Impossible?

An employee's motivation is a direct result of the sum of interactions with his or her manager.

—Bob Nelson

After studying this chapter, you should be able to

- use techniques to cultivate employee engagement;
- understand how human motivation varies;
- recognize how human resource management affects employee engagement;
- discuss personnel strategies for increasing engagement; and
- apply methods for dealing with difficult employee behaviors.

Employee engagement has become an important topic in recent years. If human resource management is about the development of policies for effective utilization of human resources in organizations, it should be doubly concerned with employee engagement, which is a key to performance—engaged workers are more committed, conscientious, and concerned with achieving outcomes, and they have less turnover, too. Leaders, managers, and psychologists alike have often pondered how they can better harness and direct people's "psychic energy" toward work objectives to increase workplace performance. Employees are also concerned about their engagement and motivation, as these often make spending time in the workplace a more attractive experience, by increasing enjoyment, learning, and effectiveness.

Employee engagement is a concept that is relatively recent, and it is not yet well-established in academia. Definitions of employee engagement typically emphasize individuals' being psychologically present and applying themselves physically, cognitively, and emotionally when performing their organizational roles (e.g., Gruman & Saks, 2011; Saks, 2006). An employee who is engaged can be characterized as enthusiastic, energetic, motivated, and passionate about his or her work, whereas a disengaged worker is one who is apathetic and withdrawn from her or his job. The concept of engagement builds strongly on **motivation**, which can be defined as the drive or energy that compels people to act, with energy and persistence, toward some goal. To say that someone "has motivation" is to say that the person has substantial energy and drive in pursuit of something. The concept of employee engagement bridges internal states of motivation with observable behaviors in the workplace.

Employee engagement and motivation are central to the work of human resource management. First, the field cannot ignore the broad impacts that classification, compensation, promotion, training, and other policies have on employee engagement. Directly or indirectly, human resource management provides employers and employees with tools for managing engagement, as discussed in this chapter. Second, in a world of tightly constrained budgets and ever-growing demands, employee engagement is increasingly relevant to human resource management as an important strategy for improving productivity and performance.

The idea of employee engagement became popularized through the work of Gallup, which began to track engagement in 2000. A 2002 study reported that only 29% of U.S. employees were engaged in their jobs, while 55% were not engaged and 16% were actively disengaged ("High Cost of Disengaged Employees," 2002). These numbers were widely reported and replicated. For example, Schwartz (2010) notes that a survey of nearly 90,000 employees worldwide found that only 21% feel fully engaged at work and nearly 40% are disenchanted or disengaged. Moreover, among those who are engaged, 59% strongly agree that "my current job brings out my most creative ideas," compared to only 17% among those who are not engaged ("Engaged Employees Inspire Company Innovation," 2006).[1] Some time ago, in a survey of public managers, Berman and West (2003b) found that in local jurisdictions in which managers had a strong commitment, 77.8% of respondents also agreed or strongly agreed that "employee productivity is high," compared with only 44.1% in jurisdictions where most managers had only mediocre levels of commitment. The numbers differ, but the conclusion remains the same: It matters that both employees and managers are committed and engaged at work. A recent Gallup (2013) study also indicates that employee engagement is strongly associated with reduced turnover and absenteeism.

These studies point to another very basic and essential truth: Employees vary greatly in their levels of engagement and motivation. Most supervisors are likely to have a mix, with some employees who are highly engaged, some who are actively disengaged, and most who are, well, somewhere in the middle. Many years ago, West and Berman (1997) found in cities with populations of more than 50,000 that 29.8% of city managers agreed or strongly agreed with the statement "Employees are highly motivated to achieve goals," 48.8% only somewhat agreed with this statement, and 21.5% disagreed in different degrees with the statement. These percentages are remarkably close to those noted above. Building on these results, the heuristic **25–50–25 rule** states that 25% of employees are highly motivated, 50% are "fence-sitters," and 25% are withdrawn or even cynical. This rule has not been rigorously validated, but many supervisors nevertheless find that it more or less accurately represents their experience. Employee engagement varies widely; that's just how it is.

The implications of the above are that organizations and their managers should be closely attentive to increasing employee engagement, recognizing that employees vary greatly in their levels of engagement and the factors that affect their tendency to engage. A reasonable goal, in an imperfect world, is to transform 25–50–25 into, say, 45–45–10, but there is no magic bullet, gimmick, or one-size-fits-all panacea that can do so. Managers need to use a diverse set of approaches, along with individualized consideration. Gallup (2013) identifies three main strategies for improving employee engagement: (1) selecting the right people, (2) developing employees' strengths, and (3) enhancing employees' well-being. Others offer much longer lists. No matter how the topic is approached, encouraging engagement requires the application of a broad tool kit and some one-on-one dialogue. As one observer has noted: "Regarding engagement, yes, we need to pay people more—pay them more attention! It's not just about the money." We need managers who can bring out greater engagement and motivation in employees.

What can be expected from human resource management? Improving employee engagement and motivation is a complex but not insurmountable challenge. First, this chapter examines the nature of employee engagement and motivation. Managers must understand the phenomena, especially the kinds of factors involved, before they can attempt to shape engagement and motivation. Second, the broad impact of human resource management policies and strategies on the climate for engagement will be explored. Third, the chapter examines specific managerial strategies for managing and motivating individual employees.

PULL, PUSH, OR DRIVE?

The concept of employee engagement is relatively new, but it is closely linked with the concept of motivation, which is well established. An engaged employee is one who is motivated and committed to achieving results that advance organizational goals and work group objectives in meaningful ways. The study of motivation is a large field with a long tradition, and the purpose in this brief space is not to summarize motivation theories—an entire book alone would scarcely do justice to such a rich topic. Rather, the goal in this section is to consider some dominant insights that lead to an appropriate appreciation of motivation for managers, and to extend this with insights about employee engagement. A basic insight is that strategies that treat employees in a one-size-fits-all way, or that assume all employees are similarly motivated, are apt to be ineffective; a bit more sophistication is needed.

Motivation theories differ according to what is emphasized. While there is general agreement that motivation is about the drive or energy (an inner state) that compels people to act with energy and persistence toward goals, the question is which factors affect this energy. Some theories focus on factors *inherent to individuals,* such as their basic needs for survival, achievement, appreciation/belonging, or development, as well as their energy level and mental state (e.g., their energy to pursue different tasks). This "needs perspective" of motivation is associated with the work of Abraham Maslow (1954), who developed a **hierarchy of needs** of basic drives around (1) survival, (2) safety, (3) belonging, (4) self-esteem, and (5) self-actualization.[2] Other theories examine components relating to the *external circumstances* in which people find themselves, such as the effects of job goals, salary, work obstructions, supervision, and leadership, which also influence motivation. HRM is involved in shaping many of these, not only through compensation but also through job design and even through selection that addresses factors inherent to individuals (U.S. Merit Systems Protection Board, 2012).

A key **principle of motivation** is that people are motivated to pursue their goals and satisfy their needs. As President Dwight D. Eisenhower put it, "Motivation is the art of getting people to do what you want them to do because they want to do it." Vroom's **expectancy theory of motivation** (1964) is a general theory that encompasses a variety of factors. Vroom's basic premise is that while people are motivated to satisfy their needs, they do so in ways that result in the greatest benefits/pleasure and minimal costs/pain. Specifically, people show effort in the expectation that this will produce performance results, which will lead to rewards that they can use to satisfy their needs; hence, efforts → performance → rewards → need attainment. This basic causal chain of events is based in three key (and obvious) assumptions:

1. The more value a person places on an outcome, the more effort he or she will put forward (valence of outcomes).

2. The more someone believes that he or she has the ability to achieve an outcome, the more effort that person is likely to put forward (expectancy of efforts).

3. The more an individual believes that rewards will be forthcoming as a result of his or her performance, the more effort the individual will put forward (instrumentality of performance).

These assumptions provide useful levers for managing motivation in others. Vroom's theory points to the need for managers to ensure that employees are committed to certain outcomes and that workers feel confident that they will be successful given their abilities and existing conditions (e.g., adequate training and resources) and the need for organizations to be reliable (e.g., not withholding rewards or creating false expectations). Research findings generally validate Vroom's assumptions and also provide useful, overarching starting points for administrators. For example, the first assumption points to managers giving employees compelling reasons to be motivated to pursue certain outcomes, helping them to achieve high valence. Employees may experience having to choose among competing outcomes—personal circumstances and nonwork motivations also affect the valuation of outcomes and efforts—and a manager's job is to help employees make effective choices. The second assumption points to supervisors providing encouraging and supportive feedback that helps employees to apply and develop themselves in pursuit of outcomes.

Underlying much of the above is the idea that people have intrinsic motivations. According to McGregor (1960), **Theory Y** states that people have adequate intrinsic motivations for work, such as needs for achievement and making a difference in the public realm. These intrinsic motivations strongly increase valance, and it is the manager's job to help workers channel and support such drives in appropriate ways, toward appropriate ends. By contrast, **Theory X** holds that people do not have adequate intrinsic motivations related to work and therefore need external inducements—that is, "carrots and sticks"—that prompt and increase their motivation to work. In the absence of external motivators, so the thinking goes, people will be inert or lazy in their approach to work. McGregor believed that in the first half of the 20th century too much emphasis was placed on Theory X, with employers motivating people by external (or extrinsic) factors (such as money, rewards, threats, and other [dis]incentives), and that not enough emphasis was placed on bringing out the internal (or intrinsic) drives (such as learning, creating, and achieving), which he believed would lead to greater creativity and performance in organizations (Theory Y). Exhibit 6.1 points to some of the cultural assumptions underlying this approach in the United States.

An implication is that today's organizations should also not put up with supervisors who are uncaring and who project an attitude that seems to say, "If employees don't like it here,

Exhibit 6.1 Cultural Roots of Motivation Theory

The views and theories presented here have their origins in U.S. culture, which includes assumptions that are not universally held. The pioneering studies of Geert Hofstede unambiguously document differences among cultures. In the United States, a motivational basis for working often lies in beliefs that work is good for people and that it is God's will that people should work, or beliefs that people find meaning in life through their work and that they should use their capabilities to the fullest extent. As Hofstede, Hofstede, and Minkov (2010) write, "These assumptions reflect the value propositions of an individualist and 'masculine' society such as the United States where McGregor grew up" (p. 329). Theory Y is grounded in Protestant values that see work as inherently good and as a path to salvation. Do people live to work or work to live? The answer for people in the United States often is the former.

Cultures vary, however. In Indonesia and other Southeast Asian societies, people believe that work is a necessity but not a goal in itself. A person's goal is to find his or her rightful place, which is to be in peace and harmony with the individual's circumstances and environment. People in these societies are also creative, but the drive is different and perhaps a bit less intense. They may also have a greater sense of being part of a group in which members support each other. There is a "work to live" view. Thus, American managers often find that employees from other cultures have different work styles, intensity, and expectations for supervisory direction. And while some people show less motivation than those in the United States, U.S. workers rank only 22nd in motivation for work on a list of 58 countries; workers from East Asian cultures show a great deal more work ethic (International Institute for Management Development, 2010). Culture affects a person's orientation toward motivation.

they can go elsewhere!" Old-fashioned carrot-and-stick approaches, when not tailored to the specific desires and conditions of individual employees, often become irrelevant irritants at best; at worst, they become fear-based management when the sticks outweigh the carrots. Such orientations do little to further employee engagement and are rightly recognized as unproductive and undesirable (Seijts & Crim, 2006). Similarly, employees are needed who bring some extra, internal motivation with them to succeed, and managers are needed who build on that to increase performance. As one manager has noted with regard to selection, "If I need to motivate you, then you are not the right person for the job" (quoted in Pink, 2009, p. 32). This may be overstated, but it surely makes the point about intrinsic motivations.

People need a degree of autonomy to solve problems, achieve high performance, and realize their intrinsic motivations. Management should ask for accountability after the fact rather than control throughout. In an academic vein, path-goal theory suggests that the job of the manager is to lay out clear and doable goals and to provide a clear path with few obstacles for employees (House, 1971; Locke & Latham, 1990). This idea has made its way into various management strategies, including management by objectives (MBO) in the 1970s, which one author sums up using five precepts (Odiorne, 1976):

1. Tell me what is expected of me in advance.
2. Give me the resources to do the job.
3. Leave me alone as much as possible to do my job.
4. Let me know how well I am doing in my work.
5. Reward my accomplishments.

This idea continues to inspire. Theory X is typically associated with a "push" style of management, whereas Theory Y and the MBO version are associated with a "pull" style of management that is especially appropriate for people who have "drive."

During the 1980s and 1990s, further progress was made on a number of fronts. Employee empowerment involves the delegation of decision making and other responsibilities to employees while holding them accountable for outcomes. Both Theory Y and MBO imply empowerment, as do other trends, such as heightened responsiveness to individualized consideration for clients. A key step in empowerment involves not only task selection (deciding what should be delegated) but also employee selection and working with people toward successful outcomes. Other advances include quality of work life (see Chapter 8) and increased customer orientation. Employee engagement builds on these advances. Analytically, though the concept of employee engagement is often defined as noted above, no standard measure of such engagement is yet in use. Academic studies typically assess aspects of vigor (e.g., "At work, I feel full of energy"), dedication (e.g., "I find the work that I do full of meaning and purpose"), and absorption ("I am immersed in my work") (Menguc, Auh, Fisher, & Haddad, 2013). Typically, multiple survey items are used to develop a composite measure of engagement, but practice-based research sometimes conflates measures of employee engagement with the drivers (causes) of employee engagement, hence engendering some confusion and criticism;[3] The distinction matters, of course.

Recent studies point to several drivers of employee engagement: (1) supervisory support and encouragement; (2) recognition, praise, and developmental feedback (e.g., "In the last seven days, I have received recognition or praise for doing good work"); (3) role clarity and resource adequacy (e.g., "I know what is expected of me on the job," and having the resources to do it); (4) supportive coworkers who are (also) committed to doing high-quality work; (5) having the opportunity to do what one does best (e.g., "My talents are used well"); (6) having opportunities to learn and grow (e.g., "Supervisors/team leaders in my work unit support employee development"); (7) alignment, support, and belief in the mission or purpose of one's work; and (8) having a voice (e.g., "My opinion counts at work"). No single factor or magic bullet is the key to employee engagement, and it is likely that all of these drivers matter. However, the actions of the supervisor do appear to be central, either directly or indirectly affecting almost all of these engagement conditions (being supportive, providing feedback and resources, encouraging development, aligning mission with employee valence). In short, organizations need to do well in appointing good supervisors and selecting the right people for particular jobs who have good intrinsic motivation ("drive") for doing high-quality work.

Context

The "big picture" of theory presented above surely raises questions and issues regarding applicability in practice. Continuing interest in the use of rewards and incentives has inspired a vast stream of research. Rewards and incentives surely induce motivation, but they should be used with caution. First, people who are motivated by rewards can quickly become dependent on those rewards: Once they have received rewards, they expect "their" rewards again, or they sharply lose motivation. In experiments, people who have had previous rewards for performing a task taken away have been found to work less hard than those who were never given rewards. Second, while rewards can put fun into work for routine tasks, rewards take the fun out of work that is intrinsically motivated. People who are creatively busy often enjoy their tasks and regard these as fun (Csikszentmihalyi, 2008). But when the goal is changed to maximizing extrinsic rewards (e.g., billable hours), intrinsic motivations are quickly "crowded out," and work becomes "just work" and is at risk of becoming dreary (Pink, 2009). Third, excessive or exclusive reliance on rewards is associated with adverse incentives, causing problems such as ethical lapses, which have been well documented in some areas (e.g., in the financial industry; Sorkin, 2009). In short, motivating by rewards is not a substitute for ensuring employee engagement.

These findings are also present in compensation. When people perceive that they lack sufficient salary (e.g., to support the lifestyle they desire), the prospect of making more money motivates. Jobs that do not bring enough salary to satisfy very basic needs fail to motivate ("Why work?"), and employee turnover in low-paying jobs is indeed very high. However, once people are able to satisfy a broad range of their needs (basic comfort and security needs), money no longer motivates quite as much.[4] While prospects of a significant pay increase will again spark motivation (allowing for meeting previously unmet needs), once a higher pay level is reached, motivation soon returns to where it was before. Thus, the motivational boost of prospective money is only temporary. Further, for some people an emphasis on pay may drive out intrinsic motivation and pleasure. In short, (1) the lack of money demotivates, (2) the prospect of making more money motivates, but (3) permanent higher salaries are not associated with permanent higher motivation.

A paradox of employee engagement is that while the public sector lacks financial inducements comparable to those available in the private sector, research suggests that money alone is not sufficient to ensure higher levels of engagement and motivation Rather, managing engagement in the public sector requires following the models discussed above, using a mix of selection, feedback, achievement, recognition, and growth opportunity. Of course, money and incentives are important. Surely it is difficult to attract good workers with below-market pay rates, and it is difficult to keep good workers if one cannot offer them advancement opportunities. All personnel, regardless of motivation, also need to be told what the limits are to their behavior. Rewards have their place—including nonfinancial inducements for performance, such as conference travel or new office equipment—but a different and broader approach is also needed.

As the importance of intrinsic and nonfinancial motivation has come to be recognized, in recent years some effort has gone into better measuring *public service motivation* (PSM), defined as a service ethic of civil servants that explains their intrinsic motivation to serve. Key dimensions of this ethic are assumed to be attraction to policy making, commitment to furthering the public interest, commitment to social justice, commitment to civic duty, compassion about the welfare of others, and commitment to self-sacrifice for public causes (Perry, 1996, 2000; Wright, Moynihan, & Pandey, 2012). The findings of the many studies of PSM in the past decade suggest to practitioners specific levers they can use to increase mission valance for employees (such as by encouraging participation in policy processes, appealing to employees' sense of social justice or interest in social welfare, and providing opportunities to further the public interest).

Researchers also note that autonomy and control should be *contingent* on tasks and people; some situations may in fact be suitable for a stronger emphasis on rewards. Some jobs really are monotonous and repetitive, offering workers little room for creativity or exploring their own intrinsic needs. Under such conditions, rewards can turn boring work into a gamelike activity (e.g., how to finish sooner) and thereby increase motivation, as can more autonomy where appropriate (e.g., flextime, relaxed dress code). Also, not everyone has abundant inner drive, and some people like to be told in great detail which procedures they should follow. Greater freedom is not always welcomed. Again, extrinsic factors such as money, instrumental power, and status (McClelland, 1985) provide clear "rules of the game" and conditions that give people an incentive and a bigger and better future to fight for. The contingency perspective acknowledges that theory needs to be applied with consideration given to specific contexts and outcomes. For example, while management control and worker autonomy are easily posited as theoretical opposites, in some jobs, such as emergency management, both are strongly present. Theory Y is preferred for employee engagement, but Theory X must at times be used.

In recent years, employers have recognized the importance of promoting an adequate level of creativity in jobs that require it. Some of the most creative and successful companies (e.g., 3M) give their workers self-directed hours in which their only task is to do something creative and different. In Seoul, the capital of South Korea and one of the world's largest cities, city managers and workers are expected to come up with creative suggestions and are given team time to develop these (Berman & Kim, 2010). Such opportunities appeal strongly to employees whose intrinsic motivation is based in creativity and are clearly consistent with increasing engagement. Another practice is to give employees opportunities for accomplishment and achievement. Some employees and managers relish pursuing especially difficult tasks. Matching the task with the right person is a key management function in taking advantage of these motivations. Exhibit 6.2 considers motivational differences across generations.

In broader context, high-wage workers can no longer compete in the world on the basis of skills or education alone, as employers can find people in India and China with similar levels of college education and skills at a fraction of the cost. Rather, high-wage workers must justify their wages by displaying creativity in bringing forth improved products, services, technologies, and other high-value-added contributions. The strategies of 3M, the city of Seoul, and other organizations reflect this. The competitiveness of cities and regions also depends on the creativity of public sector workers in developing and mining new ways of making their jurisdictions more attractive for residents and business. Additionally, high labor costs and tight tax revenues put pressure on public agencies in managing their routine work. Contracting out to private sector firms and the increased use of part-time workers put more pressure on remaining public servants to be creative, effective, and forward-looking. In Singapore, for example, senior civil servants are expected to "think ahead, think again, and think across" in their work, and they are evaluated, rewarded, and retained based on these abilities (for discussion, see Neo & Chen, 2007).

Exhibit 6.2 Motivating the Millennial Generation

Do younger employees differ from older workers in their motivations? Many managers seem to think so, and an emerging literature agrees with them. In *Motivating the "What's in It for Me?" Workforce,* Cam Marston (2007) argues that earlier generations of workers (Baby Boomers and those Marston calls "Matures") were motivated to work by making an income and having identity through their professions and employment by their organizations. They were willing to "pay their dues" and "wait their turn" in return for increasing growth opportunities. In contrast, younger workers, Generation Xers and New Millennials, are motivated to make just enough money to enjoy the lifestyles they seek. Others see Millennials as enterprising workers who are energetically following their dreams on their own terms. In any event, they have loyalty to people who can help them but not to employers (organizations did not show loyalty to workers in their parents' generation, so why should they be loyal to organizations?). Millennials are likely to stay with their employers as long as the work is interesting, is educational, and serves their needs. Young employees are far more demanding of their employers than were their counterparts of past generations, and it is a greater challenge to HRM systems to keep the most talented ones.

HUMAN RESOURCE MANAGEMENT AND THE CLIMATE FOR ENGAGEMENT

HRM affects employee engagement largely through the strategies, tools, and conditions that it provides for supervisors and employees, as well as through the specific management and supervisory processes that it champions and supports. HRM provides a broad range of strategies, tools, and conditions that employees and supervisors can apply in the pursuit of employee engagement. The workplace **climate for engagement** consists of the opportunities employees have to be engaged at work, which, in part, are determined by the range of human resource management policies and practices. An analogy would be to view human resource management practices as a cafeteria or buffet in which each employee values the selections differently. People differ in their goals and needs and what they seek and what they are willing to accommodate. Most employees, employers hope, will be satisfied by whatever selections they have made (even if some are mandatory). This section looks at the "HRM menu," while the next examines two specific strategies that supervisors can use to increase employee motivation and engagement.

From the perspective of managers and their organizations, the elements listed below constitute a general climate for engagement. Motivation is furthered when individuals have the opportunity to meet their needs, and engagement is furthered when motivation is combined with opportunities for applying that motivation in the workplace. The discussion below builds on the preceding, considering both drivers of engagement and consideration of rewards, public service motivation, and more. When all of the following efforts and conditions are present, employees, while drawn toward each to differing degrees, will likely find a combination that provides them with adequate motivation and opportunity for engagement:

- Competitive salaries and relevant benefits
- Meaningful rewards and recognition (that are fairly distributed)
- Friendly and cooperative workplace relations
- Assignments that allow workers to make meaningful contributions to society
- Feedback that provides recognition
- Opportunities for challenge and development
- Meaningful control over the work environment
- Minimization of the demotivating effect of rules and regulations that impede job performance and satisfaction
- Reduction of negative supervisory relationships
- Selection of the right people for the job

Readers can readily verify that an environment with these conditions is likely to be attractive, motivating, and engaging. Would you like to work in an organization in which these conditions are present? The factors listed above are associated with the previously mentioned groups of needs and are affected by human resource management policies and practices. These connections are shown below; many also are explored in other chapters of this book.

1. *Competitive salaries and relevant benefits.* At-market compensation helps employees meet their basic needs for physical security and more. By giving employees a sense that they are receiving a fair return for their efforts, employers also further retention. Some employers also try to give their excellent staff above-market wages. For all these reasons, it is important that remuneration is periodically adjusted to remain competitive. Beyond this, benefits assist workers to meet health care, retirement, education, and other needs. In the United States, fewer and fewer of these needs are subsidized through taxes, and employees depend on their employers to help them address these concerns. By contrast, citizens in other developed countries can often count on affordable, government-subsidized benefits. Employers now offer cafeteria-style menus of benefits that have become important. Compensation and benefits are explored in Chapters 7 and 8, respectively.

2. *Meaningful rewards and recognition (that are fairly distributed).* People need appreciation, not only that expressed by compensation but also appreciation shown through formal recognition and informal thank-yous. Appraisal systems (Chapter 10) should provide sufficient appreciation and recognition, but in practice they often fail to do so; more is needed. HRM can help to encourage alternative forms of rewards and recognition. In some organizations, workers can make instant, on-the-spot awards to others in the form of gift certificates, thus reducing delays and providing peer recognition. Workers also need to perceive that rewards are fairly distributed.

3. *Friendly and cooperative workplace relations.* Employees prefer to come to a congenial work setting. While this may or may not be associated with increased motivation, an office that is perceived as hostile is a demotivator (Cherniss & Goleman, 2001). For this reason, most organizations make "people skills" a criterion in their hiring and promotion. According to Berman and West (2008), 71.5% of city managers in U.S. cities with populations over 50,000 agree or strongly agree that they focus on people skills when hiring or promoting managers. A subsequent section of this chapter offers suggestions for how managers can increase friendly and cooperative relations on the job.

4. *Assignments that allow workers to make meaningful contributions to society.* Most people who go to work for public and nonprofit organizations do so because they are motivated to make a difference in society. This is an essential part of public service motivation, and it reflects the fundamental achievement need that many people in such organizations have. Needless to say, the task of human resource management is to design jobs that allow for having such impact, and the task of managers is to ensure that in fact they do. Some studies show that modern management practices and better agency performance increase employee motivation, presumably in part by fostering workers' needs for achievement and making a difference (Boardman & Sundquist, 2009).

5. *Feedback that provides recognition.* Feedback is not only part of formal performance appraisal (Chapter 10); the challenges of work require frequent assessment and adjustment. Feedback serves essential approval and improvement purposes, and giving it in a positive way (even when the message is not positive) is a part of the manager's job. This chapter considers how managers can do that. This skill also lies at the heart of the "one-minute manager" (Blanchard & Johnson, 1981), who provides frequent and concise feedback to employees.

6. *Opportunities for challenge and development.* Making the most of other people's strengths and the least of their weaknesses is a surefire formula for managerial success. Many employees enjoy the experience of being deeply immersed in their work, and some have a need for growth and learning (Theory Y). The lack of meaningful work challenges is a demotivator for productive and creative people. Chapter 9 discusses training and development that can be used to provide growth opportunities, which are associated with increasing engagement and career development.

7. *Meaningful control over the work environment.* Being in control is a source of motivation, as it allows people to tailor their job experiences in ways that affect their satisfaction (e.g., choosing office decor; setting flextime schedules or telecommuting, both discussed in Chapter 8). The lack of such control reduces satisfaction. More important is the extent to which the employee is subject to the whims of others, especially when preferences collide and communication is poor. Exhibit 6.3 looks at one way in which employees may benefit from having control over their work (i.e., how and when they take breaks).

8. *Minimizing the demotivating effect of rules and regulations.* The job of the manager is to make it possible for workers to accomplish their tasks, and that includes finding ways of meeting the requirements of rules and regulations or working around them when appropriate. While recognizing that many requirements have been adopted for good reason (such as to ensure accountability), Herzberg, Mausner, and Snyderman (1959) long ago noted that demotivators such as bad rules and regulations get in the way of workers' performance and motivation; the negative side effects of these rules are recognized, and a task of the manager is to reduce the impact of these effects. Increasingly, organizations are trying to meet accountability needs in post hoc and less burdensome ways.

9. *Reducing negative supervisory relationships.* People need to get along, especially with their bosses. The failure to get along with supervisors can be a source of serious stress and distraction that severely demotivates many employees (Van Wart, 2005). Traditionally, supervisory relations were thought to have more downsides than upsides, being sources of control, stress, and disappointment. The cost of supervisor–employee conflict can be high for organizations, and today's focus on employee engagement includes the recognition that supervisory relations are key and need to emphasize support, encouragement, development feedback, and opportunity.

10. *Selecting the right people for the job.* Last but not least, selecting the right person for the job is key. It should no longer be enough that applicants are qualified for jobs; they must be well motivated, accomplished, and able to get along with others in supportive and engaged ways (recruitment and selection are discussed in Chapters 3 and 4, respectively). The selection of supervisors is especially important, as supervisors set the tone for engagement for their work groups.

The conditions described above provide for a work environment in which many employee needs can be met. The entire set of these practices and policies matters, and human resource management is concerned with ensuring that the entire range of these practices is fulfilled. People vary in their needs, and while they may be unclear about them and reluctant to disclose them, the above practices and conditions provide a broad range of ways to satisfy employee needs.

In broader context, federal workers are quite satisfied with their work and their working conditions as they relate to the above factors: 90% agree or strongly agree that the work they do is important, 96% agree or strongly agree that "when needed I am willing to put in the extra effort to get a job done," 79% know what is expected of them, 80% agree or strongly agree that their supervisors treat them with respect, and 72% agree or strongly agree that employees in their work units share job knowledge with each other. Overall, 64% agree or strongly agree that they are satisfied with their jobs, and 63% would recommend their organizations as good places to work. There are, however, some areas for further improvement: 57% agree or strongly agree that their talents are well used, 46% agree or strongly agree that they are satisfied with the recognition they receive for doing a good job, and only 40% agree or strongly agree that their units are able to recruit people with the right skills. Variation surely exists. About half, 54%, also agree or strongly agree that they are satisfied with their pay (U.S. Office of Personnel Management [U.S. OPM], 2013). These survey results, while not perfect measures of engagement or even motivation, paint a favorable picture of the climate for engagement and motivation, which, in a previous report, was

Exhibit 6.3 The Effective Manager . . . Takes a Break

Being motivated does not always mean working hard at all times. Berman and West (2007) have shown that managers who take breaks report themselves as being more effective, with less stress, than those who do not take breaks. Yet U.S. culture sometimes confuses break taking with slacking off or not being motivated or serious: "Attitudes have not always been very positive about managers taking breaks. Managers experience very busy schedules . . . and they may perceive that taking a break will set a bad example, encouraging workers to work less, thereby feeding negative stereotypes of public sector employees" (Berman & West, 2007, p. 381).

Some managers take breaks during lunch, whereas others take short breaks during the day, often about 10 or 15 minutes each. Doing so clears and restores the mind. Managers also do well to encourage their subordinates to take breaks. It is not the work activity that counts, but the quality of the work that is actually completed.

found to be comparable with (or only slightly less than) conditions found in the private sector. Using workers' talents and input well is a matter not only of motivation but also of workplace performance.

Organizations can use the above items to create a **climate for engagement checklist**. For each item, managers and other employees can rate whether they strongly agree, agree, somewhat agree, somewhat disagree, disagree, or strongly disagree that each element is present in their organization or workplace. What improvements do they suggest?

TOOLS OF ENGAGEMENT

Managers have a broad array of tools at their disposal for increasing the engagement and motivation of workers. Some of these, such as compensation, promotion, and relevant benefits, are discussed in later chapters. In the remainder of this chapter, the focus is on some interpersonal strategies that help managers know and shape the goals of workers (or, in terms of motivation theory, their needs and valences), assess and address workers' "instrumentality" (the feasibility of the goal of need attainment), and assess and take corrective action to ensure performance and goal attainment. Managers and employees surely need to be proficient in the matters discussed below that affect their interpersonal relations at work.

Psychological Contracts

While the policies and practices described above set the climate for engagement, managers and employees are likely to find that some tailoring and accommodation are necessary. Managers should recognize, for example, the extent to which any specific worker desires a challenging assignment or seeks to learn a new skill. They need to find out from workers whether they are interested in flextime or telecommuting. Administrators cannot read the minds of employees, and they are apt to make errors if they assume that they know what motivates their staff. More communication can often make both workers and their managers better off. Employees are not always aware of what opportunities exist for them, nor are supervisors always clear about employees intentions and underutilized skills. Remember, too, that supervisors have good reason for ensuring that employees understand the valance of their role outcomes.

One tool for increasing employee engagement and performance is the **psychological contract** (Guest, 2007; Rousseau, 1995). It builds on the famous management by objectives insight that involvement of workers in goal formation increases buy-in and mutual understanding many times over. Whereas the original MBO efforts focused on formal and documented aspects of joint goal setting (Drucker, 1954), psychological contracts are unwritten understandings about mutual needs, goals, expectations, and procedures. Such agreements go beyond employment contracts, which typically specify salary, benefits, modes of feedback, and working hours; it can be said that psychological contracts begin where formal employment contracts leave off. These informal understandings improve the fit between individuals and the organization, and better fit is associated with increased motivation and reduced turnover (Bright, 2008).

Psychological contracts are potentially far-reaching (any issue is fair game), but they are usually limited to highly valued concerns. Topics can include the amount or nature of work, work schedules, growth opportunities, responsibilities and performance objectives, the frequency and nature of managerial feedback, preferred work styles, behaviors that are bothersome, job security, possible rewards, workplace autonomy, support in dealing with child care responsibilities, and so forth. Psychological contracts increase engagement by allowing managers to better understand the needs of individual employees, by helping to provide rewards and conditions that address individual needs, and by ensuring clarity about roles and expectations.

Psychological contracts are a relatively new tool. They can be used at any level of the organization, involving employees in the very highest or lowest positions. A decade ago, a survey of senior local government managers found that 57.3% of them established psychological contracts with employees, but only about a fifth of these (20.7%) said that they fully employed the processes described below (Berman & West, 2003a). Some administrators referred to psychological contracts as "informal agreements" or "mutual understandings." The study also found that the use of psychological contracts was associated with encouraging employees to take up new challenges and promoting a productive organizational culture. More recently, Berman, Chen, Jan, and Huang (2013) examined the use of psychological contracts between very senior civil servants and deputy ministers in Taiwan. About half of the civil servant respondents reported having psychological contracts with their deputy ministers, and among those who did, 75% agreed that their agencies frequently developed innovative programs, compared with only 46% of respondents who did not.

Managers can readily establish psychological contracts with subordinates. For example, a manager may go to an employee and note that it has been some time since their last conversation. The manager says that she would like to know how things are going and asks whether there is anything that might be done to make the employee's work go better. Following the employee's somewhat surprised response, the manager asks whether the employee has anything he would like to achieve or improve or do over the next few months. Then, as the employee answers, the manager discusses each possibility with the employee. The fact that a subordinate wants something does not mean that a manager can make it happen. Thus, the manager gives evaluative responses to the employee's ideas,

Exhibit 6.4 The Psychological Contract

	Psychological Contract	
	Expect to Get	**Expect to Give**
Worker		
Supervisor or other		

SOURCE: Adapted from Osland, Kolb, and Rubin (2000).

explaining why each (1) can be done (e.g., training or flextime), (2) cannot be met (a salary increase over which the manager might not have control), or (3) can be met in a modified form only (the manager might not have control over promotion but can help through assignments to make the employee more competitive). The manager's job is to help the employee embrace these understandings and facts.

Next, the manager informs the employee that while the list is a good one, the manager has some job-related needs as well. Perhaps some project needs to be completed, such as a pilot test on a new strategy. In addition, the manager may raise concerns she has about the employee's performance or skills. She then suggests a way to resolve the paradox of needs, for example, by asking the employee to make an increased commitment to improvement in return for her assisting him in meeting some of his needs. Thus, some employee contributions are seen as conditions for the manager's helping to meet the employee's needs. Exhibit 6.4 shows the basic give-and-take that the psychological contract entails.

After the worker and the manager have agreed on all their needs, the manager summarizes the discussion and notes that situations and other things do change. The door remains open for communication between worker and manager, especially regarding perceived misunderstandings. The manager should mention the psychological contract to the employee at least twice over the next few weeks, because people sometimes "forget" things or do not take them very seriously unless they are repeated.

While it is easier for a manager to initiate a psychological contract with a subordinate than for a subordinate to take the lead, sometimes subordinates can initiate such dialogues with their supervisors or with coworkers. Psychological contracts are also easily established within the first few weeks of employment, before routine patterns of communication set in.

Several factors make psychological contracts effective as a tool of engagement: (1) They help bring to light workers' goals or the needs that motivate them, (2) they allow managers to clarify workers' aims and evaluate the extent to which those needs can be met, (3) they are perceived as a fair balance between what workers want and what workers are expected to give, and (4) they have mechanisms for following up, ensuring that the agreement is put to work and addressing changes that may occur. The engagement properties of psychological contracts come from managers' earnest efforts to reach out and increase mutual involvement. The psychological contract process is a vehicle for strengthening expectations about mutual contributions, and performance improvement comes from agreement and information that otherwise might not be brought up.

It might also be noted that psychological contracts are rooted in modern Western culture. The assumption that employees and managers welcome talking about their needs and reaching alignment with others is not universal. In workplaces in some Confucian (East Asian) cultures, for example, it is assumed that the boss knows what is good for employees and that employees show loyalty by working hard in return. These assumptions work against communication, and young workers often leave when their needs and expectations go unmet, rather than trying to talk about them. In the United States, members of the Baby Boomer generation may not be very good at talking about these matters; they often prefer that others just do their duties and act their roles (Berman & Berman, 2011).

Such attitudes are seen as increasingly dated, furthering mediocrity, and being too incompatible with the younger generation and increased diversity in the United States. Increased communication and openness does not mean that people always get what they want, but it improves performance and alignment (see, e.g., Schwartz, 2010).

A psychological contract assumes that people can have a rational dialogue and are susceptible to reason. Making a psychological contract is especially (but not only) useful when people begin a new employment relationship. At that point there is considerable uncertainty, and interaction and communication patterns are still fluid and subject to change. Agreements can also be made among group members, or between a group and the group leader. This can be accomplished through a discussion about what the group wants to get or do and what the group is willing to give (and give up) to get what the members want. The understandings are then written down, distributed, and reviewed a few weeks later. The later review demonstrates commitment to the contract and allows for dealing with whatever may have come up in the meantime. Establishing psychological contracts is an approach that helps get agreement and alignment among group members and, hence, helps motivate workers.

Exhibit 6.5 shows an example of an actual psychological contract between a supervisor and her employee. According to Berman and West (2003a), the most common topics addressed in such contracts are workload issues (87%), working relationship with supervisor (79%), work schedules (75%), job security (70%), specific rewards and promotion (58%), responsibility or authority (56%), and work quality (52%). People who use psychological contracts often report increased communication and satisfaction. One manager who used a psychological contract provides this feedback:

> I am pleased to say that all is going well with the psychological contract entered into with Ms. Johnson, Director of Development. We have continued to meet on a regular basis and discussion continues to be open and fruitful. Our meetings include each of us going over any project we feel the other needs to know about. While my door is always open to any staff member, Gail has taken the initiative to stop in more often just to touch base on pending projects.
>
> Over this past month, we have had to deal with some difficult issues, including the postponement of our largest event of the year, due to delays in a major project. She continues to work with a great deal of autonomy that is important to her, and because I see the result of her working within this capacity, I am happy to give her more independence. It has been a good experience, one that will continue. I hope to enter into such contracts with the other five department heads.

Giving Feedback

Feedback is evaluative information given to employees about their performance or behavior, the purpose of which is to influence future performance or behavior. It is increasingly being recognized as an important element in the promotion of employee engagement. Employees should receive feedback frequently and consistently, in a timely and positive way. Effectiveness is lost when feedback is given sporadically, is far removed from the

Exhibit 6.5 Sample Psychological Contract

What supervisor wants from employee:

- Timely arrival at work
- More engagement in oversight of Web maintenance and postings
- Preparation of weekly employment scorecard
- Preparation of weekly updates of orders, account totals, and monetary shortfalls
- Ensuring that orders are processed in compliance with joint forces travel regulations

What employee is willing to give to supervisor:

- Greater attention to punctuality
- More commitment to professional training in department
- More engagement in daily operations and more frequent updates on account balances and pending orders

What employee wants from supervisor:

- Training in new IT program
- Better understanding of use of weekly and monthly products
- Time to finish associate's degree

What supervisor is willing to give to employee:

- Enrollment in off-site training for IT upgrades
- Greater visibility on internal decision-making processes as well as feedback on internal politics and how they affect products
- Time off work to finish associate's degree

moment of performance, or is presented in less than constructive ways. A common error that managers make is to assume that workers are receiving feedback, such as through others, when in fact they may not be.

The **strategy for feedback** is straightforward. Managers should take care to do the following:

- Provide balanced assessments of employees' performance (including both positive and negative aspects)
- Emphasize the objective nature of service outcomes (although some facts are indisputable)
- Establish their commitment to helping subordinates achieve positive results
- Work collaboratively with employees to develop strategies for improving performance (without imposing solutions)
- Help employees develop the perspective that they have the power to affect conditions for success

- Agree with employees on timetables for monitoring improvement
- Provide employees with strategies for obtaining support and feedback
- Offer employees future rewards for improvement

This approach helps minimize problems that occur in practice: (1) Workers do not receive sufficient feedback, (2) feedback is given that does not contain adequate information, or (3) feedback is interpreted in ways that do not result in desired changes. The lack of feedback affects motivation among those who need appreciation. Inadequate feedback can be frustrating for those who seek to do better but do not know exactly what is expected or required of them. Feedback that is curt and disrespectful is clearly dysfunctional, especially for those who seek cooperative workplace relations. Moreover, impulsive or emotional outbursts of managers are apt to have negative and demotivating effects. Such outbursts usually contain nothing that can be construed as being helpful. While they may induce short-term improvement, they can also cause long-term resentment.

People are often less skilled in giving feedback than they think they are. People who need little feedback think that others are just like them, and so they give little feedback, too. Some managers give feedback a bit too directly, perhaps with little social tact. It is therefore most helpful for supervisors to receive periodic feedback from subordinates—something some organizations now require. For example, one human resource director described her experience:

> I was evaluated by the city manager, assistant city manager, department directors, legal department, and other direct reports. Each responded anonymously to about 50 close-ended questions (scale from one to ten) and a half dozen open-ended questions. Some questions dealt with social and communication skills. The summary report by the consultant was 12 to 18 pages, outlining my strengths and weaknesses. (quoted in Berman & West, 2008, p. 747)

Such detailed feedback is useful for managers, of course, and it is sometimes quite serious when the area of feedback is also the subject of ongoing employee concerns.

Finally, individualized approaches also exist for dealing with unsatisfactory performance. There are instances in which feedback cannot wait until the next formal performance appraisal—sometimes performance is poor and needs to be corrected quickly. The nature of underlying problems can be highly diverse. A person might be in the wrong position and unable to get the work done well; perhaps the supervisor or organization would do best to find another job for that person. In other instances, however, as the 25–50–25 rule predicts, some employees stubbornly refuse to be motivated. For example, some people are just plain unhappy, and others use being upset as a tool for gaining attention and control over others. Still others bully coworkers and are a destructive influence at work. For managers, all such situations require responses, not only because they affect individual performance but also because they may have a disruptive influence on unit performance.

In short, what is a manager to do when feedback based on rational discourse and a spirit of cooperation does not produce the desired result? Limits to rational discourse must be acknowledged. The point of further interaction is to minimize the impact of unsatisfactory behaviors. The basic strategy for **dealing with difficult people** is to arrest patterns of inter-action with the difficult person through avoidance, setting boundaries, and confronting each difficult behavior in appropriate and controlling ways (Bramson, 1981; Heathfield, 2008; Lubit, 2004). Typically, after several documented interactions, managers would do well to contact their human resource directors and discuss next steps. One such action is to remove the employee from interaction with mission-critical functions until he or she demonstrates improved performance and behaviors. A second action is for the manager to stand his or her ground on boundaries, setting limits that are not to be crossed (such as speaking rudely or coming in late). Over time, consistently and immediately responding to such problems can result in a pattern of documented poor performance that can be used in subsequent discipline (see Chapter 10).

Unhappily for some supervisors and their organizations, the story seldom ends here. Difficult employees may seek to avoid being disciplined by corrupting, compromising, or

---

Exhibit 6.6 Poor People Management

Good management is not only about doing the right thing; it is often about avoiding doing the wrong things. Being a manager means being confronted with one's own ways and instincts, which may not always be right. But it is not always easy to avoid these, and most managers have a few areas of weakness, for sure. Numerous sources of information about bad management and things that managers should avoid, many of which are the flip side of those stated here, are available online. For example, Heathfield (2011) identifies 10 mistakes that managers make:

- Not getting to know employees as people
- Failing to provide clear direction
- Failing to trust
- Failing to listen
- Failing to get input before decisions are made
- Failing to react to problems
- Trying to be friends with those who report to them
- Failing to communicate and withholding important information
- Not treating everyone equally
- Blaming employees rather than taking responsibility for when things go wrong

Many of these are mentioned in this chapter—people skills are essential to performance, but when managers just do not see or correct their own deficiencies they become a source of worker demotivation and poor or mediocre performance. Getting managers to see their behaviors as problematic is often the first step toward improvement. Managers, too, can benefit from receiving feedback and making psychological contracts with others.

SOURCE: Adapted from Heathfield, 2011

blackmailing their supervisors through social or ethical embarrassment. Some threaten legal action, such as discrimination or harassment lawsuits. The possibility of people gathering "dirt" on others with whom they work over several months or years is very real, of course—everyone has said or done something that other people could try to use to their advantage. The quid pro quo of such silent agreements (or standoffs: "I won't embarrass or sue you if you don't . . .") can allow difficult employees to stay on the job for years. Sometimes organizations even deal with such people by promoting them out of their current jobs. While we do not know what percentage of employees may be "difficult," most administrators have had some brushes with such employees. A reasonable guess is that 1 out of every 20 or 30 employees could be described as difficult, depending on how one defines the term. Human resource directors earn their pay not only by creating conditions for motivation but also by being confidential aides to managers in dealing with these situations. Addressing employee motivation sometimes means dealing with the darker side of human motives. Exhibit 6.6 provides a bit more reflection on poor people management in general.

SUMMARY AND CONCLUSION

The promotion of employee engagement is an important management task. When people are engaged, they work with energy, enthusiasm, and initiative. *Engagement* is defined as being psychologically present when performing one's job and applying oneself physically, cognitively, and emotionally. The concept of employee engagement includes motivation as well as its behavioral manifestations at work. Levels of engagement vary widely among workers: The 25–50–25 rule states that 25% of employees are highly motivated, 50% are somewhat inspired, and 25% are withdrawn or cynical. While this rule has not been validated by research, many managers feel that it generally represents their experience. Studies also show that employee engagement is widely associated with increased performance and reduced turnover.

Supervisory support, encouragement, and development are frequently mentioned as drivers of employee engagement, but other drivers include role clarity and resource adequacy; supportive coworkers who are (also) committed to doing high-quality work; having the opportunity to do what one does best; having opportunities to learn and grow; alignment, support, and belief in the mission or purpose of one's work; and having a voice in the workplace. No single factor or magic bullet is the key to employee engagement, but supervisors are central, either directly or indirectly affecting almost all of these conditions.

Human resource management affects employee engagement largely through the strategies, tools, and conditions that it provides for supervisors and employees, as well as through the specific management and supervisory processes that it champions and supports. HRM provides many conditions and resources that set the stage for employee engagement. Engagement is promoted by competitive salaries and relevant benefits, meaningful rewards and recognition, friendly workplace relations, work that allows employees to make meaningful contributions to society, feedback that provides recognition and opportunity for development, opportunities for challenging assignments and learning, control over the work environment, reduction of the negative impacts of rules and regulations, reduction of poor supervisory relationships, and selection of the right people for the job. Human resource management does much to shape these factors. Both drivers and HRM conditions should be applied with consideration to specific contexts and outcomes.

Finally, HRM should champion specific management strategies that strengthen employee engagement. This chapter has discussed two such strategies that are especially relevant to employee–supervisor relations: psychological contracts and feedback. Psychological contracts help workers and supervisors to increase alignment and also provide channels for increased communication for dealing with barriers and other issues. Myriad topics are appropriate for psychological contracts, including workloads and schedules, communication styles, and responsibilities and rewards. Feedback is a key to performance, and appreciation should be factual and task oriented, with the purpose of improving outcomes.

The promotion of employee engagement is a multifaceted endeavor, and managers should understand that high levels of engagement are associated with improved performance and the retention of human capital.

KEY TERMS

Climate for engagement
Climate for engagement checklist
Dealing with difficult people
Employee engagement
Expectancy theory of motivation
Feedback
Hierarchy of needs

Motivation
Principle of motivation
Psychological contract
Strategy for feedback
Theory X
Theory Y
25–50–25 rule

EXERCISES

Class Discussion

1. Based on your experience, what levels of engagement do you see in the organizations with which you are familiar? Do you agree that the 25–50–25 rule is accurate? What are the characteristics of workplaces in which employees are actively engaged or disengaged? Do you agree with the assertion that supervisor–employee relations are at the heart of efforts to ensure employee engagement?

2. Discuss what motivates people the most in their jobs in order to verify the claims that "people are motivated to pursue and satisfy their needs," and "people vary in their needs." How can a manager motivate employees when their needs differ? Is motivation too difficult to accomplish? Is it reasonable to attempt to motivate people using mostly "carrots and sticks"?

3. Examine the list of items that promote a "climate for engagement" and develop a list of specific activities that could affect engagement. Identify those HRM activities that might do the most to increase engagement.

4. Consider the statement that "difficult employees may seek to avoid being disciplined by corrupting, compromising, or blackmailing their supervisors through social, sexual, or ethical embarrassment." Can you provide any examples of this? Can you identify any movies that show this theme? What is the impact of such employees on the engagement and motivation of others? What would you do if you were to experience such behaviors?

Team Activities

5. Assume that the members of your group are responsible for a group project, such as a group presentation for your class. Make a psychological contract for the group. Discuss what people need to give and what they expect to receive. Discuss how you would implement the agreement so that it shapes behavior and expectations.

6. Identify and discuss in your team the characteristics of supervisors that motivate and increase employee engagement. How would you recruit and select for these elements? How would you interview for these and be confident in the responses of job candidates?

7. Indicate the needs that your team members have at work. What are the most important needs for them? What are the less important needs? How important is money? Do you agree that permanent higher salaries are not associated with permanent higher motivation? If so, how would you deal with motivating workers who already make a good amount of money?

Individual Assignments

8. Give three examples of how Vroom's expectancy theory applies to situations you have experienced.

9. Identify ways in which your immediate supervisor has knowingly and unknowingly affected your motivation. Which of these increased your motivation? Which decreased your motivation? How would you like to be motivated?

10. Make a psychological contract with someone, preferably a work colleague or someone working under you. To ensure that the understanding works out, discuss what you want from that person and what that person is willing to give, as well as what that person expects to get from you and what you are willing to give. Then make the contract and put it in place for a few weeks. What are the results? Was there improvement in any sense? What might you do differently next time?

11. Think of a specific situation in which you gave feedback. What impact did it have? How can you improve the effectiveness of your feedback?

12. Job seekers usually do not have good information about the climate for engagement in the organizations of prospective employers. What questions might you ask during a job interview to better gauge this important aspect? How can you trust the answers that are given to you?

NOTES

1. Gallup (2013) has reported that worldwide only 13% of employees are engaged in their jobs, but in the United States the figure is 30%.

2. Later work cast doubt on the hierarchical order of these needs and identified other needs as well. However, the needs mentioned in Maslow's pioneering work are still relevant. For example, the need for survival can be understood to include the need to ensure survival through securing health insurance coverage as well future retirement income. It may take a little imagination to find examples, but Maslow's categories remain relevant today.

3. This includes frequently cited work by Gallup and the federal government (see, e.g., Gallup, 2013, p. 15; U.S. OPM, 2013, p. 7). Gallup argues that its measures cover primary needs, contribution, recognition, belonging, and development. These closely follow Maslow's hierarchy of needs but are not necessarily measures of engagement, as shown in the text.

4. A question is how much money that is for most people. A reasonable guess might be an annual income of $50,000 to $80,000 for most people in the United States. For example, one U.S. study found that making more than $75,000 per year is not associated with increased happiness (Luscombe, 2010).

REFERENCES

Berman, E. M., & Berman, D. (2011). *People skills at work*. New York: Taylor & Francis/CRC Press.

Berman, E. M., Chen, D.-Y., Jan, C.-Y., & Huang, T.-Y. (2013). Public agency leadership: The impact of informal understandings with political appointees on perceived agency innovation in Taiwan. *Public Administration, 91*(2), 303–324.

Berman, E. M., & Kim, C.-G. (2010). Creativity management in public organizations: Jump-starting innovation. *Public Performance & Management Review, 33*(4), 619–652.

Berman, E. M., & West, J. P. (2003a). Psychological contracts in local government: A preliminary survey. *Review of Public Personnel Administration, 23*(4), 267–285.

Berman, E. M., & West, J. P. (2003b). What is managerial mediocrity? Definition, prevalence and negative impact (Part 1). *Public Performance & Management Review, 27*(2), 7–27.

Berman, E. M., & West, J. P. (2007). The effective manager . . . takes a break. *Review of Public Personnel Administration, 27*(4), 380–400.

Berman, E. M., & West, J. P. (2008). Managing emotional intelligence in U.S. cities: A study of public managers. *Public Administration Review, 68*(4), 740–756.

Blanchard, K., & Johnson, S. (1981). *The one minute manager*. New York: William Morrow.

Boardman, C., & Sundquist, E. (2009). Toward understanding work motivation. *American Review of Public Administration, 38*(5), 519–535.

Bramson, R. M. (1981). *Coping with difficult people*. Garden City, NY: Doubleday.

Bright, L. (2008). Does public service motivation really make a difference on the job satisfaction and turnover intentions of public employees? *American Review of Public Administration, 38*(2), 149–166.

Cherniss, C., & Goleman, D. (2001). *The emotionally intelligent workplace*. San Francisco: Jossey-Bass.

Csikszentmihalyi, M. (2008). *Flow: The psychology of optimal experience*. New York: Harper.

Drucker, P. F. (1954). *The practice of management*. New York: Harper.

Engaged employees inspire company innovation. (2006, October 12). *Gallup Management Journal*. Retrieved from http://gmj.gallup.com

Gallup. (2013). State of the global workplace 2013. Retrieved from http://www.gallup.com/topic/STATE_OF_THE_GLOBAL_WORKPLACE_2013.aspx

Gruman, J., & Saks, A. (2011). Performance management and employee engagement. *Human Resource Management Review, 21*(2), 123–136.

Guest, D. E. (2007). HRM and the worker: Towards a new psychological contract? In P. Boxall, J. Purcell, & P. Wright (Eds.), *The Oxford handbook of human resource management* (pp. 128–146). Oxford: Oxford University Press.

Heathfield, S. M. (2008). Rise above the fray: Dealing with difficult people at work. About.com: About Money. Retrieved from http://humanresources.about.com/od/workrelationships/a/difficultpeople.htm

Heathfield, S. M. (2011). Top 10 mistakes managers make managing people. About.com: About Money. Retrieved from http://humanresources.about.com/od/badmanagerboss/a/mistakes-managers-make-managing-people.htm

Herzberg, F., Mausner, B., & Snyderman, B. B. (1959). *The motivation to work.* New York: John Wiley.

The high cost of disengaged employees [Q&A with Curt Coffman]. (2002, April 15). *Gallup Business Journal.* Retrieved from http://businessjournal.gallup.com/content/247/the-high-cost-of-disengaged-employees.aspx

Hofstede, G., Hofstede, G. J., & Minkov, M. (2010). *Cultures and organizations: Software of the mind* (3rd ed.). New York: McGraw-Hill.

House, R. J. (1971). *Path-goal theory of leadership.* Seattle: University of Washington.

International Institute for Management Development. (2010). *World competitiveness yearbook.* Lausanne, Switzerland: Author.

Locke, E. A., & Latham, G. P. (1990). *A theory of goal setting and task performance.* Englewood Cliffs, NJ: Prentice Hall.

Lubit, R. (2004). The tyranny of toxic managers: Applying emotional intelligence to deal with difficult personalities. *Ivey Business Journal, 68*(4), 1–7.

Luscombe, B. (2010, September 6). Do we need $75,000 a year to be happy? *Time.* Retrieved from http://www.time.com/time/business/article/0,8599,2016291,00.html

Marston, C. (2007). *Motivating the "What's in it for me?" workforce: Manage across the generational divide and increase profits.* Hoboken, NJ: John Wiley.

Maslow, A. (1954). *Motivation and personality.* New York: Harper & Row.

McClelland, D. (1985). *Human motivation.* Glenview, IL: Scott, Foresman.

McGregor, D. (1960). *The human side of enterprise.* New York: John Wiley.

Menguc, B., Auh, S., Fisher, M., & Haddad, A. (2013). To be engaged or not to be engaged: The antecedents and consequences of service employee engagement. *Journal of Business Research, 66*(11), 2163–2170.

Neo, B. S., & Chen, G. (2007). *Dynamic governance: Embedding culture, capabilities and change in Singapore.* Singapore: World Scientific Publishing.

Odiorne, G. (1976). MBO in state government. *Public Administration Review, 36*(1), 28–33.

Osland, J. S., Kolb, D. A., & Rubin, I. M. (2000). *Organizational behavior: An experiential approach* (7th ed.). Upper Saddle River, NJ: Prentice Hall.

Perry, J. L. (1996). Measuring public service motivation: An assessment of construct reliability and validity. *Journal of Public Administration Research and Theory, 6*(1), 5–22.

Perry, J. L. (2000). Bringing society in: Toward a theory of public-service motivation. *Journal of Public Administration Research and Theory, 10*(2), 471–489.

Pink, D. H. (2009). *Drive: The surprising truth about what motivates us.* New York: Riverhead Books.

Rousseau, D. M. (1995). *Psychological contracts in organizations: Understanding written and unwritten agreements.* Thousand Oaks, CA: Sage.

Saks, A. M. (2006). Antecedents and consequences of employee engagement. *Journal of Managerial Psychology, 21*(7), 600–619.

Schwartz, T. (2010, June). The productivity paradox: How Sony Pictures gets more out of people by demanding less. *Harvard Business Review,* pp. 65–69.

Seijts, G. H., & Crim, D. (2006). What engages employees the most or, the ten C's of employee engagement. *Ivey Business Journal, 70*(4), 1–5.

Sorkin, A. R. (2009). *Too big to fail.* New York: Viking Press.

U.S. Merit Systems Protection Board. (2012). *Federal employee engagement: The motivating potential of job characteristics and rewards.* Washington, DC: Author. Retrieved from http://www.mspb.gov/netsearch/viewdocs.aspx?docnumber = 780015&version = 782964

U.S. Office of Personnel Management. (2013). *Federal employee viewpoint survey results: Employees influencing change.* Washington, DC: Author. Retrieved from http://www.fedview.opm.gov/2013files/2013_Government wide_Management_Report.pdf

Van Wart, M. R. (2005). *Dynamics of leadership: Theory and practice.* Armonk, NY: M. E. Sharpe.

Vroom, V. H. (1964). *Work and motivation.* New York: John Wiley.

West, J. P., & Berman, E. M. (1997). Administrative creativity in local government. *Public Performance & Management Review, 20*(4), 446–458.

Wright, B. E., Moynihan, D. P., & Pandey, S. K. (2012). Pulling the levers: Transformational leadership, public service motivation, and mission valence. *Public Administration Review, 72*(2), 206–215.

CHAPTER 7

Compensation

Vital, Visible, and Vicious

I may be unappreciated, but at least I'm overworked and underpaid.

—A bureaucrat's lament

After studying this chapter, you should be able to

- understand why conventional wisdom about pay is often wrong;
- recognize that there is no absolute standard used to determine pay—that is, organizations do not pay people exactly what they are worth because they do not know what their employees are worth;
- explain why compensation is a key human resource function but pay programs, paradoxically, are not a management system;
- comprehend that a compensation system is the result of law and policy, labor markets, job evaluation, and personal contribution;
- understand that fair, "threshold" pay takes the issue of money off the table so that employees can focus on the work itself;
- articulate why it is difficult to resolve "the great pay debate";
- critique the claim that pay for performance is a panacea for compensation fairness;
- describe key compensation tools—cost-of-living adjustments, longevity pay, merit pay, skill-based pay, bonuses, and pay differentials—and their often paradoxical nature;
- design and calculate the essential elements of a salary survey; and
- assess and critique criteria for an ideal compensation system in the context of future trends.

If position classification and motivation define the individual–organization relationship (Chapters 5 and 6), then compensation quite literally quantifies it. Earnings affect a person—not only economically but also socially and psychologically—because they are a concrete indicator of employee value to the institution, purchasing power, social prestige, and, sadly, perhaps even self-worth. Payroll expenses, likewise, represent a substantial investment on the part of the organization; they often constitute the majority of its budget. In the U.S. Department of Defense and the U.S. Postal Service, for example—and in most other agencies irrespective of jurisdiction—labor costs often amount to more than 80% of outlays.

Accordingly, a compensation system should aim to align individual and organizational objectives, an ideal that may be difficult to achieve when many elected officials—with backgrounds in insurance agencies, real estate offices, law firms, and other small businesses—have little experience in large public organizations.[1] Nevertheless, dilemmas in managing compensation are of paramount importance. Trends in performance accountability and staff reduction suggest that supervisors and employees will determine resolution of these issues, with human resource management experts serving as consultants, not controllers. It will no longer do to blame controversial decisions on the personnel office.

Organizations have a right to expect staff to be as productive as possible, and individuals have the right to be fairly compensated. Thus, a value-added remuneration system should optimize the balance between institutional constraints and personal expectations by creating value for both the organization and its members. Program goals include attracting new workers, rewarding and retaining existing ones, providing equity, controlling budgets, and supporting the culture that the agency seeks to cultivate. The design and maintenance of a compensation system constitute a complex and prominent function in an organization; other human resource functions are important to some employees, but money is crucial to virtually everyone.

How a jurisdiction handles salaries and benefits, then, is vital (for individual sustenance and organizational credibility) and visible (personnel salaries and agency payrolls are a matter of public record), as well as vicious (actual or imagined inequities among workers breed considerable friction in organizations). Competence and performance may be hard to judge (Chapter 10), but pay and benefits are known. For instance, federal bankruptcy judges excluded from dining and transportation privileges enjoyed by other judges may well feel like "second-class citizens."

Despite—or perhaps because of—its importance, the compensation function of human resource management is the one that produces the most displeasure among both public and private sector employees. There are at least three reasons for discontent. One is that people compare themselves with others: with those doing the same job in the same office, with those performing different jobs in the agency, and with those holding equivalent positions in other departments. It is not unusual that perceived discrepancies and real discontent emerge as a result of those comparisons.

A second explanation is that remuneration is often driven more by political considerations than by economic ones. "It is completely fallacious," contend Risher and Fay (1997), "to argue that government pay programs represent a management system" (p. 14). Elected officials typically focus on personnel costs, and compensation policies become pawns in a quest for political advantage. Raising taxes, cutting services, or reallocating budget monies to fund pay increases is not politically popular. Thus, over time, salaries may be affected more by political opportunism than by objective merit—something not likely to engender confidence in compensation policies.

A final, related reason for concern over pay is that many citizens believe civil servants are overpaid and underworked—despite arguably noncompetitive salaries and increased workloads resulting from downsizing. As Risher and Fay (1997) observe, "Some people will always think that public pay levels are too high; but it is safe to say that their views have a life of their own independent of the facts" (p. 323). Stated differently, the effectiveness of compensation reforms is certain to be constrained by the culture in which they are created. These three factors—personal comparisons, political expediency, and public beliefs—tend to reinforce one another in a manner that further exacerbates dissatisfaction. At the root of these explanations is the fact that most organizations want the most work for the least money, whereas many employees want the most money for the least work. Compensation, in short, is considered crucial by employees, decision makers, and taxpayers alike.

The following pages examine factors that affect the determination of pay: law and policy, external competitiveness as it relates to labor markets, and internal consistency as a function of job evaluation and various systems of pay progression, as well as individual considerations. The analysis is framed by equity and expectancy theory and illustrated with controversial issues including pay banding and comparable worth, as well as discussion of cost-of-living adjustments; pay based on longevity, merit, and skill; bonus programs; and differential pay. Having diagnosed challenges for compensation programs, the chapter closes with a prescription for an "ideal" program and projections of future trends.

EQUITY AND EXPECTANCY THEORY

Equity theory explains that an individual's satisfaction with his or her job is largely (but not wholly) determined by the person's perception of the fairness of the balance between contributions made by the individual and the rewards received from the organization. Unfortunately, it is often the case that neither "the people who manage the (federal) systems, the managers who use them, [nor] the employees themselves" (Wamsley, 1998, p. 30) hold compensation programs in high regard. To appreciate the significance of equity theory, the weighing of contributions and rewards, consider the foundations and nature of this balance. Its basis is the presumed link between performance and pay, and its dynamic is how (or whether) this linkage operates.

While equity theory examines the effect of perceived fairness on satisfaction, expectancy theory (Vroom, 1964; see Chapter 6, this volume) examines the role of individual perceptions in determining behavior and offers insights into the choices that people make.

In terms of inducing behavior, it includes what is offered, what is likely to be provided, and what is valued by recipients. Its tenets are a three-link causal chain:

1. The value (valence) the employee attaches to a desired result (e.g., higher pay)
2. The worker's belief that rewards will actually be provided as a consequence of high performance (instrumentality)
3. The employee's understanding (expectancy) is that he or she can successfully accomplish the task that will lead to reward

Stated differently, the theory assumes that people take action based on their perception of the possible success of that action (expectancy) and the likelihood of their achieving outcomes (instrumentality) that they value (valence).

If any of the three links in this chain is weak, then the success of the pay program is reduced. Contemplate, for instance, that the parole supervisor in a state department of corrections demonstration project: He has authority to provide productivity bonuses to caseworkers who increase the number of interviews they conduct with their parolees. These officers want the bonus (valence) and understand that it will be awarded if they achieve the improvement objective (instrumentality). They are concerned (expectancy), however, that simply adding to the contacts they have with their charges, without a reduction in overall caseload, will result in superficial interviews. They are not convinced that the program is desirable (because it minimizes chances of in-depth information gathering) or feasible (overtime work is not available). Accordingly, public safety would be put at risk, and employee burnout is likely. In one such actual case, few sought the payouts, and the initiative was discontinued.

Consider a more common scenario. Although most people value money (valence), there are often significant constraints on their obtaining more of it. When local, state, or national legislative bodies regularly limit pay raises to inconsequential amounts, for example, the importance attached to those amounts is devalued (repeated raises that are below the rate of inflation in effect constitute pay cuts). Suppose instead that substantial monies are provided. Employees must then have confidence that the performance evaluation system (instrumentality) distributes rewards fairly and accurately. For reasons examined in Chapter 10, such confidence is often uncertain at best. Finally, although many Americans believe that hard work makes a difference (expectation), working smarter also counts. Thus, if training, acceptable working conditions, and up-to-date equipment are not provided, then working harder may make little difference.

As these cases demonstrate, expectancy theory can be an effective diagnostic tool to ensure that the human resource management system is administered in a manner that coherently establishes linkages among valence, instrumentality, and expectancy.

- Do employees value available rewards?
- Do workers see a link between the rewards and their performance?
- Are they confident, given their background and organizational climate, that they can complete their assigned tasks?

Equity and expectancy theories mandate, in other words, that policy makers be concerned about more than the absolute amount of money required to fund public service. They must also focus on comparative levels of pay and how these monies are distributed. Reward systems unconnected to productivity indicators motivate poor workers to stay and high performers to become discouraged and leave. The irony of such a situation is that overall compensation costs rise because more employees are needed to complete tasks that fewer conscientious ones could readily accomplish.

PAY DETERMINATION

With these theoretical—and quite real—considerations noted, this section turns to an exploration of factors affecting pay determination. Perhaps the most significant goal of any remuneration system is fairness. An organization confronts two types of decisions in the management of compensation to achieve this goal: pay level and pay adjustments. Compensation in any jurisdiction is a product of the following elements:

- Pay philosophy, as informed by law and policy
- Labor market forces (external competitiveness), as reflected by manipulation of supply and demand
- Internal consistency based on job evaluation, as tracked by different systems of pay progression
- Individual considerations, as manifested in various types of pay (see Exhibit 7.1)

Decisions about levels of pay are largely consequences of philosophy, market, and job evaluation, whereas decisions about pay adjustments emphasize employees' specific placement in the salary structure. Taken together, these judgments should represent the greater good by aligning the interests of the public and its servants.

Pay systems, then, reflect not only law and policy but also (1) comparisons of similar jobs in different organizations through salary surveys (external competition), (2) comparisons of content among jobs within an agency through job evaluation techniques (internal consistency), and (3) comparisons among employees in the same job category in the same organization through measures of seniority, merit, skill, or temporary pay (individual considerations). As each of these equity dimensions is explored below, it is important to keep in mind that "there are no absolute measures of job value. For things like temperature and weight, instruments are both reliable and valid. Job value is at best a relative or comparative measure" (Risher & Wise, 1997, p. 99). Instead, what exists in many organizations are inconsistent mixes of fair-pay criteria. A common denominator and underlying assumption shared by all forms of equity, however, is that they implicitly hold a time clock model of work (Kelly & Moen, 2007). That is, as examined in Exhibit 7.2, labor is commoditized, to be bought and sold in easily measured time units (hours, days, weeks, months, years). Time is money—or is it?

Exhibit 7.1   Determinants of Compensation

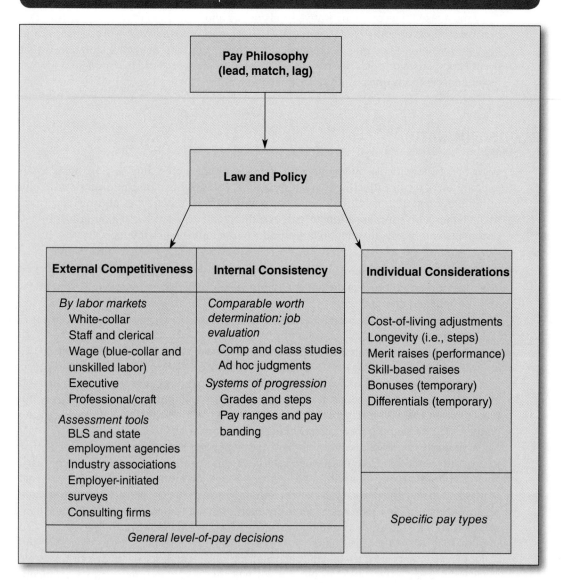

PHILOSOPHY

Lead, Match, or Lag

Organizations can lead, match, or lag behind what other employers offer employees. In sharp contrast to the strategies of governments in some other advanced democracies, the approach in U.S. governments has generally been to limit pools of job candidates to those

Exhibit 7.2 How Much Time Do You Owe the Organization?

Time isn't money; money is money.

—Anonymous

In an attempt to curb exploitative work schedules and thereby create jobs during the Great Depression, the 1938 Fair Labor Standards Act (FLSA) instituted the 5-day, 40-hour workweek—a compromise measure agreed to after the Senate passed a 30-hour workweek bill. Since that time, dramatic changes have occurred in the economy (from industrial to service), the workforce (from predominantly white and male to increasingly diverse and female), and lifestyles (from a family model consisting of a husband with a stay-at-home wife with children to singles, single parents, and married as well as unmarried dual-career families). Most organizations, however, still structure work hours as if nothing has happened in the intervening decades, a posture that has exacerbated the paradox of needs (see this volume's introduction). Indeed, under employment law any workplace rule that is not a business necessity cannot disproportionally affect one group. This can be interpreted to mean that inflexible work schedules are illegal unless it is demonstrated that they are essential to the conduct of business (Fairchild, 2014).

This is not to say that there has been no reaction to these changes.* Many organizations have experimented with **alternative work schedules**—"the joy of flex"—in the past half century. Variations are nearly infinite (e.g., compressed workweeks). In the oldest and most common approach, however, alternative schedules consist of a specified bandwidth when the office will be open (e.g., 6:00 a.m. to 8:00 p.m. Monday through Friday) and a set of core hours (perhaps 10:00 a.m. to 2:00 p.m.) around which people can arrange their 8-hour workdays (usually on a set schedule rather than with daily flexibility). Thus, early risers can come in early and leave at 3:00 p.m., and late risers can come in at 9:00 a.m. and leave late. Typically, everyone completes time sheets. Agencies may also benefit from such schedules by having offices staffed during a longer workday and by having reduced tardiness and absences.

Advantages should be evident: Employees work when they want to work, with all the personal and organizational benefits that may result from that fact. Drawbacks are of two types: inherent and practical. There is some work that is structured so that it cannot be "flexed," and there are organizations that cannot effectively implement flextime—either because record keeping becomes too burdensome or because managers lose a sense of control over subordinates. When available, flextime is often seen as an individual accommodation that deviates from standard policy instead of a recognition of the changing workforce. As a matter of fact, many private companies and government agencies indicate that they have flexible hours and telecommuting, but this does not mean that large numbers of eligible employees actually participate in these programs on a daily basis (see Chapter 8). Just 2.3% of the American workforce consider home as their primary workplace (Heathfield, 2011). As one scholar has observed, "The reality is that the full potentials of flexible work remain largely untested and unverified" (quoted in Bernard, 2014).

Generally, results are varied, but often flextime improves the quality of work life for employees more than it enhances the productivity of the organization. **Herzberg's theory of motivation** helps explain

---

*By most accounts, the numbers of employers offering flexible work hours have steadily increased. Although employers may provide these opportunities in parts of their organizations, many employees do not participate because they do not know they can; when they do know, most take advantage of them (see the Families and Work Institute's website at www.familiesandwork.org).

(Continued)

Exhibit 7.2 (Continued)

this finding (Herzberg, Mausner, & Snyderman, 1959). Flextime is a "job context" factor (such extrinsic factors focus on policies, supervision, and working conditions) that, if absent, can create job dissatisfaction. When these factors are available in desired forms, however, they normally are taken for granted. Consider university parking: If convenient, it is unlikely that it would create job satisfaction; if it is a continuous hassle, however, it can create substantial on-the-job morale problems. What really matters in explaining productivity, however, are "job content" factors (intrinsic elements that emphasize challenging work, responsibility, achievement, and the like). Flextime has nothing to do with the substance of work.

This speaks to the fundamental flaw of all forms of flextime—even if perfectly implemented. It assumes, applying the concept of **functional rationality**, that work must be a function of time instead of a function of the actual task to be performed. Indeed, exempt from the FLSA, most professionals of yesteryear[*] and today (managers, surgeons, members of the clergy, military officers) work until the work is done. They are not paid by the clock but rather for their overall contribution to the organization.

In like manner, Best Buy's Results-Only Work Environment (ROWE) was an unparalleled and viable non–time management program intended to redefine work from a place to go to something people do. Performance, not presence, was what counted at the 4,000-employee corporate headquarters. ROWE's transformational strategy completely altered the way employees worked: Because no two lives are the same, individual employees decided how, when, and where they would do their assigned tasks; they were required to put in only as much time as they needed to do the job. The program took flexibility—and accountability—to the maximum. With employees so empowered, surveys revealed, the approach

- increased productivity,
- saved significant amounts of money,
- produced higher customer satisfaction,
- resulted in enhanced recruitment and retention,
- improved morale and loyalty,
- enhanced family/work balance, and
- encouraged employees to be more focused and energized about their work as teamwork improved and the numbers of meetings declined (Kiger, 2007).

Such results encouraged the U.S. Office of Personnel Management to launch a ROWE-like pilot program, which it later terminated because of insufficient managerial support.

At Best Buy the pioneering strategy, which has been successfully adopted by at least 40 companies, lasted in its original form for nearly 10 years. In 2013, the company's new chief executive officer found the work-at-anytime-and-place innovation to be too radical, arguing that its extreme delegation of responsibility to employees was inappropriate. He instituted an "all-hands-on-deck" approach, and he now emphasizes top-down accountability and believes that "you need to feel dispensable, not indispensable" (quoted in Peterson, 2013).

[*]Samurai warriors, who refused to touch money, simply could not understand how it could be used as a substitute for expertise, discipline, and loyalty. The legacy of that feudal tradition remains, as the contemporary Japanese "salary-man" typically has his wife handle family finances.

Results-oriented programs, overall, appear to resolve the paradox of needs. When implemented effectively by leaders who focus on the long term, such methods not only promote work/life balance for individuals but also maximize the value of human capital for the organization. To the extent that New Millennials, or members of Generation Y, reject traditional workplace routines, the program acknowledges, indeed celebrates, the need for an individualized, accepting, productive workforce. As one employee said, Best Buy gave "you the opportunity to really be an adult" (quoted in Kelly & Moen, 2007, p. 497; also see Ressler & Thompson, 2013; as well as http://gorowe.com).

Further experimentation and research are needed to determine if the ROWE approach produces unintended consequences as people attempt to set boundaries on work and home commitments. Employee schedule control, for instance, could lead to employees taking on more work. In fact, employment laws are meant to protect personnel from abuses that could occur in a clockless office. With Millennials often desiring a relationship between work and life that is different from that experienced by earlier generations, increasing numbers of women in the workforce, and large numbers of Baby Boomers retiring, attempts to improve work/life balance may—or may not—be the wave of the future. Concurrent with these developments, the behaviors of growing numbers of employees are being monitored anytime, anyplace by biometric identification devices, raising questions of personal autonomy (West & Bowman, 2014).

It is not necessarily maintained that all organizations and jobs could—or should—be reconceptualized in a manner consistent with **substantive rationality**. It is suggested, however, that agencies seek a blend of functional and substantive approaches instead of an unquestioning focus on quantity time. A catalytic strategy to accomplish this is an annual hours program whereby the number of hours needed during a given year is agreed on and a scheduling format is then designed.

prepared to accept that salaries in the public sector are frequently not competitive. Compensation is *not* seen as a strategic tool to achieve organizational objectives but rather as a cost to be managed and contained (with the controversial exception of performance pay programs, discussed below). At least since the passage of the 1883 Pendleton Act (Chapter 1), public servants have been expected to forgo opportunities for wealth in exchange for opportunities to serve the citizenry, often in challenging and unique ways (e.g., environmental protection, criminal justice, teaching, foreign relations, tax collection). Self-enrichment, after all, was and is not the purpose of service. The idea, unlike that underlying the spoils system, was to create a corps of career professionals insulated from political intrigue by providing job security, career progression, and reasonable benefits and working conditions. Also important was the fact that they represented but a tiny proportion of the workforce (less than 1 % in 1900); they held little political power or ability to organize themselves into unions, and none at all to strike (Chapter 11).

By the 1960s, however, public employees were far more numerous, had fallen substantially behind in compensation, and had won the right to organize. Beginning with the 1962 Federal Salary Reform Act, attempts were made to establish the principle that federal pay would match that found in the private sector. Codified in the Federal Pay Comparability Act of 1970, the law established a mechanism to provide annual comparability adjustments unless the president directed otherwise—which whoever was in that position did virtually every year for two decades.

In 1989, the first National Commission on the Public Service (the Volcker Commission) called for significant salary increases at the federal level; the passage of the Federal Employees Pay Comparability Act of 1990 mandated that the 30% public–private sector pay gap be closed gradually by the end of the century.[2] According to the findings of the 2003 Volcker Commission II, the gap was wider than ever at that time because successive administrations repeatedly cited "severe economic conditions," irrespective of the state of the economy, as a reason to deny employees full pay raises. If the raises promised under the law had been enacted in 2008, according to the Congressional Research Service, they would have been nearly 20% (Davidson, 2008). Although the situation is more varied elsewhere (and some critics disagree with these assessments, as examined below), the difficulties experienced by the national government are manifested in many states and localities. Such conditions lend credence to the idea that employees should seek a **pay restoration**, not merely a pay raise. It should be noted that the principle of comparable pay has long been practiced for federal blue-collar hourly workers. Thus, in different statutes, it is required that wage grade as well as Postal Service workers receive compensation comparable to that received by workers doing similar jobs in the private sphere.

The paradox of needs (discussed in this book's introduction) indicates that organizational and individual objectives may not coincide. Ideally, business strategy, human resource philosophy, and compensation goals should be aligned in a manner suited to meeting the needs of both employer and employee.

A wage-led approach may reflect a belief that by "working smarter," a high-quality, satisfied workforce constitutes a cost-effective, money-saving strategy. That is, total labor costs are not the same as labor rates. It is possible to achieve high productivity from a relatively small workforce if the cost per unit of output is less with a highly efficient, though well-paid, staff. This plan, however, may be seen as counterintuitive and difficult for many cash-strapped public and nonprofit organizations to adopt in the short run.

A wage-competitive policy in effect neutralizes compensation as a factor in human resource management. It does this by paying consistently at market rates and accentuating nonmonetary amenities affecting the overall ability to attract and retain employees. These include such time-honored (and timeworn) techniques as "selling scenery" (or the area's weather), contending that the community is "family-friendly," and claiming that the organization is at the seat of power in a political capital ("Potomac fever" and its subnational equivalents). Many of these tactics, however, are available to organizations using above- and below-market pay policies. Still, a match policy does not necessarily place the organization at a disadvantage in the marketplace. Indeed, the virtue of reasonable pay is that "it takes the issue of compensation off the table" (Pink, 2009, p. 79).

Last, wage-follower plans may be indicative of unique characteristics of the occupation (military service, State Department diplomacy), a philosophy that dictates service is not about making money (Salvation Army), high unemployment in the area, short time horizons, or simply a "lean and mean" approach to human resources that involves "working harder" to get the most from as few poorly paid workers as possible. Such a strategy, to the degree that it is conscious and not a product of economic malaise, must work to mitigate low morale, higher turnover, and increased training costs. A below-market approach might—arguably—be acceptable for low-skill retailing organizations such as Walmart, but it would clearly be a "penny-wise and pound-foolish" strategy for professionally staffed organizations. For example, the federal agency with the lowest-paid workforce (despite well-paid medical staff), the Department of Veterans Affairs, has chronic problems related to poor management due to systemic underfunding (Oppel, 2014). Everyone, in any case, seems to have an opinion about what constitutes an appropriate pay policy (see Exhibit 7.3).

Exhibit 7.3   Pay Policy: A Politician, a Philosopher, and an Economist Comment

Lead

> *Labor is prior to, and independent of, capital. Capital is only the fruit of labor, and could never have existed if labor had not first existed. Labor is the superior of capital, and deserves much the higher consideration.*
>
> —Abraham Lincoln

Match

> *Under the influence either of poverty or of wealth, workmen and their work are equally liable to deteriorate.*
>
> —Plato

Lag

> *Bad jobs at bad wages are better than no jobs at all.*
>
> —Paul Krugman

The selection of an appropriate pay policy involves a complex set of factors, including the types of skills required, job market characteristics, ability to pay, desired institutional image, assumptions about employee work attitudes, and employer ideologies. The strategy chosen likely will position the organization within or across sectors of the economy. Thus, in the public arena, some cities and counties, for instance, use a wage-lead approach at least when compared with state employment. The federal government's pay policies, however, are generally superior to those of many subnational governments—but inferior to those utilized by major corporations. It should also be noted that different policies might exist within one organization. The compensation package available to public service clerical personnel, for instance, may be better than that found in many small businesses. Such a lead approach is reversed, however, for most public and nonprofit executives within the same agency, whose remuneration is the result of a wage-lag strategy.

The paradox of needs may be resolved in good measure through employee self-selection, provided that basic economic and noneconomic needs are met. Equity theory suggests, however, that if people do not perceive that a balance exists between their contributions and the rewards they receive, then they will try to relieve the tension by reducing productivity, misusing organizational resources, or seeking higher rewards either within the department or outside it.

These trends can be expected to continue as agencies: seek pay policies designed to reduce the size of the workforce, evidence less concern with competitive compensation and more with what can be afforded, and attempt incentive programs to make payroll costs more variable than fixed expense. Organizations, in the end, usually get what they are willing to pay for.

THE GREAT PAY DEBATE

Since 2010, public employee compensation—both salaries and **benefits**—has become a prominent political issue. The recession, stagnating pay, high unemployment, budget deficits, and revelations such as those in Bell, California (where the city manager momentarily and corruptly earned more than the president of the United States), have fueled controversy. One survey found that 75% of citizens think that federal employees "get better pay and benefits than people doing similar work outside of government" (Risher, 2010). For all these reasons, civil servants have become a symbol of government excess, and legislators have instituted limits on hiring, pay freezes, furloughs, salary reductions, pension benefit cutbacks, and outsourcing.

Not surprisingly, this "war on public salaries" has become highly politicized; for every claim that government pays too much, another is made that it pays too little. For example, news stories and reports from *USA Today,* the *Wall Street Journal,* the Cato Institute, the Heritage Foundation, and the American Enterprise Institute assume that the typical private sector wage package is the right one, and the country's economic problems are tied to public service pay. They charge that governmental employees are paid more than business workers (at least 20% better when benefits are included) (U.S. Government Accountability Office [U.S. GAO], 2012).

In contrast, the U.S. Office of Personnel Management, the President's Pay Agent (the directors of the Office of Management and Budget and the OPM as well as the secretary of labor), and employee unions counter that the public workforce is not only older but also more educated, unionized, and white-collar than business employees. The pay of an average private sector worker, because it masks such important factors, cannot be fairly used as the standard for public service pay. As organizational size significantly affects earnings, they also point out that an "apple-to-apple" comparison should compare large corporations with the civil service. Indeed, even with these differences, federal employees, according to official reports, are consistently underpaid by at least 26% (Losey, 2011b; on states and localities, see Bender & Heywood, 2010; Keefe, 2010). At the federal level (which is much less personnel-intensive than state and local governments), the nation's economic woes have little to do with allegedly overpaid government employees; even cutting the payroll in half would reduce spending by less than 3% (Krugman, 2010). The pay gap is likely to grow as public service salary freezes become a popular tactic among lawmakers.

Both sides of this fierce, complicated controversy believe that the other mischaracterizes the research findings, and neither has had its data independently verified. In 2010, the OPM asked the National Academy of Public Administration and the Administrative Conference of the United States to work with it, the Office of Management and Budget, and the Bureau of Labor Statistics to develop a transparent methodology to compare public and private earnings. Apparently backing away from this initiative, the OPM recently stated that performance appraisal policy should be addressed before compensation issues; without a clear connection between an individual's evaluation and compensation, pay reform is problematic.

In the meantime, critics assert that public employers should be no different from profitable private employers who have curtailed salaries, hired low-paid temporary workers, and downsized their workforces. Defenders counter that those actions are attributable to reduced demand for products and services—which is not the case in government. If services are to be reduced no matter what, then the use of well-paid contractors should be cut back and/or positions should be insourced to save money. They also point out that the focus on public salaries deflects attention from lucrative corporate compensation policies that continue to reward the kind of high-risk behavior and criminal perfidy that contributed to the 2008 economic debacle. Unions point out that they fight for workers' pensions and paychecks the same way CEOs fight for theirs. What is evident in this brouhaha is that arguing about salaries is easier than tackling the biggest sources of governmental financial problems: military expenditures, special interest tax subsidies, and entitlement programs. There is a lot less political risk in attacking bureaucrats than in reducing popular programs, although the two are hardly unrelated.

Like the debate over pay, arguments over benefits—the cost of which comes out of wages—are driven at least as much by partisan ideology as they are by fiscal responsibility. Critics of civil service benefit programs describe them as "lavish," "gold-plated," and "out of line" (e.g., Montgomery, 2011), arguing for reduction in their scope and increases in cost sharing. If less secure and more expensive 401(k) defined-contribution pensions, for instance, are good enough for business employees, then they should be good enough for bureaucrats. Indeed, private citizens—whose companies have frozen, decreased, or defaulted on their obligations—may resent the more arguably secure pensions of public employees.

Defenders of the civil service point out that the benefits civil servants receive are comparable to those found in most major corporations. In the case of pensions, converting to defined-contribution plans (typical of small and medium-size businesses and the federal government since 1984)[3] does not address funding shortfalls. The principal reasons for unfunded pension liabilities today are investment losses during the Great Recession starting in 2008 and the refusal by officials to make legally required payments;[4] these liabilities have not been caused by governmental retirement benefits that are too generous. Such benefits average $19,000 per year (Reich, 2011), representing outlays that are less than 4% of a typical state's budget (McEntee, 2011). To suggest that these costs are a primary cause of budget problems is disingenuous.

Arbitrarily cutting pensions—which are delayed salary payments promised to civil servants in exchange for lower pay—is a betrayal of those who chose public service over higher business salaries. Difficult economic times demand shared sacrifice. Indeed, recent reforms have included raising the retirement age, increasing employee contributions to pensions, cutting benefits, and abolishing retiree cost-of-living adjustments. Yet making civil servants scapegoats for economic problems—while well-heeled politicians refuse to cut their own compensation, businesses prosper, and the wealthy get tax breaks—does little to address underlying issues. It is worth pointing out that budgetary problems are largely self-inflicted, resulting from unsustainably low taxes on the ultrawealthy and corporate tax loopholes.

It is important to recognize that there may be no lasting solution to pay and benefit issues because, as even some critics acknowledge (Biggs & Richwine, 2011), government is not, and cannot be, subject to market forces in the way that business is. Rather, at least for the federal government, the legislatively mandated standard (as noted above) is comparability of employee compensation with compensation in the private sector (Chassy, 2011). What is needed is a transparent way to determine the comparisons and to assess the potential effects of changes before reform is adopted. Finally, it should be remembered that public service pensions and benefits vary substantially; while there are certainly examples of excessive benefits being approved in the "good years" prior to the recession of 2008, this is a far cry from saying that all or even most are out of line with appropriate and sustainable levels (see Exhibit 7.4).

The compensation debate, in the end, is a proxy fight for what role government should play in society, a dispute not likely to be resolved by data and sweet reason alone. In principle, pay and benefit problems should be resolvable through objective economic analysis. Yet even in this relatively quantitative issue area, relevant facts are hardly conclusive and are subject to interpretation. When interpretations are driven by conviction, and conviction becomes the basis for disagreement, consensus is unlikely. To the extent that facts are important in a political controversy, it is useful to know that at least one website, FactCheck.org (www.factcheck.org), offers an unbiased information source (see, e.g., Morse & Kiely, 2010).

Whatever may be decisive in policy change, it should meet these principles, as stated by the U.S. Office of Personnel Management: "transparency, equal pay for equal work, no

---

Exhibit 7.4   Tipping From Reasonable to Unsustainable Pension Benefits

Not all pension plans are created equal. Most California local governments had reasonable defined-benefits plans in the 1990s, with rank-and-file workers eligible for between 2% and 2.5% of their salary for each year of employment at age 60. Public safety employees were generally eligible for 2.5–2.7% per year at age 57. All local government retirement plans were paid-up-date plans. However, more than a few California cities and counties boosted their retirement plans in the late 1990s and early 2000s during "the long boom," in many cases to unsustainable levels. For example, Riverside County boosted public safety personnel to 3% at age 50 "to be competitive." This gave police officers the chance to retire after many years of service and begin second careers. Someone who came out of the academy and served 25 years could retire at 50 with 75% of his or her peak salary, which that person would then collect for the next 30–35 years on average. In other words, because individuals would be drawing a large percentage of their top salary, in many cases they might get more in retirement than they did while working. Pension benefits liabilities shot up when the economy faltered. Although California local governments were not alone in making such pension boosts, fortunately they were not common across the country.

Recently Riverside County dropped its pension formula for public safety back to 2.7% at age 57. So to get the same 75%, an employee would have to work 28 years and would expect to draw for 23–28 years. The difference is about 10 years (i.e., 3 additional working years and 7 fewer retirement years), or the equivalent of $750,000 to $1 million per officer over time in reduced costs for the county.

It should be clear that the differences between small defined-benefit multipliers are huge for the jurisdictions paying for them, as are differences in the ages when people may start drawing benefits. Changes should be made with long-term sustainability in mind; when defined-benefits plans are reasonable, their costs can easily be absorbed as a part of "doing business."

political influence, and the ability to recruit and retain a well qualified workforce" (O'Keefe, 2011). Put differently, government can act as a model employer—one that offers fair and competitive pay and benefits. That the business sector does not like competing with such an employer does not mean that private and public employees should be pitted against one another in a race to the bottom. The goal should be that every working American receives reasonable pay and benefits. Instead, those who have a living wage and modest pensions in government are being asked to give up what citizens of most advanced nations enjoy as a right. The country would be better served by improving the public service rather than serving it up as a false sacrifice for economic problems (Stier, 2011). Turning now from pay philosophy issues, the next section examines labor market forces (refer back to Exhibit 7.1).

LABOR MARKET FORCES: EXTERNAL COMPETITION

Classical economic theory holds that the "free market" determines salaries based on supply and demand for specific jobs. The obvious, if often overlooked, fact is that pay is not a function of a fanciful, pristine, abstract free market—something that has never existed and never will. Rather, occupations exist in different **labor markets**, none of which is "free." Supply and demand are affected by public policy related to levels of spending, focus of expenditures, and types of labor preferred. Another factor altering the labor market is the presence of contracts and laws that give some workers a measure of stability. Finally, private sector financial bubbles and busts certainly play havoc with labor markets.

The overall public labor market may be constituted in different ways depending on organizational needs. Five labor market dimensions, or submarkets, can be identified:

1. Governments use a lot of people who become highly skilled at the functions of government itself and who do specialized white-collar work. This submarket includes those with the appropriate educational background (almost always a bachelor's degree and a master's degree for supervisory positions) who are skilled and experienced. Frequently certification is required for specialized training. Illustrations include frontline caseworkers, procurement specialists, teachers, law clerks, employment experts, accountants, medical technicians, public affairs specialists, and inspectors, as well as the supervisors, managers, and senior directors of those units and divisions.

2. The staff and clerical labor submarket includes administrative support personnel who are responsible for maintaining local finances, processing HR paperwork, and organizing routine unit functions. While positions in this pool do not require a college education, increasingly they are filled with individuals with bachelor's and sometimes even master's degrees.

3. A third category is blue-collar wage labor, consisting of skilled laborers (requiring certifications or apprenticeships) and unskilled workers. It comprises personnel such as plumbers, electricians, carpenters, metal workers, painters, mechanics,

maintenance staff, drivers, and machinists. When employed by the federal government, these hourly staff are covered by the Federal Wage System, which mandates that pay is set according to local prevailing market rates.

4. Executives are a fourth submarket comprising both highly qualified and experienced executives, such as city and county managers, and those with political connections, policy skills, organizational change expertise, and/or public renown. While it is common to think that this pool is always flush, it becomes quite difficult for U.S. presidents to fill agency positions in the last years of their terms because such individuals are not likely to find short-term temporary caretaker roles desirable (thus, agency careerists generally take interim positions).

5. Professional and high-level craft occupations requiring licensure are the final market type, and in fact may be a series of small submarkets related to high-skill and high-demand jobs in areas such as medicine, law, engineering, and finance. For instance, while the average annual pay for federal employees is $79,374, the highest-paid agency, the Securities and Exchange Commission, is part of the well-paid submarket with an average salary of $169,039 (Hicks, 2014), a modest sum compared to Wall Street compensation. Public safety positions, in particular law enforcement positions, are sometimes in this category (rather than in the white- and blue-collar classifications that they were a part of in the past) due to the training and education required, citizen demands, and political clout associated with their unions.

There is considerable variation in the actual use and blending of these categories. To illustrate, the state of Indiana has eight pay plans: (a) one for professional, administrative, and technological, plus another for its managers; (b) one for clerical, office machine operators, and technicians, plus another for its managers; (c) one for labor, trades, and crafts, plus another for its managers; (d) one for executives but also including highly paid medical and scientific workers; and (e) one for protective occupations–law enforcement. In practical terms, compensation specialists and the management team negotiating contracts may think of markets as being roughly equivalent to bargaining units (e.g., the state of California has 21 bargaining units, so it considers the labor market as divided into 21 parts).

Pay for these different markets is benchmarked using a variety of tools. Large systems, such as the federal and state governments, normally require workforce analysis for internal purposes. For example, the Texas State Auditor's Office (n.d.) states:

> Workforce analysis is a systematic process for identifying the human capital required to meet agency goals and developing the plans and strategies to meet these requirements.
>
> As part of the strategic plan required under Texas Government Code, Section 2056.002, state agencies must conduct a strategic planning staffing analysis and develop a workforce plan. Workforce plans are completed as part of agencies' strategic plans.

The most common approach involves the use of government-supplied employment data sets. The Bureau of Labor Statistics (BLS) provides data on wage averages by sectors, industries, and regions throughout the year. Most states have equivalent agencies that furnish even more localized information, such as California's Employment Development Department. Industry-generated studies also are useful sources of data (professional organizations that conduct such surveys include the National League of Cities, the National Association of Counties, and their statewide counterparts, as well as the National Conference of State Legislatures). Organizations, in addition, do their own salary surveys, or may do them for self-defined benchmark groups. For instance, universities in the same athletic conference or region of the country may routinely survey one another—a process that becomes subject to some degree of circumlocution and professional collusion. Finally, when a high level of expertise is required, long-term planning for specialized needs is sought, or speed is required, organizations may contract with consulting firms to conduct surveys. The design and implementation of such surveys involves significant technical issues (identifying key jobs and relevant organizations, calculating benefits, data collection uncertainties). But even flawed assessments—in the absence of better data—can provide useful information, as long as it is recognized that interpretation of the information "requires a combination of the 'science' found in the calculated values and the 'art' of using these figures in alignment with an organization's strategy and pay policy" (York & Brown, 2008, p. 123).[5]

Although salaries form the foundation of most employees' perceptions of pay, accurate estimates of external equity cannot focus solely on salary data. Benefits, a trivial "fringe" in most organizations before World War II, now add an average of 41% to the payroll and account for some 29% of the total personnel compensation package. This increase is attributed largely to tax policy (both employers and employees realize tax advantages from certain types of benefits) and the rising costs of health and retirement programs.[6] An interesting paradox nevertheless exists: As the value of benefits increases, employee satisfaction can decrease (see Exhibit 7.5, as well as Chapter 8). In fact, to the extent that a selected benefit is unwanted, it is less than a benefit and more of a salary deduction. Furthermore, the utility of benefits in achieving organizational goals is limited because benefits are available to all members, irrespective of employee performance.

Historically, low public salaries have been partially offset by benefits (usually untaxed or tax deferred) because their costs can often be put off by lawmakers and are thereby less visible to voters than pay increases. These programs are reputed to be superior to those found in the private domain, as public employees are sometimes covered under more types of plans. When governments are compared with other large white-collar employers, however, such disparities all but disappear, especially because corporate executive perquisites (e.g., stock options, personal security, executive coaches, expense accounts, multiple residences, free insurance, no-cost financial and legal counseling, country club memberships, box seats at sporting events, guaranteed bonuses, moving expenses, home repairs, clothing allowances, first-class travel, spouse travel, chauffer service, personal chefs, company cars, generous severance pay, estate planning, children's education, vacations) are unusual in other sectors.[7] Indeed, government and nonprofit benefits are often inferior to those in big business, and whatever perceived advantages the public sector has held as a "benefit-rich/salary-poor" employer are being eroded by increasing employee costs and diminishing coverage.

Exhibit 7.5 Unbeneficial Benefits

Organizations have generally decided what benefit coverages were needed and that all their members wanted the same mix of programs. Especially in a diverse workforce, however, individual differences in age, sex, marital status, and number of dependents become manifest.

Rigidity, gaps in coverage, and cost shifting to employees have resulted in discontent with employer benefit programs. Some have one or more of the following elements:

- Standardized packages that require participation whether or not employees need the benefits (duplicate insurance for two employees in the family) or even desire them (inexpensive—and inadequate—group life and disability insurance)
- Considerable omissions in coverage that annoy many participants (e.g., eye and dental care, long-term care policies, legal assistance, child and elder care, domestic partner coverage)
- Cost-containment strategies in health care coverage (to the extent that insurance premiums can wipe out pay raises) and retirement plans (changing from employer-paid "defined-benefit" programs to employer/employee-paid "defined-contribution" programs)

One method of addressing such concerns is to offer flexible or "cafeteria" plans that establish employee accounts or menus equal to the dollar value of benefits. Each person can then choose a combination of appropriate benefits. Administrative barriers may exist in these programs, but they can be overcome (e.g., benefits can be bundled into selected packages to ensure balanced utilization). Such programs can resolve organization–individual conflicts, because employers no longer pay for benefits unwanted by employees—and both can save on taxes. It should be pointed out, however, that flexible programs make it easier for employers to pass cost increases to employees because the individual decides whether to pay more or take less coverage.

More radical than flexible plans would be to simply give employees the cash and tax value of their benefits, thus abolishing these programs entirely. Employer-sponsored benefit programs, after all, are largely a result of historical accident; with wage and salary controls during World War II, the only way organizations could keep people from seeking better-paying jobs elsewhere was to add benefits that were not covered by wage and salary restrictions. The logic is straightforward: An individual could obtain desired coverage by joining any number of nonemployer group programs that offer rates as low as those provided by employers. Should large organizations terminate their programs, vendors would develop even more, perhaps cheaper, options. However, making everyone responsible for all their own benefits ignores advantages of specialization and expertise; even Wall Street bankers are not good at managing investments.

Such decisions are far more complex, financially critical, and risky than decisions about most consumer purchases. Even if they were not, having to make the decisions would cause employees to spend time on issues far removed from workplace, remove an attractive way to recruit people, and change the original intent of defined-contribution programs (which were never intended to replace defined-benefit programs, but rather merely to supplement them). While it may be a useful idea to give individuals the cash value and/or some control over selected benefits, employers should retain their responsibility to offer a minimum coverage package for the most important benefits. One way to accomplish this goal, as noted, is the use of cafeteria benefit plans.

The determination of external equity, in short, should recognize that although conventional free market supply-and-demand theories seem simple, in practice there is no single labor market—there are many. And no sooner has one determined what the market is than it changes. Salary assessment tools are at once problematic and valuable; benefit programs, although hard to quantify and compare, constitute a significant, often controversial, part of compensation.

JOB CONTENT: INTERNAL CONSISTENCY

Pay decisions are made within the framework of the compensation structure. Some form of job evaluation method is used to assess the value of jobs systematically and assign jobs to salary grades, which in turn are given a range of salaries. This procedure defines an internal value hierarchy based on comparisons of jobs by their contribution to organizational objectives. Internal equity, then, rewards jobs of equal value with the same amount and pays jobs of different value according to some set of acceptable factors.

All systems of job evaluation—the most widely used of which is the point factor method (described in Chapter 5)—are premised on the need to identify criteria relative to job value (e.g., responsibility, working conditions, skill); jobs are then ranked in the hierarchy on these criteria. Despite its facade of objectivity (and resulting drawbacks), job evaluation retains a measure of face validity and thus remains the basis of internal equity in most organizations.

The scope of job evaluations varies substantially. When a single job or classification is changed based on differences between it and a job or classification in the outside market, this is called a **market adjustment** (or it may simply be the result of a counteroffer to an employee with another job prospect). When a change is made based on the fact that an incumbent is in a job that is out of alignment with other similar jobs, it is known as an **equity adjustment**. The study of a single classification or perhaps a series of jobs constituting a career ladder for modification is called a job classification or job series evaluation. Adjustments can occur when jobs of a similar nature have different classifications (because they are found in different divisions and have minor differences, but one group wants a similar, and higher, level of pay). Finally, when an organization attempts to reassess and recalibrate its entire system of job worth, it undertakes a **comp & class study**. It should be noted that requests for job evaluations do not necessarily result in studies of jobs, any more than the outcome of a job evaluation will necessarily result in a change. As noted in Chapter 5, evaluation also is done on an ad hoc basis for single positions or small systems.

Pay schedules attempt to provide fairness and some degree of predictability. While this leads to complaints about not achieving these goals (e.g., "He gets paid more than I, and I do more and do it better!") or achieving the goals too well ("Workers in Agency X are complacent because of a mechanical pay system")—no matter how flawed they are—pay schemes rationalize and organize how compensation is allocated. Pay plans fall on a spectrum from lockstep (grade-and-step systems) to integrated (pay range systems) to elastic (pay-banding systems).

A lockstep approach uses pay levels or grades. It emphasizes longevity, orderliness, and predictability. Each employee is placed into a job that has a specified grade (e.g., the state of Washington has 73 grades). Most positions that use grades have 13 steps; these are incremental increases that are automatic unless performance is designated as subpar. The full range of steps represents approximately a 31% increase of base pay over time. In the case of career ladders (e.g., Financial Analyst 1, 2, and 3), employees can be promoted from one grade to another with management approval and the technical confirmation of human resources that higher-level job requirements are being met (this is a rigorous, rather than pro forma, review). Personnel must compete for similar jobs in other agencies, and for positions not in their classification. Managers have little control in adjusting salary upon hire or as employees move through the steps in grade. They do retain substantial control in career series promotions and considerable control over competitive promotions such as supervisory positions.

Integrated systems try to balance longevity and managerial discretion. The federal government is a good example. The bulk of its 1.5 million employees are a part of the General Schedule, with its 15 grades and 10 steps. An employee is placed in a grade and can move through the 10 steps in set intervals as long as he or she does not have a negative evaluation. The first three steps are a year apart, the next three are 2 years apart, and the last three are 3 years apart. The salary range increase represented by the steps is about 30% and takes 18 years to achieve without a special "quality step increase" that accelerates the process. There are defined career ladders (usually designated as levels I to IV) that allow regular promotions in grades at lower levels but become increasingly selective at higher grades. Because steps get further and further apart as an employee progresses in a grade, there is pressure to get promotions. Because of managerial discretion in allowing promotions, there is pressure on employees to perform unless they want to see salary stagnation. Thus, while the federal system has a lockstep quality in the early part of a person's career, managerial discretion plays a large role in later advancement.

Elastic pay systems use a small number of pay levels, usually dropping the term *grade* altogether and referring only to pay *ranges*. In this procedure, to make the salary structure flexible, separate job levels are grouped into broad categories of related jobs called pay bands; the bands may have ranges of 40% to more than 100%, with only minimums and maximums. For example, the state of Virginia has only nine pay bands, with each band having a range just above 100%. This can provide managers with considerable discretion in setting pay within these levels by grouping pay ranges and adjusting pay. Some governments use different systems for different agencies. The U.S. Merit Systems Protection Board (2003) offers the following advice to federal agencies considering pay banding:

> **Grouping pay ranges.** In pay banding, [federal] agencies may collapse the 15 General Schedule grades into a smaller number of pay ranges or bands. For example, an agency could establish four bands encompassing the GS 1–5, the GS 6–11, the GS 12–13, and the GS 14–15 levels. . . . At today's rates, for

instance, the second band . . . would allow managers to set pay anywhere from $28,253 to $60,405. The number of bands and the way grades are assigned to the bands can be designed to support the organization's mission, values, and culture.

Adjusting pay. Once the pay bands are defined, the agency determines how employees move within and across pay bands. The GS system uses longevity (time-in-grade) and quality step increases [incentive pay] to move an employee within a grade, and merit promotion to move an employee to a higher grade. Pay under the GS system also is increased through general, governmentwide pay increases. In pay banding systems, the amount of a pay increase within a band is based on the employee's skills or competencies, job performance, contributions, or similar measures. Monies earmarked in the GS system for within-grade, general, and quality step increases may become "at risk" incentive pay in a pay banding system. . . . A high performing employee could move to the top salary of a pay band much more quickly than is possible in the GS system. . . . These flexibilities allow an agency to manage its workforce by rewarding highly valued behaviors that result in better mission accomplishment. (p. 3)

The technique, then, makes it easier for agencies to adjust salaries and provide managerial discretion but does little to deal with basic pay problems (indeed, when instituted, it is frequently required to be "budget neutral"). Further, at least at the national level, there is no evidence that it is cost-effective to replace the existing classification system (Blair, 2003). Pay banding, in fact, increases payroll costs, reduces promotion opportunities, and can expose agencies to charges of violations of the **Equal Pay Act of 1963** (Exhibit 7.6) if they do not have written plans detailing the method of pay progression within bands. Such problems led one federal agency to abandon its 9-year program. While it offered more horizontal movement and raises, it did not provide career ladders, promotion opportunities, and compensation controls (Rutzick, 2005). Information on employee satisfaction at agencies with these systems (e.g., the Federal Aviation Administration and the Transportation Security Administration) reveals that large numbers of employees have been dissatisfied with their raises (Losey, 2008).

Despite the paucity of concrete successes, movement to pay ranges and pay banding will be important in the future, if only because of the popularity of such systems with policy makers. At this point it seems unlikely that highly elastic systems will come to dominate most jurisdictions in the near term. However, it is clear that governments are introducing more managerial discretion over time, reforming lockstep pay systems (even when they perform well), and integrating features of both longevity and managerially defined merit. This is good news for those that want a wide variety of tools regarding individual considerations, the topic explored in the next section. However it makes the art of implementation far more complex and difficult to achieve in a world in which political figures can confound managerial plans. No matter what pay system is used, a significant challenge is to ensure that **comparable worth**—notably as it relates to gender disparities—is examined (see Exhibit 7.6).

Exhibit 7.6   Job Evaluation and Comparable Worth

> *It is difficult to get a man to understand something when his salary depends upon his not understanding it.*
>
> —Upton Sinclair

Job evaluation systems are designed to build an internal equity hierarchy based on comparisons of jobs; compensation systems assume that in setting pay, an organization should evaluate the contribution of each position to the organization. It follows, then, that equal pay should be offered for equal work; indeed, that is mandated by the 1963 Equal Pay Act (which is not always enforced; see AFL-CIO, n.d.). Job evaluation also, however, provides a way to equate jobs different in content but equal in value. Comparable worth, or **pay equity**, calls for equal pay for jobs of equal value. In concept, comparable worth is gender neutral; in reality, many of its beneficiaries have been women because jobs often held by them pay less than those held by men.

While seemingly objective, job evaluation can be undermined by the selection of factors, the way the factors are defined, and how points are assigned to them (Chapter 5). A compensation system, for example, that pays different guards in a prison at different base rates, groundskeepers at a hospital more than nurses, and county dog pound attendants more than child care workers lacks face validity.

Although the Equal Pay Act and Title VII of the 1964 Civil Rights Act deal with issues of pay equality and sex discrimination, comparable worth claims consistently have been rejected by the courts because existing law: does not mandate a job evaluation methodology, is not intended to abrogate market principles, or is relevant only in cases of deliberate discrimination. The U.S. Supreme Court has yet to hear a comparable worth case. The concept nonetheless has been implemented in state and local government through legislation, collective bargaining, and the development of more valid and reliable evaluation factors. Nearly half of the states and more than 1,500 local governments either have statutory pay equity requirements or have changed their job evaluation and salary practices to reflect comparable worth principles.

Because few argue against the desirability of pay equity (more than 100 nations, but not the United States, have ratified the United Nations' International Labour Organization convention on comparable worth), most of the controversy focuses on its feasibility. Supporters maintain that job evaluation tools—when properly utilized—advance pay equity; opponents argue that these techniques ignore the free market. Advocates counter that markets seldom operate efficiently (e.g., sex and race discrimination); critics say that job evaluation technology is inherently arbitrary. Although the debates of the 1980s have subsided (job security being a higher priority than pay equity in an era of downsizing), many pay equity issues remain unresolved (not the least of which is a legal definition of the term). Indeed, legislation has been proposed in each congressional session since 2001, and by initiatives in state legislatures—where the percentage of women lawmakers is twice as great as it is in Congress. It is unlikely that comparable worth concerns will disappear in the years ahead.

The infamous "wage gap" between men and women has remained largely intact in the overall economy in the past few decades. Women earn approximately 77 cents for every dollar a male employee earns in the general economy, although the wage gap is much smaller in most government settings (U.S. Office of Personnel Management, 2014). Two explanations—human capital factors (e.g., differential experience, education, job longevity, occupational choice, work/life views) and sex discrimination—contribute to the disparity. Women with the same experience, education, occupation, and union status as men earn 88% of the male wage (the public service wage gap is less than it is in business, e.g., the median salary for federal female employees is 93% of that for male employees; Tully, 2011).

Some commentators hold that women have different standards for fair pay, expect less than men, choose part-time employment, and often work for government and nonprofit employers that have less ability to pay than do corporations. Susan Pinker (2008), for instance, argues that women limit the time they spend at work as well as their efforts to find meaning in it—a phenomenon Jennifer Lawless and Richard Fox (2008) call the "ambition gap." A related dimension is that women's "leaning in" (Sandberg, 2013) to negotiate as hard as men for higher pay may be counterproductive. Cultural expectations are powerful, and even women penalize women for doing so; thus, women may be more reticent to bargain than men for good reason (Konnikova, 2014). Although women work fewer hours for less status and money, Pinker (2008) reports—perhaps paradoxically—that women find greater satisfaction in their careers than do men. Indeed, one study found that over a 10-year period, 1,500 companies that had women in executive positions performed better than those without female executives (Neal, 2011). Michele Singletary (2008), summarizing a number of studies, notes that women sometimes experience a "confidence gap," and also, despite their desire to learn and earn more, they may be so overwhelmed by short-term priorities (e.g., child and elder care) that they postpone long-term career and financial planning.

The pay gap may be slowly closing, but it is evident that cultural attitudes, even in the face of lawsuits, are difficult to change. In the meantime, better enforcement of existing laws, as well as increasing availability of on-site child care, flextime, and paid family leave, may help to address gender-based inequities (Giapponi & McEvoy, 2005–2006; see also Labaton, 2014). In addition, as noted above, the pay gap is typically narrower in government than it is in other sectors. For a compilation of data on women in the workforce, with multiple links to original sources, see Heathfield (2008).

INDIVIDUAL CONSIDERATIONS: FAIRNESS AND INDIVIDUAL CONTRIBUTIONS

Once job evaluation has established a salary structure and each grade is assigned a range of salaries, attention shifts from external equity with the market and internal equity in the agency to individual equity. That is, job evaluation then needs to determine the pay level of each employee in the range and, by so doing, the base for subsequent pay adjustments. Individual considerations require ensuring that there is fairness between current and future employees, and that the contributions of those personnel in the same job are rewarded proportionately. Six approaches are examined here. Four of them affect base salaries: cost-of-living adjustments (to keep abreast of inflation), longevity pay (to recognize expertise gained), merit pay (to reward excellence), and skill-based pay (to acknowledge new competencies). Two approaches provide temporary raises: bonuses (one-time increases usually based on performance) and differentials (additions for performing special functions or working under exceptional conditions).

While the six categories are distinct, organizations may use several by combining different logics under a single name. For example, they may rely on either longevity or merit increases, but not both. When the speed of longevity can be varied, it is a merit-like consideration; when the merit increases are spread out evenly, it is more about longevity.

Cost-of-Living Pay Adjustments

Cost-of-living adjustments (COLAs) are given annually to maintain external equity since inflation is characteristic of modern economies. They are a way to maintain the compensation system with no developmental dimension. These adjustments are provided to all employees, and simultaneously all salary grade scales are adjusted for new hires. In economic terms, failure to provide a cost-of-living adjustment is the equivalent of a pay reduction. Thus, many in the workforce today are not earning as much, on an inflation-adjusted basis, as they did earlier in their careers.

Exhibit 7.7 provides an example of inflation and cost-of-living adjustments and their effects on federal General Schedule salaries (the Consumer Price Index [CPI] is equated to the inflation rate). Using the 25-year period from 1989 to 2014, the year-to-year inflation rate averaged 2.75%. In one exceptional year, 2009, there was a negative inflation rate of −0.3% (this has happened only about 10 times in the past 100 years, primarily during the Great Depression). However, inflation rates during the 25-year time frame were as high as 5.4% in 1990, 4.8% in 1989, and 3.85% in 2005. The compounded inflation rate during that period was nearly 100%.

In practice, COLAs often lag at least a year behind inflation. While some governments try to keep up with inflation annually, it is typical for policy makers to provide either an adjustment less than inflation or none at all. In the case of the federal government since 1989, no COLAs were budgeted (that is, salary freezes were in place) in 1994, 2011, 2012, and 2013.

The sentiment of both the citizenry and lawmakers has become less supportive of cost-of-living adjustments for a number of reasons. First, there is a public perception that these adjustments are rare in business, and that they should be reduced or eliminated in government. When this is coupled with the view that civil servants should not get merit increases "for doing their jobs," it means that the citizenry simply wants salaries to be reduced overall. Second, not only is there support for reducing or skipping COLAs in tight budget years, but also there has not been much interest in making up the salary inflation losses to keep employees "whole." Since merit-based pay is politically more palatable, a single pool of funds based primarily on merit may be approved. Suppose a 3.5% raise pool is offered, but inflation is 2.75%. Merit monies are extremely limited—unless most people get raises less than inflation, relatively few employees can get increases in excess of 3.5%.

Longevity Pay

Longevity pay (also known as seniority pay) is furnished on the basis that an employee's value has increased for the organization as a result of experience, training, and professional development (Chapter 8). Such raises recognize that recruitment and training are expensive, institutional knowledge is valuable and difficult to replace, loyalty to the organization is important, and a team ethic with relatively equal raises should not be ignored (e.g., employee competition could focus on moving from one grade to the next).

The most common approach to rewarding longevity is through the use of step increases, which are increases within each grade. As discussed above, the exact amount of steps and

Exhibit 7.7 An Example of a Federal Career and the Accompanying Salary Progression

Sarah earned her MPA in 1989 and got a job with the federal government. Like most employees with master's degrees, she started at grade 9, step 1, with a salary of $24,705. That was enough for her to live in her own apartment and have a car in a moderate-sized city. She got step increases each of the next several years, and in 1992 received a promotion to grade 11, skipping grade 10 (which is common). She continued in that position for 7 years, increasing four steps, and benefited from the introduction of **locality pay**, which brought her a 20% raise based on the cost of living in her moderately expensive metropolitan area (she retained that same locality pay differential because she did not move).

In 2000 she was promoted to grade 12 (having substantial professional, but not supervisory, responsibilities); her salary went from $56,346 to $71,570. With the acceptance of supervisory duties in 2006, Sarah moved to grade 13, progressing through step 6 by 2014. With her locality pay, her salary was $101,347. Her overall pay, in summary, went up because of three promotions, five step increases in the last grade, a substantial pay differential, and 21 COLAs. Because of promotions her salary had more than doubled. However, the portion of her salary increases based on COLAs had barely kept pace with the cost of living, as the CPI nearly doubled over the course of her 25-year career.

Year	Sarah's Grades/ Steps in Her Career	Other Increases[a]	Sarah's Salary at the Time	Current Salary of the Position	CPI of the Salary Compared to Today[b]
1989	9; step 1		24,705	41,979	47,007
1991	9: step 3	COLA	28,288	44,777	49,076
1992	11; step 1	COLA	32,506	50,790	54,746
1999	11; step 5	COLA; locality pay (20%)[c]	51,331	69,074	72,804
2000	12; step 1	COLA; locality	56,346	73,052	77,318
2005	12; step 4	COLA; locality	71,570	80,357	86,592
2006	13; step 1	COLA; locality	75,486	86,868	88,476
2014	13; step 6	COLA; locality; pay freezes	101,347	101,347	101,347

a. Cost-of-living adjustments varied over Sarah's career, from a high of 4.2% in 1992 to none in 1994, 2011, 2012, and 2013.

b. The Consumer Price Index adjusts for inflation (that is, $24,705 in 1989 would be equivalent to $47,007 today).

c. Locality pay was introduced in 1993 to help the federal salary schedule aid in adjusting salaries for agencies in expensive areas and catch up with the pay gap at the time.

amounts of pay are determined in salary schedules. A new employee is expected to start at the first step unless there is special authorization. The minimum time for the step increase is defined across the agency or government; the time between steps can be as short as 6 months or as long as 3 years, or it can be set to become longer as an individual progresses through the system.[8]

If an agency uses a lot of grades and fewer steps, there may not be overlap between the top step in one grade and the first step in the higher grade. However, when fewer grades and more steps are used, higher steps in one grade may overlap with the initial steps in the next grade (employees promoted to a higher grade are placed in the next-highest salary step in the new grade). Step systems are used by most federal agencies, and in many state and county governments, but less so in municipal and special district governments, including education. Most true step systems provide for little management input except for judgments about whether an employee is functioning at an acceptable level, and therefore eligible to receive an increase.

An example is the state of New York, which uses a variety of pay systems, most of which rely heavily on grade-and-step structures. A major category is the professional/scientific/technical pay plan, which has 38 grades and 5 steps (step increases are expected, unless unfunded in a fiscally stringent year, but career ladder increases require positive approval). The city of Seattle has 350 grades; each has 5 steps, with the first after 6 months and the later ones being a year apart. The state of Kansas has 34 grades and 13 steps. The attractiveness of inflation adjustments and longevity pay, in sum, lies in their simplicity, objectivity, predictability, and perceived fairness, as well as their ability to encourage workforce stability.

Nevertheless, many organizations believe that performance should be rewarded and report using some form of pay-for-performance, incentive, or variable pay plan. Such approaches depend on output, personnel, and organizational contingencies (see Exhibit 7.8) and work best in an environment of harmonious labor–management relations characterized by easy-to-understand payouts, high morale, and budgets sufficient to provide rewards. For staff personnel to see a link between pay and performance, their work must be evaluated by objective and/or subjective criteria in which they have confidence. Incentive pay also must be clearly distinguished from regular compensation and cost-of-living adjustments.

In contrast, as Hogler (2004) observes,

> simplistic notions of pay for performance that reject the concept of seniority tend to discount fundamental notions of fairness and loyalty, and managers who condemn seniority as having no value in the modern workplace may overlook the virtues of a neutral, wholly objective standard of distributing awards and the advantages of accumulated training and experience. Indeed, it could be argued that if a manager's subordinates do not improve their performance with length of service, the manager should be terminated. Used properly, seniority offers a means of avoiding arbitrary action and the appearance of favoritism. (pp. 161–162)

"The core fallacy of pay for performance," as Bob Behn (2004) observes, "is that money is not a great a motivator. . . . Most people . . . do not choose to work in government to maximize their income" (p. 2). To illustrate the paradoxical interplay of intrinsic and extrinsic motivations, one study of artists revealed that those who accomplished their

Exhibit 7.8   Pay for Performance: Reality or Illusion?

Pay for performance is a wonderful theory. . . .
Unfortunately, as with most government activities, the details matter.

—Bob Behn

The pay-for-performance idea is so widely accepted that most organizations say they use it and most employees believe that pay should be tied to performance. An analysis of economic, management, and social psychological research by two Harvard University faculty members, however, demonstrates that what is supposed to occur with these plans in theory seldom occurs in reality. The conditions for success for these programs—(1) the output produced, (2) the people who do the work, and (3) the organization where it is done—"are generally not met in the private sector, and even less so in the public sector" (Bohnet & Eaton, 2003, p. 241).

First, pay for performance runs well if (1) an employee has to complete one well-defined task, (2) the output is clearly measurable, and (3) the result can be attributed to one person's efforts. These overlapping and mutually reinforcing factors are difficult to achieve. Most white-collar employees are faced with multitasking problems, hard-to-measure work products, and team-oriented work environments, none of which fit well with individual incentives.

Second, assumptions about human nature and motivation are key to pay-for-performance plans. These programs may be effective if (1) employees work primarily for cash and (2) they care about absolute pay levels. Yet people are interested not only in money but also in job satisfaction and challenge, something not subject to performance pay. Indeed, most research suggests that humans do not want to believe that they work only for money, a finding that is especially true for public servants. Employees can even be offended when treated as if they can be manipulated by transparent monetary incentives, as payments create the idea that work is all about money, not the work itself.

Furthermore, personnel are less interested in absolute pay than in comparisons relative to some reference point, such as others' salaries, the jurisdiction's budget, or the state of the economy, considerations not germane to pay for performance. In fact, although everyone wants to be a winner, incentive plans usually mean that this is not possible. The result is "the silver medal syndrome, based on a study of Olympic champions, [which] shows that the most disappointed people are those who come in second" (Bohnet & Eaton, 2003, p. 248). A system that guarantees that most will be losers is not a useful motivational tool.

Third, institutional factors affect pay-for-performance programs. They operate best when employees know what to do and whom to serve. Knowledge of an organization's objectives, however, is not a given for the rank and file; the absence of clear goals is a result of multiple or changing leaders with different goals. This problem, known as "multiagency," is especially evident in government, where staff may serve many masters: chief executives, legislators, political appointees, judges, and senior career executives.

The university researchers do not claim that incentives are not effective under the right conditions, but only that "ideal conditions are rarely met in empirical reality" (Bohnet & Eaton, 2003, p. 251). They endorse the belief that "the rising and falling tides of interest in the various incentive plans have more to do with changing social, political, and economic fashions than with accumulating scientific evidence on how well the plans work" (Blinder, as cited in Bohnet & Eaton, 2003, p. 241). Nonetheless, most managers, for motivation and cost-control reasons, believe that performance should be an important part of the compensation system. More than 80% of nearly 1,000 private firms surveyed in 2003 said that they "pay for performance," although often for small parts of their workforces (Hewitt Associates,

(Continued)

Exhibit 7.8 (Continued)

2003). A meta-analysis of 39 empirical research projects in the private sector found that financial incentives were not related to performance quality (Jenkins, Mitra, Gupta, & Shaw, 1998). Indeed, in 2004 Harvard University Press published a book on business executive compensation titled *Pay Without Performance* (Bebchuk & Fried, 2004). Lane, Wolf, and Woodard (2003) assert that "there is an utter lack of empirical evidence in the private and public sectors that pay for performance has any positive effect on either morale or productivity" (p. 138). Careful investigation—not intuitive reasoning, common sense, and misguided confidence—is needed to understand how performance pay operates, as managers often have little in-depth understanding of compensation complexities (Ariely, 2010, p. 37).

Pay-for-performance programs, in short, are deceptively difficult to achieve, both technically and politically. The idea of paying for performance may be good in principle but difficult to enact, as indicated by past experience with the federal general pay schedule as well as reform attempts in the 1970s, 1980s, 1990s, and the first decade of this century. First, as Gage and Kelly (2003) point out, the federal GS is, in fact, a performance-based system that has never been correctly implemented. Supervisors do not take advantage of available incentives—cash awards, within-grade increases, quality step increases—because there are insufficient funds for them to do so. When this traditional approach was nonetheless modified to emphasize incentive pay, it had to be repealed as unworkable.

Second, as Risher (2002) notes, performance compensation was tried "first for managers under the Civil Service Reform Act of 1978 and then under the Performance Management and Recognition Act starting in 1984. [The] experience was so bad . . . that [the laws] were allowed to sunset . . . and the idea of pay for performance was all but forgotten" (p. 318). These attempts led to consternation and delay, paperwork, and appeals, and they cost more money while still not rewarding the best employees. Third, in 1996, the Federal Aviation Administration implemented pay for performance. By 2004, it was dubbed "a failure" that led to inequity and poor morale (Kauffman, 2004).

Fourth, following the implementation of a "best practices" reform program at the U.S. Government Accountability Office, it was reported that 81% of employees believed that morale was worse than before pay restructuring (Ballenstedt, 2008a). Another program once viewed as a model for the rest of government, that of the Senior Executive Service, was found after 4 years to have little effect on performance while hastening retirements and discouraging midlevel managers from applying to the SES. The U.S. Department of Homeland Security's MaxHR program as well as the Department of Defense's national security personnel system produced so many productivity problems, court defeats, and widespread dissatisfaction that both abandoned pay for performance (Haga, Richman, & Leavitt, 2010; Tiefer, 2008). To date, no one has developed lessons from these failures.

In a triumph of hope over experience, pay for performance nonetheless remains as popular in management circles as ever. Thus, the 16 agencies constituting the intelligence community began implementing pay for performance in 2008, building on a little-known effort by the National Geospatial Intelligence Agency—a program that, according to the National Academy of Public Administration, had no influence on productivity or performance (Losey, 2010). In addition, an OPM report claimed success for the federal government's pay incentive plans, lauded more than 25 years of successful experiments with all existing alternative pay systems, and later announced performance pay pilot projects at five agencies (Walker, 2008). A union official, however, noted, "The patchwork of pay programs across government cannot be collectively or individually characterized as a success; the reality is that each is terribly flawed," leading to increases in grievances, litigation, attrition rates, and low morale (quoted in Walker, 2008). At the Federal Deposit Insurance Corporation, for example, just 12% of employees believed that pay for performance reflected actual performance. Indeed, an arbitrator ruled that the

Securities and Exchange Commission performance pay plan discriminated on the basis of sex and race (Ballenstedt, 2008b). An influential congressman, nonetheless, declared his intent to establish a pay-for-performance program for all federal employees based on a U.S. Postal Service program, an initiative that is under investigation for its problematic nature (Losey, 2011a).

At best, it remains to be seen if these initiatives will overcome inherent problems typically found in these incentive plans. Even Howard Risher (2004), in an enthusiastic endorsement of performance pay, admits that the technique "may well prove to be the most difficult change any organization has ever attempted" (p. 46). As if to make the point, he offers no fewer than 29 recommendations.

Not to be overlooked, the National Institute of Standards and Technology reported that its long-standing pay-for-performance project has enabled the institute to "compete more effectively for top talent, retain more of its high performers, and expand managers' authority over hiring and pay decisions" (Kirkner, 2008, p. 23). Hays (2004), in addition, has written about two cases in state and local jurisdictions where the approach apparently works. For this to occur, the plans must be well designed, meet expectations for pay gains, and be implemented in an atmosphere of high trust and employee morale. Such success stories tend to be isolated, temporary, and/or constrained; if confirmed by independent research, they must nonetheless contend with a substantial body of evidence on performance pay failure. As the U.S. Merit Systems Protection Board (2006) stipulates, such systems can be effective only if the following factors are present:

- A supportive organizational culture
- Fair-minded, well-trained supervisors
- A rigorous performance appraisal system
- A system of checks and balances
- An ongoing system of program evaluation

One expert recommends that pay for performance be introduced first for managers. Among the criteria that should drive their salary increases is their mastery of the skills needed to manage employee performance.

While an organization's compensation system reinforces good performance, the focus on pay for performance, paradoxically, should not emphasize only money. Incentive compensation is neither quick nor easy. Other factors—public service motivation, good management, importance of work—affect job satisfaction; many professionals do not work for profits, stock values, or commissions. Jauhar (2008) provides an account, and a devastating critique, of the unintended consequences that can happen when physicians are paid for performance.

As Perry (2003) observes, "The reality is that pay for performance is likely to be of little benefit to organizations with serious performance problems and may actually be harmful" (p. 150). If not well implemented, a demoralized, embittered, unmotivated workforce can result. Brown and Heywood (2002, p. 10) cite an official who identified two common attributes of these plans—they involve huge amounts of management time and make everyone unhappy. Indeed, pay-for-performance programs—since they are often required to be "budget neutral"—can become an excuse to resist fair pay in the first place. Money can get people to work, but it cannot get people to want to work. The evidence suggests that incentives are seen as bribes and thereby reduce employees' self-respect. According to a federal incentive pay consultant, reform-minded officials should look at the culture of the agency, the kind of work it does, and the resources needed to deploy a new program. "Instead of saying, 'we want [it] because everyone else has it,' agencies should ask themselves, 'What are we trying to accomplish?'" (Hewitt Associates, 2003, p. 6).

SOURCES: Ariely (2010); Ballenstedt (2008a); Bohnet and Eaton (2003); Brown and Heywood (2002); Gage and Kelly (2003); Hays (2004); Hewitt Associates (2003); Jauhar (2008); Jenkins et al. (1998); Kauffman (2004, 2005); Kellough and Selden (1997); Kirkner (2008); Losey (2010, 2011a); Perry (2003); Risher (2002, 2004); Tiefer (2008); Walker (2008); Zeller (2004).

work more for its sheer pleasure than for rewards were found to be socially recognized as superior. "It is those who are least motivated to pursue extrinsic rewards who eventually receive them" (J. Carney, cited in Pink, 2009, p. 49).

Merit Pay

Like longevity pay, **merit pay** involves annual incremental increases to base salary, an annuity that compounds for as long as the employee remains with the department. In "true" merit systems, managers have flexibility about who gets how much (not just when there are grade or classification promotions). Typically, organizations opt for either a longevity or a merit category, although raises may use both criteria simultaneously. One common practice, noted earlier, is to divide the pool of funds for raises into COLAs and merit. However, sometimes merit is designated as the sole determinant; in such cases the portion going to performance is in lieu of the cost-of-living portion and longevity is implicitly eliminated. Those who are underperforming receive no merit, but generally, those individuals would be deprived of their step increases in most step systems as well. Merit systems jurisdictions may use pay ranges rather than steps for job classifications and their related grades, with minimums, midpoints, and maximums. The important feature is that the amount paid out is at the administrator's discretion. New employees are expected to start at the minimum pay in the range, but line managers may have more discretion than in step systems. In addition, most merit systems have fewer grades and move to broader pay bands with more than a 40% span rather than the 20% to 35% range more typical in step systems.

The use of merit has an intuitive attractiveness supported by conventional wisdom as well as leading motivation theories (economic, need, expectancy): Incentives lead to improved performance. Increases are based on managers' decisions relating to the quantitative and qualitative factors of employment (e.g., amount of results, accuracy of results). The explicit values of merit pay are competition and promotion of individual striving. The implicit values are that significant pay inequality is fair and that individual contributions are more important than teamwork.

It is not surprising that public and private organizations claim to give great deference to merit; the civil service is even named for it. A substantial discontinuity exists, nevertheless, between rhetoric and reality, as merit pay (outside of sales and commissions jobs) "may not be as desirable, as easy to implement, or as widely used as commonly believed" (Fisher, Schoenfeldt, & Shaw, 2006, p. 512).[9] In the national government, the results are at best disappointing (Kellough & Lu, 1993; Perry, Engbers, & Jun, 2009). The cardinal paradox is that performance pay is offered as a replacement for traditional pay systems that themselves are supposed to be merit based. That is, there is nothing under those approaches that obligates managers to give time-in-grade raises. Thus, while merit pay is a powerful cultural symbol and a source of control for managers over employees, they are reluctant to use it (Bowman, 2010).

For merit pay systems to be successful, certain conditions must be present: trust in management, a valid job evaluation system, clear performance factors, meaningful and consistent funding, and accurate personnel appraisal (Chapter 10). Even if these exist, merit compensation may perversely (1) focus on the short term at the expense of the long term,

(2) encourage mediocrity by setting limits on expectations, (3) reduce creativity and risk taking, (4) promote self-interest above other interests, (5) destroy teamwork by increasing dependence on individual accomplishment, (6) generate counterproductive win–lose competition among employees for merit monies, (7) encourage sycophancy ("do as I say performance pay"), and (8) generally politicize the compensation system. Employees may "eventually come to see merit pay as a kind of punishment" (Gabris & Ihrke, 2004, p. 504), as rewards ultimately penalize employees when they are not received.

Merit pay, in theory, has the potential to produce high performance, but in practice it is difficult to administer in a way that personnel perceive as fair, as the example below illustrates:

> When a municipal government received political pressure to implement a pay plan, the city manager and professional staff contracted a consultant to develop a first-rate, by-the-book, technically sophisticated design. This new system should have worked.
>
> Originally, the total money available from the compensation pool was to be divided, with about 60% going for cost-of-living adjustments and automatic pay increases and 40% reserved for merit pay. When the elected officials heard this, they reversed the formula to 75% reserved for merit pay and 25% for cost-of-living increases. These political officials clearly wanted a strong merit message sent to employees.
>
> The city's employees resisted such intense merit pay strategies, and the police department, to avoid the merit program, unionized that same year. After the efforts of cooler heads and the making of various compromises, the merit distribution went back more or less to the original 60–40 split. Why was this so important to the rank-and-file employees? Why did they not want more resources put into the merit pool on the premise that if they performed well, they stood to receive considerable pay increases?
>
> By and large, these employees, like others in the public sector, were more concerned with external and internal equity than with individual equity. Merit raises, although helping, usually do not bring public agency base salaries up to market. What happens instead is that employees find their base salaries compressed in relation to what the market would currently pay someone with their level of skills and experience. This **pay compression** happens when people stay in the same jobs for long durations, receiving generally small base salary increases and only periodic merit raises. Ineluctably, these workers find new hires starting with base salaries not much below, and even in some cases above (pay inversion), their salaries. (Gabris, 1998, p. 649; emphasis added)

Even business admirers like Risher and Fay (1997) have concluded:

> Despite policy statements that make individual merit important, salaries have been managed in a lock step manner. . . . The most aggressive corporate programs rarely give meaningful recognition to outstanding employees. The underlying merit philosophy is solidly entrenched . . . but the typical private sector employee can expect an annual salary increase with almost as much certainty as the typical public sector employee. (pp. 3, 43)

In order for a merit pay system to operate as advocated, the differences in pay must be substantial. For example, given a pool of dollars for distribution, the top 10% of employees get a 10% raise, 60% of employees get 5%, and 30% of employees do not get any raise. Such a system is motivating for those who are in the top group, there will be mixed reactions in the middle group (some will be satisfied, but since most people think they are above average, there may be resentment), and there will most likely be dejection and anger in the lowest group.

Overall, merit plans seldom provide enough funds to reward exceptional employees without unfairly penalizing valued satisfactory ones. It is a major administrative challenge for an organization to continuously reevaluate motivation and productivity, to identify the additional level of performance that warrants special recognition, and to provide those incentives on an equitable and timely basis. Bob Behn (n.d.; also see Behn, 2004) identifies more than 20 key design and perceptual issues found in these programs: (1) who gets rewarded (e.g., eight design questions based on rewarding individuals and/or teams), (2) the nature of the reward (four questions on whether the reward is intrinsic or extrinsic; if the latter, what is its size, is it a one-time bonus or added to base pay, and what is the source of funds?), (3) what is rewarded (eight questions on how rewards are determined), and (4) how the plan is perceived (three questions on advocates' motivation, whether the plan appears to reward or punish, and whether the plan is regarded as fair).

Merit pay, in short, should never be oversold as a panacea for organizational problems; if used, it should be merely one part of the compensation system (Gabris & Ihrke, 2004, p. 506). So long as government salaries are inconsistent with the expectations of job candidates, those motivated by money will find better alignment of individual and organizational needs in the for-profit sector. Performance pay, even well implemented, cannot address such inconsistencies. It is easy to understand why simpler, "set-it-and-forget-it" compensation systems are so widespread. Indeed, it is telling that performance pay promoters have not sought to apply the technique to presidents, members of Congress, agency secretaries, or the uniformed services. Further, it is not surprising that among the many techniques employed by Sloan workplace award winners, performance pay is not one of them (Galinsky & Eby, 2008). As well, two important books on civil service reform reject pay for performance (Bilmes & Gould, 2009; Donahue, 2008).

In spite of—or perhaps because of—such problems, there is no indication that decision makers are ready to abandon merit pay, an idea that has become a kind of management's "fool's gold."[10] Indeed, OPM, the second National Commission on Public Service (Volcker II), and the National Academy of Public Administration have recommended a new federal governmentwide compensation system.[11] Widespread and consistently discouraging results inevitably raise questions about the efficacy of performance pay itself. Undaunted, compensation reformers, as a result, sometimes resort to tactics such as the following ("Don't Abandon Performance-Based Pay," 2007; National Academy of Public Administration, 2004; Partnership for Public Service, 2005; Risher, 2008; Schuster & Zingheim, 2007):

- Suggesting that technical concerns deflect attention from performance
- Conceding that the evidence does not confirm that pay enhances performance
- Claiming that alternatives are worse
- Blaming critics for not creating better compensation systems

- Arguing that pay for performance is not actually that important since it is not an end in itself
- Declaring that the real problem is not pay at all, but rather personnel appraisal, performance management, "communication," or something else

However ingenious (or disingenuous) and wishful (or desperate) these arguments might be, they are certainly effective in the realpolitik of public pay plans. There is a deeply ingrained belief in pay for performance, one encouraged by vendors promising that however difficult the technique may be it nevertheless can be done with their guidance. A pretense of assumed future benefits seems better than the prospect of exposing actual past and present failures.

Officials are generally reluctant to admit mistakes, and administrators tend to use merit monies to reward things other than performance (see below and Chapter 10). Performance pay can become a substitute for good management: Manipulating compensation packages is far easier than designing meaningful jobs and paying everyone fairly. Merit is simply too oceanic a social myth to reject outright; to do so would suggest that individuals do not make a difference. Instead, as Gabris (1998) suggests, because merit plans fixate on individual equity, every effort should be made to ensure that the total compensation system strives to align individual, internal, and external equities. This balance must include attention both to how much people receive (distributive justice) and to the processes used to decide how much (procedural justice). Failure to address these issues exacerbates the vicious, visible, and vital aspects of pay, a topic about which few hold neutral feelings.

Skill-Based Pay

Criticisms of merit schemes have triggered a high level of interest in **skill-based pay** (also known as knowledge or competency pay). Such plans analyze the job knowledge a competent employee needs to possess. As new skills are (1) learned, (2) used, and (3) demonstrated by results, employees qualify for salary increments.

Skill compensation can be consistent with longevity and/or merit principles and is compatible with broad pay banding because employees are recognized for gaining additional competencies in a wide array of job practices. It is person centered rather than job centered because, unlike job evaluation, it focuses on how well the individual is doing the job, not on how well the job is defined. For example, the Riverside, California, police department provides pay increases for becoming bilingual, qualifying for the sniper team, and learning hostage negotiation skills. Skill-based pay is common in education (e.g., substantial increases in pay for a master's, master's + 30 credits, various certifications), public safety (e.g., courses and certifications for firefighters in emergency medical training, aerial operations, trench rescue, associate's, bachelor's, and master's degrees), health, and other areas where constant skill upgrading is important. The state of California has five pay ranges for psychologists depending on whether incumbents have a master's degree only, 2 years of doctoral work, 3 years of doctoral work, 3 years of doctoral work plus the completion of comprehensive exams (indicating work on a dissertation), or the completion of a doctoral degree.

The technique of basing pay on skill promises to improve productivity: Instead of focusing on minimal qualifications, it emphasizes competencies that a fully performing, multi-skilled employee is expected to demonstrate. In so doing, it specifies what the organization needs (a capable, flexible workforce) and what people want (control over compensation and job success). As an added benefit, it also helps resolve a nettlesome problem for both employers and employees—that of traditional performance appraisal (Chapter 10), as the individual either does or does not progress in skill level. It should be noted that this form of pay may add to labor costs, at least in the short run, until increased productivity manifests itself.

Although few studies have validated skill-based pay systems, they are growing in popularity, especially in organizations that focus on participatory management and teamwork. Englewood, Colorado, for example, has developed a skill-based pay system that updated all job descriptions, verified each job position's current salary, and formulated career development plans. Implementation of the strategy involved developing a new pay line (determining the skill bases for jobs and assigning a monetary value to each skill category), establishing an individualized career development program for employees, and giving employees a choice as to whether or not they would participate in the plan. The program resulted in higher individual satisfaction, better-defined personal and professional goals, increased employee empowerment, and cost-effectiveness (Leonard, 1995).

The Virginia Department of Transportation's skill-based program failed, however, because it lacked supervisory or union support, compelled all employees to participate (many of whom then complained to legislators), and neglected to redesign human resource systems needed to support the change (e.g., classification and appraisal). A significant factor was the use of business consultants who did not understand the sensitive political milieu in which the agency operated (Shareef, 2002). Between the experiences of the Englewood and Virginia programs are those of the Veterans Benefits Administration, the Federal Aviation Administration, and the North Carolina State Transportation Department, each of which had to undertake major changes in their skill-based initiatives to make them work (Thompson & LeHew, 2002).

These plans are not, then, a panacea for two reasons. First, intrinsic concerns include the frustration that occurs when newly achieved skills go unused or when employees "top out" of the program with no further opportunity to earn raises, as well as the complex bureaucratic processes that are likely to develop to monitor and certify employee progress. Second, extrinsic impacts include effects on complementary personnel functions (short-term training and long-term payroll costs increase) and the dynamic political atmosphere (electoral cycles, employees as voters, unions, rank-and-file versus managerial pay).[12] Note also that it is far more difficult to determine external equity in this approach to pay.

Bonus Programs

As noted earlier, when employees receive a temporary pay increase, a type of **bonus** program is in effect (Exhibit 7.9). Bonuses can be awarded based on high levels of individual productivity (performance awards) or can result from the distribution of savings to the organization (gainsharing, where the benefits are disbursed to groups or even whole organizations).

Exhibit 7.9   Employee Bonuses: Compensatory, Contemptible, or Comical?

Money costs too much.

—Ralph Waldo Emerson

A growing compensation trend is the use of bonuses, one-time payments sometimes made instead of awarding more costly permanent pay increases. To encourage high performance, the payouts must be noticeable—at least 10% of salary is common in Europe—because smaller amounts may be demoralizing and counterproductive. For the organization, this technique provides an economical, flexible method to control salary expenditures but nonetheless still reward employees. For the individual, one lump sum may seem like more money than a comparably sized raise spread over an entire year. At least in the short run, then, bonuses appear to resolve the paradox of needs.

Unfortunately, such plans are subject to political processes that frequently undermine them because the politicization of compensation often results in program underfunding. Administrators, then, are faced with two unattractive options: giving a few employees relatively large amounts and other deserving staff nothing, or providing virtually everyone with trivial rewards. At the federal level, the average award in 2007 was $577; most personnel believe that their agencies' programs do not provide incentives to encourage performance (Method, 2008). A similar result can be found at the state level, as the case below illustrates:

> Some politicians are fond of blustering about making government run "like a business" and they often stereotype public employees as do-nothing bureaucrats. So when the government does run "like a business," that, one might think, would make them happy.
>
> The Florida Department of Revenue took state lawmakers up on a challenge issued when the legislature passed a law allowing monetary rewards—bonuses—to state employees who go above and beyond the call of duty and save the state money. The department saved state taxpayers $9 million. Not bad.
>
> Having accomplished this, the agency's executive director, Larry Fuchs, asked the legislature to appropriate enough to give half of his deserving staff $100 bonuses. Save $9 million. Spend $250,000. But that's when another stereotype came into play: the stereotype of the conniving, forked-tongue, hypocritical politician. The Senate refused to give Fuchs the bonus money.
>
> Some lawmakers say the state should not pay its employees extra for simply doing their jobs. Others have questioned whether the agency met performance standards, but Fuchs says he was never told why the Senate refused to pay the bonuses. If the Senate does not want to offer financial incentives for meeting higher work standards in state government, it should say so. But government leaders have an obligation to keep their promises. Pay the $100 bonuses. (Cotterell, 2004)

In the same state, many departments paid identical amounts to eligible staff (e.g., $371, although some payouts ranged from $76 to $2,000 for a small number of employees; Cotterell, 2004). For different reasons, most personnel—those receiving and those not receiving the monies—found such payouts to be depressing. In Wyoming, $400 annual performance bonuses were allotted to state

(Continued)

Exhibit 7.9 (Continued)

agencies for distribution in 12 monthly installments. In some departments, awards were given to a few people who then gave the money to others, threw a party, or refused to accept it. In other offices, employees drew straws for the money (Behn, 2000, p. 4). Thus, while these programs are a tool in the pay raise quiver, they are much less suited to widespread use than in the private sector, especially in areas like sales, executive pay, and Wall Street, where they predominate.

Another concern is that performance awards incentivize inappropriate behavior. In 2014 an outcome-driven performance management system at the Veterans Administration (VA) created unrealistic goals that ultimately put the health of veterans at risk. The program led managers to falsify wait-time records to make it appear that veterans were being seen by medical personnel sooner than they actually were. At the height of the scandal, an agency official testified before Congress that annual bonuses were a vital tool in recruiting and retaining top employees (nevertheless, the bonus program was canceled). The episode was ironic since the VA had been seen as a success story; in the 1990s reformers cut back middle-management ranks and began using performance data. The overall result was that patients received high-quality, low-cost care and did not appear to wait longer than nonveterans in private hospitals (the satisfaction rate among patients was over 80%; Fahrenthold, 2014).

Incentive payout schemes like bonus programs, even if adequately funded, should not be used to cover up more fundamental problems in the workplace. There are settings in which bonuses make sense if the work offers employees no opportunity to find satisfaction and fulfill intrinsic needs. And, yes, there should be public acknowledgment of extra performance. The offer of bonuses, however, implies that employees are not working hard, cannot be trusted to do their work, and need extra incentive to do their jobs well. It is for these reasons such plans are often counterproductive. Promoting the idea that no one will do anything right unless it is required is no way to run an organization.

SOURCES: Behn (2000, 2004); Lee and Straus (2004); "State Should Keep Promise" (1996), © Copyright 1996 by Tallahassee Democrat. Reprinted with permission.

Performance awards are akin to merit increases in that they are competitive and unequally distributed; the difference is that they must be earned each year and they do not contribute to base salary. They are used extensively at the federal level and for executive pay in state and local governments. In the federal government case, discretionary bonuses are capped at "no more than 1 % of an agency's aggregate salaries of rank-and-file employees, and no more than 5 % of the aggregate salaries for its senior executives" (Mullen, 2014). This category topped out in 2011, when the payout was $439 million, but has declined dramatically since then (due to strong political criticism), with a payout of only $177 million in 2013. In addition, the Presidential Rank Awards were suspended in 2013. Ironically, the use of this type of raise has increased in the private sector, where it is called variable pay.

In a **gainsharing** pay plan, the organization and its employees divide greater-than-expected gains realized through productivity and/or cost reductions. Typically, half of the savings revert to the agency general fund and the balance is allotted equally among the people involved. Several interesting variations of gainsharing have been used by city governments. For example, under a popular program in Loveland, Colorado, the provision of funds to city personnel depended on the results of citizen satisfaction surveys and the amount of funds left over in the budget; this program was terminated, however, because managers found it to be problematic. Charlotte, North Carolina, has a "competition-based program" that distributes monies either to employees when they competitively bid and win projects or to city departments when they exceed benchmark performance standards (Jurkiewicz & Bowman, 2002).

Gainsharing, in short, is designed to accomplish the same objective as individual incentives: the linking of rewards with performance. The difference is that in gainsharing performance is measured as a result of group effort, thereby reinforcing team cohesion, promoting a problem-solving culture, and reducing perceived internal inequities. Individual and group incentives are not mutually exclusive but can be blended through concentration on individual behavior consistent with gainsharing (i.e., contributions to teamwork). To succeed, the technique requires a high degree of organizational trust as well as widespread information distribution. Focusing on employee empowerment and quality improvement, a number of experiments in the U.S. Department of Defense since the 1980s have had varying degrees of success. One concern with gainsharing is that it may be quite successful in the program's first several years, when the potential for savings is high, but this potential can decline over time.

Although not widely used, gainsharing carries genuine potential to create a flexible, proactive, problem-solving workforce (Masternak, 2003). This is one of many areas, however, where rhetoric and reality collide. As Sanders (1998) has ruefully observed, lawmakers may argue that "bureaucrats are already paid (perhaps too much) to efficiently use public funds, and that they should not be offered more money to do what they should be doing anyway" (p. 239). The idea is that base salary and just having a job should be adequate incentive (a notion that progressive businesses rejected long ago). Accordingly, when an agency attempts an incentive plan such as gainsharing or bonuses, its payroll may subsequently be reduced by the amount of savings generated.

For incentive programs to be successful, a cultural change is required to overcome the suspicion and cynicism with which these plans are currently viewed. Yet, should such a change occur, these approaches, when used as partial or complete substitutes for other plans, can mean less money for most employees than that provided under other approaches to individual equity.

Differential Pay

Differential pay is additional pay for special work conditions based on time, location, responsibilities, or deference to special needs or employee considerations. It is considered temporary and not a part of the base pay; however, employees may be eligible for differential pay for long periods or even their entire careers, and some compensation systems allow differentials to be used in calculating pensions (a practice curtailed by recent pension reforms). The implicit values of this type of pay are to motivate people to take on less desirable assignments, locations, or responsibilities, and to hold them harmless for job-incurred expenses.

Shift differentials, for example, are common where hours extend considerably beyond the normal 8:00-to-5:00 workday and the Monday-through-Friday workweek (e.g., the evening or swing shift, 4:00 P.M. to midnight; the late-night or graveyard shift, midnight to 8:00 A.M.). It is typical for agencies to give employees hourly shift differentials for working these shifts, as well as to provide a larger differential for the graveyard shift. The federal government customarily pays 7.5% and 10% differentials for the second and third shifts, respectively.

Location pay is typically provided to employees working in high-cost areas or unattractive regions and those with undesirable duties. The national government pays up to a 35% premium in the most expensive cities (e.g., for the San Jose–San Francisco area), but with a norm of 20% to 28% for most other urban sites, including, ironically, the minimum 14% location pay provided to all U.S.-based federal employees. Undesirable assignments, common in the armed forces and U.S. State Department, are also eligible for location differentials, such as hazardous duty pay, hostile-fire-and-imminent-danger pay, hardship pay, and assignment-incentive military pay (for extending tours in less desirable locations). The equivalent for civilian personnel is danger pay, which can be as high as 35% in war-ravaged areas.

Overtime pay is for time beyond the 40-hour workweek and is provided at one and a half times the worker's regular pay rate. Holiday pay is a special type of overtime, requiring work on a state or national holiday; it is usually double time in recognition of this work's onerous nature. Although overtime is rarely allowed in many agencies except in extraordinary conditions, it is common and desired in public safety and corrections, where staffing limitations and the need for trained personnel require agencies to use large amounts of overtime routinely. Such departments regularly have standing overtime allocations built into their budgets. Overtime among employees in fire and corrections can be so extensive that a few individuals nearly double their salaries. Since overtime is not a part of the base salary, it normally does not count toward pension benefits. Special variants of overtime are standby pay for availability to work in extreme circumstances and call-out pay for being on duty during nonnormal hours for an emergency.

Allowances are monies to pay for costs imposed by employment or as part of the job. They can be relatively small (food, clothing, dislocation, moving, and family separation) or large (cars, housing). Allowances can be considered either reimbursements or income: Most travel and uniform allowances are considered reimbursements and not taxable, whereas automobile and housing allowances are regarded as a type of income and have tax ramifications. The military makes extensive use of allowances; they are also common in executive positions and public safety. A variant of an allowance is when an employee gets benefits from a job that reduce costs and may not be taxable (e.g., food eaten on the job or a "take-home" car for an employee who is on call).

Finally, differentials are also provided for assumption of special responsibilities (special duty or assignment pay). They may be awarded for assignments that are difficult, filled on a crisis basis, or hard to fill because unusual skills are needed. For example, the U.S. Navy has 23 standing special duty pay areas, ranging from being a recruiter to working on the USS *Constitution* to being a military attaché to being a brig officer.

IMPLICATIONS

The above discussion has examined the similarities and differences among pay systems awarding raises based on cost of living, longevity, merit, skill, bonuses, and differentials. These provide a set of compensation tools that can be precise and purposeful. In practice, they are often conflated, used too bluntly, ignored, and/or simply misrepresented, with the result that the similarities engulf the differences. Any reasonable increase becomes a symbolic lightning rod for criticism. Consequently, available resources are often so trivial that managers have little choice but to use the "peanut butter" approach: spread the funds more or less equally among employees to help keep everyone from losing ground to inflation.

This is perhaps most clear when cost-of-living allowances not only are used as a substitute for incentive pay but also are doled out below living costs. When there is little consistent attempt to "keep employees whole" against inflation, the real issue is not raises (seniority, merit, skill, or gainshare) but the size of the pay reductions. When the economy improves, many lawmakers paradoxically, if predictably, see even less reason to provide raises—to say nothing of furnishing "catch-up" monies.[13] Indeed, they often argue against raises as a way to keep inflation under control.

This strategy serves as an indicator of elected official "toughness" and responsiveness to taxpayers. Thus, equity—external, internal, individual—is simply replaced by the amount of lost purchasing power as the years go by. Nowhere is the dilemma between organizational and individual goals more evident: Employees wish to be treated fairly at the same time that public compensation systems often act to deny that need. The depth of the problem was illustrated in 1999. Rather than pay soldiers salaries sufficient to keep them off public assistance, the military again lowered recruiting standards, and some elected officials advocated reinstating the draft.[14] The value to the public of this conundrum is limited: Employees in an inequitable situation, according to equity theory, seek to reduce the inequity by decreasing performance, increasing absenteeism and tardiness, or simply quitting.

Although it may be true that relative pay levels will not drive government out of business, it is also true that a noncompetitive salary structure has very real consequences for public service. It serves as an impetus to hire peripheral labor—low-paid, often poorly trained, part-time employees, temporary workers, and even volunteers, many of whom are likely to leave as soon as they find full-time positions.[15] It also acts as a stimulus to privatization—the functional equivalent of going out of business—sometimes at a higher cost to the taxpayer.

In this context, then, debates over pay reform plans, although intellectually interesting, are diversionary because they miss the fundamental point: inadequate pay for all employees—women, men, black, brown, yellow, red, and white alike. The actual problem is decidedly not the type of pay technique; rather, the real, substantively rational issue is the amount of pay. It is not unexpected, therefore, that incentive systems often do not produce expected gains. Rather than focusing on fundamental problems—insufficient funding, inaccurate evaluations, incomplete feedback, ineffective leadership—agencies introduce incentive pay, thought to be a quick way to increase effort, while not understanding that in reality it is a complex, expensive, questionable enterprise.

Pay in all sectors has been stagnant for several decades; gross compensation has increased slightly largely because of health care costs (Bureau of Labor Statistics, 2014). Productivity has grown 80% since 1973, but incomes have grown only 10% on average, and that was before 2000. Indeed, mean income (including market earnings) has continued to rise slightly, yet because 65% of that income went to the top 1%, overall median household income has actually slid by more than 10% since 2000 (Greenhouse, 2013). In the federal case, ideological factions see the gap differently and cite different studies to argue either for reducing pay and benefits (Congressional Budget Office, 2012; House Budget Committee, 2014) or attempting to keep federal workers' incomes from slipping due to inflation and reducing pay gaps (President's Pay Agent, 2011; U.S. GAO, 2013). Because government employees tend to be substantially better educated and slightly older than their counterparts in the private sector, as well as the complexity of factors to consider, different methodologies come to different conclusions. There is general agreement that federal employee benefits are better than benefits in the private sector (largely because some businesses provide few or no benefits) while the salaries of federal employees are lower (U.S. GAO, 2012). State and local studies and debates have mirrored these arguments.

Pay stagnation or decline has not been the sole problem for government workforces in the United States. In addition to the pay gap perceived by many public sector workers, there has been an increase in the level of frustration and burnout due to workforce downsizing and political criticism. This means that the careful use and articulation of individual salary allocations is all that much more important, even as such allocations have become more politically and publicly debated.

SUMMARY AND CONCLUSION

Pay policies and programs are a significant—and problematic—dimension of management (Zingheim & Schuster, 2000). Pivotal to the employment relationship, compensation decisions can further fulfillment of individual goals as well as organizational goals. Because compensation represents a powerful symbol of an institution's overall beliefs, employees need to know that the organization is looking out for their interests as well as for its own. Without this understanding, pay becomes a target for a wide variety of work-related problems.

This chapter has focused on the elements that influence pay determination. Equity in external competitiveness (labor markets), in internal consistency (job evaluation leading to different types of pay determination systems), and in individual considerations (cost of living, longevity, merit, skill, bonuses, and differential compensation) has been examined within the context of policy (lead, match, lag) and law (e.g., the 1963 Equal Pay Act and the 1990 Federal Employees Pay Comparability Act). Among the controversial issues in this important human resource management arena are pay dissatisfaction, the public–private sector pay gap, time and money, and benefits. Reading between the lines, key principles characterize this vital, visible, and vicious topic: (1) Compensation, perhaps more than any other personnel function, is a people issue; (2) pay is a nonverbal but loud and powerful form of communication; (3) pertinent strategies are contingent on the culture of the jurisdiction and the vision of its organizations—one size does not fit all; (4) pay systems must support and be consistent with all other aspects of the agency; and (5) determination of pay is more art than science (also see Flannery, Hofrichter, & Platten, 2002).

Public and nonprofit employers, far more than business employers, need to be able to demonstrate that compensation systems are managed effectively and treat people fairly. Failure to honor competitive pay in law and policy in the name of political expediency does little to foster trust in the democratic process or to ensure productivity. This is dramatically illustrated by the substitution of contract workers for public employees (see Exhibit 7.10).

Exhibit 7.10   Contractors and Compensation: Politics and Policy

Public employees constitute only a fraction of today's government workforce; contractors perform much of government work. While no clear estimate is available of how many such employees there are, most observers agree that the number has dramatically expanded in recent years, creating a "silent revolution" in an increasingly hollowed-out government. By one 2006 estimate, there now exists a "shadow government": The number of personnel on federal contracts and grants is 10.5 million, compared with 1.9 million federal civil servants. The Counterintelligence Field Activity, for example, is staffed 70% by contractors, joining other agencies, such as the U.S. Department of Energy and NASA, that function as "holding companies" for a consortia of corporations. According to the U.S. Government Accountability Office, 15 of 21 U.S. Department of Defense program offices are staffed primarily by contract workers. Even the government's online database, the Federal Procurement Data System, was initially contracted out. A prime example of this contracting phenomenon is Edward Snowden, the low-level but high-clearance CIA consultant who divulged thousands of top-secret documents in 2013.

To the extent that contracting is based on ideology rather than cost-benefit analysis, it is simply assumed that government should be run like, and increasingly by, business. Yet Paul Light, an expert on the subject, has pointed out, "We have no data to show that contractors are actually more efficient than the government" (quoted in Shane & Nixon, 2007). Every contract, in fact, includes handsome executive salaries, campaign contributions, marketing expenses, and profit margins—monies that could be used to provide goods and services if offered by the public service. Privatization, in fact, is often used as a way to outsource problems (e.g., Hurricane Katrina recovery, tax collection, detainee torture, and prison management) to organizations whose actions are frequently unchecked and therefore unaccountable. Simultaneously, the federal government's contract-monitoring workforce, now handling a record number of contracts, is experiencing high turnover due to low pay, retirement, and legislative demands for more reports, restrictions, and inspections. The U.S. Army, for example, admitted in 2008 that it turned to contractors, even for inherently governmental work, because it could not fill employee vacancies in any other way. The contracted jobs were paid more than federal positions.

At the peak of the conflicts in Iraq and Afghanistan, the U.S. Department of Defense estimated that there were 196,000 contract personnel involved, more than the number of troops deployed. While they performed a wide variety of tasks, some carried out duties that paralleled combat roles along with prisoner interrogation and intelligence gathering. The U.S. State Department paid $1,222 per day for private security guards in Iraq, compared with the $200 per day that would be paid to a

(Continued)

Exhibit 7.10 (Continued)

soldier. American military veterans working for a private security company were compensated about $135,000 a year, the same as a U.S. Army two-star general. (Other contractors, often from developing nations, are offered about one-tenth of that amount to perform mundane work.) With billions of dollars in contracts, companies become a powerful lobbying group whose pursuit of profit may not coincide with the national interest. In Iraq, allegations of war profiteering, work stoppages, and human rights violations by contracting corporations were so widespread that a nonprofit watchdog group maintained an extensive contractor misconduct database as a number of high-level scandals erupted.

The use of contract workers can be effective, however, provided that the overuse and abuse of contracting authority does not undermine the legitimacy and accountability of public institutions. The Acquisition Advisory Panel (appointed by the White House and Congress) concluded in 2007 that the contracting trend "poses a threat to the government's long-term ability to perform its mission" and could "undermine the integrity of the government's decision making" (quoted in Shane & Nixon, 2007). The advantages of contracting, then, are often overstated, while the disadvantages are understated. In fact, the Pentagon was later given authority to insource because so many contracts had been awarded without competition or resulted in poor performance. It is, of course, ironic that a private firm can lure highly trained federal personnel away from public service so it can then sell their services back to the government at a premium.

SOURCES: "Blackwater's Rich Contracts" (2007); Castelli (2007, 2008); Hedgpeth (2008); Matthews (2008); Seahill (2007); Shane and Nixon (2007); Strivers and Hummel (2007); Watkins (2008).

The success or failure of organizations is related in large part to their reward systems. Fortunately, as this chapter has outlined, there are many compensation techniques available that can support organization success. Unfortunately, none of them is as simple as it may appear. From a technical perspective, the folly is the myth of universal applicability; the ultimate mistake, however, is the failure of political will to provide just salaries so that the public can be faithfully and honorably served.

To put it differently, there is no single agreed-upon way to determine compensation; *no* job has intrinsic economic worth, simply because human reality is socially constructed. Compensation certainly cannot be determined by the free market, if for no other reason than there is no such thing. It is possible, however, to suggest criteria that could define an ideal compensation system. Although such standards are neither mutually exclusive nor exhaustive, they do suggest a starting point from which any plan can be assessed. These criteria, which strive to align employee and employer goals, include the following:

1. *Stakeholder involvement in system design or reevaluation.* Because equity is often in the eye of the beholder, it is vital that all stakeholders—taxpayers, elected officials, nonprofit contributors, managers, and employees—have meaningful voice in the policy. For example, Kansas commissioned a state pay study that involved 16 focus

groups of randomly selected employees, a survey of 3,000 additional employees, and group meetings with legislators and middle managers. It was, no doubt, a difficult process, but responsible democratic governance demands no less.

2. *Simplicity in base pay and diversity in benefits.* As the basis of most people's perceptions of the entire compensation system, the structure of base pay—which must be competitive—should be readily comprehensible to all. (For instance, Wyoming condensed 37 state pay grades into 11 broad pay bands in 1998.) Although the principle of clarity should also pertain to benefits, given the diversity of the 21st-century workforce, there should be variety and choice among them. The options must be offered in such a manner that no one can gain advantage or suffer disadvantage, something that occurs with uniform benefit packages.

3. *Salary progression tied to continuous improvement.* Whether through seniority or through merit, skill, or bonus pay, people need to be rewarded as they become more valuable to the agency. If these systems, singly or in combination, cannot be properly designed, implemented, or funded, then either (a) cost-of-living adjustments, in the name of fairness, should be seen as an automatic cost of doing business or (b) the number of hours worked should be reduced (e.g., Pennsylvania, Tennessee, and South Carolina require 37.5-hour workweeks). Employees might then seek promotional opportunities and/or second jobs to increase their income.

4. *Job security.* Precisely because compensation is vital, visible, and vicious, and political cronyism is endemic in systems that do not have strong rules and cultures against it, some form of job security for core employees, linked to productivity and due process, is necessary. People must know, as Winston Churchill stated in a speech to the House of Commons on June 18, 1940, "that they are not threatened men, men who are here today and gone tomorrow." The more employees are expected to have creative ideas and solve difficult problems, the less their agencies can afford for them to feel that a single mistake may be their last.

5. *Market match pay philosophy.* While recognizing that market match, lead, and lag policies can all exist in one organization, an overall competitive approach neutralizes compensation as it largely takes the issue off the table. It avoids not only the self-defeating (and expensive) dimensions of the market-follower strategy but also the politically toxic (if less costly) market-led philosophy.

Ideally, a compensation system should seek to achieve external, internal, and individual equity. In so doing, it should foster self-managed employees, reward innovation, and focus on citizen service; a successful policy is one that facilitates excellent public service (Bilmes & Gould, 2009; Stier, 2011). The above standards do not guarantee that every paradoxical problem will be resolved. The denigration or absence of any of them, however, ensures that an equitable system is unlikely.

As the new century unfolds, traditional pay practices ("automatic" merit increases derived from cost of living, few bonuses, small employee earnings differentials, salaries based on hierarchical position and the number of people managed, vague performance criteria) are being challenged by new practices (no pro forma annual increases, large bonuses earned for performance, substantial personnel salary differentials, pay based on results with some staff earning more than their managers, defined performance criteria). More specifically, a number of trends in base pay, salary progression, and employment benefits are evident. To make base earnings more attractive, at least in the short run, pay-banding experiments are likely to continue. Automatic increases in salary probably will be minimized in favor of individual or team incentive and variable pay systems. Finally, although more benefits (especially in the arenas of health and family) may become mandatory in the future, what is evolving is a system in which the employee is increasingly responsible not merely for benefit choices but also for their cost.

Overall, then, low-salary budgets reflect a general trend toward cost containment sparked by global competition for jobs, technological displacement of staff, and increasing use of contingent workers. The traditional social contract at work—hard work justly compensated in exchange for job security and loyalty—has been dramatically eroded as more organizations want less responsibility for their workforces. This portends a turbulent environment for employers, employees, and society in the years ahead. To help readers navigate this environment, the appendix to this chapter discusses the economic value of a graduate degree in public affairs and administration.

KEY TERMS

Alternative work schedules
Benefits
Bonus
Comp & class study
Comparable worth
Cost-of-living adjustments
Equal Pay Act of 1963
Equity adjustment
Federal Employees Pay
   Comparability Act of 1990
Functional rationality
Gainsharing

Herzberg's theory of motivation
Labor markets
Locality pay
Longevity pay
Market adjustment
Merit pay
Pay banding
Pay compression
Pay equity
Pay restoration
Skill-based pay
Substantive rationality

EXERCISES

Class Discussion

1. Discuss the following statement, employing "Leonardo's parachute" (see the book's introduction): "We need to pay people based on their value-added contributions to their organization as well as to the nation."

2. If teamwork, process improvement, and citizen service are hallmarks of quality management, then discuss the most appropriate pay system for an agency pursuing quality.

3. To what extent do flexible benefit programs resolve individual–organization compensation dilemmas? Would it be better to abolish benefits altogether (Exhibit 7.8)? Identify the conditions necessary for that to occur.

4. At the end of the chapter, it was suggested that the number of work hours be decreased in the name of employee fairness. Actually, European economists have long claimed that organizational productivity increases as hours decrease. Discuss how "less can be more."

5. According to U.S. Senator Paul Sarbanes, "As much as it is a disservice not to support the federal workforce, at the end of the day it's a disservice to the public." Explain.

6. Explain why it is so difficult for "the great pay debate" to be resolved. Hint: Pay systems receive criticism from both those who think employees are paid too much and those who think they are paid to little.

7. Discuss the following statement: "From Enron to Global Crossing, from BP to Mining and Minerals Service (in the Interior Department) from the Veterans Administration bonus issue to the latest scandal, it is evident that money corrupts the workplace."

8. In 2011, Transocean, whose drilling rig exploded in the 2010 Gulf oil disaster, awarded employee bonuses in recognition of the company's "best year in safety performance." Comment.

9. The head of a public interest group observed in 2011 that "a lengthy pay freeze, increased employee pension contributions, limited bonuses for outstanding employees, and a hiring freeze will inevitably result in a demoralized, depleted, and ultimately less talented and less effective workforce." This situation will "lead to operational failures . . . and cause increased disillusionment with government." Discuss.

Team Activities

10. This chapter claims that pay is important because it is vital, visible, and vicious in organizations. Divide into groups and analyze, from the perspective of the paradox of needs, at least three strategies to ensure (a) external, (b) internal, and (c) individual equity for employees.

11. Resolved: "If recruitment and placement functions of human resource management are done well, then incentive pay plans are irrelevant—even harmful." One team should argue the affirmative position, one the negative.

12. Analyze the importance of and controversies surrounding benefits from the perspective of the employee (one team) and the employer (another team). If some governments use benefit programs to attract and retain employees, is this ethical?

13. Because managers typically lack flexibility to increase employee pay (except to a limited extent in performance appraisal; Chapter 10), they may resort to finding ways to upgrade jobs (Chapter 5) instead. Discuss the ethics of this tactic and whether or not pay banding is a genuine solution to low pay in government.

Individual Assignments

14. There are many paradoxes in the human resource management compensation function. Identify at least three and discuss ways to resolve them. To what extent do they relate to the fundamental paradoxes discussed in this book's introduction?

15. Your division has been selected as a demonstration project that will establish a pilot program to ensure individual equity. Top management has created an employee advisory committee to recommend how this can best be established, and you are the committee chair. Which strategy would you recommend for the first committee discussion? Why?

16. Discuss the following paradox: American employees work longer hours than they did a generation ago and work longer hours than employees in most other advanced nations, yet they are among the least protected and often the worst paid. The wages earned by the "working poor," in business and in government, in fact, do not lift them out of poverty.

17. Examine this paradox: One of the most robust findings in social science research is one of the most ignored—managers use rewards hoping to get the benefit from motivated employee behavior, but they often get the unintentional cost of destroying individuals' intrinsic motivation in their jobs.

18. Comparable worth is an important issue in rank-in-job classification systems. Why is it irrelevant in rank-in-person systems (Chapter 5)?

19. Reformers advocate performance pay to replace longevity systems. Ironically, the federal General Schedule longevity system is performance based. It has never been properly implemented because its performance incentives (within-grade increases, quality step increases, cash awards) have been subject to insufficient funding. Discuss.

20. In the context of the importance of distributive and procedural justice in pay determination, consider these observations:

    - "How do leaders serve their people? They pay good wages and treat employees with respect."
    - "We apply rigorous discipline to learn how to earn a living, but not how to live."

APPENDIX

COMPENSATION FOR GRADUATE DEGREES IN PUBLIC AFFAIRS AND ADMINISTRATION

Although people vary in their motivations for pursuing graduate work, when graduation nears most students become interested in using their degrees for career advancement. Such advancement is a means to increase income, and, at least in the aggregate, higher education is associated with higher income.

Of course, no one can guarantee a payoff from education. The first step is to get a job that is consistent with your degree—one that requires and rewards having that specific degree. Previously, advice has been offered on the importance of networking and on improving interviewing skills and résumés to improve chances of getting a desired position. You should also be able to express clearly what difference or contribution you want to make, and how that relates to the needs of potential future employers.

As a second step, however, it is also useful to look strategically at compensation as the result of career choices. Variation exists in compensation among those who have graduate degrees in public affairs, such as master of public administration (MPA) or master of public policy (MPP) degrees. In general, there is consensus that this may be a propitious time to enter public service. First, as increasing numbers of Baby Boomers retire, numerous career opportunities will open up. Management positions will be available to qualified people at a much earlier time than in the past, though it might take another 5 years for this to become evident. Second, the link between public service and employment has weakened. People can do service while working for government, nonprofits, and even for-profit organizations. Indeed, careers are no longer tied to any one employer or sector. For example, if a person wants to specialize in environmental regulations, he or she can work almost anywhere. In a market-based economy, this means opportunities for career and salary advancement.

Third, in the public sector the historic gaps between federal, state, and local government salaries have narrowed in recent years. Historically, federal salaries have been greater than those in state government, which have been higher than those in local jurisdictions. But for some jobs, local government management salaries are more than those in state government, and sometimes on par with those in the federal government. The change is attributed to strong growth of local government since the 1990s and, hence, increased demand for talent. However, the economic downturn of 2008 has (temporarily?) reduced local hiring, allowing state governments to sometimes catch up. Beyond this, salaries are sometimes highest in public enterprises, special districts, and other single-purpose public organizations like universities, public hospitals, and transit agencies.

Fourth, competition between the sectors for scarce talent also means that salaries in public organizations are sometimes on par with those of the private sector. In some professions they are higher in government (accountant, librarian, microbiologist), in others they are higher in the private sector (medical doctor, human resource director, chief executive officer). On average, the public and private sectors pay managers about the same, but there is a lot of variation. Further, while business sometimes pays more (such as in some high-growth technical firms that offer substantial performance bonuses), job security, benefits, and working hours should also be considered.

With so much change and variation, graduates would do well to examine data relevant to their specific situations. Information about salaries in public administration is available on the website of the Network of Schools of Public Policy, Affairs, and Administration (NASPAA) at www.naspaa.org/students/careers/salary.asp, and the Bureau of Labor Statistics presents a much more thorough look at salaries in public and nonprofit organizations at www.bls.gov/oes/current/oessrci.htm (for information on government, scroll down and select Sector 99; on nonprofits, see, for example, Sector 62). NASPAA offers an interesting look at careers, and especially alumni profiles, at www.naspaa.org/students/careers/careers.asp. This site also includes a link to job resources. Federal jobs are the focus at the Go Government website (http://gogovernment.org), which has information about positions and how to find them as well as links to sites with jobs.

Figures 7.1 and 7.2 provide data on the salaries associated with particular positions. Many federal employees earn about $70,000 to $80,000 annually. Federal managers earn between $80,000 and $130,000, with an average of about $111,000. Agency directors (chief executives) in the federal government earn $165,000, whereas those in state and local government earn about $125,000. Further analysis shows that there are payoffs from

1. having technical or specialized skills (e.g., budgeting, HR, IT);
2. working for federal agencies, higher education, and some advocacy or lobbying organizations; and
3. being a manager rather than a senior employee.

The advantage in each instance may be $10,000 to $15,000 per year; motivated, skilled people are often rewarded. State governments had been losing ground in compensation for well over a decade, but they are now beginning to catch up to local governments, which

Figure 7.1   Mean Salaries of Selected Occupations in Federal Government (2013)

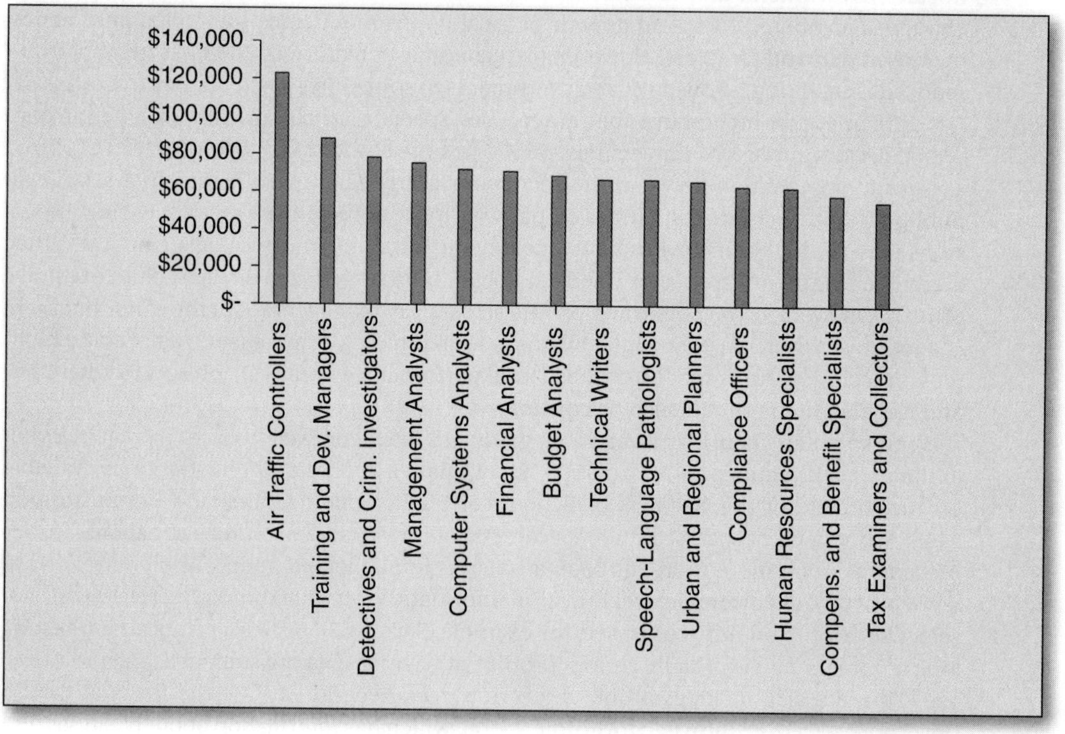

SOURCE: Bureau of Labor Statistics (2013).

Figure 7.2 Mean Salaries of General and Operations Managers (2013)

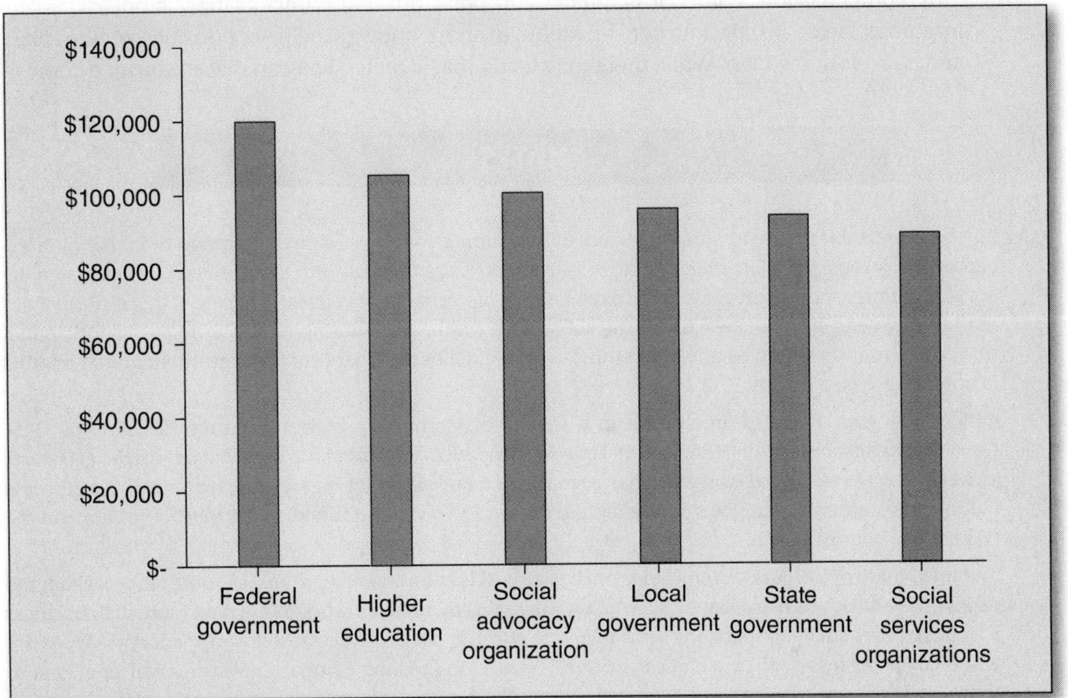

SOURCE: Bureau of Labor Statistics (2013).

had increased salaries as they sought to expand (until recently, when they cut back due to adverse budgets). The importance of having additional specialized knowledge, skills, or experience beyond the MPA or MPP degree should not be overlooked. Many public sector managers with graduate degrees who now make top salaries worked for several years in entry-level positions; they paid their dues and developed positive reputations for success. Others have specialized skills and knowledge in information technology or accounting (both high-demand fields) or second graduate degrees, such as in law or social work. Indeed, some individuals with dual graduate degrees and some professional experience have accepted jobs with exceptional salaries immediately after graduation. In short, top salaries go to those who have made an investment in their careers.

Also, the federal government has a program designed to attract top MPA graduates into federal service. The 2-year Presidential Management Fellows Program (www.pmf.gov) provides salaries, in Washington, D.C., of about $51,000 to $74,000, depending on the grade in which an individual is hired. Upon completion, departments vie for these professionals, who can then be hired at higher grades and earn more, likely in the $75,000–$90,000 range, depending on qualifications and prior experience.

Whether just starting out or ready to take advantage of prior experience, opportunities await. The above discussion is not intended to advocate that you make career choices solely to maximize compensation. Rather, it is intended to point out that compensation is one of several important factors to take into consideration. In short, know thyself! Set priorities, make a plan, and then work the plan. While there may be no magic bullet, you can make informed choices.

NOTES

1. Furthermore, their tenure in office, in an era of term limits, may be of shorter duration than that of many career employees. Decision-making horizons, therefore, are likely to differ, and elected officials may be apt to maximize short-term goals at the expense of long-term effectiveness. Nowhere is this more evident than in compensation policies. Given the substantial funds devoted to payrolls, it might be anticipated that compensation would be one of the most carefully deliberated aspects of government policy, but this is not the case (see Exhibit 7.1).

2. Official pay gap estimates are subject to a variety of technical criticisms (see Kauffman, 2000; U.S. Government Accountability Office, 1995). For a more political interpretation, one that denies the gap exists and claims that the federal workforce has become an "elite island" of highly paid personnel, see Edwards (2006), who contends that government should not set the pace as a model employer but rather lead the "race to the bottom."

   The magnitude of the gap and/or its existence is also fodder for interest groups, as some studies claim the gap is 23% and others place it at 17%. Another maintains that federal workers are paid more than business executives. Any such comparisons must take into account the fact that most governmental positions are white-collar professional or technical jobs (relevant comparisons compare governmental positions to those found in large corporations), where public employees generally earn less money. See also the section of this chapter headed "The Great Pay Debate."

3. In contrast to traditional pensions, where the amount of the benefit is defined, most workers today participate in defined-contribution plans like 401(k)s. In such plans, as their name indicates, the amount of the contribution is defined rather than the amount of the benefit.

4. In fact, pensions can be essentially self-funding in good economic times.

5. It should be noted that many governments, although committed by law to external equity, actually emphasize an internal labor market strategy in recruitment. That is, except for entry-level positions, most career service job opportunities are filled from within. Governments resort to the outside market when no internal candidates can be found. (For data on selected public service salaries, consult the *Government Executive* website at www.govexec.com.)

6. The importance of benefits can be seen in employee recruitment and retention. Some individuals seek employment precisely because comprehensive health insurance and retirement programs are offered. Both discourage turnover and thereby provide employers with the opportunity to recoup training costs (Chapter 9). The best example of this is U.S. military personnel, who benefit from "socialized medicine" and are able to retire at half pay at age 40. In fact, by a margin of nearly two to one, Americans favor a government system of national health care over a private-employer-based system (Akst, 2003).

7. Note, however, that legislators, especially at national and state levels, often give themselves very generous benefit programs, as well as substantial perquisites and access to campaign funds.

8. Time-in-grade restrictions were established in the early 1950s as a cost-control measure: during the Korean War, Congress was concerned that federal employees would rapidly progress through pay levels (as they had in World War II).

9. An estimated one in seven business employees are under performance pay, and most of them work in real estate and sales (Wojcicki, 2010).

10. It has been said that the definition of insanity is doing the same thing over and over again while expecting a different result.

11. One federal official who worked for 5 years under a pay-for-performance demonstration project claimed: "The incentives of the new [Department of Homeland Security] system are a joke, because they are so small. [T]hey constitute a zero-sum game, in that so little money is available for incentive pay that large increases for some translate into small increases for everyone else, regardless of how they performed" (quoted in Kauffman & Ziegler, 2004, p. 4). Most experts suggest that an increase of 7% to 10% in an employee's annual pay is necessary to serve as a motivator. Ironically, the typical "employee likely would earn about the same as under the current system" if the DHS approach was adapted government wide (p. 4). The DHS system was dismantled in 2010.

12. These drawbacks may be moderated by a variation of skill pay in which one-time, skill-based bonuses are awarded without permanently increasing the pay base.

13. With the end of the postwar social contract at work, there is no doubt that a full-time job with benefits is a precious commodity in today's America. If the logic in the private sector is "Business is great—you're fired," then in the public sector it is "Expect nothing—you may be the next to be downsized" (see, e.g., Bowman, 2002).

14. Indeed, in 2004, thousands of soldiers were forbidden to return to civilian life when their contracts expired. This was an attempt to stanch the loss of troops from a military stretched thin by the war in Iraq. Some experts found these "stop loss" orders to be inconsistent with the principle of voluntary military service.

15. The Florida Highway Patrol was so strapped for funds in the 1990s that it could not even employ peripheral labor. Instead, one year it purchased department store mannequins, dressed them in uniforms, and put them in official vehicles on the roadside. Although this technique may have had some deterrent value, it is not to be mistaken for effective law enforcement in a high-crime state.

REFERENCES

AFL-CIO. (n.d.). Working women. Retrieved from http://www.aflcio.org/Issues/Civil-and-Workplace-Rights/Working-Women

Akst, D. (2003, November 2). Why do employers pay for health insurance, anyway? *New York Times.* Retrieved from http://www.nytimes.com/2003/11/02/business/on-the-contrary-why-do-employers-pay-for-health-insurance-anyway.html

Ariely, D. (2010). *The upside of irrationality.* New York: Harper.

Ballenstedt, B. (2008a, March 14). Lawmakers seek remedy for GAO pay reform. *Government Executive.* Retrieved from http://governmentexecutive.com/story_page.cfm?filepath = /dailyfed/0308/031408b1.htm

Ballenstedt, B. (2008b, January 31). OPM touts success of performance-based pay. *Government Executive.* Retrieved from http://governmentexecutive.com/story_page.cfm?filepath = /dailyfed/0108/013108b1.htm

Bebchuk, L., & Fried, J. (2004). *Pay without performance: The unfulfilled promise of executive compensation.* Cambridge, MA: Harvard University Press.

Behn, R. (2000). Performance, people, and pay. *Bob Behn's Public Management Report,* pp. 1–10. Retrieved from http://www.ksg.harvard.edu/TheBehnReport/PerformancePeopleAndPay.pdf

Behn, R. (2004, January). On the limitations of: Pay for performance. *Bob Behn's Public Management Report, 1*(5), 1–2. Retrieved from http://www.hks.harvard.edu/thebehnreport/January2004.pdf

Behn, R. (n.d.). *Twenty design questions about any approach to pay for performance plus three perception questions that are answered by these design choices.* Unpublished manuscript, Harvard University.

Bender, K. A., & Heywood, J. S. (2010). *Out of balance? Comparing public and private sector compensation over 20 years.* Washington, DC: National Institute on Retirement Security.

Bernard, T. S. (2014, May 19). For workers, less flexible companies. *New York Times,* p. B1.

Biggs, A., & Richwine, J. (2011, February 14). Yes, they're overpaid: The truth about federal workers' compensation. *Weekly Standard.* Retrieved from http://conservativeoutpost.com/node/4798

Bilmes, L., & Gould, W. S. (2009). *The people factor: Strengthening America by investing in public service.* Washington, DC: Brookings Institution Press.

Blackwater's rich contracts [Editorial]. (2007, October 3). *New York Times.* Retrieved from http://www.nytimes.com/2007/10/03/opinion/03wed2.html?_r = 0

Blair, B. (2003, August 18). Experts debate pay rules for a new personnel system. *Federal Times,* p. 8.

Bohnet, I., & Eaton, S. (2003). Does performance pay perform? Conditions for success in the public sector. In J. D. Donahue & J. S. Nye Jr. (Eds.), *For the people: Can we fix the public service?* (pp. 238–254). Washington, DC: Brookings Institution.

Bowman, J. S. (2002). At-will employment in Florida government: A naked formula to corrupt public service. *WorkingUSA, 60*(2), 90–102.

Bowman, J. S. (2010). The success of failure: The paradox of performance pay. *Review of Public Personnel Administration, 30*(1), 70–88.

Brown, M., & Heywood, J. S. (2002). Paying for performance: Setting the stage. In M. Brown & J. S. Heywood (Eds.), *Paying for performance: An international comparison.* Armonk, NY: M. E. Sharpe.

Bureau of Labor Statistics, U.S. Department of Labor. (2010, October 1). *May 2010 national industry-specific occupational employment and wage estimates.* Washington, DC: Author. Retrieved from http://www.bls.gov/oes/current/oessrci.htm

Bureau of Labor Statistics, U.S. Department of Labor. (2013, May). National industry-specific occupational employment and wage estimates. Retrieved from http://www.bls.gov/oes/current/naics3_999000.htm

Bureau of Labor Statistics, U.S. Department of Labor. (2014, April). *Employment Cost Index historical listing* (Vol. 4). Washington, DC: Author.

Castelli, E. (2007, October 8). The case for insourcing. *Federal Times.*

Castelli, E. (2008, June 16). DoD redirects contracting support work. *Federal Times.*

Chassy, P. (2011, March 14). *Can you compare federal government vs. private sector pay?* Washington DC: Project on Government Oversight. Retrieved from http://pogoblog.typepad.com/pogo/2011/03/can-you-compare-federal-government-vs-private-sector-pay.html

Congressional Budget Office. (2012). *Comparing the compensation of federal and private-sector employees.* Washington, DC: Author.

Cotterell, B. (2004, July 26). Money talks when handing out bonuses. *Tallahassee Democrat,* p. 1B.

Davidson, J. (2008, August 14). Promises of pay parity—dashed again. *Washington Post,* p. D3.

Donahue, J. D. (2008). *The warping of government work.* Cambridge, MA: Harvard University Press.

Don't abandon performance-based pay. (2007, May 14). *Federal Times,* p. 20.

Edwards, C. (2006, May). Federal pay outpaces private-sector pay. *Cato Institute Tax and Budget Bulletin, 35,* 1–2.

Fahrenthold, D. A. (2014, May 30). How the VA developed its culture of coverups. *Washington Post.* Retrieved from http://www.washingtonpost.com/sf/national/2014/05/30/how-the-va-developed-its-culture-of-coverups

Fairchild, C. (2014, July 24). Is there a legal case for work–life balance? *Fortune.* Retrieved from http://fortune.com/2014/07/24/work-life-balance-legal

Fisher, C. D., Schoenfeldt, L. F., & Shaw, J. B. (2006). *Human resource management.* Boston: Houghton Mifflin.

Flannery, T. P., Hofrichter, D. A., & Platten, P. E. (2002). *People, performance, and pay: Dynamic compensation for changing organizations.* New York: Free Press.

Gabris, G. T. (1998). Merit pay mania. In S. E. Condrey (Ed.), *Handbook of human resource management in government* (pp. 627–657). San Francisco: Jossey-Bass.

Gabris, G. T., & Ihrke, D. M. (2004). Merit pay and employee performance. In M. Holzer & S. Lee (Eds.), *Public productivity handbook* (2nd ed., pp. 499–514). New York: Marcel Dekker.

Gage, J., & Kelly, C. (2003, November 10). Unions support smart performance pay for homeland. *Federal Times*, p. 21.

Galinsky, L., & Eby, L. (2008). *Guide to bold new ideas for making work work*. New York: Families and Work Institute.

Giapponi, C., & McEvoy, S. (2005–2006). The legal, ethical, and strategic implications of gender discrimination in compensation: Can the Fair Pay Act succeed where the Equal Pay Act has failed? *Journal of Individual Employment Rights, 12*(2), 137–150.

Greenhouse, S. (2013, January 12). Our economic pickle. *New York Times*. Retrieved from http://www.nytimes.com/2013/01/13/sunday-review/americas-productivity-climbs-but-wages-stagnate.html

Haga, B., Richman, R., & Leavitt, W. (2010). System failure: Implementing pay for performance in the Department of Defense's national security personnel system. *Public Personnel Management 39*(3), 211–230.

Hays, S. W. (2004, September). Trends and best practices in state and local human resource management: Lessons to be learned? *Review of Public Personnel Administration, 24*(3), 256–275.

Heathfield, S. M. (2008). Women and work: Then, now, and predicting the future for women in the workplace. About.com: About Money. Retrieved from http://humanresources.about.com/od/worklifebalance/a

Heathfield, S. M. (2011). Reasons why teleworking belongs in your future. About.com: About Money. Retrieved from http://humanresources.about.com/od/workschedules/a/teleworking.htm

Hedgpeth, D. (2008, July 24). Pentagon auditors pressured to favor contractors, GAO says. *Washington Post*. Retrieved from http://www.washingtonpost.com/wp-dyn/content/article/2008/07/23/AR2008072301437.html

Herzberg, F., Mausner, B., & Snyderman, B. B. (1959). *The motivation to work*. New York: John Wiley.

Hewitt Associates. (2003, September 15). OPM official: Performance pay has staying power. *Federal Times*, p. 6.

Hicks, J. (2014, May 12). Median federal salary increased 1.4 percent last year, despite pay freeze. *Washington Post*. Retrieved from http://www.washingtonpost.com/blogs/federal-eye/wp/2014/05/12/median-federal-salary-increased-1-4-percent-last-year-despite-pay-freeze

Hogler, R. (2004). *Employment relations in the United States: Law, policy, and practice*. Thousand Oaks, CA: Sage.

House Budget Committee. (2014, April). *The path to prosperity: Fiscal year 2015 budget resolution*. Washington, DC: Author.

Jauhar, S. (2008, September 9). The pitfalls of linking doctors' pay to performance. *New York Times*. Retrieved from http://www.nytimes.com/2008/09/09/health/09essa.html

Jenkins, C., Jr., Mitra, A., Gupta, N., & Shaw, J. (1998). Are financial incentives related to performance? A meta-analytical review of empirical research. *Journal of Applied Psychology, 83,* 777–787.

Jurkiewicz, C. L., & Bowman, J. S. (2002). Charlotte: A model for market-driven public-sector management. *State and Local Government Review, 34*(3), 205–213.

Kauffman, T. (2000, April 3). Studies delay pay locality reform. *Federal Times*, pp. 1, 18.

Kauffman, T. (2004, December 13). Pay reform failure: How FAA's bold experiment led to inequity, poor morale. *Federal Times*, p. 1.

Kauffman, T. (2005, January 3). OMB to push performance pay governmentwide in '05. *Federal Times*, p. 11.

Kauffman, T., & Ziegler, M. (2004, May 2). National Academy of Public Administration: Pay reform for all. *Federal Times*, pp. 1, 4–5.

Keefe, J. (2010, September 10). *Debunking the myth of the overcompensated public employee* (Briefing paper). Washington, DC: Economic Policy Institute.

Kellough, J. E., & Lu, H. (1993). The paradox of merit pay in the public sector: Persistence of a problematic procedure. *Review of Public Personnel Administration, 13*(2), 45–64.

Kellough, J. E., & Selden, S. C. (1997). Pay-for-performance systems in state government: Perceptions of state agency personnel managers. *Review of Public Personnel Administration, 17*(1), 5–21.

Kelly, E., & Moen, P. (2007). Rethinking the clockwork of work: Why schedule control may pay off at work and at home. *Advances in Developing Human Resources, 9*(4), 487–506.

Kiger, P. J. (2007, June 19). Throwing out the rules of work. *Workforce Management.*

Kirkner, R. (2008, July 21). Pioneering performance pay. *Federal Times,* p. 23.

Konnikova, M. (2014, June 10). Lean out: The dangers for women who negotiate. *New Yorker.*

Krugman, P. (2010, December 2). Freezing out hope. *New York Times.*

Labaton, V. (2014, July 25). Myths about the gender gap. *Washington Post.*

Lane, L., Wolf, J., & Woodard, C. (2003). Reassessing the human resource crisis in the public service. *American Review of Public Administration, 33*(2), 123–145.

Lawless, J. L., & Fox, R. L. (2008, May). *Why are women still not running for office?* (Issues in Governance Studies 16). Washington, DC: Brookings Institution. Retrieved from http://www.brookings.edu/~/media/research/files/papers/2008/5/women%20lawless%20fox/05_women_lawless_fox.pdf

Lee, C., & Straus, H. (2004, May 17). Two thirds of federal workers get bonus. *Washington Post,* p. A1.

Leonard, B. (1995, February). Creating opportunities to excel. *HRMagazine,* pp. 47–51.

Losey, S. (2008, August 25). Better performers net bigger payouts. *Federal Times,* p. 6.

Losey, S. (2010, May 23). Intel workers' pay system unfair, study says. *Federal Times.*

Losey, S. (2011a, April 5). Key lawmaker wants to bring pay for performance to feds. *Federal Times.*

Losey, S. (2011b, November 4). Pay gap grows in private sector's favor. *Federal Times.*

Masternak, R. (2003). *Gainsharing: A team-based approach to driving organizational change.* Phoenix, AZ: World at Work.

Matthews, W. (2008, March 3). State pays $1,222 per day for contractor security guards. *Federal Times,* p. 8.

McEntee, G. (2011, January 18). Today's debate: Pension envy. Don't blame public pensions. *USA Today,* p. 6A.

Method, J. (2008, June 23). Few bonuses paid to federal employees, survey shows. *Federal Times,* p. 6.

Montgomery, L. (2011, May 15). Federal worker pensions emerge as target in debt-reduction talks. *Washington Post.*

Morse, M., & Kiely, E. (2010, December 1). Are federal workers overpaid? Both sides in great pay debate are misleading the public. FactCheck.org. Retrieved from http://www.factcheck.org/2010/12/are-federal-workers-overpaid

Mullen, S. (2014, May 4). Bonuses for federal workers cut in half, figures show. *USA Today.* Retrieved from http://www.usatoday.com/story/news/politics/2014/05/04/federal-employee-bonuses/8708305

National Academy of Public Administration. (2004). *Recommending performance-based federal pay.* Washington, DC: Author.

Neal, M. (2011, September 20). In the workplace, what can women learn from men? Huffington Post. Retrieved from http://www.huffingtonpost.com/2011/09/19/in-the-workplace-where-ca_n_969842.html

O'Keefe, E. (2011, March 9). Federal pay and benefits back in the spotlight. *Washington Post.*

Oppel, R. A., Jr. (2014, May 8). V.A. officials subpoenaed for inquiry into wait list. *New York Times.* Retrieved from http://www.nytimes.com/2014/05/09/us/politics/house-committee-subpoenas-veterans-affairs-secretary.html

Partnership for Public Service. (2005). *Pay for performance* (Issue Brief PPS-5-01). Washington, DC: Author.

Perry, J. (2003). Compensation, merit pay, and motivation. In S. W. Hays & R. C. Kearney (Eds.), *Public personnel administration: Problems and prospects* (4th ed., pp. 143–153). Englewood Cliffs, NJ: Prentice Hall.

Perry, J., Engbers, T., & Jun, S. (2009). Back to the future: Performance-related pay, empirical research, and the perils of persistence. *Public Administration Review, 69,* 39–51.

Peterson, G. (2013, March 12). Cutting ROWE won't cure Best Buy. *Forbes.* Retrieved from http://www.forbes.com/sites/garypeterson/2013/03/12/cutting-rowe-wont-cure-best-buy

Pink, D. H. (2009). *Drive: The surprising truth about what motivates us.* New York: Riverhead Books.

Pinker, S. (2008). *The sexual paradox: Men, women, and the real gender gap.* New York: Scribner.

President's Pay Agent. (2011). *Report on locality-based comparability payments for the General Schedule.* Washington, DC: Author.

Reich, R. (2011, January 5). The shameful attack on public employees. *Washington Post.*

Ressler, C., & Thompson, J. (2013). *Why managing sucks and how to fix it: A results-only guide to taking control of work, not people.* Hoboken, NJ: John Wiley.

Risher, H. (2002). Pay-for-performance: The keys to making it work. *Public Personnel Management, 31*(3), 317–332.

Risher, H. (2004). *Pay for performance: A guide for federal managers.* Washington, DC: IBM Center for the Business of Government.

Risher, H. (2008). Adding merit to pay for performance. *Compensation and Benefits Review, 40*(6), 22–29.

Risher, H. (2010, November 2). Analysis: More twists in the federal pay debate. *Government Executive.* Retrieved from http://www.govexec.com/dailyfed/1110/110210an1.htm

Risher, H., & Fay, C. H. (Eds.). (1997). *New strategies for public pay: Rethinking government compensation programs.* San Francisco: Jossey-Bass.

Risher, H., & Wise, L. R. (1997). Job evaluation: The search for internal equity. In H. Risher & C. H. Fay (Eds.), *New strategies for public pay: Rethinking government compensation programs* (pp. 98–124). San Francisco: Jossey-Bass.

Rutzick, K. (2005, September 30). Agency decides pay banding is not the answer. *Government Executive.* Retrieved from http://www.govexec.com/dailyfed/0905/093005r1.htm

Sandberg, S. (2013). *Lean in: Women, work, and the will to lead.* New York: Random House.

Sanders, R. P. (1998). Gainsharing in government. In S. E. Condrey (Ed.), *Handbook of human resource management in government* (pp. 231–252). San Francisco: Jossey-Bass.

Schuster, J., & Zingheim, P. (2007). Do colleges and universities really pay for performance? *Workspan, 50*(7), 46–52.

Seahill, J. (2007, August 13). Flush with profits from the Iraq war, military contractors see a world of business opportunities. AlterNet. Retrieved from http://www.alternet.org/world/59571

Shane, S., & Nixon, R. (2007, February 4). In Washington, contractors take on biggest role ever. *New York Times.* Retrieved from http://www.nytimes.com/2007/02/04/washington/04contract.html?pagewanted = all&_r = 0

Shareef, R. (2002). The sad demise of skill-based pay in the Virginia Department of Transportation. *Review of Public Personnel Administration, 22*(3), 233–240.

Singletary, M. (2008, August 24). Despite strides, women still tripped up by confidence gap. *Washington Post,* p. F01.

State should keep promise. (1996, December 12). *Tallahassee Democrat,* p. 10A.

Stier, M. (2011, January 9). Restoring worth to our public servants. *Washington Post.*

Strivers, C., & Hummel, R. (2007). Personnel management: Politics, administration, and a passion for anonymity. *Public Administration Review, 67,* 1010–1117.

Texas State Auditor's Office. (n.d.). Workforce analysis. Retrieved from http://www.hr.sao.state.tx.us/Workforce

Thompson, J. R., & LeHew, C. W. (2002). Skill-based pay as an organizational innovation. *Review of Public Personnel Administration, 20*(1), 20–40.

Tiefer, C. (2008, April 4). Re-evaluating pay for performance. *Federal Times,* p. 23.

Tully, M. B. (2011, June 20). MSPB: Glass ceiling for female federal employees "fractured," not shattered. FedSmith. Retrieved from http://www.fedsmith.com/2011/06/20/mspb-glass-ceiling-female-federal-employees

U.S. Government Accountability Office. (1995). *Federal/private pay comparisons* (OCE-95-1). Washington, DC: Government Printing Office.

U.S. Government Accountability Office. (2012, June). *Federal workers: Results of studies on federal pay varied due to differing methodologies.* Washington, DC: Government Printing Office.

U.S. Government Accountability Office. (2013, June). *Federal recruiting and hiring: Making government jobs attractive to prospective employees.* Washington, DC: Government Printing Office.

U.S. Merit Systems Protection Board. (2003, February). Pay banding in the federal government. *Issues of Merit* (newsletter). Retrieved from http://www.mspb.gov/studies/newsletters.htm

U.S. Merit Systems Protection Board. (2006). *Designing an effective pay for performance compensation system.* Washington, DC: Author.

U.S. Office of Personnel Management. (2014, April). *Governmentwide strategy on advancing pay equality in the federal government.* Washington, DC: Author. Retrieved from http://www.chcoc.gov/files/governmentwide_strategy_on_advancing_pay_equality_in_the_federal_government.pdf

Vroom, V. H. (1964). *Work and motivation.* New York: John Wiley.

Walker, R. (2008, February 1). Union disputes OPM claim of success in new pay systems. *Federal Computer Week.* Retrieved from http://fcw.com/articles/2008/02/01/union-disputes-opm-claim-of-success-in-new-pay-systems.aspx

Wamsley, B. S. (1998). Are current programs working? In S. E. Condrey (Ed.), *Handbook of human resource management in government* (pp. 25–39). San Francisco: Jossey-Bass.

Watkins, S. (2008, March 17). An eclipsing shadow. *Federal Times,* p. 2.

West, J. P., & Bowman, J. S. (2014). *Electronic surveillance at work: An ethical analysis.* Unpublished manuscript, University of Miami.

Wojcicki, E. (2010, May 17). New research shows merit pay for teachers a poor idea. Huffington Post. Retrieved from http://www.huffingtonpost.com/esther-wojcicki/new-research-shows-merit_b_577886.html

York, D., & Brown, T. (2008). Salary surveys. In L. A. Berger & D. R. Berger (Eds.), *The compensation handbook: A state-of-the-art guide to compensation strategy and design* (5th ed., pp. 111–124). New York: McGraw-Hill.

Zeller, S. (2004, September 8). Union's opposition to pay-for-performance systems unrelenting. *Government Executive.* Retrieved from http://www.govexec.com/dailyfed/0904/090804sz1.htm

Zingheim, P. K., & Schuster, J. R. (2000). *Pay people right! Breakthrough reward strategies to create great companies.* San Francisco: Jossey-Bass.

CHAPTER 8

Employee-Friendly Policies

Fashionable, Flexible, and Fickle

People are assets whose value can be enhanced through investment.

—David Walker

After studying this chapter, you should be able to

- understand the composition of the workforce and trends that drive employee-responsive programs;
- identify different employee-friendly initiatives and their applications;
- determine the relative merits of proposals for resolving work/home conflict;
- develop a telecommuter agreement for use in a public organization;
- assess the impact of employee-friendly policies on agencies and their staff;
- identify not-so-employee-friendly policy trends in pensions and health benefits; and
- recognize relevant paradoxes.

Career demands often conflict with personal pressures, and juggling the two poses problems in both settings.[1] Work/life balance is a top career priority for many: 73% of 3,278 U.S. workers surveyed by Spherion Corporation in 2003 said that they "strongly agree" with the statement "I am willing to take a back seat in my career in order to make time for my family" (Kleiman, 2003). However, the United States actually ranks 28th among advanced nations (9th from the bottom) in the category of "work–life balance" according to the Organisation for Economic Co-operation and Development's (2013) Better Life Index. Some employers, responding to employee expectations, especially among younger, Generation X (those born between 1960 and 1980) and New Millennial (those born after 1980) workers, have introduced employee-friendly policies to reduce home/work conflict and help people achieve a better balance between work and home. These policies make the workplace more attractive and help employers to attract and retain younger workers, who are increasingly mobile. Organizations also expect a return on this investment in the form of improved productivity at work. In the past, critics maintained that such organizational initiatives were unjustified, uneven, and extravagant in a period of declining resources, but employee- and family-friendly policies are increasingly accepted and even expected among today's workers.

Proemployee policies are fashionable (stylish and responsive to trends), flexible (adaptable to the unique needs of a diverse workforce), and fickle (unstable and subject to the fluctuating fortunes of the economy). For example, paternity leave is currently offered to employees at the Federal National Mortgage Association (commonly known as Fannie Mae), a government-sponsored enterprise. This policy allows fathers to take up to 4 weeks of paid leave spread out over an extended period to care for newborn or newly adopted children. The availability of such policies might change with downturns in the economy.

Worker-responsive policies include a variety of initiatives to address employees' needs and to advance organizational interests. Individuals' needs are addressed when agencies introduce work schedules and benefit plans tailored to employees' ages and stages of life. Organizational interests are served if staff performance improves as a result, or if recruitment is enhanced. Experience suggests, however, that "win–win" outcomes are not easy to achieve. Reflecting the paradox of needs (see the book's introduction), institutional goals of efficiency and productivity may conflict with employees' goals of a supportive workplace. For instance, flextime might be a boon to some, enabling them to care for young children or ailing parents, but in practice it may create problems, such as insufficient office coverage and unreliable on-time project completion.

This and other paradoxes help explain why employers often hesitate before they undertake large-scale programs of this type and why employee-friendly policies might exist on paper but lack top-management support when people seek to implement them. Organizations may not trust employees who are working in remote locations, or they might resist change that reduces on-site staff and redefines managerial roles. Paradoxes also help explain why personnel may lobby for specific worker-responsive programs but then underutilize them once they are available. This might result from management that does not "walk the talk" of employee-friendly policies. Alternatively, people may like to know the policies exist (e.g., access to child care or elder care, wellness programs, options for telecommuting) whether or not they use them at the moment. Employees often fear that taking advantage of flexible work options signals to their supervisors that they do not take their careers seriously.

Consistent with the distinction between personnel administration and human resource management, this chapter focuses on the person as a whole by considering the characteristics and use of employee-friendly programs. The social trends that may make such programs popular are summarized, and organizational responses to these trends and the challenges they pose are explored. Several family/work initiatives, health/wellness programs, flexible benefit plans, and relocation assistance efforts are considered. The impacts of such programs on employee and organizational performance are discussed, together with selected implementation issues. Some not-so-employee-friendly policy trends regarding pensions and health benefits are also examined. Finally, the chapter highlights paradoxes that agencies may encounter when implementing specific programs.

WORKFORCE AND WORKPLACE TRENDS

Characteristics of the changing American workforce and work/life benefits have been widely discussed (Cayer & Roach, 2008; Galinsky, Aumann, & Bond, 2009; West, 2012). Projections suggest that coming decades will bring more women, older workers, temporary employees, minorities, and immigrants into positions in both the public and private sectors (Guy & Newman, 1998; West, 2014).[2] For example, in 2011 the labor force participation rate of mothers with children under 18 years was 70.9% (Bureau of Labor Statistics [BLS], 2013d). The participation of women in the labor force overall has increased significantly, from 33.9% in 1950 to 69.9% in 2013 (BLS, 2014). This feminization of the workforce has had numerous ripple effects on life at home and at work. Workforce composition has changed in other ways as well:

- Seven in ten working husbands are married to women in the labor force.
- More than one-eighth of U.S. full- or part-time employees have elder care responsibilities.
- Nearly six in ten caregivers for family members (58%) are employed (46% work full-time and 11% work part-time) (National Alliance for Caregiving & AARP, 2009).
- Women (10.4 million) are more than four times as likely as men (2.5 million) to be in charge of single-parent families, but the numbers of fathers responsible for their children are increasing more rapidly than the numbers of mothers with this responsibility (Leonard, 1996; Levine, 1997; Peterson, 1998; U.S. Bureau of the Census, 2007).

The rise in dual-career couples and **nontraditional families**, along with the need to consider both work and caregiving for dependent children and elderly parents, adds to the stress of home and career.

As the workforce grows more diverse, pressures will intensify for policies that address the special needs of these employees. Thus, employer assistance in meeting child care and elder care responsibilities will be priority concerns for members of the **sandwich generation** (those with responsibilities for both children and elderly parents), as will flextime and parental leave programs. Telecommuting might have particular appeal for the more technologically sophisticated members of Generation X and New Millennials. Those in nontraditional families (including gay and lesbian couples, unmarried couples in committed relationships, single-parent families, and reconstituted families) will be especially interested in domestic partner benefits.

Alternative work arrangements and cafeteria-style benefit plans (which allow workers to choose among benefits to best suit their needs) will appeal to employees who seek a better balance between job and home life and whose benefit preferences may change over the life cycle of their employment. As of 2007, according to a Bureau of Labor Statistics (2007) survey, one-third of state and local government workers had access to flexible benefit plans. Workers who are **downshifting** (scaling back their career ambitions and giving more time and attention to their family and personal needs) may find part-time work or job-sharing options appealing. Those losing their positions because of **downsizing** (e.g., caused by government reductions in force, outsourcing, or base closure) will press employers for employee relocation assistance.

These trends will come up against countervailing pressures in the workplace. There is a need for organizations to consider adopting employee-friendly policies to attract and retain staff. This will help public employers remain competitive with private employers, who may offer a variety of workplace alternatives. To the extent that jurisdictions continue to face resource scarcity, competition, and taxpayer demands that they be lean, mean, and productive, they will avoid expenditures on all but the most essential programs. Indeed, as public organizations are becoming flatter, more nimble, and more automated, they are simultaneously downsizing as well as increasing use of temporary workers and contractors. These trends will lead to lower investments in human capital.[3] Worker-responsive policy proposals, especially absent hard evidence of pending benefits, will be a hard sell in such an atmosphere.

Public officials and managers need to respond to these competing, often contradictory demands of the workforce and workplace in crafting policies. The menu of options available to promote supportive employee relations is broad, tempting, and rich with possibilities; the options, however, can be costly, and there is a risk that personnel may not come away satisfied. The three sections that follow discuss this array of possibilities: (1) family/work programs; (2) health, safety, and wellness programs; (3) flexible work arrangements; and (4) traditional benefits.

FAMILY/WORK PROGRAMS

For employees, it is important to know what work/family conflicts might exist and how they can be resolved. For employers, the issues are what programs, if any, to provide and how to implement them. This section briefly examines these questions from both perspectives. Employees with dependent children or elderly parents are concerned about their home/family responsibilities. They want to know about the support and benefits the organization might provide to reduce conflicts. Employers need to decide how best to respond to work/family conflicts and whether such responses require institution-sponsored services or modifications in benefits packages.

Five programs address these dual employee and employer concerns: (1) child care, (2) elder care, (3) parental and military leave, (4) adoption assistance, and (5) domestic partnership coverage. These program types, plus those discussed subsequently, illustrate that one activity (e.g., child care service) represents a small part of a much broader approach to "holistically" and strategically managing employee-responsive policies. Each of these initiatives is discussed in turn below.

Child Care

Former U.S. Representative Pat Schroeder (1998) reports a conversation with a colleague early in her career in Congress. Asked how she would juggle her responsibilities as a mother and a legislator, she replied, "I have a brain and a uterus, and they both work" (p. 128). Many women (and men) want what Schroeder wanted—to use their mental and physical endowments to be both parents *and* employees. This raises the thorny and much-discussed question of what to do about dependent children while parents are working.

The issue touches most people in one way or another. Consider this fact: In 2011, 64.2% of mothers with children under 6 years of age participated in the labor force (BLS, 2013d). In a majority of single-parent families the parent is in the workforce, and 59% of two-parent families have both parents employed (Society for Human Resource Management [SHRM], 2013), so child care benefits are crucial.

Research from the U.S. Government Accountability Office (2007) indicates that 54% of federal government employees have dependent care needs, and 19% more expect to have such needs in the future. Most parents at one time or another have experienced problems with child care arrangements that interfered with work. Tardiness, absenteeism, and productivity are all affected. Even if employees who are parents arrive on time and work throughout the day, they may be subject to the **3 o'clock syndrome**—their attention to work-related tasks wanes as they begin thinking about their children ready to leave school and return home. Employers can minimize these disruptions and distractions by providing child care benefits.

The types of benefits employers make available to working parents vary. A relatively small percentage of private and public employers provide child care on or off the premises (BLS, 2010). A far larger proportion offer financial assistance for off-site child care, and many more provide information and referral services. Paradoxically, a majority of federal agencies offer on-site, near-site, or referral services for child care, but a very small percentage of eligible employees use these facilities. By contrast, only 10% of private employers surveyed in 2014 said that they provided direct-cost on- or near-site child care. The same survey found that 61% of all employers provided dependent care assistance plans, and 37% offered referral services for child care (Matos & Galinsky, 2014). Exhibit 8.1 lists some of the specific family benefits provided to full-time employees in private industry as well as in state and local government.

Eligibility for such benefits is greater in state government than in either private industry or local government. President George W. Bush signed a law (P.L. 197-67) in 2001 authorizing the use of appropriated funds by executive agencies to provide child care services for federal civilian employees. Exhibit 8.2 identifies several types of employer-sponsored child care options.

Two examples from local governments suggest creative approaches to child care. The city of Westminster, Colorado, formed a public–private partnership with other area employers to provide child care for employees. The local school district and private businesses are members of the partnership consortium. It provides in-home backup care for ill children, subsidizes school vacation child care programs, and has a resource or referral program for child care. The South Florida Water Management District provides child care for personnel at no cost to the agency as a result of negotiations with a developer who agreed to build a

Exhibit 8.1 Eligibility for Specific Family Benefits by Full-Time Employees in 2014

Benefit	Private Sector (%)	State Government (%)	Local Government (%)
Full or partial reimbursement for on-site or off-site child care	10	27	8
Flex-place	6	N/A	2
Long-term care insurance	16	48	22
Paid family leave	12	18	15
Wellness programs	35	69	46
Employee assistance program	48	84	70

SOURCE: Bureau of Labor Statistics (2013d).

Exhibit 8.2 Employer-Sponsored Child Care Options

1. Child care facility
   - On- or near-site center
   - Consortium center
   - Family day care home or network
   - Expansion of local centers

2. Financial assistance
   - Child care subsidies
   - Dependent care assistance plans

3. Resource and referral service
   - Referrals for parents
   - Quality improvements

4. Mildly ill/emergency/special-needs child care
   - "Get well" rooms in child care program
   - Satellite family day care homes
   - Home visitor program
   - Special program just for mildly ill children
   - Backup care when school is not in session

5. Flexible benefits
   - Flextime, part-time work
   - Flex-place
   - Job sharing
   - Voluntary reduced time

6. Parental leave

7. Investment in community resources
   - Creation of new supply
   - Funding of provider training programs

child care facility on property owned by the agency. The developer is leasing the land from the district for a nominal fee ($1 a year for 25 years) and rents the building to a child care operator. The facility will be turned over to the district after 25 years and will be paid for using the rent paid by the child care operator.

Another child care issue—breast-feeding of infants in the workplace—has resulted in public policy changes at the state and federal levels and in foreign settings (see Exhibit 8.3). In Great Britain, a flexible work program has been established that allows employees with children under the age of 5 to request changes in their work schedules and requires employers to consider their requests, at least. The program provides flexibility to employees that may allow them to create a better balance between work and family responsibilities. At the same time, employers may be more able to maintain skilled staff, reduce absentee-ism by increasing staff morale, and develop efficient techniques for responding to changes in market conditions. It is estimated that 25% of employees seeking this option have been successful in their jobs, without businesses losing any productivity. Due to the program's success, in 2007 the right to request flexible working hours was extended to adults in some careers and in 2009 to parents of children under 17. In 2011 an impact assessment was conducted in anticipation of further extending the right to request flexible working hours to all employees (Department for Business Enterprise and Regulatory Reform of U.K., 2008; Modern Workplaces Consultation, 2012; Obama, 2006, p. 343). Exhibit 8.4 reports on the extent of government support for child care in Denmark.

Elder Care

Caring for elderly relatives is an increasingly common, time-consuming, expensive, and stress-inducing problem. A MetLife (2011, p. 2) study reports that the percentage of adult children providing personal care and/or financial support to a parent has more than tripled in the past 15 years; a quarter of adult children currently provide such care to a parent. The aggregate lost wages to these caregivers (totaling wages, pensions, and Social Security ben-efits) is estimated to be nearly $3 trillion. The total individual amount of lost wages due to

---

Exhibit 8.3 Breast-Feeding at Work

Currently, 24 U.S. states have laws protecting breast-feeding in the workplace: Arkansas, California, Colorado, Connecticut, Georgia, Hawaii, Illinois, Indiana, Maine, Minnesota, Mississippi, Missouri, New Mexico, New York, North Dakota, Oklahoma, Oregon, Rhode Island, Tennessee, Texas, Vermont, Virginia, Washington, and Wyoming. Further, 45 states, the District of Columbia, and the Virgin Islands have laws allowing women to breast-feed in any public or private location. There is considerable variation in the content of the state laws, however. For example, in some states (California, Illinois, Minnesota, and Tennessee) employers are required to provide reasonable break time and to designate a place to pump breast milk, but such breaks should not be unduly disruptive of daily operations. Less restrictive legislation in Rhode Island merely states that employers "may" provide such breaks. Other states (Connecticut and Hawaii) do not mandate breast-feeding breaks but prohibit employers from refusing to allow women to use existing breaks to breast-feed and from discriminating against such workers. California's is the only state law that authorizes fines for violators of the workplace accommodations law (Oakley, 2008; Vance, 2005). Other state laws protect breast-feeding in any public or private location (44 states, Washington, D.C., and the Virgin Islands), exempt breast-feeding from the public indecency laws (28 states), and exempt breast-feeding mothers from jury duty (12 states; National Conference of State Legislatures, 2014; Oakley, 2008).

Breast-feeding in public in a federal building (e.g., museum, courthouse, federal agency) or on federal property (e.g., national park) is protected by a federal law passed in 1999, provided the woman and her child are authorized to be present at the site. The federal Patient Protection and Affordable Care Act (widely known as Obamacare), passed in 2010, requires employers to provide reasonable break time for an employee to breast-feed her child for one year following the child's birth; however, employers are not required to compensate an employee receiving reasonable break time for any work time spent nursing. Employers must also designate an area for the purpose of breast-feeding. Employers with fewer than 50 employees are excused from meeting these requirements if doing so would impose undue hardship on the employers. If a state law provides greater protection than the federal legislation, the federal requirements do not preempt state law. Around the world, 107 other countries protect the right of mothers to breast-feed in the workplace (Project on Global Working Families, 2007).

SOURCES: Adapted from Oakley, 2008; Project on Global Working Families, 2007; Vance, 2005, Breastfeeding Laws, 2011.

Exhibit 8.4 Child Care in Denmark

Denmark has granted the right to public child care for all families since 1976, when the Social Assistance Act was put into law, creating a system that recognizes local autonomy and universal concerns for equity. The system allows mothers to work outside the home by providing a mostly publicly funded (parental fees are capped at 25% to 28% of operation expenses; parents who have several children receive sibling discounts and can apply for free or reduced-cost day care) child care system that is operated at the local level, providing flexibility that helps communities meet their individual needs. All children 26 weeks or older are entitled to day care until they are school age: 91% of children 1–2 years old and 97% of children 3–5 years old attend government-supported day care facilities (Danish Ministry of Social Affairs and Integration, 2012).

It is estimated that 70% to 75% of child care services in Denmark are provided by 98 municipalities and five regions, which set the agenda and framework for the services, including facility locations, opening hours, and overall goals. More general guidelines were established in the 1999 Social Services Act, which states that the goal of child care services should be to provide an environment for good development, well-being, and independence for children.

The child care system also includes the right to pregnancy leave 4 weeks before birth, maternity leave for up to 14 weeks after birth, paternity leave for up to 2 weeks after birth, and another 32 weeks of parental leave to be shared between the father and mother after the first 14 weeks following birth, all with 50% pay. Families are also provided pay allowances and annual child care allowances, paid for by the state, until a child reaches 18 years of age.

SOURCES: Coalition of Child Care Advocates of BC (2007); Danish Ministry of Science, Technology, and Innovation (2008); D; Walter (2005).

leaving the workforce to provide elder care averages $303,880 for a caregiver age 50 or older. According to a study published by the Families and Work Institute, 42% of persons in the workforce, or about 54.6 million employees, have provided elder care in the past 5 years; 17% are currently providing such care (Aumann, Galinsky, Sakai, Brown, & Bond, 2008, p. 2). Women are slightly more likely than men to provide elder care (AARP, 2004); 35% of Baby Boomers have been or are responsible for care of their aging parents. Employers have responded to this need: As of 2007, 25% to 50% were offering some form of elder care assistance services for their workers (SHRM, 2007). It should be noted, however, that many elder care policies are informal.

According to the U.S. Office of Personnel Management (U.S. OPM, 2011), 25.8 million Americans spend an average of 18 hours a week caring for a relative. Studies conducted by MetLife and AARP in 2006 and 2007 found that the cost to U.S. business from the lost productivity of employees caring for elderly family members is more than $33 billion per year (AARP Public Policy Institute, 2007; MetLife, 2006). The cost factors include replacing employees, absenteeism, workday interruptions, supervisor time, unpaid leave, and employee transitions from full-time to part-time.

Caregivers face additional concerns that take a personal toll. They have reduced time for leisure activities (hobbies, vacations) and are more likely than their noncaregiving counterparts to report physical or mental health problems such as diabetes, high cholesterol, hypertension, pulmonary disease, heart disease, cancer, kidney disease, depression, and stress (MetLife, 2010).

This issue is pervasive and costly to the workplace as well, given that two-thirds of caregivers are full- or part-time workers (Levine, 1997). The 2006 MetLife caregiving study found that 15% of employees who had caregiving responsibilities left their workplaces (6% quit their jobs entirely), 3% retired early, and another 10% reduced their schedules to part-time work (Dobkin, 2007). Among caregivers, 1 in 10 quits his or her job, a similar proportion takes a leave of absence, and 6 in 10 display sporadic attendance at work. Increased absenteeism, abbreviated workdays, diminished productivity, and excessive turnover linked to caregiving for dependent elderly persons add to costs employers must bear. As Exhibit 8.1 shows, state government personnel are more likely than those in local government or the private sector to be eligible for long-term care insurance.

Elder care programs address both employees' and employers' needs to reduce work/ family conflict by providing staff with some combination of the following: social work counseling, financial assistance, subsidies to service providers, leave policies, information and referral sources, support groups, and other forms of aid. Approximately one-third of large employers nationwide offer elder care programs. Employers were much more likely to do so in 2014 than they were in 2008; for example, a survey of employers with 50 or more employees found the proportion providing elder care resource and referral increased from 31% to 43% from 2008 to 2014, and the percentage providing access to respite care went from 3% to 7% (Matos & Galinsky, 2014). Surprisingly, 75% of employers say they allow employees to take paid or unpaid time off to provide elder care without putting their jobs in jeopardy. Among the best practices in employer elder care programs are increased reliance on technology to provide information and support services, use of internal staff and multiple vendors, availability of paid time off, resource and referral services, discounted backup home care for emergency needs, geriatric care management services, and assistance with insurance paperwork. Several best-case examples of employers offering effective elder care programs are Aetna, the American Psychological Association, Duke University, Johnson & Johnson, and Pfizer (National Alliance for Caregiving, 2012).

Parental and Military Leave

The Family and Medical Leave Act of 1993 guarantees eligible workers up to 12 weeks, during any 12-month period, of *unpaid* leave for childbirth or adoption; for caregiving to a child, elderly parent, or spouse with a serious health problem; or for a personal illness. These FMLA provisions apply to private employers with at least 40 employees and all government agencies (local, state, and federal), as well as elementary and secondary schools, regardless of the number of employees. Six in ten members of the U.S. labor force work for employers covered by the Family and Medical Leave Act (American Association of University Women [AAUW], 2007). Nonetheless, the United States lags behind much of the rest of the world in providing some form of paid maternity leave: It is one of only 5 countries, out of 173 surveyed, lacking paid maternity leave (AAUW, 2011). Furthermore, nearly one in five employers appear to be out of compliance with the FMLA (Matos & Galinsky, 2014).

Thus, it is not surprising that **parental leave** policies are among the most prevalent of the five items discussed in this section for subnational governments and private sector organizations. McGill University's Institute for Health and Social Policy (2007) estimates that more than 50 million Americans have taken advantage of the parental leave program since 1993 (AAUW, 2007). As Exhibit 8.1 shows, paid and unpaid leave for full-time employees is more available in state government than in local government. Paid leave (maternity and paternity) is much less common in the private sector. Surveys conducted by the International City/County Management Association (ICMA) indicate that 19% of cities offer paid maternity leave, whereas less than 9% offer paid paternity leave. Where paid maternity or paternity leave is available, cities typically make it available to all staff.

Managing parental and family leave programs involves costs of various types at different stages:

- Before leave (absenteeism and productivity impacts)
- During planning (securing and training potential replacements)
- During leave (disability pay and stakeholder impacts)
- While staffing (temps or replacement costs, overtime)
- After leave (retraining, possible turnover costs)

Estimates of the costs associated with parental or family leave, according to five surveys analyzed by Martinez (1993), most frequently range between 11% and 20% of annual salary. Employee gains in flexibility and support must be weighed against employer costs in subsidizing parental leave programs.

In 2002, California became the first state to offer paid parental leave when it introduced an employee-funded program that allows up to 6 weeks of paid family leave to care for a child after birth or to care for a seriously ill family member. The leave is funded by employees who pay $27 a year into the state's disability insurance program, which transfers the funds to the participants. Program benefits include increased employee retention and, as a result, reduced hiring costs; increased bonding time for parents who may not otherwise be able to afford time off from work, which results in the healthy development of children; and fewer dollars in welfare spending (California Employment Development Department, 2011; Equal Rights Advocates, 2008; Houser & Vartanian, 2012). Since California's introduction of this initiative, other jurisdictions have followed: San Francisco (in 2006), Washington, D.C. (2008), Milwaukee (2008, later rescinded), and Seattle (2011) all approved paid leave policies (AAUW, 2011). Between 2002 and 2012, more than a million workers took advantage of the California program; in 2012 the average benefit per week was $497, with an average of 5.35 weeks per claim (Engeman, 2012). In 2008, New Jersey adopted the California model, becoming the second state to institute a paid family leave program (Appelbaum & Milkman, 2011).

Federal and state laws also protect employees who serve in the military. The Uniformed Services Employment and Reemployment Rights Act of 1994 prohibits employer discrimination against those in the military or the reserves. Negative job actions against employees because they are in the armed forces or reserves are prohibited. Furthermore, employers are required to reinstate any person who leaves his or her job to serve in the armed forces so long as certain conditions are met (e.g., advance notice, time limitations, honorable release). In 2008 the National Defense Authorization Act was signed into law, expanding the FMLA to include employees caring for injured service members as well as employees who have family members called to active military duty. In addition, most states have laws that forbid employer discrimination against those in the state's militia or National Guard (Nolo, 2003).

Adoption Assistance

Adoption assistance includes benefits ranging from time off to reimbursement of expenses following adoption of a child. Although employees who give birth to a child typically enjoy paid leave and medical coverage, this may or may not be the case for those adopting a child. The expenses associated with adoption can be substantial, sometimes up to $40,000 (for, e.g., medical costs, legal fees, travel expenses; Adoption.com, n.d.). Employers are beginning to recognize that adoptive parents need assistance. Three key issues need to be considered: eligibility, leave time, and reimbursement. Factors related to eligibility are length of employment, age of the child, and whether coverage includes stepchildren and/ or foster care children. Regarding leave, considerations are the length of time available for unpaid leave; the permissibility of using sick leave, annual leave, or personal leave; and whether those who take leave are guaranteed job reinstatement. Reimbursement issues concern the coverage of legal or medical expenses.

During the period 1990 to 2013, the number of large U.S. employers offering some type of financial adoption benefit increased from 12% to 52%, and 16% now offer paid adoption leave (Meinert, 2013; SHRM Online Staff, 2013). For example, Dow Chemicals USA, Wendy's International, and Campbell Soups provide adoption benefit programs. The city of Philadelphia is a public sector pioneer in making such coverage available. The state of Washington passed a law establishing 5 weeks of partially paid leave for the adoption of a child (Reddick & Coggburn, 2008). Reimbursement of up to $10,000 for adoption expenses is not unusual in the private sector (Adoptive Families, 2008). Local government employees are less likely than either private sector or state government employees to be eligible for assistance. The rationale for employers to provide such benefits is linked to equity: If parents giving birth are entitled to benefits, why not adoptive parents? Two other reasons are also important: cost factors (adoption benefits are low cost because few use them) and stakeholder loyalty (support for adoptive parents can increase loyalty, morale, and retention). Similar equity, cost, and loyalty issues surround questions of domestic partner benefits.

Domestic Partnership Coverage

Domestic partnership coverage consists of the benefits—such as health insurance, retirement benefits, and sick or bereavement leave—that may be made available to a person designated as a domestic partner of an employee. Employers with 50 or more employees were much more likely to provide health insurance for unmarried partners of employees in 2014 (43%) than they were in 2008 (29%) (Matos & Galinsky, 2014). Less encompassing policies might involve little more than public recognition of cohabiting couples; more encompassing plans include dental and vision benefits, employee assistance programs, and posttermination benefits for domestic partners. The need for such coverage has increased in recent years because of changes in the American family and workforce, the importance of benefits as a key component in an employee's total compensation package, and efforts to avoid discrimination against gays and lesbians. As of 2010, according to the U.S. census, 7.5 million opposite-sex unmarried couples were living together, and 620,000 same-sex unmarried couples were living together.

New York City provides benefits for domestic partners of employees, and San Francisco goes even further, requiring private organizations that contract with the city to provide such benefits. In response, the U.S. House of Representatives took steps to deny federal housing dollars to cities that require organizations doing business with them to provide same-sex domestic partner benefits to the organizations' employees. The experience at the Salvation Army (see Exhibit 8.5) suggests that granting domestic partner coverage can be controversial in the nonprofit sector: It may please some stakeholders and anger others. Additional obstacles to domestic partner benefits are rising costs of health care coverage and reluctance by insurance companies to cover unknown risks. As workforce diversity continues to expand, however, pressures for such benefits will mount.

Exhibit 8.5 A Flip-Flop at the Salvation Army

In November 2001, the Western Branch of the Salvation Army announced it would extend health benefits to same-sex partners of employees. This new policy would affect employees in 13 western states plus Guam, Micronesia, and the Marshall Islands. The company said it was acting in compliance with San Francisco's landmark 1998 Equal Benefits Ordinance. Previously, the Salvation Army had forfeited $3.5 million in contracts for noncompliance. According to Colonel Phillip Needham, chief secretary for the Salvation Army's Western Corporation, the action "reflects our concern for the health of our employees and those closest to them, and is made on the basis of strong ethical and moral reasoning that reflects the dramatic changes in family structure in recent years" (quoted in People for the American Way, 2001). In response to this action, the national offices of the Salvation Army received 10,000 e-mails and 1,500 phone calls in protest. Groups such as the American Family Association, Focus on the Family, Concerned Women for America, the Traditional Values Coalition, and the Family Research Council loudly decried the act and began protesting. Vociferous negative reactions were also voiced on Christian radio and television and by the evangelical branch of the Salvation Army.

Two weeks following the announcement, the Salvation Army's national Commissioners' Conference rescinded the policy, stating, "We will not sign any government contract or any other funding contracts that contain domestic partner benefit requirements" (quoted in Gordon, 2001).

In response, Parents, Families and Friends of Lesbians and Gays (PFLAG) organized a protest supporting reversal of that decision. Opponents to rescinding the policy placed fake money (phony $5 bills), printed from an Internet site, in the Salvation Army's Christmas season collection kettles. They claimed their actions were intended more to send a message than to do harm. The Salvation Army maintains the protest did not hurt the organization's collection efforts.

In 2013, in an attempt to counter those who criticize the organization's anti-LGBT stances, the Salvation Army began removing links from its website to sites promoting so-called conversion therapy, aimed at changing sexual orientation from homosexual to heterosexual. While the organization's efforts to change its image included statements of clarification (e.g., "The Salvation Army embraces employees of many different faiths and orientations and abides by all applicable anti-discrimination laws in its hiring"), critics point out that it continues to maintain antigay religious stances and to discriminate against its own employees and their partners (Jones, 2013).

This example shows that implementation of domestic partner plans can raise complex and contentious political and social issues. National support for (or opposition to) such plans is linked to broader gay rights issues.

SOURCES: Gordon (2001); Heredia (2001a, 2001b); Jones (2013); King (2001); People for the American Way (2001); Price (2001).

According to a survey by the Society for Human Resource Management (2013), 24% of organizations offer same-sex domestic partner benefits (excluding health care), and 20% provide opposite-sex domestic partner benefits (excluding health care). Rapidly changing legal and policy provisions regarding same-sex and opposite-sex partners, especially since the overturning of the Defense of Marriage Act in 2013, illustrate the challenges in this area. For example, in 2014 President Obama announced his support for expanded health insurance coverage and full retirement survivor benefits for same-sex spouses in response to the Supreme Court decision overturning DOMA (Yoder, 2014). Furthermore, currently the District of Columbia and 17 states—California, Connecticut, Delaware, Hawaii, Iowa, Illinois, Maine, Maryland, Massachusetts, Minnesota, New Hampshire, New Jersey, New Mexico, New York, Rhode Island, Vermont, and Washington—authorize the issuing of marriage licenses to same-sex couples. Another 4 states offer different legal protections short of marriage: Colorado recognizes civil unions, Oregon and Nevada have broad domestic partnership laws, and Wisconsin has a limited domestic partnership law (Defining Marriage, 2014; Freedom to Marry, 2014). In 33 states, state law defines marriage as a relationship between a man and a woman, thus prohibiting same-sex marriage. Of these states, 29 have similar language in their state constitutions. Many public and private sector benefit plans have been restructured to add flexibility and take into account these and other changes. For instance, in state and local government, one-third of civilian workers have access to health care benefits for same-sex partners, and 28% have access for opposite-sex partners; the comparable figures for defined-benefit retirement survivor benefits are 50% and 48% (BLS, 2013c). Results of employer surveys indicate that health benefit coverage for domestic partners is no more costly than coverage for spouses or other dependents (Employee Benefit Research Institute, 2009). Human resource managers need to take a strategic perspective and keep abreast of this rapidly changing policy terrain so that they can adapt accordingly.

Each of the five work/family programs discussed in this section is likely to appeal to a different group of employees. Jurisdictions that provide a smorgasbord of offerings will be most responsive to a diverse workforce. Some policies have broad appeal; others are important to a narrower clientele. Potential gains in loyalty and productivity may warrant investments in these areas. The main reasons employers provide such supportive programs are to improve recruitment, retention, and productivity; to aid employees in managing work and family life and meet employee needs; and to improve morale and job satisfaction (Matos & Galinsky, 2014). It is imperative that performance-minded employers know what motivates their employees, periodically review organizational policies and communications, revisit their talent management programs and work/life policies regularly, and create opportunities for diverse elements in the workforce to network and learn from each other. Health and wellness programs, covered in the next section, promise similar returns on human capital investments.

Family-Friendly or Single Hostile?

Some single employees may harbor resentment against their employers regarding policies designed to benefit their married coworkers. They may feel shortchanged or overburdened when employers expect them to "take up the slack" for absent coworkers who are given "special help" in dealing with spouse- or child-related problems. An example of this sentiment appeared in a letter published in the popular "The Ethicist" column in the *New York Times Magazine,* in which the writer questioned whether his employer's paid "family days" discriminated against single people (Cohen, 2002). If single or childless workers receive fewer benefits than others, subsidize benefits provided to others for which they are ineligible, and are expected to assume more responsibilities than others, friction will likely result. In seeking to help their employees achieve work/life balance, employers should be careful to design "lifestyle-friendly" policies that are inclusive and flexible, and that offer choices to workers (Gannon, 1998; Kirkpatrick, 1997; Lynem, 2001).

A new twist in this area is what the Families and Work Institute terms "the **new male mystique**" (Aumann, Galinsky, & Matos, 2011). This is the male version of the "feminine mystique," a concept articulated by Betty Friedan in 1963 in her work addressing the role tension that women face in juggling work and family responsibilities. Now, five decades later, men face some of the same tensions as they try to satisfy both the traditional expectations of men as financial providers for their families and the expectations accompanying emerging gender role values that they be more nurturing husbands/partners, fathers, and sons. Some of the factors that put men at risk for experiencing work/family conflict are spending more time at work; attitudes about work, family, and appropriate gender roles; increasing job demands; being more work-centric than family-centric; holding traditional gender role values; and having children under the age of 18 at home. Among factors that reduce family/work conflict for men are supportive coworkers and supervisors; access to workplace flexibility options; and a workplace culture that supports the use of available workplace flexibility (Matos & Galinsky, 2011). Human resource managers as well as line administrators need to be aware of this new dynamic that has implications for organizational performance and employee well-being.

HEALTH, SAFETY, AND WELLNESS PROGRAMS

As society has become increasingly health conscious, employees have taken greater interest in the health-promoting activities made available by their employers. Typical personal concerns are the accessibility of **wellness programs**, the range of activities offered, cost-sharing arrangements, convenience, and privacy. Employers are inclined to focus on issues of program demand and productivity returns on whatever funds are invested. Four relevant initiatives are stress reduction programs, wellness programs, safety initiatives, and employee assistance programs, each of which is discussed in turn below.

Stress Reduction Programs

The causes and consequences of stress at work have been widely discussed, and the human resource management implications of stress are important. Too much stress impedes individual and organizational performance, but too little stress also can be counterproductive. The challenge to managers is to create optimal levels of stress and promote employee well-being while avoiding practices that lead to chronic mental or physical problems that reduce performance. Such "negative stress" is often characterized by high levels of absenteeism and turnover. Because it has been estimated that more than 10 million people in the nation's workforce experience stress-related problems, it is not surprising that some organizations have responded with stress reduction programs. An Aon Hewitt (2013, p. 9) employer survey recently identified these top stressors: financial situation, work changes, work schedule, work relationships, influence/control over how I do my work, personal relationships, and family member's health condition.

The prevention, detection, and management of negative stress are beneficial for both employees and employers. The following are some ways of reducing stress, linked to human resource management functions:

- Using effective screening devices in recruitment to ensure a good person–environment fit
- Avoiding individual–organization "misfits" in selection by matching the right person with the right job
- Orienting employees in ways that reduce the gap between job expectations and reality
- Providing assessment, observation, feedback, counseling, and coaching in career planning and development
- Offering worker support systems that foster attachments among employees
- Furnishing crisis intervention counseling (including emotional support and problem-solving strategies) to employees who experience difficult moments
- Tracking organizational indicators of stress to identify problem areas
- Training employees in behavioral self-control skills to increase relaxation on the job
- Equipping staff with cognitive problem-solving skills to reduce stress in problem solving
- Offering workshops and short courses on time management to reduce stress

Stress reduction programs incorporating some or most of these strategies are found in a majority of local governments (64%) and private sector settings (52%) (Mercer, 1996; West & Berman, 1996). Exhibit 8.6 suggests further stress reduction strategies for managers and employees.

Wellness Programs

The goals of wellness programs are to alter unhealthy personal habits and lifestyles and to promote behaviors conducive to health and well-being. Employers offer such services as health assessment (first aid and emergency), risk appraisals, screenings (blood pressure checks, blood sugar and cholesterol tests), injections (allergy, immunizations), and health and nutrition education or counseling. They may provide exercise equipment and facilities or negotiate health club discounts and reimburse employees for participation. Health promotion activities often focus on physical fitness, weight control, smoking cessation,

Exhibit 8.6 Tips for Managers and Employees on Ways to Reduce Work-Related Stress

What can managers do?

- Follow a consistent management style.
- Avoid actions that erode the competence or confidence of employees.
- Treat all employees fairly.
- Give positive feedback whenever appropriate.
- Support flexible work schedules and job sharing.
- Clarify objectives and communicate them to employees.
- Establish performance targets that are challenging but realistic.
- Make sure tasks are well defined and responsibilities are clear.
- Introduce some variety if jobs are extremely monotonous or boring.
- Establish good two-way communication.
- Increase employees' decision latitude.
- Avoid work overload or underload.
- Decrease role conflict and ambiguity.
- Promote career development and career security.
- Develop job content that avoids narrow, fragmented tasks with little extrinsic meaning.
- Promote participation and control.
- Avoid under- and overpromotion.

What can employees do at work?

- Schedule time realistically.
- Avoid setting unrealistic expectations for themselves.
- Do one thing at a time.
- Avoid depending on memory to keep track of all tasks.
- Ignore situations they cannot control.
- Get away from their desks at lunchtime.
- Identify sources of stress.
- Mentally rehearse stressful situations.
- Allow extra time when traveling.
- Review their priorities and lifestyles.

What can employees do at home?

- Exercise regularly.
- Explore ways to reduce caregiving and work conflicts.
- Take advantage of community support networks.
- Build fun into their schedules.
- Express feelings openly.
- Be prepared to wait.
- Begin to rid their lives of clutter.
- Spend time each day in relaxing activity.
- Set aside time to eat leisurely, well-balanced meals.

and health awareness. These activities can be emphasized at brown-bag lunches or wellness fairs. Psychological and physiological benefits and resulting reductions in insurance premiums have been reported for participating employees. Improved morale, organizational commitment, sense of belonging, recruitment and retention, and productivity are potential benefits to organizations that emphasize wellness. Overall, studies have shown that wellness programs are usually successful investments, reducing health care costs and providing returns to the employer (Aon Hewitt, 2013; Goetzel & Ozminkowski, 2006).

Availability of wellness programs is more than twice as likely in state government and local governments (52%) as in the private sector (25%) (BLS, 2011). When Aon Hewitt (2013) surveyed employers about top health care outcomes they would like to achieve, the top-ranked response was to increase participation in wellness, health improvement, and disease management programs (76%). The five highest-ranked behavioral foci for health improvement in the study were physical inactivity, poor diet, smoking, lack of health screening, and poor stress management. Nevertheless, benefit eligibility figures for full-time employers are lower than these figures, preferences, and rankings would suggest (see Exhibit 8.1).

The city of Loveland, Colorado, has an innovative wellness program called Healthsteps. It offers bonus points to those with positive medical history and healthy lifestyle choices. Based on the number of bonus points employees earn, they are eligible for distributions of up to 50% of any annual health plan savings. Attending the annual health fair and undergoing tests there can earn employees lifestyle points. Lifestyle points can also be earned for having test results that meet targets for blood pressure, weight, and cholesterol, and for participation in various fitness activities (walking, jogging, running). Medical points can be awarded for all premium dollars paid for employees and their families (with points subtracted based on the dollar value of claims paid). Employees are never penalized for heavy use of medical care because point totals do not fall below zero. Some other cities have similar creative, incentive-based initiatives.

Stress reduction and wellness plans promote healthy lifestyles and reduce the likelihood of serious illnesses. Such preventive activities may be buttressed by employee assistance programs designed to address health-related problems when they appear.

Safety Initiatives

Federal and state laws protect employees from being endangered by unsafe workplaces. Provisions of the Occupational Safety and Health Act provide employees with several rights if they are concerned about unsafe conditions or practices in the workplace (see Exhibit 8.7). State laws typically conform closely to the federal legislation.

Employee Assistance Programs

Organizations with **employee assistance programs (EAPs)** use them to improve employee health and help employees cope with personal problems such as difficulties resulting from work/family conflict. Such plans usually offer counseling or referral services for people having problems with alcohol or drug abuse, personal debt, domestic abuse, or

Exhibit 8.7   Worker Rights to a Safe Workplace Under the Occupational Safety and Health Act

Workers have the right to the following:

- Receive training from employers on the health and safety standards that the law mandates
- Receive training from employers on any dangerous chemicals workers are exposed to and on ways employees can protect themselves from harm
- Receive training from employers on any other health and safety hazards (e.g., construction hazards, blood-borne pathogens) in the workplace
- Receive information from employers regarding OSHA standards, worker injuries and illnesses, job hazards, and workers' rights
- Make direct requests to employers to cure any hazards or OSHA violations
- File complaints with OSHA
- Make a request that OSHA inspect the workplace
- Find out the results of an OSHA inspection
- File a complaint with OSHA if the employer retaliates for asserting employee rights under the act
- Request the federal government to research possible workplace hazards

SOURCE: Nolo (2003). *Providing military leave: State and federal laws protect workers who take leave to serve in the military.*

other problems that impede job-related performance. The objective of EAPs is to improve employees' competence, performance, and well-being. Eligibility for EAPs in state and local governments is reported in Exhibit 8.1.

A profile of a comprehensive EAP would include the following:

- Counseling and referral for employees and their families
- Staff with solid clinical background and knowledge of providers for referral
- Broad health coverage (including mental health) in the benefits package
- Staff familiarity with the health package to ensure that provider services are covered
- Confidential services
- A training component for employees, supervisors, and managers
- Reference checks on all service providers

A national survey of employee benefit offerings in the United States in 2013 found that 77% of surveyed organizations currently had EAP benefits and another 2% planned to begin offering EAP services in the next 12 months (SHRM, 2013). Many local governments—including Ventura County, California; Chesterfield, Missouri; and Middletown, Rhode Island—have EAPs reflecting several of the above "ideal" characteristics. One legal caution: Employees and managers need to be aware that information gathered during EAP sessions may belong to the employer, not the employee. Furthermore, decision makers designing EAPs need to weigh both ethical principles and economic imperatives (see Exhibit 8.8).

> **Exhibit 8.8** Employee Assistance Programs: Ethical Principles and Economic Imperatives
>
> Weighing ethical principles and economic imperatives involves viewing choices in terms of their ethical right and wrong as well as their economic good and bad. *Right–good* decisions are ethically correct and economically efficient, *wrong–bad* decisions are ethically incorrect and economically inefficient, *right–bad* decisions are ethically correct but economically inefficient, and *wrong–good* decisions are ethically deficient but economically efficient. This fourfold framework can be applied to EAPs.
>
> Right–good EAP policies provide comprehensive services in recognition of the ethical and economic gains from such an approach. A right–bad strategy would not be sustainable (at least without a healthy investment of funds), a situation evident in some government jurisdictions. A wrong–good strategy would fail to meet legitimate employee (and arguably organizational) needs given the priority of saving money, a condition characterizing some small firms. A wrong–bad plan would be a lose–lose strategy that is ineffective ethically and also economically costly.
>
> From a utilitarian perspective, an EAP would be morally justified if the benefits most clients experience (reduced health expenditures, workers' compensation and disability costs, and reduced risks of workplace violence, sexual harassment, and other behavioral problems) outweigh the costs. Overall, EAPs can promote both utilitarian and altruistic objectives, but ethical dilemmas and fiscal concerns, especially in an era of widespread outsourcing, require that decision makers do some adroit juggling to assure individual well-being and organizational productivity.

SOURCE: Adapted from West and Bowman (2008).

Institutional sponsorship of health and wellness programs signals to individuals that the organization is concerned about their well-being. Another way that agencies can communicate such concern as well as address workforce diversity is by offering more flexible work arrangements, the subject of the next section.

FLEXIBLE WORK ARRANGEMENTS

Flexible policies go a long way in reducing work/family conflict. Worker surveys indicate that substantial portions of the workforce support practices like flextime (80%), job sharing (48%), and telecommuting (48%) (Workplace Flexibility, 2010). During the economic instability and recession in 2009, employers maintained or increased flex options offered to employees as a strategy for promoting employee engagement (see Chapter 6) and retention (Matos & Galinsky, 2014). Employees are interested in the range of options available to them at work that might minimize problems at home: Will they have any control over the hours and location of work? Are there possible alternatives to leaving home at 8:00 A.M. and returning at 6:00 P.M., Monday through Friday, year-round? Can they work at home? Can they choose their benefits? Can they negotiate alternatives to full-time work? Are job- or leave-sharing arrangements permissible? These are important issues in management. Employers are interested in getting the work done. They have to weigh the pros and cons of flexible arrangements before making such options available to large numbers of employees. Seven alternative work arrangements are briefly considered below: flex options, telecommuting, part-time work, voluntary reduced work time, temporary work, leave sharing and pooling, and job sharing.

Flex Options

Flextime work schedules allow differential starting and quitting times but specify a required number of hours within a particular period. According to the Bureau of Labor Statistics (2005b), about 27 million full-time wage and salary workers (27.5%) had flexible schedules in 2004, down from 29 million in 2001. Only about one in ten workers is actually enrolled in a formal, employer-sponsored flextime program. In the private sector, flexible schedules are most prevalent in financial activities (37.7%), professional and business services (37.6%), and information (34.9%). In the public sector, flexible schedules are more prevalent at the federal (28.8%) and state levels (28.4%) than at the local level of government (13.7%). Formal flextime programs are more prevalent in the public sector than in private industry: More than half the workers in the public service with flexible schedules are in formal programs. Nearly three-fourths of federal employees with flextime participate in formal programs, whereas only about one-third of private sector workers with flextime participate in such programs.

Another flex option is the **compressed workweek**, in which the number of hours worked per week is condensed into fewer days. For example, employees work a set 160-hour schedule per month but do it in fewer than 20 workdays by working more than 8 hours a day and fewer than 5 days a week. According to the SHRM (2013) employee benefits survey, more than one-third of organizations offer compressed workweeks. In 2003, the U.S. Office of Personnel Management reported that 357,326 federal personnel were using compressed schedules. Compressed workweeks enable employers to extend hours of operation and enable employees to reduce commuting costs and gain leisure time. They may introduce problems of employer supervision and employee fatigue, however. (These two flex options are discussed in Chapter 7—see Exhibit 7.2—so treatment here is limited.) In 2008, Utah became the first state to institute a mandatory 4-day workweek for most state employees (Copeland, 2008), but it has since moved back to a 5-day workweek (Kerrigan, 2011). Research by Facer and Wadsworth (2008) on the impact of a compressed workweek in a small, growing Utah city found that employees working the 4-day, 10-hour (4/10) schedule reported higher levels of job satisfaction, higher perceived productivity, and lower levels of work/family conflict than their non-4/10 coworkers. Other cities (e.g., North Miami and Tamarac, Florida) also have instituted 4-day workweeks. However, Condrey, West, and Ledvinka's (2010) national survey of large cities suggests that there are both upsides and downsides to the 4-day workweek and that jurisdictions considering making the switch should proceed with caution. Organizations are more likely to offer flextime than compressed workweek options. Overall, it is estimated that 50% of employees in the United States are eligible for flextime (Galinsky, Bond, & Hill, 2004; Stockwell, 2006).

Among federal agencies, 92% have implemented flexible work schedules, and one-third of the federal workforce participates in compressed and flexible work schedules. Only 14% of states (California, Illinois, Maine, Massachusetts, Minnesota, Missouri, and Tennessee),

79% of federal agencies, and 60% of firms offer compressed workweek options. In the U.S. Department of Labor, eight in ten employees work flexible schedules (Daniel, 1999). In California, air quality regulations provided the impetus for many governments to try alternative schedules as a way to decrease pollution and traffic congestion. A bare majority of cities (52%) nationwide offer flextime to some employees. It may take various forms:

- Core hours (required presence at work)
- Band of flexible hours (typically at the end or beginning of the day)
- Variable lunch hours
- Sliding schedule (variation in the start or stop times daily, weekly, or monthly)
- Bank time (variable length of workday; hours from long days can be banked for short days later on)

The number of employees with the core hours option increased from 29% in 1992 to 43% in 2002.

Clearly, the greatest flexibility is present when combinations of options are available. Implementation problems can result when employees are expected to work as a team, when unions or supervisors resist the move to flextime, and when laws (e.g., maximum hours and overtime requirements) introduce complications. Care needs to be taken to ensure that there is adequate staffing during noncore hours. Compressed schedules may be less successful in smaller governments, where staff coverage for leave-taking employees may be inadequate. Telecommuting, discussed next, is another type of flexible benefit.

Telecommuting

Telecommuters are people who work away from the traditional work locale (e.g., at home, at satellite locations, or on the road). It is estimated that 45 million employees in the United States telecommute at least one day a week, and their numbers are increasing (Levit, 2010). The Families and Work Institute's 2014 survey of employers with 50 or more employees found that more employers were offering the option of occasional telecommuting (67%) for at least some employees than were doing so in 2008 (50%) (Matos & Galinsky, 2014). Three-fourths of telecommuters work for private sector firms, a reduction from 81% in 2005, due in part to increased telework among state and federal employees (Heathfield, 2011). More than 8 in 10 of *Fortune*'s "100 Best Companies to Work For" allow employees to telecommute at least 20% of the time (Heathfield, 2011). The American Community Survey found that telecommuting increased 79% between 2005 and 2012 and now involves 2.6% of the American workforce, or 3.2 million employees (cited in Tugend, 2014). In 2008, according to the Partnership for Public Service (2010), while 62% of 1.9 million federal employees were eligible to telework, less than 6% of full-time federal workers did telework at least one day a week. Among the reasons for underutilization of telework are managerial worries about limited productivity, inaccessibility of teleworkers, access to classified information in nonsecure settings, uncertainty about who provides equipment, lack of accountability, limited face-to-face contact, and potential for abuse (ICMA, 2012; Partnership for Public Service, 2010). Despite these concerns, several agencies have experienced success with telework. A successful federal case study is presented in Exhibit 8.9.

Exhibit 8.9 Federal Case Study of Telework

At NRC, Leadership Support for Flexibility Is the Key Ingredient

For senior leaders at the Nuclear Regulatory Commission (NRC), the satisfaction of being named the "best place to work in the federal government" in 2007 lasted only briefly before a major question surfaced: How to stay on top?

NRC leadership knew the agency's likelihood of remaining a "best place to work" rested largely on its ability to maintain a satisfied, engaged workforce. To learn more about the issues facing employees, NRC leaders authorized a work/life committee represented by 8 to 10 office directors and deputies. The committee's first step: evaluate employee responses to the Federal Human Capital Survey (now called Federal Employee Viewpoint Survey) and NRC's Internal Safety Culture and Climate Survey to identify ways to improve employee work/life. Two major issues arose: desire for more flexibility in work hours and desire for more flexibility in work location.

To address these concerns, the work/life committee implemented the NEWFlex (NRC Employee Workschedule Flexibilities) pilot program in a large office for 3 months. The program offered all employees more flexible work hours (the workday could begin as early as 5:00 A.M. and end as late as 11:00 P.M.) and the opportunity to telework.

Once implemented, the NEWFlex pilot quickly gained popularity. With its success, the pilot was expanded to other parts of the agency and finally was offered agencywide in 2009. In addition to countless anecdotal success stories from the agency's employees, the federal Human Capital Survey results suggest that NEWFlex is having positive impact: NRC's work/life balance score increased from 73.2 in 2007 to 76.6 in 2009, and employee satisfaction with telework increased from 52.2 in 2006 to 61.5 in 2008.

Keys to Success

Senior Leadership Support

The implementation of the agencywide NEWFlex program would not have been possible without the support of the NRC leadership. As one employee stated, "Leaders see past the barriers that exist and make every effort to ensure that all employees have the opportunity to participate in work/life programs." NRC leaders paid more than lip service to the NEWFlex program: Many senior leaders in the agency use NEWFlex themselves.

Peer-to-Peer Information Sharing

Despite support for the NEWFlex program by senior management, the work/life committee soon had to address objections from first-line supervisors, who play a critical role in the success of any flexibility program. NRC found that sharing success stories and best practices was best done on a peer-to-peer basis. With this knowledge, the agency arranged an all-supervisors meeting featuring a panel of managers who participated in the pilot. This meeting gave managers an opportunity to ask difficult questions, hear honest answers, and learn more about NEWFlex from peers who could relate to the challenges facing them. The peer-to-peer interaction and information sharing addressed the concerns of managers and enhanced the credibility of the program for first-line supervisors.

(Continued)

Exhibit 8.9 (Continued)

Commitment to Organizational Values

NRC's success as an organization rests on seven overall values that affect the work of the agency. Prominent among these values is "respect for individuals' diversity, roles, beliefs, viewpoints, and work/life balance." These values are supported across the organization, from entry-level employees to senior executives.

Culture

According to NRC employees, the agency has a very social culture. The overlap of work and life in the agency was a contributing factor to the success of the NEWFlex pilot and still plays an important role in work/life programs today. NRC was ranked number 4 in 2013 and number 6 in the *2014 Best Places to Work in the Federal Government*® rankings.

SOURCE: Reprinted with permission from *On Demand Government: Deploying Flexibilities to Ensure Service Continuity*, July 2010. Partnership for Public Service and Booz Allen Hamilton.

In 2010, President Obama set a goal of 150,000 federal employees teleworking by 2011, and the Partnership for Public Service (2010) set a goal of 600,000 federal civil servants teleworking by 2014. Also in 2010, Obama signed the Telework Enhancement Act. Among other things, the act requires the head of each federal agency to (1) establish a telework policy clarifying employee eligibility to telecommute, (2) identify employees eligible to participate in telework, and (3) notify employees of their eligibility. The specific elements of a telework policy are outlined, the relationship between telework and employee performance is addressed, and training requirements are covered in the legislation. Further, each agency is directed to designate a telework managing officer and qualifications; duties and reporting requirements are specified.

The most recent status report on telework in the federal government indicates that 1,020,034 employees are eligible to telework (out of 2,157,668 federal employees), 267,227 employees have telework agreements, 209,192 employees were teleworking in September 2013, and 301,372 employees were teleworking in fiscal year 2012 (U.S. OPM, 2013, p. 11). Each of these figures is an increase from 2011. The Government Accountability Office's (2013) analysis of the OPM's 2012 report on the status of telework points out that full compliance with the Telework Enhancement Act has not yet been achieved. Unfortunately, the flexibility provided by telework options can lead to abuse. For example, the Patent and Trademark Office had received accolades for its telework program until a recent report provided evidence that half of the 8,300 patent examiners who were telecommuting had lied about the hours they worked and were awarded bonuses for work they did not perform (Clark, 2014). Equally troubling in this case, supervisors who had obtained evidence of fraud and asked higher-ups for further investigation to document wrongdoing were bluntly rejected by top agency officials, who thereby undercut efforts to discipline the cheaters.

Between 2005 and 2011 the number of telecommuters in local government grew by 67% (ICMA, 2012). Experience with telecommuting in the city of Richmond, Washington, suggests that the tasks most suitable for work at home include writing, reading, telephoning, data analysis or entry, computer programming, and word processing. As of 2007, at least 34 states allowed some of their employees to telecommute (Council of State Governments, 2007). According to a 2011 publication titled *The State of Telework in the U.S.* (Lister & Harnish, 2011), 82 of the top 100 companies on *Forbes* magazine's list of "Best Companies to Work For" at that time offered telecommuting, and 76% of telecommuters were working in the private sector. Although by 2007 many private companies offered the telecommuting option (World at Work, 2007), only 2% of employees were using it (International Public Management Association for Human Resources, 2007). In 1995, a 50-state survey found that most states had no formal telecommuting programs, but informal arrangements often existed in selected agencies (Kemp, 1995). Currently, 19 state governments mention telecommuting on their websites. Advantages of telecommuting programs include increased productivity, flexibility, economy, and satisfaction. Disadvantages or impediments include loss of management control, inadequate technology, absence of policy guidance, stakeholder resistance, concerns about customer complaints, insufficient office coverage, problems scheduling meetings, and insufficient funds. (See Appendix A at the end of this chapter for a list of questions for employers and employees regarding telecommuting arrangements.) Subsequent sections of this chapter discuss the implementation of telecommuting in detail.

Part-Time Work

Some employees might prefer working a specific number of hours fewer than the traditional 40 during the workweek on a recurring basis. Part-time employment is defined by the federal government as involving fewer than 35 hours per week. The part-time employment rate in the United States is 13.4 %; the country with the highest part-time employment is the Netherlands at 37% (Organisation for Economic Co-operation and Development, 2013). In 2013, the number of persons in the United States who were employed part-time for economic reasons (i.e., involuntary part-time workers) was 7.5 million (BLS, 2014). By law (5 U.S.C. 3402), nearly every federal agency is required to have a program for part-time employment. According to the U.S. OPM (2003), 92% of federal agencies have implemented part-time work, but data from the Partnership for Public Service (2010) show that only 3.3% of workers pursue this option.

In Florida, one-fifth of the state government workforce consists of part-time employees. Working part-time might be an attractive option for new parents, who may want to cut back on work hours temporarily as a transition between family leave and a 40-hour workweek, but part-time workers receive no benefits despite the fact that many of them work nearly full-time hours. Another downside of part-time work is that it is frequently accompanied by unpredictable and on-call work schedules, which often make it difficult for workers to know when they will be working the next week or the next month. Lacking a firm, steady, and predictable schedule makes it difficult to plan for child care, college classes, or doctor appointments. As employers have to cope with fluctuations in supply and demand, some part-time and on-call workers often have to be available every minute of every day (Greenhouse, 2014). At the time of this writing, legislation has been proposed in Congress that would ensure employees get their work schedules two weeks in advance and extra compensation for last-minute changes ("New Rules for Part-Time Work," 2014).

Voluntary Reduced Work Time

Selected full-time employees want to reduce their work hours and their pay, and some employers prefer this option as a way to reduce labor costs. Such reductions often range from a few hours a week up to 20 hours. Typically, health benefits are prorated. Voluntary reduced time (**V-time**) enables parents to meet caregiving responsibilities, provides an alternative to layoffs or use of part-time replacements, and helps phase workers into retirement. These arrangements are often negotiated.

Temporary Work

The rise of the contingent workforce is tied to employers' need for flexibility and to employees' desires for variable work schedules and employment. For individuals, temporary employment enables them to meet family responsibilities, complete education or training, master new skills, or compete for full-time positions. For organizations, temporary staffing provides a source of specific skills for only the time they are needed, allows for development of a core workforce while supplementing it as budgets fluctuate, and controls labor costs by moving labor from a fixed to a variable expense. The number of temporary workers employed nationwide on an average day in the first quarter of 2011 was 2.62 million (American Staffing Association, 2011).

The hiring of "temps" has been a common accompaniment of downsizing in business, and it is becoming more evident in government as belt-tightening occurs. For example, the state of Texas has put a legal employment cap on full-time positions to restrain personnel costs. The cap does not cover temporary employees or outside workers. In 1997, Texas had more than 20,000 consultants, contractors, and temps working in state government, a 300% increase from just a decade earlier. This so-called **hidden workforce** cost $41 million; of that amount, $24 million was spent on temporary workers (Gamino, 1997). The movement from full-time permanent workers to the "contingent" workforce is likely to continue in both the public and private sectors, and it may raise issues about performance quality, legality, and work alienation (West, 2012). Organizations should weigh gains in flexibility carefully against potential losses in effectiveness before proceeding with new workplace initiatives.

Leave Sharing and Pooling

Leave sharing and pooling are types of employee-to-employee job benefits whereby healthy workers donate sick time or other benefits to coworkers in crisis. Unlike some employee-friendly policies common in the private sector, leave sharing and pooling are found more often in government. For example, although only 8% of companies nationwide offer such sharing benefits, the federal government, more than two-thirds of state governments, and many municipal jurisdictions and public school districts allow leave sharing and pooling (Camp, 2006; Council of State Governments, 2007; Murphy, 2005; Suttle, 1998; U.S. OPM, 2007). Despite its availability, only 1% of federal employees use it (Daniel, 1999).

Direct donation of leave to individual employees is permitted in 22 states, and 18 states have collective leave banks. Delaware, Montana, and Tennessee offer both options. Massachusetts has leave banks that allow state employees to assist colleagues confronting long-term illness. The state's sick leave bank allows all workers who donate 1 day to the bank to collect up to 120 extra days off. This is an important benefit for employees confronting catastrophic illness, enabling them to keep their jobs and avoid spending down their savings to qualify for Medicaid (Murphy, 2005). The federal government's Voluntary Leave Bank Program allows individuals to pool their hours to provide time off to others (Zielewski & Boots, 2010). Leave sharing under this program allows employees facing personal or medical emergencies who have exhausted their own leave to benefit from voluntarily donated annual leave from other federal workers (U.S. OPM, 2005). Overall, organizations offering leave sharing, like those offering V-time, provide examples of addressing the paradox of needs.

Job Sharing

Job sharing enables two employees to split the responsibilities, hours, salary, and (usually) benefits of a full-time position. In a recent national survey, 10% of organizations reported offering job sharing (SHRM, 2013). A 1997 status report to the president on federal workplace family-friendly initiatives found that 63% of federal agencies offered job sharing. However, job sharing is rarely used in the federal government: 0.02% of federal employees job shared in 2010 (Partnership for Public Service, 2010). In part, this low usage is related to a lack of awareness among managers about the job-sharing option. In 2010, a study conducted by the University of California, Los Angeles, found that 18 states had job-sharing programs. Colorado's website says that it has had job sharing since 1977. According to the Families and Work Institute, the option for job sharing has been reduced in organizations with 50 or more employees, from 29% in 2008 to 18% in 2014 (Matos & Galinsky, 2014). Where job sharing has been used successfully, that success has been partially attributable to careful planning, supervisory training, and highly motivated workers; problematic results have been linked to supervisory resistance and state-imposed restrictions on participation. Examples of positions where job sharing is used include nursing, social work, law, and mental health. Job sharing offers employees the advantages of balancing home/work responsibilities, earning professional wages, and maintaining a career while cutting back on hours.

Job sharing is less frequently reported as a benefit in local government (11%), although some governments may be willing to approve such arrangements in response to specific proposals. The city of Redmond, Washington, uses job sharing to fill secretarial, street maintenance, financial analyst, and recreation coordinator positions. Agencies see potential advantages in job sharing, especially when they are facing severe financial constraints, possible layoffs, or the needs of working mothers. Employers may also see job sharing as a way to reduce absenteeism and turnover and to heighten productivity (Appelbaum & Tilly, 2011). However, benefit levels, promotion implications, and seniority issues remain problematic under this arrangement.

To summarize, two factors influencing the employee-friendly and flexible policies discussed so far are important determinants of work/family conflict and of whether employees use benefits: employers' attitudes and "the power of peers." The importance of employer attitudes is apparent from research that shows that work/family conflict is greater for employees whose supervisors put work first, regardless of the worker-friendly or flexible benefits provided. The power of peers is evidenced in research findings showing that employees more frequently use alternative work schedules when those in their work groups are already using them (Clay, 1998). Contrary to critics' claims that encouraging individuals to use employee-friendly policies will erode employee commitment and loyalty, research by the Families and Work Institute, drawing on a national sample of 2,877 employees, found that support from employers, as demonstrated by flexibility and family-friendly policies, was the most important factor in job satisfaction (Clay, 1998). Clearly, the employment context is crucial.

In addition to employers' attitudes and peer pressures, the costs of employee-friendly policies are important. Although costs may be offset by employee gains in flexibility and support, they can be substantial. This leads to two key problems. First, unlike the private sector, public organizations cannot pass the costs through to the marketplace. Second, managers are, with some exceptions, usually not in a position to authorize these programs; appropriate governing bodies must approve them. That usually means that they become part of negotiations of overall compensation, benefits, and work rules. The complexity of adopting, financing, and implementing such programs requires careful consideration. Furthermore, initiatives can become politically volatile (e.g., domestic partner benefits), suggesting that organizations need to consider intangible costs in addition to tangible ones.

The preceding sections have highlighted different strategies managers can use to minimize family/work conflict and promote employee well-being. Employers need to experiment to discover the appropriate mix of such plans as they search for the best "fit" between employee needs and organizational requirements (see Exhibit 8.11). OPM opened the Family-Friendly Workplace Advocacy Office in 1999 to encourage these programs. Resource scarcity might limit the range of options available for some jurisdictions and agencies, but workforce diversity will provide a counterweight pushing for reform. Jurisdictions will be more likely to respond if the proposed changes meet pressing needs and if payoffs are evident.

The Alfred P. Sloan Awards for Excellence in Workplace Effectiveness and Flexibility seek to identify leading employers who replace command-and-control and control authority systems with productivity and organizational results outcomes. The focus on results is evident from the fact that 98% of the 2012 winning employers identified employees' accomplishment as very or extremely important, and only 11% of these winners described the number of hours that employees spend at work as very or extremely important (Galinsky & Jackson, 2012). While workplace flexibility is increasing, it is nuanced and changing. A number of developments have taken place regarding workplace flexibility since 2008, as summarized by the Families and Work Institute's report on its 2014 National

Study of Employers (Matos & Galinsky, 2014, p. 22):

- Employers are less likely to provide reduced-hours options and career flexibility.
- Employers are more likely to provide flextime and flex-place, options in managing work time, and time to meet personal needs during the workday without loss of pay.
- Greater variety is available in flexibility options that enable employees to work longer hours or modify work time to meet both personal and work needs.
- Fewer flexibility options are available that involve employees spending less time working for the organization.
- Employers are less inclined to reward those within the organization who support effective, flexible work arrangements.
- Employers are less inclined to encourage supervisors to assess employees' performance by what they accomplish and not just by "face time."
- Employers are less inclined to train supervisors in managing employees of different ages.

Among the best predictors of workplace flexibility initiatives, according to this Families and Work Institute study, are the presence of a large proportion of women in the workforce and the presence of large proportions of women and racial/ethnic minorities in executive leadership positions or reporting directly to persons in those positions.

TRADITIONAL BENEFITS: NOT-SO-EMPLOYEE-FRIENDLY TRENDS

Because employee benefits account for a large part of employee compensation, often upward of 40%, they are a prominent part of a jurisdiction's financial management and human capital strategy (Reddick & Coggburn, 2008). Funds saved on benefits can greatly affect a jurisdiction's bottom line. Benefits can also be viewed by workers as deductions from salary monies; retirement benefits, for example, are likely viewed as delayed salary by employees. Spending on benefits has grown more rapidly than wages, due primarily to spiraling costs for public employee pensions and health care benefits. Given the economic downturn and the upswing in labor costs, public jurisdictions are increasingly shifting costs away from employers and onto employees, reducing or dropping benefits and requiring higher employee benefit contributions. This is especially true in the traditional benefit categories of pensions and health care benefits, discussed in turn below.[4]

Retirement Security

The news media are filled with headlines highlighting a growing crisis in public sector employee pension liabilities. Virtually all public sector plans calculate pension benefits based on the previous 1 to 3 years of work, with typical benefits equal to about 60% of pay after 30 years (with generally higher percentages for public safety) (Edwards, 2010), a significant financial commitment by government. While the private sector relies primarily on defined-contribution plans, the public sector at all levels of government has been more reliant on defined-benefit pension plans. Some government jurisdictions have begun shifting from **defined-benefit pension plans**, which guarantee preset lifetime pension payments, to **defined-contribution pension plans**, such as 401(k) accounts, with their attendant risks of vulnerability to a volatile stock market. Some have created hybrids of defined-benefit and defined-contribution systems. Indeed, 15 states have passed legislation implementing either mandatory or optional defined-contribution plans for some public employees (Thom, 2013). Others have reduced pension benefits for all future employees. One reason for the movement to defined-contribution plans is the pressure many governments are experiencing because of longer employee life spans and the numbers of employees taking early retirement. However, resistance to such reform can be strong, as Governor Arnold Schwarzenegger learned when he attempted, unsuccessfully, to reform the California state pension plan in 2005 by shifting from a defined-benefit to a defined-contribution approach. Flaws in traditional defined-benefit pension systems in some instances have included lax accounting standards and unrealistic assumptions about likely investment returns, which have resulted in public pension systems with huge unfunded liabilities (McMahon, 2011).

As the number and size of public pension funds have increased, there have been claims of waste, fraud, and abuse, leading to calls for reform. Elected officials like Governor Chris Christie of New Jersey have battled with employee unions and their supporters to overcome pension deficits (a deficit of $46 billion in New Jersey's case). Governor Rick Scott of Florida proposed that public employees contribute ("buy in") 5% of their pay to their pensions (matching the state's contribution), causing an outcry among workers who have modest salaries, who have not received pay raises in years, and who previously had not been required to pay for their pensions. The law that passed in Florida requires state workers to put 3% of their salaries toward retirement and eliminated cost-of-living increases on benefits earned after July 1, 2011. In New York, employees are required to give up 3% of their salaries to fund their pensions over a 10-year period (Smiley, McGrory, Teproff, & Brown, 2011), but Governor Andrew Cuomo has proposed that future state and New York City employees pay 6% of their salaries toward their pensions. By 2010, 12 states had mandated higher employee contributions; by mid-2011, another 8 states had done the same and 10 other states were proposing pension changes (Greenhouse, 2011). When state pension deficits are totaled nationwide, the unfunded liabilities facing the states amount to $3.2 trillion, and this occurs at a time when states' annual budget shortfalls total more than $100 billion (Issa, 2011).

Pension funding levels suffer from inadequate contributions, in part because governments do not make required contributions and in part because required contributions are insufficient to ensure adequate funding. Among other reasons for depleted contributions are the Great Recession and selective tax breaks. A report by the Pew Center on the States titled *The Widening Gap: The Great Recession's Impact on State Pension and Retiree Health Care Costs* (2011) states that "the gap between the promises states made for employees' retirement benefits and the money they set aside to pay for them grew to at least $1.26 trillion in fiscal year 2009," up 26% in one year (Pew Center on the States, 2011). The U.S. Government Accountability Office recommends that states maintain at least an 80% funding level. However, declining revenue has depleted states' coffers, hampering their ability to pay for annual retirement costs. It is important to note that attacks on public service benefits are often decoupled from the actual situation with benefits. For example, it could be argued that in some states the problem either did not exist (e.g., Florida) or was self-inflicted through tax cuts (e.g., Wisconsin).

In fiscal year 2012 the state-run retirement systems nationwide had a $915 billion shortfall; total pension debt rose to more than $1 trillion when promises by local government were added in. While several states passed reforms following the fiscal crisis, only 15—Alabama, Arizona, California, Delaware, Georgia, Maine, Mississippi, New Hampshire, New York, Rhode Island, South Carolina, South Dakota, Tennessee, Utah, and Wisconsin—consistently made at least 95% of the full actuarially required contributions to their pension plans from 2010 through 2012; the other 35 states fell behind in at least one year (Pew Charitable Trusts, 2014). At the local level, a Pew study found that 61 cities' retirement systems faced a $217 billion gap (Pew Charitable Trusts, 2013b). Clearly, strategic human resource management requires a balancing act to both meet the fiscal imperative of funding retiree benefits liabilities and meet the human capital challenge of recruiting and retaining a professional workforce (see Coggburn & Kearney, 2010).

Beginning in 1985, newly hired federal workers had a three-tiered retirement plan that included Social Security, a fixed-benefit plan, and a 401(k) plan. At the state and local levels, prohibitions exist making it virtually impossible for jurisdictions to change retirement benefits already promised to current employees (Tumulty, 2011). Utah now requires new state and municipal workers to select between a defined-contribution plan and a hybrid defined-benefit plan with a 401(k). The hybrid plan is the default choice for those who do not make their preference explicit (Borowski, 2011; Snell, 2010). Kentucky created a new pension plans for anyone hired after January 1, 2014, that requires future cost-of-living adjustments to be paid for prior to distribution (rather than occurring automatically) and commits lawmakers to full funding of promises in future years (Pew Charitable Trusts, 2013a). Other states are considering similar reforms.

A related issue is retiree health care and related benefits. Here, the Pew Center on the States (2011) reports that in fiscal year 2009 states had a total liability of $638 billion but had saved less than 5% ($31 billion) of total costs. Indeed, 19 states had not set aside any funds to pay bills for retiree health care and other nonpension benefits, and 7 states had funded only one-fourth of their liability. Leaders in this area included Alaska (104%), Arizona (100%), and North Dakota (106%). Further, only 2 states, Arizona and Oregon, had 50% or more of their liability for retiree health benefits funded. In 2013 99% of state and local government workers had access to retirement and medical care benefits (BLS, 2013a). If state retirement systems and health benefit contributions continue to accelerate more rapidly than overall general spending, competition for resources for other policy priorities (e.g., criminal justice, education) will intensify. These developments have increased the policy salience of pension and retiree health care benefits and increased pressure to reduce benefits, increase employee contributions, or both. Indeed, Pew reports that in the first 10 months of 2010, 18 states reduced pension liabilities via paring benefits or boosting employee contributions, 11 states did so in 2009, and 8 did so in 2008. Clearly, the trend in this area is much less employee-friendly than in the past. However, passage of the Patient Protection and Affordable Care Act (ACA) provided some relief by establishing the Early

Retiree Reinsurance Program (ERRP) to assist employers in continuing retiree health plans for employees age 55 or over but still ineligible for Medicare, along with their spouses and dependents. The program provided a bridge to 2014, when major provisions of the ACA took effect (Costello, 2013).

Two perspectives on public employee pensions can be related to the hard and soft approaches to human resource management. The **hard HRM** (utilitarian–instrumental) view sees employees as costs to be minimized and resources to be used for maximum return; the **soft HRM** (developmental–humanistic) view regards employees as assets worthy of investment and resources of competitive advantage. As West and Bowman (2008) have noted, from the soft HRM perspective, "reneging on promised pensions (or severely cutting them) is theft, robbing employees of their investment; the principle of 'fidelity of purpose' is crucial in building enduring, trustworthy relationships with workers. The obligation to pay for 'human depreciation' has been likened to the responsibility to pay replacement costs for worn-out equipment" (pp. 38–39).

But there is another point of view. As West and Bowman (2008) stress, from the hard HRM perspective,

> pensions are viewed as a voluntary and expensive obligation of management. Stewardship of stockholder and taxpayer resources requires prudent decision making, especially in an era of rising costs, competitive pressures, and an unpredictable future. If the benefits of pensions (e.g., employee loyalty, recruitment and retention edge) do not outweigh the costs, then the reality of doing business requires moving away from paternalistic policies of the past and insisting that employees assume more personal responsibility for their financial future. (p. 39)

Reconciling these two competing philosophies is difficult, and currently it is increasingly evident that hard HRM policies are gaining traction at the expense of softer policies.

Health Care

Similar less-than-employee-friendly trends can be seen in the health benefits area. Health care expenditures have grown considerably over the years, and as of 2014, 13.4% of Americans were without health care coverage (Levy, 2014). For most people, health insurance is a crucial benefit, yet the percentage of employers offering this benefit has been declining over the past decade. In addition, employers are increasingly reluctant to assume the full cost of individual and family health insurance premiums; instead, they are modifying their plans and expecting employees to absorb the costs via higher premiums, copays, and deductibles (Hacker, 2006, p. 139). Employers are also using carrot-and-stick approaches to improve employee health: Carrots include sponsoring health promotion activities (wellness programs, smoking cessation, and exercise promotion) and encouraging healthy lifestyles, and sticks include increasing premiums or limiting/eliminating coverage to deter high-risk behaviors (smoking, excessive weight, high cholesterol, participation in risky activities) (Wojcik, 2007).

The emergence of a "two-tier labor force" (core and peripheral) has led to the cost-saving strategy of "load shedding," whereby part-time, temporary, or sometimes newly hired employees are provided inferior benefits compared to those offered to current first-tier employees. In the public sector, nearly all federal agencies offer part-time work, and in local jurisdictions 15.4% of employees work part-time (Roberts, 2003). As noted earlier, approximately 20% of Florida's state government workers are part-time, and many of those work 35 hours per week. As organizations downsize or "rightsize" to economize, temporary employees with minimal benefits have become more commonplace, and this trend is likely to continue.

With continuing increases in health-related expenses, cost shifting away from employers and onto employees has become more prevalent, mandating employee benefit contributions like copays and deductibles or dropping employer-provided benefits altogether (Bens, 2005). Other strategies include switching from health insurance coverage to offering flexible spending accounts or health care savings accounts, the inherent tax advantages of which are attractive to some fiscally concerned public officials. Mail-order drug plans can result in cost savings, given the expense of prescription drugs, and audits of medical claims may also lower costs. It is possible for jurisdictions to participate in regionally funded benefit consortia to reduce costs. In other words, a smorgasbord of options is available to employers seeking to address exploding health care expenses.

Exhibit 8.10 displays the results of a survey concerning the actions taken by large cities to curb rising health benefit costs. West and Condrey's (2011) data indicate that cities are moving on several fronts to cut benefit costs. They are using preventive strategies by providing wellness programs that encourage healthy behavior and educational programs to increase employee awareness of ways to improve their overall health. As noted, sharing costs with employees (e.g., cost-shifting or displacement strategies) is one method of controlling benefit costs, and a third of the cities surveyed did this by increasing employee benefit contributions, increasing copays and deductibles, and/or imposing lifetime limits. Several cities have adopted the less frequently used approaches of offering mail-order drug plans, offering health care savings accounts, auditing medical claims, and reducing health care coverage levels. Cities are both reducing benefits and increasing employee contribution levels. They are also offering the alternative of flexible spending accounts, whereby they help employees to cope with increased costs by enabling them to pay for rising expenses with tax-free dollars. Very few of the cities surveyed have dropped specific benefits or participated in regionally funded benefit consortia.

As is the case with philosophical differences over pension reform, there is a gap between soft and hard HRM perspectives regarding health care benefits. As West and Bowman (2008) note, "Hard strategies look to the bottom line and managerial prerogatives, supporting health benefits so long as they promote business objectives and conserve resources. Proponents of this approach advance shareholder value theory and focus on the expense of obligation to the workforce" (p. 36). By contrast, the soft HRM approach seeks "coverage that expresses 'caring' by addressing employee needs, respecting individual rights and promoting healthy lifestyles." The authors conclude that while "the language used to support health policies is often linked to the soft approach, the reality of what is offered . . . is more closely aligned with the hard perspective of HRM" (p. 36).

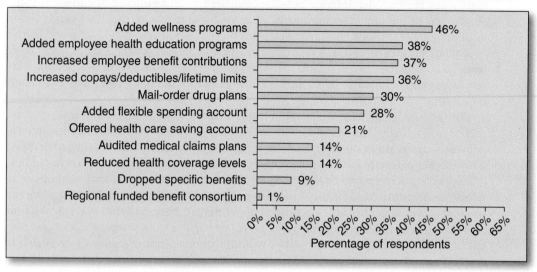

Exhibit 8.10 Strategies and Adjustments to Benefits

SOURCE: West and Condrey (2011). Used by permission.

IMPLEMENTATION, ASSESSMENT, AND EVALUATION

Organizations seeking to help workers become more effective and employees seeking supportive workplace relations have a convergence of goals. Strategic human resource managers can jump-start these efforts. The trick is to design a program that meets the objectives of both employers and employees while avoiding the paradoxes described previously. Before embarking on flexible work options or deciding on the mix of employee-responsive policies to pursue, an agency should conduct a needs assessment. Appendix B at the end of this chapter lists some of the questions employers should consider as they assess the needs of their agencies. At a minimum, data should be gathered on workforce demographics, the range and utilization of existing programs, employee-identified problem areas, satisfaction levels and program preferences, and so forth (data sources include employee personnel records, surveys, interviews, and focus groups). Once the needs, resources, values, and issues have been clarified, the agency needs to assess the benefits and risks of acting or not acting. Professionals in the human resource office are the most likely candidates to collect, analyze, and interpret relevant data and to present recommendations to officials.

The activities and stages involved in implementing employee-responsive policies (Collins & Magid, 1990; Hall, 1990; Mikalachki & Mikalachki, 1991; Stanger, 1993) can be grouped as follows:

- *Setting of policies and values for the program:* task force or advisory committee, values clarification, issue framing, needs and resource assessment, policy formulation and adoption, program management

- *Identification of options or models:* personnel policies, benefit plans, work restructuring, information and referral, parent education and counseling, direct service, career paths, dependent care
- *Articulation of program objectives:* goals, expectations, eligibility, benefits, participation levels, advantages, external factors, planning estimates
- *Planning for implementation:* involvement of key stakeholders, pilot or phased projects, breadth and depth of change, modification of work environments, costs, timetables, communication system, building support, overcoming resistance, training
- *Specification of outcomes and benefits:* benefit or cost projections, impact on key indicators, negative side effects
- *Measurement and evaluation:* data sources, tracking of outcomes, employee surveys, focus groups, cost accounting, program evaluation, data analysis and use

Research by McCurdy, Newman, and Lovrich (2002) on worker-friendly policies in Washington State's local governments found a paucity of measurement and evaluation efforts. Roberts's (2001) findings from a study of local governments in New Jersey reiterate this concern regarding the need for better documentation. Becerra, Gooden, Dong, Henderson, and Whitfield (2002) have also stressed the need for employers to assess the "intergroup variations in the worklife needs of their employees" (p. 315).

AVOIDING AND COPING WITH HOSTILITY AT WORK

Another challenge facing managers is that of developing and implementing programs to deal with hostility in the workplace. In seeking to create a proemployee environment, employers must remove threats to worker well-being. This includes reducing the likelihood of intimidation, harassment, threats, conflict, or violence. Chapter 2 discusses sexual harassment (in the context of legal requirements prohibiting it). Here it is important to emphasize that managers and officials committed to employee-friendly policies need to consider ways to avoid or cope with hostility. Not to do so is to invite disruption, damage to the lives and health of workers, and loss of productivity. In 2004, it was reported that in an average U.S. workweek, violent assaults by current or former coworkers at work resulted in 1 employee killed and 25 seriously injured (Armour, 2004). In one 10-day period in 2007, the nation experienced the Virginia Tech mass murders, killings in offices in Troy, Michigan, and killings at the offices of the National Aeronautics and Space Administration (NASA) in Houston, Texas.

Indeed, workplace violence is so pervasive, according to the U.S. Department of Justice, that the Centers for Disease Control and Prevention (CDC) classifies it as a national epidemic. The Bureau of Labor Statistics reports 13,827 workplace homicide victims between 1992 and 2010, an average of more than 700 homicides annually. The most vulnerable occupational classifications for workplace homicides are sales and related occupations, protective services, and transportation and material moving occupations. During the period 2003–2010, 130,290 nonfatal occupational injuries and illnesses took people away from work; the majority of these occurred in the health care and social assistance fields. In 2009 alone, it is estimate that the number of nonfatal violent crimes committed against workers age 16 or older was 572,000 (CDC, 2013).

What can employers do to prevent such attacks from occurring? It is important that they recognize those most at risk, the warning signs or red flags that deserve attention, the various types of workplace violence and rationales, and the steps necessary for appropriate action. First, those most at risk are employees who are in regular contact with the public and strangers coming into the workplace, those working with unstable or volatile persons (e.g., health care, law enforcement), and employees in mobile workplaces (buses, police cruisers). Other employees who may be at risk are those transporting people or goods to unfamiliar locales, working alone or in small groups, exchanging money, or guarding valuable property or possessions. Time of day (late at night or early morning) and place (high-crime areas) can also affect the level of risk.

Second, some warning signs of a potential for workplace violence include poor workplace situations (stress, discrimination); the presence of individual, family, or social problems (finances, illness); aggressive behavior in the workplace (intimidation, bullying); discussion about or presence of a weapon or threat of its use in the workplace; and statements suggesting fascination with violent workplace incidents. Third, where workplace violence occurs, it can take various forms, including violence by strangers lacking any relationship between the worker and the violent person, violence by customers or clients (complaints turned violent, prisoner resisting arrest), and violence by coworkers (response to bullying, response to layoff) (International Association of Chiefs of Police [IACP], 1995).

Finally, why and how might organizations best respond to workplace violence? The rationale for action is linked to several concerns, including the costly nature of violent incidents (potential liability suits, reduced productivity); zero tolerance for abusive, threatening, or violent workplace behavior; and anticipated changes in the workplace environment (layoffs, higher workloads). Justification may also be related to research findings indicating the negative impact of workplace violence on employees and employers' desire to ensure safe workplaces for employees, citizens, and visitors.

What form should action take? Here policies, plans, programs, and procedures are needed. Personnel policies stressing thorough preemployment screening and background checks might help to reduce the likelihood of hiring individuals who have the potential to commit violent acts at work. Organizations can forge cooperative relationships with law enforcement officials to help inform workers on ways to prevent and avoid workplace violence. Security procedures can be reviewed and updated, and security devices (silent alarms, metal detectors) can be installed and maintained. The increasing use of electronic surveillance and monitoring systems in the workplace (West, Bowman, & Gertz, 2014) may help employers to detect or correct potentially volatile situations before violent outbreaks occur. Management can develop threat plans offering guidance on how to respond to workplace threats, as well as postincident plans to be implemented in the aftermath of violent events (debriefing, grief counseling) (IACP, 2008). The Bureau of Labor Statistics (2005a) conducted a survey in 2005 examining the prevalence of workplace violence prevention programs and policies in state and local governments and found that most jurisdictions had such policies or programs (58.3%), usually written (52.4%) but sometimes only verbal (16.0%); 41.6% had no programs or policies.

It is imperative that managers be alert to the warning signs, violence types, rationales for action, and policy options if they are to help their agencies avoid and cope with hostility at work. There is a paradox in implementing both workplace violence and sexual harassment policies, however. Many organizations have policies on these subjects, there is widespread agreement about what constitutes harassing and threatening or violent behavior, and there are numerous instances of such behaviors at work—yet the number of reported violations is low (Duncan, Estabrooks, & Reimer, 2000; McPhaul & Lipscomb, 2004). Implementing the general guidelines and action steps outlined above, with special attention to protecting those who report violators, will help resolve this paradox. Clear policies regarding threats, harassment, and disruptive and dangerous behavior—and specific procedures to follow in case of a critical incident—will reduce the risk of hostility and help employees to cope with it when it occurs (IACP, 2008). Preventing workplace violence, sexual harassment, and other forms of hostility is consistent with strategic human resource management and with creating a proemployee environment.[5]

BEST PLACES TO WORK

In an attempt to identify exemplary workplaces in the federal government, the OPM conducts the annual Federal Employee Viewpoint Survey, collecting data from thousands of federal employees (Partnership for Public Service, 2013). Staff rank their agencies on 10 categories of workplace characteristics, two of which are "work/life balance" and "family-friendly culture and benefits." Exhibit 8.11 reports the rankings for these categories from the survey in 2013. Among the top large agencies (15,000 or more employees) in both rankings were NASA (rank 2, 1), the Department of Commerce (4, 2), and the Department of Health and Human Services (5, 5). NASA ranked first in both 2012 and 2013 in large agency overall rankings in the 10 workplace categories.

SUMMARY AND CONCLUSION

Management fads come and go. Are family- or employee-friendly policies just another passing and politically correct fad? This is not an easy question to answer. The subtitle of this chapter refers to proemployee policies as fashionable, flexible, and fickle. The reader may have the impression that most jurisdictions are responding to changes in the workforce with "fashionable" policies that will reduce work/family conflict, promote employee health and wellness, build flexibility into the workplace, and assist in employee relocation. This is not the case. Some public sector environments are more accurately described as family- or employee-unfriendly, in that they do not offer the type and range of programs discussed here to all or most employees. Instead, the experiences highlighted above are those of progressive jurisdictions. Many of these experiments are informal, are restricted to a limited number of areas, involve small numbers of employees, and may come and go as budgets rise and fall.

Exhibit 8.11   Best Large Agencies to Work for in the Federal Government in 2013

Agency	Work/Life Balance Ranking	Family-Friendly Culture and Benefits Ranking
Intelligence Community	1	NA
National Aeronautics and Space Administration	2	1
Department of Transportation	3	9
Department of Commerce	4	2
Department of Health and Human Services	5	5
Office of the Secretary of Defense, Joint Staff, Defense Agencies, and Department of Defense Field Activities	6	4
Department of Justice	6	16
Department of the Treasury	8	3
Department of the Navy	9	12
Department of State	10	10
Department of the Air Force	11	11
Department of the Army	12	13
Social Security Administration	13	15
Department of Labor	14	7
Department of Veterans Affairs	15	18
Environmental Protection Agency	16	6
Department of Agriculture	17	8
Department of Homeland Security	18	16
Department of the Interior	20	14

SOURCE: Adapted from Partnership for Public Service (2013).

NOTE: Rankings based on survey data collected by the Office of Personnel Management.

Evidence is mounting (although incomplete) that employee-friendly policies can lead to important positive outcomes that "ideally" would catch the attention of public employers—improvements in job satisfaction, absenteeism, productivity, morale, recruitment and retention, and loyalty. On the other hand, some studies show negligible to no effects from such policies because of underutilization or effects that do not benefit the intended groups (Bruce & Reed, 1994; Shuey, 1998). Paradoxes abound and should not be overlooked by employers tempted to undertake such policies or by employees who push for them. Key among the paradoxes is that, once adopted, programs might not be used. When funding for new programs is limited, as is often the situation, a persuasive case must be made to skeptical budget guardians that the returns on investments will be substantial.

It is important to keep in mind, however, that employee-friendly policies encompass a broad range of initiatives, and a holistic view is needed in the assessment of their value and effectiveness. Failure or underutilization of one program should not diminish the value of others. Some plans may appeal to or be relevant to a relatively small segment of the workforce (telecommuting, domestic partner coverage, adoption assistance, leave sharing, job sharing, spousal employment assistance, outplacement services). Others have much broader appeal and relevance (child or elder care; parental leave; wellness, stress reduction, and employee assistance programs; flex options; cafeteria plans; and other than full-time work options). Some plans are provided in-house, but many (such as EAP services) are often purchased from private and third-sector providers. Furthermore, the forms that selected programs (e.g., flextime) take differ based on organization size and service demands. Large organizations that need not address widely varying walk-in service requests have more management flexibility than small organizations in this regard. They can handle leaves of absence better and accommodate flextime more easily than other jurisdictions.

Large, innovative, and resource-rich organizations are more able to provide both the broad and narrow ranges of worker-responsive programs. Unfortunately, most governmental jurisdictions in the United States are small or midsize, traditional, and strapped for funds. They may be able to offer a few of these programs, but not a complete set. Nevertheless, strategic human resource management practices, even in an era of limited resources, can contribute to reducing work/family conflict and to meeting both individual and organizational obligations. Employers need to explore ways to help make this happen.

KEY TERMS

Adoption assistance

Compressed workweek

Defined-benefit pension plans

Defined-contribution pension plans

Domestic partnership coverage

Downshifting

Downsizing

Employee assistance programs (EAPs)

Flextime

Hard HRM

Hidden workforce

Job sharing

Leave sharing

New male mystique

Nontraditional families

Parental leave

Sandwich generation

Soft HRM

Telecommuters

3 o'clock syndrome

V-time

Wellness programs

EXERCISES

Class Discussion

1. Create two columns on a whiteboard or chalkboard headed "Buzzwords of Government Success" and "Ideal Friendship and Family Life." Brainstorm and write down words for each topic, one column at a time. Compare and discuss the words in the two columns. Discuss the reasons that none or only a few words appear on both the lists.

2. Form groups and let each group select one of the family-friendly policies discussed in this chapter. Discuss the following: (a) the advantages, (b) the disadvantages, (c) the outcome indicators you would use to judge program success, (d) the obstacles that you would expect to encounter in implementing this program, and (e) the types of employees most likely to benefit from the program. Present a group report on your results to the class.

3. Review examples of employee-friendly policies discussed in this chapter. Identify as many paradoxes related to those policies as you can and discuss ways to resolve them.

4. Identify other not-so-employee-friendly policies that are not addressed in this chapter.

Team Activities

5. Separate into four or five different groups. Within each group, select three to five of the worker-friendly programs covered in this chapter, and have each group member interview someone who is currently using one of these programs regarding its pros and cons from the user's perspective. Write up the individual interviews (each no more than two typed pages) and then compile them into an integrated group report.

6. Have each team member create a hypothetical employee profile by identifying that individual's personal characteristics on each of the following dimensions: age, gender, dependent children, marital status, sexual orientation, distance from work, health status, emotional health, stress level, and job security. Have each member then choose three employee-friendly policies that would be most helpful to the hypothetical employee and justify his or her choices. As a team, compile the personal profile analyses from the individual student papers and add a group analysis section making some generalizations about which policies appeal most to particular types of employees.

Individual Assignments

7. Choose any one of the employee-friendly policies mentioned in this chapter and outline the implementation steps that are most important at each of the six stages from the point of view of the individual public manager or supervisor. Develop your response in a four-page paper.

8. Identify each of the paradoxes mentioned in this chapter and consider various ways to resolve each paradox. Can you identify additional paradoxes related to these topics?

9. Select one of the programs discussed in this chapter and conduct an online search for additional information on this subject. Share the information you find with the class.

10. Review the questions for telecommuters in Appendix A and then do one of the following assignments:

    a. Develop a written telecommuter agreement for a particular public organization to be signed by both the employer and the employee. Make sure the agreement adequately addresses each of the questions listed in Appendix A.

    b. Obtain a written telecommuter agreement used by a specific organization and write a brief paper showing the degree to which the agreement you have obtained responds to each of the questions in Appendix A. Attach a copy of the agreement to your paper.

APPENDIX A

Questions for Employees and Employers Regarding Telecommuting Arrangements

- Has a pilot program been conducted?
- What are the results of the pilot program?
- Who is eligible to telecommute?
- If telecommuting is not to their liking, can employees return to their office work location?
- If the program is terminated, can employees return to their office work location?
- If an employee's performance deteriorates, will he or she be asked to return to the office work location?
- Will salary, job responsibilities, or benefits be changed because of employee participation in the program?
- Will the total number of work hours change during the program?
- How will employees account for time worked?
- Can employees vary their hours to suit their preferences?
- How can employers be assured that employees are accessible during working hours?
- Will employees divide their time between days at the office location and at the off-site location?
- Will employees be expected to come in to the office as requested when the workload requires it?
- Will employers provide the equipment required for the job?
- Does the employer retain ownership of property provided to telecommuters?
- Who absorbs costs (installation, monthly service) of telephone lines installed for use during the program?
- Who is responsible for off-site-related expenses (e.g., air conditioning, renovation)?
- Who is responsible for travel expenses to and from work on days when employees come in to the office?
- Who provides needed office supplies?
- Who absorbs costs of insurance to protect equipment from theft, damage, or misuse?
- How will confidential or proprietary materials be protected?

- Does the employer have the right to visit the off-site location to see if it meets health and safety standards?
- Will the employer provide assistance to ensure the adequacy or safety of the off-site work area?
- Will the employer be liable for injuries resulting directly from off-site work activities?
- Is telecommuting viewed as a substitute for dependent care?
- Will the employer provide income tax guidance to employees who maintain an off-site office area?

SOURCE: Adapted from Gil Gordon Associates (1998). © Copyright 1998 by Gil Gordon Associates.

NOTE: These are suggested items to include; actual agreements must be tailored to the needs of specific employers and their employees.

APPENDIX B

Some Questions to Answer When Considering Implementation of Employee-Friendly Policies

- What is the percentage of females employed?
- What is the size of the organization?
- What is the age profile of the employees?
- To what extent are resources available to recruit and train employees?
- What education levels are required of qualified employees?
- What are current dependent care arrangements, costs, and satisfaction levels?
- What special work/family problems are employees facing?
- How many employees have young children, and how many days have those employees missed work to care for an ill child?
- How many employees care for elderly dependents, and how many days have those employees missed work to provide elder care?
- What is the percentage of employees who currently engage in a variety of wellness-related activities?
- Which employees are more likely to prefer flextime?
- Which employees are more likely to prefer telecommuting?
- What is the percentage of employees who indicate that they experience high levels of work-related stress?
- What are the main sources of work-related stress?
- What is the percentage of employees who have adopted children?
- What is the percentage of employees who are unmarried with domestic partners?
- What is the percentage of employees who are dissatisfied with the current range of employee benefits?
- What is the percentage of employees who are being displaced as a result of downsizing?

APPENDIX C

Family-Friendly Policies

Class Exercise

Background:

The expansion of family-friendly policies has accompanied the redefinition of today's family. "Family" now means something more than just a married man and woman and their biological offspring. Today, family responsibilities may include caring for stepchildren or foster children, elderly parents, or a domestic partner.

Employees today are often juggling work and family responsibilities. Demands on their time can leave them feeling dissatisfied with the quality of both their work and their personal lives.

Faced with the constant struggle to balance work responsibilities with personal commitments, more and more employees are looking for employers that will be supportive of their need for a healthy work/life balance. They are attracted to organizations that offer flexibility in an environment where they can have an interesting career.

Consider:

You are the human resource director of the county Parks and Recreation Department. The organization consists of the following:

- More than 5,000 employees
  - Frontline manual labor employees (e.g., landscapers)
  - Transactional-level employees (e.g., credit and collections)
  - Professional-level administration support (e.g., finance, marketing)
  - Management and executive management

You are challenged to develop a business case to support the following premises:

- Organizations that promote family-friendly workplaces have an edge when it comes to recruitment and retention of skilled employees.
- Family-friendly policies are a way to support and recognize the changing needs of employees at different points in their lives and careers.
  - They are good for business.
  - They are good for employees.
  - They are good for families.

Assignment:

Complete the following outline for this business case proposal.

Family-Friendly Policy Proposal

Objective(s) or Purpose

- State what you are trying to achieve and why.
- Strategic vision—what will this do for the organization?
- What are the specific objectives of your proposal?
- What are the high-level benefits?
  - To the employee
  - To the organization

Technology Assessment

- What technology improvements or alternatives need to be considered?

Change Analysis

- What implications to the business do you anticipate?
- What business reengineering issues will arise?

Cost and Benefit Estimate (Nonfinancial)

- What benefits to the employee and employer will result?
- What intangible benefits may change, for better or worse?

Cost and Benefit Estimate (Financial)

- What current costs and cost structures will change?
- What new costs will be incurred?
- Can you estimate costs? ($10, $100, $1,000, $10,000, etc.)

Risk Assessment

- Identification of organization risks to
  - do nothing
  - move ahead
  - phased approach
- Identification of high-level risk mitigation plans for each potential risk

Measures and Metrics

- Outline how you measure success.
  - What would you need?
  - How would you position it?
- What counterarguments would you anticipate?

Example Family-Friendly Initiatives

Flexible Work Arrangements

- Telework—working from home or a remote office
- Flextime—changing the start and end times of the workday
- Job sharing—splitting a full-time position between two employees
- Compressed workweek—working full-time hours in fewer than 5 days
- Part-time—reducing the number of hours worked each day or week

Employee Assistance Programs

- Counseling support on a range of issues from financial to legal to personal

Child Care and Elder Care Services

- Options range from on-site child care centers to emergency or backup child care, to resource materials for new parents.

Health and Wellness Initiatives

- Programs range from health club facilities to smoking cessation initiatives to stress management workshops.

Leaves of Absence

- Regulatory leaves like parental leave and jury duty as well as additional options for time away from work such as educational leave, community service leave, and sabbaticals

NOTES

1. This chapter is titled "Employee-Friendly Policies" instead of "Family-Friendly Policies" because it addresses the needs of single employees as well as those of employees in both traditional and nontraditional families (see Hoyman & Duer, 2004).

2. Although this chapter focuses primarily on the changing workforce in terms of gender, it is important to note that cultural diversity introduces a range of different issues in addition to those covered here. For example, gender stereotypes and familial relationships vary from culture to culture; these differences have important significance for the workforce. The existence of extended families may have changed dramatically over the past four decades for white, middle-class families of European heritage, but the situation is quite different for families in other cultural groups and socioeconomic status categories.

3. Human capital consists of the knowledge, skills, and abilities characterizing a workforce. Investments in human capital (e.g., training, development) are expected to bring improvements in performance and thus to provide a competitive advantage to individual workers and employing organizations. In contrast, human resources traditionally have been viewed primarily as costs to be minimized rather than as assets worthy of investments. Investments have been made in other assets, such as land, capital, and raw materials.

4. The discussion in this section draws on work found in West and Bowman (2008) and West and Condrey (2011).

5. Some examples of local governments with innovative workplace violence programs are Phoenix, Arizona; Ventura County, California; Broward County, Florida; Evanston, Illinois; and Cary, North Carolina (ICMA, 1994).

REFERENCES

AARP. (2004). *Baby Boomers envision retirement 11: Survey of Baby Boomers' expectations for retirement.* Washington, DC: Author.

AARP Public Policy Institute. (2007). *Valuing the invaluable: A new look at the economic value of family caregiving.* Washington, DC: Author.

Adoption.com. (n.d.). Adoption costs. Retrieved from http://costs.adoption.com

Adoptive Families. (2008). Making it work: Top adoption-friendly companies. Retrieved from http://adoptivefamilies.com/articles.php?aid = 832

American Association of University Women. (2007). *Family-friendly workplaces: Expand family and medical leave and paid sick leave.* Washington, DC: Author.

American Association of University Women. (2011). *Balancing work and Life: Family-friendly workplace policies.* Washington, DC: Author.

American Staffing Association. (2011). 2011 analysis. Retrieved from http://www.americanstaffing.net/statistics

Aon Hewitt. (2013). *2013 health care survey.* London: Author.

Appelbaum, E., & Milkman, R. (2011). *Leaves that pay: Employer and worker experiences with paid family leave in California.* Washington, DC: Center for Economic and Policy Research.

Appelbaum, L. D., & Tilly, C. (2011, April 4). Job sharing lessens pain of unemployment on workers. UCLA Newsroom. Retrieved from http://www.today.ucla.edu/portal/ut/share-the-job-200056.aspx

Armour, S. (2004, July 15). Managers not prepared for workplace violence. *USA Today.* Retrieved from https://www.mosaicmethod.com/documents/USATODAY.com % 20- % 20Managers % 20not % 20prepared % 20 for % 20workplace % 20violence.pdf

Aumann, K., Galinsky, E., & Matos, K. (2011). *The new male mystique.* New York: Families and Work Institute. Retrieved from http://familiesandwork.org/downloads/NewMaleMystique.pdf

Aumann, K., Galinsky, E., Sakai, K., Brown, M., & Bond, J. T. (2008). *The Elder Care Study: Everyday realities and wishes for change.* New York: Families and Work Institute. Retrieved from http://familiesandwork.org/downloads/TheElderCareStudy.pdf

Becerra, R., Gooden, S., Dong, W., Henderson, T., & Whitfield, C. (2002). Child care needs and work-life implications. *Review of Public Personnel Administration, 22*(4), 295–319.

Bens, C. (2005). The municipal health cost crisis. *National Civic Review, 94*(3), 42–52.

Borowski, J. (2011, January 20). Utah shows how to solve the looming public pension crisis. FreedomWorks. Retrieved from http://www.freedomworks.org/blog/jborowski/utah-shows-how-to-solve-the-looming-public-pension

Bruce, W., & Reed, C. (1994). Preparing supervisors for the future workforce: The dual-income couple and the work–family dichotomy. *Public Administration Review, 54*(1), 36–43.

Bureau of Labor Statistics, U.S. Department of Labor. (2005a). *Survey of workplace violence prevention.* Retrieved from https://www.bls.gov/iif/osh_wpvs.htm

Bureau of Labor Statistics, U.S. Department of Labor. (2005b). *Workers on flexible and shift schedules in May 2004.* Retrieved from http://www.bls.gov/news.release/pdf/flex.pdf

Bureau of Labor Statistics, U.S. Department of Labor. (2007). *National Compensation Survey: Employee benefits in state and local governments in the United States, September 2007.* Retrieved from http://www.bls.gov/ncs/ebs/sp/ebsm0007.pdf

Bureau of Labor Statistics, U.S. Department of Labor. (2010). *National Compensation Survey.* Washington, DC: Author.

Bureau of Labor Statistics, U.S. Department of Labor. (2011, June). *Employment situation summary* [News release]. Washington, DC: Author.

Bureau of Labor Statistics, U.S. Department of Labor. (2013a, July 17). *Employee benefits in the U.S.—March 2013.* Washington, DC: Author.

Bureau of Labor Statistics, U.S. Department of Labor. (2013b, March). *National Compensation Survey: Employee benefits in the United States.* Washington, DC: Author.

Bureau of Labor Statistics, U.S. Department of Labor. (2013c, September). *Unmarried domestic partners benefit fact sheet, March 2013.* Washington, DC: Author.

Bureau of Labor Statistics, U.S. Department of Labor. (2013d, February). *Women in the labor force: A databook.* Washington, DC: Author.

Bureau of Labor Statistics, U.S. Department of Labor. (2014, April 25). *Employment characteristics of families—2013.* Washington, DC: Author.

California Employment Development Department. (2011). Disability: About the program. Retrieved from http://www.edd.ca.gov/disability/About_the_Program.htm

Camp, S. (2006). The influence of organizational incentives on absenteeism. *Criminal Justice Policy Review, 17*(2), 144–172.

Cayer, N. J., & Roach, C. M. L. (2008). Work–life benefits. In C. G. Reddick & J. D. Coggburn (Eds.), *Handbook of employee benefits and administration* (pp. 309–334). Boca Raton, FL: CRC Press.

Centers for Disease Control and Prevention. (2013). Occupational violence: Training and education. Workplace violence prevention for nurses, CDC Course No. WB1865, NIOSH Publication No. 2013-155. Retrieved from http://www.cdc.gov/niosh/topics/violence/training_nurses.html

Clark, C. S. (2014, August 11). Report: Agency leaders protected teleworkers who lied about their hours. *Government Executive.* Retrieved from http://www.govexec.com/management/2014/08/report-agency-leaders-protected-teleworkers-who-lied-about-their-hours/91142

Clay, R. (1998, July). Many managers frown on use of flexible work options. *APA Monitor,* p. 29.

Coalition of Child Care Advocates of BC. (2007, November 16). *Good governance of child care: What does it mean? What does it look like?* Vancouver: Author. Retrieved from http://www.cccabc.bc.ca/cccabcdocs/governance/ggcc_combined.pdf

Coggburn, J. D., & Kearney, R. C. (2010). Trouble keeping promises? An analysis of underfunding in state retiree benefits. *Public Administration Review, 70*(1), 97–108.

Cohen, R. (2002, September 8). The ethicist. *New York Times Magazine,* pp. 29–30.

Collins, R., & Magid, R. (1990). Work and family: How managers can make a difference. *Personnel, 67*(7), 14–19.

Condrey, S. E., West, J. P., & Ledvinka, C. B. (2010). Making the switch: Implementing the 4-day work week in America's largest cities. In R. R. Sims (Ed.), *Change (transformation) in government organizations* (pp. 137–157). Charlotte, NC: Information Age Press.

Copeland, L. (2008, June 30). Most state workers in Utah shifting to 4-day week. *USA Today.* Retrieved from http://www.usatoday.com/news/nation/2008-06-30-four-day_N.htm

Costello, A. (2013). Early retiree reinsurance program: Bridge to 2014. *Benefits Quarterly, 29*(2), 54–59.

Council of State Governments. (2007). *The book of the states.* Lexington, KY: Author.

Daniel, L. (1999, April). Feds and families. *Government Executive,* pp. 41–46.

Danish Ministry of Science, Technology, and Innovation. (2008). *Maternity leave.* Copenhagen: Author. Retrieved from http://www.workindenmark.dk

Danish Ministry of Social Affairs and Integration. (2012). *Social policy in Denmark.* Copenhagen: Author.

Defining Marriage. (2014, March 26). *State defense of marriage laws and same-sex marriage.* Washington, DC: National Conference of State Legislatures.

Department for Business Enterprise and Regulatory Reform of U.K. (2008). *Flexible working and work-life balance.* Retrieved from http:www.berr.gov.uk/employment/workandfamilies/flexible-working/index.com

Dobkin, L. (2007, April 10). The costs of caregiving. *Workforce.* Retrieved from http://www.workforce.com/articles/the-costs-of-caregiving

Duncan, S., Estabrooks, C. A., & Reimer, M. (2000). Violence against nurses. *Alta RN, 56*(2), 13–14.

Edwards, C. (2010, January). *Employee compensation in state and local governments* (Tax & Budget Bulletin 59). Washington, DC: Cato Institute. Retrieved from http://www.cato.org/pubs/tbb/tbb-59.pdf

Employee Benefit Research Institute. (2009, February). *Domestic partner benefits: Facts and background.* Washington, DC: Author. Retrieved from http://www.ebri.org/pdf/publications/facts/0209fact.pdf

Engeman, C. D. (2012, September). *Ten years of the California paid family leave program: Strengthening commitment to work, affirming commitment to family* (Policy brief). Retrieved from http://www.femst.ucsb.edu/projects/crwsj/engagements/pdf/Engeman-PFL-Policy-Brief.pdf

Equal Rights Advocates. (2008). California paid family leave. Retrieved from http://www.equalrights.rog/professional/fmla.asp

Facer, R., & Wadsworth, L. (2008). Alternative work schedules and work family balance: A research note. *Review of Public Personnel Administration, 28*(2), 166–177.

Freedom to Marry. (2010). Where state laws stand. Retrieved from http://www.freedomtomarry.org/pages/where-state-laws-stand

Galinsky, E., Aumann, K., & Bond, J. T. (2009, revised 2011). *Times are changing: Gender and generation at work and at home.* New York: Families and Work Institute. Retrieved from http://familiesandwork.org/downloads/TimesAreChanging.pdf

Galinsky, E., Bond, J. T., & Hill, E. J. (2004). *Workplace flexibility: What is it? Who has it? Who wants it? Does it make a difference?* New York: Families and Work Institute.

Galinsky, E., & Jackson, H. (2012). What's new? What's newsworthy? In When Work Works, *2013 Guide to bold new ideas for making work work* (pp. 4–12). New York: Families and Work Institute and Society for Human Resource Management. Retrieved from http://familiesandwork.org/downloads/2013GuidetoBoldNewIdeas.pdf

Gamino, D. (1997, December 28). State makes use of "temps" despite job cap. *Austin American-Statesman.* Retrieved from http://www.austin360.com/news/12dec/28/temps28.html

Gannon, J. (1998, June 19). Single and childless workers say they're not getting fair share of benefits. *Pittsburgh Post-Gazette.* Retrieved from http://www.postgazette.com/businessnews/19980619bbenefits1.asp

Gil Gordon Associates. (1998). Generic telecommuter's agreement. Retrieved from http://www.gilgordon.com/downloads/agreement.txt

Goetzel, R. Z., & Ozminkowski, R. J. (2006). What's holding you back: Why should (or shouldn't) employees invest in health promotion programs for their workers? *North Carolina Medical Journal, 67,* 428–430.

Gordon, R. (2001, November 2). Salvation Army OKs partner benefits: Charity's reversal to allow ties with S.F. *San Francisco Chronicle.* Retrieved from http://sfgate.com/cgi-bin/article.cgi?file = /chronicle/archive/2001/11/02/ MN128788.DTL

Greenhouse, S. (2011, June 15). States want more in pension contributions. *New York Times.* Retrieved from http://www.nytimes.com/2011/06/16/business/16pension.html

Greenhouse, S. (2014, July 18). Part-time schedules, full-time headaches. *New York Times.* Retrieved from http://nyti.ms/1yEup7e

Guy, M. E., & Newman, M. (1998). Toward diversity in the workplace. In S. E. Condrey (Ed.), *Handbook of human resource management in government* (pp. 75–92). San Francisco: Jossey-Bass.

Hacker, J. S. (2006). *The great risk shift: The assault on American jobs, families, health care, and retirement and how you can fight back.* New York: Oxford University Press.

Hall, D. (1990). Promoting work/family balance: An organization change approach. *Organizational Dynamics, 18*(3), 5–18.

Heathfield, S. M. (2011). Reasons why teleworking belongs in your future: Advantages, impediments, and who's teleworking? About.com: About Money. Retrieved from http://humanresources.about.com/od/workschedules/a/teleworking.htm

Heredia, C. (2001a, December 22). Gays spurning Salvation Army: Rights groups protesting benefits policy. *San Francisco Chronicle.* Retrieved from http://articles.sfgate.com/2001-12-22/news/17632470_1_bell-ringer-red-kettles-partner-benefit

Heredia, C. (2001b, November 14). Salvation Army says no benefits for partners: National panel overturns regional OK. *San Francisco Chronicle.* Retrieved from http://sfgate.com/cgi-bin/article.cgi?file = /chronicle/archive/2001/11/14/MN143620.DTL

Houser, L., & Vartanian, T. P. (2012). *Pay matters: The positive economic impacts of paid family leave for families, businesses and the public.* New Brunswick: Center for Women and Work, Rutgers, The State University of New Jersey. Retrieved from http://www.cww.rutgers.edu

Hoyman, M., & Duer, H. (2004). A typology of workplace policies: Worker friendly vs. family friendly? *Review of Public Personnel Administration, 24*(2), 113–132.

Institute for Health and Social Policy. (2007). *The Work, Family, and Equity Index: How does the US measure up?* Montreal: McGill University.

International Association of Chiefs of Police. (1995). *Combating workplace violence.* Washington, DC: Author.

International Association of Chiefs of Police. (2008). *Combating workplace violence.* Washington, DC: Author.

International City/County Management Association. (1994). Focus on violence. *HR Report, 2*(8), 3–6.

International City/County Management Association. (2012). *The benefits of telecommuting.* Washington, DC: Author.

International Public Management Association for Human Resources. (2007). *Personnel practices: Telecommuting policies.* Alexandria, VA: Author.

Issa, D. (2011, January 14). A federal carrot and stick to ease public pension crisis. Sign on San Diego. Retrieved from http://www.signonsandiego.com/news/2011/jan/14/a-federal-carrot-and-stick-to-ease-public-pension

Jones, Z. (2013, December 11). The Salvation Army's history of anti-LGBT discrimination. Huffington Post. Retrieved from http://www.huffingtonpost.com/zinnia-jones/the-salvation-armys-histo_b_4422938.html

Kemp, D. R. (1995). Telecommuting in the public sector: An overview and a survey of the states. *Review of Public Personnel Administration, 15*(3), 5–14.

Kerrigan, H. (2011, July 13). Utah's demise of the four-day workweek. *Governing the States and Localities.* Retrieved from http://www.governing.com/columns/utahs-demise-of-the-four-day-work-week.html

King, M. (2001, November 3). Salvation Army allows health-care access for domestic partners. *Seattle Times.* Retrieved from http://archives.seattletimes.nwsource.com/cgi-bin/texis.cgi/web/vortex/display?slug = salvation03m&date = 20011103&query = %22Salvation + Army%22

Kirkpatrick, D. (1997, April 2). Child-free employees see another side of equation. *Wall Street Journal* (Interactive ed.).

Kleiman, C. (2003, October 8). Workers willing to put family ahead of career advancement. *Tallahassee Democrat,* p. 3E.

Leonard, B. (1996). Dual-income families fast becoming the norm. *HRMagazine, 41*(8), 8.

Levine, S. (1997, March 24). One in four U.S. families cares for aging relatives. *Washington Post,* p. A13.

Levit, A. (2010, April 26). Convince the boss that you should telecommute. *Forbes.* Retrieved from http://www.forbes.com/2010/04/26/telecommute-flextime-work-home-leadership-careers-jobs.html

Levy, J. (2014, July 10). In U.S., uninsured rate sinks to 13.4% in second quarter. Gallup. Retrieved from http://www.gallup.com/poll/172403/uninsured-rate-sinks-second-quarter.aspx

Lister, K., & Harnish, T. (2011). *The state of telework in the U.S.: How individuals, business, and government benefit.* San Diego, CA: Telework Research Network.

Lynem, J. (2001, May 13). Family-friendly or single-hostile? Unwed employees feel shortchanged by policies aimed at helping parents. *San Francisco Chronicle.* Retrieved from http://sfgate.com/cgi-bin/article.cgi?file = /chronicle/archive/2001/05/13/AW152151.DTL

Martinez, M. (1993). Family support makes business sense. *HRMagazine, 38*(1), 38.

Matos, K., & Galinsky, E. (2011). *Workplace flexibility in the United States: A status report*. New York: Families and Work Institute. Retrieved from http://familiesandwork.org/downloads/WorkplaceFlexibilityinUS.pdf

Matos, K., & Galinsky, E. (2014). *2014 National Study of Employers*. New York: Families and Work Institute. Retrieved from http://familiesandwork.org/downloads/2014NationalStudyOfEmployers.pdf

McCurdy, A., Newman, M., & Lovrich, N. (2002). Family-friendly workplace policy adoption in general and special purpose local governments. *Review of Public Personnel Administration, 22*(1), 27–51.

McMahon, E. J. (2011, December 7). On pensions, a cure or a bandage? *New York Times*. Retrieved from http://www.nytimes.com/roomfordebate/2011/02/06/will-new-york-citys-pensions-be-cut/on-pensions-a-cure-or-a-bandage

McPhaul, K., & Lipscomb, J. (2004). Workplace violence in health care: Recognized but not regulated. *Online Journal of Issues in Nursing, 9*(3). Retrieved from http://www.nursingworld.org/MainMenuCategories/ANAMarketplace/ANAPeriodicals/OJIN/TableofContents/Volume92004/N03Sept04/ViolenceinHealthCare.aspx

Meinert, D. (2013). Families first. *HRMagazine, 58*(9), 33–36, 38.

Mercer, W. M. (1996). *Mercer work/life and diversity initiatives benchmarking survey 1996*. New York: Author.

MetLife. (2006). *The MetLife Caregiving Cost Study: Productivity losses to U.S. business*. Westport, CT: Author. Retrieved from http://www.caregiving.org/data/CaregiverCostStudy.pdf

MetLife. (2010, February). *The MetLife Caregiving Cost Study of working caregivers and employer healthcare costs*. Westport, CT: Author.

MetLife. (2011, June). *The MetLife study of caregiving costs to working caregivers*. Westport, CT: Author.

Mikalachki, A., & Mikalachki, D. (1991). Work–family issues: You had better address them! *Business Quarterly, 55*(4), 49–52.

Modern Workplaces Consultation. (2012). *Government response on flexible working*. London: HM Government.

Murphy, K. (2005, June 14). Leave-sharing helps retain state workers. *American City & County*. Retrieved from http://americancityandcounty.com/resource-center/leave-sharing-helps-retain-state-workers

National Alliance for Caregiving. (2012, March). *Best practices in workplace eldercare*. Bethesda, MD: Author.

National Alliance for Caregiving & AARP. (2009). *Caregiving in the U.S.* Westport, CT: MetLife Foundation. Retrieved from http://www.caregiving.org/data/04finalreport.pdf

National Conference of State Legislatures. (2014, June 11). Breastfeeding state laws. Retrieved from http://www.ncsl.org/research/health/breastfeeding-state-laws.aspx

New rules for part-time work. (2014, July 23). *New York Times*. Retrieved from http://www.nytimes.com/roomfordebate/2014/07/23/new-rules-for-part-time-work

Nolo. (2003). Providing military leave: State and federal laws protect workers who take leave to serve in the military. Retrieved from http://www.nolo.com/legal-encyclopedia/providing-military-leave-29897.html

Oakley, M. (2008, April). *The bottle, the breast, and the state: Breastfeeding rights policy and the role of grassroots and traditional women's rights groups*. Paper presented at the annual meeting of the Midwest Political Science Association, Chicago.

Obama, B. (2006). *The audacity of hope*. New York: Crown.

Organisation for Economic Co-operation and Development. (2013). OECD Better Life Index. Retrieved from http://www.oecdbetterlifeindex.org

Partnership for Public Service. (2010). *On demand government: Deploying flexibilities to ensure service continuity*. Washington, DC: Author.

Partnership for Public Service. (2013). *The best places to work in the federal government: 2013*. Washington, DC: Author.

People for the American Way. (2001). Salvation Army rescinds domestic partner benefits after right wing backlash. Retrieved from http://www.pfaw.org/pfaw/general/default.aspx?oid = 4162

Peterson, M. (1998, July 18). The short end of long hours. *New York Times*, pp. B1–B2.

Pew Center on the States. (2011, April). *The widening gap: The Great Recession's impact on state pension and retiree health care costs*. Washington, DC: Author. Retrieved from http://www.pewtrusts.org/en/research-and-analysis/reports/0001/01/01/the-widening-gap

Pew Charitable Trusts. (2013a, September). *Kentucky's successful pension reform*. Washington, DC: Author. Retrieved from http://www.pewtrusts.org/ ~ /media/legacy/uploadedfiles/pcs_assets/2013/20130927Kent uckyPensionReformBriefpdf.pdf

Pew Charitable Trusts. (2013b, January 16). Pew study finds 61 cities' retirement systems face $217 billion gap [News release]. Retrieved from http://www.prnewswire.com/news-releases/pew-study-finds-61-cities-retirement-systems-face-217-billion-gap-187097561.html

Pew Charitable Trusts. (2014, March). *The fiscal health of state pension plans: Funding gap continues to grow*. Washington, DC: Author. Retrieved from http://www.pewtrusts.org/ ~ /media/Assets/2014/03/31/ PewStatesWideningGapFactsheet2.pdf

Price, J. (2001, December 10). P-FLAG targets Salvation Army: Drops fake money in kettles over repeal of "partner" perks. *Washington Times,* p. A6.

Project on Global Working Families. (2007). Work, Family, and Equity Index. Retrieved from http://www.global workingfamilies.org

Reddick, C. G., & Coggburn, J. D. (Eds.). (2008). *Handbook of employee benefits and administration*. Boca Raton, FL: CRC Press.

Roberts, G. (2001). New Jersey local government benefits practices survey. *Review of Public Personnel Administration, 21*(4), 284–307.

Roberts, G. (2003). Municipal government benefits practices and personnel outcomes: Results from a national survey. *Public Personnel Management, 33*(1), 1022.

Schroeder, P. (1998). *24 years of housework and the place is still a mess*. Kansas City, MO: Andrews & McMeel.

Shuey, P. (1998, October 19). Few use flexible benefits. *Federal Times,* pp. 1, 4.

Smiley, D., McGrory, K., Teproff, C., & Brown, J. (2011, February 6). Battle shaping up over pension proposal. *Miami Herald*. Retrieved from http://www.miamiherald.com/2011/02/06/2054211/battle-shaping-up-over-pension.html

Snell, R. (2010, June). *State defined contribution and hybrid pension plans*. Washington, DC: National Conference of State Legislatures. Retrieved from http://www.aztreasury.gov/wp-content/uploads/2013/1609_final_report/State_DC_and_Hybrid_Pension_Plans.pdf

Society for Human Resource Management. (2007). *2007 employee benefits survey*. Alexandria, VA: Author.

Society for Human Resource Management. (2013). *2013 employee benefits survey*. Alexandria, VA: Author.

Society for Human Resource Management Online Staff. (2013, September 5). *More employers provide adoption-friendly benefits*. Alexandria, VA: Author.

Stanger, J. (1993). How to do a work/family needs assessment. *Employment Relations Today, 20*(2), 197–205.

Stockwell, M. (2006). *Flexible work for strong families*. Washington, DC: Democratic Leadership Council. Retrieved from http://www.dlc.org/ndol_ci.cfm?kaid = 114&subid = 144&contentid = 254111

Suttle, G. (1998, March 8). Solidarity in sickness. *News Tribune,* p. F1.

Thom, M. (2013). Politics, fiscal necessity, or both? Factors driving the enactment of defined contribution accounts for public employees. *Public Administration Review, 73*(3), 480–489.

Tugend, A. (2014, March 7). It's unclearly defined, but telecommuting is fast on the rise. *New York Times*. Retrieved from http://ntyi.mas/P6a8GK

Tumulty, K. (2011, March 8). State and local workers: Gone but not off the books. *Washington Post*. Retrieved from http://www.washingtonpost.com/politics/state-and-local-workers-gone-but-not-off-the-books/2011/03/03/ABpnU70_story.html

U.S. Bureau of the Census. (2007). *Single-parent households showed little variation since 1994*. Washington, DC: Author.

U.S. Government Accountability Office. (2007, March 30). *An assessment of dependent care needs of federal workers using the Office of Personnel Management's survey*. Washington, DC: Author. Retrieved from http:// www.gao.gov/assets/100/94749.pdf

U.S. Office of Personnel Management. (2003). *Part-time employment and job-sharing guide*. Washington, DC: Author. Retrieved from http://www.opm.gov/employment_and_benefits/worklife/officialdocuments/ handbooksguides/pt_employ_jobsharing/index.asp

U.S. Office of Personnel Management. (2005). *Work arrangements and quality of work/life.* Washington, DC: Author. Retrieved from http://www.opm.gov/policy-data-oversight/human-capital-management/reference-materials/talent-management/qualityworklife.pdf

U.S. Office of Personnel Management. (2007). Voluntary leave bank program. Retrieved from http://www.opm.gov/oca/leave/html/VLBP.asp

U.S. Office of Personnel Management. (2011). *The handbook of elder care resources for the federal workplace.* Washington, DC: Author. Retrieved from http://www.opm.gov/Employment_and_Benefits/WorkLife/OfficialDocuments/HandbooksGuides/ElderCareResources/elder02.asp

U.S. Office of Personnel Management. (2012). *2012 status of telework in the federal government.* Washington, DC: Author. Retrieved from http://www.telework.gov/Reports_and_Studies/Annual_Reports/2012teleworkreport.pdf

U.S. Office of Personnel Management. (2013). *2013 status of telework in the federal government.* Washington, DC: Author. Retrieved from http://www.telework.gov/Reports_and_Studies/Annual_Reports/2013teleworkreport.pdf

Vance, M. R. (2005). Breastfeeding legislation in the United States: A general overview and implications for helping mothers. *Leaven, 41*(3), 51–54. Retrieved from http://www.llli.org/llleaderweb/lv/lvjunjul05p51.html

Walter, L. (2005). *Social welfare in Denmark.* Contribution to the SCD Senior Seminar: Welfare and the Welfare State, University of Wisconsin–Green Bay. Retrieved from http://www.uwgb.edu/walterl/welfare/denmark.htm

West, J. P. (2012). Employee-friendly policies and development benefits for millennials. In W. I. Sauser Jr. & R. R. Sims (Eds.), *Managing human resources for the millennial generation* (pp. 201–228). Charlotte, NC: Information Age.

West, J. P. (2014). Combating age discrimination: Legal and regulatory issues, challenges, and opportunities. In R. R. Sims & W. I. Sauser Jr. (Eds.), *Legal and regulatory issues in human resources management.* Charlotte, NC: Information Age.

West, J. P., & Berman, E. M. (1996). Managerial responses to an aging municipal workforce: A national survey. *Review of Public Personnel Administration, 16*(3), 38–58.

West, J. P., & Bowman, J. S. (2008). Employee benefits: Weighing ethical principles and economic imperatives. In C. G. Reddick & J. D. Coggburn (Eds.), *Handbook of employee benefits and administration* (pp. 29–53). Boca Raton, FL: CRC Press.

West, J. P., Bowman, J. S., & Gertz, S. C. (2014). Electronic surveillance in the workplace: Legal, ethical, and management issues. In R. R. Sims & W. I. Sauser Jr. (Eds.), *Legal and regulatory issues in human resources management.* Charlotte, NC: Information Age.

West, J. P., & Condrey, S. E. (2011). Local government strategies for controlling personnel costs. *Journal of Public Budgeting, Accounting and Financial Management 23*(3), 423–454.

Wojcik, J. (2007, July 17). Employer to fine unhealthy workers. *Workforce.* Retrieved from http://www.workforce.com/articles/employer-to-fine-unhealthy-workers

Workplace Flexibility. (2010). Flexible work arrangements. Retrieved from http://workplaceflexibility2010.org/index.php/policy_components/flexible_work_arrangements

World at Work. (2007). *Telework trendlines for 2006.* Scottsdale, AZ: Author.

Yoder, E. (2014, January 2014). Key federal-employee policies have changed during Obama administration. *Washington Post.* Retrieved from http://washingtonpost.com/blogs/federal-eye/wp/2014/01/29/key-federal-employee

Zielewski, E. H., & Boots, S. W. (2010). *Exploring policy models for extended time off* (Memos and Fact Sheets 26). Washington, DC: Georgetown University Law Center. Retrieved from http://scholarship.law.georgetown.edu/legal/26

CHAPTER 9

Training, Learning, and Development

Exploring New Frontiers

Excellence is an art won by training and habit.

–Aristotle

You get the best efforts from others not by lighting a fire beneath them, but by building a fire within.

—Bob Nelson

After studying this chapter, you should be able to

- understand why organizations often underinvest in training and development;
- use adult learning theories to improve training and development activities;
- describe the development of learning organizations and the role of human resource management;
- recognize seven relevant training strategies and their applications; and
- develop methods for evaluating the effectiveness of this management process.

All workers require some way of staying abreast of the latest industry and workplace changes. Who could have imagined 5 years ago that government agencies would be developing their own specialized apps? Who knew that social media would become an expected way for public agencies to communicate with citizens? New skills are needed, and organizations know that they must help their workers and managers keep pace with change. Training and development (T&D) is one of several strategic ways that organizations help ensure that their workforces have the requisite skills for today and tomorrow.

Training and development has undergone considerable change—indeed, almost a paradigm shift. Gone are the days of large in-house training staffs, but so too are the days when learning was synonymous with contracting out for training programs delivered to employees. While training is still delivered in this way, a lot of training is now presented online, offered through webinars and video, and employees and managers are responsible for identifying and using such sources. Training and learning are not always physical, in-class experiences. Even more fundamental is the growing emphasis on how organizations can improve their efforts through self-learning and self-assessment. Instead of being told what to do, managers and their groups need to figure that out for themselves. Training is increasingly used to support people coming up with new ideas and implementing them. T&D is increasingly seen as a strategic investment in present abilities and future leadership. Organizations may track which employees take advantage of these development opportunities as a signal of their professional commitment and, hence, value to the organization.

All of this has implications for human resource management, which is being shaped and reshaped. For HRM staff, the challenge is profound, from ensuring that training is delivered to staff and managers to making self-learning and improvement the focus of training strategies and outcomes that have implications as criteria in recruitment, selection, evaluation, appraisal, promotion, and retention. It also means that HRM staff helps managers with their staffing and organizational needs, such as assisting with employee transfers. For individuals, it means figuring out what is now expected of them. Some officials pay close attention to employees who seek to increase their value to the organization, show leadership potential, and take advantage of training and development opportunities to help them do their current jobs better and prepare for new ones.

Training is the effort to increase the knowledge, skills, and abilities (KSAs) of employees and managers so that they can better do their jobs. Employees often begin new jobs with the expectation that they will receive sufficient training, but this is seldom the case, at least in terms of training in any formal sense. In traditional organizations, KSAs are often imparted by existing employees and managers who know the work and how to get it done; in learning organizations, this is even more likely to be the case. Indeed, much KSA acquisition occurs in informal ways, but training continues to be important. T&D is also used as a strategy for increasing the capacity of broad occupational categories, such as ensuring adequate numbers of procurement and program management officials (Clark, 2013).

Whereas training focuses on improving performance in present jobs, **development** consists of efforts to improve future performance by providing skills to be used in subsequent assignments. Development increases staff potential, assists in succession planning, and is tied to strategic organizational development, ensuring that agencies have employees with relevant skills. The distinction between training and development is somewhat inexact because many developmental activities have immediate uses. To illustrate, leadership training for employees can be regarded as a developmental activity, but the skills learned are likely to also improve current employee teams as personnel gain new knowledge about and insights into group dynamics and processes.

In recent years, **learning** has been emphasized as a third category. While learning is inherent in training and development, the new focus on learning stems from the recognition that participating in training and development activities does not necessarily equate with actual learning, mastering, and application of KSAs that employees need. *Learning organizations* are organizations that have recognizable processes in place for the ongoing assessment of what they are doing and how they are doing it, and whether and how they might do better. For HRM, this includes supporting processes of developing, applying, and reinforcing learning processes among individual and organizational units, such as through training and development, among employees as well as managers. The first books on the topic of the learning organization were written in the 1990s (e.g., Peter Senge's *The Fifth Discipline,* 1990), and such practices have become increasingly commonplace.

The use of training and development varies across organizations. At a minimum, organizations use training to ensure that existing staff are familiar with new technology, work procedures, and rules, as well as to assist in onboarding new workers. Beyond this, training and development is also associated with talent management and leadership development, ensuring that future leaders have required knowledge and a broad range of development experiences before they assume positions of responsibility. Training and development can also be part of strategic efforts to attract and retain talented workers and managers who are looking for career growth. T&D is also associated with high-performance organizations that frequently change and expect workers to acquire new skills. The need for training is well expressed in the following exchange: "What if you train people and they leave?" "Worse still is if you do not train them and they stay."

The environment for training, learning, and development reveals key paradoxes. The first is that almost everyone, from presidents and management gurus to shop stewards and department heads, emphasizes the importance of training, learning, and development; all agree that in the past and in the present, these have been insufficiently emphasized. For example, it was more than 20 years ago that the Winter Commission recommended that state and local government expenditures for training and development activities be about 3% to 5% of salaries (National Commission on the State and Local Government Public Service, 1993). One estimate placed these federal expenditures at just 1.3% (Kettl & DiIulio, 1995), and a decade later, in fiscal year 2005, a similar proportion was estimated (about 1.4%). In a later survey of federal employees, only 50% reported being satisfied with the training they received in their present jobs, only 57% agreed that their talents were well used, and 35% agreed that creativity and innovation were rewarded (U.S. Office of Personnel Management [U.S. OPM], 2013), all of which suggests that training is still not where it needs to be.

The second paradox is that as training, learning, and development become more important to the organization, responsibility for fulfilling these needs is shifted downward to individual employees, supervisors, and units. That is, **decentralization of training** has been occurring, and many organizations have cut back or even eliminated training staff in human resource departments. At the same time, however, only a few organizations have taken steps to ensure that this responsibility is indeed met by lower levels, though HR directors should take a strategic perspective about the role of HRM in organizations and ensure that training needs and participation are tracked. The lack of training at lower levels has sometimes resulted in key service shortfalls, including in frontline services (e.g., among 911 emergency operators; Crummy & Olinger, 2012).

The third paradox is that as their responsibilities increase, employees have less time to focus on training, learning, and development. They may recognize their need for increased KSAs and complain about not getting enough training and development, but that does not mean that they have the time or energy to pursue KSAs. Many people work extra hours, and most have substantial outside obligations. It is probable that only when organizations make learning, improvement, and creativity a priority will employees have the time and structure within which to pursue their development. Some organizations invite or even require employees and managers to work with higher administrators to formulate professional development plans in which training and development activities are identified.

Difficult economic times intensify these crosscurrents affecting training, learning, and development through tighter budgets, overworked staff, deferred technology investments, and staffing reductions. But the above fundamentals remain: Technology develops, jurisdictions must still increase their competitiveness, and employees still seek to improve their careers and salaries. Neither good times nor bad times make these things go away. Employees and managers who seek ways to increase their value to organizations will find training, learning, and development relevant to their efforts.

GENERAL PRINCIPLES OF LEARNING

Learning theories provide a foundation for successful training and development and are based on principles gleaned from cognitive psychology, behaviorism, and social learning, which focus, respectively, on the roles of information and understanding, feedback and incentives, and role modeling and tasks. These **principles of learning** are relevant to both individual and group efforts (e.g., Noe, 2012; Van Wart, Cayer, & Cook, 1993). They are discussed with an eye toward **adult learning theory**, which emphasizes the extensive experience of adults, a preference for active participation, an interest in self-improvement and problem solving, and the exercise of some control in learning styles and methods. Consistent with these principles, motivation, relevance and transference, repetition and active participation, underlying principles, and feedback and positive reinforcement are discussed in turn below.

Motivation

A key principle in successful training and development, **motivation in training** holds that people learn better when they are eager to acquire new KSAs, are encouraged to seek out application opportunities and make them work, and are not readily discouraged by obstacles that are part of every learning experience, especially in organizations. For this reason, the literatures of individual training and organizational change and development all emphasize the importance of ensuring worker motivation. Though these literatures developed separately, they show clear convergence on this topic. Motivation is the drive or energy that compels people to act with energy and persistence toward goals, and the question is how to encourage that drive in the matter of training, learning, and development.

One strategy for motivation is to ensure that workers understand the *need* for what they are to do, or how T&D fits in with larger agency purposes. At a minimum, managers should explain the reasons for training, such as the need to meet changed requirements, master new technology, or adapt to a more efficient approach to service delivery (International City/County Management Association [ICMA], 2003). If the purpose is to support how training furthers organizational change, then an explanation is needed of why the old ways are no longer good enough (e.g., unable to meet demand, associated with a major incident or legal matter, delivery makes clients unhappy, policy preferences of politicians, media). Either way, understanding that a given change is critically needed is a key extrinsic motivation for workers (see Chapter 6).[1]

A second strategy for worker motivation is *management support* for dealing with the consequences of training. Employees often have concerns about how new approaches will be put into practice, whether they will have the opportunity to use any training or adjust it to specific conditions or concerns, and how subsequent workplace changes might affect their jobs or job security. For instance, will the new procedures interfere with their flextime arrangements or opportunities for career advancement? How will managers deal with initial failures (all learning and new efforts have setbacks) and people who cannot master the new skills? How will managers and other employees deal with those who cannot carry their weight? Because people have varied concerns, trainers and managers often must have open discussions prior to and during learning events in which these issues can be discussed. Path-goal theory states that the job of the manager is to state (and gain acceptance for) goals and lay out a viable pathway to those goals; addressing employee concerns clarifies both goals and path, as well as ensures management support for dealing with whatever adjustments are necessary. It can also help to align the needs of the organization with those of employees (see Chapter 6 on motivation).

Relevance and Transference

Managers and trainers must explain how training or the intended organizational learning and development effort relates to a specific task or problem at hand. When people are unclear about the relevance of what they are doing, some will lose motivation, and few will be able to take advantage of whatever skills and knowledge are imparted. This is quite obvious, but nevertheless it frequently occurs due to contracting out, managerial skills deficits, and time pressure. Contracting causes organizations to use external trainers and consultants who have little knowledge of the actual problems that workers face. Though it seems clear that trainers should solicit the input of employees and their supervisors, they do not always do so. Managerial skills deficits are seen in the inability of some managers to explain things well to trainers and workers, such as what is to be accomplished and exactly how materials are to be used—managers need to be good "teachers," too, but some simply are not.

Time pressure in training also reduces employees' understanding of relevance. Sometimes, training periods are of such short duration that instructors can provide only overviews of their topics or stick to general concepts rather than address specific applications and problems that have greatest relevance to workers. Training or a one-shot learning effort with no follow-up later does not provide workers with opportunities to discuss with the trainer subsequent application problems. A problem with **transference** may occur when training is conducted in a setting other than the work environment; for training to be effective, the new knowledge and skills must be readily transferred into the workplace. This is a problem not only with technology applications but also with management applications that do not consider specific restrictions and conditions. Exhibit 9.1 discusses the relevance of training for managers in the world's largest democracy.

Exhibit 9.1   Training and Development Among Civil Servants in India

Meghna Sabharwal

With 10 million employees in the Indian central and state-level governments, the importance of training and development in the world's largest democracy cannot be overstated. The civil service in India is broadly classified into three main categories: (1) All India Services, (2) Central Services, and (3) State Services. The All India Services comprise officers that belong to the Indian Administrative Service (IAS), Indian Police Service (IPS), and Indian Forest Service (IFS); these are typically supervisors or managers who can serve in both central and state governments. The IAS cadre is most involved with the day-to-day service delivery and policy-making functions of government. To handle matters of policy formulation, implementation, and evaluation, these officers undergo regular training at various points in their careers. New IAS officers spend their first 2 years in training, and additional training is required at the 12th, 20th, and 28th years of service. In between, they also get training.

Yet, despite mandatory training requirements and several institutions offering these programs, the perceptions of civil servants belonging to All India Services and Central Services regarding their training programs do not paint an encouraging picture (Government of India, 2010). Approximately 65% of these civil servants report training programs to be general and not matching the specific needs of their jobs. Additionally, 85% express dissatisfaction that their posttraining job postings do not take training into account, and 75% state that there is a lack of procedures for selecting officers into training programs. Anecdotally, many training programs are also very theoretical and lack efforts to integrate and promote useful applications.

In broader context, officers state that much of their knowledge is learned on the job (81%) and through self-development and self-study (71%). Additionally, 29% mention mentoring by senior managers. Only 30% of officers over 50 years of age use the Internet as a source of learning, and only 16% identify training programs as a source for acquiring knowledge. The current state of training and development among public managers in India certainly points to deficiencies in the training system and the need to take a broader perspective on what public managers learn, how they avail themselves of up-to-date information and practices, and how they put new ideas into practice. Despite being touted as one of the world's rising economies, India could do more to ensure the abilities of its civil servants.

SOURCE: Used by permission.

Repetition and Active Participation

Most people do not immediately retain complex information and use new skills. The **rule of three** states that people hear things only after they have been said three times, and the **rule of seven** states that people must practice something seven times to master it. These are heuristic rules, only, but they do contain a kernel of truth. Managers and trainers often need to explain several times why something needs to be done and mastering new skills really well takes trial and error. Beyond this, workers also need to experience applications with slightly different variations, under slightly different conditions, and with slightly different issues in order to master skills a bit more broadly. It takes time to learn things and master skills.

Most adults are active learners who prefer to learn through participation in learning processes. Adults prefer to participate in discussions about the meaning of concepts and how they might be correctly applied rather than sit passively listening to an instructor talk. Repetition and multiple examples increase opportunities for active involvement, especially when applications occur out of class and training is scheduled over multiple sessions, allowing reflection on what has been learned. People also experience **learning plateaus**, or periods during which they must first fully absorb and assimilate newly presented material before they are able to learn more. One implication of this is that employees should first learn skills and solve problems that are relatively easy before moving on to progressively more difficult and complex matters.

Overlearning is the assimilation of material so that it becomes second nature—that is, so that new KSAs are completely integrated into an individual's repertoire. Overlearning is an important aspect of training when high levels of performance mastery are needed. People must apply new skills and knowledge repeatedly before these become ingrained: Practice makes perfect. Overlearning is particularly important in workplaces where mistakes could be expensive or dangerous. Overlearning aids performance later, when employees must perform under time constraints or substantial psychological pressures.

Underlying Principles

People are more effective at their jobs when they can understand why the methods they are using work, but some people can do little more than repeat the models or procedures given to them. To know why something works is to understand the principles that lie behind it, and knowledge of these principles opens the door to finding new applications as well as problem solving when something goes wrong. Matters of computer security, customer relations, and ethical conduct usually require a clear understanding of the principles that give rise to specific protocols and procedures that vary from situation to situation. Understanding the underlying principles helps employees deal with situations that they have not previously encountered. Organizational learning is often an exercise in applying general principles to specific situations (e.g., finding new ways to increase client choices, wherein the idea that clients should have choices is a general principle).

The effort to gain a working knowledge of the principles underlying "higher-order" tasks is challenging to some workers and managers, taxing their ability to be creative and imagine new applications. Increasingly, training techniques emphasize the development of insight, understanding of principles, and creativity in seeking new applications (Lucas, 2003; Newstrom, Scannell, & Nilson, 1998). Providing adequate guidance to workers and managers to develop these skills is one of several current challenges.

Feedback and Positive Reinforcement

Training and learning are enhanced by feedback that is immediate, direct, and positive (or constructive) in nature. Immediate and direct feedback helps guide activities toward correct goals and supports people in quickly mastering new skills. Immediate and direct feedback also reduces the buildup of wrong habits and viewpoints. Generally, positive feedback is used to reinforce actions, whereas negative feedback is designed to arrest them. Although negative feedback is important (e.g., pointing out an incorrect application or faulty outcome), it must be constructive in nature to be successful. As discussed in Chapter 6, feedback should be "objective" in nature (focusing on processes and outcomes rather than on people and their qualities) and should be part of a "collaborative" approach to developing new strategies for improving performance. For many employees, managers should balance negative feedback with **positive reinforcement**, providing encouragement through acknowledgment, praise, and acceptance. As the saying goes, "What gets measured gets done," and some employees surely use the extent and nature of feedback as a measure of their organization's commitment.

However, some people do not want to learn, and some have learning deficits. Others have low levels of creativity and imagination, and require specific guidance to apply new knowledge or skills to unique tasks. They need to be told what to do. Still others have low levels of perseverance and need to be encouraged to "try and try again" when they are not immediately successful. How feedback is given, and what is done to make the most of a person's contribution and role in the organization, often sends a powerful message to other workers about the importance, support, and consequences that workers can expect.

In sum, the principles discussed above provide important points for ensuring the effectiveness of training, learning, and development. Participants need to be motivated to learn and apply that which is taught, and management must address participants' concerns. The material should be relevant to their work and illustrated through multiple examples and opportunities for practice and application. Participants must understand both the specific applications and the underlying principles that may be relevant to future uses. Finally, employers need to follow through by providing feedback and encouragement about the importance and appropriateness of workplace applications. Exhibit 9.2 examines some situations in which these principles are not met.

TRAINING STRATEGIES

Training and development serves a variety of sometimes strategic purposes that support performance, risk management, and human capital purposes. This **strategic focus** includes the following:

1. Helping existing staff to adapt to new tasks as a result of promotion, restructuring, or other reassignments (performance)

2. Assisting new employees to get up-to-date on the unique procedures, equipment, or standards of the organization (performance and risk management)

3. Confirming that employees are kept abreast of new laws, procedures, or knowledge pertinent to the organization, the environment, or their jobs (risk management)

4. Ensuring that personnel in jobs critical to the organization's performance—and that have high costs of failure—perform in satisfactory ways (risk management)

5. Using T&D as a tool to ensure that desirable employees and managers stay current and develop themselves for future roles, and hence stay committed to the organization (retention of human capital, talent management)

6. Ensuring that all employees have KSAs that are consistent with what they need to help the organization move forward (planning)

The importance of these responsibilities is readily seen. For example, security has become an important focus for organizations in the past decade, and training and development is a cost-efficient and effective way to increase abilities (Perry & Mankin, 2005). Consultants can be brought in to train employees, ensuring that they have new KSAs while also ensuring that they are kept abreast of new laws and procedures that address risk management. T&D also can make sure that employees' and managers' skills are consistent with the organization's future needs, and it can help the organization keep or even promote talented key staff. It might be noted that purposes 1, 2, and 3 above reflect broad organizational needs (all employees have some training requirements, especially recent hires, the newly promoted, and those dealing with new technology or procedures), whereas purposes 4, 5, and 6 reflect needs that, in practice, often are special or less routine.

Exhibit 9.2   Training and Culture

The training principles discussed in this chapter reflect learner-centric assumptions that are common in the United States. That is, it is assumed that people want to learn and that they will use creativity and resourcefulness in applying whatever general and specific knowledge is offered, provided that they are supported and given useful information and feedback.

Yang, Zheng, and Li (2006) suggest that some learner orientations and limitations may be culture based. They found that learners from mainland China are more instructor-centric: They seek to absorb the expertise and knowledge of the instructor, sometimes through rote memorization, and do not use the information and encouragement of the instructor to develop their own expertise and knowledge. Traditional learners in China may be more likely to focus on providing the right answer than on providing the answer that reflects their own creativity.

Instructors know well that these orientations are readily found among some U.S. employees and students, too, and that they certainly are not found among all Chinese learners in a modern world. Rather, Yang et al.'s findings point to the need for trainers to examine their assumptions about learning and to work with employees in addressing their limitations, such as lack of creativity, leadership, or perseverance, regardless of their culture.

A broad range of training and development strategies are available to meet these needs. The following approaches are discussed below: on-the-job training, mentoring, in-house seminars, Web-based learning, innovation and development hubs, professional conference attendance, simulation and role-playing, and formal education.

On-the-Job Training

On-the-job training (OJT) is perhaps the most common training technique—and not what most people associate with training! OJT is not "sink or swim" for new employees, nor is it an employer giving an employee a manual and the name of a supervisor to contact if there is a problem. Bona fide OJT involves a thoughtful and guided approach to learning the job as it is performed. The approach involves the application of formal knowledge, regulations, and other general principles to actual tasks, as well as the acquisition of often-idiosyncratic information linked to specific jobs, such as evolving technology systems, regulations, or agency procedures. Because OJT concerns knowledge tied to specific positions, it follows that such training is often best delivered by those currently or recently in the positions that new employees are asked to fill. **Coaching** involves assigning an experienced employee to help other employees to master their job situations (see also the discussion of mentoring below). This approach is usually regarded as a cost-effective way of transferring essential job skills and knowledge, although part of the appeal lies in the fact that it seldom requires a separate budget. Existing staff are simply asked to supply training as a temporary, additional duty.

Although associated with employees assuming new positions, OJT also can be used when employees face changes in job responsibilities or new technology (Lawson, 1997; Wu & Rocheleau, 2001). Further, OJT can be used for **cross-training**, the practice of training employees to fulfill multiple job functions. OJT has the potential to meet many of the requirements for effective learning: New employees are often highly motivated, the knowledge is relevant, and transference is usually not an issue; there are ample examples that can be repeated as necessary; and employees have opportunities to receive feedback. But there are also threats to the success of OJT. The effectiveness of this approach depends heavily on the credibility of the "manager as teacher" as well as that person's ability to transfer his or her job-specific KSAs to the "employee as student." OJT is best provided by employees who are respected for their abilities in the organization, including the ability to teach. In addition, the "students" must be motivated and able to learn. Finally, OJT is no substitute for formal training. When students lack formal knowledge, such as essential accounting or IT skills, OJT will not be successful because teachers cannot build on critical foundations. Also, employees sometimes are not motivated to learn their jobs—for instance, they might have been involuntarily transferred to new assignments.

Although it may seem obvious that managers can improve the effectiveness of OJT by carefully selecting and training experienced employees to fulfill the instructor role, they do not always do so. Expert employees do not always make for expert OJT coaches, and it may be useful for managers to send some employees acting as OJT coaches to "train the trainer" workshops in which instruction methods are taught. Trainees may request more examples that facilitate their learning, and managers need to ensure that their "teachers" have sufficient time to train employees properly. Administrators must develop a realistic time schedule for acquisition of job skills and develop realistic expectations about the abilities of employees to complete tasks correctly. The success of OJT ultimately is judged by the eventual ability of employees to perform new duties with minimal supervision.

Mentoring

Mentoring is a developmental approach through which inexperienced employees learn and develop their career potential through ongoing, periodic dialogue and coaching from senior managers. Whereas the issues that are dealt with in OJT are usually fairly technical and immediate, mentors often assist in dealing with long-term goals, complex skill development, and professional socialization. Typically, the mentor–employee relationship evolves into one that is both personal and professional. Many officials report having mentors who were key to their career success. Employees and beginning managers, accordingly, are encouraged to reach out and identify potential mentors. A mentor can help to shape an employee's career, help the employee to avoid pitfalls, and help expand the employee's network by opening doors and offering opportunities. Women and minorities report that they find it useful to select mentors who themselves are women or minorities because such people are particularly able to understand and address their needs. Many personnel prefer to choose their own mentors or at least have the opportunity to influence the selection.

Similar to OJT, mentoring reflects the principles of adult learning. Mentors and coaches provide employees with examples (e.g., making the right career moves or preparing for a job interview), and discussion usually focuses on their application and relevance. Mentors and coaches also often use feedback on performance to reinforce important principles. Both mentoring and coaching assume that employees are motivated to advance their careers and job skills, but the issues of career development and professional development involved in mentoring are somewhat more abstract than the KSAs imparted through OJT and thus require more opportunity for reflection, clarification, and feedback through trial and error.

A principal barrier to the use of mentors is the failure of employees to cultivate relationships with more experienced managers. Individuals need to identify prospective mentors rather than wait for mentors to volunteer. Recognizing this, some organizations take a proactive approach by asking senior administrators to volunteer as mentors. For instance, in some health care agencies, senior managers mentor nurses as they transition to supervisory positions. But few organizations are proactive in this area, and employees do well to seek their own mentors. Exhibit 9.3 discusses supervisory training, in which good mentoring is important.

Mentoring, with on-the-job learning and feedback, is also a key part of talent management schemes. Talent management is the activity of identifying (spotting) employees and supervisors with potential for current and future contributions. Such assessment involves not only demonstrated competencies but also, and especially, the potential for adaptation, strategic insight, team collaboration, and results orientation—in short, leadership. Talent management usually involves providing employees and supervisors with developmental,

Exhibit 9.3 Supervisory Training

Employees frequently are promoted to supervisory positions on the basis of their technical accomplishments, time in service, and perceived ability to get along with others. None of these qualifications, however, offers much of the know-how and skills that are necessary to succeed as a supervisor. Few employers provide their managers and supervisors with training prior to promotion, and usually few persons are available who are able and willing to help new supervisors learn the ropes of supervision. Promotion to the rank of supervisor is often an exercise in "hitting the ground running."

The main challenges of supervision concern (1) getting work done through staff, in a productive way; (2) dealing with employee discipline, conflict management, and other personnel matters; (3) implementing various policies (e.g., promoting workforce diversity); (4) nurturing a unitwide perspective and efforts to move the unit forward; (5) learning how to develop and administer budgets; (6) ensuring the safety and cleanliness of offices; (7) ensuring adequate information and other technology; (8) ensuring adequate employee training and development; and (9) developing administrative and legal expertise in dealing with employee discipline. Finally, supervisors must continue to develop their interpersonal competencies.

Organizations may assist new supervisors by providing orientation guides. The problem is that, despite good intentions, such manuals may go unread or be forgotten in the heat of everyday managing. Supervisors need to learn how to learn from employee feedback. Some agencies also provide 1- or 2-day seminars on supervision and leadership. Although these seminars do provide and reinforce important information, "trainees" may be hesitant to share their ignorance of this information with those of similar rank. Selected departments send new supervisors to off-site workshops and seminars. Although the presence of strangers from other organizations ensures some anonymity, such off-site training efforts may lack follow-through.

Perhaps a more effective strategy is the use of mentors. In this approach, a new supervisor is asked to identify a mentor, either inside or outside the organization, with whom the supervisor then meets on a regular basis. These confidential conversations allow the new supervisor to receive feedback and advice from someone who has held a similar job in the past. Mentors can help new supervisors deal with a variety of challenges. They can also offer guidance regarding how supervisors can respond to employee feedback and prepare themselves for higher functions. Through mentoring, new supervisors get real-time feedback that helps them to progress quickly on the learning curve.

"stretch" experiences with mentors, who offer feedback and assessment. Though many examples of formal talent management are found outside the United States (e.g., Fernández-Aráoz, 2014; Poocharoen & Lee, 2013), organizations also informally offer developmental opportunities with mentoring for talented staff. Some younger employment candidates explicitly ask about such opportunities during the recruitment process.

In-House Seminars

In-house **seminars and presentations** are more widely associated with the idea of training for many people than are the approaches discussed above. Seminars and presentations are widely used to communicate information such as new developments, expectations, or rules and policies to groups of employees. Management arranges for training on topics that cut across different units, such as (1) generic workplace practices (e.g., supervision), procedures (e.g., travel reimbursement), or computer skills; (2) legal workplace matters affecting employees (e.g., sexual harassment and discrimination seminars); and (3) benefits (e.g., retirement planning seminars, presentations on health care expenses). Often the human resource department is responsible for ensuring that these crosscutting training efforts are in fact carried out (ICMA, 2002; Reese & Lindenberg, 2003; Ugori, 1997).

Seminars, though information based, may lack important elements of effective learning. When seminars are mandatory, staff may not be motivated to learn what is presented. Information taught is often general and not job specific; employees may struggle to see its relevance. Because seminars are often short, there is little time for repetition or hands-on application. For these reasons, seminars are sometimes regarded as inadequate except for strictly one-way communication by management to staff. Their impact is even weaker when supervisors fail to follow up and ensure that the information is used. When limited to small groups, seminars often include opportunities for clarification, application, and feedback. Indeed, an important trend is the tailoring of seminars to the needs of small work units rather than auditorium-size groups.

The effectiveness of seminars can be increased in several ways. Lecturing can be kept to a minimum, and opportunities can be increased for participants to discuss training materials and actual, real-life problems. Managers and trainers can gauge employee interest and concerns beforehand and address these during seminars. Trainers might offer to follow up with groups of employees or to assist in application. Exhibit 9.4 provides suggestions for making effective presentations. A cutting-edge topic is training for very senior managers and political appointees, discussed in Exhibit 9.5.

Exhibit 9.4   Effective Presentations

Effective oral presentation is key in the delivery of in-house seminars. The following guidelines can help ensure the success of an oral presentation:

- State why the topic is important and how it benefits employees.
- Keep eye contact with the audience.
- Discuss the topic in "bite-size," manageable pieces.
- Use notes as reminders of what material must be covered, but do not read verbatim from notes.
- Provide multiple relevant examples and applications of new concepts or procedures.
- Invite comments at appropriate intervals and provide clarifications as needed.
- Defer tangential comments to the end of the seminar.
- Consider the use of small groups to discuss problems or generate solutions.
- Practice keeping the presentation as short as possible.
- Summarize main points and discuss implementation or follow-through as appropriate.

Seminars increasingly use slides (typically in PowerPoint format) and printed materials that have a professional appearance and that facilitate the communication and dissemination of information. Handouts should help participants focus on the presentation and minimize their need to take notes (Duarte, 2012).

Exhibit 9.5 Training for Ministers and Political Appointees in South Korea

---

Pan Suk Kim

In South Korea, the Central Officials Training Institute (COTI) provides a National Agenda Workshop for ministers and equivalent-level political appointees in collaboration with the Office of the President. This workshop is not a typical form of training. Instead, it is seen as a necessary vehicle for ensuring that top-level officials and political appointees have a full understanding of national agendas and the necessary competencies for realizing the goals of the administration and also promoting a culture of innovation throughout agencies. Even the president of South Korea often attends and leads dialogues with ministers and/or deputy ministers.

Ministers often come into office with little experience in managing key relationships with their stakeholders: the Office of the President, the National Assembly, political parties, the Office of the Prime Minister, other ministries, the mass media, the policy community (academia, think tanks), local governments and councils, civil society, and the business community. The training consists of several hours of dialogues, including presentation and discussion of difficult issues and problems, a "practice break" of several weeks, and a second meeting in which application experiences are discussed.

Political appointees also get training that focuses on task competency (organizational management, vision, leadership, problem solving, external relations, expertise), governing (undertaking the president's vision and mandates, learning to apply executive core national agendas), and morality (personal integrity, organizational integrity, accountability, transparency). Training for appointees and ministers also addresses public administration failures and how to deal with them and learn from them for innovation. Training also discusses dealing with family and friends who may jeopardize officials' integrity or ethical standards through their requests. This kind of training is particularly needed during regime changes, which come with massive reshuffling in key positions.

Senior officials also get training. In addition to dealing with the some of the above, training also contributes to realizing the goals of the administration, including policy objectives, core values such as fairness, and performance management strategies. Candidates for the Senior Civil Service (SCS) and senior members of the SCS, in particular, take training courses at COTI.

The idea of training high-level officials is still uncommon in many countries. Sometimes it is said that these officials are already "very excellent" and, hence, not in need of training. The typical perception of training is that it is needed by middle- and lower-level officials, while no emphasis is placed on the needs of higher-level officials. It is time to recognize that high-level officials need more learning opportunities to deal effectively with big surprises as well as other nonroutine affairs, including economic stagnation, pandemics, climate change, natural disasters, and glocal (global + local) issues.

SOURCE: Used by permission.

Web-Based Learning

Web-based learning is increasingly used in employee training and continuing education. While some older workers still prefer traditional face-to-face instruction, many people have now become familiar with Web-based learning and appreciate the advantages of remote access (reducing travel time and costs), convenient participation times for employees, and rapid access to information. Some prior disadvantages of Web-based learning, such as lack of immediate instructor feedback, are rapidly disappearing as technology enabling real-time interactions has become widely available. Content in some advanced subject areas is not yet well developed, but content and modalities are becoming increasingly available for both one-time events (e.g., webinars) and short courses. Online learning is indeed here to stay, and it is likely to expand further (Lin & Edvinsson, 2011; U.S. Government Accountability Office [U.S. GAO], 2003). Additionally, some employers provide employees with a range of Web-based developmental opportunities, such as free online language classes for those who wish to improve their Spanish or Chinese.

Innovation and Development Hubs, Centers, and Labs

Recognizing the need for organizational learning and development, and encouraging work units not only to adopt new procedures and technologies but to also take an active hand in identifying the need for them and tailoring them to their circumstances, some jurisdictions have created innovation hubs, the purpose of which is to provide spaces in which groups of employees and managers can discuss common challenges and find support in implementing new solutions. These are small offices staffed by a few employees who are able to assist in the development, awareness, and diffusion of new processes. Such efforts acknowledge that while mentoring, in-house presentations, and Web-based learning are largely individual centered, group support is also needed to help foster organizational change.

For example, the U.S. Office of Personnel Management opened its Innovation Lab in 2013; the lab, located in the subbasement of the OPM's Washington, D.C., headquarters, occupies a classroom and several offices for about six staff members. The Innovation Lab seeks to generate concrete solutions for problems in HRM, driven by users; its work involves iterative testing of new services, products, and processes at the front end of the design process as a way of avoiding large, expensive failures upon implementation. Initial efforts of the lab have addressed ways to improve the attraction and retention of science, technology, engineering, and mathematics (STEM) talent; redesign of the Presidential Management Fellows Program; issues of cybersecurity; action planning for chief financial officers; international affairs communications; interagency communities of practice on innovation; usability training; new employee onboarding; diversity and onboarding; and more (U.S. GAO, 2013).

Such efforts recognize the importance of providing time and space for employees and managers to step away from their day-to-day work to offer one another support and to share in thinking through possible solutions to problems they have in common. Additional organizational-level approaches to learning are discussed further later in this chapter.

Professional Conference Attendance

Professional conference attendance is an old mainstay in training and development. Though participation has fallen in recent years as employers have cut back on travel benefits and Web-based learning has become a cheaper alternative, conference attendance is unlikely to go away anytime soon. Conferences are still very important venues for learning about new developments in one's field and for networking and meeting new people in one's field. One of many reasons managers attend professional conferences is to become better informed and to learn where they can acquire new skills. Those with hands-on experience often make presentations at professional conferences, and although discussion times at panels are too short, attendees can easily walk up to presenters afterward and follow up on key points. Beyond this, the network building that attendees do at conferences is often vital to their career development, as well as for providing them with essential contacts who can help with real problems they may encounter at work. Top local government managers often attend annual meetings of professional organizations, and many managers send their employees, as well. Conference attendance may be expensive, but it can be invaluable to those who are seeking to increase their professional development and widen their networks.

Simulation and Role-Playing

Simulation allows managers and employees to replicate on-the-job experiences without disruption of ongoing work processes. It is appropriate when employee learning through OJT could result in unacceptable outcomes. For example, pilots use flight simulators to hone their skills and practice difficult maneuvers. NASA's astronauts simulate entire missions, and firefighters practice blaze control in simulated settings because they cannot risk on-the-job learning. Antiterrorism units practice in mock settings, and technicians use simulation to learn new tools and procedures that would be inappropriate to try out in the real world. *Vestibule training* is the use of separate areas where workers practice skills or processes without disrupting ongoing work activities. Budget analysts use computer simulations of alternative fiscal scenarios to predict revenue shortfalls and to learn how to solve a variety of operations and inventory control problems. Finally, managers test staff by presenting them with simulations of real-life examples. The military, for example, simulates attacks without informing personnel that these events are actually simulations. Such exercises help managers to assess staff performance under real-life conditions (Gillespie, 2002).

Some widely used simulation applications are in customer service and employee relations. During customer orientation training, staff members are advised of new expectations and are provided opportunities to discuss how they can best handle service challenges. Role-playing and simulation are part of these efforts. Typical exercises include dealing with irate customers and dealing with contingency situations that upset client expectations. Prison personnel, for example, may have to explain to family members of inmates why they will not be able to visit their relatives during scheduled visiting hours. Role-playing is most useful when it closely matches or exceeds the intensity of emotions and behaviors that occur in real-life incidents. Video recordings of role-played scenarios are also used, so that trainees can watch and learn from their own reactions. Through repeated interactions until they "get it right," employees increase their skills without risking the adverse consequences of getting it wrong in the workplace.

Whatever the virtues of simulation and role-playing techniques may be, it should be noted that they have important limitations. For instance, in the largest such exercise ever conducted, 13,000 troops accompanied by sophisticated computer simulations pitted U.S. military forces against a Middle Eastern enemy. When the enemy inflicted serious damage during the ensuing attacks, the American "dead" were ordered back to life, the "sunk" fleet was refloated, and the enemy was ordered to stand down while the Marines performed a victorious amphibious landing (Borger, 2002; Peters, 2005). In another case, Louisiana emergency management planners did not simulate mass civilian evacuations and did not include levee breaches for Category 4 or 5 hurricanes in their training exercises due to lack of funding. Finally, the FBI's Critical Incidence Response Group developed a computer-based training program because commanders resisted simulations conducted by real people. The reason? Poor performance in simulations would damage careers.

Formal Education

Advanced academic degrees are increasingly required for management positions, so many employees hoping to advance in their careers return to universities. **Education** prepares people for the future. It differs from training in that it is concerned with broad principles of knowledge and practice rather than the technical details of work. Training makes people more alike because they learn the same skills. Education, because it involves self-discovery, makes them more different; it emphasizes not merely information but also formation. This includes better understanding of the context of personal choices, a perspective on human affairs, and ideas about what is important—a passion for living well. The master of public administration (MPA) is the degree of choice for those in the field of human resources because MPA course work provides students with telling viewpoints on the role of agencies as democratic institutions, the structure of public budgeting and personnel systems, the role of leadership, and many other vital topics. Individuals who receive the MPA are assumed to have the appropriate background to quickly apply their education. Education has become increasingly accessible to full-time employees through distance learning and outreach efforts (branch campuses, off-site education) as well as the growing trend toward certificate programs that involve sets of courses from graduate or undergraduate curricula.

At least two contrasting views exist about the use of education as a training and development strategy. Some organizations view education benefits as excessively expensive and uncertain in their returns. Current graduate school fees range from several hundred dollars to more than $1,200 per credit hour at private universities; employees who receive tuition benefits usually pay only a share of the cost of their tuition bills. Organizations cannot be wholly certain how they will gain from enabling employees to pursue education, as some employees who use tuition benefits may fail to be promoted and others may leave. To avoid the latter, some agencies require staff who receive such benefits to continue working with the agency for up to 3 years following program completion. Some other agencies view education benefits as useful instruments for attracting and retaining highly qualified personnel. Motivated employees are likely to stay for the duration of their education (often pursued on a part-time basis over many years), and this gives their employers first crack at retaining them on graduation, even if competitive, market-based salary increases are required. Employees are also motivated by knowing that their agencies offer education benefits, and this motivation contributes to creating a favorable work climate.

Two perennial questions asked by organizations are (1) How much training do we need? and (2) How can we measure the returns from our training investment? The unique and individualized nature of employee and employer needs implies that decisions about which training approaches to use must almost always be made on a case-by-case basis, driven by employees' needs and goals as well as specific employer needs or conditions. At an organizational level, managers do well to consider the strategic purposes of training mentioned above (helping new employees get up to speed, ensuring familiarity with laws and procedures, addressing risk management, developing existing employees, furthering retention, and providing access to KSAs), assess whether these strategic purposes are being met, and weigh how each of the training and development approaches described above can further these purposes. The two questions above are meaningful, but answering them defies a quantifiable formula.

At an individual level, all best practices advise workers and managers to periodically discuss workers' goals and their needs for T&D. The very best organizations take managers' commitment to identifying and meeting their units' and workers' T&D needs seriously. This is a one-on-one activity that results in agreed-upon individual KSA goals, and workers' fulfillment of their training goals is seen as a meaningful part of their performance appraisals. As one senior public executive states:

> I do not spend much time worrying about measuring the effectiveness of our training dollars. I require that our managers examine how training and development can benefit each employee, and participation in training activities is tied to employees' annual performance appraisal. It is very difficult to determine what the right amount of training is for any department, and the right amount must be argued on a case-by-case basis in terms of staff development needs. It is important that managers and supervisors talk with each employee about their training and development needs.

This senior manager then explains that he uses follow-up discussions with lower managers about the T&D needs of their lower units as well as discussions with some individual employees to ensure that these managers have indeed done so. This is a practical and time-tested strategy for dealing with the intractable questions above, however imperfect it might be in some settings. Thus, determining what training, and how much training, often begins with an assessment process. For organizations that are thought to be underinvesting in T&D (which, as previously noted, is very common), enhancing the assessment processes is a useful step for increasing awareness. The appendix to this chapter provides some assessment questions that can be asked organization-wide, such as on employee surveys. It also includes a short discussion on training evaluation and a brief evaluation instrument.

ORGANIZATIONAL LEARNING STRATEGIES

While the emphasis in training is on helping employees do their existing jobs better, and sometimes also preparing them for next ones, the above discussion does not deal with a more basic and fundamental matter—helping organizations to assess whether they should be doing something different. The purpose of **organizational learning** is to get agencies, departments, and individuals thinking about what and how they are doing and what and how they could or should be doing differently or better. Organizational learning concerns these processes. The public hopes that public organizations will respond quickly to change and be forward-looking and efficient in their ways—and it is rightly disappointed when agencies do not meet these standards. But training strategies are seldom concerned with these purposes; training is not expected to lead to the redefinition of a person's job tasks, though information could lead to discussion. The strategies discussed in this section reflect current thinking on keeping organizations vibrant and receptive to change. The training and development strategies discussed above can be adapted and put in service of organizational learning purposes.

Much has been written on organizational learning; the academic lineage is deep (e.g., Argyris & Schön, 1978; Nonaka & Takeuchi, 1995; Senge, 1990). At issue are (1) encouraging individuals to be willing and able to see that things could be done differently and better, and (2) getting buy-in from different groups of people in the organization to support change. The first issue involves a spark of creativity. This is not only about finding a better solution to a current problem (say, an overburdened delivery process) but also about suggesting new policies or services that are cost-effective or attractive in some other way. For example, to increase funding for local nonprofits, one city installed in its subway stations machines through which people could make small charitable donations using their smart cards. New ideas come in many shapes and forms; people often need to be encouraged and sometimes trained to think in new ways.[2]

The second issue is getting support from within one's own unit, higher levels of management, and rival departments. New ideas often call into question something about existing goals, methods, policies, and assumptions. Common (2004) notes that organizational learning in the United Kingdom public sector is often hindered by (1) inadequate links between processes of idea creation and processes of power, (2) cultures of conformity and blame finding in which change is risky at best, and (3) overemphasis on individual rather than organizational performance. These problems also exist in the United States. Some cultures are very rule bound, and some governments make extensive use of political appointees whose short tenures and political agendas usually do little to promote cultures of learning and change. A key lesson from these experiences is that senior management support and involvement in organizational learning change is needed to (1) keep the forces of resistance to change in check and (2) give legitimation and support to new ideas.

In recent years, a number of organizational practices and policies have evolved that encourage departments and work units to engage in learning, creativity, and change. Though born from practice, most are consistent with the above principles of learning.

Idea Development

A very simple and effective approach is asking employees, as individuals and as groups, to submit ideas for improving their own work, that of their work units, or that of the agency. The practice of workers generating and submitting ideas for improvement has roots in "quality circles," which originated in Japanese production processes. In the 1960s and 1970s, workers in Japan would form groups and discuss ways of improving quality and performance, leading to that nation's famed zeal for quality in automaking and electronics. These efforts show that idea development and creativity can work well when they are part of organizational processes that have management support, such as production processes, new product development processes, and strategic planning. Some basic questions for organizations are whether they can add greater creativity to existing processes, whether they can increase the number of processes that generate improvement and adaptation, and whether they can create new processes that spur employees into doing these things.

A practical illustration is seen in Seoul Metropolitan Government (SMG), where employees are expected to come up with ideas for improvement for their work, their unit, or their city. HRM provides training that introduces employees to processes and expectations regarding creativity. The training is a 2-day workshop in which trainers share examples of past ideas and employees engage in role-playing, helping each other to develop new ideas and solutions. People can submit ideas individually, and some departments also encourage employee teams to meet once every 2 weeks to propose new ideas or improve the implementation of new ideas. Such groups are sometimes known as "communities of practice." Commitment to idea generation is underscored in that creativity (idea generation) is part of SMG appraisal processes for employees and managers, and all levels of management are involved in idea review and implementation processes.

Seoul is the world's eighth-largest city (more than 10 million residents), and SMG has 15,700 workers. On average, workers submit 3,000 ideas per month—smaller jurisdictions would have far fewer ideas, of course. As Berman and Kim (2010) describe, over a 2-year period employees and managers proposed 62,666 ideas (about 2.2 ideas per year per worker), of which 13% were selected for implementation. Selected ideas include both big and small ones, such as creating a website where people can upload pictures of city defects, holding subsidized concerts for persons with disabilities, creating a waterfall from a bridge, hosting a design conference, creating a digital wall for marriage proposals, constructing underground roads, and organizing a bicycle festival. Results of surveys of both managers and employees also show that the proportion of officials who view their divisions as innovative more than doubled (from 13% to 33%), suggesting that such efforts can indeed jump-start innovation in the public sector.

A process was created to manage the evaluation of the large number of ideas. Ideas are submitted electronically and are evaluated by a pool of midlevel managers based on creativity (possible maximum 40 points), feasibility (30 points), and effectiveness (30 points). Ideas are selected for implementation in separate processes, thus separating rewards for good ideas from their actual use. Creativity management is also supported by appraisal processes in which idea submission and evaluation are appraisal and award criteria. For employees, creativity elements related to planning, overcoming obstacles, and developing customer-oriented approaches now account for up to 25% of total appraisal points. Managers' appraisal criteria include whether their departments have activities for generating and evaluating ideas, number of ideas their departments submitted to the city's intranet, and implementation of creative ideas as well as programs and workshops for knowledge and creativity. Highly rated ideas get additional awards, too. The mayor of Seoul made this approach a priority of his administration, and it has continued beyond his tenure.

Organizations are still experimenting with different ways of getting new ideas and initiatives from their employees and managers. Above, we discussed the use of innovation hubs. Some years ago, Vince (2000) reported on an approach that involves a cross section of staff from all levels of the organization in five workshops. In the first three of these, the emphasis is on gathering thoughts, ideas, and issues. Participants in the fourth workshop are given a summary and work on refining these ideas as well as their own. The final workshop is used to generate further agreement about change, and a later "development team" of staff involved in the workshops is created to further initiatives. As Vince notes, this approach suffers from a lack of management buy-in—at some point, management support and constructive feedback are necessary for any set of ideas that employees propose. Idea development is not enough, but organizations that adopt significant numbers of new ideas are likely to increase their responsiveness, performance, and innovation.

Leaders' Thinking

Any system is only as good as its leaders, so how leaders and managers are selected and evaluated matters greatly in determining the nature of an organization. A learning organization needs managers and leaders who support learning and the search for improvement that implies. The U.S. federal government emphasizes core qualities for leadership that include the abilities to bring about strategic change, to lead people, to build coalitions, to manage business functions, to be results driven, to apply technical knowledge, to calculate risks, to be decisive, and to be customer focused (U.S. OPM, 2010). While these are necessary leadership skills and abilities, they do not emphasize those qualities associated with learning organizations, such as being forward-looking, open to innovation, able to implement change, and able to bring out these qualities in others.

Singapore is a very small country (smaller than the state of Rhode Island) with a population of about 5 million. It is one of Asia's miracle growth economies, developing from modest levels in 1965 (when it separated from Malaysia) to achieve the world's third-highest gross domestic product per capita in 2010. Singapore's story is one of strong state direction of business and other areas of life. Since 1983, Singapore has come to evaluate and select public managers based on both their recent performance and their potential for senior management, based on a system developed by Shell.[3] In 1994, Singapore modified its system to include the so-called **HAIR qualities**, also based on Shell's system (Vallance, 1999). The acronym HAIR stands for

- *helicopter* (the ability to look at things from a higher vantage point while still seeing the details on the ground and being able to zoom in on those),
- *analysis* (a superior ability for rational analysis, logic, and judgment),
- *imagination* (the ability to develop fresh and creative approaches to problems), and
- *reality* (the ability to develop grounded and realistic solutions).

The HAIR elements are considered necessary "intellectual qualities" of senior managers. Additionally, managers are evaluated on "results orientation" (achievement motivation, business sense, and decisiveness) and "leadership qualities" (capacity to motivate, delegate, and communicate). These other qualities are obviously also important (see below), but the HAIR qualities add some specificity for what leaders and managers need to be able to do in forward-looking and innovative organizations.

More recently, Singapore has adapted a model of "dynamic governance" that further specifies the above qualities. *Dynamic* implies a world with changes to which public agencies need to adapt and give leadership, which requires the ability to understand how one's organization interacts with it. Leadership capabilities for doing this are as follows (Neo & Chen, 2007):

- *Thinking ahead* (developing foresight into the future, drawing implications from the likely future to the present, and identifying strategic actions and options that might be needed)
- *Thinking again* (exercising hindsight for understanding how we got to where we are, what our strategies and capabilities really are, and having candid conversations about what changes are likely needed)
- *Thinking across* (developing insight that comes from thinking across boundaries and learning through others' experiences that suggest new strategies, options, and connections)

Practitioner examples are slowly but surely beginning to show how managers should think in order to create forward-looking organizations that adapt to change well. Above we noted that a key issue is encouraging individuals to see that things could be done differently and better. Leadership development has become increasingly important in this regard. Exhibit 9.6 provides an example from New Zealand, which is moving toward an integrated development effort.

Managing Changes

A lot has been written on managing change. Though some of this concerns one-shot, major change efforts used to steer organizations in new directions, the literature is increasingly adapted to learning organizations that have many ongoing changes that are often more modest in nature. Change is to be expected and ongoing. Which organization today can afford not to be constantly changing in some way? Listed below are the major elements of managing change (Cameron & Green, 2009; Collins, 2001; Hayes, 2010; Hiatt, 2004; Kotter, 1996):

1. Having insightful analysis about forces prompting change and organizational strategy
2. Being clear about the nature and scope of change
3. Involving or consulting people and addressing their concerns at an early point
4. Wisely choosing feasible operational targets (or picking the low-hanging fruit first)
5. Wisely choosing those who are tasked with implementing change

6. Declaring and celebrating success

7. Adjusting and learning from initial efforts

8. Having plans for dealing with setbacks, learning curves, and resistance

While this list builds on the lessons learned from change management, in learning organizations many new ideas are supported by the strategic purposes of public agencies but will not always lead to major changes in broader purposes. Organizations make a lot of small changes, too.

The point here is not to recap the voluminous change management literature, but rather to focus on some T&D aspects. No book can adequately prepare any manager for the vicissitudes of events that pop up in change processes, and there is no substitute for having stood

---

Exhibit 9.6 Leadership Development in New Zealand

A number of countries are taking a renewed, strategic look at how supervisors and managers are selected and developed for more senior roles. Leadership matters, and the performance of the public service depends in part on having excellent leaders at the top. One of these countries is New Zealand, an island nation in the Pacific that has only 4.5 million people but that is renowned for the quality of its public services. A review of agency performance found that internal leadership was among the least satisfactory factors. Good leaders are scarce, and the public sector finds itself competing with the private sector for scarce talent.

The talent management focus is now increasing efforts to identify and develop emerging leaders as well as invest in developing existing leaders for complex and challenging roles and deploying them where they are suited best. The strategy rests on the identification of future leaders through career boards—cross-agency panels of senior public officials who work within their agencies to identify talent at different levels. Differentiations are made between those who have shown clear ability for making significant career steps and those who have shown only some (potential) or little ability. Differentiations are also made with regard to individuals' aspirations. "Star performers" do not always aspire to become agency chief executives and interact with political appointees, for example. Some are quite satisfied with professional positions.

Those who are selected for leadership development are put through assignments across agencies to ensure they that have broad appreciation and knowledge of the New Zealand public sector. They are assessed on an ongoing basis and provided with challenging experiential learning opportunities. While they receive some formal training, it is less than 10% of their developmental investment; more important is the feedback they get from supervisors, mentors, and coaches. They also participate in action learning with peer groups that discuss common experiences and challenges. In this way, public managers get diverse experiences, feedback and assessment, and a positive environment created for the development and retention of New Zealand's most talented public managers. Supporting this work is the NZ Leadership Development Center, a public agency that works closely with the New Zealand State Services Commission (2013b).

Young staff and students often ask how they can be chosen for leadership development. The answer: Ask to be assessed and provided with feedback about one's leadership potential.

SOURCES: New Zealand State Services Commission (2013a) and author interviews.

in the line of fire. Even minor changes can have major unforeseen consequences (e.g., a new bicycle path affects the environment, access to underground cables and pipes, school safety, and long-term traffic and future development). In-house training courses can give only an overview and familiarization with the issues that may come up; real learning requires the presence of a mentor or other experienced manager who has been through the process and who can be there in real time for questions that inevitably come up. Mentoring is about passing on the lessons that have been learned and developing skills for handling the unexpected (which is always expected). Learning organizations help managers acquire such skills by ensuring people-to-people knowledge and skills transfers. Officials do a lot of on-the-job learning, and they benefit from access to management generalists as well as specialists in their field who can answer questions. Mastery is about paying attention to everything.

T&D is also helpful in creating cultures of good followership among employees. People need to be told what is expected of them. There is a time for giving new ideas, a time for helping to develop someone else's idea, and a time for being a loyal organizational citizen by helping to make the implementation of a new effort go smoothly and well. There are different roles to be played. The flip side of urging managers to not build resistance and to be supportive is to have employees who are willing to go along with that. In-house seminars are good vehicles for explaining how things work, and some films are also available, but these approaches inevitably need follow-up and follow-through from trainers and managers, too. T&D can help smooth the process of organizational learning and change.

APPLICATION: ETHICS TRAINING

Concerns about ethics violations have prompted many organizations to provide ethics training for their employees and managers. Agencies believe that an emphasis on values and ethics is consistent with building up a modern and desirable workplace. Negative reports of personnel being caught up in unethical conduct tarnish the images of organizations. When overseas U.S. military personnel were caught in unethical conduct, the secretary of defense ordered ethics review and training for all staff, from high to low (Alexander, 2014; Bumiller, 2012). But ethics is obviously difficult to shape, let alone control. What can organizations realistically expect from ethics training? How can an organization learn from its ethical failings and do better next time?

The purposes of training and development mentioned earlier are well applied to ethics training. Ethics training to ensure that both new and existing employees are aware of important laws and practices—in relation to, say, gift taking, conflict of interest, fraud, and harassment—can be made mandatory, with employees required either to attend workshops or to complete online training. Organizations can hope to reduce their legal exposure and improve their risk management by ensuring that all personnel have been made duly aware of critical laws and policies.

Beyond general topics, employers can also tailor some ethics training to special circumstances or tasks of their employees. For example, law enforcement involves concerns for the rights of alleged offenders and their victims. Those in police custody have the right to be treated with respect and dignity, regardless of alleged crime, and this aspect of police work has certainly received heightened interest in recent years. Other concerns in law enforcement include issues of bribery and criminal wrongdoing by officers themselves, as prolonged exposure to criminal activity can have a corrupting influence. Other areas of public service have their own unique ethics challenges, such as those relating to health care and fund-raising for nonprofits. The list of possible ethics training topics is long and can include the following:

- Working with contractors
- Government travel
- Gifts
- Misuse of government office
- Post–government employment
- Conflicts of interest
- Use of government resources
- Security, data, and intellectual property
- Sexual harassment
- Hiring
- Fraud

Ethics training also reinforces retention and performance strategies by emphasizing the "value basis" of the modern workplace—specifically, efforts to create heightened emphasis on objectivity, equality, and concern for stakeholders and the environment. For instance, ethics training can be used to raise awareness of and promote discussion about the impact of a unit on the environment. What is the ethical obligation of an agency toward the environment? How well is it meeting its environmental obligations? These types of discussions further awareness that may resonate with workers.

While the purposes noted above support the strategic aims mentioned earlier, the general principles of learning and specific training strategies suggest that ethics training is most likely to be effective when it is part of a broad effort to instill awareness and reinforce behavior; one-time, isolated training events are likely to have less effect. For example, the rule of three, discussed above, suggests that employees will likely need to hear several times from managers that a new ethics policy or practice is important, especially if it is very different from previous policies or practices. Repetition of this message might be needed to overcome a certain skepticism. Also, the complexity of many ethical dilemmas suggests that decision making and application may not always be as self-evident as training scenarios suggest. It is not always easy to recognize or to resolve ethical issues (e.g., when should residents be forewarned of planned street closures?). The rule of seven suggests that employees and managers may need some practice, trial and error, and discussion before the new practices are well ingrained. The concept of the learning organization suggests that workers should discuss a broad range of matters and offer ideas for improving how specific ethics issues are addressed. Learning is also about workers discussing with managers and among themselves the issues that come up and finding solutions by sharing information and experiences. Indeed, best practices of ethics training include repeated and open discussions—some as part of training, with exercises, and others as part of ongoing department operations.

Rather than looking at ethics training as a panacea or silver bullet, managers should view it as one of several tools that they use—along with role modeling, appraisals, and feedback—to instill or change ethical conduct. Training alone is not enough. Some organizations use a multifaceted approach, and increasing numbers are beginning to apply the well-known acronym POSDCORB (planning, organizing, staffing, directing, coordinating, reporting, and budgeting) to ethics as well. Managers can plan for ethics ("What behaviors do we expect?" "What behaviors do we discourage?"), organize for ethics ("How are offices to be made responsible for implementing ethics objectives?"), staff for ethics (making ethics a criterion in hiring and promotion, assigning responsibilities for ethics objectives), budget for ethics (supplying resources for training), and report on ethics accomplishments and violations. Many organizations are now putting such elements in place, supported by training (Berman, 2008; Menzel, 2007, 2010; Svara, 2015; West & Berman, 2007). Ethics leadership means not only that managers now bring new ethics to their employees but also that changes in ethical awareness start with managers themselves. Not surprisingly, some agency heads have made ethics reform a top priority for all of their managers. Training can make use of videos and role-playing scenarios. At the end of the day, though, ethics training is likely to be most effective when it is integrated into how the organization is run (Williams, 2007).

Research is providing evidence that supports the above propositions. In an award-winning article, West and Berman (2004) report on their research into the use of ethics training in U.S. cities, in which they found that about two-thirds of cities with populations over 50,000 use some form of ethics training and that such training is mandatory in about one-third of cities. However, the mean duration of such training is only about one-half day per year. In a sophisticated empirical analysis, West and Berman show that "targeted" ethics training (i.e., training oriented toward specific applications and practices rather than toward general awareness) is integrated with broader management efforts. They note, "Training is part of a jurisdiction's ethics management practices, and the results indicate that it provides managers with leverage as they seek to attain their ethics goals" (p. 202). Note also that Exhibit 9.7 shows that the source of organizational improvement begins with "moral leadership by senior managers," which affects or even drives all other ethics activities.

Finally, although ethics training is useful and needed, we should not overstate its effectiveness; no amount of training can eliminate human folly and misconduct. Who among us has not done something best left unspoken? "There but for the grace of God go I" is a shared sentiment. The human mind is subject to finding itself in a fog and beset by misjudgment. Yet the fact that human error cannot be avoided does not mean that managers should not seek to minimize it—indeed, they should do so. Training reinforces the message that ethical conduct matters, and it tells employees what to do and what not to do. Ethics training, in some form or practice, is likely here to stay, but it cannot replace the need for vigilance by managers; appraisal and discipline are necessary as well. After all, the next ethical misstep is just a step away.

SUMMARY AND CONCLUSION

Training and development is undergoing some major changes, from being a provider of training services that strengthen an individual's SKAs to taking a broader perspective that includes all ways through which individuals learn and strengthen their abilities, as well as ways that organizations and work groups learn and develop. While traditional

Exhibit 9.7   Structural Equation Model of Ethics Training, Leadership, and Outcomes

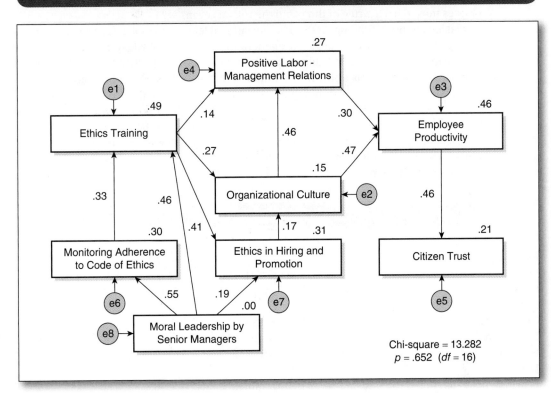

SOURCE: West and Berman (2004). Used with permission.

T&D supports individual and organizational learning, emphasis on the latter inevitably brings in a broader range of HRM issues as well, to which T&D can also contribute.

Training is no longer confined to in-house seminars but takes a broad view of how workers learn. Thus, it includes on-the-job training strategies and the use of people-to-people interaction to transfer and develop SKAs. Mentoring and coaching are part of these approaches. While some organizations identify mentors for new employees, such relationships do not always work out—employees do well to develop mentorship relations themselves. T&D also includes Web-based learning, education, and simulation strategies. As the new century unfolds, increasingly workers and their managers must take responsibility for identifying and meeting their T&D needs. The need for training in basic skills—such as those relating to writing, public speaking, and teamwork—also remains important.

Training can be improved. Effective T&D builds on the principles of adult learning, ensuring that participants are motivated, that material is relevant and transferable to the specific problems and settings at hand, that training includes numerous examples and opportunities for practice and application, that training addresses the underlying principles of whatever material is being taught, and, finally, that participants receive sufficient feedback to encourage their correct application and use of the material. Application of these principles should guide how different training approaches are used. In short, if training is to be effective, managers and employees must heed the rule of three and the rule of seven.

Increasing attention is being given to organizational learning, because change is normal. This chapter has discussed strategies for generating new ideas in organizations as well as for increasing forward-looking leadership from managers. A main HRM challenge is how to help workers at all levels apply better thinking in their jobs; the chapter has discussed the leadership capabilities of thinking ahead, thinking again, and thinking across as an example. The upshot is that "mindware" will be at least as important as hardware and software in the years ahead. Managers and employees also need to be familiar with processes for managing and experiencing continuous change. The focus on learning has the potential to transform this area, putting greater emphasis on how and how much organizations expect their managers and employees to keep learning.

KEY TERMS

Adult learning theory
Coaching
Cross-training
Decentralization of training
Development
Education
HAIR qualities
Learning
Learning plateaus
Mentoring
Motivation in training
Needs assessment
On-the-job training

Organizational learning
Overlearning
Positive reinforcement
Principles of learning
Rule of seven
Rule of three
Seminars and presentations
Simulation
Strategic focus
Surveys
Training
Training evaluation
Transference

EXERCISES

Class Discussion

1. Discuss how the principles of learning apply to a training program to improve the effectiveness of (a) agency trainers, (b) frontline customer service personnel, and (c) supervisors.

2. To what extent is your organization a "learning organization"? In what ways is it such an organization? In what ways is it not? Make a list on the board of things that make up a learning organization.

3. Examine how the paradoxes and trends discussed in the introduction to this book are present in the agencies where students in the class are employed.

4. Discuss the following statement made by Polish writer Stanisław Lec: "You will always find some Eskimos ready to instruct the Congolese on how to cope with heat waves."

Team Activities

5. Explore the paradoxes in the following statement: "We don't want to invest money in training because it is lost when employees leave."

6. Identify three objectives of a training program for new police officers. Focus on what participants should be able to do on completion. What should be the relative emphasis of OJT, in-house seminars, cross-training, simulation, and formal education? Why?

7. Analyze a training program for first-time supervisors. Identify some competencies for which overlearning is relevant.

8. Many employees complain about a lack of positive reinforcement. Design a training program to increase its use, and link it to performance appraisal.

9. Consider the following statement in the context of the paradox of needs: "Never let your professional development be governed by your organization."

Individual Assignments

10. Identify job-related skills and knowledge that you think your employer should provide. How likely is it that your employer will actually help you acquire these skills? How will not acquiring these skills or knowledge affect your job performance and career? What can you do to acquire these KSAs?

11. Develop some ideas for improving performance in your workplace. How might you go about getting these accepted and implemented? Should you be disappointed if not all of your ideas find acceptance?

12. You have been appointed the training director in a large state agency to develop and implement programs for staff personnel. Paradoxically, insufficient monies are budgeted for this training. Can you resolve this dilemma? How?

13. Develop a skills acquisition plan for yourself. Identify specific skills that you would like to acquire and when you will be acquiring them over the next 24 months. Try to identify at least one additional skill to be acquired every 6 months.

APPENDIX

Needs Assessment and Evaluation for Training

Needs Assessment

Needs assessment is undertaken to determine training requirements that are (1) organization- and unitwide, (2) related to improving specific work processes, and (3) concerned with the training needs of individual employees (Balisi, 2014; Jacobson, Rubin, & Selden, 2002). At the organizational level, assessments can reflect a variety of different purposes from which training and development needs are inferred. Van Wart (2010) discusses seven types: (1) ethics assessments; (2) mission, values, vision, and planning reviews; (3) customer and citizen assessments; (4) employee assessments; (5) performance reviews; (6) benchmarking; and (7) quality assessments. Each of these areas may suggest different needs for employee training.

Many organizations conduct comprehensive employee **surveys** involving 50–100 items that address working conditions, supervisory relations and collegiality, access to technology, policies and procedures, salary and benefits, availability of training and development, and many other areas. To ensure that employees participate in such surveys, managers may instruct them to complete the questionnaires during work hours; to ensure confidentiality, employee names are not attached to their responses. Exhibit 9.8 presents a sample of a survey instrument. Low ratings in any area are obviously cause for concern and may prompt further inquiry and future training. Such employee surveys are increasingly common. Their development and implementation is often led by human resource staff; results are disseminated to managers and employees through a succession of meetings.

Needs assessments are also sometimes conducted before work process improvements are undertaken. Top managers may require lower units to rigorously assess their performance by collecting performance data and by evaluating their delivery processes to detect shortfalls or bottlenecks. In addition, they may also require units to increase performance. Such improvement processes may require skills that employees currently do not have. Justification for training and development usually follows from the context in which the assessment is made: concern for general workforce development, strategic concern for retention and development, future needs of departments, or efforts to ensure or improve organizational processes and functions. These justifications can be augmented by the following efficiency-focused analytical techniques: comparing the cost of training and follow-up to that of recruiting new employees or using consultants, or comparing the cost of continuing to use outdated technology to the cost of dealing with resulting errors. Managers can also compare the costs of different training methods to further justify their preferred training approaches. Such analyses can help to further bolster the case for using training (Fitz-enz & Davison, 2001).

Evaluation

Training evaluation aims to assess the effectiveness or impact of training and typically involves feedback from employees and managers. Different evaluation approaches can be distinguished: (1) subjective assessments of training seminars (obtained immediately after completion), (2) subsequent assessments about on-the-job improvements (obtained some period, usually 1 to 3 months, after completion), and (3) controlled pre- and posttraining evaluations.

It is common to obtain information on employees' perceptions of training immediately afterward. Exhibit 9.9 presents a sample evaluation instrument that can readily be adapted for organizational use. Human resource departments sometimes use such forms for soliciting input about their service from other departments. The advantage of collecting

Exhibit 9.8   Selected Survey Questions for Needs Assessment

Please note your level of agreement with the following statements, using the following letter codes:

SA	=	Strongly Agree
A	=	Agree
DK/CS	=	Don't Know, Can't Say
D	=	Disagree
SD	=	Strongly Disagree

A. Rules and Regulations

I am familiar with the laws and policies concerning workplace discrimination.
I am familiar with the laws and policies concerning workplace harassment.
I am familiar with workplace leave policies.
I am familiar with my benefit options.
I am familiar with the workplace safety rules of my unit.
I am familiar with ethics requirements and expectations.

B. Workplace Relations

My unit needs to improve its teamwork.
My supervisor is considerate and supportive.
I can approach my supervisor to discuss almost any work-related issue.
In our unit, we conduct ourselves in ethical ways.
Colleagues support one another in carrying out their duties.

C. Training Needs

Please identify three specific areas about which you would like to receive training:

1.
2.
3.

D. Performance Management

I know the vision and mission of my department.
We maintain high standards.
We regularly survey our customers about their needs.
We regularly compare our performance to that of similar organizations.
We regularly measure and discuss our performance.
My supervisor tells me what is expected from me.
My supervisor provides adequate, ongoing feedback about my performance.
My skills are well used.
Colleagues discuss new or better approaches for improving operations.
Overall, my coworkers have solid professional skills.

Exhibit 9.9   Questions for Evaluating Training Seminars

Please note your level of agreement with the following statements, using the following 5-point scale:

5 = Strongly Agree

4 = Agree

3 = Don't Know, Can't Say

2 = Disagree

1 = Strongly Disagree

The training accomplished the stated objectives.

The training was useful.

The level of difficulty was about right.

The material was presented in a way that facilitated learning.

The training included practical examples.

The training material was up-to-date.

The trainer tried to address our needs.

The trainer was approachable.

The supplemental materials were relevant and useful.

Overall, I am satisfied with the training I received.

. . . and please answer the following questions, too:

What was the most helpful thing that you learned today?

Would you like a follow-up session? If so, when?

What suggestions do you have for improving this session?

students' perceptions is that they are easy to obtain. Although low levels of satisfaction indicate that training has not met the employees' needs, high satisfaction levels do not necessarily mean that the training has met either employee or organizational needs. Management may fail to follow up, and there may be problems of transference that obstruct application. Furthermore, in some settings employees generally give positive ratings to trainers, reducing the effectiveness of this approach. It is also problematic that some training evaluation assessments focus on the delivery style rather than on the content and usefulness of the material; the former information is useful to trainers rather than to managers.

Evaluations should take place after employees have opportunities to apply the training material. Such evaluations emphasize changes in on-the-job behaviors as well as results obtained through training (Kirkpatrick & Kirkpatrick, 2007). For example, training on hazardous materials should include behaviors associated with safe handling, such as the use of protective devices and the consultation of handbooks to better familiarize the employee with properties of chemicals. Considerable effort has been made to improve the evaluation of training's effectiveness, such as for health professionals who are involved in terrorism response efforts (e.g., Markenson, Reilly, & DiMaggio, 2005) and in many other areas and in other countries as well (McElhatton, 2013; Yang, Wu, Xu, & Chen, 2012).

Discussion of evaluation frequently conjures up images of carefully controlled, scientific approaches. However, it is seldom feasible to find equivalent groups for evaluation purposes in training, and measurement of pre- and posttraining capabilities cannot conclusively prove that skill increases are caused by training—skills could be affected by other learning that is not part of formal training. Still, many examples show how evaluation can be used to improve training initiatives and program performance. In one instance, a county jail faced numerous complaints from inmates' families about visitation and release procedures. The jail director suspected that part of the problem was inadequate client orientation. A client satisfaction survey was conducted among inmates' family members before a customer service training improvement effort was undertaken, and a second survey was conducted shortly thereafter. By comparing the scores, the director was able to determine the effect of the training on the families' satisfaction with service. Such cases show how training evaluation is used for program decision making and improvement of future training (Fitz-enz & Davison, 2001; Phillips, 1997).

NOTES

1. Some workers also have strong intrinsic desires for pursuing training and improvement. Though these workers will need little extrinsic motivation, they may face the task of persuading others of the critical need for them to pursue T&D.

2. Argyris (1990) distinguishes between single-loop learning, or processes that lead to the achievement of better alignment and expected outcomes, and double-loop learning, which calls into question the "fundamentals" of expected goals, methods, values, and so on.

3. Singapore's public service has long used management tools developed by Shell, one of the first foreign companies in Singapore and chosen partly for its management practices.

REFERENCES

Alexander, D. (2014, March 12). U.S. Navy bars 151 sailors from jobs after sex assault review. Reuters. Retrieved from http://www.reuters.com/article/2014/03/12/us-usa-defense-assault-idUSBREA2B28H20140312

Argyris, C. (1990). *Overcoming organizational defenses: Facilitating organizational learning.* Boston: Allyn & Bacon.

Argyris, C., & Schön, D. (1978). *Organizational learning: A theory of action perspective.* Reading, MA: Addison-Wesley.

Balisi, S. (2014). Training needs assessment in the Botswana public service: A case study of five state sector ministries. *Teaching Public Administration, 32*(2), 127–143.

Berman, E. M. (2008). Implementing ethics. In E. M. Berman (Ed.), *Encyclopedia of public administration and public policy* (2nd ed., pp. 461–464). New York: Marcel Dekker.

Berman, E. M., & Kim, C.-G. (2010). Creativity management in public organizations: Jump-starting innovation. *Public Performance & Management Review, 33*(4), 619–652.

Borger, J. (2002, September 6). War game was fixed to ensure American victory, claims general. *Guardian*. Retrieved from http://www.guardian.co.uk/world/2002/aug/21/usa.julianborger

Bumiller, E. (2012, November 15). Panetta orders review of ethics training for military officers. *New York Times*. Retrieved from http://www.nytimes.com/2012/11/16/us/panetta-orders-review-of-ethics-training-for-officers.html?_r = 0

Cameron, E., & Green, M. (2009). *Making sense of change management: A complete guide to the models, tools and techniques of organizational change.* London: Kogan Page.

Clark, C. S. (2013, June 12). Program managers too scarce in the federal government, survey concludes. *Government Executive*. Retrieved from http://www.govexec.com/management/2013/06/program-managers-too-scarce-federal-government-survey-concludes/64787/

Collins, J. (2001). *Good to great: Why some companies make the leap . . . and others don't.* New York: Harper Business.

Common, R. (2004). Organisational learning in a political environment: Improving policy-making in UK government. *Policy Studies, 25*(1), 35–49.

Crummy, K. E., & Olinger, D. (2012, April 8). Handling of 911 calls in metro Denver spurs look at training, policies. *Denver Post*. Retrieved from http://www.denverpost.com/ci_20349414/handling-911-calls-metro-denver-spurs-look-at

Duarte, N. (2012). *HBR guide to persuasive presentations.* Boston: Harvard Business Review Press.

Fernández-Aráoz, C. (2014, June). 21st-century talent spotting. *Harvard Business Review*, pp. 46–56.

Fitz-enz, J., & Davison, B. (2001). *How to measure human resources management* (3rd ed.). New York: McGraw-Hill.

Gillespie, G. (2002). High tech training for military air traffic control. *Summit, 5*(4), 25.

Government of India. (2010). *Civil services report.* New Delhi: Ministry of Personnel, Public Grievances and Pension, Department of Administrative Reforms and Public Grievances. Retrieved from http://darpg.nic.in/darpgwebsite_cms/Document/file/Civil_Services_Survey_2010.pdf

Hayes, J. (2010). *The theory and practice of change management* (3rd ed.). New York: Palgrave Macmillan.

Hiatt, J. M. (2004). *Employee's survival guide to change.* Loveland, CO: Prosci Research.

International City/County Management Association. (2002). *Supervisory skills for improving employee performance* [Training package]. Washington, DC: Author.

International City/County Management Association. (2003). *So, now you're a trainer!* Washington, DC: Author. Retrieved from http://bookstore.icma.org/freedocs/NowYoureATrainer.pdf

Jacobson, W., Rubin, E. V., & Selden, S. C. (2002). Examining training in large municipalities: Linking individual and organizational training needs. *Public Personnel Management, 31*(4), 485–506.

Kettl, D. E., & DiIulio, J. J., Jr. (Eds.). (1995). *Inside the reinvention machine: Appraising governmental reform.* Washington, DC: Brookings Institution.

Kirkpatrick, D. L., & Kirkpatrick, J. D. (2007). *Implementing the four levels: A practical guide for effective evaluation of training programs.* San Francisco: Berrett-Koehler.

Kotter, J. P. (1996). *Leading change.* Boston: Harvard Business School Press.

Lawson, K. (1997). *Improving on-the-job training and coaching.* Alexandria, VA: ASTD.

Lin, C. Y.-Y., & Edvinsson, L. (2011). *National intellectual capital: A comparison of 40 countries.* New York: Springer.

Lucas, R. W. (2003). *The creative training idea book: Inspired tips and techniques for engaging and effective learning.* New York: AMACOM.

Markenson, D., Reilly, M. J., & DiMaggio, C. (2005, November). Public health department training of emergency medical technicians for bioterrorism and public health emergencies: Results of a national assessment. *Journal of Public Health Management & Practice, 11*(Suppl.), S68–S74.

McElhatton, J. (2013, April 16). GAO questions metrics of training effectiveness for contracting staffs. *Federal Times.* Retrieved from http://www.federaltimes.com/article/20130416/ACQUISITION03/304160007/GAO-questions-metrics-training-effectiveness-contracting-staffs

Menzel, D. C. (2007). *Ethics management for public administrators: Building organizations of integrity.* New York: M. E. Sharpe.

Menzel, D. C. (2010). *Ethics moments in government: Cases and controversies.* New York: Taylor & Francis.

National Commission on the State and Local Government Public Service. (1993). *Hard truths/tough choices: An agenda for state and local reform.* Albany, NY: Rockefeller Institute of Government.

Neo, B. S., & Chen, G. (2007). *Dynamic governance: Embedding culture, capabilities and change in Singapore.* Singapore: World Scientific Publishing.

Newstrom, J., Scannell, E., & Nilson, C. (1998). *The complete games trainers play: Vol. 1.* New York: McGraw-Hill.

New Zealand State Services Commission. (2013a). *Leadership strategy for the state services.* Wellington: Author. Retrieved from http://www.ssc.govt.nz/sites/all/files/leadership-strategy-for-state-services.pdf

New Zealand State Services Commission. (2013b). *Strengthening your career: Senior leader development across the public service—A guide to the Senior Leader Career Development programme and career boards.* Wellington: Author. Retrieved from http://www.ssc.govt.nz/sites/all/files/strengthening-your-career-2013.pdf

Noe, R. A. (2012). *Employee training and development* (6th ed.). New York: McGraw-Hill/Irwin.

Nonaka, I., & Takeuchi, H. (1995). *The knowledge-creating company: How Japanese companies create the dynamics of innovation.* New York: Oxford University Press.

Perry, R. W., & Mankin, L. D. (2005). Preparing for the unthinkable: Managers, terrorism and the HRM function. *Public Personnel Management, 34*(2), 175–193.

Peters, K. M. (2005, November 1). Testing their mettle. *Government Executive.* Retrieved from http://www.govexec.com/story_page.cfm?filepath = /features/1105-01/1105-01s2.htm

Phillips, J. J. (1997). *Handbook of training evaluation and measurement methods.* Houston, TX: Gulf.

Poocharoen, O. O., & Lee, C. (2013). Talent management in the public sector: A comparative study of Singapore, Malaysia, and Thailand. *Public Management Review, 15*(8), 1185–1207.

Reese, L. A., & Lindenberg, K. E. (2003). The importance of training on sexual harassment policy outcomes. *Review of Public Personnel Administration, 23*(3), 175–191.

Senge, P. M. (1990). *The fifth discipline: The art and practice of the learning organization.* New York: Doubleday/Currency.

Svara, J. S. (2015). *The ethics primer for public administrators in government and nonprofit organizations* (2nd ed.). Burlington, MA: Jones & Bartlett.

Ugori, U. (1997). Career-impeding supervisory behaviors. *Public Administration Review, 57*(3), 250–255.

U.S. Government Accountability Office. (2003). *Strategic planning and distributive learning could benefit the special operations forces foreign language program.* Washington, DC: Author.

U.S. Government Accountability Office. (2013). *Agency needs to improve outcome measures to demonstrate the value of its innovation lab.* Washington, DC: Author.

U.S. Office of Personnel Management. (2010). *Guide to Senior Executive Service qualifications.* Washington, DC: Author. Retrieved from http://www.opm.gov/ses/references/GuidetoSESQuals_2010.pdf

U.S. Office of Personnel Management. (2013). *Federal Employee Viewpoint Survey results: Employees influencing change.* Washington, DC: Author. Retrieved from http://www.fedview.opm.gov/2013files/2013_Governmentwide_Management_Report.pdf

Vallance, S. (1999). Performance appraisal in Singapore, Thailand and the Philippines: A cultural perspective. *Australian Journal of Public Administration, 58*(4), 78–95.

Van Wart, M. (2010). Increasing organizational investment in employee development. In S. E. Condrey (Ed.), *Handbook of human resource management in government* (3rd ed.). San Francisco: Jossey-Bass.

Van Wart, M., Cayer, N. J., & Cook, S. (1993). *Handbook of training and development for the public sector: A comprehensive resource.* San Francisco: Jossey-Bass.

Vince, R. (2000). Learning in public organizations in 2010. *Public Money and Management, 20*(1), 39–44.

West, J. P., & Berman, E. M. (2004). Ethics training efforts in U.S. cities: Content and impact. *Public Integrity, 6*(3), 189–206.

West, J. P., & Berman, E. M. (Eds.). (2007). *The ethics edge* (2nd ed.). Washington, DC: International City/County Management Association.

Williams, R. L. (2007). [Review of the book *Ethics management for public administrators: Building organizations of integrity,* by D. C. Menzel]. *Public Integrity, 9*(4), 389–391.

Wu, L., & Rocheleau, B. (2001). Formal versus informal end user training in public and private organizations. *Public Performance & Management Review, 24*(4), 312–321.

Yang, B., Zheng, W., & Li, M. (2006). Confucian view of learning and implications for developing human resources. *Advances in Developing Human Resources, 8*(3), 346–354.

Yang, K., Wu, F., Xu, X., & Chen, T. (2012). The challenge of civil servant training in China: A case study of Nanning City. *Review of Public Personnel Administration, 32*(2), 169–191.

Appraisal

A Process in Search of a Technique

If anyone can solve the performance evaluation problem, he should be entitled to the Nobel, the Pulitzer, and the Heisman in the same year.

—Federal personnel official

After studying this chapter, you should be able to

- explain why personnel appraisal is at once important and paradoxical;
- weigh the advantages and drawbacks of typical types of appraisals;
- understand that appraisal accuracy may not be an important goal;
- appreciate why the root problem is not technical in nature;
- demonstrate and apply appraisal interview skills in a self-study exercise;
- discuss why an annual formal evaluation may be the least important component in an effective appraisal system;
- recognize the value of an exit interview;
- suggest ways to improve the appraisal process;
- assess alternative approaches to employee discipline;
- evaluate an appraisal system, through fieldwork, in the light of the characteristics of a "litigation-proof" process; and
- explore future trends in this arena.

After having been hired, classified, paid, and trained, an employee will have his or her work reviewed as the organization seeks to assess the extent to which the individual's and the collective's needs coincide—or conflict.[1] Employees may value the appraisal process for both intrinsic reasons (as a validation of their workplace efficacy) and extrinsic ones (recognitions and rewards). Because many decisions can hinge on these ratings, the process of personnel evaluation is central to strategic human resource management; indeed, the success of an organization depends on the success of its workforce. Playing key functions in employee compliance, performance improvement, and system validation, appraisal reviews are mechanisms for reinforcing organizational values. They provide data on the effectiveness of recruitment, position management, training, and compensation (where such information is most frequently used). In the absence of this feedback, executives may have difficulty understanding how well other management functions are working. Likewise, judgments about individual conduct may be needed if performance-contingent decisions in such areas are to have a rational basis.

Clearly, then, employee evaluation is central to strategic importance for the agency and a chief activity of management. It is also a complex function that includes administrative decisions (e.g., pay), developmental recommendations (e.g., training), technical issues (system design), and interpersonal skills (superior–subordinate appraisal interviews). Although a well-designed assessment process can benefit an agency, creating, implementing, and maintaining such a process is not easy. Programs serving multiple purposes, in fact, may serve none of them in an effective manner.

An emotional, inexact, human process, appraisal is a complicated, difficult task— one that most organizations do not do well. A review of performance reviews reveals that they are not good at what they are meant to do: evaluate performance. Two-thirds of employees receiving the highest scores in a typical appraisal system were not actually the organization's highest performers (Thompson, 2014). In business, for instance, one survey revealed that 87% of managers and employees believed that performance appraisals were neither useful nor effective (Williams, 2012). A meta-analysis of more than 600 studies found that at least 30% of evaluations *decreased* employee performance (Kluger & DeNisi, 1996). Furthermore, less than 10% of organizations judge their appraisal systems to be effective (Grensing-Pophal, 2001). Not surprisingly, some organizations have elected to eliminate appraisals; SAS Institute, the software industry leader, ended its policy of conducting annual reviews and held a bonfire celebration to burn its appraisal forms.

There is no reason to believe, as discussed below, that the situation is any different in government. Indeed, only 20% of federal employees indicate that the appraisal system motivates them to do a better job (U.S. Merit Systems Protection Board [U.S. MSPB], 2003). Donna D. Beecher (2003), a founding member of the federal Senior Executive Service, has written that "performance management systems are rarely effective in communicating specific expectations, providing helpful feedback, engaging and energizing the workforce and raising levels of employee satisfaction" (pp. 463–464). It is highly ineffective for organizations to conduct individual evaluations if their systems are problematic. It is premature, for instance, to install a pay-for-performance plan if a sound appraisal system is not in place.

Personnel appraisal, in short, is one of an administrator's most difficult issues, precisely because it is both important and problematic. Few other managerial functions have attracted more attention and so successfully resisted solution (Halachmi, 1995, p. 322). Personnel systems predicated on rewarding merit are undermined when questionable appraisal practices take place. What these widely used and intensely disliked systems reveal is that instead of being a solution, they are often part of the problem; in point of fact, many authorities agree that appraisal can contribute to Enron-style corruption (Meisler, 2003; Spector, 2003) or workplace violence (Exhibit 10.1).

It follows that paradoxes abound:

- People are often less certain about "where they stand" after an assessment than they were before.
- The higher an individual rises in a department, the lower the likelihood that he or she will receive high-quality feedback; most employees perceive little connection between performance and pay.
- Although the communication of negative information is difficult, not communicating it can be much worse.
- Because it is impossible to have good ideas without also having a lot of bad ones, rewarding success is not enough; failure should also be recognized, especially if it results in valuable lessons.
- While authorities recommend that appraisal be kept separate from salary decisions (appraisal is supposed to be a developmental function; see, e.g., DelPo, 2007), most organizations link them tightly.
- The more appraisal systems are made objective, the more it is evident that there is no way to avoid their inherent subjectivity.
- If a manager does not effectively address an employee behavioral problem, the manager may be regarded as a problem.

Despite—or perhaps because of—the vexing, intractable nature of personnel review, political pressures to "just do it and get it over with" are substantial. Although members of the general public know about the problems with appraisals from their own work experiences, they nevertheless make an odd assumption: Because evaluations are done successfully (somewhere) in business bureaucracies, they should especially be used in government agencies. For this human resource function, myth is not merely more important than reality—it often seems to be reality.

This chapter begins with a discussion of the evolution, as eerie as it is, of the appraisal function. Common types of appraisals, who does them, and typical—if robust—rating errors are then examined. That section climaxes with a discussion of the fundamental and beguiling reason for these problems. Diagnosis completed, attention then shifts to ways to design and improve evaluation programs, including an examination of disciplinary systems. This leads to a specification of the characteristics of a system that could withstand legal scrutiny. The chapter closes by sketching future trends in this administrative function. The overall objective is to describe the processes, problems, and paradoxes, as well as to critique the premises on which many appraisal systems are built.

Exhibit 10.1 Preventing the "Ultimate" Evaluation Solution

The work site definitely has become leaner and meaner in the last generation. The traditional social contract between employers and their minions has been broken: Organizations downsize, management turns over, employees wonder if they are "next," pay stagnates, benefits become more expensive, and computers monitor humans (see discussion later in this chapter). Beginning in the 1970s (with blue-collar employees) and continuing since the 1980s (with white-collar personnel), organizations have regarded employees not as valuable assets but rather as a flexible cost to be excreted as necessary. It is perhaps no coincidence that violence at work has become an important issue (U.S. MSPB, 2012).

About half of workplace violence is employee on employee; the balance involves citizens or family members entering offices. One in four employees has been harassed, threatened, or assaulted. Homicide is the leading cause of occupational death for women, the second for men. The costs of abuse to personal well-being, organizational productivity, and American society as a whole are substantial in terms of counseling, turnover, litigation, security measures, insurance premiums, and the social fabric of the nation.

Although many people—incorrectly—feel secure at work, offices, courts, schools, and hospitals are no longer safe havens; occupational violence is a serious and underreported public health problem. Indeed, defense mechanisms such as denial ("It can't happen here") actually put employees at risk and impede preventive measures.

Management policies, including personnel practices, can both provoke and help prevent violence in organizations. Factors such as poor job design, inadequate space, outdated equipment, demanding schedules and workloads, and weak interpersonal skills can lead to aggressive behavior. A key critical incident provoking danger, for instance, is performance appraisal, with its possible consequences: close supervision, layoff, and termination.

In 2007, following a negative performance review, a National Aeronautics and Space Administration employee shot his supervisor and took another employee hostage before killing himself. In an already tense workplace, the evaluation method used, how it is employed, and the way people learn about its results can produce paroxysms of shock and sorrow, anger, and rage. For example, not long ago a newly elected speaker of a southern state house of representatives distributed Christmas cards to all house employees on December 24. Those who received their cards in green envelopes still had their jobs; those whose cards were in red envelopes were told to clear out their desks by 5:00 P.M. Similarly (albeit without the Christmas cheer), a private corporation called the police to secure the premises and then asked 200 employees to go to the auditorium. They were told to turn in their building keys and were escorted from the company property. Neither of these cases, luckily, resulted in violence, but abandoned employees sometimes return to their former workplaces months or years later to exact retribution.

Although it is not possible to prevent violence entirely in American culture, the probability of crisis incidents in organizations can be lowered through proactive and reactive planning:

- Establishing a violence prevention team to conduct a needs assessment that includes a review of personnel recruitment, training, and appraisal practices, as well as employee assistance programs (see Chapter 8)
- Training managers to identify risks and to defuse problems that can precipitate incidents (perpetrators often evidence early warning signs, such as talking about retribution, threatening supervisors, and showing weapons to other employees)

- Developing a plan comprising a clear agency policy on workplace violence, a penalty schedule for violations, a mechanism to report incidents, and employee training on topics such as stress management, problem solving, and negotiation
- Forming a crisis management group, to be mobilized when needed, with defined procedures and role definitions in key areas such as employee communication (e.g., rumor hotlines), media relations, and counseling (see, e.g., Minor, 1995).

As an official in a security firm observed, "A written plan may not work, but an unwritten plan never works." A carefully designed approach can mean the difference between acting decisively to cope with and defuse incidents and reacting haphazardly in a manner that may exacerbate a difficult situation. Yet prevention is a low priority in many organizations, as many employers remain unprepared to deal with dangerous episodes.

Likely to increase in the years ahead, trauma at work is related to management practices as well as to all the experiences employees bring to the organization. Still, effective human resource management makes it easier to contain than violence in the streets. It is the agency's responsibility to provide a safe working environment—and the Americans with Disabilities Act (see Chapter 2) specifies that reasonable accommodations must be made for those who exhibit stress-related symptoms that may lead to aggressive conduct. Is this duty being fulfilled in your jurisdiction? To help answer this and other questions, see Bates (2007) for a comprehensive prevention and response strategy. Also see Kelloway, Barling, and Harrell (2006), Lewis (2006), and Chapter 8, this volume.

Contrary to popular perceptions, the U.S. Postal Service—a very large, visible, hierarchical, and high-pressure organization—does not have a higher rate of dangerous incidents than other organizations. Indeed, it has an effective prevention program that has reduced the amount of workplace violence (Trimble, 1998, p. 12).

EVOLUTION

The paradoxical nature of service ratings—rarely do they deliver in practice what is promised in theory—stems from the legacy of the spoils system (Chapter 1). Aghast at widespread looting, plunder, and corruption during the spoils system era, good-government groups, armed with scientific management techniques such as job analysis (Chapter 5), sought to guarantee competence by insulating employees from political influence. Reformers established merit systems, which were closely monitored by nonpartisan civil service commissions. As these systems evolved, the emphasis was on recruiting meritorious people (Chapter 3) and protecting them from partisan entanglements. Less attention was devoted to divining ways to evaluate their work; after all, the system was designed to select competent workers in the first place.

It should not be surprising, then, that although concern for employee appraisal has existed for a long time (Congress mandated evaluations as early as 1842), the topic for decades was a stepchild slighted by both academicians and managers. The dramatic growth of government during the Great Depression and World War II, however, culminated in considerable interest in appraisal programs, so that by the 1950s many jurisdictions had adopted them.

Characteristic of the times, an underlying faith in science to control, direct, and measure human performance resulted in the continuing search for the perfect evaluative scheme—or, if not the perfect scheme, then at least ways to improve existing technology. Thus, many of the early systems, based on personal traits (discussed in the next section), were widely criticized for failing to differentiate among employees: Virtually everyone received a "satisfactory" rating.

Aiming to correct this problem, the 1978 Civil Service Reform Act sought to evaluate employees not on subjective characteristics but on objective, job-related performance standards. This effort, in turn, produced its own set of problems, so that the National Performance Review (NPR, 1993, p. 36) declared it to be dysfunctional and detrimental to the success of governmental programs. In calling for simplified, decentralized, team-based evaluation, the NPR de-emphasized the need for results-oriented appraisals. This approach, as discussed below, has not been any more successful than it has been in business. Today, service ratings remain as the most criticized area of human resource management and seem to be endured only because realistic alternatives are not currently in wide use.

Abandoning the function altogether may not be a solution, however, because human beings have always made informal or formal evaluations of others. The challenge is to decide what to appraise in a manner that meets the needs of the organization and the individual. Ironically, "the primary problem supervisors encounter is not *knowing* who are the best performers, but rather *measuring* and *documenting* performance differentials" (Perry, 2003, p. 147). Recognize that in appraisal there is no "objective reality," or ways to measure it, on which everyone agrees. What can be said is that the best are very good, the worst are very bad, and the middle is very large.

APPRAISAL SYSTEMS

You probably wouldn't worry about what people think of you if you could know how seldom they do.

—Olin Miller

Designing and implementing a good assessment system takes not only planning but the achievement of a realistic balance as well. Some of the problems of appraisal are excessive subjectivity leading to various types of bias, lack of clarity, absence of preparation, over-reliance on annual assessment, use of forms that are too simple or too complex, and systems that are too ambitious. A well-thought-out evaluation process can reduce, but not eliminate, these concerns.

The Appraisal Process

The supervisor who comes to the annual review period and realizes that he or she had better get started has already failed. Appraisal is a yearlong endeavor, and no amount of last-minute work can make up for the preparation that a sound evaluation entails. The process should comprise a minimum of four elements: initial goal setting, monitoring and data availability, continuous feedback, and annual assessment.

- *Initial goal setting.* All employees should have goals. Many of these may simply be to meet productivity and quality guidelines, which, depending on the level of resources and level of competence, may be easy or hard to attain. Other goals may be to improve in select areas; still others may be to take on new projects. Goals may also concern improving competencies (knowledge, skills, and abilities) and thus be developmental in nature. No matter what the goals are, however, they should be specified in the beginning of the year. Ideally this is done as the result of the previous evaluation. Exceptions occur when there is a new employee, someone is given a new assignment, or an individual has performance issues during the evaluation period. If goals are assumed and not clarified, the subordinate has a legitimate reason to dispute the annual assessment review.

- *Monitoring and data availability.* Monitoring should occur throughout the year: Frontline personnel should be monitored regularly, and supervisors, specialists, lead workers, and managers intermittently. Data may come from observations, discussions with the employee, performance information, work products, complaints or compliments about the individual, work communications, and multirater evaluations. These data provide the basis for the annual review, which should include performance averages and comparisons as well as critical incident data. Performance averages reflect simple outputs (e.g., how many cases did the employee handle?), while comparisons reflect quality dimensions (e.g., what was the error rate of the cases handled and how did that rate compare with requirements or the rates of other personnel?). When such data are not available, the assessment will ultimately become more subjective.

     The **critical incident technique** identifies unusually superior or inferior events (not routine performance). The approach is usually required to assign the highest or lowest ratings in a category in a comments section. It can also be used developmentally for midyear improvements. A critical incident log may be helpful in supporting other appraisal formats provided that the anecdotal nature of the method is understood as both a strength and a weakness (e.g., people's mistakes, rather than achievements, may be more likely to be recorded because employees are supposed to be competent).

- *Continuous feedback.* All employees should get regular feedback. When positive, it should take the form of supportive gestures (e.g., "good job" comments, or subtle indications that work is being properly done). When minor or operational adjustments are necessary, appropriate directions should be provided, with opportunities for clarification and verification if necessary. When significant corrections are necessary, candid (but polite) feedback and coaching are required and should be documented. This ensures that there are no "surprises" in the annual assessment. If feedback has not been clear and no attempt has been made to coach an employee, then the individual may dispute a low ranking. Some organizations require formal midyear assessments for new employees or for all staff. These should be standard procedure for first-year recruits because of their new context; midyear assessments for all veteran employees, however, need to be balanced with supervisors' spans of control as well as their other duties (accordingly, decisions regarding midyear reviews are generally up to the appraisers).

- *Annual assessment.* Yearly reviews may all be completed in a single period or on individual employees' anniversary employment dates. Some organizations may stipulate the use of particular forms or provide choices of formats. No matter what the format and organizational culture, however, all personnel deserve annual assessments to know how they are doing; likewise, the organization deserves the accountability that comes with a process that affects other HRM functions. The types of annual assessments vary. The basic types, in their pure form, are discussed below.

Because there are few jobs with clear, comprehensive, objective output measures that eliminate the need for judgment, the most widely used evaluation methods are judgmental in nature.[2] What differentiates them is the degree of subjectivity that is likely in the judgments made. The approaches can readily be grouped as trait-, behavior-, and results-based systems. It should be noted, however, that there is considerable variety in available techniques. Not only are they frequently combined with one another, but also different systems may be used for various types of employees.[3] Only the most familiar are examined here, and even these, albeit in differing degrees, can produce either **deficient evaluations** (not all pertinent factors are considered) or **contaminated evaluations** (irrelevant considerations are included).

Trait-Based Appraisals

Trait-based appraisals require assessments concerning the degree to which someone possesses certain desired personal characteristics deemed important for the job (Exhibit 10.2). These could include factors such as dependability, adaptability, productivity, communication, teamwork, continuous improvement, analytic ability, citizen service, professional development, stewardship, and cultural sensitivity.[4] Descriptors must avoid being either too vague or not job related. Vagueness occurs when there are too few categories to evaluate and when definitions of categories are not provided. To emphasize job relatedness, forms should avoid the inclusion of traits that elicit personal feelings. Accordingly, categories such as friendliness (ambiguous), enthusiasm (amorphous), manner (open to multiple interpretations), and drive (can mean many different things unless better articulated) should not be used.

The strengths of trait rating are considerable. First, the appraisal form can be used across the organization with relative ease as a "default" assessment instrument; thus, it is an efficient method. Second, when the instrument is well constructed, the characteristics can address most major areas of work in a generic way; opportunities to provide additional factors make it possible to avoid oversights. Third, the form can be completed quickly and is readily computerized and electronically filed. Fourth, it is particularly appropriate for many frontline jobs in which the functions are mechanical, repetitive, and/or standardized.

The weaknesses of this type of format are also considerable. First, it is not customized, so everyone is evaluated using the same categories. Second, the potential to add categories is rarely taken advantage of, no matter how desirable it might be to expand the categories. Third,

Exhibit 10.2 Example of Trait Appraisal

Appraisal Categories		Unsatisfactory	Needs improvement	Satisfactory	More than satisfactory	Outstanding	Not applicable
Dependability	Follows instructions; responds to management direction						
	Is punctual						
	Attends regularly; absences are not problematic						
	Comments:						
Adaptability	Adapts to changes in the work environment						
	Manages competing demands						
	Performs well under pressure						
	Comments:						
Productivity	Meets productivity standards						
	Completes work in a timely manner						
	Works accurately						
	Achieves established objectives						
	Comments:						
(Etc.)	(6 to 12 additional categories)						
Other	(filled in by evaluator)						
Overall comments and evaluation	Comments:						
	Signature: _____						
Person evaluated	Response: (not required) Signature: _____						

ironically, the ease of filling out the form can be a major problem. Since the annual evaluation may be the single most important event in an employee's year, rushing to get it done can lead to complications when judgments are made without care and documentation. Fourth, the format is not particularly good at capturing the essence of nonroutine and managerial work. When it is used for managers, additional specialized categories are often included. Fifth, as a sole assessment strategy, trait-based methods are reactive and past oriented.

There are colorful iterations of such graphic rating scales based on the characteristics chosen, their definitions (if any), and the number of categories (adjective or numeric) used. None, however, overcome serious validity and reliability questions. Thus, because it is difficult to define personality characteristics (much less the extent to which someone has them), subordinates may become suspicious, if not resentful, especially because this technique has little value for the purpose of performance improvement. Human traits, after all, are relatively stable aspects of individuals.

This is not to suggest that vivid personal characteristics are unimportant in job performance; individuals can hardly perform without them. And people routinely make trait judgments about one another, because this can be a powerful way to describe someone, so powerful that recalling something about a person typically elicits mention of a personal trait. Indeed, the use of flexible, subjective criteria seems inevitable, especially for ambiguous managerial jobs. Such characteristics often provide a shorthand way of describing an individual's behavior and performance. This may explain why some experts contend not only that personal rating scales are reasonably valid and reliable but also that they are more acceptable to both employers and employees (Cascio, 2009; Gomez-Mejia, Balkin, & Cardy, 2011). And the use of informal (if not formal) subjective criteria seems inevitable. It follows, then, that "courts do not reject subjectivity" (Barrett & Kernan, 1987, p. 489) so long as raters focus on behavior and support judgments with facts. If they are consistent in their subjectivity, a defensible judgment has been rendered. As Grote (2011) notes:

> This deference by the courts to employers has been stated as the *business judgment rule* and has been acknowledged by the courts plainly: "We do not assume the role of a 'super-personnel department,' assessing the merits or even the rationality of employers' nondiscriminatory business decisions." . . . the appraisal is a record of a manager's opinion. If the employee and the manager disagree about that opinion, the manager wins. (p. 10)

If personal attributes are a more natural way to think about other people (Gomez-Mejia et al., 2011), then requiring supervisors to use nontrait techniques—as most organizations do—is a sleight of hand that introduces well-known psychometric mistakes (discussed below). Many employees tend to believe that their supervisors' liking of them influences evaluations, and to the extent that managers like good workers such compatibility can represent "true" performance levels. Attempting to minimize or remove subjectivity may not improve accuracy (Hauenstein, 1998).

Despite the inherent subjectivity of the trait-based format, it continues to be practiced because human beings frequently make trait judgments about others in daily life. The approach, although often inscrutable, seems intuitively sensible as a result.

When used with accurate job descriptions and trained evaluators, such ratings may become more credible. Even when the traits measured are job related (e.g., job knowledge, dependability), however, a landmark court opinion (*Brito v. Zia Co.,* 1973) criticized their subjective nature because the results were not anchored in or related to actual work behavior.[5]

Just as trait rating is no longer likely to be used alone, neither is the narrative essay technique; in fact, in one form or another written descriptions often supplement most appraisal formats. Because individuals are unique, thoughtful commentary can provide personal, intimate, and detailed information. Done well, such an essay includes discussion of an employee's strengths and weaknesses, developmental needs, and potential for advancement. The premise of this approach is that a candid statement is at least as useful as more complicated techniques. Or maybe not.

The "anything goes" nature of such essays lends them to rater idiosyncrasies, subjectivity, and pop psychology. Their interesting, sometimes ambiguous, statements (e.g., "When it comes to self-improvement, Van Westman has great potential") make comparisons virtually impossible. Subject to a wide variety of rater errors (see discussion in a later section), essay-type appraisals are often deficient and contaminated, and thereby unreliable and invalid. Although they may be of value to the employees reviewed, they are of limited use to anyone else. In their pure, stand-alone form, then, narratives are rarely used.

Behavior-Based Systems

Unlike trait-focused methods, which emphasize generic personal characteristics, **behavior-based evaluation systems** attempt to discern what a person actually does. The relatively tangible, objective nature of these systems makes them more legally defensible than personality scales. In point of fact, civil rights legislation enacted in the middle of the 20th century led to the development of tools that concentrate on behavioral data.

A **behaviorally anchored rating system (BARS)** defines the dimensions to be evaluated in behavioral terms and anchors or describes different performance levels (Exhibit 10.3). When introduced in the 1960s, BARS was claimed to be a breakthrough technology because raters could match observed activity on a scale instead of judging it as desired or undesired (Halachmi, 1995, p. 330). Because the scales are developed from the experience of employees, it was also thought that user acceptance was likely. As a job-related system, BARS remains relatively invulnerable to legal challenge.

Such a rating system relies on a customized analysis of the specific job and a breakdown of its component parts. Behavior-based assessments are used in many professions, such as teaching. In a teaching-oriented college, for instance (see Exhibit 10.3), three categories are usually identified and defined with possible metrics: teaching, service, and research. Such categories are in use throughout higher education, but their relative importance and definition differ (e.g., publication may be de-emphasized in a community college but emphasized in a research institution). At the K–12 level, categories might include planning skills, lesson plan implementation, communication with students, student evaluation activities, knowledge of curriculum and subject matter, alignment with prescribed curriculum, setting of high student expectations, evidence of academic growth, maintenance of discipline, collegiality with other teachers and parents, and following regulations.[6] Behavioral assessments

Exhibit 10.3 Behaviorally Anchored Rating Scale Using a Faculty Evaluation at a Teaching-Oriented Institution

Appraisal Categories		Unsatisfactory	Needs improvement	Satisfactory	More than satisfactory	Outstanding
Teaching	Teaching is the single most important function for this faculty position, constituting approximately 50% of the job responsibilities. Elements of quality teaching include the syllabus, lectures, tests, projects, writing assignments, practice assignments, timely feedback, use of appropriate technology, teaching innovation, etc. Teaching quality is assessed by peer evaluations, student evaluations, instructor self-assessment, external assessments where appropriate, among others. A self-assessment of teaching is required.					
	Evaluation statement:					
Research	Research is approximately 30% of a faculty member's responsibility for this position. Elements of a quality research agenda include a regular output of publications, the overall quality of publications, and professional contributions of a scholarly nature. Demonstration of quantity is provided by a portfolio of published work. The quality of work can be demonstrated by the number of citations of publications, journal impact factor, journal ranking, publisher reputation, etc. Demonstration of professional contributions can include roles as editor, advisory board member, symposium editor, etc. Pedagogical, applied, and artistic contributions are relevant as defined by the department.					
	Evaluation statement:					

Appraisal Categories		Unsatisfactory	Needs improvement	Satisfactory	More than satisfactory	Outstanding
Service	Service is approximately 20% of a faculty member's responsibility for this position. Service must include university service but may include service to the community as appropriate. University service includes support of general departmental operations (e.g., faculty meetings, convocation, commencement, etc.), faculty governance on various committees at various levels in the university, and student support (e.g., club adviser), as well as special administrative assignments. Community service should be related to the university, such as positions on municipal advisory boards, consulting (pro bono or paid), and speaking to or serving on professional organizations related to one's discipline. Demonstrations of these activities should be included in a written statement, with documentation as appropriate.					
	Evaluation statement:					
Overall comments and evaluation						

are common for many professional groups—including police, fire/EMS, attorneys, accountants, social workers, analysts, medical staff, human resource management, and computer support staff—where job components can be identified for large employee groups. However, tailored behavior-based assessments are possible for any job or job group in which the position description is translated into an appraisal instrument.

In contrast to trait-based formats, then, behavior-based methods tend not to suffer from either vagueness or lack of job specificity. In fact, that is their strength—they are customized for a job or job group: The categories fit the work environment. The use of seemingly concrete data suggests that vagueness may be reduced. Finally, behavior-based systems tend to suit professional jobs, because they provide nuanced language and categories that professions themselves use.

Yet this method is often not practical because each job category requires its own BARS; either for economic reasons or because of a lack of employees in a specific job, the approach is often infeasible. An agency may not have personnel who have the time or inclination to design the instrument and then get it approved in a large bureaucratic setting. Indeed, many organizations prefer standardization partly because behavior-based forms can reduce uniformity and allow for perceptions of potentially unequal criteria.

Gomez-Mejia et al. (2011) argue that if personal attributes are a more natural way to think about other people, then requiring supervisors to use BARS (or, for that matter, any nontrait technique) is merely a sleight of hand that introduces psychometric errors (discussed in the "Rating Errors" section below). Indeed, these authors cite research findings indicating that both employers and employees prefer trait-based systems. Other studies have demonstrated that managers and staff personnel do not make much of a distinction between BARS and trait scales (e.g., Wiersma & Latham, 1986). Not surprisingly, there is little evidence to support the superiority of the behavior-based technique over other approaches.

Finally, most experts do not find that the potential gains in using BARS warrant the substantial investment the system requires in time and resources. Thus, where this technique is used, it may play a residual role, limited either to a small number of selected job categories or to the developmental function of personnel appraisal. Overall, then, whatever else trait- and behavior-based systems may do, they are largely silent on the question of what an employee is to accomplish, as they do little to ensure the alignment of goals and future plans except in areas denoted as deficient. For that reason, like trait-based assessment instruments, behavior-based instruments are often combined with a future-oriented or developmental component, similar to the appraisal type discussed next.

Results-Based Systems

Measuring neither personal characteristics nor employee behaviors, **results-based systems**, or outcome-oriented approaches, attempt to calibrate employees' contributions to the success of the organization. Although "results" have always been of keen interest to administrators, **management by objectives (MBO)** promises to achieve substantial organization–individual goal congruence.[7] Introduced in the 1950s, this most common results-focused approach establishes agency objectives, which are followed in cascading fashion by derivative objectives for every department, all managers, and each employee. Such linkages promise not only to minimize distortions common in the appraisal process (see below) but also to mitigate the paradox of needs. MBO systems require specific, realistic objectives, mutually agreed-upon goals, interim progress reviews, and comparison between actual and expected accomplishments at the end of the rating period. One format is to provide a form to be completed (Exhibit 10.4); another is to require an essay describing what has been accomplished during the year, how it matches with the employee's predetermined goals, and an outline of future goals (Exhibit 10.5). The process may be facilitated through the use of specific, measurable, achievable, relevant, time-bound (SMART) criteria to guide objective setting and completion (Yemm, 2013).

Exhibit 10.4 Management-by-Objectives Appraisal: Predetermined Format

Appraisal Categories		Unsatisfactory	Needs improvement	Satisfactory	More than satisfactory	Outstanding
Goal 1 (Selected by supervisor and person evaluated)	Describe the goal, project, or operational function to be accomplished. Describe the progress made. Discuss challenges met and challenges overcome. Describe future progress needed. (To be completed by person evaluated)					
Goal 2 (Selected by supervisor and person evaluated)	Describe the goal, project, or operational function to be accomplished. Describe the progress made. Discuss challenges met and challenges overcome. Describe future progress needed. (To be completed by person evaluated)					
Goal 3 (Selected by supervisor and person evaluated)	Describe the goal, project, or operational function to be accomplished. Describe the progress made. Discuss challenges met and challenges overcome. Describe future progress needed. (To be completed by person evaluated)					
Goal 4 (Selected by supervisor and person evaluated)	Describe the goal, project, or operational function to be accomplished. Describe the progress made. Discuss challenges met and challenges overcome. Describe future progress needed. (To be completed by person evaluated)					
Goal 5 (Selected by supervisor and person evaluated)	Describe the goal, project, or operational function to be accomplished. Describe the progress made. Discuss challenges met and challenges overcome. Describe future progress needed. (To be completed by person evaluated)					
Comments and overall evaluation						

The advantages of results-based systems are substantial. First, they ensure that there are in fact goals as well as linkage among individual and organizational goals. These systems encourage striving for higher goals. Second, they provide plans for accomplishment against predetermined objectives. Therefore, they are future oriented rather than past oriented. Third, the results-based approach emphasizes manager–subordinate interaction and joint planning. Finally, it is well regarded as a method by managers, executives, and employees who have project-based work flows.

Exhibit 10.5   Management-by-Objectives Appraisal: Narrative Format

---

Instructions to the person being evaluated. Write an essay about (a) your objectives for this year, (b) progress made in meeting those objectives, and (c) objectives for next year.

a. In discussing objectives, be sure to include all the major areas or elements of your job, as well as personal developmental goals. What concrete plans were made in the beginning or during the year to maintain or improve performance/quality/innovation, introduce new programs, discontinue nonfunctioning activities, and other issues? When appropriate, be sure to delineate where objectives fit into multiyear projects or initiatives and identify when the overarching goal is projected to be completed.

b. What is the status in meeting objectives? Provide concrete data on both process efforts (e.g., training sessions provided, number of individual coaching sessions) and actual results (outputs and/or outcomes). What unplanned challenges occurred? What unexpected opportunities occurred and were taken advantage of?

c. What are your objectives for next year? Specify the steps that will be used to achieve them and the way(s) in which achievement will be measured.

Despite its rationality and evidence of effectiveness, MBO, like other appraisal techniques, also has serious drawbacks:

- Although development of objectives may not be as technically demanding as it is in BARS, the process nevertheless is quite time-consuming; an effective program takes 3 to 5 years to implement. (Accordingly, few agencies adopt the formal hierarchical process to ensure organization–department–manager–employee linkage.)
- There are likely to be conflicting objectives, differing views on the appropriateness of the objectives, and disagreements about the extent to which objectives are mutually agreed upon—and fulfilled.
- Because it focuses on short-term goals, a compulsive "results no matter what" mentality can produce predictable quality and ethical problems, as anything that gets in the way of the objective gets shunted aside. (How a job is done often is as critical as output.)
- Not only is it difficult to establish equally challenging objectives for all people, but also expectations that they will invariably improve (an MBO-induced "treadmill") can lead to user acceptance problems.
- The technique can stifle creativity because employees may define their jobs narrowly (as they "work to quota"), leaving some problems undetected and unresolved.
- Teamwork is likely to suffer if people become preoccupied with personal objectives at the expense of collegiality. (They may fulfill their goals but not be good all-around performers.)
- The method may not assist in the employee development function because performance outcomes do not indicate directions for desired change.

In short, results-oriented approaches are susceptible to contamination errors when results are affected by factors beyond employee control and deficiency problems. When results are emphasized, important "organizational citizenship" behaviors may be discouraged. Further, the considerable effort that supervisors must devote to results-based performance schemes often provokes comments like this one from a federal manager: "I don't have time to do evaluations, now, so how would I have the time to do this?" (quoted in Ziegler, 2004, p. 6). The sort of rational planning embodied in MBO is seldom effective; the human condition is too complicated and human reason too frail. "MBO works," Peter F. Drucker, the founder of the technique, wrote, "if you know the objective; 90 percent of the time you don't" (quoted in Gilson, 2007); the law of unintended consequences likely will prevail. Treating people like the responsible professionals they are, instead of like rational robots, will probably produce superior results. "You can be totally rational with a machine," wrote Akio Moriata, founder of Sony. "But, if you work with people, sometimes logic has to take a back seat to understanding." Nevertheless, MBO in particular remains a popular technique for appraising managers because their roles are often ambiguous, and it does provide a measure of accomplishment against predetermined objectives.

Commentary

> *Man plans, God laughs.*
>
> —Yiddish proverb

To summarize, Exhibit 10.6 specifies the promise, problems, and prospects of the three categories of appraisal. Although the intuitive appeal of trait rating is considerable, this method is highly susceptible to both contamination and deficiency errors. Its future potential, accordingly, is limited to a supplemental role in the review process because of subjectivity and vulnerability to court challenge. Systems based on employee behavior hold substantial promise because they are job related—something most judges expect. They, too, are likely to play a modest role in the years ahead, however, largely because of their susceptibility to deficiency errors and, in the case of BARS, high technical demands coupled with limited applicability. Results-derived approaches,

Exhibit 10.6   Promise, Problems, and Prospects of Person-Centered Appraisal Systems

System	Promise	Characteristic Problems	Prospects
Trait based	High (intuitive appeal)	High (contamination and deficiency errors)	Low (supplemental role)
Behavior based	High (job related)	Average (susceptible to deficiency errors)	Average (high technical demands)
Results based	High (face validity)	Average (deficiency problems)	Average (emphasizes accomplishments)

like the others, have face validity but often suffer from a host of deficiency and implementation problems. Still, they do emphasize actual accomplishments, as opposed to personalities or behaviors, and therefore may survive litigation.

Although combinations of techniques can offer advantages, available research does not support a clear choice among methods. Because each has its own strengths and weaknesses, selecting one to cure a problem likely will cause a new problem; there is no foolproof approach. Notice, too, that all three systems are backward-looking. Because there is no systematic continuous improvement process, they may be self-defeating as they perpetuate the organizational status quo. The more efficiently traditional appraisals are done, paradoxically, the more likely it is that the organization will remain the same. Hauser and Fay (1997, p. 193) wistfully argue that the search for the perfect instrument—a goal that has eluded industrial psychologists for more than 70 years—is now largely regarded as futile. Instead, they suggest, efforts to improve the overall process likely will provide much larger returns than attempts to develop (and redevelop) seemingly better rating forms every time a new high official takes office.

The technique used, then, is decidedly not the central issue in personnel appraisal, because the type of tool does not seem to make much difference (Cardy & Dobbins, 1994). A National Research Council study found no conclusive evidence to support claims that distinguishing between behaviors and traits has much effect on ratings. Psychologically, supervisors form broad opinions that affect their evaluation of actual work behaviors. There is little research evidence that rating systems using job-specific factors produce results much different from those using general dimensions (Milkovich & Wigdor, 1991).

That is, available data indicate that judgments about performance are not necessarily correlated with results (Murphy & Cleveland, 1995) precisely because these decisions rely on cognitive abilities that are notoriously prone to error (see "Rating Errors" below). Compromised evaluations are common. Not surprisingly, the choice of tools is less significant than the fact that employees often have little confidence in the abilities of managers to implement the tools effectively. It is not the assessment technique that fails to yield an accurate evaluation, it is the manager. The NPR (1993) found, for instance, that "performance ratings are unevenly distributed by grade, gender, occupation, geographic location, ethnic group, and agency" (although shoe size was not mentioned) (p. 32). That is, technically sophisticated and well-designed systems do not operate in a vacuum; organizational culture, leadership credibility, employer–employee relations, and levels of trust affect the efficacy of appraisal processes. Stated differently, it is important to ensure that there is an alignment between organizational performance and individual performance (Riccucci & Lurie, 2001). The exact evaluation method used is less relevant than building a goal-oriented organization where people have productive attitudes toward work and each other (Palguta, 2001).

Appraisal software programs nonetheless promise to (1) enable managers to select predigested forms (or to design their own), (2) walk them through form completion (including tips and hints, provision of preprogrammed phrases and prompts for examples, and even reminders when appraisals are due), and (3) verify their work with arithmetical, logical consistency and legal checks before printing out professional-looking reports. Prospective customers are assured by one enthusiastic vendor that using an automated system is "a snap." A balanced review of these programs, however, reveals that they run on algorithms with no knowledge of organizational culture, job standards, or individual performance—elements whose importance is likely to intensify in a virtual workplace. Indeed, such programs make the process too easy; managers should devote real thought to appraisals, and not simply point and click. The software contributes nothing to the most important part of service ratings: the manager–employee interview (discussed in a subsequent section).

RATERS

Given that common appraisal methods are judgmental in character, an important question is, Who makes this judgment? Traditionally, there was one answer: the subordinate's immediate supervisor. Other knowledgeable information sources include the ratee, peers, computers, and outsiders.

Self-appraisals, based on the belief that employees have important insights about how their jobs should be done, can provide valuable data, particularly when supervisors and subordinates engage in joint goal setting. These evaluations are, however, subject to distortions, including self-congratulation and, less likely, self-incrimination. (For a devastating critique of this technique, see Kunreuther, 2008.) People tend to be inadequate judges of their own performance. Inept individuals are often self-assured because they are deficient in self-monitoring skills; their incompetence robs them of the aptitude to realize their own incompetence. Such employees lack the ability to see that they lack ability: They confuse confidence with competence. It is well established, for instance, that many people attribute their good performance to their own efforts and blame their poor performance on other factors. These biases can be moderated if objective standards exist and the ratee is regularly provided candid feedback. Still, because self-evaluations tend to focus on personal growth and motivation, they are best used for developmental rather than administrative purposes.

As work in some organizations has changed from a stable set of tasks done by one person to a more fluid ensemble of changing requirements done by groups of employees, **peer evaluations**, also known as team evaluations, have become appropriate. In an agency culture high in trust, where coworkers develop rating scales and have access to relevant information, such assessments can be accurate. When these conditions do not exist, supervisors likely will be reluctant to give up control, and subordinates will often see these techniques as a disruptive competition that can easily be sabotaged by lenient ratings or converted into "popularity contests." Thus, these reviews are often most useful when done anonymously and for developmental reasons.

The objective of **electronic monitoring** (via e-mail and video surveillance, website blocking, GPS tracking) is to increase productivity, improve quality, and reduce costs by continuously collecting performance data, pinpointing problems, and providing immediate feedback (Flynn, 2008). To illustrate, in one form of such monitoring, sensor-rich lapel badges transmit data about the wearers' frequency of, and gestures during, conversations. When electronic monitoring provides objective performance appraisals, employee satisfaction and improved morale could result. Today, computer-generated statistics are the basis for evaluations of millions of office workers. The virtual work site of the future is almost certainly going to expand the collection and use of such information. Indeed, as software becomes more sophisticated, a wide variety of occupations (e.g., medicine, engineering, accounting) are likely to undergo electronic scrutiny. Harrah's casinos, for instance, track the smiles of workers on the grounds that they affect customer satisfaction. When implemented without reasonable safeguards (e.g., employee access to data, rights to challenge erroneous records, rating decisions made on the basis of nonelectronic as well as electronic information), such a program can create an "electronic sweatshop" environment that is damaging to employee creativity, morale, and health. If personnel feel helpless, manipulated, and exploited, then they will eventually find ways to circumvent most monitoring techniques.[8] Overall, the majority of employers monitor the activities of their subordinates in some form, and clandestine observation is widespread; the trend is toward more surveillance, more loss of privacy, and greater control by management (West & Bowman, 2014).

Finally, multirater systems, or **360° evaluation systems**—those that gather information from superiors, subordinates, peers, and citizens—by definition provide more data than other approaches. More data may produce more reliable, but not necessarily more valid, information. The administratively complex and time-consuming nature of these systems is compounded by distrust among peers and a lack of convergence among the different information sources. That is, managers may be confronted with a host of seemingly conflicting opinions—all of which may be accurate from the opinion holders' respective viewpoints. Systems that assure respondent anonymity and encourage participant responsibility, nevertheless, no doubt supply some useful feedback for improving both management processes and employee development.

The value of the method reveals itself, paradoxically, when it is used as a developmental—not an evaluation—technique, an approach that reduces fear and encourages honesty. Organizations that use multirater systems in this way foster a "development culture" that, in turn, results in higher performance (Carson, 2006). In short, although an employee's immediate supervisor is apt to play an important role in the rating process, seeking feedback from other sources is increasingly seen as a way to obtain a more holistic understanding of performance (Society for Human Resource Management, 2000). Currently, one-third of American organizations use multirater systems. An effective program is one that has been developed in a participatory manner, has been pilot tested, and provides adequate training to both managers and employees. There has been little critical evaluation of 360° appraisal systems.

RATING ERRORS

The use of ratings assumes (rather naively) that the definition of job performance is clear, that direct measures are available to assess the employee, and that evaluators are reasonably objective and exact. With the misguided conviction that objective criteria are possible, necessary, and desirable, "precise imprecision" is sought. This illusion of manageability encourages officials to believe that personnel can be manipulated to contain, correct, and/or reverse their behaviors if only they devote a little extra effort to their work. Yet regardless of the appraisal instrument used, a large number of well-known kinds of errors (examined below) occur in the process. These errors result from four primary causes: cognitive limitations, intentional manipulation, organizational influences, and human nature. When errors happen—and they are difficult to prevent—not only is the rater's judgment called into question, but also the resulting evaluation may leave the ratee unable to judge his or her own performance accurately.

Cognitive Limitations

When confronted with large amounts of information, people generally seek ways to simplify that information. **Cognitive information processing theory** maintains that appraisal is a complex memory task involving data acquisition, storage, retrieval, and analysis. To process data, people employ subjective categories that in turn produce no less than six problems. Thus, **compatibility error** (also known as similarity or liking error) is potent because both compatibility and ratings are person focused. Indeed, as noted above, most employees believe that their supervisors' opinions of them influences evaluations (Cardy & Dobbins, 1994). When the Wei dynasty in China rated the performance of its household members in the third century, the philosopher Sin Yu noted, "An imperial rater of nine grades seldom rates men according to their merits, but always according to his likes and dislikes." This error may be tempered, however, to the extent that managers like good performers. In other words, flaws in rating can represent, paradoxically, "true" performance levels, and removing such errors may not improve accuracy (Hauenstein, 1998).

The second mental shortcut is the **spillover effect** (also known as the halo effect or black mark effect); that is, if the ratee does one thing exceptionally well (halo) or poorly (black mark), then that unfairly reflects on everything else he or she does. Third, the **recency effect** occurs when a major event has taken place just prior to the time of the evaluation and overshadows all other incidents. Fourth, **contrast error** exists when people are rated relative to other people instead of against performance standards. Fifth, **outcome bias** is the tendency of raters to see the result of performance as the most important consideration in an evaluation regardless of whether or not it was the consequence of factors beyond the employee's control. Finally, **actor/observer bias** (partially alluded to earlier) occurs when subordinates, as actors, point to external factors to explain their weak performance, whereas supervisors, as observers, attribute that weak performance to the employees. Ratings, in short, are as much a reflection of raters as they are of those being evaluated.

Intentional Manipulation

The second general source of rating problems is that appraisals in many organizations are adroitly seen as a political, not necessarily a rational, exercise. Results are deliberately manipulated to be higher or lower than employees deserve. The goal is not measurement accuracy, but rather management discretion and organizational effectiveness. The Nuclear Regulatory Commission, for instance, "made a conscious decision to be more generous with its *performance* ratings" (Losey, 2008, p. 1; emphasis added) in order to boost retention, acknowledge increased workloads, and be more competitive with private industry. As one expert has noted: "It would be naive to think of performance appraisal as anything other than a political process. . . . Rating accuracy is not always the goal of appraisers . . . , and there are many situations where providing *inaccurate* appraisal data is sound management" (Hauenstein, 1998, p. 428, emphasis added; also see Tziner, Murphy, & Cleveland, 2005).

Accordingly, **leniency error**, also known as friendliness error or the "Santa Claus effect," is the consequence of a desire to maintain good working relationships, maximize the size of a merit raise, encourage a marginal employee, show empathy for someone with personal problems, or avoid confrontations (and appeals) with an aggressive worker.[9] This type of error is exacerbated when raters think that other supervisors are inflating their employees' evaluations. There is a consensus that when reviews are done for administrative purposes (as opposed to for developmental reasons) they tend toward leniency (Curtis, Harvey, & Ravden, 2005). The aphorism "We'd rather be ruined by praise than saved by criticism" seems apropos.

Fair appraisals, in short, are not necessarily accurate. Indeed, **severity error** (the "horns effect") may be present when an appraisal is used as a way either to send a message to a good performer that some aspect of his or her work needs improvement or to shock an average employee into higher performance. More than 70% of managers in one survey reported that they deliberately inflated or deflated evaluations for such reasons (Longenecker & Ludwig, 1990). Note that the inherent conflict of interest present in supervisory evaluations is a powerful political reason likely to make the leniency effect prevail over other psychometric errors. That is, if all (or most) subordinate evaluations are inflated, then the supervisor may look like an effective manager; if the appraisals are not so inflated, then his or her management abilities may be called into question.[10]

The employer, however, has an obligation to conduct appraisals with due care. This duty may be violated (as a result of the Santa Claus effect) when a poor performer receives satisfactory ratings and subsequently is subjected to attempts at termination. The importance of proper diligence is illustrated by a 2000 Federal Bureau of Investigation report that pointed to concerns about Arab nationals training to fly aircraft with no interest in learning how to land them. The report was rejected, unread by an FBI official who in 2002 received a cash award for performing his duties in safeguarding the American people.

Organizational Influences

This leads to an examination of a set of organizational influences that cause a variety of problems. The first of these is insufficient management commitment to performance appraisal. In light of the difficulties with various evaluation schemes, much skepticism, a sense of futility, and even doubts about the possibility of performance appraisal exist (Nigro, Nigro, & Kellough, 2007, p. 170). For some administrators, then, investing heavily in these systems does not make a lot of sense. One Florida school superintendent, referring to legislative dictates, noted that "we have changed proficiency standards 21 times in the last six years," and 100% of teachers were rated "highly effective" or "effective." Stated differently, the daily press of business makes evaluations a peripheral, not a central, responsibility. According to the U.S. Merit Systems Protection Board, "When the work being evaluated involves more than counting widgets, human judgment will always come into play. Therefore, spending inordinate amounts of resources trying to objectify the evaluation of performance will likely not be successful" (Crum, 2009, p. 3). Appraisals are often isolated not only from getting the job done but also from strategic organizational planning and budgeting.

Overall, then, there are few incentives—and sometimes there are genuine disincentives—to use appraisal as a management tool. To illustrate, higher management may not support an assessment, it could be reversed on appeal, and/or the supervisor could be falsely accused of sex, age, or racial discrimination. Why convert an acceptable worker into a hostile one when it can be stated that the person meets expectations? Employee reviews, then, are often done for the sake of evaluation: an irrelevant, once-a-year formality to complain about, complete, and forget in the service of administrative rules. Such programs quickly become "organizational wallpaper," existing in the background but not necessarily expected to add value.

Such an attitude can produce the **error of central tendency** (if not leniency), where nearly all employees are rated as satisfactory—if for no other reason than that higher or lower scores may require time-consuming documentation. This "error," in turn, is reinforced by the **no money effect**—that is, either there are insufficient funds to distribute or they are awarded on an across-the-board basis (see also Chapter 7). All of these problems are exacerbated if reviews are tied, as they often are, to salary decisions. When mandated by organizational policy, appraisals tend to be less accurate and helpful for developmental purposes as employees and managers focus on monetary rewards. Performance pay plans (Chapter 7) raise the stakes in appraisal, making the already existing problems more severe. Evaluations, in fact, may be done to support decisions to offer raises, rather than the other way around.

Human Nature

Overall, cognitive, political, and organizational limitations help explain the reasons for rater error. Although some of these constraints can be addressed in training (see "Improving the Process" below), something more fundamental lies at the root of personnel appraisal difficulties: human nature. Its pertinent aspects are revealed by risk aversion, implicit personality theory, conflicting role expectations, and personal reluctance.

Defending judgments in open court is not something most people relish; as a result, it is natural for supervisors to try to reduce risk by being aware of all possible pitfalls in the appraisal process. Because reviews are often tied to pay, the well-known tendency to avoid supplying negative feedback is exacerbated (especially in performance pay programs) when supervisors seek to avoid inflicting financial harm on employees. When managers must convey negative information, they have three options: avoid giving it, delay giving it, or distort it. The last option is often the most viable, if inaccurate (Curtis et al., 2005, p. 45). A paradox arises, however, when playing safe through leniency may invite a legal challenge on the grounds that appraisals do not differentiate employees by performance (Halachmi, 1995, p. 325).

Second, **implicit personality theory** suggests that people generally judge the "whole person" based on limited data (stereotyping based on first impressions, or the spillover effect); ratings then tend to justify these global opinions rather than accurately gauge performance. Third, conflicting role expectations are inherent in the appraisal process because evaluators must reconcile being helpful coaches with acting as critical judges. In playing these roles, administrators (as noted earlier) also, in effect, evaluate themselves. Human nature suggests that better-than-deserved ratings will occur because a manager's own skills may be called into question should his or her employees receive poor evaluations.

Finally, appraisal systems are complicated by the understandable distaste that people have for formally evaluating others. Because there is no such thing as infallible judgment, when administrators must take responsibility for judging the worth of others, "it is dangerously close to a violation of the integrity of the person" (McGregor, 1957, p. 90). Most people, especially in light of all the other questions about the reliability and validity of personnel appraisal, are as reluctant to judge others as they are to be judged themselves. It is onerous, in other words, to "play God."

Given the human condition, it is unwise to expect much from the appraisal function. It is little wonder, then, that many share the sentiment expressed in this aphorism: "Appraisal is given by someone who does not want to give it to someone who does not want to get it." More formally: "Employees and supervisors alike dread the end-of-the-year annual performance appraisal cycle, when productivity plummets for several weeks and hard feelings translate into grievances. The paperwork, damage to self-esteem, and drops in productivity are simply not worth [it]" (Beecher, 2003, p. 464).[11] Indeed, since evaluations typically occur once a year and paydays are at least once a month, employees are regularly reminded of the real and perceived problems with appraisals. Such problems are not confined to U.S. institutions, as the Chinese experience suggests (Exhibit 10.7). Lest one think that human nature in its various forms inevitably makes personnel review a hopeless task, Exhibit 10.8 presents a balanced defense of this human resource function from one veteran county manager (see also McElveen, 2000).

To summarize, because many jobs are not amenable to objective assessment and quantification, ratings typically incorporate nonperformance factors—for all the reasons discussed above. When this occurs, of course, it leads to a violation of the most revered

---

Exhibit 10.7   Personnel Appraisal in Chinese Public Service

As a result of the economic boom during the last generation, China is seen as an important model in a globalizing world economy. Reforms in Chinese government, accordingly, have sought to more appropriately fit a market economy. Key factors animating change include these:

- Hierarchical loyalty is a highly prized cultural value.
- The Chinese Communist Party (CCP) plays a leading role in the management of the civil service, including maintenance of complete personnel files on each public servant.
- Decentralization of personnel management decision making, following international trends, has taken place, but the hegemonic role of the CCP ensures that the civil service remains more centralized than in many other nations.

Reforms have been problematic because employees tend to be rewarded on the basis of organizational loyalty and political reliability, at the expense of technical competence. A gap exists between national policy makers (who look to increase economic gains) and agency managers (who emphasize organizational harmony, a cultural factor threatened by use of foreign personnel techniques). Indeed, China as a whole may be understood as a conflict and convergence of Confucianism, socialism, and capitalism, with the first having the most enduring effect.

In 1993, the State Council launched civil service reform aimed specifically at personnel evaluation to improve administrative efficiency, enhance government capacity, and reduce corruption. The Ministry of Personnel directed that appraisals should be based on merit (work ability and accomplishments) and political integrity (support and understanding of CCP ideology). The linkage of salary to rank and years of service indicates that seniority is a significant factor as well. The goal of good relations with superiors and coworkers in Chinese culture suggests that personal loyalty complements these criteria.

The changes included appraisal committees, self-reviews, and supervisory evaluations in an attempt to institutionalize openness, fairness, and participation. Employee reviews soon experienced many of the problems discussed in this chapter. The system was rife with inaccurate data, and supervisors were not held responsible for falsifying records. Exacerbating the situation was that government found it difficult to retain and motivate personnel when more lucrative careers were available in China's surging business sector.

Although leaders understand the significance of performance appraisal, the changes underestimated the importance of maintaining organizational harmony in a collectivistic culture. The prevailing system is characterized by authority networks composed of reciprocal relations and mutual obligations. Managers reward loyal followers with career opportunities, raises, training, and moral support, while subordinates aid superiors during occasions such as performance ratings or political strife. To maintain goodwill, harmony is critical. In an environment valuing interpersonal associations and personal trust, people tend to avoid confrontation and to save face. Social accord and stability are seen as priorities more important than individual rights; individuals are regarded as part of a network of social connections (*guanxi*) where personal interests are subordinated to the group's interests.

This conflicts with more discriminating evaluation techniques used in Western societies, notably the United States. Because both managers and employees in China find the cost of revealing each other's performance weaknesses too high (i.e., the disruption of comity), foreign systems that assess performance by pointing out weaknesses have not been used effectively. The impact of the reform is undermined when managers cover up deficiencies of subordinates and manipulate appraisal results. In return, workers overlook the faults of managers. Nearly all civil servants are rated excellent or satisfactory and receive merit awards because pointing out each other's problems risks deep resentment and, in the end, conflict. When systems are attempted that require that some employees be rated as less than satisfactory, in practice it is newcomers who receive poor ratings. If there are no junior employees, then everyone in the office takes turns getting a low score.

In countries that focus on harmony, appraisal systems might be designed to bring out the importance of each person to the organization by treating each one as a stakeholder. Perhaps gainsharing systems (Chapter 7) would be beneficial so that the gains derived from department productivity could be distributed among managers and staff. An approach that emphasizes the positive aspects of employee performance, in any case, likely will be more efficacious than one that damages agency well-being and interpersonal relationships. While it may be true that as the market economy expands the importance of personal relations may diminish, it is also true that a nation's cultural heritage cannot be easily transformed; reforms can only be adapted to that heritage.

SOURCES: Benson, Debroux, Yuasa, and Zhu (2000); Black, Gregersen, and Mendenhall (1992); Burns (1999); Chou (2008); Gregersen, Hite, and Black (1996); Muñoz (2006); Yang and Zheng (2003); Yang, Zheng, and Li (2006); Zhao (1994). See also Liu and Dong (2012).

Exhibit 10.8 A Manager's View of Performance Appraisal: Theory in Practice

Mary L. Maguire
Assistant to the Chief/Public Affairs Officer
Department of Fire and Rescue Services
Loudoun County, Virginia

Having over 30 years' experience with city and county government agencies, I have been on the giving and receiving ends of a wide array of evaluation methods. From early forms where we were judged on appearance to the more modern ones where we are judged on contributions to the organization, each has had its merits. The one that seems to be the most promising is our current performance management system. It is a multifaceted tool aimed at improving individual employee job performance. It is anticipated that through the effective use of this system managers and supervisors will be better equipped to help with the enhancement, motivation, and retention of employees (the county's most valuable resource), while achieving the goals of the organization.

From the moment new employees set foot through the door, they are provided instructions on the finer points of the system. Through classes and written guidelines, managers and subordinates are told that emphasis on the following skill sets is essential to be successful:

- Performance planning
- Coaching
- Counseling
- Documenting
- Recognizing and motivating employees
- Handling unsatisfactory performance
- Assessing performance

Although each piece is equally important, the attention focuses heavily on the beginning and end components: planning and assessment. This, so to speak, is where the "rubber meets the road"—where the employees believe they will be rewarded for their efforts. As one of many tools in the managerial toolbox, the planning and assessment components provide opportunities for the organization to show its commitment to its employees, while recognizing them for their contributions. The system is designed to ensure that all parties involved know up front what is expected. Through the other components— coaching, counseling, documenting, recognizing and motivating employees, and addressing unsatisfactory performance—supervisors are provided with additional tools for guiding and evaluating their employees. By effectively outlining expectations, maintaining open dialogues between manager and subordinate, keeping employees apprised of their progress, and redirecting them when improvement is needed, everyone knows what to expect when it comes time for the year-end evaluation.

All this looks good on paper, but how does it really work? Annually, employees outline their goals as they relate to the department's mission and that of the county. The goals are then weighted based on relative importance. Both the employee and the supervisor develop and sign this plan; it can be modified as the person's duties evolve. In this way, there will be no surprises by the end of the evaluation cycle.

As the year draws to a close, the subordinate is asked to prepare a self-evaluation, while the manager develops a separate assessment. When they meet, an open dialogue helps clarify areas where the supervisor may have some concern. If consensus is reached and the employee has met the goals and objectives, he or she may receive a merit increase. If expectations were exceeded, then he or she may be nominated for a performance bonus. (If the employee is not in agreement with the evaluation, then he or she can make an appeal. It is interesting to note that employees are also afforded the opportunity to anonymously evaluate their supervisor.) During the meeting, a development of the upcoming year's plan will begin. Although this process can be quite time-consuming and cumbersome, it is effective.

I was a bit dismayed, however, when I actually began comparing this process with a list of common appraisal defects. For every effort made to fight these defects, I could find example after example where the defects still exist. For instance, the system was designed so that we would not be evaluating for evaluation's sake. Although great pains were taken to eliminate this problem, many agencies find themselves scrambling at the end of the year to get the paperwork done. In addition, while the system was set up so that it can be modified at any time, this does not really occur. Employees continually find themselves being evaluated with respect to the goals found in outdated plans.

Managers also continue to pit people against one another and have a tendency to grade everyone the same, whether positively or negatively. And employees, not only supervisors, become victims of the halo effect. Employees might do a bang-up job on one little project: Because they were recognized for their work on that assignment, the employee believes that he or she has exceeded the expectations on every other aspect of his or her evaluation, which can lead to great disappointment during the evaluation phase.

Furthermore, during economic downturns there is often little to nothing left with which to reward employees. Bonuses for exceptional performance are thrown out the window in an effort to cut taxes. Employees are given minuscule or no increases in salary for cost of living and even less for performance. Therefore, the exceptional performer who strives to do his or her best may receive the same increase as the average employee who is just meeting expectations. There is no incentive for doing well. Even more devastating is the fact that one of the organization's core values of recognizing its personnel as the primary resource for service delivery is compromised. The entire process, as a result, becomes suspect.

Despite its faults, there are benefits to this process. It provides guidance for future performance and is used to help further develop your staff. People at all levels have been involved in its design. Furthermore, they play an active role in the actual development of individual plans. The approach tries to use valid and reliable standards that are usually based on past performance. In addition, the standards are often measured against criteria established in the county. For instance, there are specific criteria for processing purchase orders. If met, then the employee would be rated fully successful. If able to complete the purchase order accurately in less time than allocated, thereby reducing costs, then the employee may be seen as exceeding the criteria. Supervisors are also provided ample opportunity to conduct the evaluation, and they are trained so that they are capable of doing it. Finally, the process provides for continual feedback. When properly documented this would, I believe, stand up in court. Although far from perfect, the performance management system still exceeds many of the subjective alternatives based on perception not performance. In light of the problems, why even bother with appraisal systems? We take the time because, when done correctly, they will provide an effective mechanism that can recognize and reward employees while providing the necessary documentation that shows the organization is successfully meeting its goals.

SOURCE: Performance Appraisal, J. Smither, © 1998 JosseyBass-Wiley. Reprinted with permission of John Wiley & Sons, Inc.

principle of the human resource management field: Appraisals evaluate performance, not the person.[12] Verisimilitude trumps veracity. When this happens, issues of law and liability arise (see the key legal principles and their relationship to appraisals identified in Exhibit 10.9). Suggestions for limiting liability in the personnel evaluation process based on selected problems include the following:

- *Harassment or constructive discharge.* Require employees to notify employer of any conditions related to job, job performance, or appraisals (e.g., supervisor bias or improper conduct) that allegedly are so severe as to require quitting. Establish and consistently follow procedures to promptly investigate and eliminate any such offending conditions or conduct by supervisors or other employees to avoid the claim that employer tacitly accepted or approved of harassment.
- *Age discrimination.* Train supervisors to avoid age-loaded comments in verbal or written appraisals. Update performance criteria as technology changes to avoid pretext claims when older workers are laid off for lack of newer skills.
- *Disability discrimination.* Review recommendations and appraisal results for evidence of perceived ("regarded as") discrimination. Ensure that only essential functions are evaluated. Train supervisors to identify reasonable accommodations in performance criteria and appraisal procedures on an interactive basis in a discrete and confidential manner.
- *Defamation or misrepresentation.* Establish procedures to control or avoid providing false performance information (favorable or unfavorable).
- *Negligence.* Keep employees advised if performance is poor so they cannot contest discharge by claiming performance would have improved but for faulty evaluation process (adapted from Malos, 1998, p. 78).

If these issues are successfully confronted, and the evaluation and discipline process improved as discussed below, then it may be more realistic to take such steps to reduce potential problems than to abolish personnel reviews entirely.

IMPROVING THE PROCESS

How would you like a job where every time you make a mistake, a big red light goes off and 18,000 people boo?

—Jacques Plante, hockey player

Designing an appraisal system requires not only establishing policies and procedures but also obtaining the support of the entire workforce and its union or unions. Top officials need to commit to the program publicly by devoting sufficient resources to it and by modeling appropriate behavior. Managers, in turn, need to be convinced that the system is relevant and operational. Employees likewise should see it as in their interest to take it seriously. A profile (or "slice") task force, representing all these groups from different parts of the department, should conduct a needs assessment by collecting agency archival and employee attitudinal data. It should then revise the existing system (or create a new one) based on the

Exhibit 10.9   Selected Legal Principles and Laws Relating to Performance Appraisal

Legal Principle or Law	Summary	Relationship to Appraisals and the Employment Relationship
Employment at will	Status under which the employer or employee may end an employment relationship at any time	Allows the employer considerable latitude in determining whether and how to appraise
Implied contract	Nonexplicit agreement that affects some aspect of the employment relationship	May restrict manner in which employer can use results (e.g., may prevent termination unless for cause)
Violation of public policy	Determination that given action is adverse to the public welfare and is therefore prohibited	May restrict manner in which employer can use appraisal results (e.g., may prevent retaliation for reporting illegal conduct by employer)
Negligence	Breach of duty to conduct performance appraisals with due care	Potential liability may require employer to inform employee of poor performance and provide opportunity to improve
Defamation	Disclosure of untrue information that damages an employee's reputation	Potential liability may restrict manner in which negative performance information can be communicated to others
Misrepresentation	Disclosure of untrue favorable performance information that causes risk of harm to others	Potential liability may restrict willingness of employer to provide references altogether, even for good former employees
Fair Labor Standards Act (FLSA)	Imposes (among other things) obligation to pay overtime to nonexempt (nonmanagerial) employees	Fact that employee appraisals may influence determination that employee functions as supervisor or manager and is therefore exempt
Family and Medical Leave Act (FMLA)	Imposes (among other things) obligation to reinstate employee returning from leave to similar position	Subjecting employee to new or tougher appraisal procedures upon return may suggest that employee has not been given similar position of employment

SOURCE: Adapted from Smither, 1998, p. 52. © Copyright 1998 by Jossey-Bass. Adapted with permission.

findings and test the system on a trial basis. This could be done in jurisdictions that allow customization to agency needs (more than half of state governments, for example) or as part of a government-sponsored pilot program.

It is, of course, possible to marginalize formal requirements entirely. In one major unit of a large hospital, a charismatic department manager decided that whatever the administration of the hospital did, he was going to run his facilities department on the basis of en quality management principles. Well in advance of the hospital's annual tedious performance appraisal drill, he gathered his troops together, reviewed the hospital's sorry and told the employees that what it represented was the starting point for them to practice their *kaizen*—continuous improvement—skills. "What do we need to do, given the fact that this basic form is mandated, in order to complete it well enough to keep the personnel monkeys off our backs but also get some good out of the process for ourselves?" he asked his team. He funded a series of weekly pizza meetings for a task force of facilities employees who were charged with developing an answer to his question that everyone supported enthusiastically (Grote, 1996, p. 351). He then dispensed with the corrupt appraisal charade that blames employees for the management-designed evaluation system.

Finessing the system may be faster, more flexible, and just as effective as formally reforming it. The design chosen involves numerous key technical questions, many of which were discussed earlier. These include selection of the most useful tool(s), as well as raters, based on system objective, practicality, and cost. Training is needed to minimize the various kinds of errors previously examined. It is generally acknowledged, however, that mere awareness of these problems is unlikely to affect behavior. Instead, raters must engage in and receive feedback from role-plays, simulations, and videotaped exercises. Evaluators also need training in interpersonal skills to conduct appraisal interviews effectively.

Monitoring performance in the period between plan approval and formal appraisal includes frequent positive or corrective feedback based on performance, not personality. When performance is monitored conscientiously throughout the year, the actual evaluation simply confirms what has already been discussed.[13] Stated differently, the process of performance management is a continuous one involving coaching, development, accountability, and—both last and least—assessment. In fact, the traditional competitive approach to personnel appraisal is misplaced if the goal is to develop people and promote strong working relationships among managers and employees.

Bersin (2007) identifies seven elements that should constitute appraisal (goal setting, alignment of individual and organizational goals, self-assessment, 360° reviews, managerial appraisal, competency assessment, development planning), six of which emphasize coaching and development and only one of which (managerial appraisal) does not. The job of the manager is to identify strengths in employees and move them into the right positions. A coaching-based, goal-centric, employee-engaged approach can change the way one thinks about performance management and the role of appraisal. In fact, Samuel Culbert (2010) recommends performance *previews* as a way to address the paradox of needs: Instead of top-down reviews, the administrator and subordinate together are held responsible for establishing goals and achieving results. Supervisors truly manage in an effort to ensure that everyone can succeed because it is their job to produce desired outcomes. The emphasis is on the future and what both the supervisor and the employee need from each other to accomplish what they both want.

Finally, the evaluation process culminates in the appraisal interview. In preparing for the meeting, the employee may do a self-assessment, and the manager should collect necessary information and complete, in draft form, the rating instrument. Although a collaborative problem-solving approach is effective, most managers use a one-way "tell-and-sell" technique in which they inform subordinates how they were rated and then justify the decisions (Wexley, 1986). No matter the approach, the supervisor should use the event to support the policies and practices of the entire system and gain training in goal setting, communication skills, and positive reinforcement.

Thus, before the interview, the supervisor should communicate frequently with the subordinate, get training in appraisal interviewing, and use a problem-solving approach. During the session, the superior should share judgments of specific performance (not personality), be an active listener, avoid destructive criticism, and work with the employee to set mutually agreeable future objectives. Afterward, the supervisor should periodically assess the employee's progress toward goals and make rewards contingent on performance (Cascio, 2009). Although conducting a good interview requires a great deal of skill and effort, many managers say that having an honest exchange is the hardest part of the entire process. Most do not do such interviews (Pickett, 2003), and those who do see little or no value in doing them (London, 1995). Yet, as Amy DelPo (2007, pp. 121–122) points out, constructive criticism is exactly that: a positive force for change. Straightforward, specific, balanced, and encouraging feedback fulfills the developmental function of performance appraisal. This feedback role can be enhanced if the manager selects a good time and place to present the feedback, gives the employee a chance to brace for potentially embarrassing information, explains the problem's importance by indicating how it affects the organization, and reaches agreement with the worker on how the issue will be addressed as well as when any change will be implemented (Heathfield, 2014).

An important purpose of this human resource management function is to retain good workers. Most of the factors that cause people to stay or leave—training, open communication, flexible working arrangements, participation in decision making, authority, responsibility—are under the purview of the manager. While attrition may be lower in the public service than in the private sphere, turnover among mission-critical employees is high (Partnership for Public Service & Booz Allen Hamilton, 2010). One-on-one conversations aimed at addressing the paradox of needs could focus on opportunities for training, career development, promotion, and participation on task forces, as well as praise from agency leaders. Employees must be reassured that they are valued and that the administrators who rate their performance believe in them. If managers do not take such measures seriously, the appraisal interview of any given employee could be that person's last one (see Exhibit 10.10). Manager interviews with employees, in fact, need not be restricted to evaluation reviews. As a retention technique, "re-recruitment" has been suggested; this practice involves seeking to keep employees out of a rut by redesigning their jobs or offering them new positions (Sullivan, 2013).

Like appraisal, employee discipline and discharge (discussed in "Disciplinary Systems" below) can be awkward and difficult. Indeed, secondary only to personnel appraisal, managers dislike taking disciplinary actions, generally for many of the same reasons (cognitive limitations, intentional manipulation, organizational influences, human nature). The process can be excruciating because administrators

- may not have kept good records, which are needed as a basis of discipline;
- do not want to spend any more valuable time dealing with poor performers than they already do;
- prefer to avoid putting the office climate at risk by taking action;

- might believe that disciplinary actions will not be effective, partly because the employee likely has years of satisfactory evaluations; or
- may have been corrupted by the subordinate, who could have evidence of inappropriate or wrongful managerial behavior, most often involving money, power, and/or sex.[14]

Paradoxically, when the need for adverse action is obvious, it may be less likely to occur. Thus, in the wake of the worst security failure in American history, the 2001 terrorist attacks on New York City and Washington, D.C., no one was disciplined, no one resigned, and no one took responsibility. The same can be said of the torture of detainees during the Iraq War and the aftermath of the 2010 BP *Deepwater Horizon* oil spill. Likewise, despite widespread unethical and illegal transactions during the 2008 financial debacle on Wall Street, few firms disciplined their employees and only a very small number of miscreant low-level financiers were brought to justice. Indeed, some retired with "golden parachutes," and most continued on the job, receiving extraordinarily high salaries and bonuses. In government, the Securities and Exchange Commission ended its discipline process in 2011 without terminating any personnel for the failure to stop Bernard Madoff's massive Ponzi scheme. More broadly, a federal judge called the Justice Department's lack of prosecutions of banks and their executives "technically and morally suspect," as out-of-court settlements typically do nothing to discourage bankers from future criminal conduct (Eskow, 2014; also see Bowman & West, 2015, Chapter 9).

It is evident, then, that officials prefer to avoid taking adverse action both in response to routine daily management and in reaction to major crises. That may be understandable, but it is unacceptable. Estimates vary, but between 3% (OPM) and 14% (MSPB) of federal personnel perform below expectations (Losey, 2011). Not only are the problem individuals thereby trained to believe that inappropriate behaviors are condoned, but also other employees become demoralized and lose respect for management. The goal, accordingly, should be first to reduce the need for adverse action, second to take corrective steps, and third, when necessary, make discharge as simple and timely as possible.

DISCIPLINARY SYSTEMS *not really for pape*

For the most part, employees discipline themselves by conforming to what is considered acceptable behavior simply because it is the sensible thing to do. Self-discipline can be encouraged when people are treated as adults—that is, when the organization uses an "open book" management style, offers employees opportunities to have input into decisions, and makes them comfortable when "speaking truth to power." Yet mistakes are made that require attention, and the test of a well-managed agency "is not how many personnel problems arise, but how effectively" the problems are addressed (Wise, Clemow, Murray, Boston, & Bingham, 2005, p. 181). The need for managers to use best practices in the disciplinary process is illustrated by the availability of professional liability insurance to safeguard managers' livelihoods and careers. That is, the administrator—not the agency's human resource or legal office—is the one accountable for the decision.

Exhibit 10.10 Final Interview: Exit and Termination Sessions

Nothing happens until it happens to you.

—Anonymous

The best time to obtain an employee's opinions is when he or she is fully committed to the agency. Oddly, not many departments use retention-oriented "stay interviews" (to elicit what people want from their jobs), a practice that might reduce the need for exit and termination interviews. Exit interviews and termination sessions, however, are unique opportunities for an organization to receive feedback on a wide variety of issues, including personnel recruitment, training, evaluation, and retention. Such interviews, when supplemented with employee satisfaction surveys, can yield interesting information.

Many organizations do not conduct exit interviews; others may use online questionnaires or have the human resource department conduct interviews. Either of these two options suggests that the employee is not important enough to be worth the line manager's time. In contrast, virtually all agencies use some form of **termination interview.**

Whether an individual is leaving voluntarily or not, it is well documented that the emotions involved in job change are comparable to those experienced in relation to divorce or the death of a loved one. Indeed, on leaving their jobs people experience a five-stage cycle of grief: shock, resistance, acceptance, exploration of other opportunities, and commitment to a new future. Thus, for a manager conducting an **exit interview**, the Golden Rule is key—that is, how would you feel if you were in the situation? What would you expect your superiors to say (Selden, 2007)? Possible interview questions, which may be adjusted depending on the reason for the termination session, include these:

- What do you value about the agency? What do you dislike?
- What would you tell the next person who does your job?
- Did you receive adequate feedback while you were here?
- What are some of the characteristics of a person most likely to succeed here?
- Do you have any recommendations for agency human resource policies?
- Was there a single factor in your decision to leave?
- If you were asked to consider working here again, what would you say?

The decision to quit a job, or the reaction to being fired, is personal and often complex, so receiving clear answers to such questions may not be a given. The emotional stress of leaving, under even the best circumstances, can produce unreliable statements. In fact, the manager may want to interview coworkers to ascertain why the person is leaving.

The following are some of the things an employee should consider before participating in a voluntary exit interview:

- Is the interview anonymous or does a document (such as a questionnaire) need to be signed?
- Is your reason for leaving any of the agency's business, or could questions about it be viewed as an invasion of your privacy?
- Why did the employer wait until now to ask your opinion?

(Continued)

Exhibit 10.10 (Continued)

- Will the organization really use your comments for improvements, or is management just trying to find out the "real" reason you are leaving?
- Might you say something in an exit interview that results in your "burning bridges," thereby putting future references at risk?

If the purpose of the meeting is termination, then the situation should be presented in a concise, considerate, final manner that avoids arguments about past behavior, explains outplacement services and how references will be handled, and includes delivery of a paycheck (Coleman, 2001). Discharges are best done at the end of the day when other staff have left, and the employee is allowed to return to his or her desk. All dismissal activities must preserve the person's dignity and privacy (see Gentry, 2005; Scott, 2007). Discussion of the adverse action with others should be restricted to those who have a legitimate need to know.

Not to be overlooked is the fact that how the final session is conducted can have an impact on the people who remain in the agency. How well this event is managed provides insight into the manager's interpersonal skills when he or she is under the strain of losing an employee.

SOURCES: Adapted from Heathfield (2007); Selden (2007).

The term *discipline* is best understood as orderly conduct at work achieved by self-control and respect for agency rules. When performance problems (failure to complete assignments satisfactorily) or misconduct issues (insubordination, document falsification, loafing, carelessness, fighting, drug use) occur, the personnel appraisal and/or discipline systems may be utilized to improve behavior. Factors that managers should consider when using these systems include problem severity, duration, frequency, extenuating circumstances, organizational policies and employee training, agency past practice, and management support.

Given the nature of the issues involved, taking action is necessary to ensure a productive workforce. Yet, paradoxically, officials may tolerate poor performers because they lack an understanding of agency rules, documentation, and top management support—to say nothing of fearing onerous employee grievances and/or false accusations of discriminatory behavior (U.S. MSPB, 1995). In point of fact, the disciplinary process involves things that many administrators try to avoid: paperwork, confrontation, and the prospect of being overruled (Lunney, 2012). Managers then may sidestep discipline procedures and write acceptable personnel reviews for marginal employees to avoid unpleasantness, something that may haunt them if there is a subsequent attempt to discharge someone for sustained inadequate performance.[15]

Simply demanding that managers "get tough" is not an efficacious approach because "a supervisor who is very effective at removing someone can nevertheless be ineffective at selecting good employees in the first place or at motivating superior performance from the majority of employees who are capable of doing good work" ("Firing Poor Performers,"

2003). Critics also ignore the fact that unsatisfactory performance needs to be addressed strategically in a larger context comprising societal and organizational culture, compensation levels, and agency HRM policies. That is, why did the poor worker get hired, how did she survive probation, why did she receive earlier satisfactory performance reviews, and why was training ineffective? Thus, in reply to demands that steps be taken to facilitate termination of personnel, one union official argued, "We do not need to make it easier to fire employees. [Instead, executives] need to hold . . . managers and senior staff accountable for their behavior . . . [and] take a hard look at the 'country club' mentality that exists within management" (quoted in Katz, 2014).

Moreover, those who focus on the difficulty of terminating workers ignore the utility of existing procedures that result in more than 10,000 separations per year in federal service—not counting employees who resign first, those who retire or are transferred, or those removed through layoffs ("Firing Poor Performers," 2003). They also overlook that performance improvement plans are often successful in rehabilitating employees. Finally, they neglect the current trend away from highly ritualized, formal grievance procedures toward alternative dispute resolution techniques. One such approach is the use of ombudsmen who can help employees get answers to questions and work to resolve disputes. The Government Accountability Office found that ombudsmen in federal agencies successfully addressed workplace problems in more than half of their cases (Bilmes & Gould, 2009, p. 213). In short, termination affects a small percentage of personnel, and this is how it should be when human resource functions such as selection and training operate effectively (Daley, 2008).

To protect both the individual and the institution, appraisal and discipline must be used only for justifiable reasons. To ensure fair treatment, actions must be derived from written guidelines; be corrective, not punitive; be based on the act, not on personality; and be timely, consistent with previous cases, and proportionate to the problem. The evaluation will be only as good as the evidence on which it is based. Documentation is the cornerstone, and it commences with a prompt and thorough investigation. Records should include the date, location, and nature of any incident; the effects on the organization; prior actions by the person and agency; the decisions made and improvement anticipated; and the employee's reaction. The agency must recognize that a manager's complaint about an employee is only an allegation until proven true; the burden of proof is on the agency to show how the employee's behavior negatively affected operations and the supervisor's actions were neither arbitrary nor capricious. If the administrator has performed his or her responsibility to train the worker and the worker fails, then appropriate adverse action is in the best interest of the organization.

Discipline regulations routinely incorporate the "Douglas factors," first articulated in *Curtis Douglas et al. v. Veterans Administration et al.* (1981), into their guidance on how to fashion an appropriate disciplinary penalty. Supervisors and managers often must complete a written response to each factor prior to taking any documented corrective action. Among these elements are (1) the nature of the offense; (2) the employee's job, past work record, and previous disciplinary actions; (3) the effect of the offense on the employee's ability to perform at a satisfactory level; (4) the consistency of the penalty with those imposed on other employees for similar offenses; (5) the clarity with which the employee was on notice of any rules that were violated in committing the offense; (6) the individual's potential for rehabilitation; and (7) the adequacy of alternative sanctions (Kunreuther, 2010).

Progressive discipline (or, more accurately, progressive punishment) and positive corrective action are two approaches used by organizations. For either to be productive, the worker must know what the problem is, what change is expected, and the consequences of inaction. **Progressive punishment**, the most common policy, is an awkward combination of retribution and rehabilitation. It involves the application of coercive measures with increasing degrees of severity: informal counseling, verbal warning or reprimand, written warning or reprimand, minor suspension, major suspension, and separation. Modeled on the American criminal justice system, this policy requires punishment following each crime. It should be evident, however, that while employees might be punished into compliance, they are not likely to be punished into commitment (Grote, 2001).

Because this policy can be autocratic, adversarial, and intimidating, some jurisdictions have replaced it with **positive corrective action**, a strategy based on the premise that adults must assume responsibility for their own conduct (see U.S. MSPB, 2008). Rather than treating people "worse and worse and expecting them to get better and better," this nonpunishment approach uses reminders instead of reprimands. More participative than punitive, the technique utilizes these steps:

- A conference between employee and manager to find a solution to the problem, with an oral agreement to improve.
- A subsequent meeting, if reform is not accomplished, to determine why the agreed-upon solution did not work, with a written reminder that the solution is the responsibility of the individual as a condition of employment.
- Paid leave time (a "day of decision"), if change is not forthcoming, wherein the employee is expected to return the next day either with a "last chance" specific written commitment or a decision to leave the agency. If the person decides to stay, it is with the condition that a future disciplinary problem will result in immediate discharge.

In brief, the employee, not the employer, is the decision maker. This responsibility-based system not only demonstrates employer good faith but also reduces the risk of workplace violence. The human resources chief of Georgia state government, which practices this approach, concluded that not one private or public organization in that state that has tried it has ever abandoned it (Grote, 2001, p. 57).

The principle underlying both progressive punishment and positive corrective action is a "just cause" standard: Was the investigation done properly? Was the employee aware of the rule violation? Was the standard reasonable? Was the rule in question violated? What mitigating circumstances merit consideration? Finally, have comparable cases occurred, and, if so, how were they addressed? The premise is that a just procedure should help ensure a fair outcome.

The purpose of such systems is not to win battles but to provide feedback and training to foster responsible employees. Managers can reduce the number of problems they experience during the discipline process through training, establishing clear work rules, following procedures, and documenting actions taken (DelPo & Guerin, 2003; Guffey & Helms, 2001). The key is to understand the scope of their administrative authority, focus on behavior (not the person), avoid decisions based on hearsay, use appropriate penalties, and follow through on the judgments made.

Although the primary objective of personnel appraisal and disciplinary systems is to ensure employee development and rehabilitation, the documentation these systems provide—including past personnel reviews—can be used to support termination decisions. Unlike in much of the private sector, where employees can be arbitrarily dismissed for no reason or for any reason not contrary to law, public servants have constitutional rights as citizens to due process.[16] In *Cleveland Board of Education v. Loudermill* (1985), the Supreme Court ruled that a civil service position is the employee's property, and the individual cannot be removed or demoted without knowing the reasons, has the right to see the evidence used, and must be given a meaningful opportunity to respond. Affording due process minimizes the chance of politically motivated sackings and maximizes the recruitment and retention of meritorious personnel. There may be good grounds for action (deficient performance or egregious misconduct such as theft), but managers nonetheless can create significant problems if they do not handle the process well (Wise et al., 2009). When an adverse action is taken, not only the employee but also any judge who may review its documentation must be kept in mind. It is imperative that administrators, in consultation with the human resources department, follow established procedures to avoid mistakes that could lead to organizational liability as well as to assist personnel whose rights might have been violated.

While it is true that there are appeal processes available to those who wish to fight termination—it is not supposed to be easy to fire employees for political or other illegitimate reasons—thousands of federal workers are discharged each year (Holan, 2007). It is also true that only 3% of workers win their jobs back using appeal and grievance systems (Gilson, 2007). Stated differently, poor performers are not a serious problem in government. The proportion of employees who coworkers believe should be dismissed is less than 4% (Nelson, 2003, p. 1). Nonetheless, in response to the 2014 Department of Veterans Affairs waiting-list scandal, President Obama signed into law a streamlined method for terminating VA executives. He suggested, in fact, that such a process should be used government-wide, only to learn that it is already "very easy" to fire leaders (Shoop, 2014). Overall, then, as a U.S. MSPB (1999) study determined, the conventional wisdom about the number of poorly performing employees, and the disposition of their cases, not only distracts consideration from the development of additional approaches to address employee performance but also diverts attention from other, more important, workforce issues.

Because discharge is a painful event for both the individual and the organization, it is critical that it be done with care and deliberation. This means that it must be approached in a humane, confidential, professional, nonaccusatory, factual way, and it must be based on substantiated, legitimate business reasons consistent with similar cases (see Exhibit 10.10). When people are treated fairly, wrongful discharge suits are unlikely to withstand legal scrutiny.[17] Employee termination is part of a manager's job: Doing it well is an opportunity to learn how to improve other human resource management functions such as recruitment, training, and appraisal. As unpleasant as dismissal may be, "it's not the people you fire who make your life miserable. It's the ones you don't" (Grote, 2011, p. 191). Officials, in brief, have the responsibility to address unacceptable behavior in a timely manner. Failure to demand even minimal competence implies that performance does not matter. This negatively affects the morale of contributing employees and can damage the reputation of the agency as a whole.

SUMMARY AND CONCLUSION

The two hardest things in life to handle are success and failure.

—Anonymous

As an aid to distilling the discussion in this chapter, the characteristics that a personnel appraisal system should contain to satisfy both employers and employees are specified below. In addition, it is important to identify preexisting conditions that can facilitate the evaluation process. These factors, as part of strategic HRM, include the need to select employees carefully, give them an important mission, empower them through training and continuous performance feedback, offer them fair compensation, and discharge them should they be unable or unwilling to contribute.

As the chapter has demonstrated, implementing the personnel appraisal function is fraught with paradoxes. Indeed, readers are invited to evaluate the extent to which the following standards are met by agencies in their jurisdictions:

1. The rating instruments, which should strive for simplicity rather than complexity, are derived from job analysis (Chapter 5).

2. Training about the systems is provided to all employees, and training in the use of the systems is given to all managers.

3. Appraisals are grounded in accurate job descriptions, and the actual ratings are based on observable performance.

4. Evaluations are completed under standardized conditions and are free of adverse impact (Chapter 2).

5. Preliminary appraisal results are shared with the ratees.

6. Some form of upper-level review, including an appeal process, exists that prevents a single manager from controlling an individual's career.

7. Performance counseling and corrective guidance services are available to employees.

Although many systems may not compare favorably to such standards, recall that the crux of the appraisal problem is not system design. Instead, because evaluation is a matter of human judgment, the conundrum is how the plan and the information it generates are used. To the extent that electronic employee monitoring is used, not only is it limited to

those behaviors that can be tracked by computer, but, more important, it also
essential nature of workplace interpersonal relations by questioning employee
privacy, autonomy, and respect.

The challenge is not to design a perfect system but, rather, in a dialectic between the
individual and the agency, to minimize the abundant problems with appraisal. Typical
barriers to effective evaluation include the absence of four elements: trust in the organization, supervisory training and top management support, rater accountability, and
overall evaluation of the system itself (Roberts, 2003). Organizations may overcome such
barriers by providing constructive, nonthreatening feedback and coaching; avoiding
numeric rating scales that pigeonhole employees and pit them against each other; ensuring multiple sources of data through use of peer reviews; and utilizing group evaluations.
It might be argued, however, that if employees are given an important mission, provided
training, and offered competitive salaries, then appraisal becomes epiphenomenal and
redundant.

The perennial, melancholy search for the best "genuine fake" technique, nonetheless,
relentlessly (sometimes shamelessly) continues. The most recent strategic performance
tool developed in the quest to drive change and facilitate federal pay for performance is
Goals-Engagement-Accountability-Results (GEAR). It is being piloted in five agencies with
the intent to expand the program governmentwide. Not only is there little difference
between GEAR and existing methods based in current law and regulations, but also the
program does not specifically address performance pay (Haga, 2014; Palleschi, 2012). After
nearly 3 years, the U.S. Government Accountability Office (2013) found that most of the
GEAR pilot programs were still in the developmental stage and that implementation plans
needed significant improvement.

"Symptom solving" is seductive and easier than genuine problem solving. Beliefs about
traditional evaluation are so deeply held that when they are repeatedly refuted they paradoxically become stronger. Dubious ideas persist because people get used to them and
prefer the certainty of misery to the misery of uncertainty. As the new century progresses,
personnel appraisal will become either more or less complex. Should the long-standing
preference for person-centered evaluations persist, both organizational downsizing and
workforce changes will likely complicate appraisals. The virtual workplace—unbound by
time and space—is likely to exacerbate this situation because it changes the fundamental
nature of interpersonal relationships, limiting them to only those behaviors that can be
monitored electronically.

Downsizing has been a one-two punch. Personnel offices have shrunk, placing more
responsibilities on line managers. At the same time, the numbers of supervisors have been
reduced, requiring the remaining ones to evaluate more subordinates. As a result, the
potential for both system design and implementation problems has increased. Several
changes in the composition of the workforce also imply a more challenging climate for
appraisals. Increasing employee diversity means that managers will be evaluating people
of all colors and cultures, a task that is surely more arduous than assessing a homogeneous
staff. Also, the fastest-growing part of the working population is made up of contingent
employees—temporary staff, short-term contract workers, volunteers—who, by definition,
present evaluation challenges.

Undaunted, reformers are encouraged, not dissuaded, by these formidable developments and are seldom deterred by past appraisal failures. After all, both employers and employees tend to support the idea of appraisals, at least in the abstract when human beings are not involved. The result is increased emphasis on evaluations, resting on the misguided belief that the employee is the primary factor in productivity. Ratings can become a control mechanism to force conformance to the status quo, as beleaguered managers find appraisals to be a convenient, if technically problematic, ideological tool. "When they sign off on them, their job is done; the responsibility for quality and productivity is returned to where, in their view, it belongs—the subordinate" (Bowman, 1994, p. 132).

Alternatively, and congruent with strategic HRM, should institutions begin to shift away from person-centered appraisal and toward **organization-centered evaluations**, or process-centered appraisals, individual evaluations may be less complex in the years ahead—or perhaps abolished altogether (see Exhibit 10.11). Indeed, in their landmark book *Abolishing Performance Appraisals* (2000), Coens and Jenkins offer 12 documented cases—including

interesting

Exhibit 10.11   Evaluating Organizations, Not Individuals

> *O body swayed to music, O brightening glance,*
> *How can we know the dancer from the dance?*
>
> —William Butler Yeats, *Among School Children*

As this chapter shows, individual appraisal is a complex issue. Even when done with great care, it can be devastating to people and destructive to organizations. Although it may be true that management practices are seldom discarded merely because they are dysfunctional, it is also true that the civil service reform movement and/or the use of pilot projects (Chapter 1) provide opportunities to reexamine orthodox approaches to appraisal.

The premise of organization-centered evaluation is that the quality of services is a function of the system in which the services are produced. Systems consist of people, policies, technology, supplies, and a sociopolitical environment within which all operate. Note that these parameters are beyond appraisee control; indeed, the employees themselves are hired, tasked, and trained by the organization. A person-only assessment, stated differently, is deficient if the goal is to comprehend all factors affecting performance. In a well-designed management system, virtually all employees will perform properly; a weak system will frustrate even the finest people.

Traditional, person-centered appraisal methods are based on a faulty, unrealistic assumption: that individual employees are responsible for outcomes derived from a complex system. Because an organization is a group of people working to achieve a common goal, the managerial role is to foster that collaboration. If the result is inadequate, then it is management's responsibility—and no one else's.

From a systems perspective, the causes of good or bad performance are spread throughout the organization and its processes. Many results in the workplace are outside the power of employees traditionally made responsible for those outcomes. When more than 90% of performance problems are the consequence of the management system (Deming, 1992), holding low-level minions accountable is a way of evading responsibility; the cause of most performance problems lies not within the individual employee but within the organization divined by its leaders.

wow!

Because employees have little authority over organizational systems, relevant appraisals should provide two kinds of feedback:

- System performance data automatically generated from statistical process controls (i.e., evaluation is built into the work process itself)
- Individual performance data—used primarily for developmental purposes—derived from anonymous multirater 360° evaluations (focusing on attributes such as teamwork, customer satisfaction, timeliness, communication skills, and attendance)

The key is to listen to customers of the process and emphasize continuous improvement. By making the system as transparent as possible, the organization can keep the focus on nonthreatening analyses of work processes and people's contributions to those processes. Such an approach would be organizationally valid, socially acceptable, and administratively convenient—key criteria for any appraisal method. Importantly, it would also change an often adversarial process to one that is more constructive.

Reflecting U.S. individualism,* the field of human resource management has focused on people rather than on systems. It is politically unlikely, therefore, that organizational appraisals will supplant individual ratings (indeed, when performance appraisals were abolished at one well-known federal government demonstration project in California, the project was terminated, partly because productivity improved). A number of public agencies (National Oceanic and Atmospheric Administration, Internal Revenue Service, Social Security Administration) and private companies (Motorola, Merrill Lynch, Procter & Gamble) have modified their approaches to appraisals. To better reflect a systems perspective, they have incorporated teamwork (in addition to individual achievements), citizen/customer feedback (in addition to supervisory opinions), and process improvement (in addition to results) dimensions into their evaluations.

A more complete reform would be to state performance standards clearly and then assume that most employees will do the jobs for which they were hired. As Greg Boudreaux (1994), a manager at the National Rural Electric Cooperative, has suggested, for the small number who do not then do their jobs: "Investigate why. Some will need further training or management counseling. Some may be an actual problem. But deal with those problems on a case-by-case, and not through a generic, faulty performance appraisal system" (p. 24; also see Eckes, 1994).

Indeed, the approach described here is partly consistent with the most recent appraisal fad: performance management (Cederblom & Permerl, 2002). This strategy emphasizes that managing performance (not merely appraisal but also planning, accountability, compensation, training) is key to institutional goal setting. Thus, performance management is a continuing cycle of goal setting, coaching, development, and assessment. From a systems perspective, however, it exemplifies the "wrong-problem problem." Yet it tries to solve the wrong problem precisely by emphasizing the individual, not the organization. It should come as no surprise, then, that just 5% of managers are "very satisfied" with their performance management process (Grote, 2011, p. 158). The same criticism can be levied at multirater 360° evaluation systems, discussed earlier in this chapter.

---

*This is an area where our myths may be more dangerous than our lies. The lone frontiersman and the outlaw gunslinger—largely products of Hollywood—were far less important in the American West than farmers raising barns together and shopkeepers settling in small towns. The myth also does not explain the wild popularity of team sports in contemporary life.

government, nonprofit, health care, retail, educational, manufacturing, and industrial organizations—that benchmark how orthodox appraisal can be successfully abolished. While each case had its own unique characteristics, these diverse workplaces that did away with evaluations shared important similarities:

- They originally had traditional, scaled performance review practices linked to pay and disciplinary systems.
- Their multiple-purpose appraisal functions did not meet objectives and were seen as counterproductive.
- The basic assumptions about employees were changed—people wanted to work and contribute—thereby empowering them to reinvent the nature of evaluations and take responsibility for their own growth.
- The focus of change was from individual appraisal to systems and processes in the organization. Improvement did not come from mandatory annual personal assessment but from educating employees to develop better work procedures.
- Formal feedback or annual meetings were not required as personnel received help "just in time" when they needed it; the emphasis was not on evaluation but on excellence.
- Individual incentive pay was dropped and raises were based on skill advancement, teamwork, market increases, and cost-of-living adjustments.
- Disciplinary processes were rarely used.

This organization-focused approach resulted in increased productivity, improved morale, and a decline in grievances and turnover—as well as an overwhelming desire never to return to the use of antiquated performance appraisal systems (also see Baker, 2013).

Less dramatic, but nonetheless useful, was one organization's decision to stop doing the orthodox top-down appraisals and institute APOP—the Annual Piece of Paper. The one-page, bottom-up review form simply summarizes ongoing daily feedback (there are no scores or future goals) by focusing on what the manager can do to make employee tasks easier and what gets in the way of accomplishing the job. Whether the appraisal function becomes more or less difficult in the 21st century, it is worth doing only if it is an integral part of the management system and if it helps both the institution and the individual develop to full potential.

KEY TERMS

Actor/observer bias
Behaviorally anchored rating system (BARS)
Behavior-based evaluation systems
Cognitive information processing theory
Compatibility error

Contaminated evaluations
Contrast error
Critical incident technique
Deficient evaluations
Electronic monitoring

Error of central tendency

Exit interview

Implicit personality theory

Leniency error

Management by objectives (MBO)

No money effect

Organization-centered evaluations

Outcome bias

Peer evaluations

Positive corrective action

Progressive punishment

Recency effect

Results-based systems

Self-appraisals

Severity error

Spillover effect

Termination interview

360° evaluation systems

Trait-based appraisals

EXERCISES

Class Discussion

1. Organizational appraisal systems typically focus on functional rationality; supervisors, however, tend to emphasize substantive rationality by filing false—but effective—evaluations. Under what circumstances can inaccurate reviews be examples of sound management?

2. "You were hired to make our organization succeed and to make your boss look successful." Do you agree with this claim? Why or why not?

3. What would be the most appropriate rating instrument for a middle manager? Staff assistant? Telecommuter? Intern? Why?

4. Visit a local agency to determine why, how, and by whom appraisals are done there. Analyze the rating form used. Is it legally defensible? Report the findings to the class.

5. In theory, personnel appraisal can provide feedback on management processes such as selection, position management, training, and compensation. Given the many problems with appraisal, however, it often does not supply this information. Accordingly, appraisal has been called the "missing link" in human resource management. Comment.

6. The problematic nature of evaluation reviews can be illustrated by this story showing the difference between a German and an Austrian: The German says that a situation is serious, but not hopeless; the Austrian calls the same situation hopeless, but not serious. Is the appraisal function in a serious or hopeless condition?

Team Activities

7. Personnel evaluations have been called a kind of bureaucratic Kabuki: elaborate, stylized, baffling—and yet predictably ineffectual. Debate this observation, with one team taking the affirmative and one team the negative position.

8. Using the "25 in 10" technique (see Exhibit 0.2 in the book's introduction), discuss this statement: "The root problem in performance rating is not technical in nature."

9. David is a star performer who frequently irritates his coworkers and managers. His agency's appraisal includes an interpersonal relations category, and David's supervisor rates him low in this category as well as in other categories. Discuss this situation in the context of the paradoxes of freedom and needs (introduction).

10. Does traditional performance appraisal help or hinder other personnel functions and their paradoxes?

Individual Assignments

11. Identify three of the most difficult rater errors. How can they be dealt with?

12. Discuss the following statement: "Most people, including supervisors, like to be liked."

13. Whenever a rating is less than the best, or less than what the employee perceives his or her contribution to be, the manager is seen as punitive. Use examples to support your agreement or disagreement with this claim.

14. Use the last examination you took in any class to discuss the reasons for using performance appraisals—and the limitations of appraisals.

15. Consider the tips presented in this chapter for conducting a performance appraisal interview. Would they have helped you—as either manager or employee—the last time you were involved in this situation?

16. Evaluate the following assertion: "Regardless of the reason, when an employee is terminated the employer should assist the person to find other employment."

17. Take an "imagination break" (Exhibit 0.2) and speculate about alternative futures for personnel appraisal.

NOTES

1. The subtitle of this chapter is purloined from Tyer (1983).

2. Whether or not such judgments should be relative (based on comparisons between employees) or absolute (based on performance standards) is largely settled because ranking is not the equivalent of rating employees. That is, relative judgments do not reveal how well someone actually performed; thus, they are not job related. The 1978 Civil Service Reform Act, as a result, does not permit ranking methods (e.g., simple rankings from best to worst or forced-distribution techniques such as the bell-shaped curve) for evaluation of federal employees. Relative approaches, however, may be used for other, related administrative matters such as promotions, pay, and layoffs. Most jurisdictions traditionally make these judgments annually to coincide with the fiscal year, although more frequent informal assessments tied to project completion are quite valuable.

3. It is neither feasible nor desirable, therefore, to discuss all these instruments. To do so would be to encourage the notion that the problem of performance measurement is merely one of technique; it is, rather, a process, not a form.

4. Depending on the size of the categories and whether they are broken into subcategories, trait-based appraisal forms generally include between 15 and 50 items to rate. An additional summative or

overall category rating is also common, with a space for global comments, accompanied by the evaluator's signature and sometimes an additional signature of the evaluator's supervisor. Space is normally allowed for "other" categories. Forms should allow space for evaluator comments for each item or set of items. Because of the generic quality of trait-based forms, a "not applicable" category is usually provided. Often the highest and lowest categories must be accompanied by explanations of organizational policy.

5. Despite all these problems, the technique has obvious intuitive appeal because traits may simply offer a shorthand way of describing a person's behavior. This may explain why some psychologists contend not only that personality rating scales are reasonably valid and reliable but also that they are more acceptable to evaluators (Cascio & Aguinis, 2005).

6. Teachers at the K–12 level are likely to be required to provide class lesson plans, lesson plans for students with special needs, examples of tests, examples of feedback, grading statistics, and attendance records.

7. MBO is fondly known in the trade as "massive bowel obstruction," precisely because such a bureaucratic hyperrational system could, in the view of critics, never work with human beings. Indeed, Dan Ariely (2008) makes a similar point: People are less rational than they think they are; in fact, their "irrational behaviors are neither random nor senseless—they are systematic and predictable" (p. 239). Just as people are tricked by visual illusions, they are fooled by illusions about how they make decisions.

8. Early examples of such circumvention include data entry personnel who, when evaluated by the number of keystrokes they made, pressed the space bar while making personal calls; and telephone operators who, when expected to fulfill a quota for calls answered in a given time period, hung up on people with complex problems. The National Institute of Occupational Safety and Health estimates that two-thirds of all video display terminals are electronically monitored (Ambrose, Alder, & Noel, 1998, p. 70). The American Management Association, which conducts annual electronic monitoring and surveillance surveys, recently found that more than three-fourths of private firms use routine monitoring of their employees' activities, a figure that has doubled since 1997.

9. According to Bernardin, Cooke, and Villanova (2000), raters who score high on "agreeableness" (trust, sympathy, cooperation, politeness) are more lenient than those characterized as "conscientious" (excellence, high performance, ability to achieve difficult goals). In academe, leniency, or "grade inflation," has been described as "the refusal by faculty members to behave like adults, that is, like people with enough integrity to disappoint other people. It is as though some professors want to believe that everybody deserves to be first. Everybody doesn't" (Carter, 1996, p. 79). This viewpoint may conflict with the expectations of Generation Yers, who, it is said, grew up receiving trophies for 7th place.

10. The saying "When you point your finger at me, remember that your other fingers are pointing back at you" is appropriate here.

11. It should be noted that those who are "high self-monitors" are more adept at deciphering cues in the environment and are more capable of adjusting their behavior to fit the context than are "low self-monitors" (Jawahar, 2005).

12. The pervasiveness of this problem accounts for the use of the term *personnel appraisal,* rather than *performance appraisal,* in many instances in this chapter.

13. In the private sector, those companies that emphasize frequent feedback have been found to outperform those that do not in all financial and productivity measures (Campbell & Garfinkel, 1996).

14. For a useful discussion on "thinking about poor performers," see Maranto (2008).

15. For example, no high-ranking American military officials were dismissed for their failures in Iraq; in fact, the only one to lose his position was the U.S. Army chief of staff, who testified before the war that hundreds of thousands of troops would be needed to secure the country. Indeed, the Presidential Medal of

Freedom was awarded to the CIA director who said Saddam Hussein had weapons of mass destruction, the general who failed to secure Iraq, and the head of the Coalition Provisional Authority, whose decisions, in effect, encouraged insurgency. Promotions, rather than punishment, were the fate of most of the torture-tainted officers in the Abu Ghraib prison scandal.

16. While social norms in public and business bureaucracies generally discourage discharge, layoffs and terminations are significantly higher in the private sector than in government (Bureau of Labor Statistics, 2005).

17. Treating employees fairly includes avoiding attempts at (a) constructive discharge (deliberately creating intolerable working conditions that compel employees to resign) and (b) retaliatory discharge (taking actions against personnel, such as demotions or denial of pay raises, when they exercise their rights under employment laws such as the Civil Rights Act of 1964).

REFERENCES

Ambrose, M. L., Alder, G. S., & Noel, T. W. (1998). Electronic performance monitoring: A consideration of rights. In M. Schminke (Ed.), *Managerial ethics: Moral management of people and processes* (pp. 61–80). Mahwah, NJ: Lawrence Erlbaum.

Ariely, D. (2008). *Predictably irrational: The hidden forces that shape our decisions.* New York: HarperCollins.

Baker, T. (2013). *The end of performance review: A new approach to appraising employee performance.* New York: Palgrave Macmillan.

Barrett, G. V., & Kernan, M. C. (1987). Performance appraisals and terminations: A review of court decisions since *Brito vs. Zia* with implications for personnel practices. *Personnel Psychology, 40*(3), 489–503.

Bates, G. (2007, July 13). It could happen here. *Workforce.* Retrieved from http://www.workforce.com/article/20070713/NEWS02/307139993

Beecher, D. D. (2003). The next wave of civil service reform. *Public Personnel Management, 32*(4), 457–474.

Benson, J., Debroux, P., Yuasa, M., & Zhu, Y. (2000). Flexibility and labour management: Chinese manufacturing enterprises in the 1990s. *International Journal of Human Resource Management, 11*(2), 183–196.

Bernardin, L., Cooke, M., & Villanova, P. (2000). Conscientiousness and agreeableness as predictors of rater leniency. *Journal of Applied Psychology, 85,* 232–234.

Bersin, J. (2007, December 6). Taking aim at performance appraisals. *Talent Management.* Retrieved from http://talentmgt.com/articles/view/taking_aim_at_performance_appraisals

Bilmes, L. J., & Gould, W. S. (2009). *The people factor: Strengthening America by investing in public service.* Washington, DC: Brookings Institution Press.

Black, J. S., Gregersen, H. B., & Mendenhall, M. E. (1992). Evaluating the performance of global managers. *Journal of International Compensation and Benefits, 1,* 35–40.

Boudreaux, G. (1994, May/June). What TQM says about performance appraisal. *Compensation and Benefits Review,* pp. 20–24.

Bowman, J. S. (1994). At last, an alternative to performance appraisal: Total quality management. *Public Administration Review, 54*(2), 129–136.

Bowman, J. S., & West, J. P. (2015). *Public service ethics: Individual and institutional responsibilities.* Thousand Oaks, CA: CQ Press.

Bureau of Labor Statistics, U.S. Department of Labor. (2005). Job Openings and Labor Turnover Survey. Retrieved from http://data.blsulov/PDQ/servlet/Surveyoutput

Burns, J. P. (1999). Changing environmental impacts on civil service systems: The cases of China and Hong Kong. In H. Wong & H. S. Chan (Eds.), *Handbook of comparative public administration in the Asia-Pacific basin* (pp. 179–218). New York: Marcel Dekker.

Campbell, R. B., & Garfinkel, L. M. (1996, June). Strategies for success in measuring performance. *HRMagazine,* pp. 98–104.

Cardy, R. L., & Dobbins, G. H. (1994). *Performance appraisal: Alternative perspectives.* Cincinnati, OH: South-Western.

Carson, M. (2006). Saying it like it isn't: The pros and cons of 360-degree feedback. *Business Horizons, 49,* 395–402.

Carter, S. L. (1996). *Integrity.* New York: Basic Books.

Cascio, W. F. (2009). *Managing human resources* (8th ed.). Boston: Irwin.

Cascio, W. F., & Aguinis, H. (2005). *Applied psychology in human resource management* (6th ed.). Upper Saddle River, NJ: Prentice Hall.

Cederblom, D., & Permerl, D. (2002). From performance appraisal to performance management: One agency's experience. *Public Personnel Management, 31*(2), 131–140.

Chou, B. (2008). Implementing reform of performance appraisal in China's civil service. *China Information, 19*(1), 39–45.

Coens, T., & Jenkins, M. (2000). *Abolishing performance appraisals: Why they backfire and what to do instead.* San Francisco: Berrett-Koehler.

Coleman, F. (2001). *Ending the employment relationship without ending up in court.* Alexandria, VA: Society for Human Resource Management.

Crum, J. (2009, July). Moving beyond performance standards. *Issues of Merit,* pp. 1–3.

Culbert, S. A. (with Rout, L.). (2010). *Get rid of the performance review! How companies can stop intimidating, start managing—and focus on what really matters.* New York: Business Plus.

Curtis, A. B., Harvey, R. D., & Ravden, D. (2005). Sources of political distortions in performance appraisals: Appraisal purpose and rater accountability. *Group & Organization Management, 30*(1), 42–60.

Daley, D. (2008). The burden of dealing with poor performers: Wear and tear on supervisory organizational engagement. *Review of Public Personnel Administration, 28*(1), 44–59.

DelPo, A. (2007). *The performance appraisal handbook: Legal and practical rules for managers* (2nd ed.). Berkeley, CA: Nolo.

DelPo, A., & Guerin, L. (2003). *Dealing with problem employees: A legal guide* (2nd ed.). Berkeley, CA: Nolo.

Deming, W. E. (1992). *The new economics.* Cambridge: MIT/CAES.

Eckes, G. (1994, November). Practical alternatives to performance appraisal. *Quality Progress,* pp. 57–60.

Eskow, R. (2014, August 7). How big is a $16 billion bank fraud settlement, really? Huffington Post. Retrieved from http://www.huffingtonpost.com/rj-eskow/how-big-is-a-16-billion-b_b_5661934.html

Firing poor performers. (2003, June). *Issues of Merit,* p. 4.

Flynn, N. (2008). *The e-policy handbook: Designing and implementing effective e-mail, Internet, and software policies* (2nd ed.). New York: AMACOM.

Gentry, J. (2005). *HR how-to: Discipline.* Chicago: CCH.

Gilson, B. (2007, May 21). Avoid getting fired: Practical advice for the likely-to-be-tanked federal employee. FedSmith. Retrieved from http://www.fedsmith.com/2007/05/21/avoid-getting-fired-practical-advice-likelytobetanked

Gomez-Mejia, L. R., Balkin, D. B., & Cardy, R. L. (2011). *Managing human resources* (5th ed.). Upper Saddle River, NJ: Prentice Hall.

Gregersen, H. B., Hite, J. M., & Black, J. S. (1996). Expatriate performance appraisal in US multinational firms. *Journal of International Business Studies, 27*(4), 711–752.

Grensing-Pophal, L. (2001, March). Motivate managers to review performance. *HRMagazine,* pp. 44–48.

Grote, D. (1996). *The complete guide to performance appraisal.* New York: AMACOM.

Grote, D. (2001, October). Discipline without punishment. *Across the Board,* pp. 52–57.

Grote, D. (2011). *How to be good at performance appraisals.* Boston: Harvard Business Review Press.

Guffey, C., & Helms, M. (2001). Effective employees: A case of the Internal Revenue Service. *Public Personnel Management, 30*(1), 111–127.

Haga, B. (2014, January 15). HR current: GEAR. Federal Employment Law Training Group. Retrieved from http://blog.feltg.com/2014/06/feb-12-2014-hr-current-gear

Halachmi, A. (1995). The practice of performance appraisal. In J. Rabin, T. Vocino, W. B. Hildreth, & G. J. Miller (Eds.), *Handbook of public personnel administration* (pp. 321–355). New York: Marcel Dekker.

Hauenstein, N. M. A. (1998). Training raters to increase the accuracy of appraisals and the usefulness of feedback. In J. W. Smither (Ed.), *Performance appraisal: State of the art in practice* (pp. 404–442). San Francisco: Jossey-Bass.

Hauser, J. D., & Fay, C. H. (1997). Managing and assessing employee performance. In H. Risher & C. H. Fay (Eds.), *New strategies for public pay* (pp. 185–206). San Francisco: Jossey-Bass.

Heathfield, S. M. (2007). Perform exit interviews. About.com: About Money. Retrieved from http://humanresources.about.com/od/whenemploymentends/a/exit_interview.htm

Heathfield, S. M. (2014). How to hold a difficult conversation: Providing responsible feedback is difficult. About.com: About Money. Retrieved from http://humanresources.about.com/od/interpersonalcommunicatio1/qt/feedback_com6.htm

Holan, A. (2007, September 5). Firing federal workers is difficult. *St. Pete Times*.

Jawahar, I. M. (2005). Do raters consider the influence of situation factors on observed performance when evaluating performance? Evidence from three experiments. *Group & Organization Management, 30*(1), 6–41.

Katz, E. (2014, August 12). Agency chiefs rebuffs union over authority to more quickly fire bad employees. *Government Executive*. Retrieved from http://www.govexec.com/management/2014/08/agency-chief-rebuffs-union-over-authority-more-quickly-fire-bad-employees/91253

Kelloway, E. K., Barling, J., & Harrell, J. J., Jr. (Eds.). (2006). *Handbook of workplace violence*. Thousand Oaks, CA: Sage.

Kluger, A. N., & DeNisi, A., 1996. The effects of feedback interventions on performance: A historical review, a meta-analysis, and a preliminary feedback intervention theory. *Psychological Bulletin, 119*(2), 254–284.

Kunreuther, R. (2008, June 23). Let us praise . . . ourselves. FedSmith. Retrieved from http://www.fedsmith.com/article/1634

Kunreuther, R. (2010, April 20). Decades and the Douglas factors. FedSmith. Retrieved from http://www.fedsmith.com/article/2404/decades-douglas-factors.html

Lewis, G. (2006). *Organizational crisis management: The human factor*. Boca Raton, FL: Auerbach.

Liu, X., & Dong, K. (2012). Development of civil servants' performance appraisal in China: Challenges and improvements. *Review of Public Personnel Administration, 32*(2), 149–168.

London, D. (1995). Giving feedback: Source-centered antecedents and consequences of constructive and destructive feedback. *Human Resource Management Review, 5*, 159–188.

Longenecker, C. O., & Ludwig, D. (1990). Ethical dilemmas in performance appraisals revisited. *Journal of Business Ethics, 9*, 961–969.

Losey, S. (2008, September 1). More execs get top performance ratings. *Federal Times*, pp. 1, 20.

Losey, S. (2011, March 22). Few employees denied step increases for poor performance. *Federal Times*.

Lunney, K. (2012, July 1). Wielding the axe. *Government Executive*, pp. 12–13.

Malos, S. B. (1998). Current legal issues in performance appraisal. In J. W. Smither (Ed.), *Performance appraisal: State of the art in practice* (pp. 49–94). San Francisco: Jossey-Bass.

Maranto, R. (2008, August). Thinking about low performers. *PATimes*, pp. 10–11.

McElveen, R. (2000, March 6). Rewards for employees reap reward for agency. *Federal Times*, pp. 1, 10.

McGregor, D. (1957, May/June). An uneasy look at performance appraisal. *Harvard Business Review*, pp. 89–94.

Meisler, A. (2003, July). Dead man's curve. *Workforce Management*, pp. 44–49.

Milkovich, C. T., & Wigdor, A. K. (1991). *Pay for performance: Evaluating performance appraisal and merit pay*. Washington, DC: National Academy Press.

Minor, M. (1995). *Preventing workplace violence*. Menlo Park, CA: Crisp.

Muñoz, V. (2006, November 27). *An examination of the failures of performance appraisal reform attempts in China's public service system.* Paper presented at the University of Miami.

Murphy, K. R., & Cleveland, J. N. (1995). *Understanding performance appraisal: Social, organizational, and goal-based perspectives.* Thousand Oaks, CA: Sage.

National Performance Review. (1993). *From red tape to results: Creating a government that works better and costs less.* Washington, DC: Government Printing Office.

Nelson, S. (2003, July). Does the solution address the problem? *Issues of Merit,* pp. 1–2.

Nigro, L., Nigro, F., & Kellough, J. E. (2007). *The new public personnel administration* (6th ed.). Belmont, CA: Wadsworth.

Palguta, J. (2001, October 1). Go beyond performance appraisal for good performance. *Federal Times,* p. 15.

Palleschi, A. (2012, January 18). Agencies try out new performance management system. *Government Executive.* Retrieved from http://www.govexec.com/oversight/2012/01/agencies-try-out-new-performance-management-system/40858

Partnership for Public Service & Booz Allen Hamilton. (2010). *Beneath the surface: Understanding attrition in your agency and why it matters.* Washington, DC: Authors.

Perry, J. (2003). Compensation, merit pay, and motivation. In S. W. Hays & R. C. Kearney (Eds.), *Public personnel administration: Problems and prospects* (4th ed., pp. 143–153). Upper Saddle River, NJ: Prentice Hall.

Pickett, L. (2003). Transforming the annual fiasco. *Industrial and Commercial Training, 35*(6), 237–240.

Riccucci, N. M., & Lurie, I. (2001). Employee performance evaluation in social welfare offices. *Review of Public Personnel Administration, 21*(1), 27–37.

Roberts, G. (2003). Employee performance appraisal system participation: A technique that works. *Public Personnel Management, 32*(2), 89–97.

Scott, G. G. (2007). *A survival guide to managing employees from Hell.* New York: AMACOM.

Selden, B. (2007). Firing someone: Does it have to be painful for them and you? National Learning Institute. Retrieved from http://www.businessperform.com/articles/human-resources/firing_someone.html

Shoop, T. (2014, August 7). Obama: It shouldn't be so hard to fire incompetent, unethical execs. *Government Executive.* Retrieved from http://www.govexec.com/federal-news/fedblog/2014/08/obama-it-shouldnt-be-so-hard-fire-incompetent-unethical-execs/90932

Society for Human Resource Management. (2000). *Performance management survey.* Alexandria, VA: Author.

Spector, B. (2003). Human resource management at Enron: The unindicted co-conspirator. *Organizational Dynamics, 32*(2), 207–219.

Sullivan, J. (2013, October 21). Winning "the war to keep your employees" requires re-recruiting your top talent. ERE. Retrieved from http://www.ere.net/2013/10/21/winning-the-war-to-keep-your-employees-requires-re-recruiting-your-top-talent

Thompson, D. (2014, January 30). The case against performance reviews. *Government Executive.* Retrieved from http://www.govexec.com/excellence/promising-practices/2014/01/case-against-performance

Trimble, S. (1998, June 8). The postal scene: Workplace violence hits a five-year low. *Federal Times,* p. 12.

Tyer, C. B. (1983). Employee performance appraisal: A process in search of a technique. In S. W. Hays & R. C. Kearney (Eds.), *Public personnel administration: Problems and prospects* (pp. 118–136). Englewood Cliffs, NJ: Prentice Hall.

Tziner, A., Murphy, K. R., & Cleveland, J. N. (2005). Contextual and rater factors affecting rating behavior. *Group & Organization Management, 30*(1), 89–98.

U.S. Government Accountability Office. (2013). *Opportunities exist to strengthen performance management pilot* (GAO-13-755). Washington, DC: Author.

U.S. Merit Systems Protection Board. (1995). *Removing poor performers in the federal service.* Washington, DC: Author.

U.S. Merit Systems Protection Board. (1999). *Poor performers in government: A quest for the true story.* Washington, DC: Author.

U.S. Merit Systems Protection Board. (2003). *Federal workforce for the 21st century: Results from the Merit Principles Survey 2000*. Washington, DC: Author.

U.S. Merit Systems Protection Board. (2008). *Alternative discipline: Creative solutions for agencies to effectively address employee misconduct*. Washington, DC: Author.

U.S. Merit Systems Protection Board. (2012). *Employee perceptions of workplace violence*. Washington, DC: Author.

West, J. P., & Bowman, J. S. (2014). *Electronic surveillance at work: An ethical analysis*. Unpublished manuscript, University of Miami.

Wexley, K. (1986). Appraisal interview. In R. A. Berk (Ed.), *Performance assessment* (pp. 167–185). Baltimore: Johns Hopkins University Press.

Wiersma, U., & Latham, G. (1986). Practicality of behavioral observation scales, behavioral expectation scales, and trait scales. *Personnel Psychology, 39,* 619–628.

Williams, R. (2012, November 13). Constructive criticism is an oxymoron we should do away with. *Financial Post*. Retrieved from http://businessFinancialPost.com

Wise, C., Clemow, B., Murray, S., Boston, S., & Bingham, L. (2009). When things go wrong. In S. F. Freyss (Ed.), *Human resource management in local government* (3rd ed.). Washington, DC: International City/County Management Association.

Yang, B., & Zheng, D. (2003). A theoretical comparison of U.S. and Chinese culture: Implications for human resource theory and practice. *International Journal of Human Resources Development and Management, 3*(4), 338–358.

Yang, B., Zheng, W., & Li, M. (2006). Confucian view of learning and implications for developing human resources. *Advances in Developing Human Resources, 8*(3), 346–354.

Yemm, G. (2013). *Essential guide to leading your team: How to set goals, measure performance and reward talent*. London: Pearson Education.

Zhao, S. M. (1994). Human resource management in China. *Asia-Pacific Journal of Human Resources, 32*(2), 3–12.

Ziegler, M. (2004, March 1). Merit pay anxiety. *Federal Times*, pp. 1, 6.

CHAPTER 11

Unions and the Government

Protectors, Partners, and Punishers

The best union organizer? Bad management.

—Anonymous

After studying this chapter, you should be able to

- appreciate the mixed views of unions held by employees and managers;
- identify differences in orientation and behavior between unions and management;
- distinguish the key issues that separate union partisans and opponents;
- determine the differences in labor–management relations between the public and private sectors; and
- understand paradoxes, contradictions, trends, and variations in labor–management relations.

Public employee unions are under fire as governments at all levels seek to cope with limited resources and budget reductions. In Michigan, for example, the state legislature adopted the Fiscal Accountability Act in 2011, authorizing the governor to appoint an emergency manager if a fiscal emergency is deemed imminent. The broad powers delegated to the appointee to address the financial emergency may include modifications to the collective bargaining contract. If such an appointed manager were to modify the terms and conditions of employment as spelled out in the union–management agreement, effectively replacing the role of elected officials and democratically selected union representatives with an unelected third party, this might well raise legal concerns under the Contract

Clause of the U.S. Constitution (Befort, 2011; Shimabukuro, 2011). Legislative actions in other states have raised similar legal, ethical, and constitutional issues. This chapter explores issues of unions and government that are highly salient now, but that have been percolating for several years. The example that follows illustrates the role of unions as protectors, partners, and punishers.

Organized labor flexed its political muscle to help repeal a controversial Ohio law, Senate Bill 5, that was passed by the Republican-led legislature and signed by Governor John Kasich, who took office vowing to curb union power. The law allowed only limited collective bargaining for the state's 360,000 public employees, and in the event of an impasse elected officials could unilaterally impose their side's final contract offer. Binding arbitration was banned, together with negotiating on pensions, health coverage, and staffing levels. Further, public workers were required to pay 15% of their health insurance costs and 10% of their salaries toward their pensions (Greenhouse, 2011a; Maher & Nicas, 2011). The law banned strikes and included provisions making it harder to collect union dues from employees who opt out of union membership. Opponents of the law were able to collect 1.3 million signatures to force a public vote before the law could take effect.

Through a vote on Issue 2 (as the ballot initiative was labeled), the law was repealed by a resounding margin: 62% to 38%. Labor groups under the umbrella organization We Are Ohio, in a vigorous $30 million no-holds-barred campaign, battled Republican-affiliated opponents of repeal. Build a Better Ohio, the opposing group, spent only $7.5 million (Huey-Burns, 2011; Weiner, 2011). Union staffing helped as well: Thousands of union members made phone calls and knocked on doors. The unions were victorious in a battle that Freeman and Hilbrich (2013) characterize as "the greatest partisan division over unions and bargaining in U.S. history" (p. 2). The unions' success in this fight shows the political power of organized labor to mobilize members and leverage public policy.

Visible opposition to Senate Bill 5 came from the AFL-CIO, the National Education Association, the Ohio Democratic Party, state public employee associations, and other unions. Union leaders, concerned about the declining economic power of unions in recent years and weakened by a schism in the national AFL-CIO, were anxious about preserving their political clout, which depended in large measure on their ability to bargain, preserve benefits, and obtain dues from their members. They detected a not-so-hidden agenda on the part of business to undermine union rights and silence the political voice of working families. Governor Kasich put his weight behind the law as part of his sweeping "reform agenda." Other prominent supporters included members of the National Tax Limitation Committee, the Ohio Republican Party, the conservative organization FreedomWorks, and other business-related groups.

Union leaders were concerned that a victory by antilabor forces in Ohio would propel further antiunion legislative initiatives onto the national agenda. They also deemed protecting the political clout of unions essential in Ohio's efforts to safeguard members' interests in the future. To succeed in repealing Senate Bill 5, unions had to "partner" with other concerned parties (public employee groups, including teachers, firefighters, nurses, and police). The repeal highlights another role of unions as well: They are "punishers" of those whose interests run counter to those of labor. In political campaigns business typically outspends unions by a large margin, but Ohio's unions battled valiantly to outspend their opponents as they resisted restrictions on union rights and power. They succeeded in punishing the "enemies of labor" by engineering a public and embarrassing defeat of those who supported the law. In retrospect, it is clear that legislative supporters of Senate Bill 5 overreached in their efforts to address financial deficits and weaken union power. Their case was further hurt by public sympathy for police, firefighters, and teachers who were adamantly opposed to further layoffs and budget cuts.

As this case shows, unions are adept at hardball politics: They act as protectors (defending employees' rights and interests), partners (with prolabor stakeholders), and punishers (against those perceived to be antilabor). These three roles help explain union behavior both internally (within the workplace) and externally (outside the workplace).

The defeat of Senate Bill 5, along with some union victories in the private sector, led some observers to conclude in the mid-2000s that a resurgence of union strength was occurring. Indeed, Richard Trumka, AFL-CIO president, said at the time, "Those who spend their time scapegoating workers and pushing a partisan agenda will only strengthen the resolve of the working people" (quoted in Huey-Burns, 2011); he also warned, "Governors in other states ought to take heed of this. If not, they do so at their own peril, and they may fact a backlash" (quoted in Clark, 2012, p. 204). Improved union prospects were thought to be linked to the national trend toward an "hourglass" economy, with high-wage, high-skill jobs on one end, low-wage service jobs on the other, and a shrinking middle class in between. The Ohio case also may have given the mistaken impression, however, that public sector unions are currently very strong. Although some unions in selected locales continue to exercise considerable clout, the trend has been in the opposite direction, notwithstanding the numbers of employees who belong to unions. As will be shown later in this chapter, recent state legislative actions in Wisconsin, Indiana, New Jersey, and elsewhere have been designed to turn back union gains and undercut worker rights.

This chapter examines union roles in governmental labor–management relations (LMRs). It provides background on employee relations and explores the mixed perspectives of employees and managers toward unions. Key paradoxes, contradictions, trends, and variations in LMRs are highlighted. Issues linked to collective bargaining in government are discussed in Chapter 12. In short, Chapters 11 and 12 point out that LMRs are critical to both the foundations and the functions of human resource management, now and in the future.

BACKGROUND: CONTEXT AND EVOLUTION OF EMPLOYEE RELATIONS

Given the central place of labor relations in public management, it is useful to briefly canvass its role in current public administration theory and practice.[1] Specifically, three topics are addressed in this section: contemporary history, pertinent laws, and collective bargaining processes.

The final quarter of the 20th century was a time of economic flux and uncertainty: energy crises, stagflation, and the beginnings of the demise of the labor movement during the 1970s; global competition and deindustrialization in the 1980s; and the "new economy" of the 1990s. What emerged, through programs of deregulation and privatization, were doctrines and policies advocating reliance on the market to allocate society's resources. The approach saw its fullest expression in the initial decade of the new millennium as markets were regarded as good, efficient, nonpartisan, and objective. Public provision of goods and services was seen as an obstacle to economic development as neoliberalism became the dominant ideology through which economic activity was to be understood. Government policies intended to buffer citizens from the business cycle were altered in the name of market-based strategies. New Public Management prescriptions were aimed at the welfare state and sought to reduce government's capacity to act; weaken merit system protections, job security, and worker rights; and privatize much of the civil service.

The rise and decline of unions in contemporary history is well documented: Representing more than one-third of U.S. workers by the mid-20th century, unions were a "countervailing power" against business and government in American democracy (Early, 2013; Galbraith, 1952/2010; Reich, 2007). Viewed as the champion of the underdog, organized labor was influential in many policy debates (e.g., trade, taxes, fair labor standards, social security, civil rights, public education, health care, equal pay for women, workplace safety). Its gains went well beyond on-the-job concerns, transforming the lives of all Americans and helping build the middle class. The achievements made by private sector unions did not go unnoticed by civil servants. A surge in public service unionism resulted from President John F. Kennedy's 1962 executive order authorizing federal worker unionization and limited collective bargaining rights, as well as from laws passed in 42 states granting collective bargaining or meet-and-confer rights to all or part of their workforces. Overall, compensation and productivity doubled in American society during the first 30 years after World War II.

During the next 30 years, labor's clout diminished as the effects of the 1947 Taft-Hartley Act (outlawing actions by unions not involved in a dispute and undermining unions in "right-to-work" states) and the 1959 Landrum-Griffith Act (allowing hiring of nonunion workers and permitting them to vote in union certification elections) became manifest. Historian Colin Gordon (2013) writes:

> Labor's foothold [on political power] continued to slip through concessionary bargaining of the 1970s and 1980s—an era highlighted by the filibuster of labor law reform in 1978, the Reagan administration's crushing of the PATCO strike, the Chrysler bailout (which set the template for "too big to fail" corporate rescues built around deep concessions by workers), and the passage of anti-worker trade deals with Mexico and China [in the 1990s].

The results of this erosion have been palpable and deleterious: The shift of economic risk from employers to employees has caused hardship and anxiety in the workforce as the fear of loss of benefits and/or job loss has left large segments of society feeling financially insecure (Hacker, 2006; West, 2012). The union movement, in fact, has been on the defensive to protect fair labor standards established during the New Deal, as pay and benefits have largely plateaued during the past 30 years.

A victim of its earlier success in improving compensation and working conditions, organized labor came to be viewed as just another special interest unsuited to a changing economy and unjustly protective of marginal employees. The National Labor Relations Board did little to curb business union-busting strategies. Relevant laws made it very difficult for workers to organize, union-avoidance consultants enabled firms to operate union-free, and companies were seldom penalized when offenses occurred (Bronfenbrenner, 2009; Getman, 2012; Greenhouse, 2009; Logan, 2006).

In the public arena, after a dramatic rise in the 1960s and 1970s, union membership flatlined in the 1980s and has remained stagnant since that time due to chronic fiscal stress, limited government growth, privatization, and taxpayer hostility. While these trends occurred earlier in the business sector, in both private and public administration, the market—absent a strong labor movement—does not assure that employees will share in the benefits of increased productivity and economic growth. Indeed, the suppression of employee organizations, weak enforcement of labor laws, and violations of worker rights in the United States is unique among advanced nations (Delaney, 2005; Kearney & Mareschal, 2014, p. 12). In short, important facets of labor–management relations include its evolution, legal basis, and collective bargaining procedures. These foundational elements are amplified in the analysis that follows.

DIFFERING VIEWS OF UNIONS

Most public employees and managers have definite opinions about unions—some favorable, some unfavorable. On the positive side, employees dissatisfied with their jobs or working conditions might see union membership as a way to salve their smoldering discontent, offering an avenue for championing workplace reforms. Unions might protect vulnerable workers and enable them to seek redress against arbitrary or capricious actions by employers. Workers may also think union membership can amplify their voices in the workplace and increase their influence with management. Vigilant unions can help keep management honest and ensure fair dealings with personnel. Collective action, especially in the labor-intensive public sector, sometimes yields results unattainable through concerted individual efforts. For example, unions have assumed leadership in supporting employee-friendly initiatives (Chapter 8) and in helping workers gain more competitive salaries (Chapter 7). Indeed, a public sector survey found that professional employees in collective bargaining states have weighted mean salaries nearly 20% higher than those in states without collective bargaining (American Federation of Teachers [AFT], 2004). Other compensation surveys have found higher (AFT, 2012) or lower (Freeman & Hilbrich, 2013) wage advantages in states with bargaining, but all of these identify a wage premium attendant to bargaining. Employees might also enjoy the feelings of solidarity as well as the perks (discounts, legal aid, loans, credit cards, insurance) that accompany union membership.

Workers who have negative views of unions might focus on such aspects as dues, unresponsive labor leaders, unflattering stereotypes associated with unions, and questionable benefits. Additional objections arise from distaste for the defense unions may give to nonproductive workers, negative views of unions' tendency to support one-size-fits-all solutions, and the belief that unions are unnecessary to accomplish workers' aims. Furthermore, some workers might prefer to be represented by a professional association rather than by a union.

Administrators have negative or positive attitudes toward unions as well. Some see unions as spiking up costs, pushing down productivity, impeding organizational change, and concentrating more on advancing employee interests than on serving citizen interests. Others oppose union organizing efforts, fearing that rigid, binding labor contracts alter or erode managerial rights and decrease administrative discretion and flexibility. Managers may view unions as introducing conflict, distraction, and disruption into the workplace, thus inhibiting cooperative working relationships. Unions may be viewed as reflexively proemployee and antimanagement. Also, unions may be seen to complicate or delay policy implementation. Some managers, especially those in **right-to-work states** (where mandatory union membership is outlawed), believe that current organizational policies and procedures are fair to employees. Such managers may believe that there is no need for **meet-and-confer rights** (i.e., laws requiring agency heads to discuss, but not to settle, grievances) or bargaining rights that force them to work with unions on employment matters. Those opposed to unions often combine their criticisms with proposals to privatize public services. Managers may try to inoculate employees against union appeals by quickly responding to morale concerns, establishing grievance procedures, and empowering workers. Some officials think that union organizing efforts result from management's unfair treatment of employees. Actually, proper treatment could be the best impediment to organizing. This is the view taken by the AFL-CIO, which has identified five factors that reduce the chances for union organizing: (1) bosses not taking advantage of employees, (2) employee pride in their work, (3) agency records of good employee performance, (4) avoidance of favoritism and high-handed treatment, and (5) good supervisor–subordinate relations ("What to Do," 1966). Appendix A at the end of this chapter provides a list of tips for managers when dealing with unions; Appendix B lists tips for unions when dealing with managers.

Employers with positive attitudes toward unions see them as contributing to a form of workplace democracy, enabling labor and management to join in improving conditions of employment. Such managers may want to tap employee preferences, prefer one-stop bargaining, and see unions as a way to ensure a level playing field for workers. They prefer to work with member-supported union representatives rather than disparate groups purporting to reflect worker sentiments but lacking the legitimacy of a representation election.

Managers and employees can have either positive or negative perceptions about each other. In some cases, this is most evident in relations between the chief executive officer and his or her union leader counterpart. When stereotypes threaten to poison such relationships, they are often based on negative perceptions each participant has of the other party (see Benest & Grijalva, 2002). Exhibits 11.1 and 11.2 show some of the stereotypes that might get in the way of effective relations between labor union leaders and city managers, as well as some steps that might be taken by each to enhance the relationship.

It is not surprising, then, that employees and managers react differently to unions. Working in a unionized environment prods both parties to consider how their jobs are

Exhibit 11.1   Overcoming Stereotypes and Enhancing the Chief Executive Officer–Union Perceptions

Union Leaders' Perceptions of Managers	Managers' Perceptions of Union Leaders
Managers "don't get it."	Union leaders are not management oriented.
They are "political" animals.	They are insulated, isolated.
They have no backbone in the face of political controversy.	They have a high need to be liked by their members.
They have no ethics.	They "don't do much."
They have short attention spans and are "frenetic."	They are not politically savvy.
They are shortsighted regarding labor relations.	They lack a big-picture perspective.
They are too concerned about quantity and not concerned enough about quality.	They are change resistant.
They are "cheap."	They do not promote diversity.
	They know more about their service than about managing people.
	They are poor collaborators.

Exhibit 11.2   Fifteen Ideas to Enhance the Relationships Between Chief Executive Officers and Union Leaders

Ideas for both partners:

- Acknowledge the difference in their roles.
- Put aside negative perceptions.
- Get to know each other.
- Look at the relationship as a partnership.

Ideas for chief executive officers:

- Acknowledge the benefit of improved public services.
- Support the advocacy of union leaders.
- Do not demonize the union.
- Appreciate union leaders' relationship to an active union.
- Reach out to public employees.
- Insist that union leaders develop wider perspectives.

(Continued)

Exhibit 11.2 (Continued)

Ideas for union leaders:

- Educate the managers.
- Pick your battles.
- Distinguish between facts and perceptions.
- Proactively become an asset to the larger organization.
- Broaden the perspectives of union members.

SOURCE: Adapted from Benest and Grijalva (2002).

affected by the presence of organized labor. Not only do employees and managers have different views of unions, so too do elected officials of different ideological stripes. Recently, as noted, public employee unions have been under attack by conservative governors in Wisconsin, New Jersey, and Indiana (see Exhibit 11.3). Such threats to unions are likely to continue in the foreseeable future. In today's hyperpartisan climate, issues sparked by unions and collective bargaining have generated heated disputes among labor advocates and opponents. The ideological differences are further explored in Exhibit 11.4.

Exhibit 11.3　Recent Threats to Unions in Wisconsin, New Jersey, and Indiana

As private sector unions have declined in power over the past few decades, public sector unions have become increasingly prominent. Public sector union members account for more than half of unionized American workers (Greenhouse, 2011b). Early 2011 may be remembered as the watershed moment for these unions. As state governments grappled with rising budget deficits in a recessionary period, several Republican governors aimed to handicap government unions in an effort to address budget shortfalls. Democrats charged that this was a reckless political gambit that was simply intended to demolish a bastion of traditional Democratic support (Greenhouse, 2011b). Republicans countered that Democrats were obstructing necessary cost-cutting measures because they are in bed with these unions.

In a purported effort to reduce Wisconsin's $137 billion budget deficit, the state's Republican assembly voted to limit public sector unions' bargaining rights (Spicuzza & Barbour, 2011). Now, union members (excepting police, firefighters, and state troopers) can bargain only for wage increases; they are barred from bargaining for any other concern (e.g., pensions, health care benefits, working conditions). Contracts covering state workers have a duration of one year, the state cannot collect union dues and remit them to unions, and annual elections are required to assess whether unions maintain their majority status (Clark, 2012). The law shifted the burden of paying for pensions and health care from government to employees.

In Wisconsin, 46.6% of government workers are union members (Kelleher, 2011). Governor Scott Walker, a Republican, argued that the proposed changes were the only alternative to government layoffs. Union activists countered that Walker's aim was to effectively destroy unions. More than

10,000 angry demonstrators surrounded the state capitol during several weeks of round-the-clock protests. Democratic state legislators fled to neighboring Illinois in order to stall a vote. Eventually, the Republicans were able to force a legislative victory on the 140-page bill with little time for debate, and Walker quickly signed it into law in 2011. Wisconsin's Supreme Court narrowly upheld the statute (Marley & Walker, 2011). Recall elections against those legislators supporting the governor were held. While hotly contested, the recall elections were unable to change the majority party in the legislature. Subsequently, Governor Walker survived a recall election in 2012 with 53% of the vote, a painful blow to Democrats and labor unions (Davey & Zeleny, 2012).

Governor Chris Christie of New Jersey, a Republican, lobbied in 2011 for increases in the contributions state employees make to their health insurance and pension plans. In response, union members demonstrated in the legislature and disrupted a state senate hearing; several demonstrators were arrested (Pérez-Peña, 2011). In a state where liberals have historically been the stalwart champions of unions, many Democrats nonetheless defected to join a predominantly Republican effort to reduce benefits, impose restrictions, and freeze wages and pensions (Powell, 2011). The state also enacted wage increase caps of 2% per year resulting from interest arbitration for police and fire personnel and suspended collective bargaining over health care for 4 years (Clark, 2012).

In 2005 Governor Mitch Daniels of Indiana, a Republican, rescinded a long-standing executive order that established collective bargaining rights for state employees. This action, together with Daniels's failure to approve pay raises for state employees for several years and his increased reliance on privatization of public services, resulted in a significant reduction in the numbers of state employees. As a consequence, union membership declined from 16,408 in 2005 to 1,490 in 2011 (Freeman & Han, 2012). Another Republican governor, Roy Blunt of Missouri, also reversed the executive order of his Democratic predecessor authorizing collective bargaining for state employees.

Some contend that public sector unions are a dangerous threat with no natural predator, because the forces of the market have little direct effect on public sector unions' clout. Others point out that confrontations such as those described above are part of a long-standing assault on American labor by businesses that have shipped jobs overseas, denied employees their share of productivity gains, and depressed wages and benefits. In light of these developments, what mechanisms do American public workers have to ensure their rights?

Exhibit 11.4   Government and Unions: Public Enemy or Defenders?

In times of budgetary crisis, the public may blame government excess. Government is accused of being too large and too expensive. If programs are criticized for being the embodiments of waste and graft, government employees are the human targets. They are accused of being lazy, underqualified, and overpaid. It seems it is a matter of core principle to many that public workers should never have more benefits or earn higher compensation than their private sector counterparts (McGinnis & Schanzenbach, 2010, p. 6). In the eyes of the typical American worker, public employees, who do not jump the hurdles of the free market system yet manage to live comfortably, must be gaming the political system (Weisenthal, 2011). To add insult to injury, public sector laurels are paid for with hardworking Americans' tax dollars.

(Continued)

Exhibit 11.4 (Continued)

Castigations of public sector unions by a clamorous minority may create the illusion that most Americans despise these workers. Yet polling indicates that moderate voters do not resent public sector unions. They usually do not feel a deep-seated animus against schoolteachers, police officers, firefighters, nurses, and postal workers ("Time for Second Thoughts?," 2011).

Public unions are also considered obstructions to bureaucratic reform. They may oppose policy innovations that could potentially streamline government services (McGinnis & Schanzenbach, 2010, p. 3). Prison worker unions, for example, have opposed decriminalization of drugs and a systematic reduction of prison sentences for a number of crimes in order to safeguard union members (McGinnis & Schanzenbach, 2010, p. 4). While liberals have traditionally supported unions, such efforts have the potential to alienate liberal allies (Greenhouse, 2011b; McGinnis & Schanzenbach, 2010). Indeed, at the height of the 2011 controversy in New Jersey (see Exhibit 11.3), the strong alliance that once existed between unions and Democrats in that state seemed to have partially disintegrated (Powell, 2011). Governor Christie has more recently split the labor movement in his state, with public unions as staunch opponents but private unions supportive of his spending reforms and job creation efforts (Malanga, 2013).

Conservative leaders have berated teachers' unions for their consistent opposition to firing prerogatives and wages based on merit (McFadyen, 2000, p. 131). In response, teachers' unions proffer the empirical record of failed merit pay schemes (McFadyen, 2000, p. 132). Teachers also reference the prejudicial subjectivity inherent in merit pay programs (Chapter 7). Many union advocates consider the debate on this issue to be a method of obfuscating the real issue of low teacher pay (McFadyen, 2000, p. 134). Nevertheless, as student test scores continue to drop across the United States, many see the intransigence of teachers' unions as an obstacle to needed education reform, such as the institution of charter schools (McGinnis & Schanzenbach, 2010, p. 9). This view is depicted in the 2010 documentary film *Waiting for "Superman"*—although one would not learn from this movie that charter school test scores are no better than those of traditional public schools.

Despite the negative role unions might play in reducing government costs and improving performance and efficiency, budget hawks should not label unions "public enemy number one." Unions are blamed for budget deficits while conservatives like Wisconsin governor Scott Walker simultaneously support tax breaks for the wealthy (Madland, 2011) and create self-induced budget crises. Walker and other conservative governors have severely limited collective bargaining rights, often under the guise of budget constraints—even though states that do not have collective bargaining statutes also have large deficits. In fact, three national opinion polls conducted in spring 2011 found that the public was opposed to stripping collective bargaining rights, 60% to 30% (Keen & Cauchon, 2011; Meyerson, 2011), demonstrating that Americans are reluctant to take away a right that unions have long had. Indeed, scapegoating unions deflects attention from the reckless Wall Street behavior that caused the deficits. The effect is that eviscerating unions makes both political parties even more dependent on the wealthy.

There is, to state the case differently, no other nationwide organization dedicated to fighting persistently for middle-class economic issues, no other that is able to mobilize working-class voters for a progressive agenda. Union accomplishments in the past century should not be discounted: the 8-hour workday and overtime pay, job and retirement security, a ban on child labor, family medical leave, equal pay for women, workplace safety, public education, and Social Security. In fact, the New Deal order produced the only three decades in American history when economic security and opportunity were widely shared. It was the only time when unions were powerful enough to ensure that corporate revenue was trickled down to workers to be shared (Meyerson, 2011). The paradox is that the Great Depression invigorated unions, while the Great Recession has crippled them.

Unions clearly raise contentious issues among key stakeholders. Exhibit 11.5 lists some questions that public employees and administrators are likely to ask as they sort out their thoughts on unions, labor relations, and collective bargaining. Answers to these questions will change from one work environment to another because of the complicated nature of public sector LMRs and existing trends. These complications are discussed below.

Exhibit 11.5   Questions for Employees and Employers Regarding Unions, Labor–Management Relations, and Collective Bargaining

Employees

- Should I join a union?
- What do unions do?
- Will I have a voice in a union?
- Will unions act on my complaints?
- Will unions protect my rights?
- Will unions affect my relationship with management?
- What is the downside of a union?
- Does collective bargaining affect me?
- Will unions effectively represent my interests?
- What should unions push for in negotiations?
- Should I participate in a work stoppage?

Employers

- How will a union affect my organization?
- How do unions affect the way employees work?
- Should I support or resist unionization?
- Will relationships with unions be cooperative or adversarial?
- Can I work effectively with union leaders?
- Do I have confidence in management's negotiating team?
- What should management seek to have in a contract?
- Will management prerogatives be protected in negotiations?
- Will contract provisions limit my managerial discretion?
- How will employee grievances be handled?
- How will contract or grievance disputes be resolved?

PARADOXES AND CONTRADICTIONS

As in other areas of human resource management, in LMRs paradoxes are plentiful and contradictions are unavoidable. Some examples include the following:

- High-performance work organizations require high levels of trust and cooperative activity, but zero-sum bargaining, where one side's gain is another side's loss, makes this difficult.

- Collective bargaining arrangements are crucial but may be incompatible with efficient merit system operations.
- Union and management might profess support for productivity improvement efforts, but that support might drop off when job security is threatened.
- Dispute resolution mechanisms add stability to LMRs, but such provisions in collective bargaining laws empower unelected arbitrators, which may diminish democratic accountability to citizens.
- Unions claim to compete on a level playing field with other interest groups (e.g., taxpayer associations, privatization advocates) seeking to influence government. They have a distinct advantage over these groups, however, given unions' right to bargain on wages, hours, and working conditions, as well as to lobby legislative bodies for special benefits.
- Managers are held accountable for making decisions and taking actions in the public interest, but the extent of unionization and the provisions of a management-approved labor contract may limit their discretion.
- Union approval ratings are higher among younger workers, but younger American employees are the least unionized.
- Administrators frequently profess support for employee participation in program design and implementation, but they often prefer that such participation be conducted through nonunion channels.

Three additional paradoxes and problems deserve mention. First, LMRs in government are based on old-style, private sector conflict resolution, where both sides stake out adversarial positions before negotiations commence. The traditional framework underlying the labor–management relationship actually undermines it. A new style for managing conflict would turn this old process on its head and put greater emphasis on cooperation, with labor and management representatives talking first and drafting specific policies last. Experiments in LMRs using this approach (see Chapter 12) show promising results (Balser & Winkler, 2012; Deery & Iverson, 2005; Masters, Albright, & Eplion, 2006). Strategic human resource managers need to carefully consider the pros and cons of the old style of managing conflict versus the new and decide which has the greater potential to achieve institutional goals and advance the well-being of employees given the organizational climate, available resources, and bureaucratic structures.

Second is the **free rider** problem, which is based on the distinction between union membership and union representation: Employees may benefit from unions without being members. Membership figures are often much smaller than representation figures (i.e., employees belong to bargaining units but fail to join the union). For example, in 2003 the American Federation of Government Employees had 222,000 dues-paying members, but it represented approximately 600,000 employees—a free rider rate of 64%. Thus, in many **open shop** governmental settings, workers may be the beneficiaries of union-sponsored initiatives without joining the union or paying dues.[2] Free riders avoid the pain but receive the gain from union efforts. Overall trends in union membership and representation in the federal, state, and local government sectors are shown in Exhibit 11.6, which displays the numbers of union members versus the numbers of employees represented by the unions

Exhibit 11.6   Government and Private Sector Union Membership and Representation: 2010–2013 (in thousands)

	Total Employed	Members of Unions		Represented by Unions	
		Total	Percentage	Total	Percentage
2013 government workers	20,429	7,210	35.3	7,900	38.7
Federal	3,515	932	26.5	1,096	31.2
State	6,353	1,966	30.9	2,147	33.8
Local	10,561	4,311	40.8	4,658	44.1
2012 government workers	20,385	7,328	35.9	8,072	39.6
Federal	3,552	956	26.9	1,114	31.4
State	6,279	1,968	31.3	2,190	34.9
Local	10,554	4,404	41.7	4,768	45.2
2011 government workers	20,450	7,562	37.0	8,321	40.7
Federal	3,568	1,004	28.1	1,185	33.2
State	6,261	1,973	31.5	2,189	35.0
Local	10,621	4,586	43.2	4,947	46.6
2010 government workers	21,033	7,623	36.2	8,406	40.0
Federal	3,670	984	26.8	1,154	31.4
State	6,328	1,969	31.1	2,191	34.6
Local	11,035	4,670	42.3	5,061	45.9
2013 private workers	108,681	7,318	6.7	8,128	7.5
2012 private workers	107,191	7,037	6.6	7,851	7.3
2011 private workers	104,737	7,202	6.9	7,969	7.6
2010 private workers	103,040	7,092	6.9	7,884	7.7

SOURCE: Bureau of Labor Statistics.

(these data reflect a less pronounced free rider problem than the example above from the American Federation of Government Employees).

Third is the paradox relating to the inherent value differences between unions and management. Although there has been some movement toward greater cooperation, a number of incompatibilities still exist between organized labor and management. As noted in Exhibit 11.7, unions and management differ in distinctions among organization members, involvement in decision making, basis for security, allocation of rewards, goals, and grounds for action. (These differences will become more apparent below.) The next section

Exhibit 11.7 Union and Management Value Differences

Union	Management
Egalitarian—few distinctions among members, all are treated the same.	Hierarchical—more distinctions among people, levels of control, chain of command.
Democratic decision making by members.	Decision making by few.
Security through mutual protection; "an injury to one is an injury to all."	Security based on competition; each gets what each deserves; individualism.
Seniority is basis for deciding among members.	Performance is basis for deciding among members.
Goals: job security, quality of work life, safety, better wages and benefits.	Goals: productivity, approval from voters, low tax rates, customer satisfaction.
Past practice and precedent control actions and decisions.	Actions and decisions are pragmatic—what works best now.

fleshes out the context of public sector labor relations and highlights some of the trends and variations that distinguish it from the private sector—patterns in LMRs that evolved in the business sphere were later adapted to the government arena.

TRENDS AND VARIATIONS

In business and industry union membership has been steadily declining since the 1950s, despite fluctuating growth spurts in public sector union membership. Overall, organized labor's share of the workforce dropped from 14.5% in 1996 to 11.3% in 2013, down considerably from 1954, when unions represented 35% of the nation's workers (Bureau of Labor Statistics, 2011, 2014). Still, in 2013 public sector workers were nearly five times more likely than private sector employees to be union members; it is not yet known whether this gap will close. The proportion of union membership in the public and private spheres in 1994 was 38.7% versus 10.8%, respectively; in 2013 it was 35.3% versus 6.7%. Total union membership was 14.5 million in 2013 (Bureau of Labor Statistics, 2014). Thus, nearly 4 in 10 government workers are union members, compared with fewer than 1 in 10 corporate personnel. While the unionization rate among government workers has varied little since 1983, the rate among private workers has declined (Bureau of Labor Statistics, 2010). As the Bureau of Labor Statistics reported, in 2010, for the first time in U.S. history, more public sector workers than private sector workers were unionized (Greenhouse, 2010). However, as a result of private sector gains and government cost cutting in 2013, there are now once again more private sector union members than public sector members: In that year the number of private sector union members increased by 281,0000, while public sector union membership dropped by about 118,000 (Bureau of Labor Statistics, 2014). In 2013, 7.2 million public employees and 7.3 million private sector workers were union members.

There are several reasons for the drop in private sector union membership. Among the most frequently mentioned are the growth of high-tech industries (where unions are harder to organize), heightened international and domestic competition, deregulation, bargaining outcome and process changes, the rise of antiunion advocacy groups, geographic shifts (from Frostbelt to Sunbelt), changes in the workforce (from blue-collar to pink-collar; greater representation of Hispanics, Asians, and African Americans), and changes in the workplace (downsizing, outsourcing). Other factors include management opposition in representation elections, replacement of striking workers, and reluctance by unions to push organizing drives in an era when gains in union jobs can be erased by losses (Freeman & Hilbrich, 2013; Katz, 2013; Milkman, 2013). Stanley Aronowitz (1998) attributed declining membership rolls at the end of the 20th century to the tendency of unions to cater to the least needy (steel- and autoworkers) rather than the neediest (farm and hotel workers), the self-interested parochialism of union leaders, and misplaced attention on bargaining and grievance processing rather than on organizing. Thomas J. Donahue, president of the U.S. Chamber of Commerce, put a different spin on the reasons for falling membership: "Improved employer–employee relationships, the fading appeal of labor's 'big government' politics, and persistent tales of union corruption" ("U.S. Labor Struggles," 1998). Whatever the explanation, until recently public sector unions have done a better job of maintaining membership than their private sector counterparts.

While there has been a fairly steady decline in union membership over the past several decades (primarily in the private sector), there are some signs that organized labor is undergoing reinvention. This is occurring, in part, through so-called **alt-labor groups**: workers' associations and work centers. Examples include the National Taxi Workers Alliance, Working America, National Domestic Workers Alliance, National Guestworkers Alliance, Restaurant Opportunities Centers, and National Day Laborer Organizing Network (Israel, 2014). Unlike in traditional labor organizing, where workers must find unionized workplaces or put their jobs at risk to organize workplaces eligible to unionize, alt-labor groups have been successful in signing up millions through effective organizing strategies. Operating outside the traditional sphere and unable to rely on collective bargaining, they face the challenge of obtaining sustainable revenues. Support typically comes from foundations, donors, the AFL-CIO, and membership dues. Tactics may include strikes, demonstrations, public presence, workplace justice campaigns, education, and/or training. Such groups are continually experimenting to develop a labor model that is viable on a large scale, and they are beginning to make their presence felt (Florito & Jarley, 2012; Israel, 2014; Milkman, 2013). Without abandoning traditional workplace organizing, they are pursuing a strategic shift in advancing worker interests (Meyerson, 2013).

The rise in public arena union membership has occurred in the past five decades, with the largest growth spurt in the 1960s and 1970s, moderate growth in the 1980s, and flat growth in the 1990s and 2000s. In 1960, there were 900,000 public sector union members (penetration of 10.8%). By 1980, government unions were the largest department in the AFL-CIO, and 2 out of 5 public employees had union representation. The overwhelming majority of all public sector union members, 73.4%, are currently at the state and local levels; only 26.8% are at the federal level (Bureau of Labor Statistics, 2011). This represents a remarkable turnaround from 1950, when more federal workers (69%) than state and local government employees (31%) were union members (Orzechowski & Marlow, 1995). The following are some of the reasons for subnational growth in public sector union membership:

- Changes in public policy (executive orders, statutory laws)
- Vigorous union organizing efforts
- The rise of social movements (civil rights, antiwar, feminism)
- The success of various job actions (slowdowns, strikes)
- Lagging wages
- Rising public sector employment
- Inexperience of government employers in resisting early union organizing campaigns
- Increasing threats to employee job security

Not only do membership trends vary between the two sectors, but labor law also varies. Public sector labor law has lagged behind developments in the private arena, but it draws on several concepts first codified in private sector legislation, so some familiarity with the earlier legislation (summarized in Exhibit 11.8) is important as a foundation for understanding the laws applying to the public sector. Although public sector labor relations are adapted from the business model, there are significant differences between the sectors; Exhibit 11.9 provides clarification of those differences before we turn to a discussion of public sector policy developments in LMRs.

Turning to policy at the local government level, in New York City, Mayor Robert F. Wagner Jr. issued Executive Order 49 in 1958, which recognized collective bargaining with unions, established grievance procedures, and set procedures for **bargaining unit determination** and **exclusive representation** (see Aronowitz, 1998). The evolution of public policy dealing with federal public sector legislation began 4 years later with a

Exhibit 11.8   Five Major Pieces of Private Sector Labor Legislation, 1926–1959

- **1926: Railway Labor Act.** Grants rail workers unionization and bargaining rights. Also covers resolution of disputes with, and interpretations of, any negotiated contract.
- **1932: Norris-LaGuardia Act.** Restricts injunctions and repudiates "yellow-dog contracts."
- **1935: Wagner Act.** Also known as National Labor Relations Act, or NLRA. Gives all workers the right to unionize and collectively bargain, lists unfair labor practices, describes union certification elections, and creates the National Labor Relations Board to watch over it all.
- **1947: Taft-Hartley Act.** Amended the NLRA and created the Federal Mediation and Conciliation Service to aid in dispute resolution; provides emergency procedures, lists unfair union labor practices, and gives states the right to pass right-to-work laws.
- **1959: Landrum-Griffin Act.** Also known as the Labor–Management Reporting and Disclosure Act. Requires unions to file financial and trusteeship reports and to set employee rights, including the right of union members to attend meetings and nominate/vote for candidates.

Exhibit 11.9   Public and Private Sector Differences

1. Benefits

   - *Public sector:* Many nonbargained benefits are provided via civil service statutes (e.g., employee grievance procedures, health/life insurance, sick leave, holidays), and the scope of negotiations is narrow (e.g., pay and benefits for federal employees are excluded as bargaining topics).
   - *Private sector:* The scope of negotiations is broad, with most terms and conditions of employment open for negotiation.

2. Multilateral bargaining

   - *Public sector:* Dispersed authority means bargaining involves more players (e.g., negotiators, public/taxpayers/media, elected officials, courts, other third parties) and more complex approval processes.
   - *Private sector:* Bargaining is a two-party process resulting in agreements that each party's policy body ratifies.

3. Monopoly versus competition

   - *Public sector:* Government is a monopoly and generally not subject to market forces, making product/service (e.g., police, fire) substitution difficult.
   - *Private sector:* Businesses are subject to market forces, and consumers can shop for price/availability of desired goods/services.

4. The strike

   - *Public sector:* Strikes occur, but they are often illegal and strikers/unions can be punished.
   - *Private sector:* Strikes are legal and a legitimate tool when negotiations reach impasse.

5. Sovereign versus free contract

   - *Public sector:* The **doctrine of sovereignty** maintains that government has responsibility to protect all societal interests; therefore, it is inappropriate to require it to share power with interest groups (e.g., unions in negotiations) or dilute managerial rights. Similarly, the **special responsibility theory** maintains that public employees hold critical positions in society and therefore should not be permitted to strike.
   - *Private sector:* The sovereignty doctrine does not apply.

6. Political versus economic

   - *Public sector:* Decisions have economic impacts but are based on political criteria.
   - *Private sector:* Decisions can have political impacts, but they are economic decisions.

SOURCES: Adapted from Coleman (1990, pp8–12); Denholm (197, pp. 32–33).

series of executive orders in the Kennedy (Executive Order 10988), Nixon (Executive Order 11491), and Ford (Executive Order 11838) administrations. These were then brought together and amplified with the passage of Title VII in the Civil Service Reform Act of 1978 during the Carter presidency.

This law gives federal employees (General Schedule and wage grade) the right to form unions and bargain collectively. It created the Federal Labor Relations Authority (FLRA) to oversee federal LMRs, disallowed union security arrangements, restricted the scope of bargaining (e.g., excluded wages and benefits), and banned strikes. In recent years, the FLRA has been subject to criticism by the courts and other observers (see Exhibit 11.10). The U.S. Office of Personnel Management's Office of Labor–Management Relations assists federal agencies with contract administration and technical advice.

Exhibit 11.10 Political Influences on Regulatory Decision Making

Public administration is often influenced by partisan politics. Up to mid-2001, the Federal Labor Relations Authority was meeting many of its goals, including increasing productivity and improving labor–management relationships. However, by 2007 the FLRA had faced many court defeats and failed to complete its mission adequately. U.S. courts rejected 13 out of 25 FLRA decisions between January 2004 and December 2006, and the three-member body was unable to meet any of its performance goals in 2006. Judicial decisions criticized the FLRA, saying, among other things, "analysis fundamentally misapplies the Statute, reasoning would yield 'bizarre results' or lead to an 'absurd situation'"; "standards are being deliberately changed, not casually ignored"; and "the Authority's decision . . . is premised on an entirely untenable interpretation."

The court defeats were partly a result of the "scuttling" of the FLRA. In mid-2001, a majority of members of the FLRA were Republicans, and Dale Cabaniss was appointed as chair. After Cabaniss took control, the authority's staff was reduced by 25%, and the FLRA used less of its annual appropriations. Cabaniss also reduced transparency in the agency by deleting data presumed to be embarrassing for the FLRA—for example, records of case processing times that were deemed to be too long. The professionals on the Federal Service Impasses Panel were cut by 60%: Cabaniss replaced them with a political appointee with no history in labor relations. President George W. Bush nominated her for another term in 2007.

Bush's action, together with civil service reforms in the Departments of Defense and Homeland Security, outsourcing initiatives, cutbacks, pay-for-performance plans, and concern about reducing the scope of bargaining and employee appeal rights, had at least one federal union leader claiming, "This administration is attacking the civil service, period" (quoted in "AFGE's 'Fighting Spirit,'" 2003). George Nesterczuk, vice president of Global USA, a consulting firm, supported the Bush initiative, claiming that under President Clinton's partnership policy, "unions had the power to run around management to get what they wanted" (quoted in Young, 2001, p. 17).

President Obama appointed Carol Waller Pope as the new chair of the FLRA. Pope was a longtime government employee and had been a member of the FLRA since 2000. In fact, for several months in the last year of the Bush administration, she was the only member of the FLRA. President Obama also filled the two vacancies that had existed since the Bush administration. Now fully staffed, the FLRA has finally begun to issue decisions at the rate it had prior to the Bush administration (Rosenberg, 2009). With regard to mission accomplishment, in fiscal year 2013 the FLRA reduced the number of pending cases by 87% (394 to 50), overage case inventory by 100% (260 to zero cases), and average age of pending cases by 81% (270 to 51 days). In 2012 the Partnership for Public Service recognized the FLRA as the "Most Improved Small Agency on Innovation" (U.S. FLRA, 2014).

SOURCES: Adapted from "AFGE's 'Fighting Spirit'" (2003); Ferris (2008); Rosenberg (2009); U.S. FLRA (2014); Young (2001), FLRA, 2014.

In 2009, President Obama founded the National Council on Federal Labor–Management Relations (NCFLMR) by executive order. This body advises the president on the current state of labor–management relations. The NCFLMR is made up of several federal employee union presidents, the chair of the FLRA, the president of the Senior Executives Association, and the president of the Federal Managers Association; it is chaired by the director and deputy director of the Office of Personnel Management and the Office of Management and Budget and includes several other prominent union presidents and agency heads. This body encourages cooperation among management, labor, and the executive branch to come up with mutually agreed-upon proposals to take to the president (Office of the President–Federal Register, 2009).

A bewildering array of federal, state, and local laws, regulations, court decisions, ordinances, and attorneys' general opinions shape governmental LMRs. The federal system for LMRs is different from state or local systems, which differ from state to state. Local-level developments reflect considerable variation. The vast majority of serious labor issues, however, arise in a relatively narrow range of local government unions associated with police, fire, sanitation, and education. At the state and local levels, public policy dealing with public employee labor relations is difficult to summarize. Nevertheless, state public employee labor relations laws share some key features, including responsibility to bargain, bargaining teams, bargaining relationships, agreements, union rights, civil rights, and government obligations.

Another trend involves LMRs themselves. The legal right of public employees to strike is hotly debated (see Exhibit 11.11). In recent years, there has been a decrease in **work stoppages** (strikes) and an increase in the use of third-party mediators. There were 15 major work stoppages in 2013, down from 19 in 2012 (Bureau of Labor Statistics, 2014).[3] The decline in government work stoppages in recent years may be attributable to growing anti-tax, antiunion, and antigovernment public sentiments; the discharge of air traffic controllers by President Reagan in 1981 (Exhibit 11.12); the employer practice of hiring permanent replacements for striking workers; and increased use of alternative dispute resolution mechanisms. Nonetheless, strike rights for some state employees have been established in 12 states. In 4 other states, judicial rulings have upheld strike rights for public workers (Kearney & Mareschal, 2014). Use of alternative dispute resolution mechanisms has occurred at all levels of government (e.g., Dibble, 1997). Overall, long strikes are being replaced by short walkouts, and more emphasis is placed on boycotts and on coalition building with community-based and social reform organizations (Milkman, 2013). Government structure, legal and economic factors, and cultural considerations all influence labor–management relations, strike activity, and collective bargaining.

SUMMARY AND CONCLUSION

Unions have played an important role in government for the past five decades. As signaled in the subtitle and opening vignette of this chapter, unions function as protectors, partners, and punishers. Reactions to unions are far from uniform. Employees and managers both have "love-hate" relationships with unions. One fundamental paradox in LMRs is that the doctrine of hostility from the private sector was adapted with minor modifications by the public sector, thereby inhibiting the emergence of a competing model built on the doctrine of harmony. The legal structures underlying public LMRs ensure the continued dominance

Exhibit 11.11   Arguments Opposing and Supporting Public Sector Strikes

Opponents to public sector strikes argue the following:

- Sovereignty rests with the American people, and public workers should not be entitled to strike because their doing so violates the public's will and undercuts governmental authority.
- Strikes pervert the policy process by bestowing special privileges on unions that other interest groups do not have.
- Public services are monopolistic, and labor market constraints to hold down labor costs are absent where strikes are allowed.
- Essential services are curtailed in strikes, posing a threat to public health and safety.

Supporters of the legal right of public employees to strike contend the following:

- Not all public services are essential, and the disruption of government services seldom seriously threatens public health and safety.
- Alternatives to government services are frequently available from the private sector.
- Denying the right to strike to public employees but allowing it for private sector workers performing identical work is inequitable.
- Work stoppages will occur regardless of legal strike bans.
- The incidence of strikes is no greater in states that permit work stoppages than it is in those that prohibit them.

SOURCES: Coleman, 1990, pp. 52–53; Devinatz, 1997, pp. 105–106; Northrup, 1984; McCartin, 2011, p. A25; BBC News, 2007a, 2007b, 2007c; Bennhold, 2007; M&C Business, n.d.

Exhibit 11.12   PATCO Strike: Misguided and Overreaching Strategy

The Professional Air Traffic Controllers Organization (PATCO) strike was a watershed development in federal labor–management relations in the 1980s. The strike resulted in 11,400 air traffic controllers losing their jobs, PATCO's decertification and eventual dissolution, and Ronald Reagan's signaling to public employers that they should stand firm and take a hard line against unions.

The union had been involved in rocky, bitter bargaining with the Federal Aviation Administration (FAA) from the late 1960s to the early 1980s. These negotiations took place on a range of issues despite restrictions on the scope of negotiations under Executive Order 10988. PATCO demands included substantial salary hikes, improved overtime pay rates, better night shift differentials, and more generous severance pay. Other demands were for greater union involvement in determining operational/safety policies, a shorter workweek, and lucrative early retirement plans. The FAA resisted the union's proposals. After unsuccessful haggling with the FAA, union members voted overwhelmingly in favor of an illegal strike in 1981.

President Reagan gave the strikers an ultimatum: Return to work within 48 hours or lose your jobs. PATCO did not comply. The president then delivered on his threat, dismissing and ultimately establishing a process for replacing strikers. In the end, union leadership and strategy were faulted for failing to garner public sympathy, framing the issues too narrowly, discounting the public interest, overreaching, and making insufficient effort to shore up support for the strike from AFL-CIO affiliates.

Looking back 30 years later, McCartin (2011) observed that Reagan's confrontation with PATCO,

> more than any other labor dispute of the past three decades . . . undermined the bargaining power of American workers and their labor unions. It also polarized our politics in ways that prevent us from addressing the root of our economic troubles: the continuing stagnation of incomes despite rising corporate profits and worker productivity.

By contrast, Freeman and Hilbrich (2013) attribute less importance to the PATCO strike and more to fundamental economic changes:

> [The strike] had no noticeable effect on union density. From the mid-1950s through 2010, the percentage of private sector workers in unions fell under Republican and Democratic administrations alike; in boom times and in recessions; under National Labor Relations Boards favorable to unions and Boards favorable to business. (p. 7)

SOURCES: Coleman, 1990, pp. 52–53; Devinatz, 1997, pp. 105–106; Northrup, 1984; McCartin, 2011, p. A25; BBC News, 2007a, 2007b, 2007c; Bennhold, 2007; M&C Business, n.d.

of the adversarial approach of traditional bargaining. Recent experiments, however, point the way to promising experiences with cooperative problem solving.

Dealing with unions is a way of life for many managers as they struggle to cope with thorny human resource problems. Difficulties are inevitable if administrators fail to understand the (actual or potential) role of organized labor and to heed requirements spelled out in negotiated contracts or mutual agreements. Public managers need to track trends and variations in labor relations. Managers must carefully monitor the activities associated with each phase and stage of the collective bargaining process if they are to do their job properly. At the same time, officials should be aware that alternatives to traditional bargaining exist.

By heeding the tips and avoiding the traps listed below, managers can reduce unnecessary friction in labor–management relations.

Tips

- Be willing to share power to solve problems.
- Be patient and acknowledge mistakes.
- Invest time and effort in building relationships and in resolving differences.
- Cooperate where the interests of both sides converge.

Traps

- Be unwilling to fix deteriorating relationships.
- Fail to recognize the inevitability of conflict.
- Be inattentive to cultivating a harmonious work atmosphere.
- Provide tardy and unfair response to complaints.

Given the entrenchment of existing legal structures and behavior patterns built on five decades of experience with traditional union–management relations, movement from institutional patterns built on the doctrine of hostility to those grounded in the doctrine of harmony will be slow and incremental. The savvy human resource manager will be guided by SHRM tenets (Chapter 1) in navigating a course that provides the most promise for advancing employer and employee interests. Government managers must carefully assess the organizational cultures and institutional arrangements in their jurisdictions and decide whether they should press for change in LMRs or work through existing human resource and LMRs mechanisms to achieve public purposes.

KEY TERMS

Alt-labor groups

Bargaining unit determination

Doctrine of sovereignty

Exclusive representation

Free rider

Meet-and-confer rights

Open shop

Right-to-work states

Special responsibility theory

Work stoppages

EXERCISES

Class Discussion

1. Given past trends in public and private labor relations, what do you predict the future will hold?

2. Why do some public officeholders view public unions as a dangerous threat? Is the threat real? Is curbing union power an effective strategy for dealing with budget deficits?

3. Are unions a relic of the past with little to contribute in the present environment?

4. How effective do you think the strategies outlined in Exhibit 11.2 might be in combating the stereotypes shown in Exhibit 11.1 and the value differences in Exhibit 11.7? Why do you think particular strategies may or may not be effective?

5. What should unions do to make themselves more attractive to newly hired Generation Y employees?

Team Activities

6. Should public employees have the right to strike? Is this preferable to binding arbitration? Why?

7. Divide into two groups and have one team develop arguments in favor of Ohio's Issue 2 and the other develop arguments against. Discuss both teams' arguments with the full class.

8. Debate the following question: Is mandatory union membership the best way to address the free rider problem? Why or why not?

9. Divide the class into two groups, one union organizers and the other Generation Y workers. How do Generation Y workers view unions? How do union organizers view members of Generation Y? In what ways are these perceptions relevant to the future of unions?

10. Debate the following statement: Labor relations in the public and private sectors are more similar than they are different. Provide specific examples to support your position.

Individual Assignments

11. Interview a local public sector union representative and ask about his or her bargaining priorities and strategies for attracting new members.

12. Why do some public sector employees join unions? Why do others fail to join?

13. What are the special challenges of managing in (a) a union environment and (b) a nonunion environment?

14. Why are there so many paradoxes and contradictions in public sector labor relations? Select five important paradoxes and consider how they can be resolved.

15. Why have private sector unions lost members, whereas public sector unions have gained members?

APPENDIX A

Tips for Managers When Dealing With Unions

- Reach out to all employees and let them know that their work is valued.
- Survey employee attitudes on working conditions.
- Provide a healthy and safe work environment.
- Examine pay rates and benefits packages to maintain them at or above "market" levels.
- Maintain close contact with first-line supervisors on employee relations matters.
- Develop cordial and personalized relationships with union officers.
- Work with union representatives in communicating policies to employees.
- Build trust between unions and management.
- Foster transparency in labor–management relations.
- Avoid arbitrariness in personnel and management decisions.
- Give employees a voice in their own working conditions.
- Respect employees' right to self-organization.
- Involve labor when implementing privatization plans.
- Respond promptly and fairly to grievances.
- Seek to resolve complaints about unfair labor practices informally.
- Consult with lawyers on a case-by-case basis as needed.
- Tailor your approach to unions depending on their ideology, political organization, and leaders' personalities.
- Recognize that it takes time to negotiate separately with every recognized bargaining agent.

- Accept negotiators as equals; do not underestimate them.
- Document each meeting with labor representatives by taking careful notes.
- Keep negotiators focused on giving customers (taxpayers, clients, citizens) what they want.
- Make effective use of third parties in resolving collective bargaining deadlocks.
- Develop a crisis management plan.
- Prepare a media and public relations plan.
- Create labor–management committees to discuss short- and long-term objectives of the organization.
- Agree only to those terms that are likely to be ratified by decision makers on both sides.

APPENDIX B

Tips for Unions When Dealing With Managers

- Always be honest. Never lie to or mislead anyone for any reason. Once you compromise your integrity, you cannot get it back.
- Never tell a union member to lie or intentionally mislead any authority. There is no excuse for lying.
- Always act in a professional, businesslike manner. Conducting union business is just that: business.
- Always be aware of a possible conflict of interest.
- If a member asks you a question and you are unsure of the answer, be honest. Tell him or her that you will find the right answer.
- Do not place your trust blindly. Trustworthiness must be earned through consistent follow-through on commitments.
- Take advantage of the knowledgeable, experienced people in the union. They are very familiar with many of the situations you will encounter and can save you the pains and troubles that often result from reinvention.
- Surround yourself with all types of people, including those who disagree with your views. The consideration of different points of view is an important part of the decision-making process.
- Confide only in those you feel you can trust. Remember that anything you say can come back to haunt you.
- Do not make decisions in anger. Always seek a second opinion.
- Be suspicious but respectful of management. Thoroughly analyze its possible motivation.
- Remind employees that their statements and memos are frequently used against them. Remind them to constantly be on their guard in their dealings with management.
- Keep a copy of all correspondence that you generate and receive.
- Copy all policy memoranda that the agency issues, and keep them in your filing system.
- Never meet with management by yourself. The recollections of two or more witnesses are far more persuasive than those of an individual.

- Regardless of your personal feelings, remember that you represent the interests of the entire bargaining unit.
- Pay attention to everyone who speaks up at a union meeting. Most people are there only to listen. Those who speak up may be willing to get involved.
- Delegate. Ask for help. The natural tendency is to let someone else handle the work. Do not be shy about admitting that there is too much work for one person.
- Recognize those who assist. All of us are volunteers. Praise and encouragement are often the only motivational tools we can offer. Dispense them liberally.
- Keep meticulous records of all of your dealings with management and of internal union business.
- Do not be afraid to ask questions.
- Do not be intimidated by management's fear tactics.
- If you are not sure about whether management's actions violate the contract or law, ask someone who knows.
- Beware of divide-and-conquer tactics.
- Be sure that the local union president also coordinates all of the bargaining in the sector.
- Record and keep contemporaneous notes of all conversations or encounters with management.
- Do not be afraid to request sufficient official time to perform representational functions. If the agency refuses to grant these requests, coordinate the filing of a grievance with your local.
- Do not abuse official time. If you are done using official time, you should return to work.
- Do not be afraid to call the local union president.

SOURCE: Adapted from Gilson (2008). © Copyright 2008 Bob Gilson. Reprinted from FedSmith.com.

NOTES

1. Parts of this section are condensed from Bowman and West (2014).
2. The term *open shop* refers to workplaces with unions but where union membership is not a condition of employment.
3. Federal employees do not have the right to strike. In most states, it is illegal for state employees to strike. Some states give state employees a limited right to strike.

REFERENCES

AFGE's "fighting spirit": Gage outlines challenges. (2003, December 1). *Federal Times*, p. 8.

American Federation of Teachers. (2004, June). *AFT public employee compensation survey*. New York: Author. Retrieved from http://www.ift-aft.org/news/dailynews/10-09-14/AFT_Releases_Results_of_Public_Employee_Compensation_Survey.aspx

American Federation of Teachers. (2012). *2012 compensation survey*. Washington, DC: Author.

Aronowitz, S. (1998). *From the ashes of the old: American labor and America's future*. New York: Houghton Mifflin.

Balser, D., & Winkler, A. (2012). Worker behavior on the job: A multi-methods study of labor cooperation with management. *Journal of Labor Research, 33,* 388–413.

Befort, S. (2011). Public-sector employment under siege. *Indiana Law Journal, 87*(1), 231–238.

Benest, F., & Grijalva, R. (2002, January/February). Enhancing the manager/fire chief relationship. *Public Management.* Retrieved from http://www.icma.org/upload/library/IQ/500632.htm

Bowman, J. S., & West, J. P. (2014, March). *Labor–management relations in public (and business) administration: A textbook case.* Paper presented at the annual meeting of the American Society for Public Administration, Washington, DC.

Bronfenbrenner, K. (2009). *No holds barred: The intensification of employer opposition to organizing.* Washington, DC: Economic Policy Institute.

Bureau of Labor Statistics, U.S. Department of Labor. (2010). Union members–2010 [News release]. Retrieved from http://www.bls.gov/news.release/pdf/union2.pdf

Bureau of Labor Statistics, U.S. Department of Labor. (2011, February 8). Major work stoppages (annual) news release. Retrieved from http://www.bls.gov/opub/ted/2011/ted_20110210.htm

Bureau of Labor Statistics, U.S. Department of Labor. (2014, February 12). Major work stoppages (annual) news release. Retrieved from http://www.bls.gov/news.release/wkstp.htm

Clark, R. T., Jr. (2012). Public sector collective bargaining at the crossroads. *Urban Lawyer, 44*(1), 185–226.

Coleman, C. (1990). *Managing labor relations in the public sector.* San Francisco: Jossey-Bass.

Davey, M., & Zeleny, J. (2012, June 5). Walker survives Wisconsin recall vote. *New York Times.* Retrieved from http://www.nytimes.com/2012/06/06/us/politics/walker-survives

Deery, S., & Iverson, R. (2005). Labor–management cooperation: Antecedents and impact on organizational performance. *Industrial & Labor Relations Review, 58*(4), 588–608.

Delaney, J. (2005). Ethical challenges in labor relations. In J. Budd & J. Scoville (Eds.), *The ethics of human resources and industrial relations* (pp. 203–228). Champaign, IL: Labor and Employment Association.

Denholm, D. Y. (1997). The case against public sector unionism and collective bargaining. *Government Union Review, 18*(1), 31–52.

Devinatz, V. G. (1997). Testing the Johnston "public sector union strike success" hypothesis: A qualitative analysis. *Journal of Collective Negotiations, 26*(2), 99–112.

Dibble, R. E. (1997). Alternative dispute resolution of employment conflicts: The search for standards. *Journal of Collective Negotiations, 26*(1), 73–84.

Early, S. (2013). *Save our unions: Dispatches from a movement in distress.* New York: Monthly Review Press.

Ferris, F. (2008, June 8). Scuttling the Federal Labor Relations Authority. FedSmith. Retrieved from http://www.fedsmith.com/article/1621

Florito, J., & Jarley, P. (2012). Union organizing and membership growth: Why don't they organize? *Journal of Labor Research, 33,* 461–486.

Freeman, R. B., & Han, E. (2012). The war against public sector collective bargaining in the US. *Journal of Industrial Relations, 54*(3), 386–408.

Freeman, R. B., & Hilbrich, K. (2013). Do labor unions have a future in the United States? In R. S. Rycroft (Ed.), *The economics of inequality, poverty, and discrimination in the 21st century.* Santa Barbara, CA: Praeger. Retrieved from http://nrs.harvard.edu/urn-3:HUL.InstRepos:10488702

Galbraith, J. K. (2010). *American capitalism: The concept of countervailing power.* Whitefish, MT: Kessinger. (Original work published 1952)

Getman, J. (2012). *Restoring the power of unions: It takes a movement.* New Haven, CT: Yale University Press.

Gilson, B. (2008, July 8). Can I join this union? FedSmith. Retrieved from http://www.fedsmith.com/2008/07/08/can-i-join-this-union

Gordon, C. 2013. *Growing apart: A political history of American inequality.* Washington, DC: Institute for Policy Studies. Retrieved from http://scalar.usc.edu/works/growing-apart-a-political-history-of-american-inequality/index

Greenhouse, S. (2009). *The big squeeze: Tough times for the American worker*. New York: Anchor.

Greenhouse, S. (2010, June 22). Most U.S. union members are working for the government, new data shows. *New York Times*. Retrieved from http://www.nytimes.com/2010/01/23/business/23labor.html

Greenhouse, S. (2011a, October 15). Ohio wages fierce fight on collective bargaining. *New York Times*. Retrieved from http://www.nytimes.com/2011/10/16/us

Greenhouse, S. (2011b, February 18). A watershed moment for public-sector unions. *New York Times*. Retrieved from http://www.nytimes.com/2011/02/19/us/19union.html

Hacker, J. (2006). *The great risk shift*. New York: Oxford University Press.

Huey-Burns, C. (2011, November 9). Ohio voters reject law limiting public unions. RealClearPolitics. Retrieved from http://www.realclearpolitics.com/articles/2011/11/09/ohio_voters_reject_law_limiting_public_unions.html

Israel, J. (2014, June 27). 6 groups that are reinventing organized labor. ThinkProgress. Retrieved from http://thinkprogress.org/economy/2014/06/27/3451317/labor-groups-outside-union-model

Katz, H. C. (2013). Is U.S. public sector labor relations in the midst of a transformation? *Industrial & Labor Relations Review, 66*(5), 1031–1045.

Kearney, R. C. (1998a). Labor law. In J. Shafritz (Ed.), *International encyclopedia of public policy and administration* (pp. 1241–1244). Boulder, CO: Westview Press.

Kearney, R. C. (1998b). Strike. In J. Shafritz (Ed.), *International encyclopedia of public policy and administration* (pp. 2180–2182). Boulder, CO: Westview Press.

Kearney, R. C., & Mareschal, P. M. (2014). *Labor relations in the public sector* (5th ed.). Boca Raton, FL: CRC Press.

Keen, J., & Cauchon, D. (2011, February 23). Poll: Americans favor union bargaining rights. *USA Today*. Retrieved from http://usatoday30.usatoday.com/nation/2011-02-22-poll-unions-wisconsin-N.htm

Kelleher, J. (2011, March 10). Wisconsin passes anti-union law in labor rebuke. Reuters. Retrieved from http://www.reuters.com/article/2011/03/10/us-wisconsin-idUSTRE72909420110310

Logan, J. (2006). The union avoidance industry in the United States. *British Journal of Industrial Relations, 44*(4), 651–675.

Madland, D. (2011, February 25). Public sector unions should have the right to collective bargaining. *US News & World Report*. Retrieved from http://www.usnews.com/opinion/articles/2011/02/25/public-sector-unions-should-have-the-right-to-collective-bargaining

Maher, K., & Nicas, J. (2011, November 9). Ohio voters reject public-unions limits. *Wall Street Journal*. Retrieved from http://online.wsj.com/articles/SB10001424052970204190704577026360072268418

Malanga, S. (2013, September 28). How Chris Christie split the labor movement in New Jersey. *Wall Street Journal*. Retrieved from http://online.wsj.com/news/articles/SB10001424127887342590045790667024647733782

Marley, P., & Walker, D. (2011, June 14). Supreme Court reinstates collective bargaining law. *Milwaukee Journal Sentinel*. Retrieved from http://www.jsonline.com/news/statepolitics/123859034.html

Masters, M., Albright, R., & Eplion, D. (2006). What did partnerships do? Evidence from the federal sector. *Industrial & Labor Relations Review, 59*(3), 367–385.

McCartin, J. A. (2011, August 2). The strike that busted unions. *New York Times*. Retrieved from http://www.nytimes.com/2011/08/03/opinion/reagan-vs-patco-the-strike-that-busted-unions.html?_r=0

McFadyen, D. (2000). The merit pay controversy. *WorkingUSA, 4*(3), 131–143.

McGinnis, J. O., & Schanzenbach, M. (2010, August–September). The case against public sector unions. *Policy Review*, no. 162, 3–12.

Meyerson, H. (2011, April 4). Wisconsin and beyond: How far will the backlash against union-busting go? *American Prospect*. Retrieved from http://prospect.org/article/wisconsin-and-beyond

Meyerson, H. (2013, September 10). At AFL-CIO convention, labor embraces the new America. *Washington Post*. Retrieved from http://www.washingtonpost.com/opinions/harold-meyerson-at-afl-cio-convention-labor-embraces-the-new-america/2013/09/10/cd820a54-1a2a-11e3-8685-5021e0c41964_story.html

Milkman, R. (2013). Back to the future? US labour in the new gilded age. *British Journal of Industrial Relations, 51*(4), 645–665.

Northrup, H. (1984). The rise and demise of PATCO. *Industrial & Labor Relations Review, 37*(2), 167–184.

Office of the President–Federal Register. (2009). Executive Order 13522: Creating labor–management forums to improve delivery of government services. *National Archives and Records Administration, 74*(238).

Orzechowski, W., & Marlow, M. (1995). Political participation, public sector labor unions and public spending. *Government Union Review, 16*(2), 1–25.

Pérez-Peña, R. (2011, June 16). Workers swarm Trenton on benefit changes. *New York Times.* Retrieved from http://www.nytimes.com/2011/06/17/nyregion/state-workers-swarm-trenton-to-oppose-health-and-pension-increases.html

Powell, M. (2011, January 1). Public workers face outrage as budget crises grow. *New York Times.* Retrieved from http://www.nytimes.com/2011/01/02/business/02showdown.html?pagewanted = all

Reich, R. B. (2007). *Supercapitalism.* New York: Alfred A. Knopf.

Rosenberg, A. (2009, November 1). Warming trends. *Government Executive.* Retrieved from http://www.govexec.com/magazine/features/2009/11/warming-trends/30252

Shimabukuro, J. O. (2011). *Collective bargaining and employees in the public sector.* Washington, DC: Congressional Research Service.

Spicuzza, M., & Barbour, C. (2011, February 15). Legislators mum on Walker proposal as union leaders, protesters rage. *Wisconsin State Journal.* Retrieved from http://host.madison.com/wsj/news/local/govt-and-politics/article_21da7e42-3883-11e0-acaa-001cc4c002e0.html

Time for second thoughts? A backlash against Republican attacks may be under way. (2011, March 10). *Economist.* Retrieved from http://www.economist.com/node/18335274

U.S. Federal Labor Relations Authority. (2014). Congressional budget justification fiscal year 2014. Retrieved from http://www.flra.gov

U.S. labor struggles to regain clout. (1998, September 7). *Miami Herald,* p. 7A.

Weiner, R. (2011, November 8). Issue 2 falls, Ohio collective bargaining law repealed. *Washington Post.* Retrieved from http://www.washingtonpost.com/blogs/the-fix/post/issue-2-falls-ohio

Weisenthal, J. (2011, April 29). New benefits data shows why people hate public sector unions. *Business Insider.* Retrieved from http://articles.businessinsider.com/2011-04-29/news/30033998_1_compensation-wages-and-salaries-public-sector-unions

West, J. P. (2012). Employee-friendly policies and development benefits for millennials. In W. I. Sauser Jr. & R. R. Sims (Eds.), *Managing human resources for the millennial generation* (pp. 201–228). Charlotte, NC: Information Age.

What to do when the union knocks. (1966, November). *Nation's Business,* p. 107.

Young, I. (2001, March 12). Partnership directive bewilders unions, agencies. *Federal Times,* pp. 4, 17.

CHAPTER 12

Collective Bargaining

Structures, Strategies, and Skills

Where free unions and collective bargaining are forbidden, freedom is lost.

—Ronald Reagan, 1980

After studying this chapter, you should be able to

- determine key bargaining issues that require resolution before, during, and after negotiations;
- distinguish between positive and negative behaviors at the bargaining table;
- cultivate negotiating skills to solve problems;
- understand the meaning of key terms relevant to collective bargaining;
- assess the various reform proposals dealing with public sector unions and collective bargaining; and
- recognize differences between the doctrine of hostility and the doctrine of harmony, as well as between traditional bargaining and cooperative problem solving.

In 2011, as noted in Chapter 11, many state policy makers sought to weaken collective bargaining rights of public employees as a cost-cutting measure to help them deal with distressed state budgets and declining revenues (see Shimabukuro, 2011). For example, Wisconsin lawmakers approved a budget bill that, among other things, stripped state workers of their collective bargaining rights. This controversial action was initiated by conservative Republican governor Scott Walker and was but one part of a concerted effort to diminish the power of unions. Subsequently, Republican state senators were targeted by Democrats in recall efforts against those who supported the bill, and the GOP then attacked the Democratic senators who sought to delay passage of the bill by leaving the state (Terkel, 2011). The passage of the "Budget Repair Bill" and the recall election energized organized labor in the state. Paradoxically, Wisconsin was the first state in the United States to authorize public employees to engage in collective negotiations in 1959. The battle in Wisconsin over worker rights is mirrored in Ohio, Michigan, Illinois, New Jersey, Florida, and other states. This chapter provides background on the structures, strategies, and skills required for collective bargaining.

STRUCTURE, REPRESENTATION, AND COLLECTIVE BARGAINING

The institutional structure and legal rights related to collective bargaining vary by level of government, jurisdiction, and occupational group. National labor laws that govern collective bargaining and representation rights for federal and private sector employees do not pertain to state and local government employees. State and local public employees' bargaining and representational rights are enumerated wherever authorized by state law and, less frequently, by local ordinance or executive order. Currently, 30 states and the District of Columbia authorize collective bargaining for public employees, 12 other states allow bargaining for some state and/or local employees (e.g., public safety workers, teachers), and the remaining 8 states lack collective bargaining statutes for their state and local government employees (Kearney & Mareschal, 2014). In some instances, however, executive orders or local ordinances confer rights to bargain or have representation.

Collective bargaining is the process whereby labor and management representatives meet to set terms and conditions of employment for personnel in a bargaining unit. Certain legal factors help to frame bargaining and union–management relationships. These factors are also influenced by and help to determine the strength and strategy of public unions. Identification of such factors is a necessary prelude to painting a portrait of the bargaining process. They include the nature of the bilateral relationship, the type of union security provisions, the kind of administrative arrangements, the range of **unfair labor practices**, and the existence of dispute resolution or **impasse procedures**. These legal distinctions are clarified in Exhibit 12.1.

The bargaining process itself is shaped by these factors. It typically unfolds in three phases: (1) organizing to bargain, (2) bargaining, and (3) administering the contract. Each stage is characterized by distinct activities, which are discussed in turn next.

Organizing to Bargain

Collective bargaining, as traditionally practiced, does not occur until (1) an appropriate bargaining unit is determined, (2) a representation election is held, (3) an exclusive bargaining agent is certified, and (4) a bargaining team is selected. Each step is necessary to determine who will engage in negotiations. Bargaining unit determination identifies whom a union or other association in negotiation sessions will represent. An administrative agency, a statute, a union, or an arbitrator makes this determination. Specifically, the FLRA makes unit determinations at the federal level, and **Public Employee Relations Boards (PERBs)**

Exhibit 12.1 Selected Legal and Contextual Factors Regarding Unions

Relationship Between the Parties

Meet and confer: Characterized by inequality between partners (labor and management); employer selects agenda items and is not obligated to bargain; management retains virtually all rights and exercises ultimate authority; and outcomes are nonbinding and typically skewed to management's perspective.

Collective bargaining: The rights of employees to form and join unions for bargaining purposes are recognized; an administrative agency oversees bargaining unit determination and establishes administrative procedures; unions with majority support become exclusive bargaining agents; employers are obligated to bargain; selected management rights are protected; and provisions are made for union security, impasse procedures, and unfair labor practices.

Union Security Provisions

Union shop: Employee must join the representing union after a certain number of days (e.g., 30–90 days), as specified in the collective bargaining agreement. This is rare in government.

Agency shop: Employee is not required to join the union, but most contribute a service charge to cover collective bargaining, the grievance process, and arbitration costs. Nonpayment can result in job loss. Such arrangements are infrequent in the public sector.

Maintenance of membership: Employee is obligated to maintain union membership in the representing union once affiliated during the life of the contract. Withdrawal may lead to forfeiture of job.

Dues checkoff: Employee may select a payroll deduction option to pay union dues to the representing union.

Administrative Arrangements

Public Employee Relations Boards (PERBs): State administrative agencies typically charged with determining appropriate bargaining units, overseeing certification elections, and resolving unfair labor practices. At the federal level, the three-member Federal Labor Relations Authority (FLRA) performs PERB functions. In the private sector, administrative responsibilities rest with the National Labor Relations Board (NLRB).

Unfair Labor Practices (ULPs)

Unfair employer practices: Interfering with a public employee's right to form or join a union, discriminating against public employees because of union membership, dominating a labor organization, or violating a collective bargaining agreement.

Unfair union practices: Denying union membership because of race, color, creed, and so forth; interfering with, restraining, or coercing (1) employees in exercising their statutory rights or (2) employers regarding the exercise of employee rights; refusing to meet with the public employer and to bargain in good faith; or interfering with the work performance or productivity of a public employee.

(Continued)

Exhibit 12.1 (Continued)

Impasse Procedures

Mediation: A dispute resolution procedure that relies on a neutral third party who attempts to facilitate communication and bring the parties together to reach an agreement.

Fact-finding: A dispute resolution procedure that relies on a neutral third party who conducts hearings, researches contentious issues, and makes nonbinding recommendations for consideration.

Arbitration: A dispute resolution procedure that relies on a neutral third party who reviews the facts and makes determinations that are binding on both sides.

Arbitration takes many forms:

- **Interest arbitration:** Arbitration dealing with the terms of the negotiated contract; may be voluntary or compulsory.
- **Grievance arbitration, or rights arbitration:** Arbitration dealing with outstanding disputes regarding employee grievances.
- **Final-offer arbitration:** Arbitration in which the arbitrator's decision is restricted to the position taken by one or the other of the parties—may include selection of a position taken by one side or the other on all issues taken together (by package) or selection on an issue-by-issue basis.
- **Med-arb:** Procedure that requires an arbitrator to begin with mediation, settle as many disputes as feasible, and move to arbitration only on items that remain contentious.

do so in many states. The criteria used in determining the composition of the bargaining unit vary by state, but the following National Labor Relations Board (NLRB) guidelines are typically followed:

- *Community of interest:* Common job factors, for example, are similar position classifications, duties, skills, working conditions, kinds of work, or geographic locations.
- *Bargaining history:* This includes such things as prior patterns of negotiation, representation, or LMRs.
- *Unit size:* Units that are too small can absorb too much of bargaining representatives' time, create unwieldy fragmentation, and create a **whipsaw effect** (in which gains by one union might be used to justify benefits for another); those that are too large may lack cohesion and a community of interest.
- *Efficiency of operations:* Bargaining structures may impede efficiency if they are a poor fit with existing human resource policies and procedures.
- *Exclusion of supervisory or confidential employees:* This is predicated on the idea that there is a potential conflict of interest in a unit that combines supervisors (management) with employees.

Election is the next step in this phase of the process. Identification of who is to represent the union in negotiations need not involve an election; the employer may choose to voluntarily recognize a union for this purpose. More typically, a **representation election** is held. Although either the employer or the union may request such an election, the union usually must "make a showing" that a certain percentage (e.g., 30%) of workers in the unit want representation. As the description of unfair labor practices in Exhibit 12.1 indicates, certain management tactics (intimidation, force, coercion) are prohibited during a representation election. The union must receive a majority vote in a secret ballot election to achieve recognition as the exclusive bargaining agent for workers in the unit. State laws vary regarding the definition of "majority vote" in a representation election. It can mean either a majority of votes cast (most common) or an absolute majority of eligible bargaining unit members without regard to the number of votes actually cast.

The actual certification of the union as the appropriately constituted exclusive bargaining agent for the unit is done by the relevant administrative agency (FLRA, PERB, or equivalent). **Certification of the bargaining agent** may be rescinded if workers become sufficiently dissatisfied, if the agent violates the bargaining law (e.g., decertification of the Professional Air Traffic Controllers Organization by the FLRA in 1981), or if another union "makes sufficient showing" of support to challenge the exclusive bargaining agent. In such a case, a decertification election (modeled on the same procedures described above) is held to determine who, if anyone, should represent employees in the unit.

Selection of the bargaining team is a crucial task. There is considerable variation in team composition depending on the level of government in question, the extent of professionalism existing within the labor relations office (if such an office exists), and the preferences of the labor and management leadership groups. Each side designates a chief negotiator. This may be a professional labor negotiator, a labor lawyer, or a savvy manager or union leader. In local government, the management team may include the chief administrative officer (city or county manager), someone from the legal office, or a human resource or budget professional, among others. Top union leaders often handpick their most rhetorically gifted and politically astute spokespersons as negotiators. In some states (e.g., Florida, Minnesota, and North Dakota), other stakeholders (public, media) may attend or comment on negotiations, but this is more the exception than the rule.

STRATEGIES AND SKILLS

Bargaining

Once the stage has been set and the cast determined, the curtain goes up on bargaining, although the audience is often restricted to the key participants. The great drama is usually reserved for the final scene, when negotiations become most heated. In the beginning, more mundane preparations occupy center stage. Getting prepared involves studying the lines of the existing contract, collecting and analyzing relevant comparative data (wages, salaries, benefits), and sorting through bargaining priorities. Bargaining strategy needs to be clarified. Opening gambits need to be scripted and choreographed differently from the compelling scenes in the last act. The costs and benefits of alternative bargaining proposals need to be weighed carefully. The logistical details of where, when, how, and how long to conduct bargaining sessions require attention, as does the agenda for each meeting.

Legal and behavioral considerations come into play here. Two legal requirements in particular require attention: Bargaining must be conducted in good faith, and the scope of negotiations is often prescribed. Although the term *good faith* is subject to multiple interpretations, the public sector has relied heavily on NLRB rulings and private sector case law to determine its meaning. Good faith is perhaps best understood through examples of its opposite. Employer negotiators who reject union proposals but advance no counterproposals, undermine or bypass the union, schedule meetings arbitrarily, or fail to respond to union requests for bargaining sessions are not acting in good faith (Baker, 1996). Appendix A at the end of this chapter presents a bargaining checklist and behavior observation sheet.

The scope of negotiations is often addressed in the law but contentious in practice. Conflict arises because unions want more perquisites (perks) and want to haggle over a broad range of issues. "What does labor want?" When the press asked this question of Samuel Gompers, the first president of the American Federation of Labor, he began by responding, "More . . ." and since then, his entire comment has been edited down to that single word. Gompers's unabridged response was, "We want *more schoolhouses* and less jails, *more books* and less arsenals, *more learning* and less vice, *more constant work* and less crime, *more leisure* and less greed, *more justice* and less revenge" (emphasis added). If unions want "more," management, intent on preserving its prerogatives, often wants to give "less" and takes a more restrictive, narrow view of what is negotiable. Vague statutory language frequently specifying the scope to include "wages, hours, and conditions of employment" fuels the debate over the legitimate array of discussable items. Issues fall (not always neatly) into three categories:

1. *Mandatory:* "Must do" matters that fall within the porous language of "wages, hours, and terms, or other terms and conditions of employment." Wages and hours of federal employees are excluded from bargaining, however.

2. *Permissive:* "May do" subjects about which the negotiating team may bargain if they opt to (i.e., these issues are neither mandatory nor prohibited). Disagreements are especially heated regarding the phrase "other terms and conditions of employment."

3. *Prohibited:* "Can't do" topics that authorizing statutes, administrative agencies (PERBs or FLRA), or the courts have determined are not subject to bargaining or are beyond the employer's authority to bargain (e.g., civil service laws, organizational mission).

Mandatory subjects can be pushed to an impasse: Neither team is required to concede. One novel permissive topic from the private sector that Briggs and Siegele (1994) have urged on public sector bargainers is a 13-point "ethics standards clause" for inclusion in collective bargaining agreements that would formalize a commitment to ethical behavior and discourage attempts to pursue unethical agendas incompatible with employee or organizational interests.

Negotiations can be viewed as a power game involving winners and losers. With well-honed negotiating skills, however, it is often possible to turn the power game into a problem-solving game. William Ury (1991) advises negotiators to resist power games and focus instead on problem solving that seeks win–win outcomes. Exhibit 12.2 presents a sample of his advice.

Exhibit 12.2   Negotiation Skills: Turning the Power Game Into a Problem-Solving Game

The power game:

You threaten or try to coerce the other side and then they back down. However, unless you have a decisive power advantage, they usually resist and fight back. They get angry and hostile, reversing your attempts to disarm them. They cling even more stubbornly to their position, frustrating your efforts to change the game. They become increasingly resistant to reaching agreement, not only because you may be asking for more but because agreement would now mean accepting defeat. . . .

You are thus forced at great cost to try to impose a solution on the other side. As they strike back, you typically escalate into a costly struggle. . . . you spend a great deal of time and money, not to mention blood, sweat, and tears. (Ury, 1991, p. 131)

Turn the power game into the problem-solving game:

- Instead of seeking victory, aim for mutual satisfaction. Use power to bring them to their senses, not to their knees.
- Let the other side know the consequences of not reaching an agreement. Ask: "What do you think we will do?" and "What will the absence of an agreement cost you?"
- Warn, don't threaten. Always have your "Best Alternative to a Negotiated Agreement" (BATNA) in mind; warn your negotiating partner how you will satisfy your interests through BATNA if an agreement is not reached.
- Use the minimum power necessary to persuade your opponent to return to the negotiating table; exhaust all your alternatives before escalating.
- Neutralize your opponents' ability to coerce you by anticipating possible reactions and preparing for them.
- Build a coalition of supporters to help constitute a potential "third force" in the negotiations.
- Let your opponents know they have a way out. For every ounce of power you use, you need to add an ounce of conciliation.
- Let them choose. Paradoxically, just when the other side seems to be coming around, you are well advised to back off and let them make their own decision.
- Keep implementation in mind. Design an agreement that induces the other side to keep their word and protects you if they don't.
- Reaffirm the relationship. It is in your interest for your counterpart to feel as satisfied as possible at the conclusion of the negotiation. Although you may feel elated at your success, don't crow.

Principled negotiations, or integrated bargaining, sometimes characterize proceedings at the bargaining table; at other times distributive bargaining prevails. In distributive bargaining, hostility is high, relationships are conflictual, bargaining parties are viewed as adversaries, and one side's gain is the other side's loss. Principled bargaining is less prevalent and more consensus oriented. It stresses identification of common ground, focuses on cooperative problem solving, and thrives in an open, trusting environment (Walton & McKersie, 1965). Fisher and Ury's (1981) well-known version of integrative bargaining (or principled negotiations) lays out a list of suggested guidelines:

- Separate the people from the problem.
- Focus on interests, not positions.
- Invent options for mutual gain.
- Insist on use of objective criteria.

Where both parties to negotiations are committed to pursuing partnership strategies, such approaches find fertile ground to take root; where more abrasive and conflictual relations prevail, principled bargaining may lack the nurturance necessary to bear fruit. Nonetheless, sometimes by reframing the problem it is possible to turn an opponent into a partner. How does this work? When dealing with a thorny problem, leaders often must be creative in order to move beyond impasse or avoid a breakdown in negotiations. Here, William Ury (1991) suggests reframing the problem to get one's bargaining opponent invested in a solution that brings beneficial results. The steps involved in reframing begin with viewing one's opponent more as a partner by taking the actions suggested in Exhibit 12.3.

Prevailing economic conditions influence bargaining strategy. In recent years, belt-tightening, downsizing, and privatizing have led to two related trends: concession bargaining and **productivity bargaining**. Negotiators on management teams are responding to taxpayer concerns that sometimes require "givebacks" from unions or promises to "do more with less" (heightened worker productivity in the future). Unions in such environments have had to switch adroitly from offense to defense, fighting a rearguard action to preserve past bargaining victories or to protect their flanks from onerous threats (e.g., reductions in force, two-tier wage structures, benefit copayments). Management may demand greater productivity (e.g., incentive-based plans) or changes in performance-impeding work rules (e.g., staffing ratios). Unions may agree with such changes to avoid concessions on less palatable alternatives. Organized labor's productivity-related demands might include worker autonomy, flextime, or gainsharing.

As labor relations have become more formalized, there has been greater reliance on written agreements and less on verbal understandings or symbolic handshakes. Indeed, state bargaining statutes specify that written contracts must be drawn up on the mandatory issues of wages, hours, and working conditions; most agreements go beyond these topics, covering a broad range of additional matters. Verbal agreements are too easy to squeeze out of and are subject to (sometimes intentional) misinterpretation. Legal contracts are written to minimize this problem. Skillful lawyers can be contortionists who may use legalese to obscure meaning and preserve "wiggle room" or loopholes to slip through when formal contracts contain objectionable provisions.

Exhibit 12.3 Negotiation Skills: Reframing the Problem With an Opponent-Turned-Partner

When dealing with an intractable problem, leaders and managers often have to take creative steps to break an impasse or prevent the breakdown of negotiations. One approach recommended by William Ury (1991) is to reframe the problem in order to get one's negotiating opponent invested in a mutually beneficial outcome. A good beginning is to view one's "opponent" more as a "partner." Reframing consists of the following steps:

1. Ask problem-solving questions. Instead of making demands, ask questions that help your partner help you.

2. Ask "Why?" Treat your partner's stance as an opportunity rather than an obstacle.

3. Ask "Why not?" If your partner won't directly answer "Why?" propose your own solution.

4. Ask "What if?" Lay out a list of possible solutions without undermining your partner's position and engage in a mutual brainstorming session.

5. Ask for your partner's advice. Acknowledge your partner's competence and status by asking his/her opinion as a way to establish trust and help him/her become invested in a mutually beneficial outcome.

6. Ask "What makes that fair?" If your partner makes what seems to you to be an unreasonable proposition, don't reject it outright; rather ask why he/she considers that to be fair. This establishes an expectation of fairness and puts the burden on your partner to justify his/her stance.

7. Make your questions open-ended. Use questions such as "How?" "Why" "Why not?" "What?" or "Who?" rather than words such as "Is?" "Isn't?" "Can?" or "Can't?" that can be answered with a simple negation, leading nowhere. Open-ended questions require answers that produce more information that can help you negotiate a mutually beneficial solution.

8. Tap the power of silence. Allow your partner creative time to answer your questions. Avoid the temptation to jump in and help break what are sometimes uncomfortable silences. Both the time and the discomfort may result in information that can further the negotiations.

SOURCE: From *Getting Past No: Negotiating with Difficult People* by William Ury, published by Random House Business Books. Copyright © 1991 by William Ury. Reprinted by permission of The Random House Group Ltd., and by Bantam Books, a division of Random House, Inc.

Written contract provisions may create inflexibility. This may occur with policies like pattern bargaining, in which every union receives the same percentage raise. Such policies have been contentious in some cities. For example, in New York City certain unions (e.g., police, teachers) have called for an end to pattern bargaining, arguing for more flexibility in job categories like theirs, where noncompetitive salaries make it difficult to attract enough qualified personnel (Greenhouse, 1998). Scrapping the pattern bargaining approach to union contracts, they argue, would help put salaries on par with those in adjacent communities. In the New York City case, however, eliminating pattern bargaining would likely sour relations between city hall and other municipal unions, and among the unions themselves.

Once the parties have reached agreement on key sticking points and contractual language has been approved, both sides must seek ratification of the contract. Members of the union bargaining team must convince their membership that the final product of negotiation deserves their consent; managers must seek ratification from the relevant governing body (e.g., city or county council, state legislature). If negotiators have assiduously maintained open lines of communication with their respective constituencies, ratification is likely to be pro forma. Where information sharing has been more sporadic, negotiators could be told that their work product is deficient and that they need to reopen negotiations. When dealing with an intractable problem, leaders and managers often have to take creative steps to avert an impasse or salvage negotiations. As noted above, William Ury (1991, Chapter 3) has suggested that one useful approach is to reframe the problem to get one's negotiating counterpart to "buy in" to a mutually beneficial outcome, as a partner rather than an opponent.

Impasse procedures are triggered when bilateral negotiations come to a standstill. If contract disagreements cannot be resolved in the course of normal bargaining, mechanisms of "first resort" or "last resort" may be necessary. Most states use **mediation** as a first step in dispute resolution. Neutral third-party mediators seek to serve as catalysts to keep the parties talking and suggest alternative proposals to reach voluntary agreement on outstanding issues. If mediation fails, the next step is **fact-finding**. Appointed by the FLRA or the PERB, fact finders hold hearings, sift through arguments, and issue advisory opinions laying out proposed grounds for settlement.

If such "first resort" options do not succeed, "last resort" alternatives may be needed. These include **interest arbitration** (distinct from **grievance arbitration** or rights arbitration) and strikes, where available. Because strikes are prohibited in most public sector jurisdictions (and are declining in use where permitted, as noted earlier), binding arbitration (conventional arbitration and **final-offer arbitration**) is the most common means of achieving final resolution. Exhibit 12.1 defines **arbitration** and lists the various forms it can take. Public sector arbitration cases most frequently deal with discharge, wages, suspensions, and benefits (Mesch & Shamayeva, 1996). Critics express reservations about binding arbitration, contending that (1) settlements are imposed by outsiders, which runs counter to voluntary two-party contract bargaining; (2) arbitrators lack political accountability (i.e., they are neither directly nor indirectly accountable to the electorate); and (3) parties may drag their feet in negotiations or "first resort" stages of dispute resolution in hopes of succeeding with favorable arbitration decisions (Tomkins, 1995).

Administering the Contract

Contract administration is the third phase of the bargaining process. The principal mechanism here is a grievance procedure, typically provided for in the negotiated agreement. Grievance procedures lay out the available steps or levels to resolve disputes about contract interpretation or implementation. Binding arbitration typically is the last step in this process.

Two key players in contract administration are the union steward and the first-line supervisor. Both must be intimately familiar with the provisions in the contract and well trained in interpersonal skills and cooperative problem solving if contract administration is to proceed smoothly. Despite the knowledge, skills, and best intentions of stewards and supervisors, there are bound to be disagreements that lead to the filing of grievances. Grievance mechanisms provide a peaceful and fair way to address these contentious issues with minimal disruption of the workplace. It is important for such mechanisms to observe due process and to resolve issues definitively. Binding arbitration of grievances provides finality to the resolution of disputes. Although some writers portray arbitration as a low-cost and impartial alternative to litigation, others contend that arbitration is more costly, tilts in favor of defendants, and yields lower monetary awards to plaintiffs (Vinson, 2002).

The Great Recession has provided an opportunity for reform-oriented critics to challenge the status quo and push reforms to undercut public employee collective bargaining. Recent articles highlighting criticisms of current labor–management relations and proposals for reform have included titles with phrases such as "The War Against Public Sector Collective Bargaining," "The Attack on Collective Bargaining," and "Unions Under Siege." Attention now turns to these contemporary developments.

BARGAINING-RELATED REFORMS

The sentiment expressed in 1980 by Ronald Reagan ("Where free unions and collective bargaining are forbidden, freedom is lost") in the quote that opens this chapter is diametrically opposed to the proposals of many Republicans and some Democrats today that seek to curb union power and undermine collective bargaining.

Indeed, in recent years unions have been under siege (Befort, 2011) for reasons discussed in Chapter 11. Conservative reformers have criticized traditional labor–management relations, including collective bargaining, contending that bargaining is an obstacle to solving the state and local budget crises caused by the 2008–2011 recession. These criticisms have resulted in a set of reform proposals that reflect concerns identified with the liberation management tide mentioned in Chapter 1. While these right-leaning reform proposals are multiple and varied, they have been a guide to action for many state and local government officials seeking to address fiscal issues while also echoing the New Public Management theme of "let managers manage." The Freedom Foundation has succinctly summarized many of these reform ideas. Exhibit 12.4 lists the Freedom Foundation's top 10 reform ideas for government unions.

The ideas underlying these proposals have been translated into legislation. The National Conference of State Legislatures' Collective Bargaining and Labor Union Legislation Database (2014) shows the large number of public sector collective bargaining and labor union bills currently under consideration. As of mid-2014, there were 516 bills in 35 states relating to public employee unions, 62 bills relating to union dues/agency fees, 21 bills on political activities and contributions, 118 bills for public safety employees, and additional bills in other categories making a total of 1,034 bills in 45 states. The majority of these bills in most states sought to weaken unions and collective bargaining rights, with the lone exception of public safety employees. The volume of such legislation, while large, is down somewhat from 2012, but public sector labor issues continue to occupy a significant portion of the state and local government policy agenda.

Exhibit 12.4 Ten Reform Proposals for Government Unions From the Freedom Foundation

1. **Union dues:** Revise mandatory payment of union dues as a condition of employment; preserve workers' rights to choose on the matter.

2. **Political speech:** Require employee permission before unions use mandatory dues to advance political purposes.

3. **Choice of representation:** Prevent union monopoly by allowing employees to choose representation from a variety of unions or associations.

4. **Payroll deduction:** Prohibit government payroll systems from collecting union political funds.

5. **Financial disclosure:** Require unions to disclose financial information to their members.

6. **Sunshine bargaining:** Mandate that collective negotiations be open to the public.

7. **First Amendment:** Impose requirements on unions to notify employees of their rights to obtain refunds for union expenditures on political activity.

8. **Public resources:** Prohibit states from subsidizing union bargaining costs.

9. **Union security:** Require frequent reelection campaigns for unions representing public employee groups.

10. **Political donations:** Prohibit union contributions to political campaigns of elected officials who may represent management in negotiations.

SOURCE: Adapted from Malandra (2011).

Union supporters adamantly oppose the Freedom Foundation's reform proposals and bills curbing labor power and weakening the collective bargaining process. Their view is reflected in the phrase "United we bargain, divided we beg," and they strongly resist efforts to curtail labor rights. As Befort (2011) reminds us, many conservative reformers view public employees as having "first-class obligations, but only second-class rights" (p. 238). The principle of fairness suggests that workers who opt with a democratic vote to have a union represent them should also be responsible for paying for the expenses of bargaining and administering a labor agreement. Creamer (2014) points out a similar truth related to city government, where ordinary citizens democratically elect the government and, even if they voted against municipal officials, they still are obligated to pay city taxes. Labor advocates argue that public sector collective bargaining is a tool to help resolve the budget crisis and to improve the well-being of workers as the economy improves. They further point out that unions made substantial concessions on wages and benefits during the 2008–2011 period (Freeman & Han, 2012).

Nonetheless, the salience of several of the right-leaning reform proposals was recently reflected not only in the actions of governors and state legislators in the Midwest and beyond, as described in Chapter 11, but also in the 2014 U.S. Supreme Court decision in the case of ***Harris v. Quinn*** (see Exhibit 12.5). In addition to Michigan and Indiana (which passed right-to-work legislation in 2012) and Wisconsin (which passed a law eliminating collective bargaining rights for most employees), the AFL-CIO predicts that 22 states will soon consider bargaining process restrictions (e.g., prohibiting specific types of government employees from joining bargaining units).

As of this writing, a sampling of the AFL-CIO watch list of states where antiunion legislation has been proposed includes New Hampshire (considering a proposal that enlarges management authority over public employees by restricting the scope of negotiations), North Carolina (attempting to enshrine language in its right-to-work legislation in the state constitution), and Iowa (proposing modifications of work rules governing grievances, bumping rights, and prohibiting voluntary payroll deduction of union dues) (Maynard, 2013).

Several states enacted reforms earlier, such as Washington and Idaho (which adopted "paycheck protection" laws in 1992 and 1997, respectively, requiring employees to give

Exhibit 12.5   The *Harris v. Quinn* Decision

The key issue at stake in the *Harris v. Quinn* case was whether thousands of home health care workers serving Medicaid recipients can be forced to pay fees to help subsidize the union's cost of collective bargaining if they are not union members. For approximately 40 years prevailing policy had been that government workers could not be required to join a public employee union or contribute to its political and ideological activities, but they could be obligated to pay union expenses ("agency fees") for collective bargaining and contract administration (Estland & Forbath, 2014).

On June 30, 2014, the U.S. Supreme Court, in an ideologically divided 5–4 decision, said that for this class of public employees requiring "agency fees" violates the First Amendment free speech rights of nonmembers whose views are contrary to the positions taken by the union. While the Court could have gone further and supported the plaintiff's broad request to overturn the 1977 decision in *Abood v. Detroit Board of Education,* which authorized payment of such fees, the decision was more narrowly framed to this particular segment of workers ("partial public employees") (Greenhouse, 2014). Nonetheless, labor advocates fear that this might be the first step in that direction. The consequences of *Abood* being overturned, should that occur, would be potentially devastating for public sector unions, undercutting their membership and financial bases and essentially requiring open shops in public sector bureaucracies.

To better understand the issues involved in what has been called "arguably the most important labor law case the court has considered in decades" (Rogers, 2014), recall concepts covered previously: Following a representation election the exclusive bargaining agent for employees in a specific unit has received support from a majority of workers in the unit. When negotiating or administering the collective bargaining contract, the union must represent all workers in the unit, members and nonmembers alike. This creates "free riders," members of the unit who receive negotiated contractual benefits without contributing to costs by paying their "fair share" of fees. Currently, about half of the states require union fees from government workers even if they are not union members (Markon & Barnes, 2014). The earlier *Abood* decision upheld government efforts to prevent free riding and promote labor stability, but the *Harris* decision is a setback for unions because it makes the fate of *Abood* look "potentially gloomy" and it "may mean something worse down the line" (Morrissey, 2014).

annual written consent before unions could collect money for political activities) and Utah (which passed a law in 2001 banning public agencies from diverting employee wages to political entities and requiring public sector unions to collect funds through voluntary member contributions) (Williams, 2012). In an effort to control its state budget, Nebraska passed reform legislation in 2011 that substantially revamped the procedures and criteria for resolving public bargaining impasses. In 2011, Oklahoma repealed a law that had required cities with populations larger than 35,000 to grant collective bargaining rights to nonuniformed municipal employees (Clark, 2012). Republican governors in Indiana and Missouri issued executive orders in 2005 to rescind previous executive orders of their Democratic predecessors that had established state-level collective bargaining (Freeman & Han, 2012). In Indiana a law passed in 2011 barring any governor from granting state workers the right to collective bargaining.

Other reforms linked to public sector budget deficits that have harsh impacts on public employees are in the areas of pension and health benefits. Rising pension and health care costs create a major budgetary drain on state and local governments. In response, from 2009 through 2011, 43 states reduced pension benefits, increased employee contributions, or both (Snell, 2012). Two other reforms have adversely affected public employees: (1) the move toward defined-contribution pension plans and away from defined-benefit plans, and (2) adoption of two-tier pension benefit plans, with new hires receiving less generous benefits than those available to current retirees and employees. States and localities have also sought to reduce unfunded retiree health care costs (see Chapter 8). The very nature of the collective bargaining process has led some to question whether it is able to respond in a timely manner to crucial fiscal challenges linked to such subjects (Clark, 2012; Freeman & Han, 2012).

In short, public sector collective bargaining is at a crossroads as states pursue structural changes that weaken the negotiating power and political influence of unions. Some observers suggest there is a need to rethink the ideas and inflexible structures associated with adversarial bargaining and to consider alternative approaches. Such approaches are the focus of the next section.

HOSTILITY VERSUS HARMONY

Ideas shape institutions. The ideas undergirding public sector collective bargaining are borrowed from models previously designed for the private sector. A critical view of public unionism and collective bargaining has been put forward by David Denholm (1997), publisher of the journal *Government Union Review*. Denholm contends that key concepts in labor–management relations drawn from the private sector are inappropriate when applied in government because of differences between the two sectors. Concepts such as competition, market economy, and free contracts are defining characteristics in the private sector, whereas government is characterized by monopoly, politics, and sovereignty. The **doctrine of hostility** between parties is fundamental to traditional collective bargaining (adversarial, conflictual, confrontational). The **doctrine of harmony**, critics argue, offers a more appropriate set of ideas and behaviors to guide public sector LMRs (cooperation, service orientation, participation) and advance the public interest. Denholm posits that the public interest in public employment includes the following:

- Maintaining a peaceful, stable employer–employee relationship
- Safeguarding the rights of all public employees
- Protecting the right of the citizenry to control government policy and costs through their elected representatives
- Providing services in the most efficient and orderly manner possible

Denholm (1997) argues that collective bargaining is ill suited to government and that the common interest is ill served by it. His conclusion: "It is time to move beyond the failed nostrums of the past into a better future for public employees and the public they serve" (p. 52).

Cardinal distinctions between these two approaches are outlined in Exhibit 12.6. Exciting recent developments in LMRs are those guided by the doctrine of harmony. They take the form of collaborative problem solving, participative decision making, and partnerships (Bilmes & Gould, 2009; Fretz & Walsh, 1998; Parsons, Belcher, & Jackson, 1998; U.S. Department of Labor, 1996). Instructive examples of such creative experiments are found at all levels of government. Selected examples of **cooperative problem solving** in state and local jurisdictions indicate the various issues tackled by joint labor–management collaboration. These include ways to improve employee safety (Connecticut), reduce health care costs (Peoria, Illinois), resolve conflict between city building inspectors and private electrical contractors (Madison, Wisconsin), settle disputes between managers and firefighters by developing joint annual plans (Phoenix, Arizona), and achieve win–win solutions for a city mayor and municipal union at loggerheads over privatization (see Fretz & Walsh, 1998; Osborne & Plastrik, 1998; Parsons et al.,1998; U.S. Department of Labor, 1996).

Cooperative problem solving is more likely to succeed when there is mutual trust, commitment, and leadership from all participants as well as from flexible, adaptive organizational structures (Levine, 1997; Rubin & Rubin, 2001). Among the improvements attributed to partnerships of this kind are better service, lower costs, improved quality of work life, fewer grievances, speedier dispute settlement, increased use of gainsharing, more effective discipline, and more flexible negotiated agreements (Lane, 1996). Although it is important not to oversell win–win bargaining and harmony-based solutions or to undervalue the merits of traditional bargaining (see Lobel, 1994), these examples suggest that public unions and managers should explore diverse paths and think strategically about ways to improve LMRs and citizen services in the future.

While collective bargaining can be vulnerable to the "low trust–high conflict" trap, consensus decision making potentially offers a "high trust–low conflict" alternative (Masters, Albright, & Eplion, 2006, p. 371). The labor–management partnership is one form of consensus decision making (see Beck & West, 2012). President Bill Clinton mandated the federal government's partnership initiative in 1993 with the issuance of **Executive Order 12871**; however, his successor, President George W. Bush, rescinded that order in 2001 (with Executive Order 13201). Bush's rescission emphasized the need for managerial flexibility, consistent with the tide of liberation management (Chapter 1), as justification for curbing labor rights.

Exhibit 12.6   Traditional Bargaining Versus Problem-Solving Bargaining

Traditional bargaining: Opposing bargaining teams engage in zero-sum posturing and demands.

Problem-solving bargaining: Discussion is resolution oriented, leading to mutually agreeable and beneficial answers to common problems.

In traditional bargaining, each side has but one goal—to wring the maximum number of concessions from the other side in exchange for the minimum amount of effort, focusing on short-term gains over long-term benefits. There are several key avenues to reaching that goal:

- Emphasizing form over substance
- Using highly legalistic language
- Obscuring real wants and needs
- Using a hierarchy to limit communication

Although traditional bargaining can be functional, it is rarely efficient, as the process itself necessitates repetition every few years.

Problem-solving bargaining repudiates the antagonistic stance of the traditional model and seeks to forge long-lasting agreements based on the needs of all stakeholders. There are several courses of action that accomplish this:

- Honestly appraising what needs to be changed
- Informing other stakeholders of these basic needs
- Encouraging exchange of possible solutions
- Reaching agreements on specific solutions

Problem-solving bargaining creates real, self-sustaining solutions to problems that benefit all stakeholders.

Examining results of the 8-year experience under the Clinton mandate, Masters and his colleagues (2006) studied 60 partnerships covering several hundred thousand federal employees to document the advantages of cooperative problem solving. Partnerships offered many of the same benefits noted above in state and local government experience: a forum for collaborative communication and joint decision making, improved organizational performance, and an enhanced labor relations climate that curtailed labor–management disputes (p. 367). While benefits can potentially be achieved through collaborative labor–management structures, costs need to be considered as well. Exhibit 12.7 presents a summary of the potential benefits and costs of consensus decision making for employers and for employees and/or union representatives.

Each party must weigh whether the gains exceed the costs and whether the benefits of harmonious relations outweigh those of the traditional adversarial relationships often associated with collective bargaining. However, it should be emphasized that various forms of collaboration can coexist with collective bargaining. Indeed, as Masters and colleagues

Exhibit 12.7   Potential Benefits and Costs of Cooperative Partnerships for Employers and Employees

	Employers	Employees/Union Representatives
Benefits	• Improved productivity and service/product quality • Reduced waste, costs, and inefficient overhead • Better use of equipment • Improved employee commitment and financial performance • Lower employee turnover and absenteeism • Enhanced stakeholder satisfaction • Fewer labor–management disputes and grievances	• Better financial benefits and improved quality of work life • Less painful employee cuts, negotiation efforts, and wage reductions • Increased employee/union involvement in operations • Greater member support if employees recognize benefits result from cooperation • Ongoing communication and decision making with employee/union input
Costs	• Loss of managerial authority, power, and status • Questionable compromises to achieve consensus • Unproductive time and energy spent in meetings	• Co-optation by management • Weakening of collective bargaining role • Reduction of member loyalty • Undermining of grievance procedures and resolutions • Need for technical training and skill development

SOURCES: Adapted from Deery and Iverson (2005); Masters et al. (2006).

point out, collective bargaining takes place around the time contracts expire, so without a mechanism like labor–management partnerships there are few occasions for ongoing communication (p. 370). This allows an informal form of "mutual gains bargaining" to occur outside the formal collective negotiations process (see Deery & Iverson, 2005).

One way to think about LMRs, proposed by James Flint (2002), is to visualize a relationship continuum. This continuum is depicted in stages that vary based on dimensions of control and effectiveness (most to least). Exhibit 12.8 maps the stages across the relationship continuum, with Stage 1 (Healthy Workplace Environment) at one end, with most control and greatest effectiveness, and Stage 5 (Resort to Litigation) at the other end, with least control and least effectiveness. The continuum is both a diagnostic tool to isolate where LMRs are in a jurisdiction at a given point in time and a prescriptive device that helps participants see what is necessary to move from where they are (e.g., acrimony) to where they want to be (e.g., cooperation).

Masters et al. (2006, p. 368) mention a different but related continuum of labor–management relations with comanagement arrangements on one end (left) of the continuum and joint labor–management committees on the other extreme (right). Strategic

Exhibit 12.8 Effectiveness and Control on the Relationship Continuum

Most Effective				Least Effective
<--->				
Healthy Workplace Environment	Need for Problem Solving	Need for Mediation	Arbitration Required	Resort to Litigation
Stage 1	Stage 2	Stage 3	Stage 4	Stage 5
Most Control				Least Control
<--->				

Stage 1. Healthy Workplace Environment: Commitment to leadership by both management and labor; commitment by both to build a positive, trusting relationship; collaboration; creating an organizational infrastructure to ensure accountability and employee development.

Stage 2. Need for Problem Solving: Training in problem-solving skills; investment in employees and the organization; selection of problem-solving tools; recognition of inevitable conflict and decisions on proactive responses.

Stage 3. Need for Mediation: Incurring moderate expenses; reliance on external problem solving; expending additional time to reach agreement; recognizing that an acceptable result may not occur; damaging labor–management relationship.

Stage 4. Arbitration Required: Absorbing increasing expenses; accepting arbitrator's decision without appeal; relinquishing control for resolution to arbitrator; creating a more confrontational environment; producing a result that may be unsatisfactory to one or both parties; altering labor–management relationship; reducing effective communication.

Stage 5. Resort to Litigation: Requiring the often expensive process of rebuilding the labor–management relationship; heightening of adversarial relations; relying on experts who lack knowledge of in-house relationships; creating win–lose decisions; injuring labor–management relations; blocking effective communication.

SOURCE: Adapted from Flint (2002).

partnerships are nearer the comanagerial end of the spectrum, but all three approaches are distinct from collective bargaining, even though their deliberations can affect negotiations. Even further to the continuum's right extreme would be meet-and-confer arrangements or Tennessee's nonbinding "collaborative conferencing" approach. Germany provides an example of codetermination bargaining, or "democratic corporatism," that would be even further to the left end of the continuum than comanagement (Exhibit 12.9). Such structural

Exhibit 12.9   Labor–Management Relations in Germany: Codetermination

Germany developed a consensual model of labor–management relations after World War II based on a system of "democratic corporatism," whereby labor, management, and the state work together to prevent and solve conflicts.

Since the 1950s, the system of "codetermination" (*Mitbestimmung*) has stipulated that workers participate, in some form, in both strategic corporate decisions and determination of workplace conditions. Codetermination takes place in two forms: (1) Workers are directly represented on supervisory boards in large companies, and (2) employees can (but do not always) elect works councils (*Betriebsräte*) in every company with 10 or more employees. As part of a democratic corporatist model of labor–management relations, the works councils are charged with representing workers' concerns in the context of the interests of the company as a whole. Works councils are distinct from trade unions, though there is a close relationship between them. The codetermination system is oriented toward enhancing personnel management by giving workers a voice in everything from training to improving workplace culture.

Codetermination gives workers a say in the following areas:

- Job cuts and compensation packages
- Conditions for bonuses
- Productivity targets
- Training programs
- Introduction of new technologies
- Vacation schedules
- Workplace discrimination
- Scheduling of breaks
- Monitoring of worker activity
- Hiring of apprentices
- Transfers of employees
- Plant shutdowns (Albach, 1993; European Foundation for the Improvement of Living and Working Conditions, 2007; Fulton, 2007; Library of Congress, 1995; Simon, 2007)

This is only a small part of the wide-ranging scope of worker participation in German workplaces. Trade unions are still responsible for collective bargaining and for the representation of workers along industry lines, though they are heavily involved with most works councils in facilitating training sessions and sharing information. Contentious issues between works councils and management that cannot be resolved within the workplace are settled in special labor courts that are distinct from the civil law system.

The motivation for codetermination initially revolved around a concern for the right of workers to participate in the workplace. A second motivation slowly developed as some employers, despite initial opposition, discovered that meaningful worker participation in workplace activities actually serves the long-term interests of their companies (Girnt, 1998; Patriarka & Welz, 2008, pp. 345–346). Codetermination has long been criticized by free market economists and some German employers as reducing the flexibility, and therefore the competitiveness, of German industry and of imposing undue costs on German firms. Employers must pay all the costs of works councils, including the paid work

(Continued)

Exhibit 12.9 (Continued)

time lost to council activities, copying and telephone costs, and even staff support for large councils in big firms (Fulton, 2007). On the other hand, Germany loses far fewer days to strikes than countries with contentious labor–management relations, and its workers have enjoyed a more stable workplace environment with a sense that their voice in personnel management really matters on a day-to-day basis (Simon, 2007).

Codetermination is currently being buffeted by the strong winds of economic change. The increasing number of start-up companies based on new technologies, company bankruptcies, foreign buyouts, outsourcing of production abroad, and the general impact of globalization are all making stable workplace participation increasingly problematic. Contemporary German workers must now face the problems that their counterparts in other countries have long been used to: fear of job loss, reduction in benefits and pay bonuses, and uncertainties about the future of their companies. Despite the economic pressures against worker participation, codetermination has become a fact of life in the German economy and, more recently, in the European Union as a whole, so that it is likely to remain a feature of personnel management even at the cost of the quantitative bottom line (European Commission, 2008; Girnt, 1998).

SOURCES: Sources: Albach, 1993; Fulton, 2007; "Germany: Mitbestimmungsrechte," 2007; Library of Congress, 1995; Simon, 2007.

arrangements are important to the extent that they improve the underlying dynamics of labor–management interactions. The challenge for strategic human resource management is to identify where along the LMR continuum they are currently and where they want to be to achieve long-term organizational goals and outcomes.

Appendix B at the end of this chapter presents a role-play exercise in the form of a mock disciplinary appeal board hearing, in which additional issues are raised regarding LMRs and the legal and ethical dilemmas that can arise.

SUMMARY AND CONCLUSION

One fundamental paradox in LMRs is that the doctrine of hostility from the private sector was adapted with only minor modifications by the public sector, thereby inhibiting emergence of a competing model built on the doctrine of harmony. The legal structures underlying public LMRs ensure the continued dominance of the adversarial approach of traditional bargaining. Recent experiments, however, point the way to promising experiences with cooperative problem solving.

Where LMRs are extremely adversarial and hostile, both workers and managers are likely to fail what former U.S. secretary of labor Robert Reich (1998) has called the "pronoun test." He assessed employees' feelings toward their employers by listening carefully to the way they responded to questions about their work. If they used "they" and "them" in referring to the organization instead of "we" and "us," they failed Reich's test of collective commitment. Similarly, "we–they, us–them" characterizations of

LMRs suggest an ingrained adversarial environment, making principled negotiations (win–win) and cooperative problem solving less likely. In workplaces peopled predominantly by employees who pass the pronoun test, strategies built on the doctrine of harmony and incorporating participative decision making are more likely to succeed. Conversely, in work environments where workers fail the pronoun test, strategic human resource managers need to assess the situation realistically and devise action plans to move their organizations forward so that organizational goals and employee well-being are both attainable.

KEY TERMS

Agency shop
Arbitration
Certification of the bargaining agent
Collective bargaining
Cooperative problem solving
Doctrine of harmony
Doctrine of hostility
Dues checkoff
Executive Order 12871
Fact-finding
Final-offer arbitration
Grievance arbitration
Harris v. Quinn
Impasse procedures

Interest arbitration
Maintenance of membership
Med-arb
Mediation
Principled negotiations
Problem-solving bargaining
Productivity bargaining
Public Employee Relations Boards (PERBs)
Representation election
Traditional bargaining
Unfair labor practices
Union shop
Whipsaw effect

EXERCISES

Class Discussion

1. What are the key implications of (a) the doctrine of hostility and (b) the doctrine of harmony as each pertains to public sector LMRs?

2. Which is preferable: traditional bargaining or cooperative problem solving? Why?

3. What important obstacles are likely to be encountered in each of the three phases of collective bargaining? How can each be resolved? How is this like a chess game?

4. Invite someone who is involved on a collective bargaining team to visit your class. Ask the visitor to discuss his or her experiences involving some of the negative and positive bargaining behaviors listed in Appendix A and the strategies suggested by William Ury.

5. How do you explain the increased hostility recently directed at unions and public employees? Is it justified?

6. How do you assess recent reform proposals? In what ways do you think they will improve or impede labor–management relations?

Team Activities

7. Divide into four groups representing the roles of (a) an aggrieved employee, (b) a mediator, (c) a fact finder, and (d) an arbitrator. Have the aggrieved employee group define the nature of the grievance, and then have each of the third-party neutral groups indicate how they would go about resolving the grievance.

8. Divide into four groups, each one representing a different type of arbitration (see Exhibit 12.1). Within the groups, discuss the pros and cons of the type of arbitration. Report back to the class as a whole.

9. What is the case against collective bargaining in the public sector?

10. Debate the following topic: The rights of public employees to negotiate a labor contract should be rescinded because of a downturn in the economy.

11. Brainstorm examples of how in your experience the negotiating strategies proposed by William Ury have succeeded or failed.

Individual Assignments

12. How is collective bargaining similar in the public and private sectors? How is it different from one sector to the other?

13. Identify an issue on which you disagree with another party and apply some of the negotiating strategies proposed in this chapter. Report your experience to the class.

14. Comb through your hometown newspaper for a story that provides an example of labor–management cooperation or conflict. What explains the relationship you have identified? Is it typical or atypical of labor–management relationships in your community?

15. Two arguments against public employee collective bargaining are that it is antidemocratic and that it impedes effective government. Do you agree or disagree with each of these assertions? Why?

16. What insights did you get from your experience with the role-play of the disciplinary hearing found in Appendix B? Does this seem like a reasonable process for handling such cases? Why or why not?

APPENDIX A

Bargaining Checklist and Observation Sheet

Observed Behavior	Management		Union	
A. Negative behaviors				
Did the bargaining team . . .				
Underestimate the other party?	Y	N	Y	N
Overestimate the strength of their case?	Y	N	Y	N
Seem unprepared?	Y	N	Y	N
Advance vague proposals?	Y	N	Y	N

Observed Behavior	Management		Union	
Argue among themselves?	Y	N	Y	N
Lose their tempers?	Y	N	Y	N
Make assumptions about the other party's priorities?	Y	N	Y	N
Escalate demands unrealistically?	Y	N	Y	N
Oversell?	Y	N	Y	N
Compromise too readily?	Y	N	Y	N
Act defensive?	Y	N	Y	N
Interrupt the other party?	Y	N	Y	N
Rush the proceedings?	Y	N	Y	N
React prematurely to the other party's proposals?	Y	N	Y	N
End the meeting on a negative note?	Y	N	Y	N
Make promises they could not keep?	Y	N	Y	N
Lie?	Y	N	Y	N
Break confidences?	Y	N	Y	N
B. Positive behaviors				
Did the bargaining team . . .				
Act calm and cool?	Y	N	Y	N
Show respect to the other party?	Y	N	Y	N
Demonstrate flexibility?	Y	N	Y	N
Act reasonably?	Y	N	Y	N
Listen carefully?	Y	N	Y	N
Focus on relevant issues?	Y	N	Y	N
Study alternatives and new information?	Y	N	Y	N
Caucus when needed?	Y	N	Y	N
Avoid intimidation?	Y	N	Y	N
Respect confidentiality?	Y	N	Y	N
Negotiate in good faith?	Y	N	Y	N
Exhibit careful planning?	Y	N	Y	N
Heed mutually agreed-upon deadlines?	Y	N	Y	N
Tell the truth?	Y	N	Y	N

SOURCE: Adapted from Colosi (1985).

NOTE: The negative behaviors by bargaining team members shown in section A are contrasted with the positive behaviors listed in section B. Although some of the section A examples may be "bargaining as usual" rather than legal violations of the "good faith" requirement, they are likely to be off-putting to the other side, and the temptation might be for the opposite team to respond in kind, thereby escalating the hostility.

APPENDIX B

Mock Disciplinary Appeal Board Hearing

Cast of Characters

Wilson Worker	Appellant
Loren Lawyer	Appellant's attorney
Estimate Value	Tax assessor
Guy Noir	Security director for tax assessor
Chris Counselor	Tax assessor's attorney
Fred Fair	Hearing examiner

Fred Fair:	The parties will come to order. The hearing is now open and on the record before the appeal board. Let the record show that the presiding officer for the hearing is Fred Fair. The hearing will take up the matter of the appeal from Wilson Worker, appeal number 100010, of the appellant's dismissal, effective November 1, 2014, from a supervisor's position with the Office of the County Tax Assessor. The parties will state their appearances.
Chris Counselor:	For the tax assessor's office, appearing are Estimate Value, the county tax assessor; Guy Noir, security director for the assessor's office; and Chris Counselor, legal counsel for the office.
Loren Lawyer:	The appellant, Wilson Worker, appears in person and by counsel Loren Lawyer.
Fred Fair:	Do the parties have any stipulations in this matter?
Loren Lawyer:	Yes, the appellant stipulates that notice of the dismissal and opportunity to discuss the matter prior to becoming effective followed established county rules and regulation. The appellant does not appeal the procedures followed in the dismissal but appeals the reasonableness of the tax assessor in dismissing the appellant.
Chris Counselor:	The tax assessor also stipulates that the process it followed in dismissing the appellant was in compliance with its disciplinary policies set forth under county rules.
Fred Fair:	The process followed in the dismissal of the appellant has been stipulated to by both parties and is uncontested for this hearing. Does the tax assessor wish to enter any exhibits into evidence at this time?

Chris Counselor:	Yes, we have prefiled the tax assessor's Exhibits 1 through 5. The appellant was served with copies of these exhibits in compliance with the hearing examiner's orders. The exhibits are a copy of the tax assessor's policy on the confidentiality of records, copy of the investigative report of this incident made by the tax assessor's security department, letters proposing and finalizing the dismissal, and a notarized statement from a former employee.
Fred Fair:	Does the appellant have any objections?
Loren Lawyer:	The appellant has none.
Fred Fair:	Thank you. The tax assessor's Exhibits 1 through 5 are admitted and made part of the record in this matter. Does the appellant wish to enter any exhibits?
Loren Lawyer:	The appellant has no exhibits to enter at this time but reserves the right to enter exhibits as appropriate at a later time during the hearing.
Fred Fair:	Does the tax assessor have any objection?
Chris Counselor:	The tax assessor has no objection but also reserves the right to raise objections to any appellant's exhibits as may later be introduced.
Fred Fair:	Thank you. The hearing will proceed with the presentation of evidence and testimony. The tax assessor's office will present its case first. The tax assessor may call the first witness.
Chris Counselor:	We call Estimate Value to the stand.

(Estimate Value takes the stand. Fred Fair, the hearing examiner, swears the witness in.)

Fred Fair:	Stand and raise your right hand. Do you swear or affirm that the testimony you are about to give is the truth, the whole truth, and nothing but the truth?
Estimate Value:	I do.
Fred Fair:	You may sit down.
Chris Counselor:	Please state your name for the record and where you are employed.
Estimate Value:	My name is Estimate Value. I am the county tax assessor. I was elected to office in 2000 and have been reelected to the office since then. My education includes a bachelor's degree in accounting and a master's degree in public administration.
Chris Counselor:	Are you acquainted with the appellant, Wilson Worker?
Estimate Value:	Yes, Wilson was employed in my office as a supervisor of our data entry and records processing team. Wilson supervised a team of seven data entry clerks and three file clerks. Up until this incident, Wilson had a clean record in my office and was a hardworking and trusted employee.

Chris Counselor: What are the facts in the matter that led you to dismiss the appellant?

Estimate Value: We received an anonymous tip on the "hotline" that Wilson Worker's home was listed substantially under value for tax purposes. The "hotline" allows persons to report allegations of wrongdoing, inappropriate and unethical behavior, or illegal activities involving tax assessments. I ordered the security director to investigate the allegation. I am dedicated to the integrity of tax records in my office. The public must be able to trust the accuracy of records processed by this department.

Chris Counselor: What happened next?

Estimate Value: The security director completed the investigation and gave me a copy. The security director found that the assessed property value listed on official records of the tax assessor's office for Wilson Worker's residence was approximately half of that for comparable residents in the same neighborhood with comparable homestead exemption histories.

Chris Counselor: What was the impact on Wilson Worker's tax liability?

Estimate Value: Property taxes for Wilson's residence were underassessed in 2013. Wilson's property taxes prior to 2012 were correctly assessed and paid. The report concluded that Wilson underpaid property taxes by $3,000 last year.

Chris Counselor: Did the investigation determine how the undervaluing and underassessment of Wilson's liability for property taxes could have occurred?

Estimate Value: Yes, the security director reviewed the computer records affecting Wilson's tax records during his entire tenure with the tax assessor's office, interviewed employees in the computer department, members of Wilson's work team, and Wilson. The investigative report concluded that official tax assessment records were altered under Wilson's security access password. The changes gave Wilson an illegal reduction of property taxes.

Chris Counselor: Did the investigative report conclude that Wilson acted alone or with the help of any coconspirators?

Estimate Value: The report concluded that Wilson acted alone. The security director said no other employees were incriminated.

Chris Counselor: Did the report identify who the anonymous caller was who identified Wilson's taxable property value was grossly underreported?

Estimate Value: Yes, he was identified as Tom Tenure, a former employee.

Chris Counselor: Did you confront Wilson Worker with the evidence of the investigation?

Estimate Value: Yes. I met with Wilson and gave him a copy of the investigative report.

Chris Counselor: What did Wilson say?

Estimate Value: Wilson denied any culpability. Wilson claimed to have been practicing on the software we were installing during 2012 to upgrade our computer system.

Chris Counselor:	How would that have changed tax records?
Estimate Value:	During installation of the new software, a parallel system was available for staff to practice with. Wilson claimed to have entered a lower tax assessment on the parallel system for 123 SW 57th Avenue, the address where Wilson resides. Wilson realized immediately the entry was not made on the parallel system but on the real system, and lowered the property tax liability.
Chris Counselor:	Did Wilson attempt to correct the incorrect data entry? What did Wilson say about that?
Loren Lawyer:	Your honor, I object to the form of the question. Chris Counselor asked the witness two questions and I won't be able to determine to which question the witness is responding.
Chris Counselor:	Your honor, I believe I asked one question using a two-question format. However, the intent of the question is clear and I respectfully request you overrule the objection of my worthy opponent and permit the witness to proceed.
Fred Fair:	The objection is overruled. The witness may respond to the question.
Estimate Value:	By now I've forgotten the question.
Chris Counselor:	Did Wilson try to change the incorrect data entry?
Estimate Value:	Wilson spoke with another team supervisor about the incident. Wilson said that the supervisor's advice was not to worry because record changes made during the trial period would not alter official records.
Chris Counselor:	From whom did Wilson get that advice?
Estimate Value:	Wilson said the advice was from Tom Tenure, a longtime supervisor in the tax assessor's office. Mr. Tenure retired and moved out of the area before the incorrect property value on Wilson's home was discovered.
Chris Counselor:	Did you question Mr. Tenure?
Estimate Value:	Since Mr. Tenure's testimony was so critical, we spoke to him by phone. Mr. Tenure did not recall the conversation Wilson claims they had. Mr. Tenure could not be here for today's hearing but provided his notarized statement.
Chris Counselor:	What happened next?
Estimate Value:	That left me with no other course of action than to dismiss Wilson for cause and terminate his employment with the tax assessor's office. I advised Wilson of my final decision by letter that same day. The letter also advised Wilson when he would receive his last paycheck. Information from the human resources office would follow, regarding eligibility to continue health care benefits under COBRA. I also told Wilson of the opportunity under County Employee Relations policies to appeal the dismissal within 30 days for a hearing before the appeal board.

Chris Counselor:	This concludes the direct examination of this witness. Thank you.
Fred Fair:	Does counsel for the appellant want to cross-examine this witness?
Loren Lawyer:	Yes, thank you. Estimate Value, you said that neither the investigation report nor the security director concluded that anyone other than Wilson Worker altered computer records to lower Wilson's tax liability. Correct?
Estimate Value:	That is my testimony.
Loren Lawyer:	Does that mean that only Wilson could have altered the records to obtain lower taxes?
Estimate Value:	That is what I believe.
Loren Lawyer:	And you are sure that happened in this case?
Estimate Value:	That was the conclusion reached by the security director after a thorough investigation.
Loren Lawyer:	What consideration did you give Wilson for the many years of faithful work for the tax assessor's office?
Estimate Value:	Up until this incident, Wilson had earned a reputation as a faithful, hardworking employee with at least satisfactory performance evaluations. However, I could not overlook my conclusion that Wilson breached the trust we have in employees to respect and guard the accuracy of our records. Wilson was dishonest with me and violated that trust. That is why I fired Wilson.
Loren Lawyer:	I have no further questions of this witness.
Fred Fair:	Thank you. You may return to your seat. The tax assessor's office may call the next witness.

(Estimate Value steps down from the witness stand.)

Chris Counselor:	The tax assessor's office calls Guy Noir to the stand.

(Guy Noir takes the stand. Fred Fair, the hearing examiner, swears the witness in.)

Fred Fair:	Stand and raise your right hand. Do you swear or affirm that the testimony you are about to give is the truth, the whole truth, and nothing but the truth?
Guy Noir:	I do.
Fred Fair:	You may take your seat.
Chris Counselor:	Please state your name and where you work, for the record.
Guy Noir:	My name is Guy Noir and I am responsible for internal investigations in the tax assessor's office. I am a graduate of the Private Eye Institute, located on the 12th floor of the Acme Building in downtown Minneapolis.
Chris Counselor:	How are you acquainted with the appellant in this matter?

Guy Noir:	Wilson Worker was the supervisor of the data entry and records processing team. I became personally acquainted with Wilson when the tax assessor asked me to investigate a case of fraudulent tax assessment involving Wilson's residence.
Chris Counselor:	Please tell the appeal board about your investigation.
Guy Noir:	I asked the manager of the management information systems—the MIS computer whiz—to determine who made the alterations to Wilson's tax records. The MIS manager said that the changes to Wilson's tax records were made under Wilson's password on Wilson's office computer.
Chris Counselor:	What else did you learn?
Guy Noir:	The MIS manager said that during the installation period of the new software system entries on the system were "live" while entries on the parallel system were not. The manager thought that was made clear to all employees during the installation period.
Chris Counselor:	Whom else did you interview?
Guy Noir:	I interviewed Wilson. He admitted making the entry lowering the residential tax liability but said a longtime employee in the office advised that no entries made during the trial period would take effect. Wilson denied willfully lowering the tax liability. When I asked Wilson who said that entries during the trial period would not become effective, Wilson identified Tom Tenure, a former employee, now retired and living out of the area.
Chris Counselor:	Did you contact Mr. Tenure?
Guy Noir:	Yes. He could not recall the conversation with Wilson. In fact, I got the impression that Mr. Tenure and Wilson were not the best of friends and had difficulties working together at the tax assessor's office.
Chris Counselor:	Why is Mr. Tenure not present today to offer his testimony?
Guy Noir:	He refused to travel back here because of the expense. A subpoena would be invalid because he lives out of state. He cooperated by providing a notarized statement of his testimony.
Chris Counselor:	The tax assessor's office calls your attention to its Exhibit 5, the statement by former employee Tom Tenure. I have no further questions of this witness.
Fred Fair:	Counselor Loren Lawyer, do you have any cross-examination of this witness?
Loren Lawyer:	Yes.
Fred Fair:	Thank you. I remind the witness you are still under oath. Counselor, you may proceed.
Loren Lawyer:	You testified that the tax records for Wilson's residence were fraudulent. Are you a criminal law expert?

Guy Noir:	No.
Loren Lawyer:	Did you report the incident to the county attorney or seek the assistance of the state's attorney?
Guy Noir:	No.
Loren Lawyer:	Why, then, do you testify that Wilson committed an illegal act?
Guy Noir:	I did not say it was illegal, just fraudulent.
Loren Lawyer:	What's the difference?
Guy Noir:	That's a question you should address to an attorney.
Loren Lawyer:	Then why didn't you ask an attorney before recommending the tax assessor fire Wilson?
Guy Noir:	That was the tax assessor's call, not mine.
Loren Lawyer:	Passing the buck!
Chris Counselor:	I object!
Fred Fair:	Sustained. The comment will be stricken from the record.
Loren Lawyer:	Are you sure that all employees knew that records changed during the trial period could become final at the end of the trial?
Guy Noir:	The MIS manager said there was a general distribution of a note advising employees to be careful with data entries during the trial period.
Loren Lawyer:	Did the MIS manager say he had personal knowledge that Wilson received the note and understood the importance of entries made during the trial?
Guy Noir:	No.
Loren Lawyer:	So you can't be sure that Wilson understood the consequence of the entry?
Guy Noir:	Well, no, but Wilson should have known.
Loren Lawyer:	What was the relationship between Mr. Tenure and Wilson when they worked together?
Guy Noir:	I gather it was not friendly. Tenure said that he and Wilson had serious disagreements at work. Tenure complained that his retirement pension was lowered because Wilson got more overtime work than he did. There was bad blood between the two over the issue.
Loren Lawyer:	I have no further questions for this witness.
Fred Fair:	Thank you. The witness may step down from the witness stand.
	(Guy Noir steps down from the witness stand.)
Fred Fair:	Does the tax assessor have any further evidence or witnesses?

Chris Counselor: No, your honor. The tax assessor rests.

Fred Fair: Wilson Worker may now present evidence.

Loren Lawyer: I would like to call Wilson Worker to the stand.

(Wilson Worker takes the stand and is sworn in.)

Fred Fair: Stand and raise your right hand to be sworn in. Do you swear or affirm that the testimony you are about to give is the truth, the whole truth, and nothing but the truth?

Wilson Worker: I do.

Fred Fair: You may be seated.

Loren Lawyer: Please state your name and where you were employed.

Wilson Worker: My name is Wilson Worker and I was employed as the supervisor of the data entry and records processing team at the county tax assessor's office.

Loren Lawyer: Tell the appeal board about your qualifications.

Wilson Worker: I was employed by the tax assessor's office for 15 years. I rose from a data entry clerk to team supervisor after completing the associate's degree in computer operations and supervision management from County Community College in 2000.

Loren Lawyer: Let's get right to the heart of this matter. Did you change the tax records for your residence and lower the tax liability?

Wilson Worker: Yes.

Loren Lawyer: Why?

Wilson Worker: I was practicing on a new software system being installed in the office on what I thought was a parallel version of the software. After I entered a taxable value for my property that cut it in half, I discovered that I had mistakenly made the change in the real version, not the parallel. I was horrified.

Loren Lawyer: Then what did you do?

Wilson Worker: I asked my coworker, Tom Tenure, if I should report this to the tax assessor. Tom said "no" because all record changes made during the practice period would not change any permanent records. "Don't worry," he said to me.

Loren Lawyer: What about your relationship with Mr. Tenure?

Wilson Worker: It wasn't good but I trusted him in this case because of his many years of experience in the office and his reputation for honesty. Later, I learned that he had given me very bad advice, advice that he knew was false. I had no idea he would deceive me, threaten my employment, and ruin my reputation.

Loren Lawyer:	Were you aware of the memo from the MIS manager that changes made to the tax database during the trial period would be converted into official records later?
Wilson Worker:	I remembered the memo but understood it to say that no record changes made during the trial period would convert into the official database afterward. Besides, I thought I changed my records in the parallel system. Anyway, Mr. Tenure certainly did not warn me of it when we spoke about the incident.
Loren Lawyer:	Were you surprised to learn that Tom Tenure was the "anonymous" person who reported you had falsely altered your own tax records?
Wilson Worker:	No, we never got along. Tom retired and left the area knowing that I inadvertently changed my records. The "anonymous" informant knew that I would not realize my taxes were undercalculated until the tax payment information arrived from the mortgage company. Tom had the motivation and opportunity to do me in.
Loren Lawyer:	So, you deny any wrongdoing in this case?
Wilson Worker:	Absolutely and emphatically, yes. I deny doing anything wrong or illegal.
Loren Lawyer:	What do you ask the appeal board to do for you in this appeal?
Wilson Worker:	I believe I did nothing wrong and should not have been fired. However, if the appeal board finds that my actions violated any policy, then I will accept a suspension without pay and then be returned to my supervisor's position.
Loren Lawyer:	Thank you. I have no further questions of the appellant.
Fred Fair:	Does counsel for the tax assessor's office wish to cross-examine the appellant?
Chris Counselor:	No, your honor.
Fred Fair:	Does counsel for the appellant have any additional testimony or evidence to present?
Loren Lawyer:	No, your honor. Wilson Worker rests.
Fred Fair:	The appellant may step down from the witness stand.
	(Wilson Worker returns to the appellant's seat.)
Fred Fair:	The tax assessor may make a closing statement.
Chris Counselor:	Thank you. Members of the board, Wilson Worker breached the trust the tax assessor places on employees. The public must be able to rely on the accuracy of tax records to accept the property tax bills we all receive yearly. The public may be unhappy with the amount of their taxes but never question its accuracy. Wilson Worker falsified tax records for personal gain and deserves to

be fired. We ask that you affirm the decision of the tax assessor to dismiss Wilson Worker and restore public trust in the property tax assessment process.

Fred Fair: Thank you. The appellant may make a closing statement.

Loren Lawyer: Thank you. Honorable board members, Wilson Worker is an honest person. The deceitful action of a coworker made Wilson appear a liar and possibly a criminal. A terrible wrong was committed against my client. At worst, Wilson may have stumbled in following office procedures when trying to learn a new computer system. That's not a crime. Wilson does not deserve the punishment that was given. I implore this board to restore Wilson to the supervisor position. The evidence in this case justifies your decision to do just that. Thank you.

Fred Fair: The appeal board thanks both parties for their conduct throughout this proceeding. The board will now recess to discuss the matter and try to reach a decision.

SOURCE: Conceived by Jeff J. Montague, Human Resources Manager, Kansas Department of Commerce, and adapted by John T. Collins, Office of Civil Rights and Labor Relations, Miami-Dade Transit. Used with permission, 2011.

REFERENCES

Albach, H. (1993). *Culture and technical innovation: A cross-cultural analysis and policy recommendations.* Berlin: Walter de Gruyter.

Baker, J. G. (1996, April). Negotiating a collective bargaining agreement: Law and strategy. *Labor Law Journal,* pp. 253–266.

Beck, M. A., & West, J. P. (2012). Millennials in the workforce: Unions and management battle for the soul of a generation. In W. I. Sauser Jr. & R. R. Sims (Eds.), *Managing human resources for the millennial generation* (pp. 355–397). Charlotte, NC: Information Age.

Befort, S. (2011). Public-sector employment under siege. *Indiana Law Journal, 87*(1), 231–238.

Bilmes, L. J., & Gould, W. S. (2009). *The people factor: Strengthening America by investing in public service.* Washington, DC: Brookings Institution Press.

Briggs, S., & Siegele, M. H. (1994). The ethical standards clause: A lesson from the private sector for the public sector. *Journal of Collective Negotiations, 23*(3), 181–186.

Clark, R. T., Jr. (2012). Public sector collective bargaining at the crossroads. *Urban Lawyer, 44*(1), 185–223.

Colosi, T. R. (1985). The negotiating process. In R. D. Helsby, J. Tener, & J. Lefkowitz (Eds.), *The evolving process: Collective negotiations in public employment* (pp. 217–232). Fort Washington, PA: Labor Relations Press.

Creamer, R. (2014, July 9). Why collective bargaining is a fundamental human right. Huffington Post. Retrieved from http://www.huffingtonpost.com/robert-creamer/why-collective-bargaining_b_5570047.html

Deery, S., & Iverson, R. (2005). Labor–management cooperation: Antecedents and impact on organizational performance. *Industrial & Labor Relations Review, 58*(4), 588–608.

Denholm, D. Y. (1997). The case against public sector unionism and collective bargaining. *Government Union Review, 18*(1), 31–52.

Estland, C., & Forbath, W. (2014, July 2). The war on workers: The Supreme Court ruling on *Harris v. Quinn* is a blow for unions. *New York Times.* Retrieved from http://www.nytimes.com/2014/07/03/opinion/the-supreme-court-ruling-on-Harrisv.Quinn-is-a-blow-for-unions

European Commission. (2008). *European works councils: Consultation of the European Social Partners on the revision of Council Directive 94/45/EC of 22 September 1994 on the establishment of a European works council or a procedure in community-scale undertakings for the purposes of informing and consulting employees.* Brussels: Author. Retrieved from http://ec.europa.eu/employment_social/labour_law/docs/2008/ewc_consultation2_en.pdf

European Foundation for the Improvement of Living and Working Conditions. (2007, October 31). Germany: Mitbestimmungsrechte des Betriebsrats [Codetermination rights of the works council]. Retrieved from http://www.eurofound.europa.eu/emire/GERMANY/CODETERMINATIONRIGHTSOFTHEWORKSCOUNCIL-DE.htm

Fisher, R., & Ury, W. (1981). *Getting to yes.* New York: Penguin Books.

Flint, J. (2002, August). Mending labor–management relationships. *Public Management.* Retrieved from http://www.icma.org/upload/library/IQ/500289.htm

Freeman, R. B., & Han, E. (2012). The war against public sector collective bargaining in the US. *Journal of Industrial Relations, 54*(3), 386–408.

Fretz, G. E., & Walsh, D. E. (1998). Aggression, peaceful coexistence, mutual cooperation—it's up to us. *Public Personnel Management, 27*(2), 69–76.

Fulton, L. (2007). Germany: Workplace representation, European Union, National Industrial Relations, European Trade Union Institute (ETUI). Retrieved from http://www.workerparticipation.eu/layout/set/print/national_industrial_relations/countries/germany/workplace_representation

Girnt, C. (1998). A sense of reality and pragmatism: An interview with industrial relations guru Wolfgang Streeck. *Mitbestimmung* (International edition). Retrieved from http://www.boeckler.de/164_29131.html

Greenhouse, S. (1998, October 12). Friction seen in future talks on city labor. *New York Times,* p. B1.

Greenhouse, S. (2014, June 30). Supreme Court ruling on union fees is a limited blow to labor. *New York Times.* Retrieved from http://www.nytimes.com/2014/07/01/business

Kearney, R. C., & Mareschal, P. M. (2014). *Labor relations in the public sector* (5th ed.). Boca Raton, FL: CRC Press.

Lane, C. M. (1996, February). Unions and management are finding common ground, but cultural change is slow and difficult for these former adversaries. *Government Executive,* p. 41.

Levine, M. (1997). The union role in labor–management cooperation. *Journal of Collective Negotiations, 26*(3), 203–222.

Library of Congress. (1995, August). Germany: Codetermination (Federal Research Division, Country Studies Series). Retrieved from http://www.country-data.com/cgi-bin/query/r-4945.html

Lobel, I. B. (1994, December). Realities of interest-based (win–win) bargaining. *Labor Law Journal, 45*(12), 771–778.

Malandra, T. (2011, June 13). Top 10 reform ideas for government unions. National Federation of Independent Business. Retrieved from http://www.nfib.com/article/top-10-reform-ideas-for-government-unions-57271

Markon, J., & Barnes, R. (2014, June 30). Supreme Court: Home health-care workers can't be required to pay union fees. *Washington Post.* Retrieved from http://www.washingtonpost.com/national/supreme-court-home-health-care-workers-cant-be-required-to-pay-union-fees/2014/06/30/ed23c622-f733-11e3-8aa9-dad2ec039789_story.html

Masters, M., Albright, R., & Eplion, D. (2006). What did partnerships do? Evidence from the federal sector. *Industrial & Labor Relations Review, 59*(3), 367–385.

Maynard, M. (2013, January 28). Collective bargaining likely to be a big issue in legislatures this year. *Governing the States and Localities.* Retrieved from http://www.governing.com/news/state/sl-collective-bargaining-likely-to-be-big-issue.html

Mesch, D., & Shamayeva, O. (1996). Arbitration in practice: A profile of public sector arbitration cases. *Public Personnel Management, 25*(1), 119–131.

Morrissey, E. (2014, June 30). *Harris v. Quinn* more important than Hobby Lobby? Hot Air. Retrieved from http://www.Hotair.com/archives/2014/06/30/harris-v-quinn-more

National Conference of State Legislatures. (2014). Collective Bargaining and Labor Union Legislation Database. Retrieved from http://www.ncsl.org/research/labor-and-employment/collective-bargaining-legislation-database.aspx

Osborne, D., & Plastrik, P. (1998). *Banishing bureaucracy: The five strategies for reinventing government.* New York: Plume.

Parsons, P. A., Belcher, J., & Jackson, T. (1998). A labor–management approach to health care cost savings: The Peoria experience. *Public Personnel Management, 27*(2), 23–38.

Patriarka, M., & Welz, C. (2008, March 20). *European Works Council in practice: Key research findings.* European Foundation for the Improvement of Living and Working Conditions. Retrieved from http://www.eurofound.europa.eu/pubdocs/2008/28/en/1/ef0828en.pdf

Reich, R. B. (1998). *Locked in the cabinet.* New York: Vintage.

Rogers, J. (2014, April 14). Why *Harris v. Quinn* has labor very, very nervous. *The Nation.* Retrieved from http://www.thenation.com/article/179033/why-harris-v-quinn-has-labor-very-very-nervous

Rubin, B., & Rubin, R. (2001). *Labor–management partnerships: A new approach to collaborative management.* Arlington, VA: PricewaterhouseCoopers Endowment for the Business of Government. Retrieved from http://www.businessofgovernment.org/sites/default/files/LaborManagementPartnerships.pdf

Shimabukuro, J. O. (2011). *Collective bargaining and employees in the public sector.* Washington, DC: Congressional Research Service.

Simon, P. (2007, April). Germany: Freedom of association and labour law. Organization for Security and Cooperation in Europe, Office for Democratic Institutions and Human Rights. Retrieved from http://www.legislationline.org/?tid = 221&jid = 21&less = false

Snell, R. (2012, March). *State pension reform, 2009–2011.* Denver, CO: National Conference of State Legislatures.

Terkel, A. (2011, July 20). Wisconsin recalls 2011: Democrats say elections are not just about collective bargaining. Huffington Post. Retrieved from http://www.huffingtonpost.com/2011/07/20/wisconsin-recalls-collective-bargaining_n_ 904645.html

Tomkins, J. (1995). *Human resource management in government.* New York: HarperCollins.

Ury, W. (1991). *Getting past no: Negotiating with difficult people.* New York: Bantam.

U.S. Department of Labor. (1996). *Working together for public service.* Washington, DC: Author.

Vinson, J. (2002, May–June). Report debunks arbitration's low-cost myth. *Public Citizen,* pp. 1, 5.

Walton, R. E., & McKersie, R. B. (1965). *A behavioral theory of labor negotiations.* New York: McGraw-Hill.

Williams, B. (2012, December 5). Why government employee collective bargaining laws must be reformed now. State Budget Solutions. Retrieved from http://www.statebudgetsolutions.org/publications/detail/why-government-employee-collective-bargaining-laws-must-be-reformed-now

Conclusion

The Future as Opportunity, Not Destiny

There are costs and risks to a program of action, but they are far less than the long-range risks and costs of comfortable action.

—John F. Kennedy

Peering into the 21st century, it is clear that the future is already here. At the beginning of the 20th century, the public service was dramatically transformed by the merit system (Chapter 1), undergirded by bureaucratic structures and the scientific management principles of the Machine Age. In the context of spending cuts and demands for better service delivery, contemporary times have witnessed fundamental challenges to these ideas—privatization (provision of public services by business for corporate benefit), devolution (transfer of federal functions to subnational jurisdictions), and personnel reform (human resource management innovation)—in the name of smaller, more flexible, and more efficient government. What is needed is a systemic approach to such initiatives that deals with the overall role of government, the place of civil and military servants in that role, and the root causes of workforce problems. Strategies that focus on citizen needs, process improvement, and employee involvement likely will generate appropriate approaches, thereby enhancing the quality and productivity of government.

One hundred years ago, the public sector in all its size and diversity was an ideal laboratory for merit system innovations; in developing best practices, it became a model employer for the nation. Although remnants of such practices remain, notably in areas such as equal employment opportunity and employee-friendly policies, the public sphere has largely ceded its leadership position in the last several generations. How or whether that proud heritage will be restored depends on the responses to at least two major societal changes now under way: (1) rapidly expanding technologies and (2) the demand for human competency.

NEW TECHNOLOGIES, HUMAN COMPETENCIES, AND REFORMS

Most obvious among the changes currently taking place is the explosion of office technology. What was once seen as merely a productivity measure is now affecting the definition of work and how it is organized: Tasks done by a roomful of personnel in an earlier era can be handled by one person—anytime, anywhere. These technologies have only begun to be tapped, but the "death" of time and distance in a virtual work environment has already substantially altered the flexibility and speed of policy making—and who may be involved in decisions. These developments have affected a wide range of human resource functions with the advent of virtual recruitment centers, online job analysis systems, just-in-time computer-based training, and personnel appraisal software. Although information technologies may advance faster than human capacities to use them responsibly, they can foster broad participation on the part of the workforce. To the extent that this occurs, pathways through the paradoxes of competing needs and democracy may be discovered.

As technologies become widely accessible, requirements for human competency expand. These requirements range from technical know-how such as client server technologies, virtual teaming, and Web-based videoconferencing to personal qualities such as genuine trust and sincere service. Indeed, in a high-tech atmosphere the only way that public agencies may be able to distinguish themselves from private providers is through the performance of their employees. Downsizing and disrespect have made it clear that individuals must anticipate change, add value, and be responsive to reform. Unless or until employees are seen as an asset worthy of investment, beginning with their selection, it is difficult to see how the public interest will be served effectively. When labor is regarded as a cost to be reduced rather than an asset to be enhanced, quality, productivity, and citizen service usually are sacrificed.

Indeed, despite significant (if underappreciated and taken-for-granted) successes in the post–World War II era, highly salient governmental failures appear, according to two systematic studies, to be increasing in the new century: the 9/11 terrorist attacks, the *Columbia* space shuttle accident, Iraqi weapons of mass destruction, the Abu Ghraib prison abuses, the Hurricane Katrina response, flu vaccine shortages, the Minneapolis bridge collapse, the Madoff Ponzi scheme, the BP oil spill, the Benghazi attack, Secret Service misconduct, the Boston Marathon bombing, the Internal Revenue Service targeting incident, the Department of Veterans Affairs waiting-list exposé—along with some two dozen other documented events (Light, 2014; Schuck, 2014). Paralleling these incidents have been troublesome HRM trends discussed in this book: personnel and funding cutbacks, proliferation of political appointees, dependence on contractors, stagnant pay, and erosion of human resource capacity in general and information technology in particular.

While multiple factors contribute to such failures, employees were confronted with policies that were, as Paul C. Light (2014) notes, "virtually impossible to deliver" (p. 14), given persistent lack of resources and understaffing, overlayered chain of command, poor leadership, and organizational culture contaminated by confusing missions, corruption, or little performance monitoring. Light offers as an example "the disastrous launch of the healthcare.gov website":

> Designed as the portal for delivering a complex policy, healthcare.gov was highly dependent on a poorly coordinated collection of 55 outside vendors; delegated to an understaffed, underfunded agency; connected to antiquated information technology; embedded in a highly diffuse, over-layered, and poorly coordinated organizational structure; led by the first Senate-confirmed administrator in seven years; leashed to a deadline that required nearly flawless delivery; and aggressively monitored by a House of Representatives that wanted it to implode. (p. 20)

While in his 2011 State of the Union address, President Obama promised a government for the new century, that goal was overshadowed by budget cuts, hiring freezes, and sequestration. Yet a strategic approach emphasizes that because other issues are more important than civil service reform, reform, paradoxically, is more important than any issue. That is, it provides the precondition for making and implementing public policy. For now, and despite evidence of significant governmental successes (Goodsell, 2011, 2015; Schuck, 2014, Chapter 11), Light believes that political dysfunction is not only worse than it looks but also more destructive than imagined.

Change is likely to occur in one of several ways: It may result from the long-term cumulative effects of frequent and repeated "routine" breakdowns, from a sudden cataclysmic failure, or, more likely, from a series of disasters in a short period. In any case, such debacles could overcome the central problem inhibiting reform: Those with interest in the civil service have little authority, and those with authority have little interest. Should interest and authority converge, blueprints for success are available. Perhaps the most thoughtful is Linda J. Bilmes and W. Scott Gould's book *The People Factor* (2009), which explains why reform is needed and details what must be done, including how to implement and fund the new system—one that would be largely self-financed because of the return on the initial investment.

More recently the nonpartisan Partnership for Public Service and the consulting firm Booz Allen Hamilton (2014) published a summary of past proposals.[1] This "new civil service framework" "articulated a vision for creating a federal government that acts as a single, integrated enterprise . . . [for] tackling the nation's biggest problems and challenges" (p. 3). Although the 40-page report, released in the spring of 2014, generated some interest, by the end of that year it had faded into the background. Some observers thought the 2014 Department of Veterans Affairs debacle, could be an opportunity not only for fixing VA-specific problems but also for introducing more comprehensive civil service changes (Katz, 2014).

Former federal human resource official and consultant Ronald Sanders (2014) proposed in an op-ed that the governmentwide information technology/cybersecurity workforce is an "ideal first candidate" for reform:

> [Take] all of the thousands of programmers, systems architects, cybersecurity experts, database administrators, across every agency in the federal enterprise . . . and modernize the way we hire them, classify them, pay them, promote them, and hold them accountable. There's a way to do all that without an act of Congress, with authorities that are on the books today.

According to Sanders, the business case for doing so includes the mission-critical nature of the occupation, the failure to be competitive in this essential labor market, strong bipartisan support for these analysts, and a robust management infrastructure—the federal Chief Information Officer Council—that is already in place to take the lead.[2] Sanders believes that this is the most promising way for systemic change to occur in the civil service: Start here with an eye to inclusive reform to follow. In fact, the country's largest cybersecurity employer, the National Security Agency, already has a program that complements Sanders's proposal: The National Centers of Academic Excellence in Cyber Operations program supports 13 universities to help prepare and place graduates.

The key to reform, however, is not simply in good ideas but also in their implementation. The nation is experiencing the ill effects of a remarkable lack of concern with managing the government—despite the fact that the long-recognized "quiet crisis" in the civil service (National Commission on the Public Service, 1989) has not been quiet for quite some time. The Obamacare (healthcare.gov) website collapse was simply a reflection of the disinterest in public administration—the machinery of government—among too many top executives. Questioning why, for instance, the Department of Veterans Affairs had not been over-hauled—as the president had vowed it would be—prior to the 2014 waiting-list scandal, a senior White House official conceded, "We don't do the small stuff well. And the small stuff is the important stuff" (quoted in Fournier, 2014). Yet management is a domain over which executive branch officials have, if not complete control, at least considerable leverage. As Shoop (2014) observes:

> The president obviously is not directly responsible for the day-to-day management of federal agencies. . . .
>
> But the president is responsible for setting up a structure in which appropriate decisions are made and carried out. Mostly, this is a matter of devoting time and attention to management. That means setting clear priorities, requiring those down the chain of command to establish appropriate goals for reaching them, and evaluating their progress.
>
> That is, much of the time, a thankless endeavor.

Not taking action will result in an even greater lack of public trust in government (Kettl, 2014; Ornstein, 2013)—a self-defeating condition for a self-governing people that could become a self-fulfilling prophecy. Effective governance—the foundation of a stable polity in which democracy and freedom can flourish—would thereby be undermined.

TAKING RESPONSIBILITY FOR PARADOXES

The scope and diversity of these technological and human capacity changes and structural reforms mandate that there is no one best way to manage people. Management is a highly individualized art, and managers must discover what works in difficult circumstances. Any number of techniques can succeed when aligned with the strategic needs and goals of an agency, its employees, the populace they serve, and the manager's own natural style. Readers having come this far have ideas about what to do and why, but only those who have a strong desire to influence the performance of others and get real satisfaction in doing so will learn how to manage effectively.

Tom Morris (1997) examined what might happen if four key dimensions of the human experience were used to run a modern organization. He urged conscious recognition of the four philosophical transcendentals that enrich life: intellectual (truth), aesthetic (beauty), moral (goodness), and spiritual (unity). Each dimension—which Schwartz and Porath (2014) have empirically documented in a parallel work—contributes to individual and organizational excellence.

Truth—disturbing or comforting—is the foundation of all relationships; one must be true to self and in interactions with others. There is no greater source of waste than the speculation, gossip, and rumor that arise in the absence of truth. Ironically, "the simplest truths," as Frederick Douglass observed, "often meet with sternest resistance and are slowest in getting general acceptance." People cannot flourish without ideas; without truth, they intellectually perish. The world is too dangerous for anything except the truth. As Helen Keller wrote, "Knowledge is happiness, because to have knowledge—broad, deep knowledge—is to know true things from false, and lofty things from low."

While essential, truth is not enough for fulfillment, since humans are not mere intellects. They must also have something attractive to motivate them—beauty. Indeed, paraphrasing Keats, truth is beauty and beauty is truth. The aesthetic dimension includes not only external, observable beauty (e.g., flowers) but also internal, performance beauty (e.g., quality work). Ralph Waldo Emerson perhaps said it best: "We ascribe beauty to that which is simple, which has no superfluous parts; which exactly answers its end; which stands related to all things; which is the mean of many extremes." Beauty liberates, refreshes, inspires, and thereby increases productivity; in contrast, ugliness depresses the spirit. If employees are to do a good job, then they must have a good job, a career, or, even better, a calling (see below).

Doing true, beautiful things, though, is incomplete, Morris (1997) argues. Leaders must be convinced of the essential morality of what they are doing. Indeed, goodness might be considered a special kind of truth and beauty. Paradoxically, humans are the only species capable of ethical awareness—and the only one capable of ignoring that awareness. People are at their best when engaged in a worthy task, one in which they can make a genuine difference, doing both a job that the world needs done and one that people want to do. As Emerson said, "I pass this way but once; any good that I can do, let me do it now."

Truth, beauty, and goodness are still not sufficient: Humans also must perceive a sense of wholeness, that they are a part of something greater than themselves. It is often difficult to do something well if we do not know the reasons we are doing it. People yearn to know that their efforts contribute to a larger whole; a way to gain that context is to spend less time asking who, what, where, and how and more time asking why. Matters of spirit, then, are connected to truth, beauty, and goodness—the worth of person and the collectivity to which he or she belongs. The Athenian Oath from ancient Greece, taken by all 17-year-old citizens, captures the idea:

> We will ever strive for the ideals and sacred things of the city, both alone and with many; we will unceasingly seek to quicken the sense of public duty; we will revere and obey the city's laws; we will transmit this city not only not less, but greater, better and more beautiful than it was transmitted to us.

The oath constitutes a public spirit, ethic, and mission that is neither liberal nor conservative, Republican nor Democratic.

Teddy Roosevelt observed that "far and away the best prize that life has to offer is the chance to work hard at work worth doing," work that provides the opportunity to fulfill the four dimensions of excellence. If Aristotle had run a modern organization, he would have created strength and integrity throughout the institution by nourishing a culture based on those four transcendental values. Living life centered on truth, beauty, goodness, and unity is ideal for the resolution of the signature paradoxes that have animated this book: Organizations need the brains, bodies, and hearts of all individuals within them—and vice versa. Transforming the organization—internalizing and institutionalizing the four dimensions—is anyone and everyone's job, but one that must be assumed by leaders. The keys to excellence lie before us: "The difference between what we do and what we are capable of doing," Mohandas Gandhi believed, "would suffice to solve most of the world's problems." Indeed, public service can be seen as a calling.

PUBLIC SERVICE AS A CALLING

Our greatest fear should not be of failure, but of succeeding at something that doesn't really matter.

—Anonymous

The role of work in life has been viewed in many ways throughout history—as curse, punishment, salvation, social duty, and self-actualization (Bowman, 2011–2012; Donkin, 2001; Hardy, 1990). Work has been denounced as a necessary evil and praised as essential for human dignity, and legacies of these perspectives affect today's understanding of work as either degrading and demoralizing or enriching and ennobling. It follows that work, as a central life interest, varies considerably in its purposes for people. It may be seen as a way to secure survival, success, or significance—that is, as a job (a means for financial gain), a career (an avenue for advancement), or a calling (one's true place in the world).

In contrast to a mere job or even a career, a calling provides a sense of deep meaning at and authentic engagement in work. Such a belief, identity, and commitment is not reducible to self-interest, especially for the responsibilities inherent in public service. The linkage between basic questions about the purpose of life and work is found in the Latin word *vocare,* "to call," the root of the English word *vocation.* Clearly transcending having a job or a career, to have a *vocatio* is to embrace a sense of direction stemming from sacred or secular sources. It lights the way for an individual to perform personally and socially significant labor, which in turn contributes to a better world.

Each person's calling, while not easily ascertained, is unique and fits his or her abilities (Novak, 1996, pp. 34–35). The enactment of a vocation is a product of situational factors and individual talents. Components of vocation include introspection, exploration, and assertion—discerning one's path on earth and pursuing the calling with passion and urgency. A calling is a way of life, a raison d'être that contributes to one's identity; fitting work is what the individual needs to do and what society needs done. Public employment is a vocation because the creation of democratic governance is largely dependent upon citizens taking up this station in life. In devotion to the public, for example, the federal civil servant takes the oath of office, pledging to help achieve "government by, for, and of the people."

Since the founding of the United States, the belief has persisted that an enlightened citizenry is concerned about the well-being of the whole country. Modern bureaucracy, accordingly, was a response to the deterioration of government during the 19th-century spoils system, when public service was a means to promote self-interest (Chapter 1). Service to the nation is, or should be, imbued with values that display a sense of mission and character that sustains duty and creates social capital.

Public service as a public trust is manifested in principles of political neutrality, incorruptibility, honesty, fairness, responsibility, and accountability. Such ideals can inspire and direct civic-spirited employees and form criteria for their attitudes and actions in work life. Public administration, as a distinct vocation, is particularly critical because officials represent and exercise the power of the state. Key to sustaining these values is a disinterested civil service committed to excellence but subject to hierarchical control to ensure responsiveness to the populace.

Prior to the 1980s, the notion of public service as essentially altruistic, while not unchallenged, was largely taken for granted. Since that time, however, the New Public Management (NPM) movement swept across Western democracies and transformed bureaucracies (Chapter 1). The civil service was not seen as an institution to protect democracy from moneyed interests and political corruption. Instead, reformists saw a self-centered elite that created a culture of big government, one out of touch with the people. The response was to defund, deregulate, and decentralize public institutions in the belief that they interfered with free markets. Employment was nothing more than an economic transaction; government work would be a commodity to be controlled and outsourced whenever possible. The distinctiveness of the civil servant as a custodian of constitutional values was further undermined as public administration became diffused both everywhere and nowhere in a hybrid enterprise of private companies, nonprofit organizations, and government agencies.

As a result, much has been lost in recent years in terms of public service values as NPM has shifted governmental administration toward managerialism, entrepreneurism, and efficiency and away from promotion of, as the Preamble to the U.S. Constitution calls it, the "general welfare." With reform predicated in economics, the value base of change was one-dimensional, with the outcome that the ability of officials to shape government—except to emphasize efficiency and cost containment—was limited. The objective seems to be to shield the market from society's needs rather than to safeguard society from market demands and failures. An economic system that marginalizes human beings—the society serves the economy instead of the other way around—is a society at risk. Joanne Ciulla (2000) says it well, arguing that "when *commitment* is reduced to time at work, *loyalty* to something one pays for, and *trust* to a legal contract, these terms are emptied of their meaning" (p. 154).

While socioeconomic conditions that once sustained vocations may have diminished, "the aspiration to find a calling has not" (Muirhead, 2004, p. 11). A new interest in finding a calling (even though the term may not be used) could be occurring as people search for more humane and robust ways to comprehend work life. In seeking "lives that matter," many are now asking hard questions about how best to make a living and what work has to do with self-identity (Schwehn & Bass, 2006). With the erosion of the traditional social contract, thoughtful people are now expecting, if not demanding, significant work.

Instead of government mimicking business techniques, the values that animate a calling can act as a beacon for those who wish to integrate what they do with who they are. The lack of integrity in private and public institutions in the initial "lost decade" of the new century—a litigated presidential election; the Enron era; preemptive war, secret prisons, and torture; influence peddling and sex scandals; reckless banking industry practices and lack of oversight—has caused people to seek a deeper sense of national purpose. In the wake of the Great Recession, for instance, citizens have raised doubts about the efficacy and benevolence of the private sector and questioned whether the market is efficient and self-regulating (Martinez, 2009). Privatization, for example, does not eliminate government; it institutes government by corporations for corporate profit, not for the benefit of citizens.

It seems a propitious time to rebuild the public service on the basis of calling. Indeed, public servants confront extraordinary challenges: international conflicts, immigration, economic inequality, financial regulation, health care, unemployment, climate change, and the energy predicament. It is evident that the United States faces a protracted test as it seeks to sustain both domestic harmony and world leadership. It should not be assumed that the citizenry is barren of anything but selfish values. A recognition that public administrators are "the *only* officials that pay attention to governmental activities all the time," and as such hold a special duty to protect and serve the public interest (Goodsell, 2006, p. 630), may be growing.

Government is a morally serious calling, and men and women are needed to respond to it. The failure of individuals to do so damages the integrity of the citizenry itself as well as the foundations of self-government. Philosophers have long proposed that *eudaimonic* well-being is the doorway to human flourishing. "The only way to achieve success," as Aristotle observed, "is to express yourself completely in service to society." Let it be resolved, then, that people will come alive to the true meaning found in pursuits that command conviction and commitment in public service. Democracy is one of the great achievements of the world. Calling—that wonder from antiquity—gives voice to an abundant life by discerning purpose in what one does in government.

THE YEARS AHEAD

Turning this page marks the end of the beginning for the keen student of the management of human resources. As an introduction to the subject, this book represents an invitation to be both an informed participant and a critical observer of the field. Common and surprising, confusing and understandable, the paradoxes, processes, and problems pondered here will continue to animate theory and practice throughout your career. "The art of progress," wrote Alfred North Whitehead, "is to preserve order amid change and to preserve change amid order." It is only fitting, then, that the book stops where it started, with the paradoxes of democracy and needs.

Striving for excellence means dealing with conflicting organizational and individual needs, and individuals may do that by emphasizing democratic values at work. The workplace is in transformation as agencies are attempting to maximize use of technology and human capacities by revamping hiring strategies, refiguring job designs, broadening employee skill bases, and redesigning reward systems. When examined from the perspective of strategic human resource management, such changes can be assessed and used to build on the key recruitment, compensation, training, and evaluation functions discussed in earlier chapters.

Indeed, the management of government confronts many problems and prospects as the second decade of the new century continues. The widely anticipated retirement tsunami of Baby Boomers leaving the workforce offers an opportunity to rethink the nature and character of public service, as a whole new generation of talented employees will be needed. Will Americans, both those just beginning and those at the ends of their careers, see the civil service—the nation's largest workforce—as an opportunity to make a genuine difference? Is the increase in contract workers and political appointees in the last generation healthy for the country? In the end, will there be a renaissance in public service in response to a call to serve and sacrifice for the common good?

Answers to such questions are important for both policy and management reasons. Thus, among the key stakeholders who will deal with the numerous policy issues in the years ahead—deficits, alternative energy sources, Medicare, education, immigration, climate change—are public employees. Should we fail to deal with these challenges, they will deal with us; if that happens, then, as White Feather, chief of the Bear clan, observed, "the past grows longer as the future grows shorter."

Nothing happens in government without people. How they are managed, then, will determine investments in new technologies and human capital that drive the future. When citizens are treated as ends for which government exists rather than as means to be manipulated, when the economy serves society, the quality and productivity of public service can only improve. The purpose of government is to secure the blessing of liberty and to promote the common good; a government does not best serve the public interest by becoming a servant to corporate interests. Look for more initiatives and innovations in public human resource management. Some of these programs will be successful, and some will not. Those with the greatest value are likely to be cognizant of past experience and research data. Changes that seek partisan advantage with little interest in or knowledge of the complexities of governance can do a great deal of damage and ultimately can become self-defeating (Bowman & West, 2007).

ENVOI: "DREAM WHILE AWAKE"

What a long, strange trip it has been! As you close this textbook, dear reader, you may not be the same person you were at the beginning of the term. Because of your studies, your understanding, compassion, and ability to engage others in informed discussion of human resource management have grown. The challenge is not to "tell it like it is" but instead to "tell it as it may become"—to eliminate hypocrisy and live up to cherished values. It does not matter where you start, so long as you start now. Unless the disconnect between autocratic organizational values and societal democratic values is bridged, human resource problems will only intensify. The entire range of an agency's human resource functions—selection, recruitment, position management, compensation, training, appraisal, and labor–management relations—must be aligned with the norms of democratic culture if the dilemmas and contradictions discussed in this volume are to be resolved. The alternatives are either to accept the status quo as fate or to abandon ideals for the security of authoritarian institutions. Either way, life will surely be a series of collisions with the future.

Dr. Jonas Salk, who developed the first vaccine against polio more than half a century ago, reflected on his achievement:

> Ideas came to me as they do to all of us. The difference is I took them seriously. I didn't get discouraged that others didn't see what I saw. I had trust and confidence in my perceptions, rather than listening to dogma and what other people thought. I didn't allow anyone to discourage me—and everyone tried. But life is not a popularity contest.

This book has sought to provoke new ideas and to encourage readers to create their own futures. In so doing, it has offered few facile solutions, for to do so would be to defeat the purpose. Instead, general principles and specific propositions have been suggested, leaving the discerning individual to align, adapt, and apply them to make the public service, in the words of John F. Kennedy, "a proud and lively career."

EXERCISES

Class Discussion

1. Discuss the following statement: "Those with interest in civil service have little authority and those with authority have little interest."

2. Comment on this claim: "If Aristotle ran Walmart, he would create strength and integrity through the company by nourishing a culture based on the four transcendental values (truth, beauty, goodness, unity)."

3. In light of the many existential problems confronting the nation and the world, is this a propitious time to rebuild the public service?

4. Will there be a renaissance in public service in response to a call to service and sacrifice for the common good?

5. Simply because a textbook ends does not mean that learning stops; our end is your beginning! The future belongs to those who are prepared. There are many ways to continue inquiry into human resource management; indeed, the possibilities are nearly endless. You are an echo of the future. Identify at least two reform initiatives, then share these ideas with the entire class. What are some things that can be done in your school, in your community, and in your workplace? What might be done today, this week, this year to enhance the public service?

NOTES

1. Unfortunately, the compilation not only overlooks many of Bilmes and Gould's recommendations but also endorses changes that have been repeatedly shown to be unworkable.

2. A recent survey of federal IT professionals confirmed that there is a "desperate" need to upgrade technical and human resources in government (TechAmerica & Grant Thornton, 2014).

REFERENCES

Bilmes, L. J., & Gould, W. S. (2009). *The people factor: Strengthening America by investing in public service.* Washington, DC: Brookings Institution Press.

Bowman, J. S. (2011–2012). Public service as a calling: Reflections, retreat, revival, resolve. *Journal of Workplace Rights, 16*(1), 47–61.

Bowman, J. S., & West, J. P. (Eds.). (2007). *American public service: Radical civil service reform and the merit system.* New York: Taylor & Francis.

Ciulla, J. B. (2000). *The working life: The promise and betrayal of modern work.* New York: Three Rivers Press.

Donkin, R. (2001). *Blood, sweat, and tears: The evolution of work.* New York: Texere.

Fournier, R. (2014, June 9). "I've had enough": When Democrats quit on Obama. *National Journal.* Retrieved from http://www.nationaljournal.com/white-house/i-ve-had-enough-when-democrats-quit-on-obama-20140609

Goodsell, C. T. (2006). A new vision for public administration. *Public Administration Review, 66*(4), 623–635.

Goodsell, C. T. (2011). *Mission mystique: Belief systems in public agencies.* Washington, DC: CQ Press.

Goodsell, C. T. (2015). *The new case for bureaucracy.* Thousand Oaks, CA: CQ Press.

Hardy, L. (1990). *The fabric of this world: Inquiries into callings, career choice, and the design of human work.* Grand Rapids, MI: Eerdmans.

Katz, E. (2014, June 4). A VA fix that goes beyond banning bonuses. *Government Executive.* Retrieved from http://www.govexec.com/pay-benefits/pay-benefits-watch/2014/06/va-fix-goes-beyond-banning-bonuses/85831

Kettl, D. (2014, May 9). The reluctant executive. *Government Executive.* Retrieved from http://www.govexec.com/magazine/features/2014/05/reluctant-executive/84109

Light, P. C. (2014, July). *A cascade of failures: Why government fails, and how to stop it.* Washington, DC: Brookings Institution, Center for Effective Public Management. Retrieved from http://www.brookings.edu/research/papers/2014/07/14-cascade-failures-why-government-fails-light

Martinez, M. A. (2009). *The myth of the free market: The role of the state in a capitalist economy.* Sterling, VA: Kumarian Press.

Morris, T. (1997). *If Aristotle ran General Motors.* New York: Holt.

Muirhead, R. (2004). *Just work.* Cambridge, MA: Harvard University Press.

National Commission on the Public Service. (1989). *Leadership for America: Rebuilding the public service.* Washington, DC: Author.

Novak, M. (1996). *Business as a calling: Work and the examined life.* New York: Free Press.

Ornstein, N. (2013, October 24). The Obama White House's original sin: A failure of effective management. *Atlantic.* Retrieved from http://www.theatlantic.com/politics/archive/2013/10/the-obama-white-houses-original-sin-a-failure-of-effective-management/280838

Partnership for Public Service & Booz Allen Hamilton. (2014). *Building the enterprise: A new civil service framework.* Washington, DC: Authors. Retrieved from http://ourpublicservice.org/publications/viewcontentdetails.php?id = 18

Sanders, R. (2014, July 17). Civil service reform: Start with IT/cyber. *Federal Times.* Retrieved from http://www.federaltimes.com/apps/pbcs.dll/article?AID = 2014307170010

Schuck, P. (2014). *Why government fails so often and how it can do better.* Princeton, NJ: Princeton University Press.

Schwartz, T., & Porath, C. (2014, June 30). The power of meeting your employees' needs. *Harvard Business Review.* Retrieved from http://blogs.hbr.org/2014/06/the-power-of-meeting-your-employees-needs

Schwehn, M., & Bass, D. (2006). *Leading lives that matter: What we should do and who we should be.* Grand Rapids, MI: Eerdmans.

Shoop, T. (2014, August 11). Does Obama have "zero control" over the bureaucracy? *Government Executive.* Retrieved from http://www.govexec.com/federal-news/fedblog/2014/08/does-obama-have-zero-control-over-bureaucracy/91163

TechAmerica & Grant Thornton. (2014). *CIO/CISO insights: Achieving results and confronting obstacles.* Alexandria, VA: Authors. Retrieved from http://www.grantthornton.com/ ~ /media/content-page-files/public-sector/pdfs/surveys/CIO-2014-survey.ashx

Glossary

Actor/observer bias: A form of bias that is present when an actor sees his or her behavior as blameless, but, when the actor observes the same behavior by another, he or she finds it blameworthy.

Adoption assistance: Employee assistance that includes benefits ranging from time off to reimbursement of expenses following adoption of a child.

Adult learning theory: A theory of employee training that integrates employee experience, active participation, motivation for self-improvement, problem solving, and control over the learning material.

Adverse action: An employer's sanction against an employee for unsatisfactory performance or misconduct.

Affirmative action: A strategy that aims to overcome barriers to equal employment opportunities or remedy the effects of past discrimination.

Age Discrimination in Employment Act of 1967 (ADEA): Federal law that prohibits discrimination in employment decisions based on age. Applies to workers 40 years and older.

Agency shop: A workplace in which employees are not required to join the union but must contribute a service charge to cover collective bargaining, grievance processes, and arbitration costs.

Alternative work schedules: Arrangements of hours of the day, days of the week, and/or places of work that differ from the traditional 8:00-to-5:00 hours, Monday-through-Friday days, and the in-office work site.

Alt-labor groups: Workers' associations and work centers. Examples include the National Taxi Workers Alliance, Working America, National Domestic Workers Alliance, National Guestworkers Alliance, Restaurant Opportunities Centers, and National Day Laborer Organizing Network.

Americans with Disabilities Act of 1990 (ADA): Federal law that prohibits discrimination in employment decisions based on disability and requires employers to provide reasonable accommodations.

Arbitration: A dispute resolution procedure that relies on a neutral third party who conducts hearings, researches contentious issues, and makes nonbinding recommendations for consideration.

Assembled tests: One or more tests used in the selection process in addition to experience and education, such as a typing exam, psychological test, or work sample.

Assessment center: A location where employees and job applicants take job-related tests and perform exercises so that a potential employer can assess their skills, competencies, and character traits.

At-will employment: A doctrine by which both employer and employee can sever their employment relationship at a moment's notice. The bulk of the public sector provides tenure rights that require a demonstration of appropriate cause, due process proceedings, and internal and external appeals processes.

Authorized salary range: The range of pay stipulated in the pay plan of the jurisdiction. The range is generally provided in a series of step increments. In the past, new employees were required to start at the first step of the range and then generally moved along it according to time in position. Today there is more willingness to grant exceptions to experienced employees or where employee shortages exist. Broadbanding essentially increases the authorized salary range to include several positions.

Banding: The treatment of numerous job applicants within a certain range of test scores as having identical scores.

Bargaining unit determination: Identification of whom a union or other association in negotiation sessions will represent.

Behaviorally anchored rating system (BARS): A behavioral approach to appraisal consisting of a series of scales based on key dimensions of performance.

Behavior-based evaluation systems: Systems in which the evaluation of performance is based on specific behaviors.

Benchmark jobs: Jobs identified through a comprehensive pay study that compares a portion of the total number of positions with jobs outside the organization to ensure external equity. That is, these positions become pay benchmarks for the entire compensation system. These positions are anchored to general market salary ranges as indicated by reliable compensation information gathered directly, either by those conducting the pay study or by organizations that periodically provide compensation survey information.

Benefits: All indirect payments provided to employees as part of their membership in the organization.

Biodata: Detailed information or examples, including important accomplishment dimensions (i.e., competencies), of employees or candidates related to the jobs they are applying for.

Bonus: A one-time payment made as a supplement or replacement for a raise that is added to base pay.

Broadbanding: The combination of several grades to create a broader salary range for a position. Formal promotions are not required for substantial pay movement (as is the case with more traditional—and narrow—classification series that limit pay movement). Broadbanding has the effect of allowing greater discretion at the agency level, offering more organizational flexibility, and providing incentives for long-term development. It may increase total employee costs to the organization over time.

Certification of the bargaining agent: Action by the appropriate administrative agency (Federal Labor Relations Authority, Public Employees Relations Board, or equivalent) recognizing that an exclusive bargaining agent for a unit is appropriately constituted.

Certified lists: Lists of technically qualified individuals from which a hiring authority may officially select. Certified lists in the past were limited to the top three candidates when civil service commissions ranked all candidates. Today, it is more common for human resource departments and hiring departments to assemble lists of all eligible candidates and then pull from the top of the lists as needed.

Character fit: An individual's fit with an organization in regard to generic work habits such as conscientiousness, motivation, initiative, resilience, service motivation, and self-discipline. Also includes the absence of dysfunctional behaviors and characteristics such as substance abuse, theft, and violent tendencies.

Civil law system: A scheme in which the law is based primarily on a code of laws that is applied by judges.

Civil Rights Act of 1964: Broad federal law that prohibits employers from discriminating against employees in hiring, promotion, and termination decisions based on their race, color, religion, national origin, or gender.

Civil service: The branches of the public service, excluding legislative, judicial, or military, in which positions are typically filled based on competitive examinations. A professional career public service exists with protections against political influence and patronage.

Civil service commissions: Governing bodies authorized to oversee civil service employment systems. Originally, civil service commissions administered all competitive examinations, reviewed qualifications for technical merits, provided certified lists, and acted as judicial review boards for hiring abuses. Today, most selection functions have been moved to human resource departments in the executive branch or to the line agencies themselves. Where they continue to exist, civil service commissions tend to be policy and review boards.

Civil service reform: Efforts to modify the structures, processes, and functions of the civil service system, such as the Pendleton Act of 1883, the Civil Service Reform Act of 1978, and the New Public Management movement of the 1990s.

Civil Service Reform Act of 1978 (CSRA): Federal law that replaced the Civil Service Commission with two agencies: the U.S. Office of Personnel Management as the staff arm of the chief executive and the U.S. Merit Systems Protection Board to adjudicate employee appeals. It also created the Federal Labor Relations Authority to oversee federal labor–management policies.

Class series: Job classifications that are linked developmentally, such as Secretary I, II, III, and IV.

Climate for engagement: A relatively enduring set of perceived conditions at work that affect workers' motivation and behavior.

Climate for engagement checklist: A list of perceived conditions at work that affect workers' motivation and behavior, used to assess the current state of such conditions in an organization.

Closed personnel systems: Systems in which few opportunities exist for lateral entry for those outside the organization; typical in rank-in-person systems. Ideally, such systems encourage employee development through job rotation and foster employee loyalty. See also *Open personnel system.*

Coaching: The training practice of assigning an experienced employee to help other employees master various job situations.

Cognitive information processing theory: A theory that maintains that appraisal is a complex memory task involving data acquisition, storage, retrieval, and analysis. When data are processed, subjective categories are employed that in turn can produce rating errors.

Collective bargaining: A process whereby labor and management representatives meet to set terms and conditions of employment for employees in a bargaining unit.

Common-law system: A scheme in which the law is developed primarily by decisions of courts rather than by codifications of legislatures or by executive actions.

Comp & class study: A study that attempts to reassess and recalibrate an entire system of job worth by examining compensation rates for all job classes.

Comparable worth: The theory that employees doing different jobs of equal value to the organization should be paid the same.

Compatibility error: Error that occurs when appraisals reflect evaluators' tendency to rate highly those they like or those are compatible with them. Also known as *similarity error* or *liking error.*

Compressed workweek: A flex option in which the number of hours worked per week is condensed into fewer days.

Contaminated evaluations: Evaluations that include factors unrelated to actual performance.

Contingent hiring: A preliminary hiring status that can be procedurally overturned if certain contingencies intervene. Appropriate contingencies include postselection physical examinations or drug tests, funding availability, job freezes, and completion of specialized training programs. Where contingencies such as these exist, it is important that the selected candidate be informed in the letter of intent.

Contrast error: Error that occurs because of the tendency of evaluators to rate people relative to others instead of relative to performance criteria.

Cooperative problem solving: A form of labor–management relations characterized by joint deliberations and planning to address pressing workplace problems.

Cost-of-living adjustments: Across-the-board pay changes based on economic conditions, not performance.

Critical incident technique: An evaluation method in which evaluators record key acts assumed to make the difference between effective and ineffective performance.

Cross-training: The practice of training employees to fill multiple job functions.

Dealing with difficult people: Working with problem employees to arrest negative patterns of interaction. The basic strategy involves avoidance, setting boundaries, and confronting each untoward behavior in appropriate and controlling ways.

Decentralization of training: The shifting of responsibilities for training from the central human resource department to operating departments and line managers.

Defamation: The act of making a false statement, oral or written, that injures an individual's work reputation.

Deficient evaluations: Evaluations that fail to include all essential elements of performance.

Defined-benefit pension plans: Pension plans that guarantee preset lifetime pension payments.

Defined-contribution pension plans: Pension plans to which defined contributions are made, such as 401(k) accounts, which have the attendant risks of vulnerability to a volatile stock market.

Development: Efforts that prepare employees for assuming future responsibilities. See also *Training*.

Dialectic: Systematic reasoning that juxtaposes contradictory, competing ideas (theses, antitheses) and seeks to resolve them by creating a new synthesis.

Direct evidence: In a discrimination or retaliation case, proof of statements made by the decision maker that show unlawful bias against the employee at the time of an adverse decision.

Disparate impact discrimination: A theory of liability in which plaintiffs claim that a facially neutral practice has a harmful effect on a class of employees characterized by race, gender, or other protected conditions. Disparate impact is generally defined as a selection rate of less than 80% that of the group with the highest selection rate. Also known as *adverse impact discrimination*. See also *Disparate treatment discrimination*.

Disparate treatment discrimination: Discrimination in which plaintiffs claim that adverse personnel actions are based on race, gender, or other protected conditions.

Diversity policies: Employers' policies that promote an environment that allows all employees to contribute to organizational goals and experience personal growth, regardless of individual, ethnic, or other differences.

Doctrine of harmony: The principle that guides a relationship between labor and management in which both sides emphasize cooperation, service orientation, participation, and the public interest.

Doctrine of hostility: The principle that guides the relationship between labor and management under traditional collective bargaining (adversarial, conflictual, confrontational).

Doctrine of sovereignty: The principle that government has a responsibility to protect all societal interests. Therefore, it is inappropriate for government to be required to share power with interest groups (e.g., unions in negotiations) or dilute managerial rights.

Domestic partnership coverage: Benefits such as health insurance and sick or bereavement leave that may be made available to persons designated as domestic partners of employees.

Downshifting: The process of scaling back career ambitions and giving more time and attention to family and personal needs.

Downsizing: The process of reducing an organization's number of employees, often caused by actions such as reductions in force, outsourcing, or base closures.

Dress and grooming codes: Employer standards for employee appearance, including clothing, grooming, and body ornamentation.

Due process rights: Public employees' rights in regard to adverse actions, including the right to a hearing.

Dues checkoff: Employee selection of a payroll deduction option to pay union dues to the representing union.

Education: A development strategy that prepares people for the future by helping them to acquire necessary knowledge, skills, and abilities (KSAs) as well as value orientations. In the context of training and development, education differs from training in that it is concerned with broad principles of knowledge and practice rather than the technical details of work.

Education and experience evaluations: Evaluations that include review of application forms as well as requests for information about specific job competencies, which can be addressed in skill inventories (such as checklists), cover letters, and/or résumés.

80% rule: A standard for determining discrimination. Any selection process that results in qualification rates of protected groups that are less than 80% of the highest group is considered discriminatory.

Electoral popularity: The basis for representative democracy. Electoral popularity is a good method for the selection of major policy makers but an ineffective method for selecting those who primarily fill administrative functions.

Electronic monitoring: Monitoring of employees conducted via e-mail and video surveillance, website blocking, and/or GPS tracking. Employers use such monitoring in an attempt to increase productivity, improve quality, and reduce costs by continuously collecting performance data, pinpointing problems, and providing immediate feedback.

Electronic posting: The listing of jobs on agency websites or websites exclusively dedicated to job seekers.

Ellerth/Faragher **affirmative defense:** A legal doctrine in hostile environment harassment claims that provides that if an employer can prove that it exercised reasonable care to prevent and correct the harassment and that the employee failed to use its remedial procedures, the employer may avoid liability.

Employee assistance programs (EAPs): Programs usually offering counseling or referral services for employees having problems with alcohol, drug abuse, personal debt, domestic abuse, or other problems that impede job-related performance.

Employee engagement: The extent to which employees apply themselves physically, cognitively, and emotionally during their performance. While definitions vary, the concept usefully bridges previous emphases on internal states of motivation with observable behaviors in the workplace. An employee who is engaged can be characterized as enthusiastic, energetic, motivated, and passionate about his or her work.

Equal Employment Opportunity Commission (EEOC): Federal agency that processes complaints of discrimination and reviews affirmative action plans.

Equal Pay Act of 1963: Federal law that prohibits sex discrimination in compensating people doing substantially the same jobs.

Equity adjustment: A salary change made when an incumbent is in a job that is out of alignment with other similar jobs.

Error of central tendency: Error that results in all staff receiving average ratings or all dimensions of performance being rated as average.

Essential functions: The major job duties of a position. Use of the term was ushered in by the Americans with Disabilities Act, which prohibits discrimination of "an individual with a disability who, with or without reasonable accommodation, can perform the essential functions of the employment position."

Ethics Reform Act of 1989: Federal law that established uniform financial disclosure requirements, prohibited lobbying of former departments, and raised pay for executive, legislative, and judicial officials.

Exclusive representation: The right of a union that gains majority support in a secret ballot election, making it entitled to act for and to negotiate agreements covering all the employees in the bargaining unit.

Executive Order 12871: President Bill Clinton's executive order of 1993 mandating the federal government's labor–management partnership initiative; the order was rescinded by President George W. Bush in 2001.

Exit interview: A session conducted by the supervisor or human resource department in an attempt to learn why an employee is leaving.

Expectancy theory: A theory of motivation that holds that people increase effort in the expectation that this will produce performance results and rewards. Expectancy theory makes three key assumptions regarding the valence of outcomes, expectancy of efforts, and instrumentality of performance.

External equity: Equity of the pay of public sector employees with the pay of those performing similar jobs in other organizations. Generally implemented in pay plans through occasional pay studies that compare a sample of positions (benchmark positions) to anchor the entire wage scale.

Fact-finding: A dispute resolution procedure that relies on a neutral third party who conducts hearings, researches contentious issues, and makes nonbinding recommendations for consideration.

Fair Labor Standards Act of 1938 (FLSA): The basic federal statute that established the minimum wage and hours of work.

Family and Medical Leave Act of 1993 (FMLA): Federal law that guarantees eligible workers up to 12 weeks of unpaid leave during any 12-month period for childbirth or adoption; for caregiving to a child, elderly parent, or spouse with a serious health problem; or for a personal illness.

Fast-track positions: Positions that offer rapid career opportunities for training, management, exposure to a variety of techniques, and, ultimately, promotion and increased salary levels. The Presidential Management Fellows Program is an illustration at the federal level; placement as a managerial analyst in a city manager's office is an example at the local level. Fast-track positions are sometimes only informally designated.

Federal Employees Pay Comparability Act of 1990: Federal law that mandated that the 30% pay gap between the public and private sectors be closed gradually by the end of the century.

Federal Labor Relations Authority (FLRA): The federal administrative unit charged with overseeing, investigating, and enforcing rules pertaining to labor–management relations.

Feedback: Evaluative information given to employees about their performance or behavior with the purpose of influencing future performance or behavior.

Final-offer arbitration: Arbitration in which the arbitrator's decision is restricted to the position taken by one or the other of the parties. This can include selection of a position taken by one side or the other on all issues taken together (by package) or selection on an issue-by-issue basis.

Flextime: Work schedules that allow flexible starting and quitting times but specify a required number of hours within a particular time period.

Free rider: In labor–management relations, a worker in a bargaining unit who acquires a benefit from union representation without the effort or costs that accompany union membership.

Free speech rights: The rights that public employees have to speak out as citizens in matters of public debate. These rights, however, do not protect them from adverse action when speaking out disrupts the efficiency of their workplace.

Functional rationality: A type of rationality that focuses on means or how goals will be fulfilled, sometimes at the expense of the goals themselves.

Gainsharing: The sharing among employees of financial gains that result from organization-wide performance.

General skills test: A test that provides information about an individual's abilities or aptitudes in areas such as reading, math, abstract thinking, spelling, language usage, general problem solving, judgment, proofreading, and memory.

Generation X: Those born between 1960 and 1980.

Grievance arbitration: Arbitration used to resolve outstanding disputes regarding employee grievances. Also known as *rights arbitration*.

HAIR qualities: Evaluation criteria of public managers that emphasize _helicopter_ (the ability to look at things from a higher vantage point while still seeing the details on the ground and being able to zoom in on those), *analysis* (a superior ability for rational analysis, logic, and judgment), *imagination* (the ability to develop fresh and creative approaches to problems), and *reality* (the ability to develop grounded and realistic solutions).

Harassment: The subjection of an employee to unwelcome conduct that is so severe and pervasive it creates a hostile work environment. The unwelcome conduct must be because of a criterion protected by discrimination laws. In the case of sexual harassment, it may be the subjection of an employee to tangible employment action because of the employee's gender.

Hard HRM: A perspective on human resource management that sees employees as costs to be minimized and resources to be used for maximum return. See also *Soft HRM*.

Harris v. Quinn: A 2014 case in which the U.S. Supreme Court decided that home health care workers serving Medicaid recipients cannot be forced to pay fees to help subsidize the union's cost of collective bargaining if they are not union members, because requiring such fees violates the First Amendment free speech rights of nonmembers whose views are contrary to the positions taken by the unions.

Hatch Act of 1939: Federal law prohibiting political activities by public employees. Some restrictions of this law were relaxed under the Federal Employees Political Activities Act of 1993.

Headhunting: Contracting out of the staffing function to a third party that makes the initial contact or even provides the hiring contract. Also known as *external recruitment*.

Herzberg's theory of motivation: A theory holding that the determinants of job satisfaction, such as recognition, relate to job content and that determinants of job dissatisfaction are associated with job context, such as physical facilities.

Hidden workforce: Temporary employees and outside workers (consultants, contractors). The numbers and costs of such workers are increasing.

Hierarchy of needs: A theory, associated with the work of Abraham Maslow (1954), that states that humans strive to sequentially satisfy needs related to survival, safety, belonging, self-esteem, and actualization. Later work has cast doubt on the hierarchical order of these needs and has noted other needs as well, but scholars agree that these needs are typically present and important.

Hostile environment: The situation that results when an employee is subjected to severe and pervasive abuse at the workplace because of a criterion protected by discrimination laws. This is a type of unlawful harassment.

Human capital: Productive human capabilities (knowledge, skills, abilities, attributes) that can be acquired and used to yield income and improved performance in the workplace.

Human resource management: A discipline that focuses on the relationship between the individual and the organization, with an eye to optimizing effectiveness from the views of both the organization and the individual. HRM includes (1) technical functions for the day-to-day operations of managing people in organizations (see *Personnel administration*); (2) policies and strategies that further the development, performance, and well-being of employees; and (3) a strategic perspective and focus on meeting/shaping future organizational needs. See also *Strategic human resource management*.

Impasse procedures: Procedures, typically involving third parties, established to reconcile differences between labor and management.

Implicit personality theory: A theory that suggests that people generally judge the "whole person" based on limited data (stereotyping based on first impressions, or the spillover effect); ratings then tend to justify these global opinions rather than accurately gauge performance.

Indirect evidence: In a discrimination or retaliation case, proof of actions taken by the employer that support an inference of unlawful bias against the employee.

Individual equity: The perceived fairness of individual pay decisions.

Individual versus "pool" hiring: Broad, entry-level classifications in moderately large organizations generally are filled using pool hiring, in which many positions are advertised simultaneously or in which advertising for a job classification is continuous. All other positions generally hire on an individual basis.

Inside (internal) versus outside (external) recruitment: Refers to whether recruitment and hiring is limited to organizational members. Generally, this decision is a matter of organizational tradition. Those organizations that are rank based hire internally, whereas those that are position based hire from the outside as well.

Institutional recruitment: Similar to hiring from a pool. See *Individual versus "pool" hiring.*

Interest arbitration: Arbitration dealing with the terms of the negotiated contract; may be voluntary or compulsory.

Internal equity: Equity of pay for employees doing similar jobs in an organization.

Internally based hiring: Hiring in which selection is limited to the agency or department, or sometimes the governmental body. Frequently, internally based hiring simply opens positions to internal candidates first and then to external candidates if no suitable internal candidates are found. Internally based hiring is most common in nonentry hires (with the major exception of converting interns to permanent employees). Although internally based hiring limits the merit principle, it is done in the name of increasing hiring assurance (because hires are known), improving initial hiring with better long-term promotional opportunities, and increasing employee morale.

Internship recruitment: The practice of using internship programs as a source of recruitment. Often used to attract high-quality management and professional candidates.

Job analysis: A systematic process of collecting data for determining the knowledge, skills, and abilities (KSAs) and other characteristics required to perform a job successfully and to make numerous judgments about the job.

Job classification: A cluster of individual positions with similar characteristics that are organized into a group for classification purposes. Other terms often used as synonyms are *job, classification, job class,* and simply *class.*

Job descriptions: Written statements that describe or list the typical or average duties (sometimes by using work examples), levels of responsibility, and general competencies and requirements of a job classification.

Job design: Specification of job features, primarily the duties, the quantity of work expected, and the level of responsibility.

Job duties: The term most frequently used in the past to refer to the major functional responsibilities of a position. The more common term today, because of the Americans with Disabilities Act, is *essential functions*. Job duties can be further divided into job tasks in job analysis.

Job enlargement: An increase in the scope of a job through the extension of the range of job duties and responsibilities; may be used when a job is perceived as too narrow or stifling, or when the work is too fragmented from either the worker's or the client's perspective.

Job enrichment: Job changes made in an attempt to motivate the employee by giving him or her more authority or greater independence for organizing the work and solving problems.

Job evaluation: Systematic determination of the value of each job in relation to others in an organization.

Job fit: Fit between employee and job in regard to specific traits that lend themselves to particular jobs, such as the ability to handle stress, assertiveness, friendliness, self-confidence, decisiveness, flexibility, willingness to assume responsibility, and similar characteristics, depending on what the job profile is.

Job (position) announcement: A posting, advertisement, or listing that requests applicants for a position. Generally tailored to the specific purpose to which it is being addressed. A full job announcement generally includes the job title and agency or organization affiliation, salary range, description of the job duties and responsibilities, minimum qualifications, special conditions, application procedures, notice of equal employment opportunity, and support for diversity. May also include classification, career potential, and special benefits.

Job posting: Originally, the placement of a job announcement on walls in prominent places. Many civil service systems require posting in a minimum number of public places. Today, job posting also includes listing jobs with in-house job bulletins, newspapers, and communications media such as intranet or e-mail.

Job rotation: A means of developing employees at all levels so that they understand the "big picture" and become cross-trained.

Job sharing: The splitting of responsibilities, hours, salary, and (usually) the benefits of a full-time position between two employees.

Job specialization: The narrowing of job responsibilities to just a few. Tends to promote higher levels of task mastery and thus speed, less training, and simpler incumbent replacement. In many situations, job specialization leads to more manageable jobs and greater professionalization. In other situations, however, it can be perceived as treating employees like replaceable parts in deadening, assembly-line-type jobs.

Job tasks: Elements of job duties. See also *Job duties* and *Essential functions*.

Labor markets: Geographical areas or occupational fields within which the forces of supply and demand, often constrained by political factors, interact to affect the size of workforces and their pay levels.

Labor market survey: A data-gathering tool that serves as a critical source of information about long-term staffing trends.

Lateral entry: The filling of non-entry-level positions from outside the organization. Lateral entry exists in rank-in-job systems, which tend to encourage competition based on technical qualifications.

Learning: Acquiring and using information from a broad range of sources that help a person to better do his or her job. Learning may be broader than training and development efforts and concern broader areas of interest.

Learning plateaus: Periods during which employees must first fully absorb and assimilate training materials before they can learn more.

Leave sharing: A type of employee-to-employee job benefit whereby healthy workers donate sick time or other benefits to coworkers in crisis.

Leniency error: Error in which all individuals or all performance dimensions are rated favorably. Also known as the *Santa Claus effect*.

Letter of intent: A letter that confirms the offer of a specific position and may stipulate major work conditions such as starting date, salary, and hiring contingencies (if any).

Liberation management: A reform tide with the goal of higher performance, characterized by implementation strategies such as standards, evaluations, and outcomes and typified by laws such as the Government Performance and Results Act of 1993.

Locality pay: A type of differential pay in the federal salary schedule to adjust salaries for working in expensive areas.

Longevity pay: Pay determined by length of service. Also known as *seniority pay.*

Mail (and e-mail) recruitment: A highly personalized approach to recruitment in which individuals are encouraged by letter or personal e-mail messages to apply for positions.

Maintenance of membership: The obligation of an employee to maintain union membership in the representative union once affiliated during the life of the contract.

Management by objectives (MBO): A results-oriented rating system based on how well managers achieve predetermined goals.

Market adjustment: Adjustment of pay based on a study of the pay associated with a single job or classification in the outside market.

***McDonnell Douglas* burden-shifting approach:** In discrimination and retaliation claims, a framework that explains how a plaintiff may prove that discrimination or retaliation occurred.

Med-arb: Arbitration that requires the arbitrator to begin with mediation, settle as many disputes as feasible, and move to arbitration only on items that remain contentious.

Mediation: A dispute resolution procedure that relies on a neutral third party who attempts to facilitate communication and bring the parties together to reach an agreement.

Meet-and-confer rights: Rights based in laws requiring agency heads to discuss, but not to settle, grievances.

Mentoring: A development approach in which employees develop their career potential through ongoing, periodic dialogue with more experienced personnel.

Merit-light systems: Systems that function in an orderly way on the basis of qualifications, performance, and competitive selection but, in comparison with full merit systems, allow more managerial discretion in the determination of recruitment, promotion, rewards, and punishments. Whereas full merit systems are somewhat prone to rigidity, merit-light systems are vulnerable to political and managerial cronyism.

Merit pay: A system under which permanent increases in base pay are based on performance.

Merit selection: Selection that emphasizes technical qualifications using processes that analyze job competencies and require open application procedures.

Merit system: A fair and orderly process for recruitment, promotion, rewards, and punishments on the basis of qualifications, performance, and competitive selection as judged by experts.

Moral management: Management that employs strategies to ensure integrity in organizational systems such as codes of ethics, standard reviews of compliance, and ethics audits.

Motivation: The drive or energy that compels people to act, with energy and persistence, toward some goal.

Motivation in training: A key principle in training, holding that people learn better when they are eager to acquire new knowledge, skills, and abilities (KSAs); are encouraged to seek out application opportunities and make them work; and are not readily discouraged by obstacles.

National Partnership for Reinventing Government: An initiative by the Clinton administration that sought to cut red tape, improve government performance, and hold public employees responsible for program results.

Needs assessment: A training strategy that involves surveying employees and managers about their training needs.

Negligent hiring: The failure of employers to use satisfactory screening—through reference checks, background investigations, and thorough selection processes—for positions that have a public safety dimension. Examples of such positions include driving, law enforcement, corrections, elder care, and work with children.

Neutral competence: A standard or value that early civil service reformers thought should be applied in the selection and retention of civil servants, as opposed to patronage.

New male mystique: The male version of the "feminine mystique," a concept articulated by Betty Friedan in 1963 in her work addressing the role tension that women face in juggling work and family responsibilities. Men currently face some of the same tensions as they try to satisfy both the traditional expectations of men as financial providers for their families and the expectations accompanying emerging gender role values that they be more nurturing husbands/partners, fathers, and sons.

New Millennials: Those born after 1980. Also known as *Generation Y.*

New Public Management (NPM): The introduction into public sector management of new principles, practices, and values that stress quality, competitiveness, and public entrepreneurialism.

No money effect: A result following appraisal when either the agency has insufficient funds to distribute among employee raises or raises are awarded on an across-the-board basis.

Noncompetitive recruitment: Recruitment in which a single official completes the hiring process with a formal comparison of candidates. Sometimes immediate hiring is allowed if candidates meet certain standards. At other times, the decision maker has the authority to select those people deemed appropriate, for whatever reason.

Nontraditional families: Families that do not conform to the traditional nuclear family model, including gay and lesbian couples, unmarried couples in committed relationships, single-parent families, and reconstituted families.

Occupational families: Groupings of class series (or positions that are not in class series) into large clusters. Examples include firefighters, administrative support staff, corrections personnel, and human service personnel. Occupational families are sometimes based primarily on job function (e.g., law enforcement regardless of agency affiliation) and sometimes on job mission (e.g., law enforcement related to drug enforcement).

Official immunity: A legal doctrine that prevents government employees from being held individually liable for actions within the scope of their duty.

Onboarding: The process of preparing for and supporting a new employee; includes workplace preparation, initial training, provision of a mentor, and any other assistance a new person needs to make a successful transition into the organization and to increase the likelihood of a positive long-term appreciation of the position and agency.

On-the-job training: The training that employees undergo as they master the unique requirements of their specific jobs.

Open personnel system: A system in which opportunities exist for lateral entry for those outside the organization; typical in rank-in-job systems. Ideally, such systems foster high technical qualifications, promote healthy competition, and prevent organization "inbreeding" and "groupthink." See also *Closed personnel systems.*

Open shop: A workplace in which a union can represent workers, but nonunion workers have no financial obligations to the union.

Organizational fit: Alignment of an individual's personality with cultural aspects of the organization, such as the reward and incentive system, notions of organizational citizenship, and organizational values. (When there is good organizational fit, individuals are more likely to exhibit a willingness to strive hard and to have some degree of professional passion for the job.)

Organizational learning: Efforts that get agencies, departments, and individuals thinking about what and how their organization or unit is doing and what it could or should be doing differently or better.

Organization-centered evaluations: Appraisals in which organizational processes are monitored and evaluated on the premise that employees will work effectively within the system if it is well designed by management.

Outcome bias: The tendency of raters to see the result of performance as the most important consideration in an evaluation regardless of whether or not the result was the consequence of factors beyond the employee's control.

Overlearning: The assimilation of material so that it becomes second nature.

Paradox: A set of seemingly incompatible ideas or a clash between apparent truths.

Paradox of democracy: The fact that people as citizens have many civil rights, but as employees of organizations they surrender those rights.

Paradox of needs: The fact that individuals and organizations need one another, but their respective needs are as likely to conflict as they are to coincide because people are dynamic and organic, whereas many organizations are static and mechanical.

Parental leave: Leave time granted to employees to care for family members.

Patronage: Selection decisions in which a single person is responsible for designating officials or employees without a requirement for a formalized application process. Those deciding patronage appointments may balance party loyalty, personal acquaintance, and technical competence. Such appointments may or may not be subject to a confirmation process. Although the terms *patronage* and *spoils system* are frequently used interchangeably, the concepts are not identical. In a spoils system patronage appointments are used primarily as a means of reward and where technical qualifications are noticeably lacking. *Spoils* also refers to positions in the career service handled as patronage appointments. See also *Spoils system*.

Pay banding: See *Broadbanding*.

Pay compression: The narrowing of differentials between pay grades in an agency.

Pay equity: The perception that the compensation received is equal in value to the work performed.

Pay plan: A pay schedule in which the grades, steps, and related pay are determined. In reality, most jurisdictions have numerous schedules as part of their pay plans for different occupational clusters, often based on union representation of different occupational groups.

Pay restoration: The provision of lost pay to employees. Employee advocates assert that, given the violation of the statutory principle that federal pay should match that found in the private sector, the pay gap should be closed through pay restoration.

Peer evaluations: Appraisals in which employees at the same level in the organization rate each other. Also known as *team evaluations*.

Pendleton Act of 1883: Federal law that established a system of open competition for government jobs via examinations, prohibited the firing of civil servants for partisan reasons, authorized creation of the Civil Service Commission, and empowered the president to alter the extent of civil service coverage.

Performance tests: Tests used in selection that directly assess the skills necessary for specific jobs. Includes tests of physical skills, knowledge tests of job aspects, and work samples (or assessment centers). In all performance tests, the connection between the test and some aspect of the job must be direct, unlike aptitude and skills tests in which the connection may be indirect.

Personal contact recruitment: Recruitment that occurs when recruiters, managers, or search panel members attend job fairs, conduct on-campus recruiting, or personally contact top candidates for positions.

Personnel administration: An older term and approach to human resource management that is mostly concerned with and defined by an emphasis on internal processes—staffing, position management, pay systems, benefits management, training, appraisal and discipline, contract management, and so on—and the efficient application of the rules and procedures of the civil service system.

Personnel ceilings: Limits on the numbers of positions that may be budgeted by appropriation unit or for all positions in an organization. When personnel ceilings are lowered, governments generally reduce services. Sometimes, however, services are shifted to nonpermanent workers not covered by the ceilings, nonprofits, or vendors, forestalling significant savings.

Piecemeal personnel systems: Systems that lack grades or ranks and assign salaries on an ad hoc basis. Common only in very small jurisdictions.

Point factor method: A job evaluation method that assigns points to compensable factors, which are summed to determine pay. Starts with the assumption that factors should be broad enough to apply consistently to all jobs in an organization or schedule. Differs from job factor systems, which may use only those factors directly related to specific positions.

POSDCORB: Acronym for *planning, organizing, staffing, directing, coordinating, reporting,* and *budgeting.* Originated by Frederick Taylor during the scientific management tide of reform in an effort to provide the "one best way" to administer government programs.

Position: The job of a single individual, as well as the specific duties and responsibilities of the job.

Position classification systems: Systems that provide grades or ranks for all merit positions as well as for nonmerit positions. Such systems can provide the basis for position evaluation and management on one hand and job support and design on the other.

Position descriptions: Written statements that define the exact duties, levels of responsibility, and organizational placements of individual positions.

Position management system: A system concerned with the allocation of positions for budgetary purposes.

Positive corrective action: A step-by-step participatory disciplinary procedure that encourages employees to take responsibility for correcting problems in their work behavior.

Positive reinforcement: Feedback that helps employees reduce errors and meet standards and enhances their motivation to excel.

Preemployment investigations: Various procedures used to validate applicant-provided information and to otherwise determine the suitability of candidates.

Principled negotiations: A negotiation process that stresses identification of common ground between labor and management, focuses on cooperative problem solving, and thrives in an open, trusting environment.

Principle of motivation: A principle that states that people are motivated to pursue and satisfy their needs.

Principles of learning: Tenets for the effectiveness of training that involve increasing employee motivation, relevance, transference, attention to general principles, repetition, feedback, and positive reinforcement.

Privatization: The shifting of public responsibilities for services or assets to the private sector.

Problem-solving bargaining: Resolution-oriented discussion leading to mutually agreeable and beneficial answers to common problems.

Proceduralism: An approach to work characterized by processes that are excessively detailed, complicated, protracted, or impersonal.

Process management: The management of work processes to ensure that the flow of work among individuals and units is as rational (smooth and optimal) as possible.

Process reengineering: A management activity in which radical improvements are made to existing work processes, thereby redesigning them for greater performance.

Productivity bargaining: Labor–management negotiations on matters affecting the efficiency and effectiveness of government operations.

Progressive punishment: An adverse-action approach that uses penalties with increasing severity and provides the employee with opportunities to correct problems prior to termination. Also known as *progressive discipline.*

Psychological contract: An unwritten understanding between employee and employer about mutual needs, goals, expectations, and procedures.

Psychological tests: Tests used in selection that examine the personality traits of candidates and compare them to the job requirements. Although psychological tests can include general intelligence tests and motivation tests, these have generally not met the rigorous validity standards expected in the public sector. However, tests that measure ability to handle stress, inclination toward aggressiveness, and disposition toward high standards of moral integrity have been used in the public sector.

Public Employee Relations Boards (PERBs): State administrative agencies typically charged with determining appropriate bargaining units, overseeing certification elections, and resolving unfair labor practices.

Race norming: The practice of adjusting test scores of minority groups to ensure that a sufficient number of minority candidates can be hired. Race norming is disallowed by the Civil Rights Act of 1991.

Rank-in-job: A personnel strategy in which rank and salary are determined by the job one holds. Substantial salary increases and higher status are attained only through a move to a better job (promotion or reclassification), but multiple promotions within an organization are uncommon beyond predetermined job series.

Rank-in-person: A personnel strategy that emphasizes the development of incumbents over time within the organization through the use of closed systems and movement through ranks. No matter what the assignment, the individual is generally paid according to rank. This tends to encourage the development of generalists (except in academic settings). Rank-in-person systems often have an up-or-out philosophy, in which those passed over for promotion are encouraged or required to leave the organization.

Realistic job previews: Opportunities for applicants to learn about both the positive and the negative aspects of jobs, so that some may opt out of the selection process and the eventual psychological contract will be more realistic for those who accept the jobs.

Reasonable accommodation: An employer's obligation under the Americans with Disabilities Act to modify the workplace to make it possible for disabled persons to work there. Also refers to an employer's obligation under Title VII to make workplace modifications to allow employees to observe religious beliefs and practices.

Recency effect: The tendency of evaluators to give undue weight to recent occurrences.

Recruitment process: The process of soliciting the most talented and motivated position applicants. Generally includes three major steps: planning and approval of the position, preparation of the position announcement, and selection and use of specific recruitment strategies.

Recruitment strategies: Methods used in recruiting, including posting in newspapers, trade journals, and other mass media; mail recruitment; recruitment through personal contacts; internships; external recruitment (use of a third party); and noncompetitive recruitment.

Representation election: An election to determine whether a union will be recognized as the exclusive bargaining agent for workers in the unit.

Representativeness: A factor in selection concerned with workplace representation of particular groups. Representativeness may be interpreted in numerous ways, such as by geography, social class, gender, racial or ethnic group, prior military service, and disability.

Respondeat superior: A common law doctrine that makes an employer liable for the acts or omissions of an employee committed within the scope of employment. The Latin phrase translates as "let the master answer."

Results-based systems: Rating systems that emphasize what employees produce.

Retaliation: Adverse action by an employer against an employee because of the employee's opposition to a prohibited employment practice or participation in an investigation, proceeding, or hearing.

Right-to-work states: States in which mandatory union membership is outlawed.

Rule of seven: A rule that states that people must practice something seven times in order to master it.

Rule of three (hiring): A rule, originally promulgated by civil service commissions, that restricts hiring to the top three candidates on the certified list. Recent trends have been to allow the hiring authority as much latitude as possible to choose from among all those technically qualified.

Rule of three (training): A rule that states that people truly hear or register things only after they have been said three times.

Sandwich generation: Workers who have responsibilities to care for young children as well as elderly parents.

Scientific management: A reform tide with the goal of efficiency, characterized by the use of implementation strategies such as structure, rules, and experts and typified by laws such as the Reorganization Act of 1939.

Self-appraisals: Ratings of employee performance completed by the employees themselves.

Seminars and presentations: Common training strategies for conveying information to groups of employees.

Senior Executive Service (SES): A federal government employee classification applied to top-level administrators. Comprises mostly of career civil servants and a lesser number of political appointees.

Seniority: A selection principle that uses time in the hiring organization as a primary or exclusive factor for promotion. Philosophically, seniority-based selection asserts that those already employed in the agency (1) have been through the merit process once, (2) have been screened in probationary periods and evaluation processes, and (3) have superior organizational insight and loyalty because of their history of employment.

Severity error: Error that occurs when all individuals or performance dimensions are given unfavorable ratings.

Sham recruitment: A situation in which a position is posted as open even though a candidate, usually internal, has implicitly been selected for the position. Also known as a *wired position*.

Simulation: A training strategy whereby job conditions and situations, such as responses to natural disasters, are simulated and employees must respond to them.

Skill-based pay: Compensation for skills that employees have, develop, and use in a multiple-task environment.

Social class selection: A selection philosophy that explicitly takes candidate social class into account. Generally illegal in the United States, but it does operate indirectly through proxies such as educational institutions attended and the subtle imposition of dominant-culture values on minorities in the selection process.

Soft HRM: A perspective on human resource management that regards employees as an asset worthy of investment and a resource of competitive advantage. See also *Hard HRM*.

Special responsibility theory: A theory that maintains that public employees hold critical positions in society and therefore should not be permitted to strike.

Spillover effect: The tendency for an unusually good or poor trait or performance to affect an entire rating. Also known as the *halo effect,* the *black mark effect,* or the *horns effect.*

Spoils system: A special type of patronage system in which appointment of jobs is viewed as one of the spoils of office (similar to spoils of war) to which those active in the victorious campaign are entitled. Also includes political nepotism (appointment of family members and friends to salaried positions) and assignment of contracts based on personal contacts rather than on technical qualifications. See also *Patronage.*

Staffing: The process of supplying staff for a workplace; incorporates both the recruitment and selection processes.

Stare decisis: The legal principle by which judges are obliged to abide by precedents established by prior decisions. The Latin phrase translates as "let the decision stand."

Strategic focus: An approach to training and development that focuses on meeting the performance, risk management, and human capital needs of organizations.

Strategic human resource management (SHRM): An approach to HRM that provides a strategic framework to support long-term business goals and outcomes. Concerned with longer-term people issues and macro issues such as talent management, workforce planning, employee engagement, and organizational design, many of which offer immediate benefits as well.

Strategy for feedback: A series of specific activities through which feedback is given to workers in ways that enhance performance and minimize demotivating effects.

Structured interview: An interview in which the questions are organized and refined in advance, in contrast to an unstructured interview, which tends to allow the candidate to discuss past work experiences. Structured interviews emphasize job competencies by matching past experiences to current job needs through behavioral anchoring or probe the potential of candidates by asking situational judgment questions about job-related hypothetical issues or problems.

Substantive rationality: A type of rationality that emphasizes ends, goals, or purposes, sometimes at the expense of how they are accomplished.

Succession planning: An organization's planning for the replacement of losses in its executive and senior management ranks with high-quality talent. When there is not sufficient in-house talent to ensure an adequate pool to complement the external pool, organizational succession planning provides additional training and rotational experiences to high-potential employees or employees who have been fast-tracked.

Surveys: A method of collecting information, often involving the perceptions of a target population or sample about some topic. In the context of training, surveys are used to get information about perceived training needs as well as information about the perceived effectiveness of training, often involving perceptions of employees or managers.

Talent management: The management of employees according to the idea that they are generally the most critical factor in providing quality service and in creating an environment of innovation.

The term may also be used more selectively to refer to attracting, grooming, and promoting exceptional employees for leadership positions or special assignments. Special emphasis is often placed on mentoring and succession planning.

Tangible employment action: A significant change in an individual's employment status (such as a hiring, firing, denied promotion, reassignment with significantly different responsibilities, or significant change in benefits) based on unwelcome sexual conduct. This is unlawful sexual harassment, a type of gender discrimination.

Telecommuters: People who work away from the traditional work locale (e.g., at home, at satellite locations, or on the road) by means of an electronic linkup with the workplace.

Temporary employees: Short-term employees without tenure rights and usually without benefits. A recent ruling by the Internal Revenue Service has enhanced the benefits rights of many persons formerly considered temporary employees, creating a new class of term employees. See also *Term employees.*

Term employees: Employees without tenure rights but usually with full benefits. Term employees generally have contracts for set periods of time. This is a rapidly increasing category in the public sector, in which governments seem to be seeking more flexibility for long-term position management. It is increasingly used by the federal government for multiple-year contracts (2 to 4 years) and by state governments, reducing the civil service protections for job classes such as managers.

Termination interview: A session conducted by the supervisor or human resource department informing an employee that he or she is dismissed from employment at the organization.

Test validity: A psychometric concept that addresses the question of whether a test or selection instrument measures what it is intended to measure. The three types of validity allowed by the *Uniform Guidelines to Employee Selection Procedures* are content, criterion, and construct. *Content validity* requires demonstration of a direct relationship of the test to actual job duties or responsibilities. *Criterion validity* involves the correlation of high test scores (the predictor) with good job performance (the criterion). It generally examines aptitudes or cognitive skills for learning and performing well in a given environment (e.g., the aptitude to learn a language, remember key data, or use logical reasoning). *Construct validity* requires documentation of the relationship of select abstract personal traits and characteristics (e.g., intelligence, integrity, creativity, and aggressiveness) to job performance.

Theory X: The theory that people are inherently lazy and therefore need a "stick-and-carrot" approach in order to be motivated.

Theory Y: The theory that people are inherently motivated to learn and grow. The manager's job, therefore, is to provide developmental opportunities for workers.

360° evaluation systems: Systems in which superiors, peers, subordinates, and sometimes people outside the organization rate one another.

3 o'clock syndrome: The tendency for employees' attention to work-related tasks to wane as they begin to think about their children ready to leave school and return home.

Tides of reform: Four reform philosophies identified by P. C. Light (*The Tides of Reform: Making Government Work, 1945–1995,* Yale University Press, 1997)—scientific management, war on waste, watchful eye, and liberation management—each of which has its own goals, implementation efforts, and outcomes.

Title VII of the Civil Rights Act of 1964: Federal law that prohibits employers from discriminating against employees in hiring, promotion, and termination decisions based on race, color, religion, sex, or national origin.

Traditional bargaining: A bargaining process in which two opposing teams sit across the table from each other, each side engaging in zero-sum posturing and demands.

Training: Efforts to increase knowledge, skills, and abilities (KSAs) to better meet the requirements of present jobs. See also *Development.*

Training evaluation: The assessment of the effectiveness of training efforts, usually focusing on both behavioral changes and results.

Trait-based appraisals: Appraisals of employees focusing on selected personal characteristics believed to be important in working effectively.

Transference: The extent to which training material is relevant in actual job situations.

25–50–25 rule: A heuristic that states that 25% of employees are highly motivated, 50% are "fence-sitters," and 25% are withdrawn or cynical.

Unassembled tests: Selection processes used when the initial selection is primarily based on education and experience evaluation.

Unemployment compensation: A mandatory federal–state insurance program created by law that is funded by employers through a tax on payrolls. Individuals who are unemployed through no fault of their own and who are actively seeking work are eligible for partial, temporary replacement wages.

Unfair labor practices: Practices by unions or employers that are unfair and legally prohibited.

Union shop: A workplace in which new employees must join the representative union after a certain number of days (e.g., 30–90 days) as specified in the collective bargaining agreement.

Unreasonable searches: Inspections by government officials that violate the Fourth Amendment to the U.S. Constitution.

Up-or-out philosophy: The thinking that those who are not promoted in rank-in-person systems should eventually be forced to leave the organization. For example, assistant professors who are not promoted to associate after 6 years are generally given terminal contracts.

U.S. Merit Systems Protection Board (MSPB): A body established by the Civil Service Reform Act of 1978 with responsibility to hear appeals from employees who allege that their rights under the civil service system laws and regulations have been violated.

U.S. Office of Personnel Management (OPM): The federal agency charged with the "doing" side of public human resource management—coordinating the federal government's personnel program. OPM's director is appointed or removed by the president and functions as the president's principal adviser on personnel matters.

Veterans' points: Credits that increase veterans' ratings as job candidates. Typically, veterans who served during wars are eligible for 5 points and wounded veterans are eligible for 10 points, although practices vary among the states and federal government.

V-time: Voluntary reduced time at work. Enables parents to meet their caregiving responsibilities, provides an alternative to layoffs or the use of part-time replacements, and helps phase workers into retirement.

War on waste: A reform tide with the goal of economy, characterized by the use of implementation strategies such as generally accepted practices, audits, and investigations and typified by laws such as the Inspector General Act of 1978.

Watchful eye: A reform tide with the goal of fairness, characterized by the use of implementation strategies such as whistleblowers, interest groups, and media, and typified by laws such as the Administrative Procedure Act of 1946.

Wellness programs: Programs with the goal of altering unhealthy personal habits and lifestyles and promoting behaviors more conducive to health and well-being.

Whipsaw effect: In the context of labor–management relations, a situation in which gains by one union are used to justify benefits for another.

Whistleblower Protection Act of 1989: Law protecting federal employee whistleblowers from unfair retaliation, specifying burden-of-proof requirements regarding retaliation, and outlining appeals channels.

Whistleblower statutes: Laws that protect employees who disclose wrongdoing in their organizations from retaliation by their employers.

Whole job analysis: Analysis that does not systematically break down a job into its constituent parts for purposes of setting grade and classification, but instead relies on past experience and intuition.

Whole job evaluation: Evaluation that does not systematically break a job down into its constituent parts for purposes of setting compensation, but instead relies on past experience and intuition.

Workers' compensation: A mandatory insurance program created by federal and state laws that is funded by employers. Workers who are injured on the job are compensated for medical bills and lost earnings, but they give up the right to sue for negligence.

Work samples: Performance tests that simulate actual aspects of the job. For example, having a trainer provide a demonstration is a work sample, as is having a lawyer provide examples of legal briefs from previous cases. When a variety of work samples is required to test the range of abilities of an applicant over an extended period (such as a full day), this is generally called an *assessment center.*

Work stoppages: Labor strikes.

Index

About the Authors

Evan M. Berman is Professor of Public Management and Director of Internationalization at Victoria University of Wellington, School of Government (New Zealand). Previously, he was the Huey McElveen Distinguished Professor at Louisiana State University. He is past chair of the American Society for Public Administration's Section of Personnel and Labor Relations. His areas of expertise include human resource management, public performance, local government, and international public administration. Berman is a prolific author in the discipline who has over 100 publications and 10 books. He has published in all the major journals of the discipline, is founding editor of the ASPA's Book Series in Public Administration and Public Policy, a Distinguished Fulbright Scholar, and senior editor of *Public Performance and Management Review*. He is recipient of the 2015 Fred Riggs Award for Lifetime Achievement in International and Comparative Public Administration by SICA, the Section on International and Comparative Administration of the American Society for Public Administration.

James S. Bowman is Professor of Public Administration at the Askew School of Public Administration and Policy, Florida State University. Noted for his work in ethics and human resource management, he has also published in quality management and environmental administration literatures. Dr. Bowman is author of over 100 journal articles and book chapters. In addition to *Human Resource Management in Public* Service, Bowman has co-authored *The Professional Edge: Competencies in Public Service* (2nd ed., Sharpe, 2010). His most recent book, with Jonathan P. West, is *Public Service Ethics: Individual and Institutional Responsibilities* (CQ Press, 2015). He has also edited six anthologies. He served as the inaugural editor-in-chief of *Public Integrity* (1995–2014), an American Society for Public Administration journal co-sponsored by three other professional associations. A past National Association of Schools of Public Affairs and Administration Fellow, as well as a Kellogg Foundation Fellow, he has experience in the military, civil service, and business.

Jonathan P. West is Professor and Chair of Political Science and Director of the Graduate Public Administration Program at the University of Miami. His research interests include human resource management, productivity, local government, and ethics. He has published nine books and more than 100 scholarly articles and book chapters. *Public Service Ethics: Individual and Institutional Responsibility* (2014), *Achieving Competencies in Public Service: The Professional Edge* (2010, second edition), *American Public Service: Radical Reform of the Merit System* (2007), and *The Ethics Edge* (2006, second edition) are his most recent coauthored or coedited books. His coauthored book titled *American Politics and the Environment* will be published in 2015 (second edition). He served 16 years as managing editor of *Public Integrity* and is a member of the editorial board of three other professional journals. He has experience as a management analyst working for the Office of the Surgeon General, Department of the Army.

Montgomery R. Van Wart is Professor of Public Administration at California State University, San Bernardino, as well as the former Dean of the College of Business and Public Administration. His publications include eight books and a substantial number of articles in the leading journals in his field. *Dynamics of Leadership in Public Service: Theory and Practice* (2005) was awarded "Outstanding Academic Title" by *Choice*. His research areas are administrative leadership, human resource management, training and development, administrative values and ethics, organization behavior, and general management. He also serves on numerous editorial boards and as the associate editor for *Public Productivity & Management Review.* As an instructor, he has spent as much time teaching and facilitating programs for executives and managers in public agencies as he has teaching graduate students. His training programs have been offered to individuals at all levels of government in the United States and to executives and elected officials from other countries.

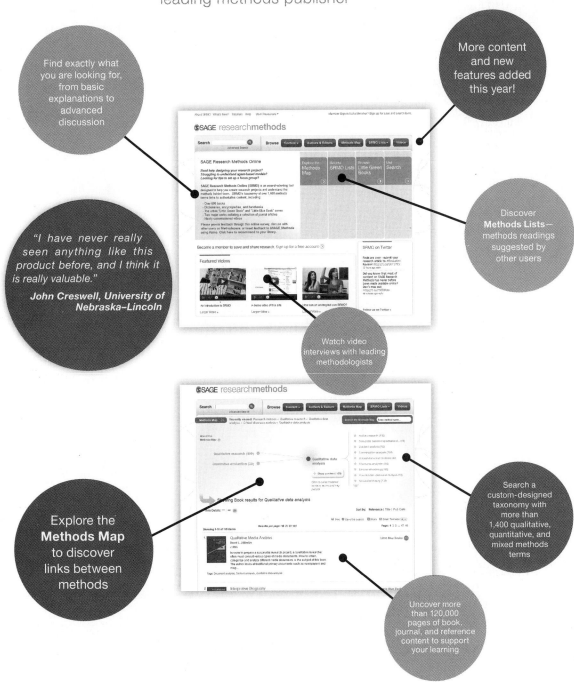

SAGE researchmethods

The essential online tool for researchers from the world's leading methods publisher

Find exactly what you are looking for, from basic explanations to advanced discussion

More content and new features added this year!

"I have never really seen anything like this product before, and I think it is really valuable."

John Creswell, University of Nebraska–Lincoln

Discover **Methods Lists**— methods readings suggested by other users

Watch video interviews with leading methodologists

Explore the **Methods Map** to discover links between methods

Search a custom-designed taxonomy with more than 1,400 qualitative, quantitative, and mixed methods terms

Uncover more than 120,000 pages of book, journal, and reference content to support your learning

Find out more at
www.sageresearchmethods.com